Commercial Real Estate Investing in CANADA

COMMERCIAL REAL ESTATE INVESTING IN CANADA

THE COMPLETE REFERENCE FOR REAL ESTATE INVESTORS AND PROFESSIONALS

PIERRE BOIRON
CLAUDE BOIRON

John Wiley & Sons Canada, Ltd.

National Library of Canada Cataloguing in Publication Data

Boiron, Pierre
    Commercial real estate investing in Canada : the complete reference for
real estate professionals / Pierre Boiron, Claude Boiron.

Includes index.

ISBN 978-0-470-83840-2

    1. Commercial real estate—Canada. 2. Real estate investment—Canada.
I. Boiron, Claude II. Title.

HD1393.58.C3B64 2007   332.63'240971   C2008-900991-3

Production Credits
Developmental Editor: Joan Homewood
Project Editor: Catherine Leek
Interior design: Adrian So
Typesetting: Lesia Hnatejko
Cover design: Mike Chan
Author photos: Heather Bertram

John Wiley & Sons Canada, Ltd.
6045 Freemont Blvd.
Mississauga, Ontario
L5R 4J3

1 2 3 4 5 TRI 12 11 10 09 08

Table of Contents

Part 2 – Understanding the Industry

Part 3 – Finance

Part 4 – Buying, Selling and Leasing

Part 5 – Managing Your Properties

Preface

Investing in commercial real estate is a very specialized form of investing. Most people are familiar with residential real estate investing, where an investor manages a portfolio of single-family and multi-family units to create cash flow and use increased values to buy more properties. The commercial real estate sector takes the form of investment in apartment buildings, office buildings, industrial buildings, warehouses, plazas or malls, and property development. The inherent risks and rewards are much different; the due diligence requirements are much different; the financial strategies are much different between these forms of real estate investment.

Through our years of experience in commercial real estate, it became apparent to us that we had gathered a body of knowledge that would be of interest to investors and professionals, such as real estate agents and brokers, financiers, lawyers, property managers, various professionals, and their tenants. We would often be called on to render an opinion or conduct research on various aspects of commercial real estate. Hence, we thought it timely to write a book that is both a primer on commercial real estate investment and a useful tool and reference guide for those seasoned professionals with a keen interest in real estate literature.

While subjective as it might be, in our opinion here are some "80-per cent facts" about commercial real estate that clearly indicate that a book such as ours could prove helpful:

- 80 per cent of commercial buildings are not properly managed, even by large landlords
- 80 per cent of landlords do not maintain a proper, rewarding relationship with their tenants
- 80 per cent of commercial properties do not generate the income they are capable of generating
- 80 per cent of landlords who are in financial trouble should not be in financial trouble, and
- 80 per cent of buildings need to be environmentally upgraded to reduce their environmental footprint, which will deliver cost savings to the owner.

Here, in broad strokes, are the main topics our book addresses:

- why you should consider investing in commercial real estate
- what to look for in each of the main types of real estate
- purchasing strategies
- a primer in real estate taxation
- how to build your team of professionals
- how Offers to Buy and Leases are structured and what you should look out for
- how commercial property financing works
- an understanding of property management, repairs, and renovations
- the requirements and responsibilities of being a good landlord
- how to conduct due diligence for prospective tenants
- ways to increase income from the property
- the pitfalls you need to avoid
- an introduction to real estate terminology, and
- sources of further information.

Please note the following:

Pronoun Usage: The pronoun "he" also encompasses "she". We respect the modern trend to use "he" and "she" but this construction can become awkward at times. For ease of reading we decided to let the pronoun "he" speak for both genders.

Measurements: We show both metric and imperial measurements as both are employed in every day real estate life.

We'd also like to invite you to visit our Web site at <www.realestatementor.ca> and contact us with questions or comments. These will be most helpful in ensuring future editions provide the most current and useful information.

Pierre Boiron
Claude Boiron
Thornhill, Ontario

PART 1

Introduction to Commercial Real Estate Investing

CHAPTER

1

Introduction

By the end of this chapter you will be able to:
- Differentiate between the three roles of real estate investors.
- Identify how this book will assist you.
- Determine if real estate investing is for you.
- Recognize that there are jurisdictional considerations.
- Know how to rise above the common obstacles to success.

1.1 TYPES OF REAL ESTATE INVESTORS

Differentiate between the three roles of real estate investors.

There are many kinds of real estate investor, ranging from the uneducated to the Ph.D., from the charming to the obnoxious, from the sophisticated to the vulgar. There are those who start out with money and those who don't (but be reassured, you don't need that much money to get started). So, do you have what it takes to be successful?

Based on many years of experience, we are convinced that you need only two things to succeed as a real estate investor: an indomitable determination to succeed and plenty of courage.

There are, however, three distinct hats that you must wear at different times to be a successful real estate investor:

1. The entrepreneur
2. The property manager
3. The technician.

1.1.1 THE ENTREPRENEUR

This is the dreamer, the person with the vision, the creativity, the desire, and the ability to make things happen. He finds, analyzes, and negotiates the deals. He will arrange financing or set up partnerships. He is the lifeblood of the business and without him nothing would be started.

1.1.2 THE PROPERTY MANAGER

This is the person who deals with the tenants, the suppliers, and employees. Without him, things might get done, but the "right" things would not get done properly and cost-effectively.

1.1.3 THE TECHNICIAN

This is the "maintenance" person who watches over the building. He decides which repairs need to be done, when, and which brands of equipment to use. The technician decides what to replace, what to repair, and which energy saving measures to implement. He also decides if major changes should be made, such as dividing a large two-bedroom apartment into two small one-bedroom units, or building an addition. The technician who starts as a small investor may do the work himself or hire and supervise others to do it.

The real estate investor must take on all three roles, whether personally or with the help of others. If your budget is generous you can hire some of this expertise, but if your budget is limited, you may have to perform all three jobs yourself, especially when starting out. The important point to remember is that you need to create these "company" positions both on paper and in your mind as part of your business plan. Each one is important to keep your real estate investments growing. You will be building on your strengths and finding outside help, where required, to compensate for your limitations.

Each position — entrepreneur, property manager, and technician — is important to keep your real estate investments growing.

1.1.4 KEY CHARACTERISTICS

Although you do need some knowledge starting out, most of this can be acquired by reading and by heeding the advice of trained professionals in the real estate industry. You don't need an MBA; street smarts are much more precious. In the end, your temperament, your personality, and, above all, your desire to succeed will be your ticket to success.

If we had only one piece of advice, it would be this: at all costs avoid associating with people who are negative and condition yourself to reject negative thoughts. How do you do that? By following the advice of the sage French pharmacist, Emile Coué, who, centuries ago, invented self-hypnosis: keep repeating to yourself what you want to accomplish. For example, repeat to yourself, "I will buy a property before the end of the month (or year)." It sounds funny, but it works.

Desire is the key. Let it burn inside of you. Become obsessed. The most important thing is to get started. Buy a property — rented or to be rented (it doesn't matter which) — but start and start small (e.g., a $100,000 property at 5% down = $5,000).

This is not to say that your journey as an investor will always be smooth; not at all. In fact, it would be a miracle if you never encountered difficult times. In all likelihood, you will have to make sacrifices and exercise self-discipline (particularly in your spending habits). As in anything new, you will make mistakes. But don't worry about any of these hurdles.

Real estate can be very forgiving of mistakes and it is through them that you will learn. Even if you make mistakes, with the help of this book, there is a 99% chance that you will break even. Remember, a property does not disappear. If you can commit yourself and survive the ups and downs, you will have demystified the process of buying and managing real estate. You will have taken the first step and started building the foundations of your real estate investment program. If by an extraordinary stroke of bad luck, you lose money on your first foray into the world of real estate investing, it will be very little because you started small. Remember, there are a number of experienced advisors to help you: lawyers, real estate agents, accountants, and appraisers.

Remember, there are a number of experienced advisors to help you: lawyers, real estate agents, accountants, and appraisers.

Virtually everyone is a little apprehensive when doing something for the first time and it becomes easy to justify not doing anything, because you can't find the "perfect property" — that is, the ideal property type, in perfect condition, at the right location, for a price you can afford, etc. The fact is the "perfect property" doesn't exist. The best you can hope for is to acquire enough knowledge to make informed decisions and act on them. All the time you spend learning about real estate investment will be wasted if you do not act on it.

You will increase your likelihood of getting started if you can find a good partner for your first venture. Sometimes, a spouse does the trick! And, if you are starting out with limited means, please, go out there and buy a rental property. When in doubt, remember the words of Wayne Gretzky: "You miss 100% of the shots you do not take".

1.2 PURPOSE OF THIS BOOK

Identify how this book will assist you.

The purpose of this book is threefold:

1. to encourage commercial real estate investing by showing that to be successful takes more courage, organization, and discipline than luck or brains;
2. to give the reader a solid understanding of how to select, acquire, lease, and manage income-producing properties (IPP), so that he can avoid trouble or deal with it at any point throughout the process; and
3. to provide investors or investors-to-be with a comprehensive reference guide that answers the "What should I do if ...?" questions when they arise.

This book is written to support a wide range of readers — from those considering or just getting started in commercial real estate investment to experienced investors and the professionals who advise them. If you are just starting out, this book will motivate you to begin by showing you that knowledge and a little bit of money go a long way. You will gain an understanding of how to do things yourself to save money.

If you have been investing in commercial real estate for years, this book can help you to become a superior investor by pointing out many things that the professionals are doing. You will discover many ideas that you had forgotten or, perhaps, never knew.

1.3 IS THIS BOOK FOR YOU?

Determine if real estate investing is for you.

This book will benefit a wide range of individuals in or near the commercial real estate industry, but especially the following:
- residential agents who want to move into commercial real estate
- students planning to acquire their real estate agent's license and intending to specialize in commercial real estate
- real estate investors and property managers, who want an easy-to-use, comprehensive reference book at hand
- residential investors, home builders, and land developers who are considering a move into IPPs, and
- financial consultants, accountants, lawyers, and lenders who work in the real estate industry.

1.4 SCOPE OF THIS BOOK

Recognize that there are jurisdictional considerations.

Real estate in Canada falls under provincial jurisdiction, which means that taxation, assessment, and legal systems are regulated or influenced by provincial law, as are many of the professionals who service the industry. Land use regulation is imposed by municipal authorities in combination with provincial and federal governments. Despite this maze of controls, there is, in fact, little variation in how business is conducted among the various provinces and territories. Although the examples in this book are Ontario-specific, readers will find that the information and advice presented apply across the country.

Indeed, there are some differences between various jurisdictions, such as condominiums (in Ontario) being called stratas in British Columbia. But this is superficial and applies mainly to the income tax and legal systems. The basic tenets of this book apply equally well to Toronto as they do to Calgary, Los Angeles, or Sydney.

1.5 OVERCOMING THE BARRIERS TO SUCCESS

Know how to rise above the common obstacles to success.

Many people view real estate investing as a great avenue to acquire wealth. While this is true, surprisingly it is not always the better-educated people who end up owning investment property. In fact, if a survey were conducted, we believe it would show that just as many, or perhaps more, truck drivers and trades workers as university professors and doctors are real estate investors.

In our experience the three most common barriers to investment success in commercial real estate are:

1. analyzing everything to death and focusing too much on the risk
2. not being aggressive or gutsy enough to make decisions, and
3. perceiving the business as being more complicated than it is.

This book will give you the information you need to approach commercial real estate investment with confidence. It will explain the risks and opportunities involved and give you the tools you need to analyze and compare investment opportunities.

Many books on real estate investing are theoretical, written by those who have little personal commercial investing experience, while many others are written by get-rich-quick artists who count more on their books to make money than on their real estate investments. This book focuses on practical advice, based on our combined 50 years of experience in the industry. It is intended to help you get started, but also to act as a one-stop resource that you can turn to again and again, either to refresh your memory about some less-often encountered detail or to help you negotiate your way through a complicated deal. We hope that it rekindles your enthusiasm and recharges your batteries for real estate investing.

The Business of Commercial Real Estate

By the end of this chapter you will be able to:
- Distinguish between real estate, real property, and other industry terminology.
- Analyze the pros and cons of various categories of commercial properties.
- Compare real estate and other types of investments.
- Consider all the factors when deciding upon the type of real estate investment.
- Evaluate the current marketplace and its near future.

2.1 SORTING OUT THE TERMS

Distinguish between real estate, real property, and other industry terminology.

"Real estate" is land in its natural state, including anything of a permanent nature on or under the land, such as trees, minerals (if allowed by law), and all the rights that go with that land. When one talks of real estate in populated areas, one is generally referring to the improvements to the land, such as the buildings, parking lots, etc. The land and its improvements are tangible property since it is quite easy to touch them.

Intangible components can include such things as zoning, the quality of a particular address, and the exposure or orientation of the buildings on the land. The term "real property" is used in this book because it includes both the tangible and the intangible components. When one buys a property, it is land only which is conveyed, from the viewpoint of the land registration system. The improvements are not shown in the deed.

2.2 COMMERCIAL REAL ESTATE DEFINED

Analyze the pros and cons of various categories of commercial properties.

Most of us are familiar with residential real estate. It includes the houses or condominiums that are our homes. "Commercial real estate" is defined in the context of this book as income producing property (IPP). However, there are many types of IPPs, ranging from farms or gravel pits to hockey arenas and shopping centres. The purpose of this book is to focus on the most common IPPs that make up the bulk of commercial real estate investing opportunities for the small- and mid-size investors. These IPPs are buildings that are leased to tenants (lessees) by landlords (lessors) and not occupied by their owners.

2.2.1 FOUR CATEGORIES OF COMMERCIAL PROPERTY

We cover four main categories of commercial real estate in this book: industrial, office, retail and multi-family residential.

(a) Industrial

Industrial buildings tend to have medium- to long-term leases (five or more years). They are the least management-intensive type of IPP, unless they comprise many small units of, say, 93-465 m² (1,000-5,000 sq ft). These are called multiple-occupancy industrial buildings.

These buildings are more frequently damaged and even abused by tenants, due to their uses, such as painting (air-borne paint deposits), steel fabricating (dust and damage to floors), woodworking (dust everywhere), and truck usage. Environmental problems or risk, due to tenants' use, is greater than in the other categories. Convenient access to freeways is important for the transportation of supplies and finished products as is availability of public transportation for the labour force.

Depending on the user, it can be very costly to move to another building at the end of a lease term. This motivates tenants to renew their leases. It is difficult to find industrial buildings for purchase for less than $1 million. It is more difficult to sell leased industrial buildings than retail or multi-family residential properties.

(b) Office

Office buildings come in all sizes (from a converted bungalow to a traditional multi-storey tower). Likewise, the size of tenancies varies enormously, starting with a one-person office to an entire building of 9,300 m² (100,000 sq ft) or more, housing hundreds of employees.

It is an advantage if the address is a well-known artery has sufficient parking, which is a large plus. Exposure is a factor too, but not crucial, and traffic count is usually of little interest. This type of tenant, particularly the larger ones, expect a higher level of involvement on the part of the property manager/owner.

We cover four main categories of commercial real estate in this book: industrial, office, retail and multi-family residential.

Office buildings are more susceptible to downturns in the economy. Therefore it is the riskiest of the four types of commercial real estate and tenant turnover tends to be greater than with industrial or retail properties.

(c) Retail

Any potential buyer of retail property must remember that appropriate location is very important and there are three key aspects: address, exposure, and traffic count. The astute buyer would do well to hire a professional to study the demographics of the property.

Analyze the tenant mix, which is poor in many plazas. Make sure that there is plenty of parking and easy access to the highway and public transportation. Ideally, if the centre is big enough, it should be anchored by a supermarket or other major retailer that will generate huge amounts of traffic for the other tenants.

In retail, leases are the most complex, as is property management (both in terms of technical complexity and multiple details). However, some landlords prefer retail over other types of commercial property because of the stability of tenants. From their viewpoint, a retail tenant who makes money is extremely reluctant to move. It is not overly expensive to enter this category as one can start with a single building containing one main floor store and one or more apartments above.

(d) Multi-family Residential

This category offers the two extremes — the least risky and the most management intensive. Also multi-family buildings are easy to sell, but good ones are hard to find.

This category is often chosen by new investors because one does not need a great deal of sophistication. However, it requires that the landlord, or the property manager, roll up his sleeves and have a great deal of patience and tolerance. It has the drawback of being subjected to rent controls and tenant turnover is quite high. This category allows for the highest loan-to-value ratio financing. Apparent returns are the lowest, but rentals can usually be increased almost every year, which is not usually the case with the other categories, since most leases are for five or more years.

Public transportation and nearby shopping (particularly a supermarket) are big pluses, as is proximity to employment. Buildings where the tenants are seniors is advantageous for landlords, as they tend to be "gentler" on the property.

2.2.2 VALUE OF COMMERCIAL PROPERTIES

Some investors want only shopping malls, others only apartment buildings, and others only office buildings. For others, the amount of money required is the key factor in determining how they are categorized as investors. Real Estate Investment Trusts (REITs), huge pension funds, such as Ontario Municipal Employees Retirement System (OMERS), and large institutions, such as Sun Life, have become significant players in the commercial real estate investment market, gobbling up expensive properties in prime locations (referred to in the industry as "class Triple A" or "A-type" locations). This trend started around 2000 and has reached such a crescendo that mid-size investors have little opportunity to compete for these properties.

Basically, we now have three categories of property values:
- over $10 million, dominated by the huge buyers mentioned above;
- between $3 million and $10 million, the hunting ground of the medium-size investor, where there is less competition than in the first category; and
- under $3 million, the stomping ground of the small, to very small, investor.

2.2.3 CAUTION: DO NOT BUY LAND

In this book we cover only properties that generate income, such as shopping centres, retail stores, industrial, office, and multi-family buildings. Many readers may wonder why we do not recommend land as an investment. There are three main reasons.

1. **Land Is an Alligator; It Keeps Eating All the Time.** This old saying means that if there is a loan on the land purchase, which is generally the case, interest has to be paid and eventually the principal of the loan. In addition, there are property taxes that, although generally quite low on vacant unzoned land, can jump significantly when or if the land is zoned. There may also be local improvement taxes for new services, development studies, etc. In other words, the cost of holding land will at a minimum remain constant, but can also increase, while there usually is no income to offset these costs.
2. **The Activist Challenge.** There are many activists, particularly environmentalists, who fight against any land development. Some would say this is an exaggeration, but it is easy to name a number of commercial real estate projects, particularly in land development, that have been hampered, delayed, or even stopped by activist intervention. One can argue about the benefits and detriments of these activists, but the fact is that for anyone who wants to develop land, they raise a spectre of incalculable costs that increase the risk of investing in land.
3. **Government Controls Are Complicated and Cumbersome.** The system controlling land development has become incredibly complex, rigid, and costly in its demands. In Ontario, the main cause is the *Ontario Planning Act*. In many places one can find the wording, "If the Municipality thinks that … it may request …" Ninety-nine per cent of the time, municipal planners replace "may" with "must."

Here is an anecdote to illustrate our point. In 1970, or thereabouts, in a small community located one hour north of Toronto, a farmer applied to subdivide approximately 20 acres of his land into residential lots. He went to see the local planner one day at 2 p.m. and at 4 p.m. had the subdivision approved, subject to having a plan of survey prepared that would show the lots. In 1985, the same farmer applied to the municipality to subdivide a 30-acre site abutting the first site. This time it took him eight years and cost him $100,000 in consultant's fees and studies to have his draft plan of subdivision approved!

To give you an idea of the complexity of taking a site through the planning process, and in case you happen to own a piece of land and want to understand what is involved, Figure 2.1 charts the typical process.

Land development is a very risky, lengthy, and costly process and often incredibly frustrating. As a result it is also often less financially rewarding. Although we concede that some very knowledgeable people make a lot of money in land development, our advice to the average investor is to avoid getting involved with land.

2.2.4 A NOTE ABOUT SPECULATION

Speculation is very different from investing. The latter is the rational analysis of risk. It generally consists of buying land or a building that has the potential to provide you with steady returns on your investment over the long term, through the income generated by the property and, upon selling, the profits realized through appreciation. Speculation is more of a "devil-may-care" approach to real estate investment — more of a gamble, less of a science. It is buying with the objective of selling quickly and "making a killing". It is buying land or a building with the hope that the market will change significantly, perhaps because of new zoning, new roads, new servicing, growth, etc., resulting in windfall profits.

Rewards in speculative ventures can be staggering, but losses can be equally severe. Generally, one has to be very patient, since the factors that cause a market to change are beyond the control of the investor and influenced by any number of unpredictable circumstances. Speculating is not for the weak of heart and ought only be attempted by those who have "play money" or money they can afford to lose.

2.3 BENEFITS OF INVESTING IN COMMERCIAL REAL ESTATE

Compare real estate and other types of investments.

There are many benefits to investing in real estate, not the least of which is that it can be an excellent way to build wealth. If you buy property that is good value for the price paid and manage your properties wisely, your investment should pay off substantially.

In truth, the commercial real estate investor has only one real enemy — an empty building.

While this seems trite, it is worth thinking about it. One of the more successful real estate investors we know, Don, always operates with this in mind. As real estate brokers, we would present him with an offer to lease, say at $32 per m² ($3 per sq ft) and he would sign it back at $40. The tenant would counter offer at $35. He would say, "OK, I'll take it." We would tell him that if he could give us a couple of hours and sign it back at $38, we thought we could get it, and 80% of the time we would be successful. The point is that Don was very conservative, always willing to accept less because he didn't want to take a chance on having empty buildings. In fact, he hated empty buildings. He was very conservative in other areas too. He financed his new buildings (he built himself) and when the mortgage was paid off, he did not refinance them.

Figure 2.1 Land Development Process

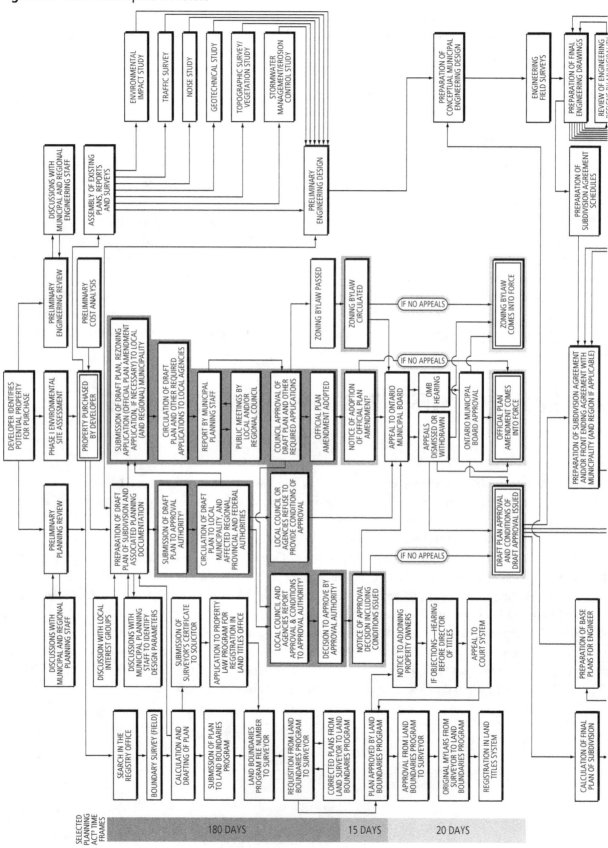

Source: Sernas Associates

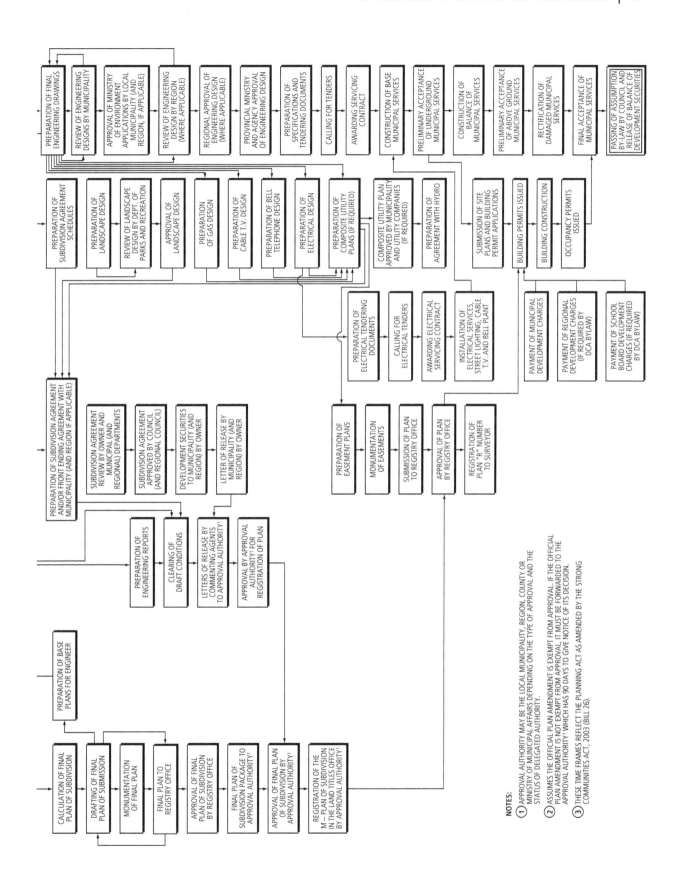

NOTES:

(1) APPROVAL AUTHORITY MAY BE THE LOCAL MUNICIPALITY, REGION, COUNTY OR MINISTRY OF MUNICIPAL AFFAIRS DEPENDING ON THE TYPE OF APPROVAL AND THE STATUS OF DELEGATED AUTHORITY.

(2) ASSUMES THE OFFICIAL PLAN AMENDMENT IS EXEMPT FROM APPROVAL. IF THE OFFICIAL PLAN AMENDMENT IS NOT EXEMPT FROM APPROVAL, IT MUST BE FORWARDED TO THE APPROVAL AUTHORITY[1] WHICH HAS 90 DAYS TO GIVE NOTICE OF ITS DECISION.

(3) THESE TIME FRAMES REFLECT THE PLANNING ACT AS AMENDED BY THE STRONG COMMUNITIES ACT, 2003 (BILL 26).

2.3.1 INVESTMENT CONSIDERATIONS

There are five main factors that you should consider when making any investment:

1. **Preservation of Capital.** How secure is the investment? What could happen if things go wrong?
2. **Liquidity.** How liquid is the investment? In other words, how easily and quickly can it be turned into cash? Real estate is not considered liquid because it can take a long time to sell it and some properties that have serious drawbacks are particularly difficult to sell.
3. **Recovery of Capital.** How will I get my money back? Will this happen only when the property sells, is refinanced, or from rentals?
4. **Stability of Income.** How predictable is the investment? Will it fluctuate considerably or be steady?
5. **Return on Investment.** Commercial real estate returns are usually excellent when one takes appreciation into account.

Some other considerations to review before making an investment are the growth of capital (through appreciation), the cost of managing the capital and the asset, amount of involvement (by you), and protection against inflation. These factors usually play less significance, but you may want to review them. See Figure 2.2 for a comparison of investment characteristics for various types of investment vehicles.

Figure 2.2
Investment Characteristics

Item	Preservation of Capital	Liquidity	Recovery of Capital	Stability of Income	Return on Investment	Growth of Capital	Cost of Managing	Amount of Involvement (by owner)	Protection Against Inflation
Government Bonds	Gilt-edged	Low, at Market Value	At Par, at Maturity	Gilt-edged	Medium	Nil	Nil	Passive	None
Corporate Bonds	Excellent	Low, at Market Value	At Par, at Maturity	Excellent	Medium	Nil	Nil	Passive	None
Debentures	Good	Low	At Par, at Maturity	Good	Low	Nil	Nil	Passive	None
Preferred Shares	Generally, good	Fair to Good	Market Value	Very Good	Medium	Nil	Nil	Passive	From None to Medium
Common Shares (Blue Chip)	Acceptable	Excellent, at Market Value	From Poor to Outstanding	Fluctuating	From Poor to Outstanding	Uncertain but Likely	Nil	Passive	Good
Prime First Mortgages	Excellent	Good, but at a Discount from Market Value	Repaid Slowly	Excellent	Good	Nil	Small	Passive	None
Real Properties	Excellent	Poor	Market Value at Time of Sale	Good	Generally Excellent	Good to Excellent	Varies with the Kind of Property	From Passive to Semi-Active	Excellent
Business	Poor	Uncertain	From Poor to Outstanding	Uncertain	Uncertain, from very high to nil	Good to Excellent	High	Active	From None to Excellent

Note: The table is a generalization. Variations within each class can be huge. For example, the security of income and of capital recovery varies considerably for each specific real property and for common stocks. Both offer the huge advantage of keeping pace with inflation.

2.3.2 KEY CHARACTERISTICS OF REAL ESTATE INVESTMENTS

Although real estate has much in common with other investment options, there are a number of characteristics that make it unique:

- Real estate is fixed in location and highly dependent upon its surroundings for its value.
- Developed real estate (improved with buildings) is not easily altered; once land is committed to a specific use, it is difficult, costly, and time consuming to change.
- Real estate development and ownership are subject to an ever-increasing amount of government control. Taxes on land sales and transfers, along with rent controls and land use controls, are expected to become an even more significant part of the Canadian real estate market.
- Most real estate investments require a great deal of money. Therefore, many investors prefer a large degree of leverage (see "leverage" at section 2.5.2).
- Real estate provides a wide variety of investment possibilities, ranging from converting a basement to a one-bedroom apartment for lease to purchasing a shopping centre.
- Real estate can often be used in whole, or in part, by the investor for his own use.
- There is a fixed, limited supply of real estate. The demand is growing as the population continues to increase (very rapidly, in some places!). This means demand will remain strong, particularly in choice locations, defying pressures from other factors such as inflation, deflation, recession, or interest rates.

> *Although real estate has much in common with other investment options there are a number of characteristics that make it unique.*

- Although certainly not recession proof, real estate tends to weather downturns much better than stocks and bonds. Since 1934, real estate has seen negative returns 5% of the time during periods of downturn while stocks and bonds were negative 25% of the time.

2.3.3 REAL ESTATE OR STOCK MARKET?

Practically speaking, the modern investor who is interested in passive or semi-passive income has two choices: real estate or the stock market. By "passive income" we mean income that is generated with no need for intervention; you make your investment and earn a return with no action required.

An investment in real estate can be fully passive if the investor buys shares of a Real Estate Investment Trust (described in Chapter 6 at section 6.7.5) or semi-passive if he buys an income property and uses a property management firm. However, if the investor manages the property directly the investment is definitely not passive. In fact, it could require a lot of involvement in the case of multi-family buildings.

Although huge fortunes have been made in the stock market, such as that enjoyed by the legendary investor, the late John Paul Getty, most large and small fortunes were realized in real estate. Even Paul Getty was active in real estate. "The first Marshall Field ... once remarked: 'Buying real estate is not only the best way, the quickest way and the safest way but the only way to become wealthy.'"[1]

People who favour stock market investments over real estate investments overlook two paramount points. There is far less risk in real estate and an investor has much more control over its condition, future, management, and results.

With real estate one has real value, not some esoteric or anticipated value, as is the case with many stocks. Most stocks trade at 15 to 30 times earnings, and sometimes much more. In fact, stocks have traded at over 150

---

1 This article appeared in *Time* magazine on April 11, 1969, and still holds true today.

times earnings in the high-tech field. Commercial real estate generally trades at 8 to 12 times earnings, and there is real, intrinsic value to it. Real estate historically also offers a higher cash flow. In support of this view, consider the case of one of our clients, a senior financial advisor and vice-president of a very large capital management firm. This company specializes in advising high-net-worth clients and investing on their behalf in the stock market, REITs, bonds, and similar items. This executive is a sophisticated professional, intimately familiar with the stock market, yet he told us that he counted on real estate to provide for his retirement. Figure 2.3 compares an investment in real estate to an investment in the stock market.

Figure 2.3
Investment Characteristics — Real Estate vs. Stock Market

Question	Real Estate	Stock Market
Is the supply limited?	Yes	No
What percentage of control do I have on running the investment?	100%	0%
If things turn sour, do I have the option of correcting them?	Yes	No
Can part of the income be sheltered through building depreciation?	Yes	No
Which percentage of high-grade investment can I finance?	85% (up to)	70%
Which percentage of low-grade investment can I finance?	60%	0%
Can I see and touch my property?	Yes	No
Which percentage of the investment do I understand personally?	100%	0-50%
Can I set the direction of the investment?	Yes	No
Can I improve the building/investment?	Yes	No
What is the percentage of volatility of my investment?	5%	70%
Can I do some of the work myself, if needed to improve the investment?	Yes	No
Can I keep a close eye on my investment?	Yes	No
Can I examine, and influence, income and expenses and decide how to increase the former and lower the latter?	Yes	No
Is my investment liquid?	No	Yes

Probably, quite a few readers will think we are biased towards real estate, and they are right. However, it is not without justification. A comparison of rates of return among a variety of investments as shown in Figure 2.4 demonstrates part of the reason we are so committed to real estate as a strong investment choice.

Figure 2.4
Comparison of Returns

Approach	Safety Level* 1-5 (5=best)	Return Before Tax**	Tax sheltering	Appreciation	Leverage	Major Advantages	Major Disadvantages
Mattress	1	0.00%		no	no	No fee of any kind. Privacy.	Can be stolen. No income.
Savings account	3	0.25% to 2.30%	no	no	no	Some flexibility.	Low interest rate.
Money Market Funds[1]	4	1.3% to 2.30%	yes/no	no	no	Short-term investments. Some provide tax free income. Parking spot for liquid capital. Offers liquidity and low risk. Less volatile than stocks. Very liquid investments.	Yields can fall sharply. May not keep up with inflation.
Government of Canada Bonds[2]	3	2.5% to 4.50%	no	no	no	Can be cashed in at any time. Prices are low if interest rates are high.	Prices are high if interest rates are low.
Guaranteed Investment Certificates (GIC)[3] (term investment)	5	0.75% to 3.50%	no	no	no	Best investment in a deflation. Absolutely safe.	Locked in. Some can be cashed if necessary. $1,000 minimum. Low yield when Bank of Canada rate is low. Fixed rate.
Treasury Bills[4]	4	2.50%	no	no	no	Many T-bills offer tax-free deferral. Highly liquid and offer security and compet. yield.	Usually, for over $250,000, gain on sale is treated as interest income.
Mutual Funds	2	6% to 12%	no	yes	no	Diversified investments (stocks, bonds, cash). Managed by professionals Minimum $500, or monthly contributions.	Will fare poorly in an economic crisis.
Real Estate	3	12% to 18%	yes (CCA)	yes	yes	You can see it and influence its performance. Appreciates 6% per year. Tax on appreciation paid only upon a sale of the property. 12% to 18% is with mortgage.	Illiquidity

Note: There are dozens and dozens of investment options, some pretty new fangled (and dangerous). This is a condensed version. Rates of Return are based on our business experience and various readings over the years.
  * Refers to safety of capital and interest levels.
** Approximate, and varying over time.

1- Money Market Fund: An open-end mutual fund that invests only in money markets, in short-term (one day to one year) debt obligations such as Treasury Bills, certificates of deposit and commercial paper. The main goal is the preservation of principal, accompanied by modest dividends. The fund's net asset value remains a constant $1 per share to simplify accounting, but the interest rate does fluctuate.
2- Bonds: Pay interest semi-annually until maturity date, when the issuing entity repays the bond's face value.
3- GICs: A GIC is a note with a fixed yield and term. Many GICs are insured by the Canada Deposit Insurance Corporation (CDIC) for interest and principal totalling up to $60,000, with a term usually from 30 to 364 days for short-term GICs, and one to five years form long-term GICs. They are sometimes called "term deposits".
4- Treasury Bills: A short-term investment issued by the federal government of one- to twelve-month duration.

People invest in real estate for economic and non-economic reasons. One non-economic reason is that most investors like the feeling of being closely involved with their investments and the pride and satisfaction in being owners of a property. The ultimate goal of investing in real estate is economic, the maximization of after-tax returns. Real estate offers an investor an average yield of one and one-half to two times that of most common stocks. However, the investor must accept the corresponding increase in risk and also give up substantial liquidity.[2]

2.3.4 ADVANTAGES OF INVESTING IN REAL ESTATE

There are a number of reasons to invest in income-producing properties (IPPs) rather than in other conventional types of investments, but the main reasons are set out below.

- **To "Park" Your Capital.** Do not squander it. For some investors, it is a benefit that real estate is not a liquid investment, that is, it is not easily converted back into cash. It forces the investor to be disciplined about the investment. Once you buy a property and sign a loan agreement (mortgage), you will do your utmost to make the scheduled payments, even if you have to keep your old car for a few more years or do without a European vacation.

- **To Be Protected Against Inflation.** Based on the Canadian Price Index (CPI), in Canada the average rate of inflation between 1914 and 2006 was 3.19% per year. Every time the cost of a square metre of land or of laying a new brick increases, every square metre of similar land or brick already laid increases in value too, although not necessarily in the same proportion. This concept disregards other factors, such as neighbourhood transitions and the economic obsolescence of buildings, but the simplistic implication is still that you generally benefit from price appreciation when you invest in real estate.

- **To Build Equity.** Assuming that you have made a wise investment, each time you collect a rental payment you will be building equity in your property by using your tenants' rent to pay a portion of your mortgage.

- **The Ease of Refinancing.** Every time your Net Operating Income (NOI) increases markedly, through increased rentals or lowered expenses, you can arrange for a higher mortgage, freeing some of your initial equity. In other words, you will recover 100% of your equity in 5 to 8 years; sometimes even sooner, with a little luck.

- **To Secure Positive Cash Flow.** This is the amount of money left after you subtract all operating and repair expenses, plus allowances for vacancies and bad debts, and mortgage payments, from the gross income. These regular monthly cheques are pretty nice.

- **To Increase your RSP Contributions.** Because rental income is considered by Canada Revenue Agency (CRA) as "earned income" for individuals, it can be used to increase the allowable amount of your Retirement Savings Plan (RSP) contributions and, thereby, defer the payment of taxes.

- **To Benefit from Income Tax Sheltering.** This is done through building depreciation (Capital Cost Allowance). In Canada, you may depreciate the building itself, not the land, at the rate of 4% (for most buildings) per year, on a declining balance.

- **To Benefit from Favourable Capital Gains Treatment.** If you sell the property, often you pay taxes on only 50% of your profits.

- **Insurance Premiums on Income Property Mortgages Are Tax Deductible.** If you have an insured mortgage, in case circumstances are such that you cannot make the mortgage payments, the insurer will do so for you, but you will lose the equity you have in the property. You may deduct the premiums from the property income, so you are protected but pay with "before-tax dollars".

---

2 E. Thomas Garman and Raymond E. Forgue, *Personal Finance*, 3d ed. Boston: Houghton Mifflin Company, 1991.

- **To Weather Economic Recessions.**
  - Leases are relatively long term, the most common being five years.
  - Staggered lease expirations are of benefit in smoothing out the impact of recessions.
  - Real estate investments enjoy relatively longer market cycles compared to other kinds of investments
  - This is due to the fact that it takes years to erect new buildings, from concept to occupancy, passing through feasibility studies, architectural plans, financing, bids, construction, and leasing.
- **Significant Future Demand.** There is the same amount of land but more and more people.
- **Greater Protection of Capital.** A prudent person would need to be consistently negligent to lose the capital he has invested in real estate.
- **Secure Higher Rates of Return.** Profits from ongoing operations, plus capital appreciation, plus leverage result in higher rates of return than most other investments.
- **Low Degree of Volatility.** Multiple tenants, staggering lease expiration dates, and long-term financing result in lower degrees of volatility.

2.3.5 DISADVANTAGES OF INVESTING IN REAL ESTATE

Since there are always two sides to any coin, you should consider the drawbacks of investing in real estate too.

- It is not a liquid investment, as it usually takes months and, in some cases, years to sell a property.
- It requires relatively large amounts of money for the initial investment.
- There may be unexpected surprises (from a cash flow viewpoint), such as a substantial tenant going bankrupt or a roof needing replacement at an inopportune time.
- It is "fixed"; that is, it cannot be moved.
- It requires management:
  - of the asset (business and property management)
  - of the money (bookkeeping, etc.), and
  - of the tenants. In addition, dealing with tenants can be unpleasant, as landlords are not liked, as a rule.
- One is at the mercy of governmental decisions: expropriation, new roads, new neighbours, new zoning, new taxes, rent controls, etc.
- The risk of financial loss, fortunately, is rare, but it can happen due to several reasons:
  - because the investor did not pay enough attention to the economy, in general, and to the real estate cycle, in particular, when making the decision to purchase the property,
  - the investor was too greedy; he took too much risk, or
  - it may be due to rotten luck. Some situations are difficult to anticipate: war, a good tenant going bankrupt, a down-turned market meaning that your building stays empty a long time before a new tenant can be found, etc.
- Insufficient knowledge or a lack of trustworthy professionals to advise the investor.

2.3.6 FACTORS INFLUENCING INVESTMENT SUCCESS

As with all investment, real estate investment comes with some risk both from controllable and uncontrollable factors. Controllable factors are those that an investor can influence, either before a property is purchased or during the ownership of the property. Uncontrollable, or external, factors are those that cannot normally be influenced by the investor. The wise investor is aware of these, but concentrates his attention on the factors that are within the investor's control.

(a) Controllable Factors

Below is a list of significant, controllable factors affecting the level of returns from a property.

As with all investment, real estate investment comes with some risk both from controllable and uncontrollable factors.

- **Location.** Find a good location for the specific use. This includes considerations regarding lot shape, neighbours, noise, odours, and natural risks such as flooding.
- **Type of Real Property.** Is the property to be used for industrial, office, or other purposes?
- **Design of the Building.** This would include the following factors:
  - attractiveness for tenants and their clients (this will keep the vacancy rate low and command higher rentals); and
  - quality of the construction (this has a direct bearing on the cost of heating, air conditioning, lighting, and maintenance).
- **Property Management.** Too often, it is not as good as it should be.

(b) Uncontrollable Factors

These are factors that cannot be influenced by an investor, either before or after a property is purchased. These are generally external factors.

- **Inflation.** Inflation is one of the most significant external factors that affect the level of real estate returns. This factor is most easily apparent in two situations – rentals of existing buildings increase if new properties cost more and the appreciation of a property's value is greater during a period of high inflation.
- **Interest Rates.** Assuming that the investor borrowed money to invest, rising interest rates will decrease the level of cash flow generated by IPPs financed at a later rate, but have a beneficial effect on the potential for long-term capital appreciation. In contrast, declining interest rates will have a positive effect on the current operating income of a newly financed property and encourage builders to expand the supply of IPPs.
- **Supply and Demand.** The supply and demand for real estate is cyclical. An over-supply will decrease rental rates and returns, while under-supply will have the opposite effect. Supply and demand must be considered on a local basis. For example, there may be a shortage of apartments in Peterborough, but an abundance of them in Goderich.
- **Governments.** We are at the mercy of new laws. In addition, governments have the right to expropriate property for a number of reasons, such as new roads or freeways, community buildings, transportation corridors, etc.
- **Income Controls.** In the case of residential properties, the government can step in and regulate possible increases via rent controls.
- **Taxation.** Again, government controls such income factors as capital gains tax, capital cost allowance, and property taxes.
- **Land Use.** Zoning regulations will impact the income producing capacity of a property. For instance a property may be located in an area that is being down-zoned so that the zoning becomes more restrictive and therefore less attractive.

- **Economy.** Like all business people, real estate investors are affected by the condition of the economy. Little, or rather nothing, can be done to control it, but many an investor with a financial cushion is able to weather a bad economic period. The one who is already stretched at the start of a downturn ends up stretched beyond his limits, financially speaking.
- **Natural Disasters.** Since these events cannot usually be anticipated, it is wise to not buy in areas that can be affected by natural disasters, such as flooding or earthquakes. In 2005, even buildings that had never been affected by heavy rainfall found their basements in four feet of water in north Toronto and Markham, due to unprecedented rainfall.

Buying real estate can be complex. To lower your investment risk, you need to acquire enough knowledge to feel quite comfortable when you purchase a property and you should consult knowledgeable professionals.

Success requires four things: time, talent, money, and good marketing. If you are weak in one area, the other three must compensate for it. Talent (people) is, by far, the most important. To invest successfully in commercial real estate you will need a pool of knowledgeable trusted advisors — including real estate professionals, appraisers, lawyers, tax advisors, investors, property managers, and various tradespeople, to name just a few. But as captain of this ship you must become knowledgeable enough to lead this crew. It is much better to have a poor ship with a good captain than a good ship with a poor captain. Obviously, if you read this book from start to finish, you will be on your way to real estate knowledge.

2.4 EVALUATING THE MARKET OUTLOOK

Consider all the factors when deciding upon the type of real estate investment.

To understand the factors that can influence real estate markets, let's look at the current market situation. The years 1996 to 2007 have been a vendor's market for real estate in much of Canada because of increased demand, due mainly to the very successful investing channel that REITs represent. During this decade, there was increased demand, but the supply remained the same because building developers erect buildings only if they can find tenants.

2.4.1 UNCERTAINTY IN THE STOCK MARKET

The stock market's quasi-meteoric rise in the second half of the 1990s appealed powerfully to the greed that is present in most people. However, the horrific crash of the market in 2001 and a few highly publicized scandals (Enron, WorldCom, Nortel) made many people leery of continuing to invest in equities. Instead, they turned to real estate, one of the few investment avenues that was maintaining its value and was substantial enough to "park" large amounts of money.

2.4.2 INTEREST RATES

During the same period, record low interest rates made borrowing to purchase more affordable, while lenders were eager to make these loans because of the tangible nature of real estate and its permanency.

2.4.3 INTRODUCTION OF REITS

REITs are public corporations that are listed on stock exchanges and sell shares to investors. They derive their income primarily from real estate as owners, property managers, lenders, or a mixture of these. Created in the United States in 1960, they grew dramatically in the early 1990s. REITs must pay 90% of their profits to shareholders.

A major appeal of REITs is that they do not pay income tax, thus eliminating the drawback of double taxation. They facilitate access to real estate investing for the small investors as well as the large ones who do not want to own real property directly or prefer to leave selection and property management to the specialists. Their diversification in terms of property types and geographic markets results in low risk.

2.4.4 STRONG ECONOMY

A boom in the resource sector, a strong export market, low unemployment, etc., means that people are employed, are well paid, and are spending on many things, including real properties.

2.4.5 SUPPLY AND DEMAND

The influx of capital into the real estate market over the 2002-2007 period, due to the above factors, fuelled by an unusually strong Canadian economy, resulted in a vendor's market that continued strong through 2007, demonstrating one of the most powerful economic laws at work: supply and demand. The real estate market remains in a state of disequilibrium because supply of new IPPs has remained constant (based on actual demand by tenants), while demand has increased enormously, fuelled by the availability of capital. This demand was mainly the result of the success encountered by REITs in raising large amounts of money. This situation continues to drive up prices in the real estate market, which benefits vendors.

2.4.6 DOWNTURN IN THE ECONOMY

While inflation has been under control for several years now, it looms large as a potential risk to real estate investment in coming years, if the equally threatening recession does not take place.

The federal banks of Canada and the US have steadily increased their rates in the 2005-2007 period, due to a fear of inflation. However, while there were a few isolated portents of a real estate slow-down in 2005, the economic (mainly real estate) numbers coming from the US in the first nine months of 2007 seemed to herald a coming cri-

Real estate represents approximately 30% of the Canadian and US national economies.

sis that could have become very serious. Canada lags the US in these matters by six to twelve months, normally. However, these fears seem to have abated. There could still be inflation, but a recession, the gravity of it totally unknown, is not very likely.

Real estate represents approximately 30% of the Canadian and US national economies. If this market segment slows down, far fewer things will be needed: wood and metal products, fuel, gas, vehicles, etc. Such a slowdown impacts the economy severely.

2.4.7 CONSEQUENCES OF INFLATION

When there is severe inflation, say, over 4% per year, people worry that their savings are being eroded. If, for example, one has $100,000 invested in Treasury Bills, or money market certificates, at 6% and the inflation rate is 5%, the following picture would emerge.

Interest earned: $100,000 x 6% =	$6,000
Income tax:	$2,300
Balance:	$3,700
Inflation @ 5%:	$5,000
Profit (Loss):	($1,300)

This is powerful motivation to find a way to avoid this loss of capital. The two main methods are the stock market and real estate. It is, indeed, easy for people to see that the value of houses and commercial buildings is increasing rapidly. This situation leads to increased demand for real estate. More demand but the same supply increases desirability and investors will accept lower rates. Therefore the value of properties will increase.

2.5 BUILDING WEALTH THROUGH REAL ESTATE INVESTING

Evaluate the current marketplace and its near future.

With knowledge and hard work, almost anyone who starts early enough in life to invest in real estate can become wealthy. There are two main reasons for this: the historical appreciation in the value of real estate over time and the benefit of leveraging your investments.

2.5.1 UNDERSTANDING APPRECIATION

Appreciation is the increase in value of a property. This can be due to inflation, increased demand, rezoning, or a number of other factors. Looking at the statistics from the Toronto Real Estate Board, as an example, we know that the average price of all residential properties sold in 1966 was $21,360 versus $355,907 in 2005. (These statistics are not available separately for commercial properties.) This is an average return of 6.36% per year (see Figure 2.5), which is why we have used 6% appreciation in the examples throughout this book. Obviously, this increase is not steady or regular; it varies from year to year (see Figure 2.6).

This means that if you bought a house in Toronto for $101,626 in 1983, it would have been worth $335,907 by 2005 (see Appreciation Table in Figure 2.5), a difference of $234,281 and a return on investment of 230.53%. When you add in rental income from the property, the picture becomes even more attractive. If we assume a net income of $9,000 per year on the same $101,626 property, we obtain a return of: 8.86%, say 9% after tax ($9,000/$101,626) + 6% appreciation = 15% return on investment.

If you start with $100,000 that gives you a return of 15%, in 20 years, in a perfect world, you will have $1,637,000 and in 40 years $26,790,000 (see Figure 2.7).

Figure 2.5
Annual Appreciation of 6.36%

Starting Value $ 21,360   Ending Value $ 335,907

Difference: $335,905 - $21,360 = $314,545; divided by 40 years equals:

Annual Appreciation of 6.36%			
#	Year	Start	% increase
1	1966	$21,360	0.00%
2	1967	$24,078	12.72%
3	1968	$26,732	11.02%
4	1969	$28,929	8.22%
5	1970	$29,492	1.95%
6	1971	$30,426	3.17%
7	1972	$32,513	6.86%
8	1973	$40,605	24.89%
9	1974	$52,806	30.05%
10	1975	$57,581	9.04%
11	1976	$61,389	6.61%
12	1977	$64,559	5.16%
13	1978	$67,333	4.30%
14	1979	$70,830	5.19%
15	1980	$75,694	6.87%
16	1981	$90,203	19.17%
17	1982	$95,496	5.87%
18	1983	$101,626	6.42%
19	1984	$102,318	0.68%
20	1985	$109,094	6.62%
21	1986	$138,925	27.34%
22	1987	$189,105	36.12%
23	1988	$229,635	21.43%
24	1989	$273,698	19.19%
25	1990	$255,020	-6.82%
26	1991	$234,313	-8.12%
27	1992	$214,971	-8.25%
28	1993	$206,490	-3.95%
29	1994	$208,921	1.18%
30	1995	$203,028	-2.82%
31	1996	$198,150	-2.40%
32	1997	$211,307	6.64%
33	1998	$216,815	2.61%
34	1999	$228,372	5.33%
35	2000	$243,255	6.52%
36	2001	$251,508	3.39%
37	2002	$275,231	9.43%
38	2003	$293,067	6.48%
39	2004	$315,231	7.56%
40	2005	$335,907	6.56%

Source: Based on Toronto Real Estate Board's average prices from 1966 to 2005 for single-family houses.

Figure 2.6
Capital Appreciation in the GTA by Year and Linear

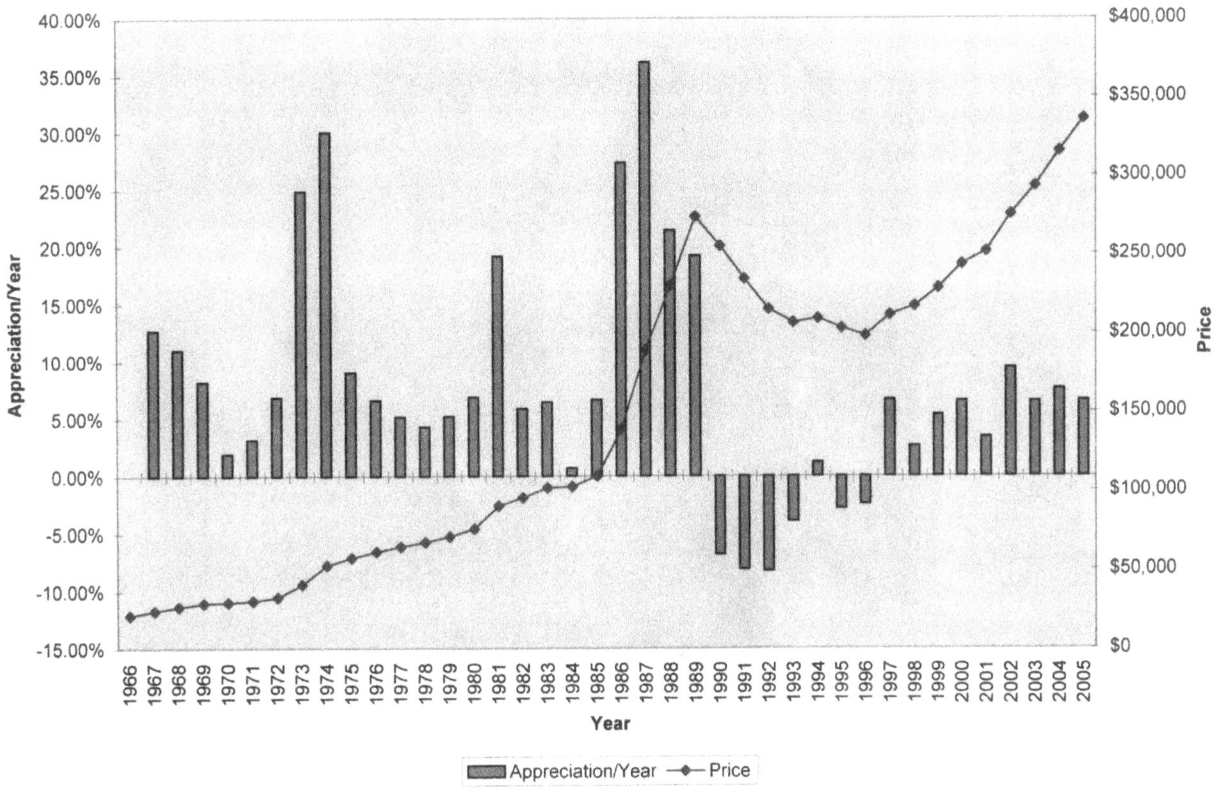

Source: Based on Toronto Real Estate Board's average prices from 1966 to 2005 for single-family houses.

Bear in mind that yearly income increases are different, depending on the type of investment. Most multi-family rentals can be increased annually (not always), depending on the economy and governmental regulations, while the owner of an industrial building leased for ten years, without any rental increase, will have to wait ten years. However, the rental may more than double at that time. Note that the return on investment would have been significantly higher if the property had been financed (see The Benefits of Leveraging at section 2.5.2).

Some people will argue that basing these calculations on rates of appreciation in residential real estate is misleading. They are wrong: commercial and residential property values move in sync with some variations and generally reflect inflation. Appreciation is not regular and can vary markedly from one year, or one period, to the next. However, given that average appreciation during the period from January 1966 to December 2005 (40 years) was 6.36%, to be conservative in this book, wherever we use a factor of appreciation, we have used 6%.

Figure 2.7
Future Value

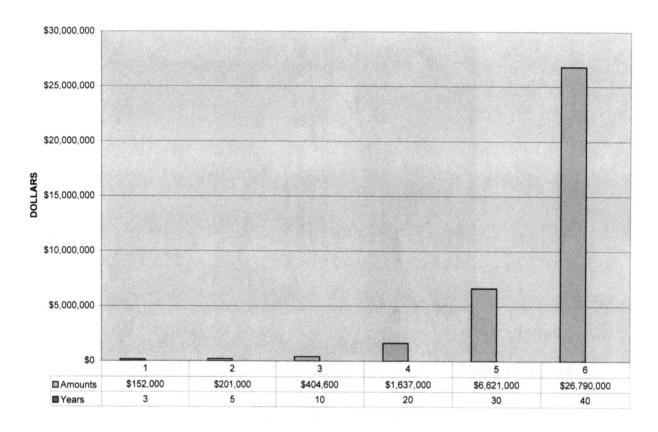

	1	2	3	4	5	6
▢ Amounts	$152,000	$201,000	$404,600	$1,637,000	$6,621,000	$26,790,000
▪ Years	3	5	10	20	30	40

Source: Based on Toronto Real Estate Board's average prices from 1966 to 2005 for single-family houses.

Frequently real property values overall are synchronized with inflation, but at a higher rate in a growing area such as the Greater Toronto Area market or lower in a depressed area. Therefore, it is important to realize that this is not the case all of the time. During a given period of time and in a given location, properties can increase in value at a rate lower, or higher, than the inflation rate, based on the factors influencing a particular local market. For example, based on the inflation rates from the Bank of Canada's Inflation Calculator (found at <www.bankofcanada.ca/en/inflation_calc.htm>) a $21,360 purchase in 1966 would cost $131,446 in 2005 versus a cost of $335,907 for a house in Toronto (see Figure 2.8). In the same 40 years, the inflation has only been an average of 4.77%/year. Why do we see housing prices rising at 6.36% in the Greater Toronto Area when the national average is so much lower? It's because the GTA has grown and prospered at a faster rate than the rest of Canada, due to strong regional economy, but mainly to its increase in population. This has created more demand for real estate, hence higher values. We have witnessed the same situation in other urban centres, specifically Vancouver and Calgary, and if current trends continue, we can expect to see real estate appreciation in the west significantly outpace the rest of Canada in the coming years.

Figure 2.8
Bank of Canada Inflation Calculator

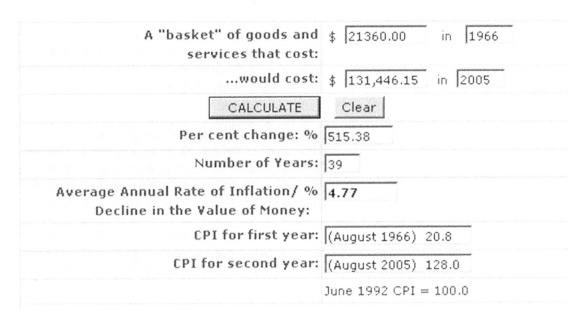

Source: Statistics Canada, Consumer Price Indexes for Canada, Monthly 1914-2006.

2.5.2 THE BENEFITS OF LEVERAGING

In commercial real estate, lenders will normally loan 60-75% of the value of the property. Therefore, a personal investment need be only 25-40% of the price of the property. This is called leveraging your investment. Leveraging can be either positive or negative. If the return, after deducting the mortgage payments, is higher than the Cap Rate (the return on money invested before deduction of the mortgage payments), the leverage is positive. If the net operating income is insufficient to cover the mortgage payments, the leverage is negative.

Negative leverage should only be tolerated for a short period of time, for example when you buy a neglected property which is under-performing and you know that you can markedly increase the income and/or reduce the expenses to turn the situation around.

Our definition of leveraging is based on cash flow. Some people prefer to say that the leverage is negative when the rate of the mortgage is higher than the Cap Rate. This implies that, in case of a blended mortgage payment, the investor will need to pay the portion representing the principal repayment from other sources. The difference between the two approaches stems from the fact that we take into account the blended payments on a mortgage, which includes the interest on the money borrowed, plus the amount of principal included with every payment. In other words, if we were talking about a mortgage that pays interest only, the two approaches would be identical.

Let's look more closely at the impact that leveraging can have, using as an example the purchase of a property for $1 million where the Cap Rate (return before financing) is 10%.

Without mortgage:
The purchase price is $1,000,000, and you pay cash.

Direct return (Cap Rate):	10%	$100,000
Plus appreciation (indirect return):	6%	$60,000
Total return:	(direct + indirect)	$160,000
Rate of return:	$160,000/$1,000,000 = 0.16 or	16%

Note that in this instance the rate of return on equity and the rate of return on investment (total value of the property) are identical.

With mortgage:
You invest $400,000 of your money and borrow 60% of the purchase price ($600,000) @ 7% interest, which amounts to interest of $42,000 per year.

Direct return:	($100,000 - $42,000):	$58,000
Rate of direct return:	($58,000/$400,000):	14.50%
Plus appreciation:	6%:	$60,000
Total return:	(direct + indirect)	$118,000
Total rate of return on equity:	($118,000/$400,000) = 0.295 or	29.50%

This example demonstrates how leveraging and appreciation can combine to make investment in commercial real estate very profitable.

Here is a formula to help you understand the impact of leverage on returns:

$$\frac{\text{rate of appreciation}}{\text{equity ratio}}$$

Note: The equity ratio is the percentage of cash (usually the down payment) an investor has in the property.

Examples for a $300,000 Property

Example 1: Down payment (equity) of $15,000 (5%)
(impossible dream!)

Appreciation:	6%		
	6/5 (equity ratio)	=	1.20 or 120%
Proof:	$15,000 x 120%	=	$18,000
Return on investment	$18,000/$15,000	=	1.20 or 120%

Example 2: Down payment (equity) of $30,000 (10%)
(almost impossible to achieve in real life!)

Appreciation:	6%		
	6/10(equity ratio)	=	0.60 or 60%
Proof:	$30,000 x 60%	=	$18,000
Return on investment:	$18,000/$30,000	=	0.60 or 60%

Example 3: Down payment (equity) of $45,000 (15%)

Appreciation:	6%		
	6/15 (equity ratio)	=	0.40 or 40%
Proof:	$45,000 x 40%	=	$18,000
Return on investment:	$18,000/$45,000	=	0.40 or 40%

CHAPTER 3

The Successful Investor

By the end of this chapter, you will be able to:
- Evaluate your tolerance for risk.
- Analyze and reduce the risk factors and create your own investment plan and strategies.
- Recognize when it is time to take the plunge.

Investors come in all shapes and forms with different means and tastes. Not all will be attracted to the same kind of assets; some look for passive investments, where they have little involvement with their properties, while others want to be involved in every little detail of managing the property; some will have higher risk tolerance, while others are income oriented and prefer lower-risk investments where the return comes primarily from cash flow from operations; and some, within the higher-risk tolerance group, may be happy with no cash flow (at least initially) and prefer properties with potential for rapid appreciation.

This was the case in Toronto when construction was announced for the Skydome (now called the Rogers Centre), the huge sports field with a retractable roof. Savvy investors bought old, small, two- or three-storey buildings in poor condition in the area and kept them rented for little income. Five or ten years later, when the Skydome went ahead, they reaped handsome profits from their vision and astuteness by selling them at much higher prices to small businesses such as bars and restaurants.

Another story that shows vision and business acumen is that of a large investment company. In 2001 it bought a Class AA, 43,850 m² (472,000 sq ft) office building in downtown Toronto for $110,000,000. The Cap Rate was outstandingly low at 4.5%. The rental rates in the building at the time ranged from $51.65 to $204.40 per m² ($4.80 to $19 sq ft) net (the building had been constructed in 1984). On the surface it appeared that this company was taking a great risk by over-paying due to low returns. However, 43% of the leases in place at the time of the sale were due to expire within two years and the rentals would then jump to market level, which was, at the time of the sale, approximately $323 per m² ($30 per sq ft) net.

The conservative investor likes the idea of investing in a large warehouse or an office building, rented for 15 years or more, to a Triple A tenant. That's great, but what happens if the tenant goes bankrupt like Enron or WorldCom, or moves out after 15 years? This investor will find himself with an empty building that must be sold or leased. He may have been happy for 15 years, but large buildings take much longer to lease or sell than smaller ones.

Basically, investing is the analysis of risk and potential returns represented by rentals and appreciation of the property. Although successful investors are skilled at recognizing value and predicting trends, the real secret of success is in knowing when making an investment is worth the risk. While some people think you can boil this down to a science — to personal discipline, organization and knowledge, we believe that it is, in great part, an art, too. We are referring to your ability to find capital, to your sensing that it is a good deal, to your ability to develop a vision for the property, and to your knowing that the location is good. Personally, we believe that the most important ingredient is the courage to take risks. Indeed, there are many would-be investors who can never go beyond the "analysis paralysis" stage, who can never take the plunge.

To become a successful and satisfied investor you need to make wise financial decisions and also understand your own investor profile so that you invest in properties that suit your style. To do this, it is important to build an investment plan that outlines your investment criteria before you buy your first property. Even for an experienced investor, a review of your current investment criteria may offer you some valuable insights as you continue to expand your real estate holdings. We will discuss your investment plan later in this chapter, but first you need to understand risk.

3.1 UNDERSTANDING RISK

Evaluate your tolerance for risk.

Basically, risk is the possibility of something bad happening. Everyone faces some risks — for example, the risk of getting sick or, if you drive a car, the risk of an accident. These risks are known as "pure risks". Pure risks offer only two possible outcomes: things stay the same or you lose something. They offer no offsetting possibility of gain.

With investment risk there are three possible outcomes: things stay the same, you lose, or you gain. When it comes to investment risk in real estate, there is the possibility that your property will decline in value or not give you the return you expect. Or you may realize a solid income stream and benefit from appreciation or other favourable market conditions, producing a stronger return on investment than expected.

Risk is present in any venture, be it marriage, career, or investing. More important than the level of risk is your reaction to it. Some people have higher risk tolerance than others. They will sleep well at night even if they have made a high-risk investment, while those with low-risk tolerance will lose sleep worrying. An investor must determine — and it is not easy — the level of risk that he can bear. Keep in mind, however, that one gets used to taking risk without losing sleep.

Risk and returns go hand-in-hand.

The ultra-conservative investor abhors risking money. The other side of the coin is that he is unlikely to ever get rich, since risk and rewards go hand-in-hand. Generally, the higher the risk, the higher the potential return, but also the greater the potential for loss. For most newcomers to real estate investments, it is better to be conservative and to start investing with a smaller property.

Your level of risk tolerance is one of the factors that will determine the type of property in which you will invest. For example, a $2-million property could have various levels of risk depending on the type of building purchased, as shown in the following (where 1 represents the lowest possible risk and 5 the highest):

- office building (5/5)
- single occupancy 3,700 m² (40,000 sq ft) industrial building (4/5)
- strip plaza with six tenants (3/5) and
- apartment building with 40 suites (1/5).

Note that office buildings pose the highest risk on this list while an apartment building with 40 suites poses the lowest. Office buildings are highly susceptible to downturns in the economy. During such downturns, people still need to live somewhere, so apartment buildings will be impacted least. Even with a 10% vacancy rate, a 40-suite building would have 36 occupied units producing rental income for the investor. Bear in mind that the risk levels shown may change over time, given, for example, vacancy rates, growth, or deterioration of an area.

Most properties are bought with the help of mortgage financing. The debt ratio (amount of debt to the value of the property), also called the Loan to Value (LTV) ratio, is an important indicator of risk. An LTV of 60% is considered reasonable and would amount to a $600,000 mortgage on a $1-million property (assuming that this price reflects its true market value). However, the amount of borrowing should be proportionate to the cash flow risk. Therefore, a property leased for 20 years to the government could be financed at 100%, while one leased to a credit risk should be financed at only 40% or 50%, if at all. It is our contention that 95% of real estate investments turn sour because of mortgages that are too large.

3.1.1 REDUCING RISK THROUGH DIVERSIFICATION

There are two ways of looking at diversification — don't diversify, but rather focus and become expert in one area, or diversify so that, as the saying goes, you don't put all your eggs in one basket. Both are defensible positions. Although there are many opportunities for diversification in real estate, geographical location and property category are the most common.

(a) Geographical Diversification

When it comes to geographical diversification in real estate, there are two schools of thought — invest in more than one market to cushion yourself from localized ups and downs, or focus exclusively on one market, which you can end up knowing extremely well.

We feel that the small- to medium-size investor should focus only on one geographical area. After you have reached a reasonably large size, it is a good idea to be in more than one market, to avoid having all your assets in one particular area that one day will no doubt go through some difficult economic times.

(b) Category Diversification

There are also two schools of thought when it comes to diversification through building class (retail, office, industrial, multi-family) — take any good deal that comes along or focus exclusively on one type of property.

We have the same recommendation here that we had for geographical diversification. The small- to medium-size investor should focus on one category of property and learn the ins and outs of that category before branching out into other property types. We view this as even more important than the geographical diversification.

The skills and knowledge required to own and manage a strip plaza are very different from those necessary for an office building or a medical building. In fact, this is one key reason why some investors do not fare as well as they should in certain investments. It is a question of personality and affinity. For example, investors who don't like detail or dealing with many small, frequently unsophisticated tenants would probably be poor at managing small, multiple-occupancy industrial units, but would fare well with large industrial buildings.

3.1.2 THE BEGINNER'S (OR START-UP) RISK

In some cases, there is less risk for a medium or large investor than a small one because the more tenants one has, the more easily one can weather a few vacancies. Another risk factor is the investor's degree of expertise. A knowledgeable investor with a "poor" property (i.e., poor quality tenants, poor location, run-down building, high vacancies, etc.) is at less risk than an investor who owns a good property, but has only limited knowledge. In other words, it is better to have a good captain than a good boat.

Indeed, the knowledgeable investor knows the "truth of the trade". He is more likely to explain (justify) to a tenant why the latter should pay a higher rental rate at renewal time and will negotiate periodic rental increases during the lease term. He is more likely to have reserves (money set aside) for the unexpected repair. The knowledgeable investor will practice preventive maintenance and allocate money intelligently to make the repairs and renovations that will attract better tenants. He appeals property tax hikes. Finally, the knowledgeable investor will be more aggressive when looking for quality tenants.

In the final analysis, how many real estate investors, honestly and truly, intelligently analyze their risk tolerance? Most are, or have been, in business running companies that manufacture peanut butter, or paper clips, or plastic parts. Or, maybe they are distributors or retailers. In their own businesses they face a myriad of risks daily: strikes, employee sickness or absenteeism, machines breaking down, obsolete inventory, staff theft, accidents of all kinds, customers who don't pay their bills, a tangle of government regulations, unreliable suppliers, etc. It's important to keep these risks in mind and how you deal with them when considering the risks of investing in real estate.

A similar approach would be to apply the diversification rule when investing in the stock market to real estate investments. For example, it is better to own four 4,650 m² (50,000 sq ft) industrial buildings than one 18,580 m² (200,000 sq ft) building. In a perfect world and with considerable financial means, an investor would have properties of different sizes, in two or three different markets, and in two or three real estate specialties. This would diminish risk considerably.

In real life, for the small- to medium-size investor, it is best to work in your backyard — that is, close to where you live or work, where you are familiar with the market, and close by to deal with problems with the property as they arise.

To summarize, there is less risk if, for a given amount invested, one has more tenants, more buildings, in more locations. However, this will vary with the times. In 2002, a sophisticated US corporation recommended, for large investors, the least risky but still financially performing real estate portfolio as consisting of the following:
- 40% multi-family
- 20% industrial
- 20% office, and
- 20% retail.

On the other hand, a high-risk portfolio might be composed of the following:
- 55% office
- 15% multi-family
- 15% industrial, and
- 15% retail.

You can now better understand why we say throughout this book that a multi-family property is low risk. Of course, this takes into account a number of factors, most of them beyond the control of the average investor, including politics, economy, vacancy rates, supply and demand, e-commerce, etc.

3.2 DEVELOPING YOUR INVESTMENT PLAN

Analyze and reduce the risk factors and create your own investment plan and strategies.

There are, of course, many steps you can take to reduce your risk of failure. The most important of these is to plan your approach. Even if you are an experienced investor, it is a good idea to periodically review your investment criteria to ensure that you are on track. Following are factors you need to consider:
- amount of investment money available
- appetite for risk
- your time investment
- desired degree of involvement
- financial investment criteria
- factors determining the ideal holding period
- real estate cycles
- get-rich-quick schemes, and
- the tortoise and the hare.

3.2.1 AMOUNT OF INVESTMENT MONEY AVAILABLE

Time and time again, when a real estate agent asks an investor how much money he has available, the answer is, "It depends". We don't think "it depends" is an acceptable answer. You should know before starting out the maximum amount of cash you have available. If you are considering involving a co-investor, you need to clarify how much the other person is willing to invest before getting started.

3.2.2 APPETITE FOR RISK

Although real estate risk is far more controllable than that of some other types of investments, it is still greater than investing in bonds or GICs. You must consider how much risk you are prepared to take and what you can do to limit your risk. In the stock market, the investor has very little opportunity to influence the value or degree of risk of his investments. Instead, the stockholder's investment return rides the roller coaster of the public's expectations. Real estate, on the other hand, when properly managed, is a significantly less volatile investment. Its value is generally based on the intrinsic worth of the investment, not other people's perceptions.

There are a number of techniques that can be used to reduce real estate risk. Examples of these factors include: the triple net lease (see sections 7.4.3 and 7.4.10(a) in Chapter 7), the number and quality of the tenants, staggered lease expiration dates, diversification of tenants, diversification of investments, and intelligent respect for timing in the real estate cycle. Of these factors, the ability to diversify is the most important.

3.2.3 YOUR TIME INVESTMENT

Consider how much time you can devote to managing your properties. If an investor does not have the time, or the inclination, to manage the property, a property management company can be hired, generally at a cost of 3-5% of the gross rental income. It is also preferable to use a property manager if you have limited knowledge. Real estate mistakes can be costly. In addition, particularly if there are multiple tenants, a professional property manager will generally achieve better results.

3.2.4 DESIRED DEGREE OF INVOLVEMENT

Consider how involved you want to be in your investments. If you buy a $20-million newly built warehouse, leased for 20 years on a net basis to an established multinational company, it will generate truly passive income. That is, you will have to do little to earn the income. However, if you buy a retail strip centre with eight tenants, you will need to be a little less passive and a little more involved with your investment property. Or you may choose to buy two multiple-occupancy industrial buildings with a total of 60 tenants and could find yourself very involved in managing the business, generating what must then be called "active income". Note that an investor always has the choice to remain a passive investor by using a property management company. This option can be costly, so if the investor has the opportunity (that is, cannot make more money elsewhere), the inclination, and the desire to learn, he may be better off performing the property management duties.

Note that in Canada, if a real estate investment corporation has five or more full-time employees throughout the year, its income will be classified as active business. This means that the corporation will not be entitled to the preferrential tax treatment, a corporate tax reduction, that applies to a Canadian-controlled Private Corporation (CCPC). This treatment consists of an annual tax credit of 16% with a maximum business limit of the corporation's active business income, which is generally $400,000.

3.2.5 FINANCIAL INVESTMENT CRITERIA

An investor needs to be cautious and follow a system in making buying decisions. The level of financial investment can be considerable and a haphazard approach or buying on impulse can lead to costly mistakes. Before you begin your search for an investment property, establish your financial investment criteria based on the investment considerations in Chapter 2 (see section 2.3.1). Write down your criteria, even if they are modest and take only a few lines. Then you must decide between three major variables.

> *An investor needs to be cautious and follow a system in making buying decisions.*

1. **Type of Property.** Do you want an office building or an industrial property; single or multi-tenancies; what size of units; total area of building; what is your price point?
2. **Geographical Area.** Is it important for your property to be close to home or can it be two hours away?
3. **Personal Preferences.** Is it acceptable to you that a property not be rented, or fully rented, when you purchase it? One of our clients bought a four-plex with three of the four units empty. It did not bother him because he wanted to renovate the three units and he knew that within three months he'd be able to rent them for more money than the vendor had been getting. Another client bought a 26-unit multi-family building with five basement units vacant. However, he felt confident he could lease the empty apartments easily, so he negotiated and was credited with the equivalent of one year of rentals in the statement of adjustments at closing time.

Here is an example of the investment criteria sent to us by a large investor, with more than $30 million to invest.

Our general investment criteria are as follows:
- Quality product of class A to B in nature
- Located in: Ontario, Quebec, and Southeast USA
- Minimum 75,000 square feet
- Cap Rates at 11% or better, or reasonable cash on cash return based on income in place with upside potential through vacancy factors and lease rollovers
- Demographics with a middle to upper class population of at least 100,000 or more within a five-mile radius, and
- Good parking ratios, traffic counts, and access.

Retail Criteria:
- Average household income $40,000 or higher
- Strip centre, with foodcourt, or other anchor
- Excellent visibility
- Good ingress/egress with median cuts, preferably located at a signalised corner, and
- Minimum 5 to 1 parking ratio (number of parking spaces per 1,000 sq ft of gross leasable area).

Industrial/Flex Criteria:
- Truck level or grade level shipping
- 18 to 24 foot — plus ceiling heights
- Minimum 3 to 1 parking ratio, and
- Close to major highway.

Office Criteria:
- Minimum 4 to 1 parking ratio, and
- Close to major highway.

Together with the expansion of our existing portfolio, we may be interested in acquiring older, near vacant properties, in need of capital expenditures. We are also interested in climate-controlled, self-storage facilities and unanchored strip shopping centres.

As investors able to conduct quick and thorough analysis together with a reputation as closers, we look forward to receiving properties for potential acquisition.

3.2.6 FACTORS DETERMINING THE IDEAL HOLDING PERIOD

The holding period refers to the length of time a property is held before it is sold. Four factors influence the holding period:

1. **Capital Cost Allowance (CCA).** The depreciation of a building (CCA) starts anew with each owner. The first year it is 2%, then 4% per year on the declining balance. This means that, as time goes by, you can shelter less and less of the income from taxes.
2. **Mortgage Amortization.** In the life of a mortgage, little principal is repaid at the beginning, but a lot of interest is paid. The inverse is true towards the end of the mortgage amortization period. This has an impact on taxes since only the interest from a property income can be deducted as an expense.
3. **Repairs.** If the building acquired is new, or in excellent condition, you can assume that you will not have any major replacements (asphalt, heating and air-conditioning systems, roof) for 10, 15, or 20 years. However, there will come a time when these replacements will have to be made, which explains why the Canadian Revenue Agency (CRA) allows the 4% yearly deduction for CCA. Of course, these capital expenditures increase the capital base in the property.
4. **Need for Cash.** If you need cash, you will sell, right? Not necessarily. You may be able to refinance, increasing your LTV ratio (see Chapter 11) and still hold onto the property. Many sophisticated investors will refinance before the end of the term of the existing financing. This frees up cash to be used elsewhere and one does not pay income tax on this refinance money.

A general rule for your investment program should be to avoid selling any property. This rule can be broken if (low) returns show that the property should not have been bought in the first place or if the property now commands a very low Cap Rate due to unusual appreciation, disequilibrium in the market, or timing in the real estate cycle. And, it could happen that you come across the "deal of a lifetime" and must sell one property to free up the cash to acquire a better property.

3.2.7 REAL ESTATE CYCLES

Develop a great deal of respect for timing. Many people, including a number of long-time investors, follow the latest "real estate fashion trend". Various types of properties (industrial, office, etc.) are more, or less, popular depending on the period. For example, apartment buildings during the 2000 to 2007 period were a popular investment in Canada and the United States, but will not stay so forever. The problem is that too many people follow the crowd, buying yesterday's winners. There is nothing wrong with buying at the beginning or in the middle of a trend, but it is not recommended that you do so at the end of it. And unless you are closely attuned to the market, you have great advisors and lots of cash, you will rarely be at the forefront of a trend.

Real estate is linked to the fortune of businesses, since most revenue-producing properties house businesses, with the exception of apartment buildings, governments, and institutions. Business goes in cycles. It is feast or famine, usually with some short periods of equilibrium between. To make significant money, you have to be a contrarian. This means that you buy when most other people are filled with pessimism, thinking that the Earth is soon going to stop spinning, and vice versa. Bargains, both in terms of price and purchasing terms, can be had only when everybody else is thinking, "Boy, things are really bad". Of course, it takes a strong personality to go against the tide, but it is only hard at the beginning!

As an example, a sophisticated businessman, Mel, borrowed money and bought a site consisting of two acres of industrial land for $110,000 per acre. The land was, in 1989, at the very height of the Toronto market, in an excellent location – "in the path of development". Four years later, in 1993, an investor, Jack, bought the piece of land abutting Mel's for $30,000 per acre. It had the same zoning, services, frontage, exposure, etc., but the vendor was in trouble. Four years hence, in 1997, both men sold their land for $110,000 per acre. The profit to Mel was zero, less carrying costs and property taxes for 8 years, which amounted to a loss of $84,750 per acre ($194,750 - $110,000). The profit for Jack was $68,000 ($10,000 - $42,000) per acre ($30,000 plus carrying charges and taxes for 4 years). See Figure 3.1 for calculations.

Figure 3.1
Market Timing

Date	Mel	Jack
1989	$110,000	
1990	Interest (at 7%) on 110,000 = $7,700 + taxes of $500 = $8,200 = $117,700 property Total invested: $118,200	
1991	7% of $118,200 = $8,274 = $126,474 + taxes of $500 = $126,974	
1992	7% of $126,974 = $8,888 = $135,862 + taxes of $550 = $136,412	
1993	7% of $136,412 = $9,548 = $145,961 + taxes of $550 = $146,511	$30,000
1994	7% of $146,511 = $10,256 = $156,767 + taxes of $600 = $157,367	7% of $30,000 = $2,100 = $32,100 + taxes of $600 = $32,700
1995	7% of $157,367 = $11,016 = $168,382 + taxes of $600 = $168,982	7% of $32,700 = $2,289 = $34,989 + taxes of $600 = $35,589
1996	7% of $168,982 = $11,829 = $180,811 + taxes of $600 = $181,410	7% of $35,589 = $2,491 = $38, 080 + taxes of $600 = $38,680
1997	7% of $181,410 = $12,699 = $194,110 + taxes of $650 = ($194,750)	7% of $38,680 = $2,708 = $41,388 + taxes of $650 = $42,038

Economists have long debated economic cycles in terms of their causes, predictability, and duration. While most agree that there are no predictable patterns to these cycles, others contend that long-term cycles are caused primarily by demographics, transportation patterns, infrastructure, and government policies. Others attribute economic trends to interest rates, general economic conditions, and consumer's confidence and, therefore, spending. Short-term cycles, which some define as lasting between 6 and 10 years,

There are four phases in a real estate cycle: development, overbuilding, adjustment, acquisition.

have a more regional impact than the longer-term cycles, which tend to have a national impact.

Real estate runs in cycles, of varying supply and demand levels, which affect prices more than any other factor, even interest rates. There are four phases to each cycle commonly known as the following:

1. development (optimism),
2. overbuilding (uncertainty),
3. adjustment (pessimism), and
4. acquisition (hesitant optimism).

- **Phase 1 – Development.** Symptoms: Inventory is low and demand is strong; developers respond by building new units; completion time lags demand; prices rise sharply; optimism prevails. Strategy: Buy very early in the phase if the price is right; sell as the phase matures for a short-term profit; remember the maxim "make your money when you buy rather than when you sell"; the late development phase, early over-building phase, is the optimum time to sell.
- **Phase 2 – Overbuilding.** Symptoms: New-construction starts exceed demand; prices level off; demand slows; optimism turns to uncertainty. Strategy: Sell and do it fast; don't hold out for top dollar; timing is more important; if you don't sell now, be prepared to wait for several more years.
- **Phase 3 – Adjustment.** Symptoms: Demand slows even more; new-construction starts to drop sharply but units already under way continue to come on line; inventory peaks and prices decline; power-of-sales are more frequent; pessimism prevails. Strategy: Hold what you have for the long-term sale; be slow to buy but start buying distress sales late in the phase.
- **Phase 4 – Acquisition.** Symptoms: New construction starts are at a virtual standstill; prices have bottomed out; demand is slow but steady; new inventory is down; resale prices firm up; pessimism is beginning to fade. Strategy: Buy now; the early part of the acquisition phase is the ideal time to invest; sell only if you can quickly roll your equity into something more valuable; the next phase will bring sharply increased prices (refer back to Phase 1).

Real estate cycles are not isolated from other economic events. In fact, usually a downturn in the real estate market follows a downturn in economic activity, which can be caused by a myriad of things. As the Canadian economy lags that of the US by about 6 to 12 months, commercial real estate, in turn, takes 6 to 12 months to reach its most critical stage. As you can see, it is difficult to pinpoint exactly when a crisis will start. In fact, it is not possible to say exactly when a specific point of the cycle took place, even after the fact.

Another school of thought relates the real estate cycles to that of a city or neighbourhood.
- **Boom (high).**
  - Everybody makes money.
  - Properties are flipped overnight for huge profits.

 – Money can be borrowed easily and at good rates.
• **Equilibrium (middle).**
 – "Normal" business situation.
• **Downturn (low).**
 – Where the "art of surviving a crisis" makes the difference.

Regardless of how you view the cycles, there is no doubt that they occur; the trick is to be aware that a change is coming before it hits you. In most cases, there are signs a turnaround is coming if you watch for them. The main problem facing many investors is that they hear and see the signs, but refuse to acknowledge and act on them. To drive our point home, you will find below a few excerpts from a popular blog that follows the housing market in the United States <www.thehousingbubble.blogspot.com/2005_05_01_thehousingbubble_archive.html>. These will be followed by taking another look at the same blog in September 2006. The following are a few comments from mid-2005:

Even before the sales numbers were released today, economists were sounding alarm bells. "I think this is actually the biggest [real estate] bubble in U.S. history and possibly even world history," Yale University economist Robert Shiller said in a telephone interview yesterday (May 23, 2005).

Princeton University economist and columnist for the NY *Times*, Paul Krugman, was open in his assessment of the US housing market while making a speech overseas. "Macro indicators suggest that the market is speculative mania. Day trading cannot be sustainable. There is a real bubble mentality in the US housing market," Prof Krugman said, adding that prices of US housing were 250% of their real values.

Hold onto your hats because the Oracle from Omaha [Warren Buffett] just threw a ton of controversy into the bubble discussion. He and Munger issued stern new warnings about the residential real estate "bubble," the destabilizing effect of hedge funds on the financial markets, and the possibility of another terrorist strike against the United States.

The following comments were taken from the blog in late 2006:

The Bakersfield Californian. "The housing market's slowdown, and the resulting loss in jobs, could mean a painful adjustment is in store for Kern County's economy, experts say. The construction industry has led the way in job creation over the past five years, said Cal State Bakersfield economics professor Abbas Grammy."

The Sydney Morning Herald in Australia. "This is Sydney's cheapest unit. The one-bedroom unit in Cambramatta sold at auction last week for $95,000. In November 2003 it cost $262,500."

From *Newsday* in New York. "For the first time in nine years, Nassau County's closed median home prices dropped over the last year, leaving experts to wonder whether the housing market's downturn could be more significant, and longer-lasting, than first thought."

"This is the turn that we've been waiting for for a long time," said Pearl Kamer, the chief economist of the Long Island Association. "This is only the beginning of the downward cycle and only the beginning of the unwinding of the housing bubble. The price declines could continue for a long time."

Finally, from a man whose name is admired in Canadian real estate circles, came a very clear message. "Reichmann knows property meltdowns: It's time to sell" read the headline in the *Globe and Mail* in the June 30, 2005, article by real estate reporter Elizabeth Church.

We are convinced, like many others, that the Reichmann family is plenty smart when it comes to real estate. The media offers a multitude of clues about when a market is about to turn, although there is never a specific date when that will start and sometimes it takes a long time. The savvy investor acts cautiously in such a market and resists the temptation to jump on the band wagon.

For example, in mid-2003, we were in the development phase. The market was riding high. It was a good time to sell, or so it seemed at the time. But, if, as an owner, you had sold then, your friends would have told you, "You sold too soon" and, with the wisdom of hindsight, they would have been right. You may have left something on the table, but you would have controlled your risk. Remember, however, that in any phase, one can find bargains. It is only harder, in the "wrong" phase.

The thing to remember is that you can find good, or at least decent, buys in any phase of a real estate cycle, but you should weigh things more carefully when the market is clearly overheating. The key is to analyze each situation in order to anticipate the needs, dangers, and opportunities that the next phase will have on the situation or specific property. The safe, and foolproof, way is to always be conservative, but many opportunities are then lost. The smart way is to take medium risks by analyzing phases, but at the same time protect yourself when you acquire each property by doing so in the name of separate corporations and risking only a decided-upon-in-advance, conservative fraction of your assets in each property.

3.2.8 GET-RICH-QUICK SCHEMES

There are many people out there who offer get-rich-quick schemes through investing in real estate. The ones that irk us most are those who advocate buying with no money down (zero down) or looking at 100 houses for each one you buy. They never tell you how much time this requires or how emotionally exhausting it would be. Too frequently, this get-rich-quick advice leads to someone being cheated. Looking to "steal" a property, with zero down, is a far-fetched dream. It may be possible, though rare, to make a decent investment on such a basis in Canada, but it is a little bit like failing to lay a solid foundation when erecting a house and jumping directly into the construction of the main floor.

> *Too frequently, "get rich quick" advice leads to someone being cheated.*

3.2.9 THE TORTOISE AND THE HARE

You know the story. The hare was so sure of his speed that he could afford to gallivant, smell the flowers, etc. The tortoise, on the other hand, knew that he was slow, that he had to be steady, to keep on pushing, and he won. Some people (most of us) would love a quick windfall, like winning the lottery. Similarly, most of us would like to make a killing in real estate in one or two years. Unfortunately, 999 times out of 1000, it does not work. The odds of such "overnight" success are astronomically low. A suitable epitaph for most failures, in real estate (and in business) would be: too big, too fast.

Make your plan; implement it; stick to it; slow and steady; and you will win — big.

Cynthia Needles Fletcher and Laura Sternwein of Iowa State University published some excellent advice on saving and investing in August 2006 ("Money Mechanics – Saving and Investing" <www.extension.iastate.edu/Publications/PM1462.pdf>). Here is an excerpt:

You may need to change your lifestyle to make savings a part of your budget.

- **Pay yourself first.** Consider savings as a fixed expense similar to the rent or utility bill. Put away some money before you do anything else with your paycheck. Have funds automatically deducted from your paycheck and put into a savings plan.
- **Save windfall income.** The theory is simple. You got along without the tax refund or gift, so why not save it? A similar tip is to save monthly loan payments after a loan is repaid.
- **Change your lifestyle.** Finding money to save may require some major changes. Moving to less costly housing or making do with one car could free up hundreds of dollars each month. Cutting back on eating out, entertainment, and daily trips to the vending machine — over time — can yield more savings.
- **Join America Saves.** Sign up for this free program that encourages you to chart your progress toward a savings goal. You'll receive a free newsletter and get free advice by phone or e-mail from financial planners. This national campaign involves more than 1,000 organizations — including Cooperative Extension — and encourages families to save and build wealth. For more information see www.americasaves.org.

If you could do with more encouragement, go to <www.ag.ndsu.edu/pubs/yf/fammgmt/fe258w.htm>.

3.3 EXCESSIVE CAUTION LEADS TO PARALYSIS

Recognize when it is time to take the plunge.

Even with your investment plan in hand you may hesitate to commit yourself to real estate investing. Perhaps you feel you don't have enough knowledge. Do not let this stop you. There are a number of real estate professionals who can advise you or even partner with you in your first venture — real estate agents, developers, appraisers, builders. Consider proposing a joint venture with someone who has a proven track record. You contribute the money and they contribute the knowledge and time, while you learn from the experience.

We offer the following advice to vacillating investors when they face the "to buy or to pass" question. It is always possible to find fault with a property and decide not to buy it. However, decades of experience have shown us that 99.9 times out of 100, buyers are glad they overcame their doubts and bought the property. There are many, many more vendors who are sorry to have sold than buyers who are sorry to have bought.

3.3.1 FINANCIAL IMPACTS OF NOT BUYING

Some people refuse to buy a property because it is too expensive, or the timing is not right, or for any other reason. Let's look at the economic consequences of this decision (to do nothing).

Usually, as an alternative, investors "park" their money in a money market fund, which pays 2-3% before taxes. The after-tax return is 1.2-1.8%. If a person has $500,000, this represents: $500,000 x 1.5% = $7,500.

Let's assume that the property to be purchased is priced at $2,000,000, the Net Operating Income (NOI) is $160,000, the down payment is $500,000, the Cap Rate is 8%, the CCA is 4% (we disregard the half-year rule), the mortgage is at 6.25%, and the tax rate is 46%.

The return for a buyer of this property is:

NOI =			$160,000

Income deductions:

Mortgage payments (interest only: $1,500,000 x 6.25%)	=	$93,750
CCA:	$1,600,00 x 4%	=	$64,000
Total:			**$157,750**
Taxable income	($160,000 - $157,750):		$ 2,250
Tax payable:	$2,250 x 46%	=	$ 1,035

Property's direct and indirect return after tax:

Direct return:			$1,035
CCA (+ tax postponing):			$64,000
Appreciation (indirect return):	$2,000,000 x 6%	=	$120,000
After-tax return:			**$185,035**

Return on Equity (ROE) after tax:
  (a) including CCA, if the building is like new (no repairs required): $185,035/$500,000 = 37.01%
  (b) excluding CCA: $185,035 – $64,000 = $121,035/$500,000   = 24.21%
Return with money market: $500,000 x 1.5%   = $7,500
Difference in:
  (a) $185,035 - $7,500 = $177,535
  (b) $121,035 - $7,500 = $113,535

Just in case you still need an extra push, meditate over the following: if you keep doing what you did yesterday, how can you expect your future to be any different? Obviously, you were doing something wrong if you did not get where you wanted to be.

3.3.2 LETTER TO A POTENTIAL REAL ESTATE INVESTOR

If we had to write a letter to somebody who was considering taking the plunge into real estate investing, it would go something like this:

You are absolutely right to want to invest in real estate, but we must warn you that unless you have a very powerful charm protecting you, you will:
- tremble with fear
- sweat big drops
- literally panic, thinking that you are finished
- despair at finding a solution
- hesitate as to what to do, and
- be forced to consider many options, then have to discard most of them.

On the other hand, you will learn to:
- overcome your hesitations
- become a stronger person and a much better manager
- be proud of your accomplishments
- become master of your own destiny
- not be afraid of empty buildings
- be successful
- acquire skills that you can use anywhere in the world
- become a better negotiator, and
- become a better businessperson.

PART 2

Understanding the Industry

CHAPTER

4

Land-Use Controls

By the end of this chapter you will be able to:
- Work within the regulatory system at any government level.
- Decipher zoning by-laws and apply for amendments.
- Walk through the steps for a site plan approval.
- Understand the purpose and process in obtaining a building permit.
- Know what Committees of Adjustment deal with and how to follow their processes.
- Recognize the purpose and scope of the Ontario Municipal Board.
- Appreciate the blessings and curses of a heritage property.
- Find a way to work with municipal planners.

Given the importance of land use to our overall economy and our quality of life, it is not surprising that all levels of government have a hand in regulating its use. This section is based on Ontario's regulatory system, which is typical of those across the country. As a real estate investor you should familiarize yourself with the overall system of controls, including the legislation around urban planning, zoning, building permits, etc., and what is involved in seeking changes or variance in these controls. This familiarity will, for example, let you avoid costly delays or missed opportunities to acquire a good (and hopefully better) tenant, who will usually increase the value of your property. You may even choose to resell the property and cash in on your investment if you feel the increased value justifies you doing so.

4.1 PLANNING IN ONTARIO

Work within the regulatory system at any government level.

In Ontario, the major controls on land use come from the *Planning Act* (R.S.O. 1990, c. P.13), Provincial Policy Statements, and Official Plans (OP). Zoning by-laws, which affect real estate investors on a day-to-day level, are passed by municipalities to regulate the implementation of the OPs.

4.1.1 THE PLANNING ACT

Provincial legislation, in the form of the *Planning Act*, regulates and controls land use and delegates certain controls to the municipalities. The Act deals with such issues as the following: the percentage of land reserved for housing, employment, and recreation; conservation of natural resources; waste management; provision of educational, health, social, cultural, and recreational facilities; and the appropriate location of growth and development. It also provides guidelines for the creation of local planning advisory committees, planning areas, and the development of OPs. The *Planning Act* is a kind of instruction manual for regional and municipal planners. Land owners are affected only indirectly by it.

4.1.2 PROVINCIAL PLANNING POLICY STATEMENTS

A new "policy" is issued by the governing political party at the beginning of a new term and is often re-cast every time the non-incumbent political party comes to power. The statement provides policy direction on matters of provincial interest related to land-use planning and development. In Ontario, it sets the policy foundation for regulating the development and use of land, while protecting resources of provincial interest, public health and safety, and the quality of the environment. Provincial plans or locally generated policies regarding matters of municipal interest may complement the Provincial Policy Statement.

4.1.3 OFFICIAL PLANS – REGIONAL, MUNICIPAL, AND SECONDARY

An Official Plan (OP) is a set of projections and studies, prepared by planners in a given area, to loosely project future growth of a community planning area. You could say that an OP is the planning of a town seen from far above, right down to the neighbourhood level. OPs are concerned with development principles, such as deciding that overall residential housing shall be no more than 100 persons per hectare (40 persons per acre) or that employment lands shall generate 200 jobs per hectare (80 jobs per acre), and identifying primary land use (residential, industrial, office, recreational, etc.) and primary land-use issues, and with phasing or timing of municipal work, such as the installation of services in a neighbourhood.

Not surprisingly, planners spend years preparing an OP, taking all possible factors into account, including demographics, geography, topography, servicing, population growth, etc. Public hearings are held for all plans, so that members of the public can have their say. The municipality or region takes into account the input it has received and modifies the plan, which is subsequently adopted by way of a by-law. OPs must be sent to the provincial Minister of Municipal Affairs for approval, but this step is no longer required of a number of Regional OPs. OPs must be updated every five years, as required by the *Planning Act* of Ontario.

There are three types of Official Plans: regional, municipal, and secondary. The Regional OP is king and must be created first because Municipal and Secondary OPs must conform to it. Although Municipal OPs follow the direction of the Regional OP, they are much more detailed. For example, the Region may designate an area "employment lands", and the Municipality will decide how much of that land will be for light industry and how much for heavy industry. Secondary Plans, or Neighbourhood Plans, take planning down to a still finer level.

There are three types of Official Plans: regional, municipal, and secondary.

Municipalities are divided into many smaller areas or neighbourhoods. Each neighbourhood is studied in detail, producing a Neighbourhood Study, also called a Secondary Study, that deals with a myriad of details for each neighbourhood, including the availability and difficulties of installing services (water, sanitary sewer, storm sewer, gas, electricity, cable TV, telephone, etc.), road networks, environmental concerns (such as retention of rain water), need for schools, libraries, public transportation, etc. Type of land use is then decided, right down to each parcel of land.

4.2 ZONING AND ZONING BY-LAWS

Decipher zoning by-laws and apply for amendments.

The more familiar investors are with zoning and zoning by-laws, the better their situation. Indeed, zoning has a major impact on property value.

Zoning by-laws are passed by municipalities and administered by planning departments to regulate the use of land at the zone level. In broad terms, they specify the type of land use permitted — such as agricultural, industrial, commercial, residential, etc. If more than one use is allowed, it is zoned "mixed use". To give you an idea of the number of zones that can exist, Figure 4.1 shows the typical zones and corresponding symbols from a city by-law.

Zoning by-laws also specify exactly what can take place on a parcel of land and how the structures are to be located. For example, a property might be given a zoning designation of "industrial, category 2, with outside storage". Permitted uses, such as "pallet manufacturing", may also be specified and listed. Maximum density and coverage (how many square metres per hectare (square feet per acre), maximum percentage of the land to be covered by the building), setbacks, maximum height of buildings, how many parking spaces, maximum percentage of the site to be hard surfaces (asphalt, concrete), minimum percentage to be landscaped, and even the number and size of trees can be specified.

Figure 4.1
Zones and Symbols

Zone	Symbol	Zone	Symbol
Agricultural 1	A1	Convenience Commercial	CC
Agricultural 2	A2	Shopping Centre Commercial	SCC
Urban Residential 1	UR1	Rural Highway Commercial	RHC
Urban Residential 2	UR2	Urban Light Industrial	ULM
Urban Residential 3	UR3	Urban Industrial	UM
Urban Residential 4	UR4	Rural Industrial	RM
Urban Residential 5	UR5	Extractive Industrial	EM
Estate Residential	ER	Institutional	I
Hamlet Residential	HR	Open Space	OS
Communally Serviced	CSR-1	Recreational Open Space	ROS
Residential	CSR-2		
	CSR-3		
Urban Commercial Core	UCC	Environmental Protection	EP
Urban Highway Commercial	UHC	Waste Management	WM

The establishment of the zoning for a particular site can vary as to its timing. According to circumstances and depending on the municipality, the zoning may be done wholesale, for an entire neighbourhood, for a particular site, or only for a site at the time a building permit is requested. If the zoning concerns only one property and differs, or has been changed, from the area zoning, it is said to be site specific.

Properties often violate zoning by-laws. It is usually for minor things, such as an industrial building being zoned to permit 10% retail, but in fact having 15% of its floor area devoted to retail. There are two main reasons for a building inspector to find a zoning by-law infraction — following a request for a building permit or other cause for inspection, or investigating a complaint from a third party (usually a neighbour).

If a change to a zoning by-law is necessary to allow a property owner to change the use of a property, erect a building that doesn't comply, or change some other standard, the property owner may apply to the city for an amendment to the by-law. The city or the Ontario Municipal Board must approve any amendment. This can be a time-consuming process, but is usually worthwhile because re-zoning can have a significant impact on the value of a property. Figure 4.2 presents a flow chart that shows the process for by-law amendment in the City of Owen Sound, Ontario. You may also find that other permits or approvals may be required, such as an OP Amendment (see section 4.2.5) if the proposed use does not conform to the OP or a site plan control application.

If you have questions about the zoning of a particular site, in theory you should be able to go to the Internet to retrieve the applicable by-laws for review. In reality, this is rarely possible. Often the municipality has not placed its by-laws online or, if it has, they are difficult to find. The best approach may be to go to city hall, but each municipality is organized differently. Some have public liaison officers who respond to the most common questions and refer you to a specialist, if necessary. Some invite you to submit your question in writing and will respond in writing, but we have not found this to be very effective, unless your question is very simple. Others divide the city into zones, with a planner assigned to each zone, in which case your best approach might be to make an appointment to meet with the planner.

Figure 4.2
Zoning By-law Amendment Process

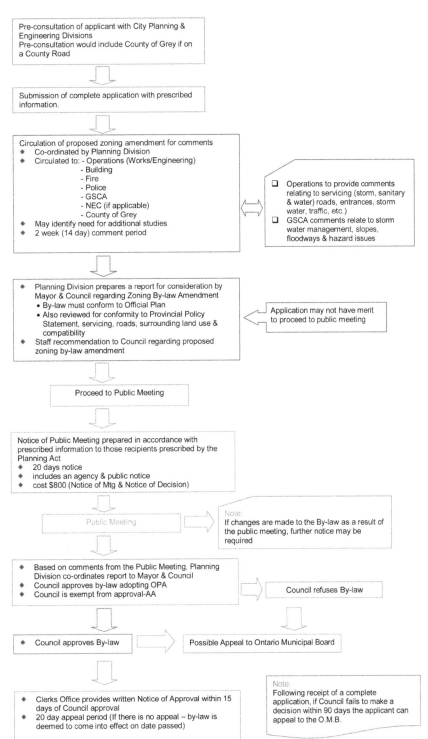

Most planners are polite and helpful, but generally do not go beyond what you ask. If you plan to meet with a planner, here are a few questions you might find useful.

- What is the exact zoning category for this property?
- Are there any exemptions to it, such as grandfathered uses or non-legal uses?
- If there is a present non-legal use, can it be continued by a new user?
- Are there any plans by a governmental or private entity that could affect the future of this property, such as a change in the OP, in zoning, projected highways, neighbourhood developments?
- From a planning viewpoint, what is the best use for this property? If you owned it, to what use would you put the property?

It is also a good idea to ask for a copy of the few pages of the by-law that are relevant to your property and the accompanying map(s) of the area.

4.2.1 ZONING COMPLIANCE REPORT

On request and for a fee, municipalities will issue a Zoning Compliance Report (also known as a Letter of Zoning Compliance or a Compliance Certificate) with respect to a specific site. Such requests are usually made by the lawyer involved when a property owner applies for a mortgage or when a property is sold. A compliance report is a document that provides detailed property information on the status of building permits or enforcement action authorized by the *Building Code Act*, 1992 (S.O. 1992, c. 23), Zoning By-law, or Property Standards By-law to property owners, their lawyers, or agents. It can also summarize the current status of development agreements. Real estate lawyers request these reports with the understanding that the purchase of a property may be impacted by various municipal by-laws and agreements.

Compliance reports are often the mechanism for addressing and rectifying violations before the completion of the sale of the property. The reports may be an alternative where title insurance is not available and where there are outstanding issues on the property. Report records can also assist city staff in determining property history when issuing building permits, reviewing zoning amendment applications, and commenting on non-conforming rights issues during zoning inspections. The compliance service also ensures that violations and deficiencies of by-law regulations and agreements are identified to prospective purchasers. Although some legal firms have opted to use title insurance in lieu of requesting a compliance report, many continue to seek these reports for greater assurance that the title to a property is clear of any encumbrances.

4.2.2 NON-CONFORMING USES

When a new zoning by-law is introduced, some existing uses of buildings may become non-permissible or non-conforming. Special provisions that permit the continued lawful use of premises that existed prior to the adoption of the new zoning by-law are referred to as "grandfathered". However, generally, if such non-conforming use of premises is discontinued for a specific length of time, any future use must conform to the new zoning.

4.2.3 PROVINCIAL ZONING ORDER

In Ontario, the province has the authority to zone any property within the province. This is referred to as a zoning order. Zoning orders are generally used in areas that are not currently administered by a local municipality and regulated by zoning by-laws (e.g., remote provincial areas).

Although, technically, a zoning order could be imposed anywhere in the province, in practice, local municipalities normally handle zoning matters.

Although, technically, a zoning order could be imposed anywhere in the province, in practice, local municipalities normally handle zoning matters.

4.2.4 PARKING

Among many other things, zoning concerns itself with the number of parking spaces to be provided for a specific use. Most developers will provide only the number of spaces required in the by-law and no more. Figure 4.3 provides an example, from the City of Barrie, Ontario, of the minimum number of parking spaces required for a specific use. In practical terms, this means that, usually, the number of parking spaces is sufficient for multi-family buildings, plentiful for industrial buildings, sufficient for retail, and insufficient for office space. An investor who has a building to sell or lease has a great advantage if there really is sufficient parking, which may actually exceed the legal minimum.

Figure 4.3
Excerpt from Parking By-law

Off-Street

Use of Building and/or Lot	No. of Off-Street Parking Spaces Required
Any residential building containing more than 3 dwelling units	1.35 spaces per dwelling unit
Any commercial uses other than those specified below	1 space for each 50 m² of gross floor area, but in no case, less than two spaces
Office	1 space for each 30 m² of gross floor area, but in no case, less than two spaces
Retail Stores, Personal Service Stores, Service Stores, Custom Workshop, Banks	1 space for every 30 m² of gross first floor area plus 1 space for 50 m² of gross floor area thereafter
Senior Citizens Homes	1 space for every two dwelling units
Service Industrial Use	1 space for each 50 m² of gross floor area up to 3,000 m² plus 1 space for each 200 m² of gross floor area thereafter
Private Clubs, Assembly Halls, Homes for the Aged, Rest Homes, Arenas	1 space for every 4 persons to be accommodated according to maximum permitted capacity

4.2.5 OFFICIAL PLAN AMENDMENT

All zoning by-laws must conform to the existing OP. Therefore, any zoning application (a request to be permitted to use the land for a specific purpose) not aligned with the OP will require an amendment to the OP. For example, if a developer with a parcel of land zoned for industrial use wants to use it for a recreational facility, say a tennis club, he must apply for an Official Plan Amendment (OPA). The procedure is identical to that required to create or modify the whole existing Municipal OP, except that generally it is for a much smaller area. It takes a minimum of six months to complete the process.

It is important for an investor to understand the OPA process, as it is up to him to make the decision to attempt to change the zoning of his land. Indeed, the land uses can be thought of as a ladder. At the bottom is agricultural use; up one rung is industrial; then, depending on location and density allowed, are retail and residential; then office. Few efforts made to improve a property will have as much financial impact as a zoning change.

Figure 4.4 presents the steps that must be followed for a Regional Official Plan Amendment (ROPA) for the Region of York. Again the same process starts with landowners' notification, erection of a sign by the applicant, public meetings, etc., and the inherent delays and costs. Figure 4.5 demonstrates some of the work completed by planners in this process. Among other things, it is their job to publicize changes made to the OP.

Many municipalities process the OPA and the zoning by-law amendment simultaneously.

4.3 SITE PLANS AND SITE PLAN CONTROLS

Walk through the steps for a site plan approval.

A site plan is a survey of the property showing existing and proposed improvements. As the name suggests, Site Plan Control is the process that is used to control or regulate the various features on the site of a development, including building location, landscaping, drainage, parking, and access by pedestrians and vehicles. Depending on the exigencies of the municipality, it may consist of only the building footprint (the area covered by the building) or include many or all of the details mentioned.

More and more often, municipalities are working with Site Plan Control Agreements. These agreements give a municipality even greater control over development of a site. Frequently, a zoning designation is followed by the letter "H", standing for "holding". A holding zone is used in conjunction with a zoning designation when the proposed uses for those lands are considered premature or inappropriate for development at a certain time or until the applicant has met certain conditions or requirements. This means that, even if the land is zoned for the use you have in mind, you will only receive the development or building permit you are seeking after the "H" has been removed (i.e., after you have submitted a site plan that satisfies the various municipal requirements). This is not a fast process. It may take from three to four months, or even longer.

The municipality may opt to register the Site Plan Agreement on a property title, so as to be able to enforce it against subsequent owners of the property, which can be an impediment to creative land use and ultimately affect the value of the property.

A site plan can be prepared by an architect, engineer or landscape architect, almost always at the request of a municipality. It permits you to see the dimensions of the property, the dimensions of the buildings and their setbacks, the number of trees, their location and drip line (the perimeter of the leaves or crown), etc. It also shows topography and the relationship of the buildings to the land, and of the buildings to each other.

The exact requirements of a site plan vary from municipality to municipality. The "10-Step Guide to Site Plan Approval" (reproduced in Figure 4.6) was created jointly by the City of Kitchener and the Ontario government. It demonstrates the intricacies, hence time and costs involved, to get site plan approval.

Figure 4.4
Official Plan Amendment Process

Pre-consultation meeting with applicant, consultants, and planning staff to discuss the details or concepts of application and provide general feedback to the applicant regarding regional policy, and *provides information on requirements of a complete application.*

Applicant/Planning Consultant or other consultants undertake required background studies, as *discussed with* staff in pre-consultation.

Applicant/Consultant completes Regional OPA application form, and submits form, required background information, application fees, draft OPA document and *all requisite information and material as prescribed in Section 22 (4) & (5) of the Planning Act and Section 2 and Schedule 1 of Ontario Regulation 543/06* to Regional Planning Department.

Within 30 days of the submission of the application, background studies, fee, etc. the Regional Planning Department will provide a letter to the applicant advising whether the application is complete.

Within 15 days of providing an affirmative notice of a complete application, the Regional Planning Department will:
1. *Circulate the application and all background studies and supporting material and information to all prescribed persons/bodies listed in Section 3 of Ontario Regulation 543/06, other external agencies, and internal departments; and*
2. *Notify the public by way of newspaper notice in Toronto Star and local newspapers that a complete application has been received and the supporting documentation is available for their viewing in the Regional Planning Department.*

Regional Planning staff prepares a Notice to Hold a Public Meeting and publish notice in the Toronto Star and local newspapers, at least 20 days prior to meeting (*This Notice may be coordinated with the Notice of Complete Application*).

A Peer Review may be required on technical background studies, such as agriculture, hydrogeology, environmental impact, retail impact, noise and vibration, and growth and settlement. The Peer Review is done at the owner's expense.

The Public Meeting is held at a regular meeting of the Regional Planning and Economic Development Committee, held monthly on Wednesdays at 1:30pm. The dates of the Planning and Economic Development Committee meetings may be accessed through this link

Planning staff prepares and presents an information report describing the application and identifying any issues that require additional analysis.

Comments from the public and agencies are received, reviewed, and a further report is prepared by Regional Planning and presented to a Planning and Economic Development Committee meeting (generally the next scheduled meeting).

Planning and Economic Development Committee's recommendation is forwarded to Regional Council, generally held once monthly. Council may recommend adoption of the amendment, or refusal of the application.

Source: Used with permission of the Regional Municipality of York.

Figure 4.5
Notice of Adoption of Official Plan Amendment

City of
BOIRONVILLE

NOTICE OF ADOPTION OF
OFFICIAL PLAN AMENDEMENT NO. 15
TO THE CITY OF BOIRONVILLE
OFFICIAL PLAN

January 29, 2008

In accordance with Section 17 (23) of the Planning Act, R.S.O., as amended, I advise that By-law 3090706 adopting Official Plan Amendment No. 15 to the City of Boironville's Official Plan was passed by the Council of the City of Boironville on the 8th day of January, 2008. (OPA 03-0013/B)

The purpose and effect of the Official Plan Amendment is to revise the boundaries of residential and open space designations on Schedule 2 – Land Use Structure, revise the boundaries of Wetlands, the Imaginary Wildlife Corridor and Shorelines and Stream Corridors on Schedule II – Resource Management, revise the Imaginary Wildlife Corridor policies and revise the Big Park Neighbourhood policies to implement the results of the Big Park Neighbourhood Study.

A copy of the Official Plan Amendment and any background material is available to the public for inspection in both the Clerk's Division and the Department, Planning and Development, Boironville Civic Complex, 123 Long Street, Boironville, ON, from 8:30 a.m. to 4:30 p.m. Monday to Friday.

Nice Guy, CMM
City Clerk
City of Boironville
Ontario
L4N 2B3

Figure 4.6
10-Step Guide to Site Plan Approval

Site plan approval is required prior to obtaining a building permit for major building renovations or additions and for the construction of a new commercial, industrial, institutional, or multiple residential building.

As some parts of this process vary according to municipality investors need to contact the local Planning Department to obtain the relevant application information.

Step 1:
Preliminary review of site plan:
The applicant consults municipal staff at the preliminary or conceptual design stage.
Most municipalities offer this service free of charge to explain the process and advise on city standards, zoning requirements, site design and time schedules.
Since each municipality may have different submission requirements, request a site plan application form as this will generally outline submission requirements.

Step 2:
Site plan application submission requirements
a) Site plan application form (completed, signed and witnessed) and fees
b) Multiple copies of existing site condition plan with the following information:
  • location of driplines and trunks of trees and their related elevation
  • location of existing driveways, paved areas, and gravel-surfaced areas
  • location of buildings to be demolished and buildings to be retained
  • existing topography of the land, showing contour lines, and clearly illustrating severe slopes, both top and bottom of banks
c) Multiple copies of a site plan showing the proposed development with the following information:
  • A key map showing the location of the property, true dimensions, bearings, and area of the property
  • The location and dimensions of all existing and proposed buildings and structures, including basements and mezzanines
  • The dimensions of all yards (i.e setbacks of all buildings and structures from property lines)
  • The location of off-street parking and loading areas including the dimensions of parking spaces and loading areas and setbacks of such areas from property lines
  • The width of driveways and aisles accessing parking stalls and loading areas
  • The dimensions detailing entrance and exit locations to and from the site
  • The location of outdoor containers and/or vaults, central storage and collection areas or other facilities for the storage of garbage and other waste or recyclable material
  • The location, height, and type of fencing and landscaped areas
  • Percentage of lot coverage of buildings and hard surface areas
  • Landscape areas
  • The location of curbing, outdoor storage areas, and existing and proposed sidewalks
  • Existing and proposed connections to municipal services
  • Storm water management areas

Additional information that maybe required:
  • Underground parking area designs shown on a separate plan
  • Preliminary storm water management concepts
  • Elevation plan
  • Traffic study

Step 3:
The Applicant submits completed application and plans to the City Hall Planning Department.

Step 4:
A letter is usually sent to the applicant accepting the complete application. If information is missing or the application is not complete you may receive a phone call or letter. Note that the application will not be processed if it is incomplete. Some municipalities may attach an example development agreement that lists the standard conditions of approval that could be registered on title as a condition of site plan approval.

Step 5:
The application is usually circulated to departments and other agencies for comments. Expect this process to take approximately ten business days.

Steps 6:
The applicants will be asked to a meeting to review the proposed site plan, comments and revisions that were received through the circulation.
Scenario a)
The application concerns an existing development with minor changes:
The site plan may simply be stamped approved (with possible conditions) and sent to the owner for their agreement.
Scenario b)
The application concerns a Greenfield development or major changes to an existing facility:
Site plan approval is issued with a summary of conditions that is usually registered on title (as per Section 41 of the Planning Act).
Scenario c)
The applicant may be requested to make changes and resubmit the plan.
Scenario d)
The application is refused with reasons.
This decision can be appealed to the Ontario Municipal Board (OMB). The Board can approve the application with or without conditions or refuse it.

Step 7:
If the approved site plan and agreement will be registered on title there will normally be a few days required to format the site plan to a registrable format and to prepare the legal documents.

Step 8:
Once the applicant agrees by signing the agreement it is registered on title. This agreement runs with the title when the property is sold. Legal Services prepares the Section 41 Development Agreement and registers the agreement after all signatures and fees are received.

Step 9:
Compliance with pre-building permit conditions:
The municipality will issue a letter of approval with the conditions, which are often registered on title.
Pre-building permit conditions may include but are not limited to the following:
- Submission and approval of grading and drainage control plan
- Submission and approval of storm water management design
- Dedication of road widenings
- Submission and approval of site lighting design
- Submission and approval of cost estimate
- Posting of a Letter of Credit
- Fulfillment of regional conditions

Step 10:
Building Permit
The permit is issued after:
- Submission, review and acceptance of the building permit application and fee. Architectural, structural, electrical and mechanical drawings to ensure that they comply with the Ontario Building Code may be required.
- All required fees[1] have been paid which may or may not include:
    - Development charges
    - Service connection fees
    - Sidewalk fee
    - Stormwater management fees
    - Damage deposit fee
    - Park land dedication fee
- Confirmation that all pre-building permit conditions, listed as part of the site plan approval process, have been met.
Start of construction.

---

1 Fees and charges vary considerably from one municipality to another and undergo regular review. For the most current information please contact the Planning Department in question.

Source: www.2ontario.com/software/facts/land_building.pdf

4.4 BUILDING PERMITS

Understand the purpose and process in obtaining a building permit.

A building permit is granted by a municipality to allow a person to erect a building or complete a renovation. This means that all electrical, mechanical, plumbing, structural, and architectural drawings must comply with the building code requirements applicable to each specific discipline. Currently there are ten areas of practice: housing, small buildings, large buildings, complex buildings, plumbing for housing, plumbing for all buildings, HVAC for housing, building services, building structural, and on-site sewage treatment systems. Designers, including professional engineers and architects, must pass exams testing their knowledge on the Ontario Building Code Act, 1992 and its administrative regulations. Failure to hire someone with the required certification will mean denial of a building permit.

Of course, getting a building permit through the building or development department of a municipality involves many steps and many months. Depending on the project, you can count on 6 to 12 months.

In July 2003, the Ontario *Building Code Act* was amended to, among other things, reduce the sluggish pace of building permit approval. The intent was laudable — to limit the time municipalities were allowed to either approve or refuse building permits to a maximum of 10 business days for residential, to 15 days for small commercial buildings, and to 30 days for large commercial buildings. In Toronto, for example, this would be one-and-a-half to two times faster than the previous rate. The final stage of the implementation was completed by January 2006; however, officials complain that they do not have the necessary staff to do it faster and, sadly, developers have not seen faster processing.

> *In July 2003, the Ontario* Building Code Act *was amended to, among other things, reduce the sluggish pace of building permit approval.*

4.5 COMMITTEE OF ADJUSTMENT

Know what Committees of Adjustment deal with and how to follow their processes.

A Committee of Adjustment is a committee at the municipal level, made up of five people, who are neither members of the municipal council or employees of the city. It deals with the following three functions:

1. zoning variance
2. change to non-conforming use, and
3. land severance.

1. **Zoning Variance.** The Committee of Adjustment has the responsibility of dealing with minor variances. Unfortunately, the *Planning Act* lets the Committee of Adjustment decide what is considered minor. In the case of zoning by-law variances, requests for variances can be made to the Committee of Adjustment if the property owner feels that the regulations of the zoning by-law harm his property. Indeed, a variance softens the rules of the zoning by-laws. For example, a variance might permit a side yard to be only 5.8 m (19 ft), whereas the zoning by-law requires 6.1 m (20 ft). This variance would be the subject of a public hearing with participation of the applicant and input available to adjacent property owners. The Committee could then:
   - approve the variance application, without conditions, or
   - reject the variance application, or
   - approve the application with some changes/conditions.

   The basic difference between a variance and a rezoning is whether the granting of a zoning variance would break the zoning rules rather then merely bend them. Theoretically, the Committee provides relief where the by-law is causing a hardship to an individual property and where strict enforcement of the by-law is not reasonable.

2. **Changes to Non-conforming Use.** The Committee of Adjustment controls changes to use. This would include alterations of a building or a change of a non-conforming use, for example when a renovation causes a side yard to be only 2.97 m (9.75 ft), instead of the required 3.05 m (10 ft).

3. **Land Severances.** The Committee of Adjustment can grant land severances to a person who has a large piece of land and wants to sell, or sever, part of it, which cannot be done without permission.

An example of a Committee of Adjustment application process is outlined in Figure 4.7. Note that any consent expires after two years if not acted upon, unless a shorter period has been imposed by the committee.

Copies of the Committee's decisions are mailed to the applicant and to such other people who appear at the hearing in person or by counsel and who file a written request with the Secretary Treasurer of the Committee for notice of the decision. Copies of the decision may also be mailed to those people who request copies in writing, prior to the date of the hearing.

Every decision of the Committee of Adjustment may be appealed to the Ontario Municipal Board (see section 4.6). However, a notice of the appeal must be filed in the manner and within the time prescribed under the *Planning Act*. The last date for the appeal will be set out in the decisions of the Committee. Note that where no appeal has been filed within the appeal period, the decision of the Committee is final and binding. This process generally takes about two months. Cost varies from one municipality to another. Whenever possible, this kind of appeal should be chosen over a zoning change because it is generally much faster, simpler, and less expensive.

Figure 4.7
Committee of Adjustment Process

```
┌─────────────────────────────────────────────────────────┐
│  APPLICANT HAS PRELIMINARY DISCUSSIONS WITH STAFF OF      │
│  THE PLANNING AND DEVELOPMENT DEPARTMENT                  │
└─────────────────────────────────────────────────────────┘
                            ↓
┌─────────────────────────────────────────────────────────┐
│  APPLICANT SUBMITS COMMITTEE OF ADJUSTMENT               │
│  APPLICATION AND SUPPORTING DOCUMENTS (i.e. SITE PLAN)   │
│  TO SECRETARY-TREASURER OF THE COMMITTEE                 │
└─────────────────────────────────────────────────────────┘
                            ↓
┌─────────────────────────────────────────────────────────┐
│  STAFF REVIEWS APPLICATION FOR COMPLETENESS             │
└─────────────────────────────────────────────────────────┘
                            ↓
┌─────────────────────────────────────────────────────────┐
│  APPLICATION CIRCULATED TO A NUMBER OF DEPARTMENTS       │
│  AND AGENCIES FOR COMMENTS                               │
└─────────────────────────────────────────────────────────┘
                            ↓
┌─────────────────────────────────────────────────────────┐
│  NOTICE OF PUBLIC HEARING IS MAILED TO ALL PROPERTY      │
│  OWNERS WITHIN 60 METRES OF SUBJECT PROPERTY            │
└─────────────────────────────────────────────────────────┘
                            ↓
┌─────────────────────────────────────────────────────────┐
│  PUBLIC HEARING IS HELD BY THE COMMITTEE OF             │
│  ADJUSTMENT TO CONSIDER THE APPLICATION AND             │
│  COMMITTEE MAKES A DECISION                             │
└─────────────────────────────────────────────────────────┘
                            ↓
┌─────────────────────────────────────────────────────────┐
│  COMMITTEE MAY DENY OR APPROVE APPLICATION.            │
│  COMMITTEE MAY ALSO RENDER A CONDITIONAL APPROVAL OF   │
│  AN APPLICATION                                         │
└─────────────────────────────────────────────────────────┘
                            ↓
┌─────────────────────────────────────────────────────────┐
│  30-DAY APPEAL PERIOD AFTER THE MAKING OF THE DECISION  │
└─────────────────────────────────────────────────────────┘
                            ↓
┌─────────────────────────────────────────────────────────┐
│  IF NO APPEAL, THE DECISION OF COMMITTEE               │
│  IS FINAL AND BINDING                                   │
└─────────────────────────────────────────────────────────┘
                            ↓
┌─────────────────────────────────────────────────────────┐
│  IF THERE IS AN APPEAL TO THE ONTARIO MUNICIPAL         │
│  BOARD, THE BOARD'S DECISION IS FINAL                   │
└─────────────────────────────────────────────────────────┘
```

Source: Used with permission of the City of London.

4.6 ONTARIO MUNICIPAL BOARD

Recognize the purpose and scope of the Ontario Municipal Board.

The Ontario Municipal Board (OMB) is an independent tribunal that deals with disputes involving municipalities. The judges, called members, are appointed by the provincial government. The OMB listens to the appeals and concerns of people, public bodies, or corporations who object to the decisions of public authorities, such as local or regional councils, committees of adjustment, land division committees, the Minister of Internal Affairs and Housing, or an expropriating authority. The Board holds public hearings throughout the province.

Some of the issues the OMB deals with include the following:
- official plans
- zoning by-laws
- plans of subdivision
- consents to convey land
- minor variances from local by-laws
- protection of rental housing
- development charges
- property tax assessment
- aggregate licences
- compensation for expropriated land, and
- applications for gravel pit licences.

Generally, any person, public body, or incorporated group, upon paying a filing fee, can appeal either a municipal decision or a failure to make a decision to the Board.

Generally, any person, public body, or incorporated group, upon paying a filing fee, can appeal either a municipal decision or a failure to make a decision to the Board. An unincorporated neighbourhood association, for example, cannot appeal in the name of the association; the association must appeal under the name of one of its members. This means that you could be granted permission by your municipality to cut down a couple of very old trees about to fall on your house and virtually anyone could appeal the decision to the OMB. This can present a number of problems.
- Expenses are generally high, since it is wise (in fact, necessary) to hire a lawyer to represent you in the hearing, and various other professionals, such as a planner, engineer, architect, and landscape engineer, will likely be required as well. Depending on the complexity of the case, a lawyer may spend considerable time preparing for the appearance in court, and then appear on your behalf.
- It is a very time-consuming process, with the hearing itself usually lasting several days, and you will want, or need, to be present.
- Delays are expensive. It can take anywhere from 3 to 9 months before a hearing is even started, depending on the schedules of OMB members, and it can take several weeks for Board members to write their decision following a hearing. The duration of the hearings vary enormously based on the complexity of the case and can cost from $30,000 to many millions of dollars.

Cases go to the OMB primarily for three reasons:

1. an activist or activist group objects to a development
2. a neighbour objects to a plan or action, or
3. a municipality does not agree with a proposed development.

If the OMB sides with the applicant, the financial benefits can be staggering, not only because it can allow a development to go ahead, but also because the OMB can order the complainant to pay the cost of the proceedings, if the case is deemed frivolous. The example below demonstrates the costs and delays that can result.

A few years ago, in Thornhill, following a woman's death, a house on a large lot was sold. It was a corner lot and the house was located at one end. The buyer asked to sever a lot at the other end. The municipality agreed to the severance. An abutting owner filed an appeal with the OMB. His reason? "If they build a house on the second lot, they will need to cut down a few trees. I object to that."

The trees were not on the neighbour's property. He had not bought them, planted them, or nurtured them but felt he "had a right to them". He neglected to mention that in the previous 5 years he had cut down three trees on his own property. He lost the case, but it took close to a year for the hearing to be held, resulting in significant expenses to the new owner of the property.

4.7 HERITAGE PROPERTIES

Appreciate the blessings and curses of a heritage property.

Most municipalities try to preserve old buildings. One can argue the merits of this on a case-by-case basis, but regardless of your stand most municipalities have some sort of Heritage Property designation. There are several Web sites that will be of help to you if you own a heritage property, including <www.nationalregisterofhistoricplaces.com> and <www.historicproperties.com>. Although these are American sites, the same principles apply in Canada. In Canada, <www.heritagecanada.org> offers some valuable information.

In February 2002, Ontario announced incentive measures to encourage heritage conservation by way of reduction of property taxes:

Once adopted by a municipality, the program provides tax reductions often to 40% to eligible property owners. Municipalities decide the amount of relief and may apply different percentages to different types of properties. The Province will automatically fund the education portion of the tax relief, while municipalities fund their portion of the tax reductions.

In Canada, there is as a rule an "Association for the Preservation of ... historic buildings", which operates under the aegis of many municipalities. If you are interested in buying an old property (say over 75 years old), call the municipality to find out if it is listed as a Heritage Property. It can be a blessing, due to its special character, personality, subsidies, etc. Or it can be a curse, due to the limitations imposed for renovations, additions, etc. Generally, it is very difficult to demolish a designated Heritage Property for a new development.

In our opinion there is no greater impediment to prolonging the life of an older building than the building code, OP, and zoning by-laws. In the early 1900s there were few or no zoning by-laws. The concept of building setback, for example, did not exist. Today's regulations, in many cases, not only restrict what can be done with a building, but make renovating a building prohibitively expensive.

4.8 WORKING WITH PLANNERS

Find a way to work with municipal planners.

A client of ours who is a builder in a large Ontario city has said about planners, "If it happened one day that I went into the planning department at city hall, and a planner smiled at me and greeted me with, 'Good morning, can I do anything to help you today?' I think that I would be so surprised that I would faint."

Unfortunately, this is a typical view of planners. They are seen as a costly road block to doing business. But, sooner or later, all real estate investors need to deal with planners, as well as other municipal employees in the planning and building departments (primarily, building inspectors). It is essential that you find a way to work well with them, in order to avoid expensive delays and minimize difficulties.

It is essential that you find a way to work well with them, in order to avoid expensive delays and minimize difficulties.

Here are a few things to keep in mind to help you develop an effective working relationship with planners and other municipal officials with whom you need to "do business":

- Understand that, as government employees, these people are subject to public scrutiny and must follow the rules. Some planners sympathize with the complexities and demands they must impose on the public. Sympathizing with their position can also help.
- Many planners are very busy. Show them that you know that and understand the pressure they are under.
- Respect their time. For example, make appointments rather than dropping in and have all the required data (and questions) ready before you telephone a planner.
- React fast. If you must do something to satisfy a planner, do it promptly and he, in turn, will be inclined to work fast on your file.
- If you have a meeting with a planner, take copious notes. When back at your office, write him a letter stating: "This is what I understood …" What you want to do is confirm what you were told. Always end your letter with, "If I have misunderstood you, please, let me know." In your letter, don't forget to thank the planner for his help and do not hesitate to apologize for taking up so much of his time.
- Planners have to be very organized because of their specialty and because they work in a political environment. You will get further if you show them that you, too, are organized.

"The proof is in the pudding" goes the saying. So, here is an example from our own experience.

> While working on a subdivision, we sent the planner in charge of the file the following e-mail: "Have you received the 40M-Plan from our engineer?"
>
> The planner answered us: "Nope."
>
> We then contacted the engineer by e-mail, and copied the planner: "I thought that you told me the planner would have the Plan by March 11. When will he have it?"
>
> The engineer answered: "The error is on my part. I have checked our files and the copies were never forwarded. I apologize for this. I have couriered two (2) copies of the latest M-Plan for the above site to the planner's attention. He should have them no later than noon, Monday. Again, I apologize for any inconvenience or misunderstanding among the parties."
>
> We forwarded the above message to the planner, writing: "My apologies for pestering you. (See above)."
>
> He answered: "That's quite alright. You're the only person who has ever apologized. And I want to move your file ahead."

Are you still skeptical? Here is another encounter with the same planner.

> We called to ask him if he could find out if the municipal council had approved a budget item the previous night. He told us that he did not know but would find out and call us back. He did call back, a few minutes later, and told us that it had been approved. We told him that we really appreciated him looking into the matter.
>
> His response? "It is a pleasure; you are always so polite. You would be surprised what it can get you. Some people who are not polite or, worse, are rude or unreasonably demanding get reactions from us that no one will ever know about, but I can tell you that they pay for their poor behaviour."

On yet another occasion, he wrote:

> "You have also kept the process moving. Every time I can remember, you have responded quickly to information or action items. And you don't leave uncertain items on the shelf. You have thereby saved yourself considerable time (and, presumably, money)".

Keep these words in mind when you enter the bureaucratic maze of planning. Because planners are frequently criticized and confronted with hostility, they appreciate politeness and courtesy more than most.

CHAPTER
5
Taxation

By the end of this chapter, you will be able to:
- Understand property taxation and:
  - appreciate how property taxes are assessed.
  - know which government offices and boards are involved in assessment.
  - take steps to reduce your property taxes.
- Unravel the intricacies of the income tax system and use such features as listed below to your tax avoidance advantage:
  - capital cost allowance, and
  - capital gains and losses.

Understanding taxation is an essential part of all kinds of businesses and investments, and real estate is no exception. Property tax is a significant expense for investors, and several aspects of income tax also come into play when you are making investment decisions. Building depreciation allows you to defer some income tax, but when you sell, you will probably be subject to recapture. Hopefully, you will be able to avail yourself of the favourable capital gains rules as well.

5.1 PROPERTY TAXES

Understand property taxes.

One can never know too much about property taxes (also called "realty taxes") because they represent such a big chunk of building ownership expenses. Yet, understanding the intricacies of the tax system can be quite challenging. As an investor, reducing tax has a tremendous impact on the bottom line, so it is essential that you have a clear picture of the taxes on a property before you make an investment decision. This includes not only property tax, but also the other taxes that appear on your property tax bill, including the education tax and, in some cases, taxes levied by a regional government.

In Ontario, the bulk of municipal revenues come from taxes on real property. The amount of tax varies with the type and value of the property. Municipalities rely on the Municipal Property Assessment Corporation (MPAC) to supply them with property market values on which property tax is based. However, not all provinces and territories base their taxes on market value.

For example, in 1997, the Ontario government introduced a new assessment system, based on current market value, in an attempt to correct the inequities in the property tax system. The most obvious disparity was the one between the City of Toronto and the surrounding areas, where the taxes were markedly lower. Prior to 1997, property assessment, and the resultant taxes paid, were not based on market value. Unfortunately, their courage in taking on this hot issue was not rewarded adequately, as many problems surfaced in the execution stage. In the years since, there has been some improvement, but certainly not as much as was desired. To provide a better idea of the differences, here are some of the rates (as a percentage of the assessed property value) that the Oakville Economic Development Alliance shows on its Web site <www.oeda.ca>:

> Commercial buildings: Burlington: 2%; Oakville: 2.4%; Mississauga: 2.5%;
> Toronto: 4%
> Industrial buildings: Burlington: 2.2%; Mississauga: 2.75%; Oakville: 3.6%;
> Toronto: 4.5%.

To present it in a more striking fashion: a $5,000,000 industrial property located in Burlington will pay taxes of $5,000,000 x 2.2% = $110,000, while a Toronto property of equal value will pay $5,000,000 x 4.5% = $225,000.

To determine how much tax each property owner will have to pay, municipalities need to know two things.

1. The assessed value of all properties in a municipality is called the "tax base". It does not include exempt properties like government, schools, churches, hospitals, and some charities.

2. The percentage of the assessed value of all the properties, or the tax rate that they will charge for property taxes, was and still is sometimes called the "mill rate". For many years, it was expressed in dollars per $1,000 (Mill) of assessed value. This percentage is determined when a municipality prepares a budget and divides the total budget requirement by the total municipal tax base, which is prepared in Ontario by MPAC (see section 5.1.1). For a simplistic example: if the municipal budget is $27M and the tax base is $800,000,000, then the mill rate is calculated as follows: $27,000,000/$800,000,000 = 0.034, or 3.34%.

Once the mill rate has been established, the municipality calculates the property taxes by multiplying its value by the mill rate.

In real life things are more complicated because there are different property tax classes (see 5.1.1(b)). This means that two properties assessed at the same value, such as industrial and multi-family, will pay different amounts of taxes.

In many jurisdictions, municipalities also collect the education tax, on behalf of school boards (Public and Separate; English and French). The education portion is determined by the provincial government. Sometimes a third tax shows up on property tax bills for the regional government (see Figure 5.1 for an example of a municipal tax bill). It is not uncommon for the municipalities themselves to receive only approximately 25% of the property taxes they collect.

Property taxes are calculated using a property's assessed value, the municipal tax rate, and an education tax rate. The formula is as follows:

- Assessed Value x Municipal Tax Rate = Amount of Municipal Property Tax
- Assessed Value x Education Tax Rate = Amount of Education Tax
- Municipal Property Tax + Education Tax = Property Taxes.

A typical municipal tax bill is shown on page 74.

Figure 5.1
Municipal Tax Bill

City of **PICKERING**

TAX BILL

THE CITY OF PICKERING
REMIT TO: CENTRAL PROCESSING
P.O. BOX 4141, STN A, TORONTO, ON M5W 3E4
TAX INQUIRIES:(905) 420-4614 NORTH:(905) 683-2760

Billing Date	JUN 19, 2002
BILL TITLE	**2002 FINAL TAX BILL**

Roll No. **030 020 13650 0000**	Group Code
Mortgage Company	Mortgage Account No.

Assessed Owner and Mailing Address	Legal Owner and Legal Description
KYPKOI-00013624 NICOU INC 63 JOHNSON ST THORNHILL ON L3T 2N9	NICOU INC CON 2 S PT LOT 34 NOW RP 40R11934 PART 1 CL TOWNLINE SWAMP COMPLEX (CW3) 21.57AC

Assessment		City of Pickering			Region of Durham			Education	
Tax Class	Value	Municipal Levies	Tax Rate (%)	Amount	Municipal Levies	Tax Rate (%)	Amount	Tax Rate (%)	Amount
RTEP	50,000	City	.375559	187.78	Region	.730904	365.45	.373000	186.50
		Lower Tier Levy $		187.78	Upper Tier Levy $		365.45		
Sub Totals					Total Municipal Levy $		553.23	Education Levy $	186.50

SPECIAL CHARGES/CREDITS		SUMMARY	
BIA	.00	Tax Levy Sub-total (Municipal + Education)	739.73
Local Improvement	.00	Special Charges/Credits	.00
		TOTAL THIS BILLING	739.73
		Less Credits (as of JUN 19, 2002)	.00
		Less Interim Billing	356.28
		Subtotal	383.45
		Arrears Due Immediately (as of JUN 19, 2002)	.00
Sub Total	.00	Total Amount Due $	383.45

1st INSTALLMENT	Due Date: JUL 15, 2002	Amount Due: $	192.00
2nd INSTALLMENT	Due Date: SEP 16, 2002	Amount Due: $	191.45

FORM 93602 (Ed. 07/01.)

Source: Used with permission of Nicou Inc.

5.1.1 MUNICIPAL PROPERTY ASSESSMENT CORPORATION (MPAC)

Appreciate how property taxes are assessed.

Municipal Property Assessment Corporation (MPAC) is a non-share capital, not-for-profit corporation. Every municipality in Ontario is a member of the Corporation, which is governed by a 15-member Board of Directors. Eight members of the board are municipal representatives, five members represent property taxpayers, and two members represent provincial interests. All members of the board are appointed by the Minister of Finance. MPAC employs 1,500 people in 35 offices across Ontario.

MPAC administers a uniform, province-wide system based on current market value assessment for over four million properties. It provides municipalities with a range of services, including the preparation of an annual assessment roll for use by municipalities in calculating property taxes. It is with MPAC that one must argue if one disagrees with an assessment. The municipalities only collect the taxes.

(a) Establishing Market Value for Assessment Purposes

MPAC analyzes market information from similar types of properties to establish property values using traditional appraisal techniques. Any one of the following three methods may be used for this analysis:

1. the selling price of a property (residential)
2. the rental income that a property generates (office building), or
3. the cost to replace a property (industrial).

Each method takes into consideration the location of a property, the size and quality of any buildings, and any features that might add to, or take away from, a property's value.

As indicated earlier, property values are updated periodically. However, the real market value is generally, but not always, higher than the assessed value. In 2007, the assessed value of an Ontario property was typically in the 80-90% range of the selling value. This is not because MPAC under-assesses properties. It is because of the changes in the market since the last base-year valuation. Frequent value reassessments produce a more accurate assessment. Indeed, over the years, values can change due to many factors such as new construction, renovation,

Property values are updated periodically. However, the real market value is generally, if not always, higher than the assessed value.

obsolescence, neighbourhoods in transition, new developments, new amenities, new services (e.g., public transportation), and new highways.

In 2004, the Ontario government changed the valuation date from June 30 to January 1. It is this valuation that is used to determine the taxes for the following year. The taxation years of 2006, 2007, and 2008 will be based on January 1, 2005, values. The 2009 taxes will be based on January 1, 2008 values, with updates on a four-year cycle from that point forward.

In order to place a correct value on income-producing properties, MPAC requests that landlords provide income and expense data through a questionnaire (see Figure 5.2) and a Tenant Verification and Rental Data Request (see Figure 5.3) that are mailed out annually to property owners.

Figure 5.2
MPAC Property Income and Expense Questionnaire (2007)

Property Income & Expense Questionnaire

HELP US GET IT RIGHT !

For assistance or information call 1 866 296-MPAC (6722) or visit our website at www.mpac.ca

MUNICIPAL PROPERTY ASSESSMENT CORPORATION

The Municipal Property Assessment Corporation (MPAC) is responsible for assessing all property in Ontario for purposes of municipal taxation. Since the value of certain properties is heavily influenced by their ability to generate revenue, it is particularly important to obtain accurate and current income information for properties of this type. MPAC requires your assistance in this regard by supplying the following information. Please sign and return this form in the enclosed postage-paid envelope. This information is collected under the authority of the *Assessment Act* and used solely for the purpose of assessing properties. Information you supply is kept strictly confidential.

Roll Number

Municipality

Location & Property Description

Fiscal Year ______ (yyyy) end of fiscal year ______ (yyyy/mm/dd)

Municipal Property Assessment Corporation
Central Processing Facility (TIP)
PO Box 9808
Toronto ON M1S 5T9

Income Received

Rents
Residential / Apartment Suites $
Laundry (Multi-Residential) $
Other residential (specify) $

Retail $
Percentage Rents $
Other retail (specify) $

Office $

Other
Storage / Basement $
Parking $
Telecommunications $
Property Tax Recoveries $
Operating Cost Recoveries $
Administration Cost Recoveries $
Other (specify)
1 $
2 $
3 $

Rental Income Loss
Vacancy $
Collection Loss $

Expenses

General
Property Taxes $
Insurance $
Land Lease Amounts $

Administration
Management $
Legal and Audit $
Professional Fees $
Leasing Commissions $
Marketing and Promotion $
Office Supplies / Equipment $
Wages & Benefits $

Utilities
Hydro $
Water / Sewer $
Heat / Ventilation / AC (HVAC) $
Cable TV $

Property Maintenance
Waste Removal / Recycling $
Snow Removal / Landscaping $
Elevator / Escalator $
Heat / Vent./ AC (HVAC) $
Parking Garage Maintenance $
Exterior Maintenance $
Security & Fire $
Janitorial $
Pools / Rec./ Tennis etc. Maintenance $
Painting / Decorating etc. $
Other (explain in 'Comments' section) $

Capital Costs Summary

Expenditure Type		Expenditure Date (yyyy)	Expenditure Type		Expenditure Date (yyyy)
Roof	$		Parking Garage	$	
Exterior Clad	$		Surface Parking	$	
Windows	$		Other Type (specify)		
Balconies	$		1	$	
Fire Retrofit	$		2	$	
Heating (HVAC)	$		3	$	

Comments (please include any additional information or explanations you feel are pertinent to this enquiry)

Name: ______ last ______ first ______ signature Date: ______

Telephone: ______ home ______ bus. ______ e-mail

Note: This information is collected under the authority of section 11 of the *Assessment Act* and is protected by the *Municipal Freedom of Information and Protection of Privacy Act* and section 53 of the *Assessment Act*. MPAC is prevented from releasing information except as authorized under provincial legislation. MPAC may contact the property owner to conduct surveys or obtain feedback regarding the collection of this and other information.

C/I -I&E-MPAC-2007

Source: 2007 forms provided by the Municipal Property Assessment Corporation. (Where words or expressions in this form differ from those used in the legislation, the legislation shall prevail.)

(b) Tax Class and Rate

MPAC has divided properties into seven major property tax classes as specified by the Ontario government (municipalities may have more optional classes). Every property is assigned a specific tax class according to its use. Some have more than one use and, therefore, more than one class. Consequently, the assessors break down the properties into a number of sub-classes. At this time, there are 14 sub-classes in Ontario.

The property owner can calculate the amount of tax that he will owe by multiplying the tax rate for the property class by the assessed value of the property. Municipalities provide Tax Rate sheets that specify the codes for various classes and the tax rate for each, such as shown in the example from the City of Cambridge, Ontario, in Figure 5.4.

Figure 5.3
MPAC Tenant Verification and Rental Data Request (2007)

Tenant Verification & Rental Data Request

HELP US GET IT RIGHT !

For assistance or information call 1 866 296-MPAC (6722) or visit our website at www.mpac.ca

MUNICIPAL PROPERTY ASSESSMENT CORPORATION

The Municipal Property Assessment Corporation (MPAC) is responsible for assessing all property in Ontario for purposes of municipal taxation. The process for establishing fair and accurate values for multi-residential properties requires information about the types of rental units and the nature of rental agreements. MPAC also collects tenant names for municipal and school board elections and determining population counts. If you received this request in the mail, please sign and return the form(s) in the enclosed postage-paid envelope. If the material was couriered to you, please call the toll-free number listed above to arrange for return delivery. You also have the option of responding to this request using our web site shown above. This information is collected under the authority of the Assessment Act and used solely for electoral purpose and assessing properties. Information you supply is kept strictly confidential.

Roll Number ______

Municipality ______

Location & Property Description ______

page __ of __

Municipal Property Assessment Corporation
Central Processing Facility (TIP)
PO Box 9808
Toronto ON M1S 5T9

This information is collected under the authority of section 11 & 15.1 of the *Assessment Act*. Section 13 of this Act provides for penalties for non-compliance. The Municipal Property Assessment Corporation is prevented from the unauthorized disclosure of this and other information under provisions of the *Assessment Act* (s.53) and the *Municipal Freedom of Information and Protection of Privacy Act*. MPAC may contact the property owner to conduct surveys or obtain feedback regarding the collection of this and other information.

In addition to the information below, MPAC requires a completed **Property Income & Expense Questionnaire** (see attached) that summarizes incomes and expenses for this property.

Include both commercial and residential tenants

✓ utilities included in rents of all units →

Office use only Sub	Seq	Apt. No.	✓ Unit Deleted	Tenant Name	Tenant Name Corrections (as of July 1, 2007)	Heat	Hydro	Water	Cable	Monthly Parking Interior No. of Spaces	Interior Amount Charged	Exterior No. of Spaces	Exterior Amount Charged	✓ Unit Furnished	Unit Type	Monthly Rent (current)	Days Vacant (Jan.1 - Dec 31 2006)	Sq. Ft. (if known)

(Heat, Hydro, Water, Cable: ✓ included in unit rent)

I certify that this and all attached information are correct

name of contact & position in organization | signature | business telephone | e-mail address | date

TVRDR-MPAC 2007

Source: 2007 forms provided by the Municipal Property Assessment Corporation. (Where words or expressions in this form differ from those used in the legislation, the legislation shall prevail.)

These rates vary by municipality, but the following rates for the city of Oakville from 2006 will give you an idea of how the rates compare:

Property Category	
Residential	0.99%
Multi-residential	1.90%
Commercial	2.43%
Industrial	3.63%
Pipeline	2.17%
Farms	0.21%
Managed Forest	0.25%

Figure 5.4

Tax Rates by Property Category, 2006

2006 CITY OF CAMBRIDGE TAX RATES

CITY OF CAMBRIDGE		TAX RATES			
CODES	DESCRIPTION OF CODES	CITY	REGION	SCHOOL	TOTAL
RT	Residential and Farm - Taxable at Full Rate	0.0042851	0.0064106	0.0026400	0.0133357
R1	Residential and Farm - Taxable at Farmland I Rate	0.0014998	0.0022437	0.0009240	0.0046675
NT	New Residential Multi-Residential at Full Rate	0.0042851	0.0064106	0.0026400	0.0133357
MT	Mult-Residential - Taxable at Full Rate	0.0100271	0.0150008	0.0026400	0.0276679
M1	Mult-Residential - Taxable at Farmland I Rate	0.0014998	0.0022437	0.0009240	0.0046675
CT	Commercial - Taxable at Full Rate	0.0083560	0.0125006	0.0204149	0.0412715
CH	Commercial - Taxable at Full Shared like PIL	0.0083560	0.0125006	0.0204149	0.0412715
CU	Commercial - Taxable at Excess Land Rate	0.0054314	0.0081254	0.0132697	0.0268265
CX	Commercial - Taxable at Vacant Land Rate	0.0054314	0.0081254	0.0132697	0.0268265
C1	Commercial - Taxable at Farmland I Rate	0.0014998	0.0022437	0.0009240	0.0046675
DT	Office Building - Taxable at Full Rate	0.0083560	0.0125006	0.0204149	0.0412715
GT	Parking Lot - Taxable at Full Rate	0.0083560	0.0125006	0.0204149	0.0412715
ST	Shopping Centre - Taxable at Full Rate	0.0083560	0.0125006	0.0204149	0.0412715
SU	Shopping Centre - Taxable at Excess Land Rate	0.0054314	0.0081254	0.0132697	0.0268265
IT	Industrial - Taxable at Full Rate	0.0111841	0.0167316	0.0261689	0.0540846
IH	Industrial - Taxable at Full Rate Shared like PIL	0.0111841	0.0167316	0.0261689	0.0540846
IU	Industrial - Taxable at Excess Land Rate	0.0072697	0.0108756	0.0170098	0.0351551
IJ	Industrial - Taxable at Vacant Land Shared like PIL	0.0072697	0.0108756	0.0170098	0.0351551
IK	Industrial - Taxable Excess Land Shared like PIL	0.0072697	0.0108756	0.0170098	0.0351551
IX	Industrial - Taxable at Vacant Land Rate	0.0072697	0.0108756	0.0170098	0.0351551
I1	Industrial - Taxable Phase 1	0.0014998	0.0022437	0.0009240	0.0046675
LT	Large Industrial - Taxable at Full Rate	0.0111841	0.0167316	0.0261689	0.0540846
LU	Large Industrial - Taxable at Excess Land Rate	0.0072697	0.0108756	0.0170098	0.0351551
LK	Large Industrial - Taxable Excess Land Shared like PIL	0.0072697	0.0108756	0.0170098	0.0351551
LX	Large Industrial - Taxable at Vacant Land	0.0072697	0.0108756	0.0170098	0.0351551
FT	Farmland - Taxable at Full Rate	0.0010713	0.0016026	0.0006600	0.0033339
PT	Pipelines	0.0049763	0.0074446	0.0130780	0.0254989
TT	Managed Forests - Taxable at Full Rate	0.0010713	0.0016026	0.0006600	0.0033339

TAXES = TAX RATE x CVA (CURRENT MARKET VALUE) OF THE PROPERTY

(c) Property Assessment Steps

Know which government offices and boards are involved in assessment.

The MPAC booklet, "Guide to Property Assessment in Ontario", provides detailed information and is available online at <www.mpac.ca>, but following is an outline of the basic steps.

1. A property is placed in MPAC's database.
2. A January 1 value is placed on the property by MPAC. Property owners may file a Property Assessment Appeal (see section 5.1.1(d)).
3. Final details, such as adjustments to value following an appeal, are dealt with.
4. A Property Assessment Notice showing the estimated value is sent by MPAC to each property owner in November. When a building has not been inspected by an assessor (they do not have enough staff to do it with every reassessment of value), it is calculated by the Automated Cost System (ACS), a computer program that makes value assumptions regarding many of the building components. The investor who values his money should scrutinize the assumptions made by the ACS. Errors do occur!
5. The information contained on each Property Assessment Notice is provided to municipalities in late December on the assessment rolls. The current value assessments on the rolls are used by municipalities to calculate the following year's property taxes.
6. MPAC addresses assessment concerns (tax appeals and errors).
7. On February 1st, the municipality follows the Assessment Notice with an Interim Tax Bill, representing approximately 50% of the previous year's taxes due and a second bill, the Final Tax Bill, follows in June, showing the amount to be paid in two instalments. In the example, shown in Figure 5.1, from the City of Pickering, the municipal taxes are $187.78, the regional taxes (Durham Region) are $365.45 and the education taxes are $186.50. These are to be paid in two instalments, July and September. If the bill is not paid by the due date, there will be a late payment fee charged. A municipality may sell a property for unpaid taxes, but usually it waits at least 3 years to do so.

(d) Property Assessment Appeal

Take steps to reduce your property taxes.

To reiterate, lowering property taxes can be the most important item in reducing expenses on a property. It is, therefore, paramount that investors understand the assessment system and appeal an assessment on a property if it seems too high. This can be achieved through a Request for Reconsideration or an appearance before the Assessment Review Board.

An excellent reason to appeal an assessment is when a property was purchased

Lowering property taxes can be the most important item in reducing expenses on a property.

close to the valuation date for a significantly lower amount than the assessed value, but there are many other reasons, such as change of use, partial or full building demolition, noxious nearby uses, decrepit condition, etc.

If a property owner feels that the property has been over-assessed when the Assessment Notice is received, he may ask MPAC to have another look at the value of the property at no charge using a Request for Reconsideration (RfR) form, which must be submitted by December 31st of that year (see Figure 5.5).

Figure 5.5

MPAC Request for Reconsideration

(mpac) MUNICIPAL PROPERTY ASSESSMENT CORPORATION

Request for Reconsideration (RfR) Form

The deadline for filing a Request for the 2007 taxation year is December 31, 2007

Roll Number:
(See the 19-digit # on your Property Assessment Notice)

__ __ - __ __ - __ __ __ - __ __ __ __ __ - __ __ __ __ __ - __ __ __ __

Municipality:	Street Address/Property Location: (See Property Assessment Notice)

Owner 1 (Name):	Agent/Representative (Name):
Owner 2 (Name):	(If an Agent or Representative is authorized to act on behalf of the property owner, a Letter of Authorization must accompany the RfR.)
Mailing Address:	Apt. #:
City/Town:	Province:	Postal Code:

Contact Information:

( )   ( )   Ext:
Home Phone Number   Other Phone #   E-mail Address

2005 *Assessed value (as shown on your Property Assessment Notice)* $_____
(January 1, 2005 Valuation Date)

You can assist our review of your assessment by providing specific reasons why you believe your assessment should be reviewed. Please take the time to provide all the relevant details that support your concerns, including property comparisons, sales information, rental data, farm leases, etc.

If the space below is not sufficient, continue on the reverse or attach additional pages. Please provide as much information as possible.

_____

_____

_____

_____

_____

_____

_____

_____

Note: This information is requested under the authority of Section 39.1 of the *Assessment Act* and your personal information is protected under the *Municipal Freedom of Information and Protection of Privacy Act.* MPAC may contact the individuals listed on this request to conduct surveys or obtain feedback.

Name: _____   Signature: _____   Date: __/__/__
       (Please Print)   YR / MO / DAY

Please mail or fax this form to:

Municipal Property Assessment Corporation
P.O. Box 9808
Toronto ON M1S 5T9 or
Fax: 1 866 297-6703

OFFICE USE:		
PAC	00	01
P_CODE	02	03

2006/11/06

Source: 2007 forms provided by the Municipal Property Assessment Corporation. (Where words or expressions in this form differ from those used in the legislation, the legislation shall prevail.)

If the reconsideration process does not result in the property owner's favour and he wants to continue to pursue the matter, he may file a complaint to an independent tribunal called the Assessment Review Board (ARB). The deadline for appeal is March 31st. The fees for this approach are $75 for a residential property and $150 for a non-residential property. Both the property owner (or his representative) and MPAC will be asked to appear before the Board at a hearing to present evidence. The owner can do this in one of three ways:

1. argue the case himself
2. hire a municipal lawyer, or
3. hire a property consultant, many of whom do this work on a contingency basis.

The Board's decision is binding on all parties — the property owner, MPAC, and municipalities.

Assessors try to be fair, but it is up to each property owner to spend time consulting the assessment rolls at the municipal offices, comparing his property to similar ones, to find out if his property is under-assessed, properly assessed, or over-assessed.

As noted on MPAC's Web site:

> Property owners have the right to know the information MPAC maintains about their property. They are also entitled to receive information and assistance to help them understand their assessment.
>
> A property owner is entitled, free of charge, to:
> - View the assessment roll available at municipal offices.
> - View details for their own property and basic assessment roll information for up to twelve properties using MPAC's secure, Internet-based AboutMyProperty™ service.
> - A Property Profile Report from MPAC that shows the assessment details for their property.
> - A comparable Property Report from MPAC, listing up to six comparable properties selected by the owner and six comparables selected by MPAC.
>
> To find out more about these reports or AboutMyProperty™, contact MPAC at 1 866 296-MPAC (6722) or visit this section of our web site [www.mpac.ca].

MPAC also offers a subscription package called Propertyline™, where for a fee, one can acquire various reports, such as Assessment Roll Report ($14), Industrial Basic Report ($9), Parcel Report ($7), and Site Service Report ($3).

(e) Reducing Taxes on Empty Buildings

If a landlord has an empty building, in Ontario, he can request a lowering of the taxes (a rebate) from the municipality for the period involved. The new rate will be 70% of the regular taxes for multi-family, retail, and office buildings and 65% for industrial buildings. Many taxpayers fail to take advantage of these provisions and pay for it dearly.

MPAC and municipalities have established a verification program for property tax rebates for vacant space. MPAC provides a vacancy verification service; however, municipalities have the option – and many use it – to hire an independent vacancy verification service company.

A building, or portion of it, may be eligible for a rebate if it meets the following criteria:
- it was empty for at least 90 consecutive days
- it was not used and was clearly delineated or separated by physical barriers from the portion of the building that was used

- it was capable of being leased for immediate occupation
- it was capable of being leased, but not for immediate occupation because it needed repairs or renovations, was under construction, or was unfit for occupation
- it was not used for commercial or industrial activity on a seasonal basis, and
- it was not, during the period of vacancy, subject to a lease or sub-lease, the term of which had started.

Applications must include the following minimum information:
- name of property owner (or of an authorized agent)
- municipal address of the property, including number, street, and municipality
- assessment roll number of the property
- dates of vacancy
- description of vacant portion (suite or unit number and floor number or location within the building), and
- square footage of vacant area.

A municipality may also request further information to substantiate an application for a rebate. If a landlord knowingly makes a false or deceptive statement in an application for a rebate, he is liable, upon conviction, to a fine of double the amount of the rebate that he sought to obtain, but not less than $500.

To substantiate a claim for a rebate, a landlord must file an application form (an example of which can be found at <www.wasagabeach.com/media/pdf>) with the municipality and be supported by the following documents:
- a copy of an expired lease and a current lease, establishing by default, the vacant period, provided that it discloses the square footage of the subject property
- a sketch/floor plan of the building and the square footage of the area(s)
- documentation showing the last day the tenant occupied the space, such as a letter of intent to vacate, a notice of eviction, or a court order, and
- evidence that the property was advertised for rent/lease, such as a copy of a real estate agent's listing agreement showing when the unit was available for rent and a copy of the subsequent lease showing the square footage of the subject property or a copy of newspaper or Internet ad corresponding to the period that a vacant unit was available for lease, provided that it shows the square footage.

If the above documentation is not available, the landlord may be required to submit a notarized statement or affidavit. Site inspections are conducted on a random basis.

Upon determining the amount of the rebate, the municipality will advise the landlord, who has 120 days to appeal the amount to the ARB. An excellent guide can be found on the Canadian Federation of Independant Business Web site (<www.cfib.ca/legis/ontario/pdf/Ontario%20Property%20Assessment-%20The%20 Ground%20Rules,%202004.pdf>).

(f) Looking at the Assessment Rolls

The foundation of the property taxation system is the assessment roll, an annually compiled list of all properties in a municipality. They include the name of the property owner and tenant and their respective addresses. They show the area of the land and the assessed value. Although each municipal office keeps a copy of its assessment roll, the masters are kept in MPAC's database.

Because real estate is fixed, tangible, and well catalogued, it is easy to tax from a government's viewpoint. In the assessment rolls, every property is recorded by MPAC's assessors and a current market value (*ad valorem*, for lovers of Latin) is attributed to each one.

Assessment rolls are kept in the clerk's department of every municipality. However, they are also accessible by computer in most town halls. By looking up the address of a particular property you can find the owner's name, the tenant(s), the use, the land dimensions and area, and the assessed value. When searching information in assessment rolls, you find, at the top left portion of the roll sheets, a number, which refers to the first property on that sheet. The numbers below represent the way the municipality is divided for assessment purposes. For example:

Cnty.	Mun.	Map	Div.	Sub-Div.
19	08	04	2	300

The explanation is:
Cnty. = County Number
Mun. = Municipality Number
Map = Map or Ward Number
Div. = Division within the Ward
Sub-Div. = Sub-Division within the Ward

This will allow you to find the block. You then have to follow the numbers within the block. Each property has a specific number in the left column to keep tenants and owners of a given property together. Remember that every assessed unit has its own number. This means that a property with four tenants will have five numbers: one for the owner and one for each of the tenants. When searching in the assessment rolls, it is a good idea to make a note of all details given for each property, such as parcel frontage or a comparison to other properties, which may come in useful in the future.

5.1.2 QUOTING PROPERTY TAX AMOUNTS

Typically, taxes are quoted by real estate professionals on a per m² (sq ft) basis. When a property is offered for sale, the agent usually indicates the amount of the property taxes on the listing — information that can be obtained from the vendor (which is not always totally reliable unless supported by a property tax bill) or from the assessment rolls. The only interesting thing, from a buyer's viewpoint, is to try to determine if the taxes are too high and could be appealed. As real estate agents, we are in the habit of asking vendors if they have appealed the tax assessment in the past few years. If the answer is "no", there is a possibility that the taxes could be lowered. Doing so can have a huge impact. An $800 annual rebate roughly amounts to an increase of $10,000 in value of the property.

The only interesting thing, from a buyer's viewpoint, is to try to determine if the taxes are too high and could be appealed.

Prior to the property tax system reform, there was a major difference in the amount of taxes paid for a property located in Metropolitan Toronto and others in the Greater Toronto Area. The difference is now less and Toronto property owners hope the gap will continue to narrow.

5.2 INCOME TAXES

Unravel the intricacies of the tax system. Use capital cost allowance and capital gains and losses to your tax avoidance advantage.

Taxes must be paid, but it is the right of each taxpayer to pay as little tax as legally possible. In most western countries the top tax bracket is currently 40-48% (46.41% in Ontario), which most taxpayers say is too much. With the help of a skilled tax expert, you can devise several effective strategies to minimize the tax you pay.

There is, however, a fine line between tax avoidance, which is legal, and tax evasion, which is illegal. Tax evasion takes place when a taxpayer does not declare income earned, for example, when a waiter does not declare tips received, when a university student tutors grade school students but fails to include the income in his tax return, or when a consultant receives a cheque but cashes it and does not declare the income. A prudent person will use tax avoidance, not tax evasion.

There is, however, a fine line between tax avoidance, which is legal, and tax evasion, which is illegal.

Generally, the best way to reduce tax is to postpone the due date for payment. For example, when a property increases in value, the property owner is subject to income tax only when the profits are realized, that is, when the property is sold. There are three obvious ways to pay less tax:

1. have less income
2. postpone the income, depending on the kind of income you have (for example, commission income, try to receive it January 1st, rather than December 31st), or
3. have greater expenses.

Each year's tax rates are available from a variety of sources. Here is some information available in early 2007, but you should not act upon it without professional advice.

In calculating the Corporate Tax Rate, you must add the federal and provincial or territorial rates together. The federal rate is calculated as follows:

- The basic rate of Part I tax is 38% of your taxable income (28% after federal tax abatement) and is subject to a 4% surtax, which works out to be 1.12% (28% x 4%[1]). Therefore the effective tax rate after federal tax abatement is 29.12% (28% + 1.12%).
- For Canadian-controlled private corporations (CCPC), which claim the small business deduction (tax credit of 16%[2]), the net tax rate is 12% (28% - 16%). This is accomplished when the CCPC retains the first $400,000 (or fraction thereof) of active business income. If, and when, that $400,000 is paid out as salary, or dividend, the recipient pays personal income tax on it.
- This is also subject to the additional surtax of 1.12%. This makes the effective tax rate for CCPCs 13.12% (12% + 1.12%).
- For other corporations, the net tax rate is 22.12%, due to the 4% surtax.

---

1 This 4% surtax will be eliminated for all businesses by January 2008 (and prorated for the fiscal years that straddled this date).
2 Will increase to 16.5% on January 1, 2008, and to 17% on January 1, 2009.

- A CCPC may postpone the inclusion of salary or bonus to its owners/managers for 1 year. It can deduct the amount involved from its income if it has a legal obligation to pay it at its fiscal year end, provided it does so within 180 days. The employee declares the income in the year he receives it. (See *Income Tax Act*, (R.S.C. 1985, c. 1 (5th Supp.)) subsection 78(4) and check out <www.taxtips.ca/filing.htm>.)

All of the above information relates to federal taxes only (see the "2006 T2 Corporation – Income Tax Guide" at <www.cra-arc.gc.ca>). In addition to federal taxes, provincial taxes are also applicable. Generally, provinces and territories have two rates of income tax — a lower rate and a higher rate. The lower rate applies to either:
- the income eligible for the federal small business deduction (SBD), or
- the income based on limits established by the particular province or territory.

The higher rate applies to all other taxable income. For Ontario, the corporate tax rate is 14% and the deduction for SBD is 8.5%, making the effective tax rate for CCPCs 5.5%. The rates vary in each province.

Navigating the Canadian income tax system is not for the faint of heart. Rates and regulations change almost every year. If you are involved with real estate investments, unless your taxable income is very low, it pays to ensure you consult a tax specialist once or twice a year.

5.2.1 TAXES ON RENTAL INCOME

Canada Revenue Agency (CRA) has many rules that must be followed to calculate rental income and expenses for income tax purposes, particularly around what should be considered capital expenses (i.e., depreciated over the years and at which rate) and what should be included in current (annual) expenses. To find the answer to these questions and many others visit the CRA Web site. This is a huge Web site and, because of its size, it is often difficult to find the item you are seeking. However, they have a wonderful list of tax guides and pamphlets listed at <http://www.cra-arc.gc.ca/menu/TGTG_T-e.html>.

5.2.2 CAPITAL COST ALLOWANCE (CCA) AND ASSET CLASSES

Use capital cost allowance to your tax avoidance advantage.

Accountants call it Capital Cost Allowance (CCA); laypeople call it depreciation. Depreciation is the loss in value of an asset over time, due to wear and tear. For example, if a new air conditioning system is supposed to last 10 years and costs $50,000, the loss in value due to this factor is $5,000 per year. There are various assets that can be depreciated for tax purposes, with the most significant for a real estate investor being the property itself. The various asset classes have different rates of CCA, with most buildings falling under the 4% rate. However, when you review Figure 5.6, which presents a sampling of asset classes and their corresponding depreciation rates, you will see a number of other assets that can be depreciated, such as fences, which can be depreciated at 10% per year.

Depreciation is the loss in value of an asset over time, due to wear and tear.

Figure 5.6
Asset Classes Determined for CCA Purposes

List of CCA rates and classes

The following chart is a **partial list** and description of the most common capital cost allowance (CCA) classes. You will find a complete list in Schedule II of the *Income Tax Regulations*.

Class number	Description	CCA rate
1	Most buildings made of brick, stone, or cement acquired after 1987, including their component parts such as electric wiring, lighting fixtures, plumbing, heating and cooling equipment, elevators, and escalators	4%
3	Most buildings made of brick, stone, or cement acquired before 1988, including their component parts as listed in Class 1 above	5%
6	Buildings made of frame, log, stucco on frame, galvanized iron, or corrugated metal that are used in the business of farming or fishing, or that have no footings below-ground; fences and most greenhouses	10%
7	Canoes, boats, and most other vessels, including their furniture, fittings, or equipment	15%
8	Property that is not included in any other class such as furniture, calculators and cash registers (that do not record multiple sales taxes), photocopy and fax machines, printers, display fixtures, refrigeration equipment, machinery, tools costing $200 or more, and outdoor advertising billboards and greenhouses with rigid frames and plastic covers	20%
9	Aircraft, including furniture, fittings, or equipment attached, and their spare parts	25%
10	Automobiles (except taxis and others used for lease or rent), vans, wagons, trucks, buses, tractors, trailers, drive-in theatres, general-purpose electronic data-processing equipment (e.g., personal computers) and systems software, and timber-cutting and removing equipment	30%
10.1	Passenger vehicles costing more than $30,000 if acquired after 2000	30%
12	Chinaware, cutlery, linen, uniforms, dies, jigs, moulds or lasts, computer software (except systems software), cutting or shaping parts of a machine, certain property used for earning rental income such as apparel or costumes, and videotape cassettes; certain property costing less than $200 such as kitchen utensils, tools, and medical or dental equipment	100%
13	Property that is leasehold interest (the maximum CCA rate depends on the type of leasehold and the terms of the lease)	N/A
14	Patents, franchises, concessions, and licences for a limited period – the CCA is limited to whichever is less: ■ the capital cost of the property spread out over the life of the property; or ■ the undepreciated capital cost of the property at the end of the tax year. Class 14 also includes patents, and licences to use patents for a limited period, that you elect not to include in Class 44	N/A
16	Automobiles for lease or rent, taxicabs, and coin-operated video games or pinball machines; certain tractors and large trucks acquired after December 6, 1991, that are used to haul freight and that weigh more than 11,788 kilograms	40%
17	Roads, sidewalks, parking-lot or storage areas, telephone, telegraph, or non-electronic data communication switching equipment	8%
38	Most power-operated movable equipment acquired after 1987 used for moving, excavating, placing, or compacting earth, rock, concrete, or asphalt	30%
39	Machinery and equipment acquired after 1987 that is used in Canada primarily to manufacture and process goods for sale or lease	25%
43	Manufacturing and processing machinery and equipment acquired after February 25, 1992, described in Class 39 above	30%
44	Patents and licences to use patents for a limited or unlimited period that the corporation acquired after April 26, 1993 – However, you can elect not to include such property in Class 44 by attaching a letter to the return for the year the corporation acquired the property. In the letter, indicate the property you do not want to include in Class 44	25%
45	Computer equipment that is "general-purpose electronic data processing equipment and system software" included in paragraph f of Class 10 acquired after March 22, 2004	45%
46	Data network infrastructure equipment that supports advanced telecommunication applications, acquired after March 22, 2004 – it includes assets such as switches, multiplexers, routers, hubs, modems, and domain name servers that are used to control, transfer, modulate and direct data, but does not include office equipment such as telephones, cell phones or fax machines, or property such as wires, cables or structures	30%

Source: Canada Revenue Agency, "T2 Corporation – Income Tax Guide 2006"

In addition to wear and tear, buildings suffer from economic obsolescence. These are the drawbacks to buildings that are not economical to improve or update. The most typical example would be an industrial building with 3.6-metre (12-foot) ceilings, which are generally less than ideal. Although the roof can be raised, it is not usually economically feasible to do so.

In Canada, buildings (not including land) are depreciated at 4% per year on a declining balance. CCA is claimed on the capital cost (or purchase price) of the building, minus the value of the land and any CCA claimed in previous years. Note, however, that in the first year of a purchase CRA allows you to deduct only 2% (half a full year). The intent of this "50% Rule" is probably to prevent investors from closing on a purchase on December 31st in order to claim CCA for a full year.

The balance (of the property value) declines over the years you claim CCA, as shown in the example following, which disregards the 50% Rule in the first year to better illustrate what happens to property value over the ownership period. The balance shows the amount that can be deducted each year, from income, for tax purposes.

Purchase price		$5,000,000
Land value		$500,000
Building value		$4,500,000
Building depreciation:		
Year 1 CCA	$4,500,000 x 4% =	$180,000
Balance		$4,320,000
Year 2 CCA	$4,320,000 x 4% =	$172,800
Balance		$4,147,200

The Depreciation Table in Figure 5.7 demonstrates the results of this approach over the years.

Figure 5.7
Depreciation Table

4% Declining Balance Over 30 Years

Year	Remaining Book Value %	Yearly depreciation	Accumulated Depreciation
1	100	4	4
2	96	3.84	7.84
3	92.16	3.69	11.53
4	88.47	3.54	15.07
5	84.93	3.4	18.47
6	81.53	3.26	21.73
7	78.27	3.13	24.86
8	75.14	3.01	27.87
9	72.13	2.89	30.76
10	69.24	2.77	33.53
11	66.47	2.66	35.16
12	63.81	2.55	38.74
13	61.26	2.45	41.19
14	58.81	2.35	43.54
15	56.46	2.26	45.8
16	54.2	2.17	47.97
17	52.03	2.08	50.05
18	49.95	2	52.05
19	47.95	1.92	53.97
20	46.03	1.84	55.81
21	44.19	1.77	57,58
22	42.42	1.7	59.28
23	40.72	1.63	60.91
24	39.09	1.56	62.47
25	37.53	1.5	63.97
26	36.03	1.44	65.41
27	34.59	1.38	66.79
28	33.21	1.33	68.12
29	31.88	1.28	69.4
30	30.6	1.22	70.62

5.2.3 RECAPTURE

When selling a depreciable property, if the sale price is greater than the purchase price plus the CCA, all or part of the CCA must be recaptured by adding it to the cost base (purchase price), as demonstrated in the following example:

Purchase Price (March 31, 2002)	**$1,100,000**
Allocation of value:	
Building	$800,000
Land	$300,000
Depreciation Taken (CCA)	
2002 2% (50% Rule) x $800,000 = $ 16,000 (undepreciated balance $784,000)	
2003 4% x $784,000 = $ 31,360 (undepreciated balance $752,640)	
2004 4% x $752,640 = $ 30,106 (undepreciated balance $722,534)	
Total CCA	**$ 77,466**
Balance available for further depreciation	$722,534
Sale Price (December 31, 2004)	**$2,000,000**
Calculation of Taxable Income upon Sale	
Sale Price	$2,000,000
Plus CCA deducted during ownership	$ 77,466
Total Value	$2,077,466
Less Purchase Price	$1,100,000
Profit (Taxable Income)	**$ 977,466**

5.2.4 DISPOSITION OF DEPRECIABLE PROPERTY

There are many intricacies in our tax laws and this is not an easy part of the investing game. We recommend that you consult a tax specialist when or if you are faced with this situation.

You cannot claim a capital loss if you sell a depreciable property for less than what you paid for it, but there is also no capital gain if a property is sold for less than its original capital cost, but more than its undepreciated capital cost. And, in fact, this situation may justify a recapture of capital cost allowance. See the example below.

Purchase price	$20,000
Less CCA taken over the years	$ 8,000
Undepreciated Capital Cost (UCC)	$12,000
Selling Price	$15,000

For income tax purposes, because the purchase price ($20,000) exceeds the selling price ($15,000), no income tax is payable, in spite of the fact that the UCC is less than the selling price.

To determine if there should be recapture of CCA:

Selling price	$15,000
Plus CCA taken over the years	$ 8,000
Total	**$23,000**
Minus Purchase Price	$20,000
Recapture of CCA subject to Income Tax	**$ 3,000**

The following outlays and selling expenses are deducted from the selling price (proceeds of disposition):
- fixing up expenses
- finder's fee
- commissions
- legal fees (incurred when purchasing and selling)
- broker's fees
- surveyor's fees
- land transfer taxes, and
- other reasonable expenses directly connected with the sale.

5.2.5 TAXATION ON INVESTMENT INCOME

The taxation levels vary depending on the type of investment generating the income.
- **Interest Income.** This type of income, when earned by an individual, is treated exactly the same as salary income. If you earn $100 in interest income and are in a 40% tax bracket, you will end up paying $40 in tax.
- **Dividend Income.** The taxation of business income often represents a compromise. Profit earned by a corporation is taxed; then, when the after-tax profit is distributed in the form of dividends, it is taxed again in the hands of the shareholder. This is called double taxation. There are special tax credits for eligible dividends from CCPCs.
- **Capital Gains and Losses.** When you sell certain investments, like real estate or stocks, under some circumstances (see CRA's IT218R in 5.2.6) a profit is considered a capital gain. Only 50% of the profit is taxable at an individual's personal tax rate. However, in the case of a capital loss, 100% can be deducted for income tax purposes. For example, if you buy a stock for $100 and sell it for $200, making a $100 profit, you will include only $50 in your income. If you're in a 40% tax bracket, you'll end up paying $20 tax on that income. On the other hand, if you sold your stock for just $50, you could deduct the $50 loss from your current, or future, year's income.

5.2.6 CALCULATION OF CAPITAL GAINS

Use capital gains to your tax avoidance advantage.

As noted above, in Canada, 50% of capital gains (and 100% of allowable capital losses) are included for income tax purposes. This means that if you (individual or corporation) make a profit on the sale of a property of, say, $500,000, you include only $250,000 (50%) of it in your income. Assuming you are in the top tax bracket, in

Ontario you would pay only 23.2% of your profit in taxes. The tax rate on capital gains varies among the provinces and territories, ranging between a low of 19.5% in Alberta to a high of 24.32% in Newfoundland and Labrador. Regardless, this is a powerful incentive to sell. Note that the capital gain preferential rate can be used by entities involved in real estate as a business, under certain circumstances.

You can even defer paying taxes on a portion of the proceeds by way of capital gain reserves. The *Income Tax Act* limits the postponement to:
- 80% of the gain, enjoyed in the year of sale
- 60% in the 2nd year
- 40% in the 3rd year, and
- 20% in the 4th year.

This can be achieved by the vendor taking back a mortgage (VTB). See the example below.

Assumptions

Amount receivable (Net Proceeds):	$2,000,000
VTB mortgage:	$ 900,000
Cash received:	$1,100,000
Tax bracket:	46%

The end result is:

Situation #1 – Without VTB
$2,000,000 x 50% = $1,000,000 (taxable profits after capital gains)
Tax due in year of sale: $1,000,000 x 46% (+/-) = $460,000

Situation #2 – With VTB
$900,000 x 50% = $450,000 (taxable profits after capital gains)
Tax due in year of sale: $450,000 x 46% (+/-) = $207,000

It is not a good idea to place a VTB mortgage on a property for a period of two years or less before selling the property because the CRA will not usually accept the decrease in capital gains. However, it is generally acceptable if done when buying, or if refinancing, more than two years before selling.

The beauty of the vendor taking back a mortgage is that, in addition to postponing the tax due, the mortgage can be used as collateral, or assigned as security, if you want to borrow money against it.

To be entitled to a capital gain treatment, it is necessary to enjoy (yes, it is enjoyable to see one's taxes cut in half) one of these situations only every few years or the CRA will disallow it, treating it as business income.

We would be remiss not to mention the once-in-a-lifetime $500,000 capital gains exemption for the sale of shares of a qualified small business corporation. Many people do not take advantage of this wonderful opportunity. Note that it is only available to individuals, not to corporations.

It is not easy to determine if one can take advantage of the capital gain provision. The following excerpt from CRA's IT218R may clarify it for you.

There is no provision in the Income Tax Act, which describes the circumstances in which gains from the sale of real estate are to be determined as being income or capital. However, in making such determinations, the courts have considered factors such as those listed below: (The list is not intended to be exclusive of any other factor.) (a) the taxpayer's intention with respect to the real estate at the time of its purchase; (b) feasibility of the taxpayer's intention; (c) geographical location and zoned use of the real estate acquired; (d) extent to which intention carried out by the taxpayer; (e) evidence that the taxpayer's intention changed after purchase of the real estate; (f) the nature of the business, profession, calling or trade of the taxpayer and associates; (g) the extent to which borrowed money was used to finance the real estate acquisition and the terms of the financing, if any, arranged; (h) the length of time throughout which the real estate was held by the taxpayer; (i) the existence of persons other than the taxpayer who share interests in the real estate; (j) the nature of the occupation of the other persons referred to in (i) above as well as their stated intentions and courses of conduct; (k) factors which motivated the sale of the real estate; (l) evidence that the taxpayer and/or associates had dealt extensively in real estate.

The CRA guide T4037, *Capital Gains 2006*, is also very helpful, particularly the comprehensive glossary, the explanation on how to determine whether or not you have a capital gain situation and how to calculate it, and the clarification of capital loss. It also contains a solid section on recapture.

You will also find good tax information for rental properties in *T4036-4, Rental Income* at <www.cra-adrc.go.ca>. You will learn, for example, that if you modify a building to accommodate persons with disabilities, you can deduct the expenses in the year incurred, rather than having to add them to the capital cost of your building and deduct them over a much longer period of time. Another interesting document is T4002-06(e), *Business and Professional Income*. In its 51 pages you will find everything you need to know about reporting income correctly.

5.2.7 CAPITAL LOSSES

Use capital losses to your tax avoidance advantage.

After covering the very pleasant subject of capital gains, further comment is needed on capital losses. Generally, you have a capital gain when you sell a capital property, such as real estate, a boat, a truck, stocks, bonds, jewelry, etc., and realize a profit. A capital loss is the opposite; you sell for less than you paid. Usually, one works hard to avoid losses, but they do occur. Although a capital loss can be used to reduce income tax, CRA looks closely at capital losses that are reported too frequently.

The tax rule says that a capital loss can be deducted only against capital gains. Capital losses can be deducted at 100% and can be carried forward 10 years and back 3 years. Let's look at an example in connection to real estate.

You bought a house 4 years ago to renovate and resell at a profit; however, you ended up losing $25,000 when you sold. One year ago, you again bought a house and everything went well. Your profit upon selling was $40,000. The $25,000 loss on the first house can be used to offset the profit on the second: $40,000 - $25,000 = $15,000 profit. It is certainly worth the effort to create a capital gain situation if one has a capital loss on the books.

5.2.8 WITHDRAWAL AT SOURCE

CRA demands that when a payment for interests, royalties, management fees, licensing fees, etc, is made to an offshore entity, the payer must withdraw a percentage (most commonly 25%) of the money and forward it to CRA. This applies to mortgage interests as well, if the mortgage is for five years or less. However, if the mortgage is for a term of more than five years, the payments made are considered to be returns of capital (until the latter has been fully repaid, of course) and, therefore, the person paying does not have to withdraw the dreaded 25%.

For example, if you buy a property in Canada and secure a six-year mortgage from an offshore lender, from the start the payments will be entered in your books as return of capital, on which no tax is due.

5.2.9 PRESCRIBED INTEREST RATES

If you make your investments using a corporation, this section will be of interest to you. The CRA periodically changes the interest rates used for income tax purposes. For the second quarter of 2007 the rates are 9% for overdue taxes, Canadian Pension Plan and Employment Insurance. Therefore you can "borrow" from the CRA at 9% interest. However, if you overpay, they will use 7% (not exactly fair, is it?).

5.2.10 GOODS AND SERVICES TAX – TAXABLE AND NON-TAXABLE ITEMS

In general, all goods and services are subject to 5% Goods and Services Tax (GST), in Canada, unless they are specifically designated as non-taxable. (However, some provinces and territories have harmonized this tax with their provincial sales tax to create the Harmonized Sales Tax (HST).) Non-taxable goods and services fall into two categories: zero-rated and tax-exempt. A supplier making a zero-rated sale is entitled to tax credits, but a supplier making a tax-exempt sale is not. A zero-rated sale has no GST at all. Zero-rated goods and services are:
- basic groceries
- prescription drugs
- certain medical devices
- exports, and
- certain agricultural and fishing activities.

Some exempted goods and services are:
- sales of existing residential properties, including multi-family
- residential rents, including parking spaces
- most health care and dental services
- day care services
- legal aid services
- many educational services
- financial services
- interests and dividends
- insurance and mortgage brokerage services, and
- most sales and long-term leases of real property by non-profit organizations.

From studying the above, it is easy to conclude that GST is due on the purchase of commercial property with an existing building. The sum due could be impressive. For example, the purchaser of a $3,000,000 property would owe $3,000,000 x 5% = $150,000 in GST. Typically, the buyer registers for GST before the closing of the transaction takes place. This assumes that the buyer has a business, or rental income, on which he will charge GST to his customers or an investment corporation, which will collect rentals, including GST. Note that this would not include residential rents, which are GST exempt. Upon purchasing the property, the buyer is usually able to claim input tax credits for the tax paid, allowing him to apply for a refund of GST. If the buyer of a property is a non-resident of Canada, he must pay the GST at closing time. Of course, many get around this by registering a provincial or federal corporation, in which case they will pay the GST due by deducting the GST they collect over time (assuming that the property owner collects GST from tenants) or by requesting a refund from CRA. Note, however, that GST is not payable on the purchase of multi-family buildings, and commissions paid to real estate agents are subject to GST.

5.2.11 TAX TIPS

For more detailed tax information visit the Canadian Tax Foundation Web site at <www.ctf.ca>. There are also a number of products available from the Canadian publisher, CCH Canadian. In addition, several major tax firms display a smorgasbord of tax information on their Web sites, along with budget information, tax calculators, and articles related to tax matters on personal and business affairs, including the following:

- KPMG <www.kpmg.ca>
- Ernst & Young <www.eycan.com> (Allows you to enter taxable income and province of residence, then determines your approximate tax due, gives your marginal tax rate for regular income, dividends, and capital gains.)
- H&R Block <www.hrblock.ca>
- BDO Dunwoody LLP <www.bdo.ca>

CHAPTER
6

Forms of Property Ownership

By the end of this chapter, you will be able to:
- Recognize fee simple as the purest form of ownership and know that it flows from the concept referred to as "bundle of rights".
- Understand that in a life estate the holder can grant another person use of the property without granting the person the right to sell it.
- Identify joint-tenancy as equal ownership by multiple people that includes the rules of survivorship.
- Determine that tenancy-in-common differs from joint-tenancy in that ownership does not end at death, but passes to the estate.
- Differentiate between the advantages and disadvantages for the tenant and landlord of a leasehold estate as opposed to ownership.
- Recognize a syndicate as a group of entities investing together and the types that might exist.
- Weigh the pros and cons of most common types of vehicles through which you can invest.

One may be the owner of a real property by acquiring it in different ways — from a legal and fiscal viewpoint. This chapter explains the most common forms of ownership.

6.1 FEE SIMPLE OWNERSHIP

Recognize fee simple as the purest form of ownership and know that it flows from the concept referred to as "bundle of rights".

The purest form of ownership of real property is fee simple, which is the highest estate or "absolute right" in a real property. It is ownership with the fewest limitations. This is the most commonly encountered form of ownership and the simplest. The owner in fee simple can be an individual (John Doe), a corporation (John Doe Inc.), or a Real Estate Investment Trust (REIT).

The highest level of fee simple flows from the concept of the "bundle of rights". The owner of a property in fee simple has the right to a bundle of rights that make up the intangible components of real property, including the right to:
- sell it
- lease it
- enter (use) it
- give it away, or
- refrain to do any of the above.

This is, of course, subject to governmental limitations, which have steadily eroded the original concept.

Remember that these rights can be subdivided. For example, a property can be divided in horizontal planes that would result in:
- surface rights
- sub-surface rights (minerals, water), and
- air rights, which stem from zoning regulations. For example a site may be improved with a two-storey building when the zoning allows for 50 storeys; in many jurisdictions, this extra density (or air rights) can be transferred to another site.

6.2 LIFE ESTATE

Understand that in a life estate the holder can grant another person use of the property without granting the person the right to sell it.

A freehold property can be held as a life estate, which means that it is limited to the life of the landholder. This rarely encountered situation would exist when the grantor in a deed, or a will, grants an interest in a property to another person, but only until the latter dies. For example, a father, in his will, grants a life estate right to his son David, but upon David's death a designated charity will inherit the property. This is a way for the grantor to permit another person use of the property, without granting that person the right to sell it.

6.3 JOINT-TENANCY

Identify joint-tenancy as equal ownership by multiple people that includes the rules of survivorship.

This is a type of ownership of real property, by two or more persons, in which each owns an undivided interest in the whole. Joint tenants have one and the same interest, accruing by one and the same conveyance, commencing at one and the same time, and held by one and the same undivided possession. The primary quality of joint-tenancy is survivorship, by which the entire tenancy, on the death of any joint tenant, remains with the survivors and, at length, to the last survivor. This would be used, for example, by two or more brothers who have no descendants, but want a property to stay in the family.

6.4 TENANCY-IN-COMMON

Determine that tenancy-in-common differs from joint-tenancy in that ownership does not end at death, but passes to the estate.

Tenancy-in-common is a form of ownership whereby each tenant holds an undivided interest in property. Unlike a joint tenancy, the interest of a tenant-in-common does not terminate upon his death but passes to his estate or heirs. Tenancy-in-common is used, for example, when two brothers want to avoid the expense of registering as a corporation to buy a property, but want the property to pass to their heirs if one of the brothers should die. In that case, the heirs become the new tenants-in-common.

6.5 LEASEHOLD ESTATE

Differentiate between the advantages and disadvantages for the tenant and landlord of a leasehold estate as opposed to ownership.

A leasehold estate is created when you don't own the land but lease the rights to it. This is rarely used with unimproved land; usually a leasehold estate applies to zoned land on which the tenant plans to erect a building. Leaseholds are frequently used by fastfood restaurants that build on pads leased to them. Some operators, Burger King for example, develop all their restaurants this way. It allows these businesses to benefit from the best possible tax structure. On the other hand, they forego the appreciation of the property.

The advantage of a leasehold for the tenant is that he does not have to buy the land, therefore reducing the financial investment. The disadvantage is that as the term of the lease comes close to its end, it becomes practically impossible to sell the leasehold interest in the property because it has very little residual value.

The advantage to the landowner is that he has marvellous security. Indeed, if the tenant defaults, the landowner will either end up with a new, hopefully stronger, tenant, or make a deal with the bankruptcy trustee and buy the leasehold interest. Very often, the land lease has periodic escalations in the rental (every 5 or 10 years, or any period agreed upon between landlord and tenant). It can also be indexed on, for example, the cost of living index. For example, a lease of land may contain the following terms:

- term: 99 years
- rental: 7.625% of the fair market value of the land, and
- increases: fair market value shall be negotiated every 10 years, except that there shall not be any increase in the last 30 years of the lease.

The disadvantage for the landowner is that the property is encumbered by a very long-term lease, is therefore difficult to sell, and the landowner has no tax sheltering since land cannot be depreciated. At the end of the lease, the improvements (e.g., buildings) will become his property. However, he can count on some serious deferred maintenance, which can represent a very large amount of money.

A land lease is virtually always "net"; that is, any expense involved with owning the land, with the exception of income tax, is paid by the tenant. The landowner must arrange to allow existing encumbrancers, if any, to postpone their interest in the title to permit the tenant/builder to place a first mortgage on the property. This means that, as part of the land lease, the landowner allows the placement of a first mortgage on the land. If the landowner did not do that, the tenant/builder would not be able to secure any financing or could do so only at an exorbitant rate of interest, because the lender would consider the risk very high.

6.6 SYNDICATES

Recognize a syndicate as a group of entities investing together and the types that might exist.

Syndicates were much in fashion a few decades ago but are less used today. Here are three definitions of syndicates:

1. associations formed for the promotion of a particular enterprise
2. combination of commercial firms associated to forward a common interest, and
3. a group of individuals or organizations, combined, or making a joint effort, to undertake some specific duty or to carry out specific transactions or negotiations.

As can be seen from the above, any group of individuals or companies joining to invest in real estate can be called a syndicate.

Syndicates can be either private or public. Private syndicates require an active involvement on the part of the investors and offer limited liability protection unless the investors form a corporation, whereas public syndicates, sometimes called Public Equity Syndicates, do not require active involvement of the investors and provide liability protection. Today, REITs are the best known kind of syndicates.

This book is written for the investor who buys real estate directly, or in association with other people, rather than purchasing shares of a public vehicle, such as a REIT. However, because an individual can start his real estate investment program with just a few hundred dollars by buying shares of a REIT, more detail on REITs is provided in sections 2.4.3 and 6.7.5.

6.7 VEHICLES TO INVEST IN REAL ESTATE

Weigh the pros and cons of most common types of vehicles through which you can invest.

The most likely types of business or legal entities through which you can make your real estate investments are the following:
- corporations
  - private and
  - public
- partnerships
  - general and
  - limited
- joint ventures, and
- REITs.

Because of the substantial level of investment involved in commercial real estate and the accompanying risk, an investor would generally look to limit his personal liability by making his investments through a corporation, usually a private one, but each entity has its advantages and disadvantages when it comes to ownership of commercial real estate. An accountant or a real estate lawyer can advise you on how best to limit your personal liability.

6.7.1 CORPORATIONS

A corporation is a type of business organization that enjoys many of the rights usually attributed to a person, with the difference being that a corporation's debts and taxes are separate from its shareholders' obligations. A corporation is owned by the shareholders and managed by directors chosen by the shareholders.

Corporations are formal legal entities that can only be created by filing articles of incorporation and various registrations, as well as by paying fees to the jurisdiction in which the business is being incorporated. Corporations are considered a distinct taxable entity. The advantages of purchasing property through a corporation include immortality, limited personal liability, ease of selling corporate shares, and tax benefits.
- **Immortality.** This is a big advantage if a property owner is of a certain age and wants to leave the property to his children. If he owns it as an individual, the property will need to change hands upon his death. That is, the children will need to acquire title to the property in their names. In addition to considerable paperwork and legal expenses, the heirs will have to pay the Land Transfer Tax and tax on any profit realized. If a corporation owns the property, only its shares will change hands, which is much simpler and less expensive in time and money.

- **Limited Personal Liability.** Because the assets of a corporation belong to the corporation and not the owners, the owners are not liable for its debts. Personal liability is limited to the money used to buy shares in the corporation. Only in special, and rare, circumstances can the shareholders be held responsible for other debts or obligations of a corporation (e.g., if the corporation commits illegal acts).
- **Ease of Selling Corporate Shares.** There are two kinds of corporations — public and private. If the corporation is public (listed on a stock exchange), the shares can usually be sold easily. Selling shares in a private corporation is more difficult and the process should be clearly set out in the shareholders' agreement, if there are several shareholders. It would be more accurate to say that transferring shares is easy, but finding an interested buyer is not.
- **Tax Benefits.** From a tax viewpoint, corporations win hands down. Dividend income is treated better than interest income. Top personal income tax hovers around 46% for interest income, but is approximately 31% for dividend income. At the same time, corporations can deduct interest expenses even on personal use properties, such as residences. This situation has led some savvy individuals to lease a home owned by their corporation.

The most favourable tax treatment is on capital gains, which is taxed at half the rate of interest or salaried income (i.e., 23%). This is powerful motivation for a real estate investor to buy, improve, and sell real estate. To present this vividly, of three entities receiving $100, one would pay $46 in taxes (personal), the second $38 (corporation), and the third $23 (capital gain)!

(a) Private Corporations

In a private corporation, shareholders generally have significant input into how the company is run and, in many cases, they work for the company as well. The shareholders' agreement should include, among other points: how the company will be organized and who will be entitled to have a nominee on the board of directors, who will work for the company and what duties each will have as employee and/or officer, under what circumstances the company will issue additional shares, and whether there will be any restrictions on the transfer of shares.

It costs $600 to $900 to register a private corporation, and the corporation must have an accountant prepare and file an annual tax return, at a cost of $1,000 to $2,000 (for a small corporation). A private corporation can also lead to double taxation (corporation and shareholders). If a corporation makes a profit, it pays taxes on it. Then, if these profits are distributed to shareholders, the shareholders pay taxes on them again. However, under most circumstances, the tax paid by the corporation combined with that paid by shareholders on dividends yields a lower amount of tax

> *In a private corporation, shareholders generally have significant input into how the company is run.*

than the individual would have paid had he received the income directly rather than through the corporate vehicle. Alternatively, if the company pays out a management fee to a shareholder, that management fee is deductible from the company income; therefore, the company pays no tax on that amount and the individual pays the entire tax on the management fee received.

(b) Public Corporations

A public corporation is much more expensive to register ($150,000 to $200,000) and to maintain ($60,000 to $100,000/year). In Ontario, the Ontario Securities Commission (OSC) has a number of hoops through which a person registering a corporation must jump. It is very costly in both time and money. A public corporation is usually created via a process called an Initial Public Offering (IPO). There is, however, another way to become a public corporation. This is by way of a merger with an existing public company, commonly known as a "Reverse Merger" of a shell company. A shell company is one that has no active business and no substantial assets or liabilities, but whose shares qualify for trading on the public securities markets provided that certain criteria are met and its filings are kept current. The advantages of a Reverse Merger over an IPO are outlined below.

- The costs of acquiring an existing company in a Reverse Merger, at $80,000 to $100,000, are significantly less than for an IPO.
- The time required is considerably shorter than for an IPO.
- An underwriter is not required while, typically, IPOs require one or more underwriters, who do not come cheap.

When a public company, or shell company, merges with an active business, the shell company eventually takes the name of the active business and the assets and liabilities of the business become the assets and liabilities of the shell company. The shareholders of the active business become the majority shareholders of the shell company. The shell then files a registration with the Exchange Commission, applies for its stock market symbol, and arranges coverage with Market Makers (dealers who use the firm's capital to buy and sell stocks they represent).

The original shareholders of the shell company usually retain a small interest in the merged company and, once it is publicly traded, they are able (within certain restrictions) to sell their stock. This allows them to make money by selling shares that, without the reverse merger, would have had no value.

6.7.2 PARTNERSHIPS

A partnership is an agreement between two or more parties to carry on a business in common with the belief that they will make a profit.

The main points to remember about partnerships are outlined here.
- The partnership will dissolve upon the death of one of the partners.
- There is no limited personal liability, however, one could achieve the best of both worlds by having a corporation (with limited liability) take title of a property as a trustee for a group of individuals, corporate owners, or partners. This is commonly done.
- Interest in the partnership cannot be sold. A new partnership must be created if one of the partners wants to sell his interest.
- It is simple and inexpensive to register.
- There is no double taxation of profits, as in a corporation. In fact, a partnership is non-taxable because the business results flow through to the partners. From this, come two implications:
  - the inception agreements between the partners should specify who gets the various tax deductions, including the Capital Cost Allowance (CCA) (who gets what, and what percentage), and
  - if one anticipates losses during the first few years of activity, these too can flow through to the partners, who can use them to reduce their taxable income.
- The CCA (depreciation of assets) can be claimed by each partner on his income tax return.

The registration of a partnership is done provincially at the Companies and Personal Security Branch of the Ministry of Consumer and Corporate Relations. In many cases it can be done by mail (6 to 8 weeks), on the

Internet, or in person. A partnership with more than five partners at any time in a fiscal period must file a partnership information return with Canada Revenue Agency (CRA) to ensure that they claim only the right amount of CCA.

The main reason partnerships (of individuals) are not used very often in real estate is that the liability of the partners is unlimited while, in a corporation, each shareholder's liability is limited to the amount he has invested when he purchased the shares. However, corporations and partnerships can present advantages:

- The pooling of resources allows for larger projects.
- The larger projects/investments may justify the hiring of an outside property management company.
- The combined financial means of several partners may permit more advantageous financing terms.
- If the partners live in different cities, it permits an easy geographical diversification.
- The pooling of business experiences may create a synergy that makes 1+1=3.
- As mentioned above, the flow-through of profit and losses may be beneficial in the sense that losses could be used to offset income from other sources.

Before any partnership is formed, the partners must consider whether they are really compatible. How well do they know each other? How will they react in case of trouble? Is everyone assessing the risks involved in the same manner? Is there agreement on the goals for investments and, most importantly, are these goals clearly specified and understood by each participant? For example, how long will the partnership hold the property before selling? five years? 10? 20?

Once the vision of the partnership is explored, it is wise for all parties to develop and sign a partnership agreement.

Once the vision of the partnership is explored, it is wise for all parties to develop and sign a partnership agreement (see section 6.7.2(c)), but first you must consider what kind of partnership you will form. There are two kinds of partnership: general and limited. Of these, general partnership is, by far, the most common.

(a) General Partnerships

In a general partnership, several people come into business together by registering a partnership under their own names, such as "Dino & Louis", or "Dino & Louis Dry-cleaning", or under an assumed name such as "Two Tall Brothers". The partners are fully liable for all debts and obligations.

(b) Limited Partnerships

Limited partnerships were in vogue a few years ago, but are rarely used now in Ontario because of the high costs in setting them up. The minimum size of an offering is $150,000 for each partner. It is also easy to spend $30,000 to $50,000 in legal costs to set up such a partnership because of the complex legal requirements. Limited partnerships fall under the Contract of Securities Commission rules.

In a limited partnership, one or more of the general partners is fully liable for all debts and obligations, and the limited partners (outside investors) are liable only for the amount of their investment. Generally, in addition to their share of the profits, the limited partners benefit from the income tax deductions, often called tax sheltering. The general partner has unlimited financial liability and is responsible for the running of the business and generally receives a salary and/or a fee. He makes all the decisions, good or bad. His actions are binding on the other partners. Usually, the general partner has only a small percentage of the shares. The main drawback of limited partnerships is that the interests in the partnership are not liquid.

A limited liability partnership (LLP) is a partnership other than a limited partnership, which is formed under section 44.1 of the *Partnerships Act* (R.S.O. 1990, c. P.5). Currently, only chartered accountants and lawyers can form LLPs.

(c) The Partnership Agreement

Although you can have a partnership without a written agreement, it is very wise to formulate and sign an agreement with the help of a lawyer. A partnership agreement is a private document, separate from the official document registering a partnership or a corporation. The primary reason for creating a partnership agreement is to protect the interests of the business and its owners. Below are some of the key points that should be considered.

- **Type of Partnership.** Will this be a general partnership or corporation?
- **Interests of the Partners.** Describe the interests of each partner, in dollars and percentages, and the contributions of each partner in terms of goods or equipment, financial, and work contributions.
- **Term of Partnership.** What is the duration of the partnership and what will happen to the partnership's assets at termination? What process will be followed if a partner dies or wants to withdraw from the partnership? Make sure there is a buy-sell clause.
- **Dispute Settlement.** What process will be followed in the event of disagreement? In the event of legal action, where will the venue be located? (This is especially important if partners live far away from each other). In the event of breach (real or imagined) of any term of the partnership agreement, what recourse/remedy will be available to the "innocent" partner(s)?
- **Location of Business.** Decide where your business will be located and the boundaries of your market area. If the business requires travelling, decide which partner will do it and the standards of expenses that will be covered (e.g., renting an economy vehicle versus renting a luxury car).
- **Financial Considerations.** How will salary amounts, profit distributions, and debt decisions (increase/pay down) be decided? How will changes to compensation be solved in the event of disagreement? (Note: It is common for one of the partners to contribute more to the success of the business than the others, particularly when it comes to sales, which is a frequent cause of conflict.) How will the kind and magnitude of perks, such as company vehicles and personal expenses, be monitored and allocated?
- **Guarantees.** It is always wise to stipulate that no partner may use his ownership in the business as security for personal commitments.
- **Day-to-day Operations.** What will each partner's role be, in the day-to-day operations of the business? Who will have the authority to sign cheques? Any limit to the amount? Who will keep the financial records? Where? How will the other partners have access to them? What kind of reporting must be made to partner(s) and by whom? How often? Who will have personnel hiring and firing authority? Who will make marketing and sales decisions? Who will make purchase decisions (capital and non-capital)? Up to what amount? Will partners' family members be allowed to work in the business or to supply to the business?

(d) A Note on Partnership/Shareholder Agreements

The majority of small business ventures start with a handshake (often, a "verbal" handshake). At this initial stage, many items have not been discussed and many assumptions are being made by each partner.

Often a projected business venture does not see the light of day and one party is left with all the responsibilities and expenses. Typically, one party devotes much more time to getting the venture off the ground and spends much more money. Nine times out of ten, if things don't come to fruition, the other party doesn't offer to pay his share of the expenses. To avoid this, it is prudent to have a "pre-nuptial" agreement or an Agreement to Form a Business Entity, even before you prepare and sign a Partnership or Shareholder Agreement. A sample of one of these is shown in Figure 6.1, offered by CCH Canadian Limited on their Web site <www.cch.com>.

It is prudent to have an Agreement to Form a Business Entity, even before you prepare and sign a Partnership or Shareholder Agreement.

A Partnership/Shareholder Agreement is a document that sets out the rules governing the behaviour, rights, and interests of the parties. It can be very long or just one page. We know of an architectural firm created in Toronto by two friends who were fresh out of school in the second half of the 1900s. The firm became a famous, very large firm that endured for 30 or 40 years. Their partnership document was less than one page long.

Even when two corporations form a partnership, there should be a Partnership/Shareholder Agreement. The Toronto law firm of Fogler, Rubinoff LLP provides some good legal advice on Shareholder Agreements.

In a closely held corporation, shareholders generally have significant input into how the company is run, and in many cases, work for the company as well.

What's in an agreement?

Issues you should cover in a shareholder's agreement depend very much on your particular situation. However, these are some of the areas you should consider:

- How will the company be organized and who will be entitled to have a nominee on the board of directors?
- Who will work for the company and what duties will each have as employee and/or officer?
- Will expenditures over a certain amount require, for instance, seventy-five percent or even unanimous approval of the shareholders?
- In what circumstances will the company issue additional shares?
- Will there be restrictions on the transfer of shares? For example, will there be a right of first refusal?
- How will the fair market value of the shares of the company be determined?
- Provide a process for the sale of shareholders' interests, in the event of death, disability or disagreement.

This list is by no means complete. Those considering setting up a closely held corporation should seek advice from an experienced lawyer on those elements that may be important for their specific situation.

It is also extremely important for each prospective shareholder to engage his own legal counsel to review the shareholders' agreement before signing.

A well-drafted shareholders' agreement will avoid those situations where owners are unable to agree on important decisions, thus causing the business to suffer.

Figure 6.1
Sample Agreement to Form a Business

The undersigned parties hereby agree to form a _____ (specify type of business entity), in the Province of Ontario, primarily for the following purposes: _____

The principal place of business is planned to be at _____

Upon formation of said entity, each of the parties intends to make the following amount and type of contribution, in exchange for the type of interest that is identified:

1- Name_____ Type and Value of Contribution. Specify Equity (Voting Capital or Nonvoting Capital) Interest or Debt Interest; and a description of the assets or services to be contributed, and the agreed value, for each type of interest:

_____

2- Name_____ Type and Value of Contribution. Specify Equity (Voting Capital or Nonvoting Capital) Interest or Debt Interest; and a description of the assets or services to be contributed, and the agreed value, for each type of interest:

_____

3- Name_____ Type and Value of Contribution. Specify Equity (Voting Capital or Nonvoting Capital) Interest or Debt Interest; and a description of the assets or services to be contributed, and the agreed value, for each type of interest:

_____

4- Name_____ Type and Value of Contribution. Specify Equity (Voting Capital or Nonvoting Capital) Interest or Debt Interest; and a description of the assets or services to be contributed, and the agreed value, for each type of interest:

_____

The costs of forming said entity, including, but not limited to, legal fees, fees paid to the Province for formation, and other expenses shall be apportioned among the undersigned parties in the following manner, irrespective as to whether the entity is actually formed:

_____
_____

Each of the parties agrees to pay his apportioned share of said costs. Each party shall be entitled to be reimbursed by the business entity for such payment, after the entity is formed.

Additional understandings among the parties (describe): _____
_____

Each of the parties acknowledges that the parties are relying on the reciprocal promises made herein in deciding to form the above-described business entity. A party who breaches this agreement shall be liable for the costs the non-breaching parties incur in enforcing this Agreement, including, but not limited to, legal fees and court costs, in addition to any other form of damages.

Remarks: _____
_____

Printed Names and Signatures   Date

_____   _____

Traditionally, Partnership/Shareholder Agreements include a provision for the disposition of the interest of one of the parties, and prevent an owner from selling his interests to an outsider without the consent of the other owners. The buy-sell agreement usually takes one of three forms.

1. **Cross-Purchase Agreement.** In this form, a selling owner agrees to sell his interest to the remaining owners. This is the simplest form of the buy-sell agreement. It is suitable especially for the small business with only a few owners.
2. **Entity-Purchase Agreement.** In this form of the buy-sell agreement, the selling owner agrees to sell his interest to the corporation itself.
3. **Hybrid Agreement.** This approach is a combination of the previous two. Typically, the selling owner must first offer his interest to the corporation. If the corporation refuses to buy the shares, they can then be offered to the other owners.

Any good buy-sell agreement should not only dictate how shares will be sold but, and this is crucial, how they will be valued. Imagine what could happen if you are the mouse that has gone to bed with an elephant. In other words, tension will likely develop between you when you, as one of the partners, has difficulty raising $200,000 and your partner can easily raise $10 million. Your shares may be worth two and a half million dollars but what can you do if he offers you only $500,000? Moral: Before tying the knot gleefully with a partner who has limitless resources, consider what will happen if the elephant gets mad.

Commonly, the main approaches for selling one's interests when there are only two partners are the shotgun and the appraisal approaches.
* **The Shotgun Approach.** If one partner (A) wants to break or dissolve the partnership, he offers to buy the shares of the other partner (B) for a specific amount. If B declines to sell his shares, he must buy A's shares, at the same price, terms, and conditions
* **The Appraisal Approach.** The partners agree that if one party wants to sell, the other one will buy at a price determined by an evaluation or, the average of three evaluations.

Most Partnership Agreements provide that if a partner wants to sell, he must first offer his shares to his partner(s). If the latter declines to buy, they can be offered to outsiders.

Some say a partnership is like a marriage: a good one is heaven, but a bad one is hell. The best precautionary measure is an arbitration clause in the Agreement (see Chapter 7).

6.7.3 MASTER BUSINESS LICENSE
If you do not want to register a corporation, be part of a partnership, or want to operate under your own name, you may register under the *Business Names Act* (R.S.O. 1990, c. B.17). If you apply personally, using "Registration Form 1" (see Figure 6.2) under the *Business Names Act*, within minutes you will receive a Master Business Licence (MBL), which is valid for 5 years. (See Figure 6.3.)

Figure 6.2
Business Name Registration Form

Ontario — Ministry of Consumer and Business Services / Ministère des Services aux consommateurs et aux entreprises

Registration Form 1
under the Business Names Act - Sole Proprietorship / Partnership
Enregistrement Formule 1
en vertu de la *Loi sur les noms commerciaux*
(Entreprise personnelle / société en nom collectif)

Print clearly in CAPITAL LETTERS /
Écrivez clairement en LETTRES MAJUSCULES

Page_____of / de_____

1. **Registration Type / Type d'enregistrement**

If B, C, or D enter "Business Identification Number" /
En cas de B, C ou D, inscrivez le nº d'identification de l'entreprise.

A ☐ New / Nouvel   B ☐ Renewal / Renouvellement   C ☐ Amendment / Modification   D ☐ Cancellation / Révocation   BIN Business Identification No./ NIE le nº d'identification de l'entreprise

2. **Business Name / Nom commercial**

3. **Mailing Address / Adresse postale**

ONTARIO

CANADA

4. **Address of principal place of business in Ontario** *(P.O. Box not acceptable)* **/**
Adresse de l'établissement principal en Ontario *(Case postale non acceptée)*   ☐ Same as above / comme ci-dessus

Street No. / Nº de rue	Street Name / Nom de la rue	Suite No. / Bureau nº	City / Town / Ville
Province / Province	Country / Pays	Postal Code / Code postal	
ONTARIO	CANADA		

5. **Give a brief description of the ACTIVITY being carried out under the business name./**
Résumez brièvement le genre d'ACTIVITÉ exercée sous le nom commercial.

6. **Type of Registrant / Type de personne enregistrée**   A ☐ Sole proprietorship / Entreprise personnelle   B ☐ Partnership / Société en nom collectif   ☐ More than 10 Partners: records at business address / Plus de 10 associés : dossiers à l'adresse d'affaires

7. **Registrant Information / Renseignements sur la personne enregistrée**

Last Name / Nom de famille	First Name / Prénom	Middle Initial / initiale 2ᵉ prénom

8. Street No. / Nº de rue   Street Name / Nom de la rue   Suite No. / Bureau nº   City / Town / Ville
Province / Province   Country / Pays   Postal Code / Code postal

Additional Information. Only complete if the registrant is not an individual. See instructions 7/8 on the form. / **Renseignements supplémentaires.** A remplir uniquement si la personne enregistrée n'est pas un particulier. Voir les instructions 7 et 8 sur le formulaire.

Ont. Corporation No. / *(For Corporate Partners Only)*
Nº matricule de la personne morale en Ontario *Pour les personnes morales associées seulement*

7. Last Name / Nom de famille   First Name / Prénom   Middle Initial / initiale 2ᵉ prénom

8. Street No. / Nº de rue   Street Name / Nom de la rue   Suite No. / Bureau nº   City / Town / Ville
Province / Province   Country / Pays   Postal Code / Code postal

Additional Information. Only complete if the registrant is not an individual. See instructions 7/8 on the form. / **Renseignements supplémentaires.** A remplir uniquement si la personne enregistrée n'est pas un particulier. Voir les instructions 7 et 8 sur le formulaire.

Ont. Corporation No. / *(For Corporate Partners Only)*
Nº matricule de la personne morale en Ontario *Pour les personnes morales associées seulement*

9. **Print name of person authorizing this registration** */ (either the sole proprietor, a partner or a person acting under a power of attorney)*
If the person is a corporation, complete **additional information** below only. /
Indiquez en lettres majuscules le nom de la personne autorisant l'enregistrement / *(propriétaire unique, associé, ou personne habilitée en vertu d'une procuration).* (Si c'est une personne morale qui autorise l'enregistrement, compléter les **renseignements supplémentaires** ci-dessous).

Last Name / Nom de famille	First Name / Prénom	Middle Initial / initiale 2ᵉ prénom

If person authorizing the registration is not an individual (eg. corporation, trust, syndicate), print name below and do not complete last, first and middle names above. /
Si la personne qui autorise l'enregistrement n'est pas un individu (c'est-à-dire une personne morale, un trust ou syndicat) ne pas remlir le nom de famille, prénom et 2ᵉ prénom.

Additional Information / Renseignements supplémentaires

MINISTRY USE ONLY - RÉSERVÉ AU MINISTÈRE

07219 (03/2003)

Figure 6.3
Master Business Licence

Ontario   Master Business Licence

Date Issued: 2003-01-22   Business Number:
(yyyy-mm-dd)

Business Name and Mailing Address:

         CA

Business
Address: SAME AS ABOVE

Telephone: Ext: Fax:

Email:

Legal
Name(s):

Type of
Legal Entity: GENERAL PARTNERSHIP   (This business has 2 partner(s) recorded on this licence)

Business
Activity: ANTIQUES & PAINTINGS

Business Information	Number	Effective Date (yyyy-mm-dd)	Expiry Date (yyyy-mm-dd)
BUSINESS NAME REGISTRATION	130083611	2003-01-22	2008-01-21

Page 1 of 1

To the Client: When the Master Business Licence is presented to any Ontario business program, you are not required to repeat information contained on this licence. Each Ontario business program is required to accept this licence when presented as part of its registration process. Call the Ontario Business Connects Helpline at 1-800-565-1921 or (416) 314-9151 or TDD (416) 326-8566 if you have any problems.

To the Ontario business program: A client is not required to repeat any information contained in this licence in any other form used in your registration process.

CB 2003-01-22

6.7.4 JOINT VENTURES

A joint venture can be defined as an association of two or more individuals, corporations, or partnerships, or some combination of the above, for the purpose of carrying on a business venture. A joint venture is not a legal entity, but rather the joining of several entities.

Joint ventures are created when two, or more, entities (something that has a real existence, such as a human being, a group of human beings, a corporation, a partnership, a trust) join forces for one project. It is an approach most frequently used for land development or the construction of a new project, where the task is considered too large for a single firm, corporation, etc., to accomplish alone. Joint ventures are typically used to allow for the pooling of equipment, skills and experience of the various groups. At the completion of the project, the joint venture is dissolved and the partners go on their own merry (hopefully) way. A joint venture is usually formed for the carrying on of one business transaction or project, while a partnership deals with several projects or continues for an extended period of time. In real estate, joint ventures are found most frequently between, or among, a landowner, a developer, a builder, and a financier.

Although joint ventures are commonly accepted in the business community as a form of business organization, the legal definition of joint venture is imprecise. The expression is sometimes used to refer to a partnership that is intended only to exist for a limited time, or for the purpose of a particular project. If the relationship between the entities of a joint venture is, in fact, a partnership, then the joint venture may be considered a partnership as a matter of law.

A joint venture may, however, refer to a relationship falling somewhat short of a full partnership, although this distinction is unclear. In these situations, the courts have relied on the laws of partnership or, where the partnership clearly does not exist, the laws of co-ownership. Taxation will depend on the legal structure chosen (corporation, partnership, etc.).

6.7.5 REAL ESTATE INVESTMENT TRUSTS (REITS)

A Canadian REIT is an open or close-ended mutual fund trust that lends money by way of mortgage, or buys, develops, manages, and sells real estate assets. REITs qualify as pass-through entities that are able to distribute the majority of income cash flows to investors without taxation at the corporate level (providing that certain conditions are met). For most REITs, business activities are generally restricted to the generation of property rental income.

REITs can be both intriguing and frustrating in terms of potential. REITs were introduced in Canada in 1993, and are generally, but not always, publicly traded companies that permit investors to invest in real estate, even if their means are fairly limited. There are three kinds of REITs:

1. equity REITs, which buy income-producing properties
2. mortgage REITs, which loan money for mortgage backed loans, and
3. hybrid REITs, which are a combination of equity and mortgage REITs.

Individual REITs tend to specialize geographically (by region, province, or metropolitan area) or in property types (such as retail properties, industrial facilities, office buildings, apartments, healthcare facilities, etc.), although some large REITs have a nationwide presence.

REITs raise money by selling units to the public through stockbrokers. They pool the capital of the investors and invest these monies in a diversified pool of mortgages or real estate. They are mutual fund trusts that own, operate, and manage real estate investments. Because of their fiscal classification, they can "flow through"[1] to investors certain gains, incomes, and expenses. From this stems the opportunity for tax reduction and tax deferral. Their income is passive although, generally, REITs manage the properties. Their assets, as a rule, are very large. Most REITs report annual returns in the 11% to 13% range, but Deloitte and Touche, in one of its annual REIT guides, show an average yield of 7% to 10%. Note that this refers to the terrific post-1996 period, which is bound to end soon. We may very well see losses instead of profits.

In order for a corporation to qualify as a Canadian REIT and gain the advantages of being a pass-through entity free from taxation at the corporate level, it must comply with the following Canada Revenue Agency (CRA) provisions:

- be structured as corporation, business trust, or similar association
- be managed by a board of directors or trustees
- have fully transferable shares
- have a minimum of 150 shareholders
- pay dividends equal to 85% to 95% of its taxable income
- hold at least 70% of its total investment assets in real estate, and
- derive at least 95% of its gross income from rents or mortgage interest.

REITs offer numerous advantages.

- **Liquidity.** A major advantage of REIT investment is its liquidity (ease of liquidation of assets into cash), because REIT shares are listed on stock exchanges, as compared to traditional private real estate ownership, where the assets may be difficult to liquidate.
- **Potential for Appreciation.** REITs that invest in real estate (equity REITs) have the potential to benefit from appreciation.
- **Strong "Hands-off" Asset Management.** This is a major advantage to investors who do not have the expertise, time, or the desire to invest directly in real estate. Investing through REITS is much less risky, due to professional management and diversification, but generally less financially rewarding.
- **Relative Diversification.** The ownership of multiple properties spreads the investor's risk.
- **Small Investment Required.** Just a few hundred dollars invested to buy a few REIT shares can constitute an initial investment for a budding investor.
- **Good Returns.** Over the long run, investors can expect good returns, although this is not always the case.
- **No Personal Liability.** Outside of the individual's capital investment, personal liability is non-existent.
- **Relatively Stable Income.**

Their disadvantages are as follows:

- too rigidly limited in a particular property type or a geographical area
- investors cannot direct their investment
- because the policy of Canadian REITs has been to distribute 95% of their taxable income to their shareholders in order to avoid corporate taxes, they may not have the funds necessary to enhance existing properties (this assures the investors (unit holders) of a steady cash flow, but may limit the potential return on investment), and
- very expensive to set up and the investors pay for these expenses. When an investor buys $100 worth of shares, $7-$8 go toward costs related to creating the REIT.

See <www.reitnet.com> for a wealth of information on REITs.

---

1 Flow-through means that the REIT corporation is not taxed, but rather each shareholder is taxed individually at his personal tax rate on the income he receives.

CHAPTER

7

Contracts and Other Legal Details

By the end of this chapter, you will be able to:

- Understand the basic forms and clauses for real property contracts.
- Know the ins and outs of the Agreement of Purchase and Sale.
- Work through an Agreement to Lease, but know the value of working with professionals.
- See both sides of a Lease Agreement – the landlord's and tenant's – and appreciate the many conditions and concepts.
- Recognize the various legal documents and their impact, including estoppel certificates and affidavits.
- Work within the court and legal system.

7.1 CONTRACTS FOR REAL PROPERTY TRANSACTIONS

Understand the basic forms and clauses for real property contracts.

The transfer of real property rights, be it a sale or a lease, is always done by way of a written and signed contract. This chapter reviews the most common contracts used in real estate transactions: Agreement of Purchase and Sale, Offer to Lease, and the different kinds of leases. In all real estate transactions, it is advisable to work with a lawyer who specializes in real estate law. However, every real estate investor should be familiar with the contracts he is signing and understand the clauses in those contracts that require particular attention. It is the fine print that can lead to problems in the future when you want to sell the property, change your tenants, or re-negotiate your mortgage.

7.1.1 CONTRACT BASICS

To ensure a contract is legally binding there are a number of points to keep in mind.

1. All contracts must be in writing. An agreement to sell land can be oral, but if there is a dispute it is not enforceable.
2. The agreement must be for a legal purpose. For example, a contract for prostitution would not be legal in most Western countries so it would not be legally binding. It is possible, however, to encounter some odd requests that are legal, such as a request in a lease for a German Shepherd to be tied close to the front door of a property from 8 P.M. to 6 A.M. every night.
3. There must be sufficient consideration by both parties, such as an exchange of money and property between the buyer and the vendor. Although gratuitous promises are unenforceable, in general the courts tend to find sufficient consideration when they want to enforce a contract.
4. The parties must be able to legally enter into a contract. This point excludes minors and mentally incompetent persons.
5. If there were conditions, such as financing or property conditions, they must have been satisfied.
6. When a non-physical entity, such as a corporation, enters into an agreement, the signatory must have the authority to commit the corporation, partnership, etc., to the agreement. Most of the time this is not verified, which is acceptable. Legislation, often referred to as the "indoor management rule" in common law, allows that a person dealing with a contracting party is not required to ascertain that the person signing for the company has the legal authority to do so. He is entitled to rely on the ostensible authority of the signing party. Ideally, the seal of the corporation is used or, preferably, a Corporate Certificate of Resolution is attached to the agreement.

7.1.2 COVENANTS

The word "covenant" is used in many places in this book, and it must be explained. There are many kinds of covenants. The *Oxford Dictionary* provides us this definition: "A solemn agreement"; with the legal definition being: "A valid promise or contract." *Black's Legal Dictionary* adds that "covenants may be classified according to several distinct principles of division," and goes on to list 34 covenants. Here are a few: express or implied, principal and auxiliary, joint or several, affirmative or negative, and absolute or conditional. Worth mentioning here is the term "usual covenants": "An agreement, on the part of a seller of real property, to give the usual covenants, binds him to insert in the grant covenants of 'seisin' (a possession of land by a freeholder/right to convey): 'quiet enjoyment,' 'further assurance', 'general warranty', and 'against encumbrances.'"

The word "covenant" is also used in a different context in business. For example one may hear, "This company has a strong covenant" or "This company has a triple A covenant". This refers to the fact that public companies are expected to respect certain business standards, including covenants (particularly financial ones), to do and not do certain things.

7.1.3 STATUTE OF FRAUDS

The *Statute of Frauds* (R.S.O. 1990, c. S.19) requires written evidence of any contract for the sale of an interest in land. More specifically, this statute prohibits the commencement of court actions under certain circumstances, including any contract for the sale of land, unless some document is presented and signed by the party to be charged. The courts have modified the strict reliance on this statute by the Doctrine of Part Performance. This doctrine also applies to contracts of land that are not in writing, where one party has actually performed part of the bargain, so as to very clearly suggest the existence of a contract. In such instances, where the person will suffer a loss if the contract is not performed, the courts may enforce the agreement. However, if no contract exists, this part performance must be very clear (e.g., construction of a building on the land or renovation of the property) and the plaintiff must clearly show that he will suffer loss.

7.1.4 POWER OF ATTORNEY (POA) FOR PROPERTY

Sometimes people find themselves in a situation where they need to execute a document but cannot do so in person. In this case, they can appoint someone else to sign for them by establishing a Power of Attorney (POA). A POA is a written document giving one (or more) person(s) the power to act on behalf of another person. It can be general, giving the other person all the powers held by the person being represented, or it can be limited, giving the other person only the right to do certain specific things. For example, the owner of a property may assign POA to another person so that person can sign an Offer to Lease.

From a legal viewpoint, a POA can fall under one of the following two Acts, and each has its own prescribed forms: the *Substitute Decisions Act* (S.O. 1992, c. 30) and the *Powers of Attorney Act* (R.S.O. 1990, c. P.20).

7.2 AGREEMENT OF PURCHASE AND SALE

Know the ins and outs of the Agreement of Purchase and Sale.

One of the most frequently encountered contracts is the Agreement of Purchase and Sale, which is used when you are buying and selling a property. The majority of Agreements of Purchase and Sale contracts used by real estate agents are standard contracts published by the local real estate board or the provincial real estate association. Standard contracts make life for everyone involved (vendor, buyer, real estate agent, lawyer) much easier. They contain the clauses most commonly required in the particular type of transaction and usually have at least two schedules appended, one for additional clauses and another for a survey or sketch. Indeed, professionals who deal with these contracts regularly know the small print well (and it is small) and do not need to read the entire document every time, permitting them to review a document in 10 minutes, instead of 2 or 3 hours.

7.2.1 STANDARD AND NOT-SO-STANDARD CLAUSES

Figure 7.1 presents an Agreement of Purchase and Sale for Commercial Property as issued by the Ontario Real Estate Association. Here are a few notes to keep in mind when using a standard Agreement of Purchase and Sale, with specific reference to the agreement headings and clauses in Figure 7.1.

- **"This Agreement of Purchase and Sale dated this"**. Enter the date that the contract is prepared.
- **"Buyer"**. Most buyers of commercial properties over $1 million will buy each property in a different corporate name. The buyer will be named "John Doe, in trust for a corporation to be registered". Some vendors object to this practice because they want the buyer to be personally liable or, if it is a corporation making the purchase, they want it to be one that owns substantial assets. Lawyers usually add a clause giving a buyer the right to assign the offer, which vendors, generally, do not like.
- **"Real Property"**. The document asks for frontage, depth, and description. Frequently, this information (or part of it) is not available, or not secured easily; however, the intent here is to make sure that the property is clearly identified, which can be accomplished by enclosing a survey, even a correct sketch will do, or a Property Identification Number (PIN).
- **"Deposit"**. Most real estate agents write that the deposit is due "Upon Acceptance". Some buyers elect to make two deposits. One deposit is made with, or immediately after acceptance of, the offer and a second upon removal of the condition(s). For example, the initial deposit may be $10,000 with a second deposit of $90,000 to be paid as stipulated in one of the schedules. Savvy vendors do not like two deposits. Buyers want the deposit cheque(s) to be made out to a broker or a lawyer because these professionals have trust accounts for such deposits. Some vendors, who have unrealistic expectations, want them made out to the vendors, which is not acceptable to buyers. Indeed it is a dangerous practice, since it could become difficult to get one's deposit back from the vendor if the deal is not completed.
- **"Schedule(s) A … attached hereto"**. This is where the attached schedules are listed. Frequently, there is also a schedule "B", which is a floor plan, survey, or sketch.
- **Clause 1: "Chattels included"**. A chattel is a type of movable personal property that is not permanently attached to the real property. This definition would cover things such as: dock plate, vacuum cleaner, electrical generator, forklift, lawn mower, etc.
- **Clause 2: "Fixtures excluded"**. A fixture is a chattel that has been attached to the building by means of bolts, screws, nails, cement, converting it to real property. There is rarely something excluded in commercial buildings. With houses, one finds things such as appliances, window air-conditioners, even plants and trees, excluded.
- **Clause 3: "Rental items"**. Commonly, this covers such things as boilers, furnaces, water heaters, alarm systems, etc.
- **Clause 4: "Irrevocability"**. In commercial real estate, an offer is usually irrevocable for 2 or 3 days. It should be noted that if a party has signed a document that an agent is delivering to the other party, he can telephone the agent and request that it not be delivered until the moment the document is in possession of the other party.
- **Clause 5: "Completion date"**. This is commonly called "closing date".
- **Clause 6: "Notices"**. Usually, one finds the fax numbers of the listing and selling brokers under this heading.
- **Clause 7: "GST"**. In previous versions of this form, there was an option to show "included" or "not included" in the purchase price. The latter being very rare, the form was changed. If, in some extraordinary circumstance, the GST is included, this can be stated in schedule "A". There is no GST due on the sale of used residential buildings — whether houses or multi-family buildings.

Figure 7.1
Agreement of Purchase and Sale – Commercial

OREA Ontario Real Estate Association

Agreement of Purchase and Sale
Commercial

Form 500
for use in the Province of Ontario

This Agreement of Purchase and Sale dated this.. day of.. 20..................

BUYER, Claude Boiron ...., agrees to purchase from
(Full legal names of all Buyers)

SELLER,..., the following
(Full legal names of all Sellers)
REAL PROPERTY:
Address..fronting on the.....................side of..................................
in the..
and having a frontage of...more or less by a depth of..more or less and legally
described as ....
....(the "property").
(Legal description of land including easements not described elsewhere)

PURCHASE PRICE: ....Dollars (CDN$)...................................

DEPOSIT: Buyer submits ....
(Herewith/Upon acceptance/as otherwise described in this Agreement)

....Dollars (CDN$)...................................

by negotiable cheque payable to... "Deposit Holder"
to be held in trust without interest pending completion or other termination of this Agreement and to be credited toward the Purchase Price on completion.
For the purposes of this Agreement, "Upon Acceptance" shall mean that the Buyer is required to deliver the deposit to the Deposit Holder within 24 hours
of the acceptance of this Agreement.

Buyer agrees to pay the balance as more particularly set out in Schedule A attached.

SCHEDULE(S) A...**attached hereto form(s) part of this Agreement.**

1. **CHATTELS INCLUDED:**...
....
....

2. **FIXTURES EXCLUDED:**..
....
....

3. **RENTAL ITEMS:** The following equipment is rented and **not** included in the Purchase Price. The Buyer agrees to assume the rental contract(s), if assumable:
....
....

4. **IRREVOCABILITY:** This Offer shall be irrevocable by..until................a.m./p.m. on the.....................day of ....,
(Seller/Buyer)
after which time, if not accepted, this Offer shall be null and void and the deposit shall be returned to the Buyer in full without interest.

5. **COMPLETION DATE:** This Agreement shall be completed by no later than 6:00 p.m. on the.....................day of.................................., 20.......,
Upon completion, vacant possession of the property shall be given to the Buyer unless otherwise provided for in this Agreement.

6. **NOTICES:** Seller hereby appoints the Listing Brokerage as Agent for the purpose of giving and receiving notices pursuant to this Agreement. **Only if the Co-operating Brokerage represents the interests of the Buyer in this transaction,** the Buyer hereby appoints the Co-operating Brokerage as Agent for the purpose of giving and receiving notices pursuant to this Agreement. Any notice relating hereto or provided for herein shall be in writing. This offer, any counter offer, notice of acceptance thereof, or any notice shall be deemed given and received, when hand delivered to the address for service provided in the Acknowledgement below, or where a facsimile number is provided herein, when transmitted electronically to that facsimile number.

FAX No..(For delivery of notices to Seller)   FAX No. ....(For delivery of notices to Buyer)

7. **GST: If this transaction is subject to Goods and Services Tax (GST), then such tax shall be in addition to the Purchase Price.**
The Seller will not collect GST if the Buyer provides to the Seller a warranty that the Buyer is registered under the Excise Tax Act ("ETA"), together with a copy of the Buyer's ETA registration, a warranty that the Buyer shall self-assess and remit the GST payable and file the prescribed form and shall indemnify the Seller in respect of any GST payable. The foregoing warranties shall not merge but shall survive the completion of the transaction. If this transaction is not subject to GST, Seller agrees to certify on or before closing, that the transaction is not subject to GST.

8. **TITLE SEARCH:** Buyer shall be allowed until 6:00 p.m. on the ....day of.................................., 20......., (Requisition Date)
to examine the title to the property at his own expense and until the earlier of: (i) thirty days from the later of the Requisition Date or the date on which the conditions in this Agreement are fulfilled or otherwise waived or; (ii) five days prior to completion, to satisfy himself that there are no outstanding

work orders or deficiency notices affecting the property, that its present use(...
....) may be lawfully continued and that the principal building may be

INITIALS OF BUYER(S): ⬭   **INITIALS OF SELLER(S):** ⬭

Form 500   04/2006   **Page 1 of 4**

insured against risk of fire. Seller hereby consents to the municipality or other governmental agencies releasing to Buyer details of all outstanding work orders affecting the property, and Seller agrees to execute and deliver such further authorizations in this regard as Buyer may reasonably require.

9. **FUTURE USE:** Seller and Buyer agree that there is no representation or warranty of any kind that the future intended use of the property by Buyer is or will be lawful except as may be specifically provided for in this Agreement.

10. **TITLE:** Provided that the title to the property is good and free from all registered restrictions, charges, liens, and encumbrances except as otherwise specifically provided in this Agreement and save and except for (a) any registered restrictions or covenants that run with the land providing that such are complied with; (b) any registered municipal agreements and registered agreements with publicly regulated utilities providing such have been complied with, or security has been posted to ensure compliance and completion, as evidenced by a letter from the relevant municipality or regulated utility; (c) any minor easements for the supply of domestic utility or telephone services to the property or adjacent properties; and (d) any easements for drainage, storm or sanitary sewers, public utility lines, telephone lines, cable television lines or other services which do not materially affect the present use of the property. If within the specified times referred to in paragraph 8 any valid objection to title or to any outstanding work order or deficiency notice, or to the fact the said present use may not lawfully be continued, or that the principal building may not be insured against risk of fire is made in writing to Seller and which Seller is unable or unwilling to remove, remedy or satisfy or obtain insurance save and except against risk of fire in favour of the Buyer and any mortgagee, (with all related costs at the expense of the Seller), and which Buyer will not waive, this Agreement not withstanding any intermediate acts or negotiations in respect of such objections, shall be at an end and all monies paid shall be returned without interest or deduction and Seller, Listing Brokerage and Co-operating Brokerage shall not be liable for any costs or damages. Save as to any valid objection so made by such day and except for any objection going to the root of the title, Buyer shall be conclusively deemed to have accepted Seller's title to the property.

11. **CLOSING ARRANGEMENTS:** Where each of the Seller and Buyer retain a lawyer to complete the Agreement of Purchase and Sale of the Property, and where the transaction will be completed by electronic registration pursuant to Part III of the Land Registration Reform Act, R.S.O. 1990, Chapter L4 and the Electronic Registration Act, S.O. 1991, Chapter 44, and any amendments thereto, the Seller and Buyer acknowledge and agree that the exchange of closing funds, non-registrable documents and other items (the "Requisite Deliveries") and the release thereof to the Seller and Buyer will (a) not occur at the same time as the registration of the transfer/deed (and any other documents intended to be registered in connection with the completion of this transaction) and (b) be subject to conditions whereby the lawyer(s) receiving any of the Requisite Deliveries will be required to hold same in trust and not release same except in accordance with the terms of a document registration agreement between the said lawyers. The Seller and Buyer irrevocably instruct the said lawyers to be bound by the document registration agreement which is recommended from time to time by the Law Society of Upper Canada. Unless otherwise agreed to by the lawyers, such exchange of the Requisite Deliveries will occur in the applicable Land Titles Office or such other location agreeable to both lawyers.

12. **DOCUMENTS AND DISCHARGE:** Buyer shall not call for the production of any title deed, abstract, survey or other evidence of title to the property except such as are in the possession or control of Seller. If requested by Buyer, Seller will deliver any sketch or survey of the property within Seller's control to Buyer as soon as possible and prior to the Requisition Date. If a discharge of any Charge/Mortgage held by a corporation incorporated pursuant to the Trust And Loan Companies Act (Canada), Chartered Bank, Trust Company, Credit Union, Caisse Populaire or Insurance Company and which is not to be assumed by Buyer on completion, is not available in registrable form on completion, Buyer agrees to accept Seller's lawyer's personal undertaking to obtain, out of the closing funds, a discharge in registrable form and to register same, or cause same to be registered, on title within a reasonable period of time after completion, provided that on or before completion Seller shall provide to Buyer a mortgage statement prepared by the mortgagee setting out the balance required to obtain the discharge, and, where a real-time electronic cleared funds transfer system is not being used, a direction executed by Seller directing payment to the mortgagee of the amount required to obtain the discharge out of the balance due on completion.

13. **INSPECTION:** Buyer acknowledges having had the opportunity to inspect the property and understands that upon acceptance of this Offer there shall be a binding agreement of purchase and sale between Buyer and Seller.

14. **INSURANCE:** All buildings on the property and all other things being purchased shall be and remain until completion at the risk of Seller. Pending completion, Seller shall hold all insurance policies, if any, and the proceeds thereof in trust for the parties as their interests may appear and in the event of substantial damage, Buyer may either terminate this Agreement and have all monies paid returned without interest or deduction or else take the proceeds of any insurance and complete the purchase. No insurance shall be transferred on completion. If Seller is taking back a Charge/Mortgage, or Buyer is assuming a Charge/Mortgage, Buyer shall supply Seller with reasonable evidence of adequate insurance to protect Seller's or other mortgagee's interest on completion.

15. **PLANNING ACT:** This Agreement shall be effective to create an interest in the property only if Seller complies with the subdivision control provisions of the Planning Act by completion and Seller covenants to proceed diligently at his expense to obtain any necessary consent by completion.

16. **DOCUMENT PREPARATION:** The Transfer/Deed shall, save for the Land Transfer Tax Affidavit, be prepared in registrable form at the expense of Seller, and any Charge/Mortgage to be given back by the Buyer to Seller at the expense of the Buyer. If requested by Buyer, Seller covenants that the Transfer/Deed to be delivered on completion shall contain the statements contemplated by Section 50(22) of the Planning Act, R.S.O.1990.

17. **RESIDENCY:** Buyer shall be credited towards the Purchase Price with the amount, if any, necessary for Buyer to pay to the Minister of National Revenue to satisfy Buyer's liability in respect of tax payable by Seller under the non-residency provisions of the Income Tax Act by reason of this sale. Buyer shall not claim such credit if Seller delivers on completion the prescribed certificate or a statutory declaration that Seller is not then a non-resident of Canada.

18. **ADJUSTMENTS:** Any rents, mortgage interest, realty taxes including local improvement rates and unmetered public or private utility charges and unmetered cost of fuel, as applicable, shall be apportioned and allowed to the day of completion, the day of completion itself to be apportioned to Buyer.

19. **TIME LIMITS:** Time shall in all respects be of the essence hereof provided that the time for doing or completing of any matter provided for herein may be extended or abridged by an agreement in writing signed by Seller and Buyer or by their respective lawyers who may be specifically authorized in that regard.

20. **TENDER:** Any tender of documents or money hereunder may be made upon Seller or Buyer or their respective lawyers on the day set for completion. Money may be tendered by bank draft or cheque certified by a Chartered Bank, Trust Company, Province of Ontario Savings Office, Credit Union or Caisse Populaire.

21. **FAMILY LAW ACT:** Seller warrants that spousal consent is not necessary to this transaction under the provisions of the Family Law Act, R.S.O.1990 unless Seller's spouse has executed the consent hereinafter provided.

22. **UFFI:** Seller represents and warrants to Buyer that during the time Seller has owned the property, Seller has not caused any building on the property to be insulated with insulation containing ureaformaldehyde, and that to the best of Seller's knowledge no building on the property contains or has ever contained insulation that contains ureaformaldehyde. This warranty shall survive and not merge on the completion of this transaction, and if the building is part of a multiple unit building, this warranty shall only apply to that part of the building which is the subject of this transaction.

23. **LEGAL, ACCOUNTING AND ENVIRONMENTAL ADVICE:** The parties acknowledge that any information provided by the brokerage is not legal, tax or environmental advice, and that it has been recommended that the parties obtain independent professional advice prior to signing this document.

24. **CONSUMER REPORTS: The Buyer is hereby notified that a consumer report containing credit and/or personal information may be referred to in connection with this transaction.**

25. **AGREEMENT IN WRITING:** If there is conflict or discrepancy between any provision added to this Agreement (including any Schedule attached hereto) and any provision in the standard pre-set portion hereof, the added provision shall supersede the standard pre-set provision to the extent of such conflict or discrepancy. This Agreement including any Schedule attached hereto, shall constitute the entire Agreement between Buyer and Seller. There is no representation, warranty, collateral agreement or condition, which affects this Agreement other than as expressed herein. For the purposes of this Agreement, Seller means vendor and Buyer means purchaser. This Agreement shall be read with all changes of gender or number required by the context.

INITIALS OF BUYER(S): ( )   INITIALS OF SELLER(S): ( )

26. **SUCCESSORS AND ASSIGNS:** The heirs, executors, administrators, successors and assigns of the undersigned are bound by the terms herein.

SIGNED, SEALED AND DELIVERED in the presence of: IN WITNESS whereof I have hereunto set my hand and seal:

....

....	.... (Seal)	DATE................................
(Witness)	(Buyer/Authorized Signing Officer)	
....	.... (Seal)	DATE................................
(Witness)	(Buyer/Authorized Signing Officer)	

I, the Undersigned Seller, agree to the above Offer. I hereby irrevocably instruct my lawyer to pay directly to the Listing Brokerage the unpaid balance of the commission together with applicable Goods and Services Tax (and any other taxes as may hereafter be applicable), from the proceeds of the sale prior to any payment to the undersigned on completion, as advised by the Listing Brokerage to my lawyer.

SIGNED, SEALED AND DELIVERED in the presence of: IN WITNESS whereof I have hereunto set my hand and seal:

....

....	.... (Seal)	DATE................................
(Witness)	(Seller/Authorized Signing Officer)	
....	.... (Seal)	DATE................................
(Witness)	(Seller/Authorized Signing Officer)	

SPOUSAL CONSENT: The Undersigned Spouse of the Seller hereby consents to the disposition evidenced herein pursuant to the provisions of the Family Law Act, R.S.O.1990, and hereby agrees with the Buyer that he/she will execute all necessary or incidental documents to give full force and effect to the sale evidenced herein.

| .... | .... (Seal) | DATE................................ |
| (Witness) | (Spouse) | |

CONFIRMATION OF ACCEPTANCE: Notwithstanding anything contained herein to the contrary, I confirm this Agreement with all changes both typed and written was finally accepted by all parties at............a.m./p.m. this...............day of.............................., 20......... ....
(Signature of Seller or Buyer)

INFORMATION ON BROKERAGE(S)

Listing Brokerage... Tel.No.(...............)....................................

....

Co-op/Buyer Brokerage.. Tel.No.(...............)....................................

....

ACKNOWLEDGEMENT

I acknowledge receipt of my signed copy of this accepted Agreement of Purchase and Sale and I authorize the Agent to forward a copy to my lawyer.

I acknowledge receipt of my signed copy of this accepted Agreement of Purchase and Sale and I authorize the Agent to forward a copy to my lawyer.

.... DATE.....................	.... DATE.....................
(Seller)	(Buyer)
.... DATE.....................	.... DATE.....................
(Seller)	(Buyer)

Address for Service..

....Tel.No.(............).............

Seller's Lawyer..

Address..

(............).................................. (............).................
Tel.No. FAX No.

Address for Service..

....Tel.No.(............).............

Buyer's Lawyer..

Address..

(............).................................. (............).................
Tel.No. FAX No.

FOR OFFICE USE ONLY **COMMISSION TRUST AGREEMENT**

To: Co-operating Brokerage shown on the foregoing Agreement of Purchase and Sale:
In consideration for the Co-operating Brokerage procuring the foregoing Agreement of Purchase and Sale, I hereby declare that all moneys received or receivable by me in connection with the Transaction as contemplated in the MLS Rules and Regulations of my Real Estate Board shall be receivable and held in trust. This agreement shall constitute a Commission Trust Agreement as defined in the MLS Rules and shall be subject to and governed by the MLS Rules pertaining to Commission Trust.

DATED as of the date and time of the acceptance of the foregoing Agreement of Purchase and Sale. Acknowledged by:

| .... | .... |
| (Authorized to bind the Listing Brokerage) | (Authorized to bind the Co-operating Brokerage) |

 **Schedule A**
Agreement of Purchase and Sale – Commercial

Form 500
for use in the Province of Ontario

This Schedule is attached to and forms part of the Agreement of Purchase and Sale between:

BUYER,.., and

SELLER,...

for the purchase and sale of...

....dated the...day of.., 20..........

Buyer agrees to pay the balance as follows:

This form must be initialed by all parties to the Agreement of Purchase and Sale.

INITIALS OF BUYER(S): ⬭   **INITIALS OF SELLER(S):** ⬭

Source: Agreement of Purchase and Sale – Commercial (Form 500) is used by permission of the Ontario Real Estate Association.

- **Clause 8: "Title Search".** For commercial real estate, we find the text dealing with the title search in this agreement awkward. Indeed, frequently, the buyer will show a closing date, but the vendor changes it significantly. It can vary so much that we are in the habit of writing "10 days before closing" for the time frame for completing a title search rather than specifying a date and time. We can make an argument for this approach because this clause addresses different things.
  - **"that there are no work orders or deficiency notices".** Lawyers check with the city building department to ascertain if there are work orders or deficiency notices against the property. Note that it would be possible to write into the Offer that the property is being sold "as is". Some people add "where is", but this statement seems superfluous for a real property.
  - **"present use".** How the property is currently being used is usually indicated as simply residential, office, retail, industrial, or, sometimes more specifically as, hotel, service station, etc.
  - **"that the principal building may be insured against risk of fire".** A savvy buyer should ask a vendor for a copy of his building insurance. It is unusual for a building not to be insured, but it can happen for a number of reasons, such as death of a principal, neglect, or lack of money. In law, a fire would represent a breach of contract. In reality, it could herald serious problems (see also item 14 in Figure 7.1).
- **Clause 10: "Title".** It is exceptional to find a title that is not "good", except for single-family homes with the few recent cases of property fraud.
- **Clause 11: "Where each of the Seller and Buyer retain a lawyer".** This statement implies that one can complete a sale/purchase, without a lawyer, which is highly risky and should be avoided.
- **Clauses 9 and 12 to 26.** These clauses are for lawyers, but a new investor should read and reread them until they are well understood. The following are a few comments:
  - **Clause 26.** If a corporation is the buyer and/or vendor, we type its name on one line and, on the line below, we enter "per" to show that the person signing does so on behalf of the corporation. Some lawyers add a statement, to be signed by the person signing on behalf of a corporation, stating that he has the "authority to bind the corporation". The signatories should hand write the date next to their signatures. Any adult person can be a witness. Note that this form instructs the vendor's lawyer to pay the real estate commission.
- **Spousal Consent.** This is required if the property is held by the vendor in his personal name, but is not necessary if it is a corporation.
- **Confirmation of Acceptances.** This is done when a final agreement has been reached and the final signatures or initials have been obtained. It is useful to have a clear starting date for conditions.
- **Acknowledgement.** Once an offer is finally accepted, both buyer and vendor receive a copy of the agreement and this is where they acknowledge this receipt. Too often, either one or both have not decided which lawyer they will use and the lawyer information is left blank. This is a warning sign, as all parties should know who is providing legal services.
- **Commission Trust Agreement.** This clause is for the protection of the cooperating/selling brokerage firm.
- **Schedule A.** This is where all representations, demands, guarantees, and conditions are detailed. Anything can be put in a schedule, even something absurd or very unusual, such as the vendor being asked to give his Rolex watch to the buyer upon closing. Anything legal can be put into a contract. The conditions most often encountered with leased properties are:
  - examination of Profit and Loss Statements for the last 3 (most common) years
  - examination of the accounting books, including invoices and receipts

– examination of leases
– examination of environmental reports, and
– review of the financing details.

For the buyer to be accepted by the mortgagor or to arrange a new mortgage, buyers usually request a minimum of 30 days, and a maximum of 90 days.

7.2.2 A FEW MORE COMMENTS

Make sure that you indicate what happens if the stated condition is satisfied and what happens if it is not. Typically, closing takes place 30 days after removal of conditions. It is difficult to do it sooner because, among other things, lawyers must secure responses from the municipal and other governmental agencies (and sometimes others). It must be noted that removal of conditions could be handled by way of promises (undertakings) made by the vendor, but it is done only in rare circumstances.

For the sake of efficiency, it has become customary for real estate agents to write a "fax clause" in all offers (e.g., "The parties herein agree to transmission of documents by fax"). Unfortunately, if an offer goes through a fax machine more than a couple of times, the documents can become illegible. As soon as legibility is difficult, we are in the habit of retyping the offer with the changes agreed to to-date, and having it re-signed by the parties, so that the lawyers can read it without problem. We do the same when a final agreement has been reached.

7.3 OFFER TO LEASE

Work through an Agreement to Lease, but know the value of working with professionals.

Like the Agreement of Purchase and Sale, the most frequently used Offer to Lease documents are standard contracts published by the local real estate board or the provincial real estate association. Virtually always, an Offer to Lease (also known as an Agreement to Lease) precedes the lease itself. The Offer to Lease covers only the main points: landlord's and tenant's name, address, area of the space, rental, occupancy date, work to be done, who pays for what, etc.

We are frequently asked by those new to the business, "Is an Offer to Lease necessary"? It is not necessary and it is possible to bypass it completely and go directly to a lease; however, the Offer to Lease accomplishes a number of things.

- It comprises all the data required for the lawyer (yes, do use one) to prepare the Lease.
- It is the tool used to negotiate the business terms of the deal that can then be transferred to the Lease.
- It superficially covers some of the legal clauses included in the Lease.
- It is much shorter than a Lease (two or three pages versus 20 to 40).

Figure 7.2 presents the Ontario Real Estate Association's Agreement to Lease for Commercial Properties. Following are a few comments on this agreement.

Figure 7.2
Agreement to Lease – Commercial

OREA Ontario Real Estate Association **Agreement to Lease** **Commercial**   **Form 510** for use in the Province of Ontario

This Agreement to Lease dated this.. day of... 20..........

TENANT (Lessee), Claude Boiron..
(Full legal names of all Tenants)

LANDLORD (Lessor),...,
(Full legal name of Landlord)

The Tenant hereby offers to lease from the Landlord the premises as described herein on the terms and subject to the conditions as set out in this Agreement.

1. **PREMISES:** The "Premises" consisting of approximately..................................square....................more or less on the.....................floor of the
(feet/metres)

   "Building" known municipally as... in the...

   of..., Province of Ontario, as shown outlined on the plan attached as Schedule "...............".

2. **USE:** The Premises shall be used only for...

3. **TERM OF LEASE:**

   (a) The Lease shall be for a term of.....................(..........) months commencing on the.....................day of..........................., 20............,

   and terminating on the...day of..............................., 20.................. .

   (b) Provided the Tenant is not at any time in default of any covenants within the Lease, the Tenant shall be entitled to renew this Lease for
   ....additional term(s) of............................months (each) on written notice to the Landlord given not less than...........................months
   prior to the expiry of the current term at a rental rate to be negotiated. In the event the Landlord and Tenant can not agree on the fixed minimum rent
   at least two months prior to expiry of the current lease, the fixed minimum rent for the renewal period shall be determined by arbitration in
   accordance with the Arbitration Act or any successor or replacement act.

4. **RENTAL:** Fixed minimum rent: The fixed minimum rent payable by the Tenant for each complete twelve-month period during the lease term shall be:

   From.................to.................inclusive, $...................per annum being $...................per month, based upon $................per sq........................
   (feet/metres)

   From.................to.................inclusive, $...................per annum being $...................per month, based upon $................per sq........................
   (feet/metres)

   From.................to.................inclusive, $...................per annum being $...................per month, based upon $................per sq........................
   (feet/metres)

   From.................to.................inclusive, $...................per annum being $...................per month, based upon $................per sq........................
   (feet/metres)

   From.................to.................inclusive, $...................per annum being $...................per month, based upon $................per sq........................
   (feet/metres)

   plus Goods and Services Tax (GST), and other tax (other than income tax) imposed on the Landlord or the Tenant with respect to rent payable by the Tenant,
   payable on: (**Check one box only**)

   ☐ the.....................day of each month commencing..

   ☐ the.....................day of the first month immediately following completion of the Landlord's Work.

   The fixed minimum rent shall be adjusted if the actual measurements of the Leased Premises differ from the approximate area. The actual measurement
   shall be agreed upon and failing agreement, calculated by an Ontario Land Surveyor/Architect using the current Building Owners And Managers
   Association standard form of measurement and shall be binding on both parties.

5. **DEPOSIT AND PREPAID RENT:** The Tenant delivers..
   (Herewith/Upon acceptance/as otherwise described in this Agreement)

   by negotiable cheque payable to.. "Deposit Holder"

   in the amount of...

   Canadian dollars (Can$...................................) to be deposited and held in trust without interest as security for the faithful performance by the
   Tenant of all terms, covenants and conditions of the Agreement and after the earlier of occupancy by the tenant or execution of the Lease to be applied
   by the Landlord against the .... and..........................month's rent and GST. If the Agreement is not accepted, the deposit is to be
   returned to the Tenant without interest or deduction.

   For the purposes of this Agreement, "Upon Acceptance" shall mean that the Tenant is required to deliver the deposit to the Deposit Holder within 24
   hours of the acceptance of this Agreement.

   INITIALS OF TENANT(S): ( )   INITIALS OF LANDLORD(S): ( )

6. **SERVICES: (Check one box only)**

    ☐ The Tenant shall pay the cost of hydro, gas, water, heating, air-conditioning and for all other services and utilities as may be provided to the premises. The tenant shall arrange with the local authority for connection of gas, electricity and water in the name of the Tenant.

    ☐ The Landlord shall pay the cost of hydro, gas, water, heating, air-conditioning and for all other services and utilities as may be provided to the premises.

7. **ADDITIONAL RENT AND CHARGES:**

    ☐ **Check this box if Additional Rent as described below to be paid by Tenant**

The Tenant shall additionally pay a proportionate share of all costs and expenses incurred by the Landlord in maintaining, operating, cleaning, insuring and repairing the property and, without limiting the generality of the foregoing, such costs and expenses shall include the costs of:
(i)   snow, garbage, and trash removal;
(ii) landscaping and planters;
(iii) heating, ventilating and air-conditioning, and providing hot and cold water and other utilities and services to, and operating the common areas of the property, and maintaining and repairing the machinery and equipment for such utilities and services;
(iv) the realty taxes, assessments, rates, charges and duties levied or assessed against the property (save any tax on the personal income of the Landlord);
(v) insuring the property and such other insurance as the Landlord will effect against public liability, property damage, loss of rental income and other casualties and risks.

(vi) ....

8. **SCHEDULES:** The Schedules attached hereto shall form an integral part of this Agreement to Lease and consist of: Schedule(s)...................................
....

9 **IRREVOCABILITY:** This offer shall be irrevocable by...................................until...............................a.m./p.m. on the.......................................
                                   (Landlord/Tenant)
after which time if not accepted, this Offer shall be null and void and all monies paid thereon shall be returned to the Tenant without interest or deduction.

10. **NOTICES:** Landlord hereby appoints the Listing Brokerage as Agent for the purpose of giving and receiving notices pursuant to this Agreement. **Only if the Co-operating Brokerage represents the interests of the Tenant in this transaction,** the Tenant hereby appoints the Co-operating Brokerage as Agent for the purpose of giving and receiving notices pursuant to this Agreement. Any notice relating hereto or provided for herein shall be in writing. This offer, any counter offer, notice of acceptance thereof, or any notice shall be deemed given and received, when hand delivered to the address for service provided in the Acknowledgement below, or where a facsimile number is provided herein, when transmitted electronically to that facsimile number.

    FAX NO. ....(For delivery of notices to Landlord)   FAX NO. ....(For delivery of notices to Tenant)

11. **LANDLORD'S AND TENANT'S WORK:** The Landlord agrees to complete the work described as the "Landlord's Work" in Schedule "................."
attached hereto. The Tenant agrees to complete any additional work necessary to prepare the Premises for the Tenant's use, described as "Tenant's

    Work" in Schedule "................." attached hereto. The Tenant shall not proceed with any work within or affecting the Premises without the Landlord's prior written approval, which approval shall not be unreasonably withheld.

12. **SIGNAGE:** The Tenant may, at its own expense, erect signage in a good and workmanlike manner, subject to municipal by-laws and government regulations and subject to the Landlord's written approval as to the design, colour, and content of any such signs, which approval shall not be

    unreasonably withheld, and to be located as follows: ....
....
....

13. **INSURANCE:** The Tenant agrees to insure the property and operations of the Tenant, including insurance for fire and such additional perils as are normally insured against, liability insurance and any other insurance as may be reasonably required by the Landlord.

14. **EXECUTION OF LEASE:** The Lease shall be prepared by the Landlord at the Landlord's expense, in accordance with the terms and conditions of this Agreement. The Lease will be signed and executed by both parties hereto prior to the commencement of work on the premises by either party and prior to occupancy by the Tenant.

15. **OCCUPANCY OR RENT TO ABATE:** In the event the premises are not completed by the Landlord for occupancy by the Tenant on the date set out herein for commencement of the Term of the Lease, the rent under this agreement shall abate to the extent of such delay, and the Tenant hereby agrees to accept such abatement of rent in full settlement of all claims which the Tenant might otherwise make because the Premises were not ready for occupancy by the said date.

16. **ASSIGNMENT:** This Agreement to Lease shall not be assignable or otherwise transferable by the Tenant. The Tenant may not sublet or assign or transfer its interest in the Lease contemplated herein without securing the written consent from the Landlord, which consent shall not be unreasonably withheld, provided however, if the consent is granted, the Tenant shall remain liable for all obligations under the Lease.

    If the Tenant is a corporation, the transfer of the majority of the issued shares in the capital stock, or any transfer, issuance or division of shares of the corporation sufficient to transfer control of the corporation shall be deemed for all purposes to be an assignment within the meaning of this Agreement and any Lease. This provision shall not apply to a corporation whose shares are listed and traded on any recognized public stock exchange in Canada or the United States.

17. **PARKING:** Unless otherwise stipulated, parking, if applicable, shall be in common and unreserved.

18. **AGREEMENT IN WRITING:** If there is any conflict or discrepancy between any provision added to this Agreement (including any Schedule attached hereto) and any provision in the standard pre-set portion hereof, the added provision shall supersede the standard pre-set provision to the extent of such conflict or discrepancy. This Agreement, including any Schedule attached hereto, shall constitute the entire Agreement between Landlord and Tenant. There is no representation, warranty, collateral agreement or condition, which affects this Agreement other than as expressed herein. This Agreement shall be read with all changes of gender or number required by the context.

19. **LEGAL, ACCOUNTING AND ENVIRONMENTAL ADVICE:** The parties acknowledge that any information provided by the broker is not legal, accounting, tax or environmental advice, and that it has been recommended that the parties obtain independent professional advice prior to signing this document.

INITIALS OF TENANT(S): ⬭   INITIALS OF LANDLORD(S): ⬭

20. **BINDING AGREEMENT:** This Agreement and the acceptance thereof shall constitute a binding agreement by the parties to enter into the Lease of the Premises and to abide by the terms and conditions herein contained.

21. **SUCCESSORS AND ASSIGNS:** The heirs, executors, administrators, successors and assigns of the undersigned are bound by the terms herein.

SIGNED, SEALED AND DELIVERED in the presence of: IN WITNESS whereof I have hereunto set my hand and seal:

....   (Seal)   DATE...............................
(Witness)   (Tenant or Authorized Representative)

....   (Seal)   DATE...............................
(Witness)   (Tenant or Authorized Representative)

....   (Seal)   DATE...............................
(Witness)   (Guarantor)

We/I the Landlord hereby accept the above Offer, and agree that the commission together with applicable Goods and Services Tax (and any other tax as may hereafter be applicable) may be deducted from the deposit and further agree to pay any remaining balance of commission forthwith.

SIGNED, SEALED AND DELIVERED in the presence of: IN WITNESS whereof I have hereunto set my hand and seal:

....   (Seal)   DATE...............................
(Witness)   (Landlord or Authorized Representative)

....   (Seal)   DATE...............................
(Witness)   (Landlord or Authorized Representative)

CONFIRMATION OF ACCEPTANCE: Notwithstanding anything contained herein to the contrary, I confirm this Agreement with all changes both typed and

written was finally accepted by all parties at............a.m./p.m. this..............day of..........................., 20......... ....
                                                                                                                                  (Signature of Landlord or Tenant)

INFORMATION ON BROKERAGE(S)

Listing Brokerage.. Tel.No.(...............)..................................

....

Co-op/Buyer Brokerage... Tel.No.(...............)..................................

....

I acknowledge receipt of my signed copy of this accepted Agreement to Lease and I authorize the Agent to forward a copy to my lawyer.

.... DATE.....................
(Landlord)

.... DATE.....................
(Landlord)

Address for Service..
....Tel.No.(...........)......................
Landlord's Lawyer..
Address...
(...........).. (...........).......................
         Tel.No.   FAX No.

I acknowledge receipt of my signed copy of this accepted Agreement to Lease and I authorize the Agent to forward a copy to my lawyer.

.... DATE.....................
(Tenant)

.... DATE.....................
(Tenant)

Address for Service..
....Tel.No.(...........)......................
Tenant's Lawyer...
Address...
(...........).. (...........).......................
         Tel.No.   FAX No.

FOR OFFICE USE ONLY   **COMMISSION TRUST AGREEMENT**

To: Co-operating Brokerage shown on the foregoing Agreement to Lease:
In consideration for the Co-operating Brokerage procuring the foregoing Agreement to Lease, I hereby declare that all moneys received or receivable by me in connection with the Transaction as contemplated in the MLS Rules and Regulations of my Real Estate Board shall be receivable and held in trust. This agreement shall constitute a Commission Trust Agreement as defined in the MLS Rules and shall be subject to and governed by the MLS Rules pertaining to Commission Trust.

DATED as of the date and time of the acceptance of the foregoing Agreement to Lease.   Acknowledged by:

....
(Authorized to bind the Listing Brokerage)   (Authorized to bind the Co-operating Brokerage)

Source: Agreement to Lease – Commercial (Form 510) is used by permission of the Ontario Real Estate Association.

- **Clause 2: Use.** From the tenant's viewpoint, the use should be as broad as possible, for example, "office and manufacturing", so that he can later add other uses or even change it within the broad category. From the landlord's viewpoint, the use should be as specific as possible (e.g., office (93 m² (1,000 sq ft) and 1,115 m² (12,000 sq ft)) for manufacturing of paint brushes made only from Canadian products). In this way, the landlord can object to uses of which he may not approve and even expel the tenant if he changes the use. In practice, if the tenant pays the rental regularly, takes good care of the premises, does not bother neighbours, and manages to keep a good rapport with the landlord, he will have no trouble changing the use, unless it is an objectional one.
- **Clause 3: Term of Lease.** A right of renewal is usually requested by tenants but is not always accepted by landlords.
- **Clause 4: Rental.** Increases in rental are optional.
- **Clause 5: Deposit and Prepaid Rent.** Tenants generally want "upon acceptance" and most landlords generally agree. A typical deposit consists of the first and last months' rental plus GST.
- **Clauses 6 and 7: Services.** We find the wording here impractical and prefer to write in the Schedule exactly what is included, or not, in the rental.
- **Clause 8: Schedules.** Usually, there are two schedules: one attached to the Agreement to Lease for additional clauses and one for a floor plan. Sometimes, the landlord's work is covered in a separate schedule.

> *As the Agreement to Lease is much more specific than the Offer to Lease, you'll find more contrasts between the tenant's and landlord's specifications.*

- **Clause 9: Irrevocability.** Usually, these agreements are irrevocable for 2 or 3 days. Note that this clause is generally not that important. It is exceptional for an Offer to Lease to be accepted by the landlord without changes and if there is just one word changed, the offer is dead and a new expiry date (irrevocability) is set by the landlord. (We should write "should be set" because it is not uncommon for the party making changes to forget to write that the offer is not made irrevocable by them.)
- **Clause 12: Signage.** Too few tenants think of signage in detail at offer time. Usually, they do so after the lease is signed and they may not be able to put up the sign or all the signs they want.
- **Clause 14: Execution of Lease. Danger.** This wording seems to allow no room for any changes to the landlord's form of the agreement. When acting for landlords, we recommend (with a lawyer's approval) use of the following wording: "The lease will be signed and executed by both parties hereto prior to the commencement of work on the premises by either party and prior to occupancy by the tenant." This can be difficult to accomplish because too many tenants wait until the last minute to secure space, then want to move in as soon as the Offer to Lease is signed. However, if a landlord allows this, and few do, he may live to regret it because once the tenant moves into the premises:
  - he is busy settling in and is not inclined to devote time to reviewing the lease and, hence, he procrastinates
  - he feels that he has the upper hand in the negotiations and keeps on asking for changes in the lease, and
  - he may flatly (right away, or after a period of negotiations) declare that he will not sign the lease.
  At this time, the landlord has little recourse because not signing the lease is not a breach of the (non-existent) lease. The relationship of the parties is then based on the Offer to Lease, which has become the governing document between them. Contrary to the lease, which is very detailed, the Offer to

Lease leaves many details unspecified. The absence of a lease is a serious drawback for the landlord, but offers many advantages and some drawbacks to the tenant.

- **Clause 16: Assignment.** As covered elsewhere in this book, when we represent the landlord, we are satisfied with this clause. When we represent the tenant, we like to specify that consent (or refusal) must be given within two or three days or will be considered to have been granted.
- **Clause 17: Parking.** This clause works to the advantage of the landlord (no headaches). Some tenants want assigned parking.
- **Clause 21 and Schedule A.** Same comments as the ones mentioned for the Agreement of Purchase and Sale.

7.4 LEASE

See both sides of a Lease Agreement — the landlord's and tenant's — and appreciate the many conditions and concepts.

A lease is a document that grants to a tenant the rights to use and occupy the property. These rights are transferred by the landlord to a tenant for a specific period of time and at a specific rent.

While there are standard lease forms published by companies such as Dye and Durham (<www.dye-durham.ca>), one of the oldest and best known legal supply companies, they are used relatively rarely, at least by real estate agents. Virtually every lawyer and landlord has his own lease form, which they tweak from time to time. While leases for a specific use, such as industrial buildings, are generally similar from one landlord to another, there are always differences between them. Leases for office, multi-unit residential, and retail tend to vary more from one landlord to the next.

7.4.1 THE COMMERCIAL TENANCIES ACT

In Ontario, the *Commercial Tenancies Act* (R.S.O. 1990, c. L.7) (the Act) regulates the responsibilities and duties between landlords and tenants. The Ministry of Municipal Affairs and Housing provides a summary of the Act regarding items you need to know. Below are a few of the key points that it covers.

It is important to be aware that a signed lease agreement may take precedence over the Commercial Tenancies Act.

…

Non-payment of Rent
When a tenant has failed to pay the rent, the landlord has two options available.

OPTION 1: Change the locks
A landlord may change the locks of the unit and evict on the 16th day after the day rent was due. The landlord is not obligated to notify the tenant that the locks will be changed.

…

OPTION 2: Seize and dispose of a tenant's property
A landlord may seize and dispose of a tenant's property that is contained within the rented premises.

…

However, landlords are required to notify the tenant of the distress and the sum of monies required to cure the default .... Before disposing of seized property, the landlord must hold it for five days.

...

The Act requires two appraisals before selling or disposing of a tenant's property.

Rent Increases

If the event that there isn't a current tenancy agreement, the landlord may increase the rent by any amount at any time.

...

Commercial Landlords:
Rights and obligations

Landlords must notify tenants in writing of specific breaches of the lease and allow a reasonable period of time for them to comply.

...

Commercial Tenants:
Rights and obligations

Tenants cannot hold back rent because a landlord has failed to fulfill their obligations as outlined in the lease.

...

Tenants have the right to take their disputes with the landlord to Small Claims Court for disputes concerning money or personal property under $10,000. Otherwise, an application must be made to the Superior Court of Justice.

7.4.2 LONG-TERM LAND LEASE

In Ontario, under the *Planning Act* (R.S.O. 1990, c. P.13), the regulations stipulate that one may not (with a few exceptions) sell, lease, or mortgage part of a property for more than 21 years, including renewals, without first obtaining a consent from a local planning committee. If this consent is not obtained, the contract (lease, transfer, or mortgage) will be void. (These consents do not come cheap. For example, the town of Orangeville, Ontario, charges $875 for the application.)

Under the *Planning Act*, a lease of more than 21 years (including renewals) is treated as a conveyance (a sale) and is subject to the Land Transfer Tax. One exception is when one deals with part of a building or structure where this regulation does not apply. For example, if a landlord owns a shopping plaza with ten stores, he may lease any one of them for more than 21 years without being subject to the aforementioned limitations. The Land Transfer Tax will be due on any building lease in excess of 50 years (including renewal options).

The above implies that there are no limitations on the lease terms for buildings. It could be 999 years.

Although there is no equivalent legislation in British Columbia to the provisions of the *Planning Act* of Ontario, the *Land Title Act* (R.S.B.C. 1996, c. 250) does prohibit the leasing of less than an entire legal lot (the lease of less than an entire building is permitted), unless the subdivision requirements of the *Land Title Act* are complied with. In Alberta, the *Municipal Government Act* (R.S.A. 2000, c. M-26) prohibits the registration of an instrument that may have the effect of subdividing a parcel of land unles the subdivision has been approved by the appropriate authority.

7.4.3 TYPES OF LEASES

Theoretically, there are two kinds of leases for real property: net and gross. In reality there are myriads of leases. Regardless of the name, the lease must state exactly who pays what. Remember that nothing is set by law. It is a question of negotiation between landlord and tenant.

- **Net Lease.** The tenant pays all expenses, except (usually) structural repairs (roof, walls, windows, and doors). This type of lease passes to the tenant all the operational expenses of the building. Other names used for this kind of lease are: triple net,[1] entirely net, or carefree to the landlord. The true Net Lease is ideal for the landlord, whose only task is to deposit rental cheques every month in the bank and, if there is a mortgage, send a cheque to the lender.
- **Gross Lease.** The tenant does not pay taxes, maintenance or insurance (TMI) or common area maintenance (CAM).
- **Semi-Gross Lease.** In a third kind of lease, a Semi-Gross Lease, the landlord pays at least the property taxes. Here, it can become complicated because he may also pay building insurance and outside maintenance (landscaping and snow removal), or he may also pay maintenance, repairs, replacement, and even utilities.

7.4.4 THE IMPACT OF THE LEASE ON FINANCING AND SELLING

As a landlord, it is important to remember that the impact of the Lease goes beyond controlling the relationship with tenants. There are two other situations where leases are of critical importance – financing and selling.

Few landlords think of selling when they are negotiating a lease. This is a mistake as one never knows when one will want, or need, to sell a property. This is why lenders scrutinize leases carefully. If a borrower defaults, the lender will have to take over the property and a poor lease will be a major annoyance. A landlord should be aware of the following:

- option to buy
- right of first renewal to buy
- right to renew
- early termination of lease
- landlord's default, and
- "going-dark".

(a) Option to Buy

Sometimes, to attract a good tenant, a landlord will grant him an option to buy. It is not too bad if it is at market value (although the way to arrive at the value may be a problem). It is definitively bad if it is at a fixed price, which can turn out to be lower than market value when the date for exercising the option arrives. An option to buy in a lease discourages prospective buyers, who often feel they will be wasting their time presenting an offer. Sometimes, this allows the tenant to sell his option. One way to avoid this is to have a clause in the option that prevents the tenant from selling the option, or reselling the property, for a long period of time if he does exercise the option to buy. In theory, this implies that if a tenant exercises the option to buy, but resells the property during the no-sale period, the property would be returned to the original vendor. In reality it will create a messy situation.

---

1 A true "triple net lease" is extremely rare, except in a Sale and Leaseback situation. Such a lease would place upon the tenant the responsibility of paying for all expenses related to the property, including: property taxes, building insurance (property, casualty, and public liability), and maintenance and/or replacements of the roof, structure, mechanical systems (heating, sprinklers, etc.), plumbing, windows and glass, etc. The lease clause might read: "The Lease shall be entirely net to the Landlord and the Tenant shall pay for all expenses, of any kind, relating to the property".

(b) Right of First Refusal to Buy

In this situation, a landlord must advise a tenant that he has received a bona fide offer to buy, and the tenant has a given period of time to decide whether or not to buy the property, usually at the same price and on the same terms as the offeror. This is a definite turnoff for potential buyers and renders the marketing of the property difficult.

(c) Right to Renew

While the right to renew may seem to be an innocuous element of the lease, it can pose a big problem if, for example, it was originally signed at a lower rental.

(d) Early Termination of the Lease

When negotiating from a weak position, a landlord may grant a tenant the right to terminate a lease before the end of the indicated term, with or without a penalty (the most commonly encountered penalty is an amount equal to between 6 and 12 months of rental).

Virtually all landlords will terminate a lease reluctantly. Indeed, if we are talking about a 5-year lease and the tenant has the right to cancel after 2 years if he pays 6 months' worth of rental, the landlord will again find himself facing the problems that every landlord of an empty building faces — cleaning and repairing, listing with an agent and paying another leasing commission, legal fees, carrying the empty building and property taxes (albeit reduced if vacancy is greater than 90 days), maintenance, building insurance, utilities, security (empty buildings seem to be a magnet for vandals), and customizing the space for the new tenant.

(e) Landlord's Default

Most leases prevent a tenant from correcting a landlord's default such as, for example, repairing a roof and deducting the cost from the basic rental or the additional rental. Here, again, in a moment of weakness, a landlord may allow such a clause in the lease and lenders will take a jaundiced eye to this right.

(f) "Going-dark"

"Going-dark" is a clause sometimes encountered in shopping centre leases, which allows an anchor tenant to close his store, while continuing to pay rent. Usually, if this takes place, the other retailers will suffer greatly because they will have fewer customers. If they have the right to pay a lower rental in this case, it will upset the landlord's income, explaining why lenders are less likely to extend a loan when there is a "going-dark" clause in the lease.

7.4.5 UNDERSTANDING OPERATING COSTS

Virtually all landlords, except those of multi-family buildings, sign net leases with "additional rent". Prospective tenants should carefully scrutinize the contents of this phrase, but frequently they do not. At first blush, operating costs include property taxes, maintenance, and building insurance (TMI). Operating costs, besides TMI, can range from $11.84 to $43.00 per m² ($1.10 to $4 per sq ft) for industrial and from $43 to $215 ($4 to $20), and higher, for office. In some situations, utilities may be included, for example, for an office building, although this is rare for most industrial buildings.

There is little to dispute when it comes to property taxes and building insurance. The latter is not expensive. For example, for an industrial building, the insurance premium runs from $0.75 to $1.08 per m² ($0.07 to $0.10 per sq ft), but the devil is in maintenance costs. A tenant should investigate maintenance costs carefully because the difference can amount to many dollars per square metre per year for industrial, and much more for office or retail space. In the last few years, it seems that more and more items have come to be included in maintenance.

Prima facia, everyone understands that maintenance should include mechanical systems (HVAC, plumbing, sprinklers, lighting), landscaping, keeping the grounds clean, and plowing the snow. Frequently, a prospective tenant who asks for more details will be told that, in addition to the above, maintenance also includes:

- maintenance and repairs of parking lot and roof, and/or
- replacement of heating units, a portion of the parking lot or roof, and/or
- security guards.

> *Everyone understands that maintenance should include mechanical systems (HVAC, plumbing, sprinklers, lighting), landscaping, keeping the grounds clean, and plowing the snow.*

Some landlords use a more transparent alternative, which is less likely to be a potential cause of arguments, and show maintenance costs as a fixed amount per square metre (or sq ft) for exterior maintenance, HVAC, and roof depreciation. The most unpleasant aspect of operating costs for the tenant is the resistance of some landlords to showing, and justifying, the detailed expenses.

Commonly, landlords use projections, made at the beginning of a year of operations, to invoice tenants on a pro rata basis every month. After the end of the year, they find out if they have over or under charged and adjust accordingly. We have seen a landlord who claimed, six months after a year-end, that his books were not quite finalized! When he submitted the "justifying" documents, they were incomplete and not detailed enough to permit the tenant to check the expenses. This example shows why tenants should spend a lot of time in negotiation of the lease if they really want to be in a position to understand and verify the details around the operating costs.

Some landlords are now aggressively trying to recover some of the capital expenditures, including renovation or improvement expenses — such as new energy-efficient lighting, new insulation, new windows, new or renovated elevators — things that in the past, landlords did at their own expense. An example would be improving or refurbishing a building to attract a tenant. These may be hidden under the "fees" that landlords charge as part of operating costs, which typically amount to 15% of the additional rent, and sometimes are as high as 20% for retail properties.

Another item that few tenants pay attention to is energy efficiency. Basically, landlords are not motivated to update their toilets, lighting, or heating systems so that they cost less (to the tenants) to operate. Because only a few tenants ask for these improvements (they should do so when they negotiate the terms of the Lease), the landlord can continue along with systems that are more expensive to operate than they could be.

7.4.6 SUB-LEASING

As a landlord, you will have to deal with sub-leases. A sub-lease takes place when a tenant moves out of his space before the end of the lease term. It is customary to have a sub-lease clause in every lease. Usually it reads as follows: "The Tenant shall not have the right to sublet the premises without the written consent of the Landlord, such consent not to be unreasonably withheld." Such a clause has two weaknesses — one for the landlord and one for the tenant.

When we act for the landlord, we like to add, "However, if the rental for the sub-lease is more than what the Tenant is paying, the excess shall be paid to the Landlord." When we act for the tenant, we like to add, following "unreasonably withheld", "or delayed, and the Landlord shall answer the Tenant within three business days. If the Landlord refuses to consent to the sub-lease, he shall give his reasons for doing so, in writing to the Tenant, within the same three business days."

(a) Refusal to Consent

The landlord has grounds to refuse to consent if the use of the property under the sub-lease is not acceptable or the tenant is not acceptable. It is difficult to refuse to accept a tenant because of its lack of financial strength, since the original tenant is still responsible to pay for the rentals.

(b) Payment of Rent

There are a few options for paying rent in these circumstances. If the sub-lease rental is the same as the original rental, or higher (and the landlord keeps the excess), the landlord may agree to receive the cheques directly from the new tenant. If the sub-lease rental is less than the original rental, the landlord will probably want to continue to receive the cheques from the original tenant. This is common because sub-lease rentals for a short term (under two years) are almost always lower than the original rental.

(c) Sub-lease Term

One of the finer points frequently not considered is that to create a true sub-lease its term should be, at most, for the length of the original (or head) lease less one day. Often, parties forget this detail, or are not aware of it. If the sub-lease is for the full remaining term of the head lease, at law it is deemed to be an "assignment" of the head lease as opposed to a sub-lease.

(d) Lease Assignment

In the signed lease, few landlords give a tenant the right to assign the lease. Indeed, if the lease is assigned, the original tenant is usually released from his obligations while, in a sub-lease, he is still responsible. This means that if the sub-tenant stops paying rent, the original tenant must keep paying it. It is important that the lease covers the question of assignment, otherwise the *Commercial Tenancies Act* takes over, which states:

> 23. (1) In every lease made after the 1st day of September, 1911, containing a covenant, condition or agreement against assigning, underletting, or parting with the possession, or disposing of the land or property leased without licence or consent, such covenant, condition or agreement shall, unless the lease contains an express provision to the contrary, be deemed to be subject to a proviso to the effect that such licence or consent is not to be unreasonably withheld. (R.S.O. 1990, c. L.7, s. 23 (1))

(e) Sub-leasing Consent

It is the landlord who sits in the driver's seat when a tenant requests consent to a sub-lease. The landlord may behave in the manners described below and still be within his rights.

- The landlord may make demands of the original tenant. For example, he may insist the payment of a certain sum of money, under one pretext or another, to consent to the sub-lease.
- The landlord may delay. Time is on his side. The tenant has found a sub-tenant who is keen. If the landlord drags his feet, the sub-tenant may, and probably will, look elsewhere. This brings about the question of reasonableness, or rather lack of it, on the part of the landlord. Indeed, there is a great temptation, at times, for a landlord to make it difficult to sublease, so that the tenant will give up his lease, allowing the landlord to lease the space for more money or to another tenant with a stronger covenant.

- The tenant is generally at a disadvantage when it comes to proving that the landlord was unreasonable and landlords can be quite creative in their reasons for delay. Indeed, can it be held against the landlord if its CEO goes on vacation the day the request for sub-lease was presented? The landlord had probably planned this trip, during which he is unreachable, for six or more months!
- However, it should be noted that an unreasonable delay in responding to a request for consent, or a refusal without providing logical reasons, may be deemed by the court to be unreasonable. The problem, from the tenant's viewpoint is that he will probably have suffered substantial damages by the time the court reaches its decision (this can take a few years) and these damages are almost always difficult to prove and quantify — another reason the sub-lease clause in the lease should be particularly well crafted and carefully scrutinized. Furthermore, most leases are for amounts of money (rental) that do not justify going to court.
- The landlord may offer a buy-out deal to the tenant. He might propose, "If you want to move out, the total of the rental due until the end of the term is $400,000. Give me a $200,000 cheque and I will cancel the lease and look for another tenant."

It is important to note that the *Commercial Tenancies Act* is quite clear that if a landlord refuses to consent to an assignment of the Lease or to a sub-lease, he should have solid grounds to do so. Indeed, the landlord exposes himself to legal action and the odds of success are against the him.

> (2) Where the landlord refuses or neglects to give a licence or consent to an assignment or sub-lease, a judge of the Ontario Court (General Division), upon the application of the tenant or of the assignee or sub-tenant, made according to the rules of court, may make an order determining whether or not the licence or consent is unreasonably withheld and, where the judge is of opinion that the licence or consent is unreasonably withheld, permitting the assignment or sub-lease to be made, and such order is the equivalent of the licence or consent of the landlord within the meaning of any covenant or condition requiring the same and such assignment or sub-lease is not a breach thereof. (R.S.O. 1990, c. L.7, s. 23 (2))

(f) Roll-and-Dump

The roll-and-dump is a two-step process used by some sophisticated tenants who want to get out of a lease economically.

In the roll, a tenant assigns his lease to a corporation that is a subsidiary (that may not have existed when the lease was signed). He can generally do so without the landlord's consent because virtually every lease permits an assignment, without landlord's consent, between a parent company and a subsidiary. The lease has been rolled over — the first step in the roll-and-dump.

In the dump, the sub-tenant's shares (the subsidiary's) are then sold to another party, generally a corporation. This can be done because most older leases do not prohibit the sale of such shares. Herein lies the danger. Often leases are just renewed or extended, rather than a new one being written. Most good lawyers, who specialize in real estate, are now aware of this roll-and-dump strategy and build safeguards into new leases. This scheme can be used to get out of a lease at low cost (cost of registering a new corporation and some modest legal fees). It can also be used to gain control of a space in a building when a landlord would never accept a specific tenant.

7.4.7 LEASE IN DEFAULT

Sometimes, a tenant is in default. It can be for any number of reasons: rental arrears, unlawful or obnoxious uses, damage to the building, etc. When this happens, a landlord asks his lawyer to send a Notice of Default (or Breach of Lease) to the tenant, as provided for in the *Commercial Tenancies Act*. The tenant has 30 days to cure the default or vacate the premises. If he fails to do so, the lease will be terminated. See a sample Notice of Breach in Figure 7.3.

A landlord has the right to seize the goods and equipment of a tenant, who is in default for arrears of rent, and to sell them. This remedy is called "distress" or "distraint." This right stems from common law and from the *Commercial Tenancies Act*. Therefore, it does not apply to residential tenants.

If a landlord seizes the company's assets, the company must pay the arrears of rent or try to come to a settlement with the landlord because the landlord has the right to sell the assets after 5 days. Note that if the company is placed into bankruptcy within the 5 days, for example, by a secured creditor who fears for his security, the bankruptcy proceedings will stop the rent distraint action.

The big appeal of distraint for a landlord is that he has the right to keep the proceeds of the sale, in priority over all the other creditors of the tenant. However, in some cases, a secured creditor could challenge this approach and the court could decide that the act of the landlord was a "fraudulent preference". A fraudulent preference could exist when a transaction takes place within three months before the bankruptcy date. This is obviously intended to prevent people from playing games. The implication for the landlord is that he must decide which creditor, if any, may elect to place the tenant in bankruptcy. This is difficult because the landlord will normally not know the details regarding other creditors.

This right to distrain applies to the goods and equipment found on the leased premises by the landlord, whether they belong to the tenant, or the sub-tenant; however, the latter has remedies (see below). This process appeals to landlords because it is relatively simple and inexpensive. There are a few rules to bear in mind.

- Tenants, even when in default, have rights. They are entitled to be given a period of time to remedy the problem as well as a redemption period.
- The landlord must make sure that what he seizes is the property of the tenant, and not that of leasing companies, vendors, or customers.
- The value of the goods and equipment, taken under the landlord's right to distrain, must be approximately the same as the money owed to the landlord. To distress more could result in a court determining that the distress was invalid. However, it is an accepted practice for landlords to seize up to four times the retail value of the goods and equipment. This is based on the fact that the goods and equipment will be sold at a fire sale, where the true value of the items will not be realized.
- Proper appraisals must be secured for the goods and equipment seized, prior to them being sold to arm's-length buyers.
- The landlord must not attempt to terminate the lease at the same time as he distrains, otherwise a court could rule that the relationship between the landlord and the tenant was not a continuing one.

Figure 7.3
Notice to Tenant of Breach of Covenant

(Pursuant to Section 19 of the Commercial Tenancies Act,

R.S.O. 1990, c. L. 7 and amendments thereto)

FROM: Industry Street Developments

TO: John Doe Inc.

                  123 Industry Street, Toronto, Ontario

TAKE NOTICE that you are in default of several covenants contained in the Lease made between Industry Street

Developments, as Landlord and John Doe Inc. as Tenant, dated March 19, 2001 (the "Lease") in respect of certain premises

located in the building known as 123 Industry Street, Toronto, Ontario (the "Premises").

THE FOLLOWING is a list of the breaches by you, of the above-noted Lease:

1.   Default of Section 3.1, 5.2, 8.2 and 12.1 of the Lease in that, notwithstanding repeated requests:

(a)   you have failed to make payment in regard to the Minimum Rent and Additional Rent totalling $289,617.05 as of

          the date hereof.

YOU ARE hereby required to remedy the foregoing breaches of Lease, within seven (7) days from the date hereof, and you are

required to make compensation in money for the foregoing breaches of Lease. This Notice is forwarded pursuant to the provi-

sions of your Lease and pursuant to Section 19(2) of the Commercial Tenancies Act, R.S.O. 1990, c. L. 7 and all amendments

thereto. If you fail to remedy the breaches of Lease within the time limit set out above, and to make reasonable compensa-

tion to our satisfaction for the foregoing breaches of Lease, we intend to proceed with the Landlord's remedies which may

include a termination of your Lease. In the event that you remedy all of the foregoing breaches of Lease to the satisfaction of

your Landlord, your Landlord will accept the sum of One Thousand Dollars ($1,000.00) as reasonable compensation in money

for the said breaches.

DATED at Toronto this 15th day of July, 2004.

"Industry Street Developments"

by its solicitors, Creative Lawyers, LLP

Per: _____

Unless the landlord secures clearance from the taxing authorities, he may have to pay the taxes on the sale of goods. Indeed, PST, GST and other taxes, such as property taxes, and obligations (payroll taxes) have priority before a

Even with good advice, the landlord's preferential claim can leave him with little or nothing.

landlord is paid. It is wise to use a lawyer who is familiar with commercial leases before seizing any goods. Even with good advice, the landlord's preferential claim can leave him with little or nothing because of the following situations:

- the goods may not be of sufficient value
- the secured creditors (government/taxes) gobble it all up
- legal fees can add up, or
- premises are occupied while the goods are offered for sale.

A sub-tenant can protect himself in two ways.

1. The sub-tenant can deliver to the head landlord a statutory declaration saying that the goods and equipment (chattels) on the premises belong to the sub-tenant.
2. There may be a clause in the sub-lease (which must be approved by the landlord) preventing the landlord from exercising this right of distress with a sub-tenant.

However, one must remember that the chattels cannot be protected from distress if the head landlord has not consented to the sub-lease.

7.4.8 TENANT BANKRUPTCY

Frequently, when a tenant is in arrears of rent, he will eventually declare bankruptcy too. Bankruptcy is a way for a corporation or an individual who cannot pay his bills to divide up all of its residual assets among its legitimate creditors and thereafter be relieved of the obligations to make any further payments. It allows the opportunity for the bankrupt to "start fresh".

Under the rules of the *Bankruptcy and Insolvency Act* (R.S.C. 1985, c. B-3) of Canada, the Governor in Council appoints a Superintendent of Bankruptcy who issues licences to trustees and one or more official receivers, who are deemed to be officers of the court in each bankruptcy division. There are three in Ontario.

A business or person can be petitioned into bankruptcy by creditors or can place itself in bankruptcy. To make a petition the services of a lawyer are necessary. The typical process involves three steps:

1. The lawyer sends a notice that a bankruptcy petition will be made if payment is not made by a certain date.
2. A trustee agrees to act as trustee in the petition.
3. If there are significant assets, a notice is placed in a newspaper, notifying the date of the meeting of creditors.

If you are involved in a bankruptcy, you will come across the terms, "Trustee in Bankruptcy" and "Receiver or Receiver/Manager". It is important to understand the difference between the two. In fact, one can encounter four possible situations.

1. **Trustee Only.** He is licensed under the Act to preserve the property of the bankrupt, for the benefit of all the creditors, but mainly to protect the interests of the secured creditor that appointed him. When a tenant becomes bankrupt, the trustee inherits all of the rights and obligations that are contained in the lease, but he has the right to terminate the lease and therefore no longer have any obligations, except three months' accelerated rent, if provided for in the lease. He must, as soon as possible, take possession of the deeds, books, records, documents, and all property of the bankrupt, and make an inventory. The trustee is in the same position as a receiver appointed by the court. Whenever asked, the trustee must report on the progress and details of the bankruptcy. He may sell the assets of the bankrupt, lease the property, carry on the existing business, borrow money, settle debts, and divide proceeds among creditors. First, he must pay the priority creditors and the costs of receivership, then the secured creditors. The trustee may appoint the bankrupt to help with the disposition of the property.

2. **Receiver Only.** The receiver liquidates the assets, collecting money due to the bankrupt, and paying what he feels should be paid. He liquidates the business if it cannot be sold. This is done at the direction of the court.

   For a long time, there were two types of receivers: one that was privately appointed by the creditor (called private receivership), with his primary duty to protect the interest of a security under which he was appointed; the other was court appointed (an officer of the court) with, or without, a wide range of powers, at the request of a security holder. It is common, now, to see an "interim receiver" that has a fiduciary duty to all parties involved.

   It is the court that appoints a licensed trustee as interim receiver. The interim receiver takes conservatory measures and may summarily dispose of items likely to depreciate rapidly in value. This approach offers more flexibility for the realization of assets. Note that the court appointment implies a more costly process.

3. **Receiver/Manager.** A receiver is appointed to run the business.

4. **Trustee/Receiver.** This is the most common situation. In this case, the receiver/trustee wears both hats and, in this capacity, he acts for all the creditors.

The remuneration of the trustee can be as voted by the creditors or 7.5% of the amount remaining out of the realization of the property of the debtor, after the claims of the secured creditors have been paid. If the trustee or receiver/manager has carried on the business, he may be allowed extra remuneration.

(a) Distribution of Money

Once all the issues have been sorted out, the monies left, if any, are distributed first to secured creditors, then to preferred ones, and finally to unsecured ones. Secured creditors have different priority rankings. For example, withholding taxes and GST come first. Landlords come behind the secured creditors, but before the unsecured ones.

This excerpt from the *Bankruptcy and Insolvency Act* (Canada) explains the priority ranking:

136. (1) Subject to the rights of secured creditors, the proceeds realized from the property of a bankrupt shall be applied in priority of payment as follows:

   (a) in the case of a deceased bankrupt, the reasonable funeral and testamentary expenses incurred by the legal representative or, in the Province of Quebec, the successors or heirs of the deceased bankrupt;

   (b) the costs of administration, in the following order,

      (i) the expenses and fees of any person acting under a direction made under paragraph 14.03(1)(a),

(ii) the expenses and fees of the trustee, and

(iii) legal costs;

(c) the levy payable under section 147;

(d) wages, salaries, commissions or compensation of any clerk, servant, travelling salesman, labourer or workman for services rendered during the six months immediately preceding the bankruptcy to the extent of two thousand dollars in each case, together with, in the case of a travelling salesman, disbursements properly incurred by that salesman in and about the bankrupt's business, to the extent of an additional one thousand dollars in each case, during the same period, and for the purposes of this paragraph commissions payable when goods are shipped, delivered or paid for, if shipped, delivered or paid for within the six month period, shall be deemed to have been earned therein;

(d.1) claims in respect of debts or liabilities referred to in paragraph 178(1)(b) or (c), if provable by virtue of subsection 121(4), for periodic amounts accrued in the year before the date of the bankruptcy that are payable, plus any lump sum amount that is payable;

(e) municipal taxes assessed or levied against the bankrupt, within the two years immediately preceding the bankruptcy, that do not constitute a secured claim against the real property or immovables of the bankrupt, but not exceeding the value of the interest or, in the Province of Quebec, the value of the right of the bankrupt in the property in respect of which the taxes were imposed as declared by the trustee;

(f) the lessor for arrears of rent for a period of three months immediately preceding the bankruptcy and accelerated rent for a period not exceeding three months following the bankruptcy if entitled to accelerated rent under the lease, but the total amount so payable shall not exceed the realization from the property on the premises under lease, and any payment made on account of accelerated rent shall be credited against the amount payable by the trustee for occupation rent;

(g) the fees and costs referred to in subsection 70(2) but only to the extent of the realization from the property exigible thereunder;

(h) in the case of a bankrupt who became bankrupt before the prescribed date, all indebtedness of the bankrupt under any Act respecting workers' compensation, under any Act respecting unemployment insurance or under any provision of the Income Tax Act creating an obligation to pay to Her Majesty amounts that have been deducted or withheld, rateably;

(i) claims resulting from injuries to employees of the bankrupt in respect of which the provisions of any Act respecting workers' compensation do not apply, but only to the extent of moneys received from persons guaranteeing the bankrupt against damages resulting from those injuries; and

(j) in the case of a bankrupt who became bankrupt before the prescribed date, claims of the Crown not mentioned in paragraphs (a) to (i), in right of Canada or any province, rateably notwithstanding any statutory preference to the contrary.

(2) Subject to the retention of such sums as may be necessary for the costs of administration or otherwise, payment in accordance with subsection (1) shall be made as soon as funds are available for the purpose.

(3) A creditor whose rights are restricted by this section is entitled to rank as an unsecured creditor for any balance of claim due him. (R.S.C., 1985, c. B-3, s. 136; 1992, c. 1, s. 143(E), c. 27, s. 54; 1997, c. 12, s. 90; 2001, c. 4, s. 31; 2004, c. 25, s. 70)

Lawyers try to protect their landlord clients by placing in the lease a clause similar to the following:

> The Tenant covenants and agrees that if the Term or any of the goods and chattels of the Tenant on the Leased Premises shall be at any time during the Term seized or taken in execution or attachment by any creditor of the Tenant or if a Receiver or Manager should be appointed for the assets or undertaking of the Tenant or if the Tenant shall make any assignment for the benefit of creditors or any bulk sale or, becoming bankrupt or insolvent, shall take the benefit of any Act now or hereafter in force for bankrupt or insolvent debtors or if any order shall be made for the winding up of the Tenant, or if the Leased Premises shall without the written consent of the Landlord become and remain vacant for a period of fifteen (15) days, or be used by any other persons than such as are entitled to use them under the terms of this Lease, or if the Tenant shall without the written consent of the Landlord abandon or attempt to abandon the Leased Premises or to sell or dispose of goods or chattels of the Tenant or to remove them or any of them from the Leased Premises so that there would not in the event of such abandonment, sale or disposal be sufficient goods on the Leased Premises subject to distress to satisfy the rent above due or accruing due, then and in every such case the then current month's rent and the next ensuing three (3) months' rent shall immediately become due and be paid and the Landlord may re-enter and take possession of the Leased Premises as though the Tenant or the servants of the Tenant or any other occupant of the Leased Premises were holding over after the expiration of the Term and the Term shall, at the option of the Landlord, forthwith become forfeited and determined, and in every one of the cases above such accelerated rent shall be recoverable by the Landlord in the same manner as the Rent hereby reserved and as if Rent were in arrears and the said option shall be deemed to have been exercised if the Landlord or its agents given notice to the Tenant as provided for herein.

(b) Rights of Sub-tenant

Many people are not clear as to the rights of a sub-tenant when a tenant defaults under the lease. If a tenant defaults and the head landlord wants to remove the sub-tenant, the sub-tenant has the right to apply to the court to remain in the space he occupies under the sublease and, generally, the court rules that he may, as covered by section 21 of the *Commercial Tenancies Act*:

> 21. Where a lessor is proceeding by action or otherwise to enforce a right of re-entry or forfeiture under any covenant, proviso or stipulation in a lease, the court, on motion by any person claiming as under-lessee any estate or interest in the property comprised in the lease or any part thereof, in the lessor's action, if any, or in any action or application in the Ontario Court (General Division) brought by such person for that purpose, may make an order vesting for the whole term of the lease or any less term the property comprised in the lease, or any part thereof, in any person entitled as under-lessee to any estate or interest in such property upon such conditions as to execution of any deed or other document, payment of rents, costs, expenses, damages, compensation, giving security or otherwise as the court in the circumstances of each case thinks fit; but in no case is any such under-lessee entitled to require a lease to be granted to him, her or it for any longer term than the under-lessee had under the original sublease.

7.4.9 LEASE-PURCHASE AND OPTION TO PURCHASE

A Lease-Purchase is a lease that contains a clause giving the tenant the right to purchase the leased property, whereas an Option to Purchase is a document giving a person, who may or may not be the tenant at the time, the right to purchase a property.

Both are generally granted by a vendor/landlord to a purchaser who does not have sufficient funds for the down payment but wants to purchase a property. Frequently, a portion of the rental is applied against the purchase price. This can also be done by way of reduced rent. Whether it is a Lease-Purchase or Option to Purchase, the big advantage for the tenant is that he controls the property and may make confident plans for the future, including renovations, etc. In the case of a Lease-Purchase, the vendor or landlord is virtually assured of a sale.

Such a situation took place in a small town located about one hour's drive from Toronto. Marty had a 1,393 m² (15,000 sq ft) industrial building on four acres that he wanted to sell for $495,000. After Alex, the real estate agent, had talked to quite a few prospects, he came across Werner who had a flourishing transport company and for whom the place was ideal, particularly the four acres that were perfect for parking his semi-trailers.

However, Werner had no money for a down payment. Alex prepared an Offer to Lease for one year at a yearly rental of $30,000, which was much less than the market rental. He also prepared an Offer to Purchase for $495,000, which was more than the vendor would have received in a conventional sale. Each was conditional on the acceptance of the other. The sale was to close on the day the lease expired. Since the tenant/buyer did not have any money to give as consideration with the Offer to Purchase, Alex set it up so that after three months Werner would pay a certain amount of money in addition to the lease payments every month that would be applied against the down payment. It worked very well and both vendor and buyer were very satisfied.

It is difficult to find an owner willing to grant an Option to Purchase, unless the consideration for the option is very high or it is a buyer's market. Many people who lease a space would like to buy a building instead, but do not have the cash to do so.

Some landlords will grant a tenant an option to buy, but it is rare and when it is done, it will often be at an inflated price. Sometimes, they will flatly refuse an option but will grant the tenant a right of first refusal. Under this scenario, if the landlord receives an offer to buy that he is willing to accept, he must notify the tenant, generally enclosing a copy of the offer, and the tenant has a set amount of time to buy the property on the same terms.

7.4.10 SALE AND LEASEBACK (S&LB)

In a sale and leaseback (S&LB) situation the owner/occupant of a building sells it and, simultaneously, leases it back, generally for a period of 10 years or more. Most of the time, there are no rental escalations during the term of the lease.

Some investors specialize, in that they only buy properties that are S&LBs. Because of the lower degree of risk (the purchaser is, in principle, assured of having no vacancy for the term of the lease), the Cap Rate is often, if not always, lower than that for empty buildings — that is, the price is higher.

Sale and Leaseback situations occur primarily with single-user industrial and retail buildings and, to a much lesser degree, with office buildings. However, nothing prevents you from selling and leasing back any property, if you can find a buyer who is interested. You may, for example, own a multiple occupancy industrial building with ten tenants. The main drawback of such a building is that its property management is relatively extensive and it goes against the essence of S&LBs, which are pursued by investors wanting clean deals with very little involvement (actual or potential) if the deal turns sour.

Nothing prevents you from doing some creative marketing, particularly with smaller properties. If you own a property and you need to lease it fast, try to find a tenant/buyer. Offer to sell and leaseback the property to him for, say, five years. As the vendor you will have no worry whatsoever, outside of depositing his cheque into your bank account every month. You will sell at a sizeable premium, if you use this strategy.

For the creation of the S&LB concept we must thank Safeway Inc., the US supermarket chain. In the 1940s, as an expanding corporation, it was quite naturally short of cash. Someone in the company had the idea that investors would be glad to own real estate leased to a tenant that was credit rated (Standard & Poor) A+ or higher. Safeway made full use of the concept to add stores at an accelerated pace by using the cash generated by selling properties with a lease-back arrangement.

For the creation of the S&LB concept we must thank Safeway Inc., the US supermarket chain.

This strategy also benefited the company by freeing up the cash that had been used to buy real estate, generating significant profits. Indeed, the reasoning was as outlined below.

- Value of an empty supermarket store was, say, $3,000,000.
- Value of the same store, based on the then current Cap Rate, and leased to Safeway at market rate was, say $4,000,000.

What has changed? The presence of a long-term lease to a credit rated tenant, often called a Triple A tenant. This lowers the risk, as an investor sees this as a very desirable investment in an investment-grade company. In other words, it was the lease, backed by Safeway's strong covenant, which was sold at a huge profit, allowing Safeway to pay not only for the store and land, but also for a few bushels of apples and oranges.

This brings us to an aspect of real estate rarely discussed. Theoretically, no business of any financial strength should initially rent a building from a developer or an owner. It should buy it, or contract for its construction, then sell it to an investor at a significantly higher price and lease it back, thus realizing a profit while also creating premises that precisely meet its needs.

In this field, as in any other, things have evolved and, use of this strategy has now spread from investment-grade companies (corporations that are very strong financially) to sub-investment-grade companies, which while not Triple A are still strong enough to interest investors.

(a) Types of Sale and Leaseback

You could say that there are two types of S&LB: tenant's credit rating oriented, which is long term (20+ years), such as described above; and real estate oriented (10+ years). Leases of less than 10 years are rare.

In real estate-oriented S&LBs, the investor's equity requirement is greater, as is the return he demands, since the perceived risk due to a less strong tenant and shorter-term lease will be higher. This shorter lease category is particularly attractive for tenants that are growing companies and may become involved in mergers and acquisitions. It gives them additional flexibility.

The advantages of S&LB for the vendor/tenant are as follows:
- higher sale price thanks to lower Cap Rates than those of an empty building
- freeing-up of capital for use in the company's area of expertise
- paying-off debt by freeing equity
- retaining control of the asset by way of a long-term lease, and
- focusing on core business competency.

The advantages of S&LB for the investor are the following:
- secure, long-term, stable cash flow
- because most S&LB are triple net leases, any increase in building operating expenses is paid by the tenant

- it is an entirely passive investment — the investor has no involvement with the management of the building, and
- by the end of the lease term most, if not all, of the mortgage principal will have been repaid, leaving the investor with an asset that is free and clear.

(b) The Evolved Leaseback

Recently, a new type of S&LB has appeared. It takes place between an investor/vendor, generally a large real estate investment company, and an investor/buyer. With this, the vendor can realize the full value of an appreciated asset that may be under-financed, due to its having increased in value significantly, and largely depreciated (CCA).

In these situations, a vendor will add its credit rating to the deal by guaranteeing the lease, thus increasing the value of the property. An example will help to explain the concept.

In 1990, ABC Real Estate Investment Corp. acquired a $6-million warehouse from Widget Co. Widget signed a 10-year lease at $440,000 per year, net (7.33% Cap Rate ($440,000/$6 million)), and with a renewal clause at fair market rental.

In 2000, Widget Co. exercised its option to renew, at a rental of $600,000 per year, net. At this time, a Cap Rate for this type of transaction was 10%, placing a value on the property of $6 million. However, the new property owner decided to guarantee the lease of Widget Co. The lease now had two covenants: Widget and ABC Real Estate Investment Corp. This enormously decreased the risk to an investor. If Widget Co. defaults, ABC will keep on paying the rent. With such strong guarantees, the Cap Rate dropped to 9%, creating a sale price of: $600,000/9% = $6,666,666. By adding its covenant to that of Widget's, ABC had increased the value of the property by $666,666.

7.4.11 SANDWICH LEASE

There is also a way to make money out of a lease without being a landlord or a tenant occupying the space. This can happen when a person leases a building from a landlord and then sub-leases it. For example, you know someone who needs to lease a 1,858 m² (20,000 sq ft) building. You also know the ideal building for him. You could enter into a lease with the landlord, for say $43 per m² ($4 per sq ft), conditional for 30 days upon your finding a sub-tenant. Then you approach the businessman who needs the space and sub-lease it to him at $54 per m² ($5 per sq ft). On a 5-year lease, you would make: $54 - $43 = $11 x 1,858 m² = $20,438 x 5 years = $102,190.

A sandwich lease is a lease in which a tenant/investor finds himself in a sandwich between the landlord (head lease) and the sub-tenant (sub-lease). This is difficult to do unless you have a tenant in mind, which generally happens through an ongoing personal relationship or if you have a business reason to support him, either because you believe in his business or in his ability as a manager. You might also be interested in investing in the business in exchange for your help.

7.4.12 COMMERCIAL LEASE

Renting new space is an expensive proposition for tenants. Finding a property and negotiating lease terms is time consuming. In addition, there are many expenses associated with any move. In fact, some can be huge. There are times when a landlord can safely overcharge a tenant who has little choice but to pay. We once were told by an automotive plastic parts manufacturing company that the cost of moving their equipment would be higher than the value of their building. In this case, the landlord could charge more than market rental, without fear of losing the tenant.

If you want to rent commercial space to a tenant, there are a few things you need to know.

1. There is no "standard" lease agreement; each lease is different and needs to be carefully reviewed.
2. The lease is the landlord's and is slanted in his favour.
3. A lease is a legally binding contract that cannot be broken easily without consequences.

Always consult a lawyer experienced in commercial properties before signing any Lease or Offer to Lease. If, by any chance, you are dealing with a property that may be badly contaminated, have the clause relating to the environmental matters written or reviewed by a lawyer specializing in environmental law. A commercial real estate lawyer may not be knowledgeable enough.

The *Land Titles Act* (R.S.O. 1990, c. L.5) states that the lessee or other person entitled to, or interested in, a lease or agreement for lease of registered land may apply to the land registrar to register notice of the lease or agreement. It is possible to register only a notice of a lease or agreement to lease by setting out the particulars of the lease in lieu of including the lease itself or agreement in the document. It is generally the lessee or his solicitor who registers the document. It is also possible to register a notice of assignment of lessee's, or of lessor's, interest in lease, and notice of sub-lease.

As previously mentioned, if a lease exceeds 50 years, for taxation purposes it is considered a sale and land transfer tax (LTT) is due. In the same vein, if a lease contains an option to purchase, the LTT is due on the value of the option consideration, if any.

7.4.13 RETAIL LEASE

Retail leases generally contain a couple of clauses that are unique to that type of property: non-competition clauses and overage or percentage rental clauses.

(a) Non-competition Clause

A good shopping centre lease will have a non-competition clause to protect both the landlord and the tenant. The landlord will want a clause saying that the tenant cannot open another store within a given radius of the centre, so as not to draw any customers away from the store covered by the lease. The radius will vary enormously depending on the type of store, for example, a convenience store versus a high-class restaurant. The tenant's non-competition clause will protect his business from competitors within the shopping centre, by restricting another store selling merchandise similar to his from operating in the same centre.

(b) Overage or Percentage Rental Clause

When a landlord wants to induce a tenant to move into a difficult-to-lease space, he may offer an overage clause or a percentage rental lease. With percentage rental leases, some, or all, of the rental is based on a percentage of the sales achieved by the retail tenant. Other retail leases require the tenant to pay a percentage rental based on his sales in excess of the minimum annual rent. This is called an "overage", and usually works in the following way: the tenant pays a basic minimum rental that usually covers all the expenses of the landlord but gives him little, or no, profit. However, the tenant must pay a percentage on every sale he makes above that. "Overage" is defined as "a percentage of the amount of sales grossed by a retail store that is paid under the terms of a lease, in addition to a fixed rent."

There are various forms of percentage leases, but most of the time the overage will not be paid concurrently with the basic rental. It will start being due only when it amounts to more than the basic rental. The considerable advantage, of course, is that this is a guarantee against inflation for the landlord since, usually, the rental remains the same for a long period of time: 5, 10, or 20 years, but if the business is successful the value of the goods sold and, therefore, the total value of them, increases over time and the landlord benefits from it.

Furthermore, usually when a shopping centre opens, it is a little "green". As it matures, sales are higher and a fraction of these sales goes into the landlord's pocket. For example, let's assume a 279 m² (3,000 sq ft) store that pays a rental of $161 per m², or $45,000 per year. The percentage rental is 5% until the store sales reach $800,000. If sales reach $1.2 million, the tenant will be paying the base rental of $45,000, plus overage: $1.2 million - $800,000 = $400,000 x 5% = $20,000, for a total of $65,000 per year.

7.5 ESTOPPEL CERTIFICATE

Recognize the various legal documents and their impact, including estoppel certificates and affidavits.

This is a legal document, generally sent by a purchaser's lawyer (though it can be sent by a vendor's lawyer) to the tenants of the building being acquired to verify the terms of their leases and various other matters, such as rental, term, security deposit, etc. An estoppel certificate may also be sent to a mortgagee to confirm the details of a mortgage. This prevents a tenant from later claiming that he paid less than was represented or had special privileges that were unknown to the purchaser. An estoppel certificate, such as the one shown in Figure 7.4, is generally required by a mortgagee from commercial mortgage tenants, but not from tenants of multi-family buildings, which are too numerous.

7.6 AFFIDAVIT

An affidavit is "a written declaration made under oath before a notary public or other authorized officer". Under the *Commissioners for Taking Affidavits Act* (R.S.O. 1990, c. C.17), certain categories of persons are automatically commissioners, for example, provincial judges, local registrars of the provincial courts, solicitors, clerks and treasurers of municipalities, and members of the provincial legislative assembly, etc. Public notaries can be appointed commissioners for taking affidavits by the Lieutenant Governor. Anyone over 18 years of age may apply for a commission.

7.7 LAWYERS AND ARBITRATION CLAUSES

Work within the court and legal system.

As a general rule, we avoid the courts like the plague. It is always very costly, what with big city lawyers charging $500 or more per hour, and most matters moving through the courts at a snail's pace. However, as businessmen, we do need lawyers. Use them without hesitation when necessary or prudent. However, give them very specific instructions to avoid excessive expense.

Figure 7.4
Estoppel Certificat of Tenant

ESTOPPEL CERTIFICATE OF TENANT

TO:

RE:

The undersigned, _____, being the Tenant of premises located at _____ of the above-noted property (the "demised premises") pursuant to a lease dated _____ (the "Lease") made between _____, as Landlord and _____, as Tenant and hereby certifies, acknowledges, and is estopped from denying the following:

1. The term as set out in the Lease commences the _____ day of _____, 200__ and expires on the _____ day of _____, 200__. There is an option to renew for a further term of _____ (___) years upon terms and conditions to be negotiated between the Landlord and the Tenant.
2. The minimum monthly rental during the first ___ years of the Lease is $_____ monthly, net net, and during the last ___ years of the Lease is $_____, net net.
3. The Tenant is in possession of the demised premises.
4. The Lease is a net net Lease and the Tenant is paying and has paid effective to the _____ day of _____, 200__, minimum rent and all other charges, including without limitation the common costs/operating costs payable pursuant to the Lease.
5. The amount of prepaid rent or security deposit held by the Landlord is $_____. No interest is payable thereon.
6. The demised premises have been completed in accordance with any obligations of the Landlord.
7. Neither the Landlord, nor the Tenant is in default in respect of the Lease.
8. The Tenant has no claims, charges, offences, right to set-off, lien, abatement or counterclaim against the Landlord in respect of the rent or otherwise.

DATED AT _____, THIS _____ DAY OF _____ 200__.

_____

PER: _____

To help avoid the costly involvement of the courts in settling disputes, we use an arbitration clause in our contracts. This is not the standard arbitration clause (under the *Arbitration Act*, 1991 (S.O. 1991, c. 17)). In our experience, many lawyers now use a clause that outlines a process that can be as costly to the client as the traditional way of settling disputes. We know of one situation where the chairman of a public company, Bill, had a contract with a world-renowned American clinic. The contract had an arbitration clause and when things went sour Bill invoked it. Both sides used lawyers. It took 2 years for the action to work its way through the arbitration process. Bill's company received what it claimed: US $1,200,000, however, their legal costs were US $400,000! This is why we suggest that the arbitration clause, presented below, be used in agreements.

> *As a general rule, we avoid the courts like the plague.*

Author's Arbitration Clause

In the event of any dispute, arising between the parties, regarding these present, they herein agree that the matter in difference be submitted to arbitration as follows:

1- Within fifteen days of the date of notice of such request for arbitration being given in writing by one party to the other, the two parties shall each appoint one arbitrator;

2- Within fifteen days of the date of the appointment of the last appointed arbitrator, the two arbitrators so appointed shall appoint a third arbitrator;

3- Within thirty days of the appointment of the third arbitrator, the three arbitrators shall reach a decision and notify the parties thereof;

4- The decision of the majority of the three arbitrators shall be final and binding upon the parties;

5- If one of the parties fails to appoint an arbitrator within the time limit in (1) above, the arbitrator(s) appointed by one, or more, of them shall reach a decision that shall be binding;

6- If the two arbitrators fail to agree upon, and appoint, a third arbitrator, both arbitrators shall be dismissed and the process started anew;

7- The arbitrators shall determine who pays the cost of arbitration; and,

8- The award and determination and allocation of costs by the arbitrators shall be final and binding upon both parties hereto and their respective heirs, executors, administrators, successors, and assigns, and each party agrees not to appeal any such award or determination.

7.8 SMALL CLAIMS COURT

There may be times when a tenant owes you money, but refuses to pay it. You should consider using the Small Claims Court system. It is designed to provide a simple, fast, and inexpensive way to settle disputes concerning money or property. There is an upper limit on the size of claim, which in Ontario is $10,000.

The more common claims at Small Claims Court are the following:

- loan not repaid
- money due because of an NSF cheque
- failure to pay rent
- failure to pay contractors
- damages caused by somebody's negligence
- failure to fulfill the terms of a written, or oral, contract, or
- claim for return of personal property, now in somebody else's possession.

In Small Claims Court, there are staff who will explain how the system works to file a claim, defend against a claim, and get an order enforced by the court. However, they do not provide legal advice. In court, you may speak for yourself or bring a lawyer.

There is a fee to file a claim, which varies with the amount claimed (generally it is $50 in Ontario), and that is added to your claim.

One of the advantages of Small Claims Court is that you can amend your claim later by filing a motion, for example, to increase the amount you are claiming, or to change something you said in your claim. You have 30 days to make an appeal to the higher court.

Enforcement, that is recovering the money the court decided you should receive, is the weakest part of the system. If the debtor is smart and does not want to pay, he won't, although there are sanctions for the contravention of a court order, which may include damages and possible incarceration. Based on our experience, this seems to have little influence for small sums.

CHAPTER 8

Real Property Registration

By the end of this chapter, you will be able to:
- Find your way through the land ownership control systems.
- Understand the importance of the Land Transfer Tax Affidavit and its role in the system.
- Acknowledge that the title of land has been transferred correctly.
- Read a Reference Plan number and break it down into a description.
- Navigate the requirements dictated by legislation.
- Identify the forms used in document registration.
- Recognize the significance of the numerous registered documents you may encounter during a title search.
- Understand the electronic land registration system.
- Decide if title insurance is appropriate for your situation.
- Choose among various online tools.

The detailed mechanics of real property registration vary from province to province; however, the general principles are the same.

1. Each individual property is given its own title and registration specifics.
2. An interested party must be able to find the details of a parcel of land and register documents affecting it, including:
   - concession and lot numbers
   - owner's name
   - date of acquisition and price
   - mortgage amount and lender, and
   - various encumbrances, registered by any other party that may have a right in the property, such as a neighbour or a government entity.

Note that there are no municipal addresses (street names and numbers) in the title registration system, and the method of cataloguing and providing this information varies with each jurisdiction.

This chapter describes real property registration in detail for the province of Ontario, but it will give you an idea of what to expect in other jurisdictions. If you are doing business in the other provinces or territories, you will have to become very familiar with that jurisdiction's system before you begin investing in real estate. Spending a few hours in a registry office would be wise.

8.1 LAND OWNERSHIP CONTROLS

Find your way through the land ownership control systems.

The goal of land registration is to catalogue real property, inform the public regarding land ownership, establish priorities of claims, and provide an efficient way to record titles to property. The province controls ownership of real property by registering each parcel in titles offices. Only the land itself is registered, disregarding any buildings or other improvements, except in the case of condominiums.

Land registration was created for several reasons. It prevents disputes as to ownership and exact parcel boundaries and it offers an official, permanent record that anyone can search. In addition, governments quickly realized that it offers an easy way to tax owners.

In Ontario, a search of title going back up to 40 years prior to the date of every sale is required by a prudent buyer and his solicitor as evidence of a good title. Additionally a good title search establishes a root of title, if there has been no conveyance, meaning no change of ownership, during the 40-year period. The "root" is the starting point of a search. It is a clean, unarguable conveyance closest and prior to the 40-year period. Typical, clean, conveyances are a grant from the Crown, a tax deed, an expropriation, etc.

There are two systems of land registration in Ontario. The *Registry Act* (the original one) was enacted in 1795. The Land Titles System was enacted in 1885. The government is slowly moving towards one system. For example, the two systems now use the same registration documents (the five forms explained later in this chapter).

You may have to search title on a property to find out details such as:
- the name of the current owner of a property
- what the current owner paid for it (usually, but not always)

- its size (sometimes)
- the existence of easements and rights-of-way, and
- if there are any mortgages, existing or discharged, and what the amounts and details were.

The system can be searched using:
- the lot and concession numbers
- the street address
- the owner's name, or
- the Property Identification Number (PIN).

Before a document can be registered, the Land Registrar of that particular office must accept it. This certifies the document. Unfortunately, there are so many exceptions to the Land Titles Certificate that many searches are still warranted.

Generally, a lawyer conducts the title search or arranges for one to be undertaken by a title searcher. If the property is in the Land Titles System, the search involves checking all information, which is on the parcel register and, perhaps, pulling instruments for review. If the property is in the Registry System, a 40-year search of the title will be conducted to ensure that the title is good and that there are no problems with it, such as undischarged encumbrances, unsatisfied claims, etc. The purpose of the title search is to establish a good chain of title that will include a description of all transactions, including any errors, gaps, or missing parties. The written history of a parcel is called a "title tree", such as the one shown in Figure 8.1. The registry and land titles searches will include looking at parties, including non-resident parties, encumbrances, expropriations, restrictive covenants, registered and unregistered easements (such as hydro easements), executions, etc.

8.1.1 METES AND BOUNDS DESCRIPTIONS

In the past, when a piece of land was irregularly shaped, a surveyor was hired to prepare a metes and bounds description. The surveyor typically would either find a marker, which is called a "monument", at one of the corners of the land or install one. Nowadays, markers consist of a solid piece of square steel, approximately 19 x 19 mm (3/4 in x 3/4 in), driven deep into the ground, with the top more or less flush with the ground. The location of the monument is called the "Point of Commencement".

Surveyors use the 360-degree angle system based on the theoretical North, not True North, which varies with the declinations. The unit used by the surveyor is the one-degree angle, which is, of course, 1/360th of a circle. The degree itself is divided into 60 minutes and each minute is divided into 60 seconds. So, a typical description using metes and bounds might be, "Commencing at the north-east corner of lot 39, Registered Plan 147, then south exactly 100 feet, then, south 13 degrees 44 minutes and 55 seconds east along the easterly limit of said lot 39, a distance of 53 feet".

Metes and bounds descriptions and *Registry Act* (R.S.O. 1990, c. R.20) lands are becoming less relevant today due to the fact that 95% of all lands are in the Land Titles System and can be accessed by electronic registration and conveyancing.

Figure 8.1
Title Tree

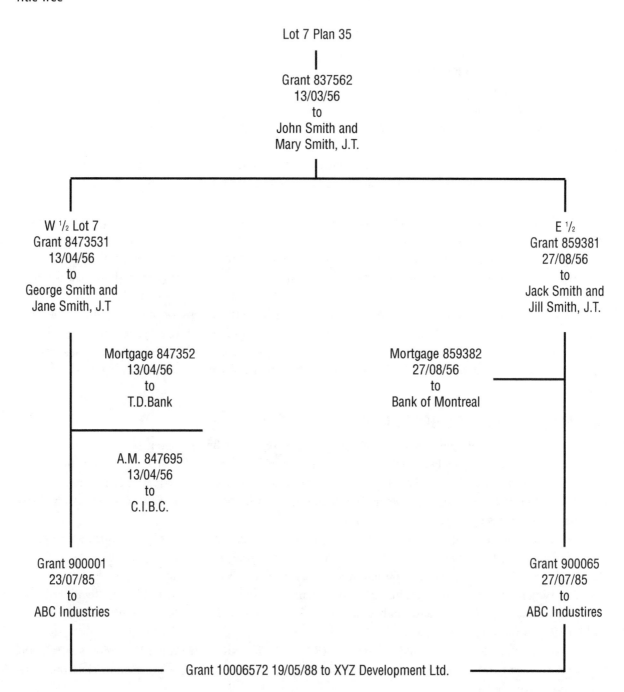

Source: MCCR Client Guide: Certification of Titles Act and Land Titles Act © Queen's Printer for Ontario, 2000.

8.1.2 THE REGISTRY SYSTEM

The original Registry System registers documents. The government runs the Registry System, but does not guarantee title and every buyer must satisfy himself that the title to the property desired is good.

The Abstract Books are the foundation of the Registry System. These books are created by the government and kept in each registry office, and cover only land situated within each office's jurisdiction. They give a publicly available written history of the title of each property, but do not guarantee that the title is good (or clean). Prior to the subdivision of lands, the Abstract Books are referred to as "Concession Books" and after subdivision as "Plan Books". In these books, every transaction (deeds, mortgages, leases, wills, liens, expropriations, etc.) that concerns a piece of land is entered chronologically (by date of registration) by the registry office staff as a summary or an abbreviated (abstracted) reference to the document involved. It shows a written history of the parcel of land. There is one book per concession and one page for each lot. Other pages are added as needed. The documents are filed for easy retrieval and are available to the public.

If the property description reads "200 acres", it is talking about one property; the lot and the concession will give you a typical grant of 200 acres. However, if the property is divided, then the description might be: "the west half", of the property in question, which would be 100 acres.

When a Plan of Subdivision is registered, a Plan Book is started, and a new page is devoted to each lot of the plan. When registration needs become complex, other books are created. Some examples of this would be the registration of the following:

- a new municipality
- condominiums
- newly installed utilities (frequently these require easements over or under a private property; these must be registered on title)
- new highways, or
- patented lands (concession lots), when the government sells a piece of Crown land.

When we are talking about a Registered Plan of Subdivision, it is the plan number that is shown. Then, the Plan Book would include the instrument, date, etc., but the description would be, for example, "Part 1 and Part 3 on R-Plan 62 R-1342, subject to an easement over Part 1". The Registry System is used less and less, but a real estate investor may, in certain circumstances, want to conduct title searches personally.

Ideally, one must know or find the numbers for the plan and lot, or concession and lot, as well as the municipality to be able to conduct a search. However, there are other aids in the registry offices and there are maps and plans to help locate a property. The originals of documents are filed in the Registry Office and can be examined by the public upon request. Locating a document is a three-step process.

1. At the Registry Office, the old fashioned way is to fill in a form that requests access to the Abstract Books.
2. Once the form is completed and the required fee is paid, an employee directs the searcher to the books.
3. Once the searcher finds the entry of interest in the book, the searcher can ask to see the document itself (remember the abstract is just a summary).

Although one can still search in this way, these days one commonly uses a computer.

8.1.3 The Land Titles System

The Land Titles System registers titles (instead of documents). In Ontario the majority of the land is registered under the Land Titles System. In this system, the government guarantees that title is vested in a certain person. If there is a mistake in this guarantee, a claim can be made to the Land Titles Assurance Fund for compensation. The counterpart of the registry Abstract Book is the Parcel Register. Both provide a similar function. Figure 8.2 presents a Parcel Register for a property in Pickering, Ontario. Looking at the column on the left of the page, following is an explanation of what this figure tells us.

- Registration No C094360 – to register a by-law affecting this property.
- Registration No DR17985 – sale of the property by Beare Estate to Nicou Inc.
- Registration No DR214914 – deletion of a prior notice No DR17986 (probably having regard to the estate).
- Registration No DR286023 – charge, that is a mortgage, in favour of The Effort Trust Company.
- Registration No 40R235333 – registration of a Reference Plan of subdivision.
- Registration No DR390222 – the owner applied to have the land placed in Land Title Absolute.
- Registration No DR457248 – charge, that is mortgage, in favour of Amos Ponds Developments Inc.
- Registration No DR457248 – charge, that is mortgage, in favour of Bank of Montreal.
- Registration No DR457249 – postponement of the Amos Ponds Developments Inc.'s mortgage, so that the Bank of Montreal is now in first position.
- Registration No DR498545 – discharge of the Effort Trust Mortgage.

(a) Plans of Subdivision

Plans of subdivision registered under this system now use the same numbering system as is applied to reference plans and, therefore, the first number is that of the particular Registry Office, followed by the letter "M", then the plan number. For example, 42M-1324 indicates the Parry Sound Registry Office.

(b) Parcels and Sections

A parcel of land in the Parcel Register may incorporate a lot, a block, a one-foot reserve, a road allowance, etc. A page is opened in the register and a particular parcel is identified by the number and section given to it, recorded at the top of each page; not by the concession and lot number as under the registry system.

Figure 8.2
Parcel Register

PARCEL REGISTER (ABBREVIATED) FOR PROPERTY IDENTIFIER

PAGE 1 OF 2
PREPARED FOR CBoiron
ON 2006/12/08 AT 15:29:42

26370-0204 (LT)

SUBJECT TO RESERVATIONS IN CROWN GRANT

Ontario — Ministry of Government Services

LAND REGISTRY OFFICE #40

PIN CREATION DATE: 2005/05/25

PROPERTY DESCRIPTION: PT LT 34 CON 2 PICKERING, PT 1 40R23533, PICKERING REGIONAL MUNICIPALITY OF DURHAM

PROPERTY REMARKS: FOR THE PURPOSE OF THE QUALIFIER THE DATE OF REGISTRATION OF ABSOLUTE TITLE IS 2005-05-25

ESTATE/QUALIFIER:
FEE SIMPLE
LT ABSOLUTE PLUS

RECENTLY:
RE-ENTRY FROM 26370-0014

OWNERS' NAMES
NICOU INC.

CAPACITY SHARE
BENO

REG. NUM.	DATE	INSTRUMENT TYPE	AMOUNT	PARTIES FROM	PARTIES TO	CERT/CHKD
** PRINTOUT INCLUDES ALL DOCUMENT TYPES AND DELETED INSTRUMENTS SINCE 2005/05/25 **						
**SUBJECT TO SUBSECTION 44(1) OF THE LAND TITLES ACT, EXCEPT PARAGRAPHS 3 AND 14 AND *						
**		PROVINCIAL SUCCESSION DUTIES AND EXCEPT PARAGRAPH 11 AND ESCHEATS OR FORFEITURE **				
**		TO THE CROWN UP TO THE DATE OF REGISTRATION WITH AN ABSOLUTE TITLE. **				
CO94360	1961/05/17	BYLAW				C
REMARKS: PLANNING ACT FOR SUBDIVISION CONTROL DELETED UNDER DR116972 *AS TO PIN 26409-0006 *ADDED 2003 01 06 BY DONNA WARREN						
DR17985	2001/08/30	TRANSFER	$875,000	BEARE, ROGER ALEXANDER-ESTATE	NICOU INC.	C
DR214914	2003/10/01	NOTICE		*** DELETED AGAINST THIS PROPERTY *** BEARE, ROGER ALEXANDER - ESTATE; BEARE, ALMA JEAN - ESTATE TRUSTEE	NICOU INC.	C
REMARKS: DR17986						
DR286023	2004/06/15	CHARGE		*** DELETED AGAINST THIS PROPERTY *** NICOU INC.	THE EFFORT TRUST COMPANY	C
40R23533	2005/05/25	PLAN REFERENCE				
DR390222	2005/05/25	APL ABSOLUTE TITLE		NICOU INC.	NICOU INC.	C
REMARKS: DR365792						
DR420522	2005/08/25	CHARGE	$2,082,937	NICOU INC.	AMOS PONDS DEVELOPMENTS INC.	C
DR457248	2005/12/09	CHARGE	$5,500,000	NICOU INC.	BANK OF MONTREAL	C
DR457249	2005/12/09	POSTPONEMENT		AMOS PONDS DEVELOPMENTS INC.	BANK OF MONTREAL	C
REMARKS: DR420522 TO DR457248						
DR498545	2006/05/09	DISCH OF CHARGE		*** COMPLETELY DELETED ***	THE EFFORT TRUST COMPANY	

NOTE: ADJOINING PROPERTIES SHOULD BE INVESTIGATED TO ASCERTAIN DESCRIPTIVE INCONSISTENCIES, IF ANY, WITH DESCRIPTION REPRESENTED FOR THIS PROPERTY.
NOTE: ENSURE THAT YOUR PRINTOUT STATES THE TOTAL NUMBER OF PAGES AND THAT YOU HAVE PICKED THEM ALL UP.
NOTE: RESULTS WERE GENERATED VIA WWW.GEOWAREHOUSE.CA

Source: Used with permission of John Dalgliesh, Director of Land Registration.

(c) Title Searching in the Land Titles System

Searching a title is easier in the Land Titles System than in the Registry System because all prior defects in title have been cleared (or are absent) at the initial registration or when the land was transferred to the Land Titles Systems from the Registry System. This is not entirely true for certain documents that may have been carried forward from the Registry System through the process of conversion.

The Registrar provides forms for requisitioning parcels, plans, and documents. It is recommended that you order a copy of the register, but if you prefer simply to study it and to make notes from it, follow the steps below.

1. Order a white print of the plan of subdivision. Verify that it matches the description in the Offer to Purchase, or the survey, and the dedication of one-foot reserves and road widenings.
2. Make a note of the parcel and section numbers for all abutting lands.
3. Get particulars of outstanding documents, such as charges and agreements.
4. Check that the Land Title signing officer's certification is on the register, after each document.
5. Order copies of all the reference plans that affect the land.
6. Check the highways and Trans-Canada pipeline registers (these entries are not made on freehold registers).

Today, almost always, searches are conducted for lawyers by title searchers they employ. Anyone with a Geowarehouse account can buy a Parcel Register Abstract over the Internet.

Because the Ontario government realized that the Land Titles System was superior to the Registry System, it decided, a few years ago, to convert properties in the Registry System to qualified Land Titles. This was done by the registry clerks, without participation or verification by property owners. The old adage "to make an omelette, one must break eggs" came true and mistakes were made. If you are buying a property whose title has been converted to a qualified Land Title, be aware that errors are not exceptionally rare.

If you are buying a property whose title has been converted to a qualified Land Title, be aware that errors are not exceptionally rare.

8.2 LAND AND TRANSFER TAX AFFIDAVIT

Understand the importance of the Land Transfer Tax Affidavit and its role in the system.

The Land Transfer Tax Affidavit, which will be completed by your lawyer (see Figure 8.3), must accompany each transfer of interest in land. The affidavit shows many details, including the consideration (the amount of money involved) and the land transfer tax (LTT) (see Figure 8.4) paid at time of registration based on the amount of consideration shown. It also shows the cash and mortgage amounts and other details. A copy of it is attached to the deed by the lawyer when he gathers documents for registration.

This is the most important document to consult when seeking information about a property sale because it gives the reader all the important points of a sale: land description, sold by X to Y, the function/position in the deal of the signatories, the price, down payment, mortgage, fair market value, value of chattels, other considerations, and other details. There are instances where the consideration is not shown, for example, with a transaction involving a gift of property ("for natural love and affection"), when no LTT is due.

Some buyers prefer that the price they pay not be shown on this form. They achieve this by paying the LTT directly to the Ministry of Finance and the Affidavit will not be available for viewing in the local registry office. Note, however, that it is possible to find out the price of the property by sending a letter to the provincial Ministry of Finance.

In the event of an exemption from LTT – trustee to trustee, trustee to beneficial owner, or beneficial owner to trustee are three prominent exemptions – the forms for registration for Ontario can be filed with the Land Transfer Tax Office in Oshawa. The short form, Affidavit of Residence and Value of Consideration, does not have to be filed with the conveyance.

8.3 TRANSFER OF TITLE

Acknowledge that the title of land has been transferred correctly.

The title of real property is the legal right of ownership interest. In real estate transactions, the title is transferred to a new owner through a deed. (See Figure 8.5 Transfer/Deed of Land.) The buyer's lawyer reviews various documents to ensure the property has clear title and to discover possible problems such as "pending" claims. Such a claim against property could be, for example, for unpaid electrical work done by a previous owner, the sale of mineral rights, perhaps 50 years ago, or, most commonly, a paid-off but undischarged mortgage. In such cases, the lawyers attempt to contact the party involved to resolve the problem. To this effect, lawyers sometimes use the Quit Claim Deed, which is a document permitting the release of any claim that a person may have in a property.

8.4 SURVEYS AND REFERENCE PLANS

Read a Reference Plan number and break it down into a description.

Figure 8.6, Plan of Survey, is a typical plan of survey showing the dimensions, lot reference plan number, acreage, and surveyor's certificate. For many decades the title searchers and the surveyors had to use old plans and often inaccurate descriptions, which easily led to errors. Now, Reference Plans have become common and all new property registration, say in the last 25 years, is done by way of a Reference Plan, unless it is the entire parcel that is conveyed. A Reference Plan is a survey that shows the boundaries of the site. This land is then divided into lots that receive a number.

Figure 8.3
Land Transfer Tax Affidavit

Ontario
Ministry of Finance
Motor Fuels and
Tobacco Tax Branch
PO Box 625
33 King St West
Oshawa ON L1H 8H9

Property Identifier(s) No.

Land Transfer Tax Affidavit
Land Transfer Tax Act

Refer to instructions on reverse side

In the Matter of the Conveyance of *(insert brief description of land)*

BY *(print names of all transferors in full)*

TO *(print names of all transferees in full)*

I

have personal knowledge of the facts herein deposed to and Make Oath and Say that:

1. I am *(place a clear mark within the square opposite the following paragraph(s) that describe(s) the capacity of the deponents)*
   - ☐ (a) the transferee named in the above-described conveyance;
   - ☐ (b) the authorized agent or solicitor acting in this transaction for the transferee(s);
   - ☐ (c) the President, Vice-President, Secretary, Treasurer, Director or Manager authorized to act for _____ (the transferee(s));
   - ☐ (d) a transferee and am making this affidavit on my own behalf and on behalf of *(insert name of spouse or same-sex partner)* _____ who is my spouse or same-sex partner.
   - ☐ (e) the transferor or an officer authorized to act on behalf of the transferor company and ☐ I am tendering this document for registration and no tax is payable on registration of this document.

2. THE TOTAL CONSIDERATION FOR THIS TRANSACTION IS ALLOCATED AS FOLLOWS:
   - (a) Monies paid or to be paid in cash ..... $ _____
   - (b) Mortgages (i) Assumed *(principal and interest)* ..... $ _____
   - (ii) Given back to vendor ..... $ _____
   - (c) Property transferred in exchange *(detail below in para. 5)* ..... $ _____
   - (d) Other consideration subject to tax *(detail below)* ..... $ _____
   - (e) Fair market value of the lands *(see instruction 2)* ..... $ _____
   - (f) Value of land, building, fixtures and goodwill subject to Land Transfer Tax *(Total of (a) to (e))* ..... $ _____ $ _____
   - (g) Value of all chattels - items of tangible personal property which are taxable under the provisions of the *Retail Sales Tax Act* ..... $ _____
   - (h) Other consideration for transaction not included in (f) or (g) above ..... $ _____
   - (i) Total Consideration ..... $ _____

   All blanks must be filled in insert "Nil" where applicable

3. To be completed where the value of the consideration for the conveyance exceeds $400,000.00
   I have read and considered the definition of "single family residence" set out in subsection 1(1) of the Act. The land conveyed in the above-described conveyance:
   - ☐ does not contain a single family residence or contains more than two single family residences;
   - ☐ contains at least one and not more than two single family residences; or
   - ☐ contains at least one and not more than two single family residences and the lands are used for other than just residential purposes. The transferee has accordingly apportioned the value of consideration on the basis that the consideration for the single family residence is $ _____ and the remainder of the lands are used for _____ purposes.

   > **Note:** Subsection 2(1)(b) imposes an additional tax at the rate of one-half of one per cent upon the value of the consideration in excess of $400,000.00 where the conveyance contains at least one and not more than two single family residences and 2(2) allows an apportionment of the consideration where the lands are used for other than just residential purposes

4. If consideration is nominal, is the land subject to any encumbrance? ☐ Yes ☐ No

5. Other remarks and explanations, if necessary.

Sworn/affirmed before me in the _____

this _____ day of _____ , 20 _____

Signature(s)

A Commissioner for taking Affidavits, etc.

Property Information Record

A. Describe nature of instrument:

B. (i) Address of property being conveyed *(if available)*

   (ii) Assessment Roll No. *(if available)*

C. Mailing address(es) for future Notices of Assessment under the *Assessment Act* for property being conveyed

D. (i) Registration number for last conveyance of property being conveyed *(if available)*

   (ii) Legal description of property conveyed: Same as in D (i) above. ☐ Yes ☐ No ☐ Not Known

E. Name(s) and address(es) of each transferee's solicitor:

For Land Registry Office Use Only

Registration No

Registration Date *(Year/Month/Day)*

Land Registry Office No.

School Support (Voluntary Election) *(See reverse for explanation)*

	Yes	No
(a) Are all individual transferees Roman Catholic?	☐	☐
(b) If Yes, do all individual transferees wish to be Roman Catholic Separate School Supporters?	☐	☐
(c) Do all individual transferees have French Language Education Rights?	☐	☐
(d) If Yes, do all individual transferees wish to support the French Language School Board (where established)?	☐	☐

Note: As to (c) and (d) the land being transferred will receive French Public School Board Election unless otherwise directed in (a) and (b).

0449K (2004-04)

Instructions

Attach this Affidavit to the conveyance tendered for registration. Provide one unattached and completed copy to the Land Registrar at the time of registration.

1. This Affidavit is required to be made by each transferee named in the conveyance. However:

    (i) Any of the transferees may have the Affidavit made on his/her behalf by an agent authorized in writing to make the Affidavit or by his/her solicitor;

    (ii) Either spouse or same-sex partner may make the Affidavit on behalf of him/herself and the other;

    (iii) If the transferee is a corporation, the Affidavit may be made by its President, Vice-President, Manager, Secretary, Director or Treasurer;

    (iv) The Minister may consent to the transferor making the Affidavit provided that the transferor is tendering the document for registration, that no tax is payable in respect of the conveyance and provided the transferor can satisfy the Minister that he has sufficient information to enable him to make the Affidavit.

    Note: The solicitor for the transferor cannot make the Affidavit.

    (v) Where any transferee (other than a joint tenant) is taking less than the whole interest in the property being acquired, then the percentage ownership of each transferee must be clearly indicated beside his/her respective name.

2. Deeming provisions: The value of consideration may be deemed to be equal to the fair market value of the lands at the date of registration where the conveyance is:

    (a) for a lease of land where the term can exceed 50 years;

    (b) from trustee to trustee where there has been a change in beneficial ownership and value of consideration was given for the change;

    (c) a final order of foreclosure or quit claim in lieu thereof due to a default under the mortgage and the fair market value is less than the total of the amounts owed under the mortgage;

    (d) to a corporation and shares of the corporation form part of the consideration; or

    (e) from a corporation to any of its shareholders.

3. Extract of Subsection 1(1) of the Act:

    "single family residence" means a unit or proposed unit under the *Condominium Act* or a structure or part of a structure that is designed for occupation as the residence of a family, including dependants or domestic employees of a member of the family, whether or not rent is paid to occupy any part of it and whether or not the land on which it is situated is zoned for residential use, and

    (a) includes such a residence that is to be constructed as part of the arrangement relating to a conveyance, and

    (b) does not include such a residence that is constructed or is to be constructed on agricultural land that is eligible to be classified in the farm property class prescribed under the *Assessment Act*.

This information is requested under the authority of s.15 of the *Assessment Act*.

Apportionment Note: Where, in respect of a conveyance of land, the value of the consideration for the conveyance **exceeds $400,000 and a part of the land being conveyed is used for a purpose other than residential purposes**, the Minister may, to the extent that he or she considers it practicable, determine what amount of the value of the consideration for the conveyance is reasonably attributable to the land used in connection with a single family residence, and the person tendering the conveyance for registration is liable to the additional tax of one-half of one per cent only upon the amount by which the value of the consideration determined by the Minister to be attributable to the land used in connection with a single family residence exceeds $400,000.

4. Insert mailing address(es) where municipal assessment notices for property being conveyed are to be forwarded after closing of this transaction.

School Support (Voluntary Election)

(a) & (b) The school support for the land being transferred will be assigned to the public school board unless otherwise directed. Only Roman Catholics can be separate school supporters. If all individual transferees are Roman Catholic and wish to be separate school supporters, the completion of items (a) and (b) will serve as notice to the Assessment Commissioner to enter the transferees on the next Assessment Roll as Roman Catholic separate school supporters.

(c) & (d) If the land being transferred is situated in an area in which a French Language School Board has been established, and all individual transferees have French language education rights, completion of (c) and (d) will serve as notice to the Assessment Commissioner to enter the transferees on the next Assessment Roll as French language school board supporters.

Individuals have French language education rights under s.23 of the *Canadian Charter of Rights and Freedoms* if the individual can answer yes to any one of the following questions:

(i) Is French the language you first learned and still understand?

(ii) Did you receive elementary school instruction in French? (This does not include French immersion or French as a second language).

(iii) Have any of your children received, or are they now receiving elementary or secondary school instruction in Canada in French? (This does not include French immersion or French as a second language).

For further information contact your local school board.

Enquiries

English (toll free)	1 800 263-7965 (Canada/U.S.)
Français (sans frais)	1 800 668-5821 (Canada et É.-U.)
TAX FAX	1 877 482-9329
TTY (Teletypewriter)	1 800 263-7776 (Ontario Only)
Ministry's website	www.trd.fin.gov.on.ca

Figure 8.4

Land Transfer Tax Statement

In the matter of the conveyance of: 26370-0204 BLOCKS 41, 43, 44 AND 45, PLAN 40M-2343, PICKERING, REGIONAL MUNICIPALITY OF DURHAM

BY: NICOU INC.
TO: THE CORPORATION OF THE CITY OF PICKERING % (all PINs)

1. CLAUDE BOIRON
   I am
   ❑ (a) A person in trust for whom the land conveyed in the above-described conveyance is being conveyed;
   ❑ (b) A trustee named in the above-described conveyance to whom the land is being conveyed;
   ❑ (c) A transferee named in the above-described conveyance;
   ❑ (d) The authorized agent or solicitor acting in this transaction for THE CORPORATION OF THE CITY OF PICKERING described in paragraph(s) (_) above.
   ❑ (e) The President, Vice-President, Manager, Secretary, Director, or Treasurer authorized to act for _____ described in paragraph(s) (_) above.
   ❑ (f) A transferee described in paragraph (_) and am making these statements on my own behalf and on behalf of _____ who is my spouse described in paragraph (_) and as such, I have personal knowledge of the facts herein desposed to.

3. The total consideration for this transaction is allocated as follows:
(a) Monies paid or to be paid in cash	2.00
(b) Mortgages (i) assumed (show principal and interest to be credited against purchase price)	0.00
(ii) Given Back to Vendor	0.00
(c) Property transferred in exchange (detail below)	0.00
(d) Fair market vale of the land(s)	0.00
(e) Liens, legacies, annuities and maintenance charges to which transfer is subject	0.00
(f) Other valuable consideration subject to land transfer tax (detail below)	0.00
(g) Value of land, building, fixtures and goodwill subject to land transfer tax (total of (a) to (f))	2.00
(h) VALUE OF ALL CHATTELS – items of tangible personal property	0.00
(i) Other considerations for transaction not included in (g) or (h) above	0.00
(j) Total consideration	2.00

4. Explanation for nominal considerations:
   (g) transfer to a municipality pursuant to a development agreement

5. The land is subject to encumbrance

PROPERTY Information Record
   A. Nature of Instrument: Transfer
      LRO 40 Registration No. DR581464 Date: 2007/02/16
   B. Property(s): PIN 26370-0204   Address   Assessment
         PICKERING   Roll No
   C. Address for Service: PICKERING CIVIC COMPLEX
      One The Esplanade
      Pickering, Ontario
      L1V 6K7
   D. (i) Last Conveyance(s): PIN 26370-0204 Registration No. DR581464 ✓
      (ii) Legal Description for Property Conveyed: Same as in last conveyance? Yes ❑ No ❑ Not known ❑
   E. Tax Statements Prepared By: Denise Bye
      1 The Esplanade
      Pickering L1V 6K7

Figure 8.5
Transfer/Deed of Land

Province of Ontario

Transfer/Deed of Land
Form 1 — Land Registration Reform Act

Do Process Software Ltd. • (416) 322-6111

A

FOR OFFICE USE ONLY

(1) Registry ☐   Land Titles ☐   (2) Page 1   of   pages

(3) Property Identifier(s)   Block   Property   Additional: See Schedule ☐

(4) Consideration   Dollars $

(5) Description   This is a: Property Division ☐   Property Consolidation ☐

New Property Identifiers   Additional: See Schedule ☐

Executions   Additional: See Schedule ☐

(6) This Document Contains   (a) Redescription New Easement Plan/Sketch ☐   (b) Schedule for: Description ☐   Additional Parties ☐   Other ☐   (7) Interest/Estate Transferred Fee Simple

(8) Transferor(s) The transferor hereby transfers the land to the transferee and certifies that the transferor is at least eighteen years old and that

Name(s)   Signature(s)   Date of Signature Y M D

(9) Spouse(s) of Transferor(s) I hereby consent to this transaction
Name(s)   Signature(s)   Date of Signature Y M D

(10) Transferor(s) Address for Service

(11) Transferee(s)   Date of Birth Y M D

(12) Transferee(s) Address for Service

(13) Transferor(s) The transferor verifies that to the best of the transferor's knowledge and belief, this transfer does not contravene section 50 of the Planning Act.
Date of Signature Y M D   Date of Signature Y M D

Signature   Signature

Solicitor for Transferor(s) I have explained the effect of section 50 of the Planning Act to the transferor and I have made inquiries of the transferor to determine that this transfer does not contravene that section and based on the information supplied by the transferor, to the best of my knowledge and belief, this transfer does not contravene that section. I am an Ontario solicitor in good standing.
Date of Signature Y M D

Name and Address of Solicitor   Signature

Planning Act – OPTIONAL

Affix Statement by Solicitor for Transferee(s) here if necessary

(14) Solicitor for Transferee(s) I have investigated the title to this land and to abutting land where relevant and I am satisfied that the title records reveal no contravention as set out in subclause 50 (22) (c) (ii) of the Planning Act and that to the best of my knowledge and belief this transfer does not contravene section 50 of the Planning Act. I act independently of the solicitor for the transferor(s) and I am an Ontario solicitor in good standing.

Name and Address of Solicitor   Date of Signature Y M D

Signature

(15) Assessment Roll Number of Property   Cty. Mun. Map Sub Par.

(16) Municipal Address of Property

(17) Document Prepared by:

Baker Schneider Ruggiero LLP
120 Adelaide Street West
Suite 1000
Toronto, Ontario
M5H 3V1

FOR OFFICE USE ONLY

Fees and Tax
Registration Fee
Land Transfer Tax

Total

Document prepared using *The Conveyancer*

160 | Understanding the Industry

Figure 8.6
Plan of Survey

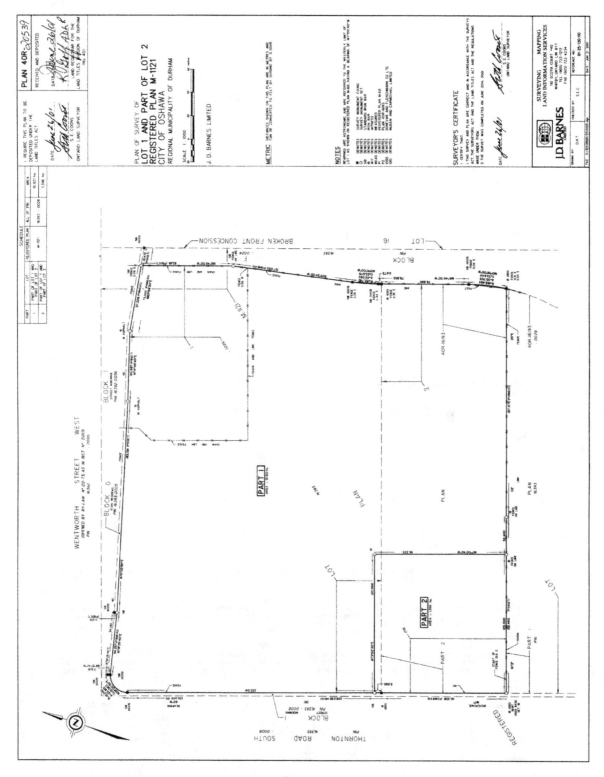

Source: Reference Plan used by permission of J.D. Barnes Limited, O.L.S.

Every new parcel of land, such as a subdivision, must be filed under a Reference Plan. Thus a lot may be described as "Part of Lots 3, 4, and 5, Plan 3911, City of Toronto" and more particularly described as "Parts, 2, 4, and 5, Plan 52R-1234". The purpose of these plans is to make it easy to describe the parcel. A Registered Reference Plan generally comprises several parts and it is then easy to describe a property by referring to "R Plan # X, Parts 1, 2, 5, and 7", for example.

Each Reference Plan is given a number when it is deposited in the Land Registration System and the number is preceded by the number of each office (there are 55) and the letter R, which stands for Reference Plan. For example, the description of "52R-1234" might read as follows: "A certain parcel composed of part of lots 2 and 4 according to Plan 2314, which parts are designated parts 5 and 9 on a Plan of Reference filed in the Land Title office at Toronto as number 52 R-1234". These plans are typically called "R-plans".

8.5 CERTIFICATION OF TITLES ACT

Navigate the requirements dictated by legislation.

In 1958, the province of Ontario passed new legislation that enabled an owner of land to apply to the Director of Titles to have the title to any land in Ontario, which was in the Registry System, investigated or certified. It has since become compulsory in many areas of Ontario for land with proposed subdivisions to be investigated and certified. Upon registration of a Certificate of Title, under the *Certification of Titles Act* (R.S.O. 1990, c. C.6), the certificate is conclusive evidence, as of the date and time stated in the certificate, that the person named therein as owner has absolute title to the lands, subject to any matter set out in a Schedule.

The Director of Titles may now certify, and therefore guarantee, the quality of the title to land included in an existing Plan of Subdivision, registered under the *Registry Act*. There is also an insurance system in place to take care of problems. See section 8.1.3.

8.6 DOCUMENTATION REGISTRATION

Identify the forms used in document registration.

Tedious and detailed work was required to register documents in the past. The province of Ontario has since created a new set of forms aimed at simplifying and streamlining the process. The following forms can be encountered in connection with document registration:

- **Form 1: Transfer/Deed of Land.** This form deals with the freehold, or leasehold, conveyance of land and replaces the traditional deed and transfer.
- **Form 2: Charge/Mortgage.** This is a form for a lien, for payment of a debt or other obligation, and it replaces the old mortgage and charge. It, too, usually has a schedule attached, for additional details.
- **Form 3: Discharge of Charge/Mortgage of Land.** This form is used when a mortgage is paid in full.
- **Form 4: Document General.** This form is a supplementary document, with 15 boxes and an attached schedule, for use when there is insufficient space in the boxes of the other forms.
- **Form 5: Schedule.** This page is used to provide additional information, plans, sketches, descriptions, etc.

Forms 1, 2, and 4 can be seen in Chapter 16.

8.7 OTHER REGISTERED DOCUMENTS

Recognize the significance of the numerous registered documents you may encounter during a title search.

There are a multitude of other registered documents that you may encounter during the course of your title search. We will deal with each of them separately.

8.7.1 NOTICE OF AGREEMENT OF PURCHASE AND SALE

A Notice of Agreement of Purchase and Sale, or its assignment, or a Notice of an Option to Purchase, or its assignment, have been registerable since 1980. These documents expire one year from the date of their registration. Anybody who registers a Notice of Agreement of Purchase and Sale on title must pay the appropriate LTT. The tax will be refunded if the closing does not take place. The notice offers great protection for a buyer holding a conditional offer or between the times of signature of an offer and closing.

8.7.2 LEASES

A leasehold interest may be created by the execution of a lease, or an Agreement for Lease. Under the *Registry Act*, it is important to note that leases for a period exceeding 7 years, or notices thereof, that are not registered on title are considered void against subsequent purchasers and mortgagees. This means that if the property is sold, be it in the usual way or under power of sale, the purchaser or the mortgagee can disregard the lease.

8.7.3 MORTGAGE/CHARGE

A mortgage is a pledging of property, to a creditor, as security for the payment of a debt. Prior to 1984, it did not transfer a legal estate (right or interest) in the land. It created only a security interest that was discharged on payment of the principal and interest.

8.7.4 DEED UNDER POWER OF SALE

Deed under Power of Sale is a grant that is identical to any other grant. The grant will contain recitals respecting the following:
- the registration date and number of the mortgage
- provision on default of payment that the mortgagee may, on a 35-day notice, enter and sell the land, and
- that the default occurred.

8.7.5 FINAL ORDER OF FORECLOSURE

When a mortgagor fails to make mortgage payments, the mortgagee is allowed to issue a final Order of Foreclosure against him. The Order is registered on title, and if the mortgagor does not redeem the property within a time period set by the Court, the mortgagee becomes the registered owner of the property. This is rarely used in Ontario (only when there is significant equity in the property).

Foreclosure is seldom used in Ontario because it would be beneficial only in those instances in which a property is worth much more than the mortgage being held, which has defaulted. A foreclosing mortgagee can be prevented from obtaining this "windfall", which he would obtain by foreclosing and becoming the owner of the property, by an owner who is entitled to make an application converting the foreclosure to a judicial sale. By making this motion (it will be successful unless the lender can prove that the value of the property is less than the value of the mortgage), the owner can ensure that the residual equity in the property will not go to the foreclosing mortgagee but, instead, to him.

> *Foreclosure is seldom used in Ontario because it would be beneficial only in those instances in which a property is worth much more than the mortgage being held.*

8.7.6 CONSTRUCTION LIEN

You may find a construction lien registered against a property (it may even be one of yours). This is a lien in favour of a person or company who supplied services or materials relating to the construction, repair, or improvement of the property, but was not paid as agreed. This lien attaches to the land upon which the construction took place.

In certain extreme circumstances, it allows the creditor to sell the property and to use the proceeds of the sale to pay his debt, with any extra money being paid to the previous owner of the property. It is possible to place a lien against leasehold interests. This could happen if a tenant does not pay contractors he hired. In certain cases, such liens affect the landlord too.

Many commercial contracts call for payment 30 days after delivery of merchandise. This is probably the reason why the owner has 45 days from the day the last goods are delivered, or the service is rendered, or a certificate of substantial performance is signed (generally by an engineer or architect representing the owner) to pay for the goods or services. If the contractor is not paid before the end of the 45-day period, he may protect himself by registering a lien on title.

The *Construction Lien Act* (R.S.O. 1990, c. C.30) says that any property owner who has signed a construction contract must hold back payment of 10% of the money owed, until all the lien expiry periods involved have expired. Therefore the holdback money is not paid until 45 days after substantial performance.

It gets a little complicated because the holdbacks may be cascading, from an owner to a general contractor, who is supposed to pay the subcontractor, who is supposed to pay his workers and suppliers of materials. All of these parties have the right to register liens. Once the 45-day period has expired, the money held back may be paid out, if there is no lien.

If there are several liens, it can become tricky. As an example, we encountered a situation where an owner received progress estimates, certified and recommended for payment by his consulting engineer. He paid them all. The construction company then went bankrupt, without fully paying its suppliers. There were three.

1. A labour union blindly filed a claim for $100,000 for its members who were employed by the construction company. After a few days of review, the claim went down to $11,825! Note that salaries have priority over other claims.
2. A material supplier filed a lien for $147,000.
3. A second material supplier filed a lien for $77,000.

In our example, the owner could have removed these liens in two ways.

1. He could come to an agreement with the three parties involved; however, if one party disagrees, all must go to court. Typically the union would be paid first, and then the remainder of the funds would be split between the other two parties according to their claims. In this case, it would look like this:
Union: $11,825
Money remaining: $49,000-$11,825 = $37, 175
Money claimed by other two parties: $147,000 + $77,000 = $224,000
Claimant 1: $147,000/$224,000 = 65.62%; this claimant would receive: $37,175 x 65.62% = $24,394
Claimant 2: 77,000/$224,000 = 34.38%; this claimant would receive: $37,175 x 34.38% = $12,781
2. If no agreement can be reached among the parties, the owner may discharge the lien unilaterally, by paying into court the amounts of all the liens claimed, plus 25% (maximum of $50,000). In this case: $11,825 + $147,000 + $77,000 = $235,825 + $50,000 = $285,825.

Lien claimants must come to an agreement within 90 days of filing or they must either perfect their liens by filing in court or abandon their claim.

As with so many legal aspects of real property, construction liens can become very complex. Here, again, it is recommended that you use a lawyer who specializes in this field, but there are not many. In southern Ontario, we would recommend Anna Esposito, managing partner of Pallett Valo LLP. She is a Certified Specialist, Construction Law.

Most large construction projects are financed by way of a mortgage (construction financing). The lenders get very nervous when they see liens coming on title. They ask for cost-to-complete updates to determine if their loans are still safe. They also ask the owner to remove these liens promptly.

8.7.7 LIS PENDENS OR CERTIFICATE OF PENDING LITIGATION

A *lis pendens* is a document that warns would-be purchasers, or any other interested party, that there is pending litigation that could affect the land. It is a caution or a warning to anyone who intends to deal with the property.

If you do get involved with a *lis pendens*, you should get a copy of these documents so you can analyze the risk and be able to discuss it with your advisors.

A certificate of pending litigation can generally be obtained *ex parte*; that is, it can be obtained without notifying the other party that an application is being made to a judge, or master, for an order to be registered against another party's land, claiming an interest in favour of the applicant. When an application is made *ex parte*, there is an obligation of complete disclosure to the court. Failure to make full and complete disclosure can in and of itself be cause for discharge of a pending litigation obtained. In fact, overlooking this requirement will usually be fatal to the application.

8.7.8 NOTICE OF SECURITY INTEREST

A creditor who has a security interest in a personal property item may register a Notice of Security Interest in a land registration office under section 54 of the *Personal Property Security Act* (R.S.O. 1990, c. P.10) (PPSA). This registration is good for a maximum of 5 years, but it may be renewed. The PPSA allows a creditor to register a security in personal property, such as cars, water heaters, appliances, equipment, inventory, which are called "collateral" under the Act. The registration is valid for the whole province and is stored in the Personal Property Security System (PPSS).

For example, if you buy a car on credit, a security agreement will be registered. This security could be a sales contract, a lease, a chattel mortgage, anything that recognizes that the creditor has an interest in the item. Usually, but not always, the date of registration will prove who has priority, if several parties claim an interest in the same item. The creditor must file a financing statement and deliver a copy of it to the debtor within 30 days of registration.

It is possible to search in-person or online under the PPSS using the names of individuals or companies, or for cars by Vehicle Identification Number (VIN). It is also possible to request a printout of all registrations against a name. Unusual in these days of user fees, one can enquire by telephone if the number of registrations is limited. This search is useful to determine what a person possesses, in terms of PPSA registerable items, and what he owes on these items. For example, if one leases a car, or a water heater, this will show on the PPSS.

Some clarification is necessary. Fixtures are chattels that are attached (fixed) to the building or land so that they become part of it. An example would be that of a suspended gas heater. This can lead to complications. Under the PPSA, if a creditor registers a security interest before the chattel becomes a fixture, he will have priority. This could be the case with a heater, for example. However, if he did not, another creditor, such as a mortgagee will claim that it is now a fixture, and he has priority of claim.

In Ontario, searches of the PPSS can be conducted at 393 University Avenue, 3rd Floor, Toronto, and at a few land registration offices (see <www.cbs.gove.on.ca/mcbs/english/57PNPL.htm>).

8.7.9 QUIT CLAIM DEED

A Quit Claim Deed is a release of any claim that a person may have in land registered under the Registry System.

8.7.10 DEED TO USES

The Deeds to Uses document is an old type of deed that was used to avoid a wife's "right to dower" in her husband's property. It was abolished in 1978. However, deeds prior to this date are still valid.

8.7.11 TAX DEEDS

Tax Deeds and Tax Arrear Certificates, registered on title prior to the new forms, were used before 1984. Now, Form 1 is used for a Tax Deed and Tax Arrears Certificate. The sale takes place under the *Municipal Act, 2001* (S.O. 2001, c. 25).

8.7.12 EXECUTOR'S/ADMINISTRATOR'S DEED

An Executor's or Administrator's Deed is similar to a regular deed except that it is registered by a representative of the deceased and is accompanied by the required statements and recitals.

8.7.13 EASEMENTS AND RIGHTS-OF-WAY

An easement is the right to use or have access to a piece of property. Easements and rights-of-way are a right or an interest in someone else's property that benefits the person who has the easement rights. Easements can be created in three ways.

1. **By Express Grant.** This is similar to a purchase of land, except that only a right, for example to bury a pipe on a neighbour's property, is involved. This type of easement is registered on title.

Easements and rights-of-way are a right or an interest in someone else's property that benefits the person who has the easement rights.

2. **By Implied Grant.** This type of easement is not registered on title, but exists by law. The two most common are the Right of Mutual Support (you cannot demolish your house if the abutting one will be harmed by your doing so) and the Right of Way of Necessity (you cannot sell a portion of your land without providing the buyer with proper access).
3. **By Prescription.** For example, someone uses a shortcut over your land for at least 20 years. By doing so, this person has created an easement for himself, provided that he can prove that the landowner knew that he was using it, and the landowner could have stopped him, but did not do so.

There are two properties involved in an easement: the dominant tenement, which is the land benefiting by the easement or the right-of-way (which is a form of easement), and the servient tenement, which is the land offering a "service" to the dominant tenement by allowing, for example, access to vehicles or a pipe to be buried.

When one of the properties is sold, the rights run with the land, not with its owner, and the rights and obligations become those of the new owner. The principle of dominant and servient easement does not apply to most utility companies or municipalities. Note that many easements are underground and one may not erect any building on top of them.

An example of a very simple and common easement would be a mutual driveway, a strip of land shared by joining neighbours. In some cities, it is common to find that, out of a 4.5 m (15 ft) access lane to rear garages, 2.25 m (7.5 ft) belong to the owner to the east and 2.25 m (7.5 ft) to the owner to the west. Each has the right to drive over the other's 2.25 m, as shown in Figure 8.7.

This is called a "positive easement" and it allows a landowner to do something to, or on, his neighbour's land. There is a second kind of easement called a "negative easement" that entitles a landowner to prevent a neighbour from doing something on that land that would be detrimental to him, such as demolishing a building or preventing a right of light. This would be the case if a person wanted to erect a building a very short distance from yours, blocking the light. We believe that this comes from an old English doctrine under which a landowner acquired, by uninterrupted use for 20 years, "an easement or right by prescription over adjoining land for the unobstructed passage of light and air" (*Black's Law Dictionary*, 5th ed., 1979).

Figure 8.7
Sample of Common Easement

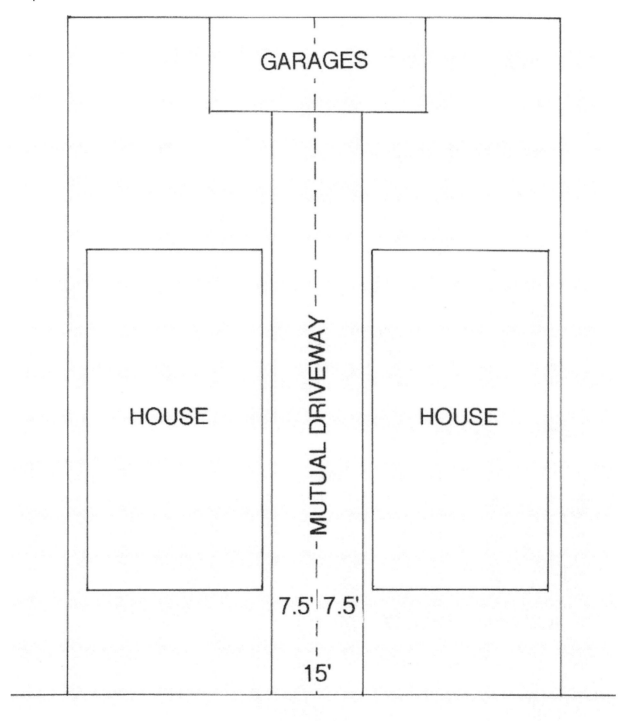

8.7.14 PUBLIC UTILITY EASEMENTS

Telephone, electricity, and gas companies can have an easement over a strip of land, commonly at the rear or the front, of each property (lot) in a subdivision. A purchaser cannot build on the easement portion of the land.

8.7.15 FREEHOLD PARCEL REGISTER

The legal description for freehold land, in each parcel, is entered at the top of the first page of the parcel registers. For example, "all of lots 1 and 2 and part of block B on plan M430 registered as plan 44R-1298".

8.7.16 LEASEHOLD PARCEL REGISTER

For example, if a piece of land is leased for 99 years by way of a ground lease and a developer intends to build a large office building on it, the registration for that piece of land is transferred to a Leasehold Parcel Register. Leasehold parcels are organized in the same way as freehold parcels, except that leasehold is noted on the register at the top of its page. If the lessee of the land acquires the freehold estate, the leasehold estate merges in the freehold.

8.7.17 CAUTIONS

Under the *Registry Act*, anyone may register a claim or agreement against a property, but under the *Land Titles Act* (R.S.O. 1990, c. L.5), a person may register only a "Caution" to protect his interest. The interesting part is that the registered owner of the land, or of the charge, cannot deal with the land, or the charge, without the consent of the cautioner. The caution automatically expires at the end of 5 years, unless it is renewed.

8.7.18 RESTRICTIVE COVENANTS

A parcel of land can be affected by way of a restrictive covenant. This is a provision that something may or, on the contrary, may not be done with the land. For example, a restrictive covenant may say that no one may have green roofs or cedar shakes or plastic siding on a house, or that the land cannot be used for a service station or a supermarket, etc. In fact, there are two different covenants – a positive covenant promises to do certain things and a negative covenant promises not to do certain things. Note that positive covenants can be written using negative words. The *Land Titles Act* provides that most restrictive covenants expire after 40 years, unless a shorter duration is indicated in the covenant.

8.7.19 ENVIRONMENTAL PROTECTION ACT

Certificates of approval regarding atmospheric emissions, waste management systems, waste disposal sites, and private sewage disposal systems are registered in Land Titles under the *Registry Act*.

8.7.20 JOINT TENANCY AND TENANCY-IN-COMMON

The main difference between a joint tenancy and a tenancy-in-common is that there is an inherent right of survivorship in joint tenancy that does not exists in tenancy-in-common. If land is conveyed to more than one person, they automatically take title as tenants-in-common, unless it is specified in the contract that they take title as joint tenants. Despite the name, this has nothing to do with being a tenant; it has to do with ownership. Under joint tenancy with two persons, upon the death of one of the owners, the other becomes the sole owner. Under tenancy-in-common, the heir(s) inherits.

8.7.21 LETTERS PROBATE AND LETTERS OF ADMINISTRATION

Probate is the procedure used by the surrogate courts to approve the validity of a will or testament of a deceased person and to confirm the appointment of the person named in the will as executor. Once the will has been probated, a copy of the letters probate is registered in the land registry office(s) involved.

8.8 ELECTRONIC LAND REGISTRATION

Understand the electronic land registration system.

In 1971, the province created a new automated (electronic) system, POLARIS (Province of Ontario Land Registration System), that catalogues real property and documents affecting it, such as mortgage, liens, and leases. In 1991, the Ontario Ministry of Consumer and Business Services entered into a partnership with private-sector companies under the name of Teranet, giving Teranet responsiblity for implementing, operating, and enhancing the POLARIS system. Teranet created a system known as "e-reg" that permits land registration documents to be created, signed, submitted, and receipted electronically without ever having to be printed out on paper. Since Fall 2003, full electronic filing is required in 18 out of 55 counties/regions. As of December 2005, 82% of registrations took place electronically.

The essential difference before and after POLARIS is that before, properties were registered by groups (concessions), while now properties are registered under individual parcels. Another difference, which represents the essence of the new system, is the fact that there is a map or plan, attached to every parcel of land. One can search the system using:

- street addresses
- owners' names, or
- property Identification Numbers (PIN).

Electronic land registration (e-reg) documents rely on encrypted digital signatures identifying the party submitting the document for registration. Lawyers create and modify documents online on behalf of the vendor and purchaser, with a property's legal description and ownership information, retrieved from Ontario's land titles database, being automatically inserted. No paper changes hands and no back-up hand-written signatures are required. Teranet has created another corporation, Teraview, whose mandate is to offer clients online access to land registration data. One can now search online electronic data of the land registration office. It is possible to find:

- owner's name(s)
- plans of survey (and print them)
- mortgagees' names
- last few recorded sales
- easements and rights-of-way, and
- details on neighbouring properties.

POLARIS consists of two databases. The title database contains abstracts of title information and the database of maps that will eventually depict over four million land parcels in the province. A database of digitized copies of instruments attached to land parcels is also being created.

POLARIS consists of two databases — the title database and the database of maps.

8.8.1 TERAVIEW SOFTWARE

The Teraview software, which can be purchased from Teranet, lets non-lawyers (real estate agents, appraisers, builders and developers) perform the following tasks:

- access the province's automated land title database, obtain the parcels registers, and view registered documents;
- confirm ownership information and determine if there are any registered encumbrances, such as construction liens;
- prepare and register mortgages, discharges, transfers, liens, by-laws, etc.; and
- access the Ministry of Attorney General's Writs of Execution database.

A solicitor, legal assistant or agent ("user") wishing to access the system must have the Teraview software, and his own electronic signature, or key, created through an encrypted disc or USB drive and a password. Only lawyers entitled to practice may make statements professing compliance with the law.

8.8.2 THE DOCUMENT REGISTRATION AGREEMENT

The Document Registration Agreement (DRA) was created to facilitate electronic closings and escrow closings, and to reduce the number of documents exchanged. It stipulates the terms of the closing arrangements, including the delivery of closing documents, building keys, and money, pending registration.

8.8.3 ACKNOWLEDGEMENT AND DIRECTION DOCUMENT

E-reg documents are completed and electronically signed by solicitors, not by a solicitor's client. Evidence of client consent and authorization is provided by an Acknowledgement and Direction Document produced automatically by the system, printed, and then signed by the client. (See Figure 8.8.)

Figure 8.8
Acknowledgement and Direction Document

ACKNOWLEDGMENT AND DIRECTION

TO: Babel Tower_____
        (Insert lawyer's name)

AND TO: Baker Schneider Ruggiero LLP_____
        (Insert firm name)

RE: Inc. sale of Lots 1-39, Plan 40-M Comprador Developments Inc.
        ("the transaction") and Take Back Mortgage to Inc. – Our File No.
        29074_____

This will confirm that:

- I/We have reviewed the information set out in this Acknowledgement and Direction and in the documents described below (the "Documents"), and that this information is accurate;
- You, your agent or employee are authorized and directed to sign, deliver, and/or register electronically, on my/our behalf the Documents in the form attached.
- You are hereby authorized and directed to enter into an escrow closing arrangement substantially in the form attached hereto being a copy of the version of the Document Registration Agreement, which appears on the website of the Law Society of Upper Canada as of the date of the Agreement of Purchase and sale herein. I/We acknowledge the said Agreement had been reviewed by me/us and that I/We shall be bound by its terms;
- The effect of the Documents has been fully explained to me/us, and I/we understand that I/we are parties to and bound by the terms and provisions of the Documents to the same extent as if I/we had signed them; and
- I/we are in fact the parties named in the Documents and I/we have not misrepresented our identities to you,
- I, _____, am the spouse of _____ _____, the (Transferor/Chargor), and hereby consent to the transaction described in the Acknowledgment and Direction. I authorize you to indicate my consent on all the Documents for which it is required.

DESCRIPTION OF ELECTRONIC DOCUMENTS

        The Document(s) described in the Acknowledgement and Direction are the document(s) selected below which are attached hereto as "Document In Preparation" and are:

❏ A transfer of the land described above.
❏ A Charge of the land described above.
❏ Other documents set out in Schedule "B" attached hereto.

Dated at Toronto, this   day of May, 2007.   Vendador Inc.

                                                    Per: _____
                                                    Name: Charmed Vendor
                                                    Title: President

                                                    I have the authority to bind the corporation

8.8.4 TYPICAL E-REG TRANSACTION

The basic concept of electronic land registration is that documents are created online by one lawyer, reviewed online by the other lawyer, then signed electronically by both lawyers. Therefore, electronic documents do not have to be printed to have legal effect.

In a typical e-reg transaction between a purchaser's solicitor ("PS") and a vendor's solicitor ("VS"), as illustrated in Figure 8.9, the sequence occurs as outlined.

Figure 8.9
Workflow through e-Reg System

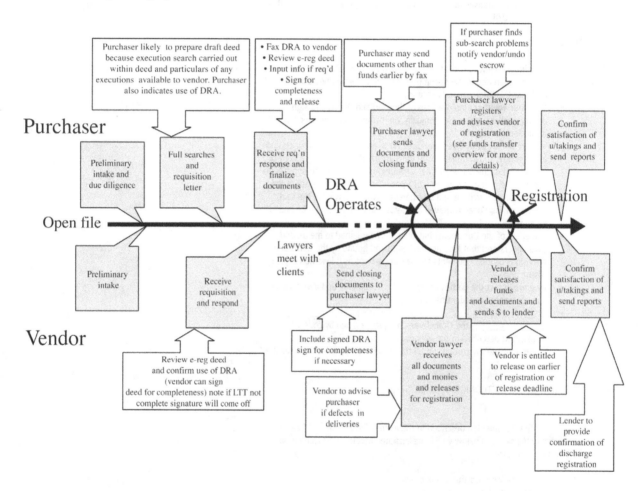

Source: Reproduced with permission of Teranet Inc.

PS and VS confirm their intention to use the DRA. PS prepares and messages the transfer to VS for review, granting VS access to the document. When both PS and VS are satisfied with the transfer, PS and VS sign electronically for completeness. PS and VS meet their respective clients who review the transaction, sign the off-title documents, and the Acknowledgement and Direction specifying the documents to be registered electronically. VS sends the off-title documents and keys to PS to be held in escrow. PS sends the closing funds to VS escrow. If VS is satisfied with the funds, VS signs Transfer for Release and notifies PS. If PS is satisfied with the off-title documents and keys, PS signs the transfer for release, searches executions, sub-searches title, electronically registers the transfer, and notifies VS of the registration so that VS can release the funds.

For those who want to delve deeper into the concept of electronic registration, visit <www.teraview.ca/resupgrades/downloads/V5_ProGuide.pdf>. This Electronic Registration Procedures Guide is 177 pages.

8.8.5 FORMS

The e-reg system has been designed to produce five different standard forms of Acknowledgment and Direction, corresponding to each of the electronic registration formats, which can be amended to suit the particular needs of any transaction.

- Transfer (Transferor)
- Transfer (Transferee)
- Charge (Chargor)
- Discharge of Mortgage/Charge (Chargee)
- Document General

Document General is now a catch-all term for the dozens of documents that used to be attached to a Document General, but which are now registered on their own.

8.8.6 SUPPORTING EVIDENCE FOR E-REG

Since supporting evidence will not be filed with the registry office when compliance statements are used, lawyers are advised to get, and keep, the evidence upon which they base their compliance statement. If litigation later arises, the material kept in their files may be the only evidence supporting compliance statements.

8.8.7 THE CLOSING

To be able to use the remote capability afforded by e-reg, an escrow closing procedure is required because there is currently no ability to electronically move purchase and sale funds between parties.

8.8.8 DOCUMENT REGISTRATION

Before a document is registered, the lawyers involved must show their approval of the document by signing for completeness. If the document contains compliance with legal statements, the e-reg system will only accept a completeness signature from a user who is authorized to practise law in Ontario.

8.8.9 TERANET ACCOUNT

Each subscribing lawyer or law firm must establish an account with Teranet to access e-reg. This account is called "the electronic registration bank account" (ERBA), from which Teranet collects the registration fees, LTT, and retail sales tax.

See <www.cbs.gov.on.ca> or <www.teranet.ca> or the Law Society of Upper Canada's Web site at <www.lsuc.ca/edrdraftdirectives_en.shtml>.

8.9 TITLE INSURANCE

Decide if title insurance is appropriate for your situation.

Title insurance is an insured statement on the condition of title or ownership of real property. For a one-time premium, the title insurance company indemnifies (compensates) both lenders and purchasers for actual loss or damage incurred in defence of the title.

Commercial title insurance serves the following purposes:
- simplifies the process and enables a faster closing
- shifts the risk from the insured to the title insurance policy
- provides coverage for known title defects, and
- provides time gap coverage for multi-jurisdictional registrations.

The following excerpt from *Canadian Lawyer* magazine (May 2002) summarizes the advantages of title insurance:

Title insurance is a no-fault financial product that compensates lenders or purchasers for any title problems. The insurer agrees to cover any defects and assumes the financial risk of a less-than-perfect title, discovered either before or after closing. Bound by a duty to defend, title insurance companies pay the insured and then, if feasible, take on the burden of recovering from any third parties who may be liable for the title defect. Policies generally do not cover non-title matters or any lawyer's advice that does not relate to title. On the other hand, title insurers protect against defects not on the public record, for example, forgery, fraud, concealed marriages, survey errors, disputed boundaries, missing heirs, unregistered easements and adverse possession.

Other than the obvious benefit of saving time and money, other advantages of commercial title insurance include:

Forgoing the requirement of proving a lawyer's negligence to succeed in claims with respect to title problems
Facilitating the closing of a potential deal
Aiding future dealings and re-financings involving the insured property, particularly when the arrangement is complicated or unconventional
Avoiding cumbersome escrows on closings

Commercial title insurance is ideal where:

There is only a short period before closing and not enough time for lawyers to do a full due diligence
The legal opinion has identified a problem that cannot be resolved or will be difficult to resolve
There is a multi-site, multi-jurisdiction transaction

There are unusual title problems or gap insurance is needed to facilitate closings, even in jurisdictions using the low-risk Torrens registration system

There are securitized mortgage pools or commercial mortgage backed securities (CMBS).

Two examples of famous title insurance cases come to mind: when SR Acquisition Corporation acquired Scott's Restaurants/KFC and its hundreds of locations, it had to insure that all locations were unencumbered and that they would be able to close quickly and simultaneously. When Sportsco International bought the SkyDome, the new owners turned to First Canadian Title for a speedy and confident closing.

Title insurance was introduced to Canada in the early 1990s and is an alternative to the conventional legal work involved in purchasing real estate. In most commercial transactions, lenders insist on an up-to-date survey or a title insurance policy. Title insurance offers full coverage to a lender in lieu of a survey, thus enabling the transaction to close as scheduled and saving the purchaser both time and money. When an existing survey reveals encroachments or other problems, a title insurance company usually can underwrite the problems and provide full coverage to the lender.

A title insurance policy is usually purchased by the lawyer, who orders title insurance on behalf of his clients and commits to a title insurance policy at the beginning of the transaction. A title insurance policy eliminates the need for title searches, resulting in cost savings for the purchaser, as well as simplifying the process, and enabling a quicker closing. In most instances, title insurance is less expensive than a survey and provides the purchaser and lender with more comprehensive coverage than that of a solicitor's opinion on title. However, remember that it is insurance and you must pay attention to what the policy says — what risks are covered and what are not. Furthermore, the insurance does not correct any defect. Hence, review the problem at hand (if any) with your lawyer to determine whether title insurance is the way to go.

A title insurance policy eliminates the need for title searches, resulting in cost savings for the purchaser.

First Canadian Title Company appears to be the granddaddy of title insurance in Canada. It was the first company to issue title insurance for commercial properties in Canada. Today, it covers real estate as diverse as vacant land zoned commercial or industrial, multi-family buildings with as few as five units, commercial towers, and everything in between, including residential.

To give you an idea of the cost of title insurance, a company's rates for commercial transactions based on the value of the property (as of 2004) are as follows:

- for a single policy of $500,000: $775;
- for a single policy of $1,000,000: $1,325; and
- for a single policy of $10,000,000: $8,825.

Additional charges are at the rate of 10% of the premium for zoning, deletion of creditor's rights, first loss, environmental lien, etc.

To date, title insurance is prevalent in residential real estate transactions, but not very common in commercial transactions. In residential transactions the cost is relatively nominal ($200 to $500) and is easily justified when compared to the savings in legal disbursements, surveys, etc. In commercial transactions, the cost is fairly high and lenders have not yet insisted on the borrowers incurring this expense as a cost of doing business.

8.10 ONLINE TOOLS

Choose among various online tools

There are a number of online services that can help a real estate investor. Some are free, such as the articles that can be found on many law firms' Web sites or on semi-public sites such as <www.lexpert.ca>, <www.lawtimenews.com>, <www.canadianlawyer.com>, or <www.lsuc.ca>. Others charge for their services. The small investor cannot justify paying thousands of dollars a year in subscription fees. However, he may impose on a subscriber (lawyer, surveyor, real estate agent or appraiser) for the occasional access.

The most outstanding tool is the Multiple Listing System (see sections 13.6.3 and 13.7 in Chapter 13), which is the preserve of members of a real estate board. In Toronto, in addition to listings, the members can access some of the services offered by Geowarehouse and Realnet directly from the Web site.

8.10.1 GEOWAREHOUSE

Geowarehouse Online Service is a web-based product offered by Teranet Enterprises. It provides stale (at least 10 days old) title data records. Aimed primarily at real estate agents, lawyers, and appraisers, Geowarehouse provides access to the Ontario Land Registry information, via the Internet, for more than three million properties. While sitting at your desk, in front of a computer, you may obtain the following:

- sales history information (price and ownership only)
- map of the parcel (most of the time), when the parcel is shown as "active"
- combined sales history and map
- neighbourhood sales report
- aerial colour photo, and
- search by block (displays all properties within an identified POLARIS block; especially valuable for users searching for condominium units).

You can search by owner name, property address, instrument number or PIN (property identification number). The data is extracted from the POLARIS system. It has nothing to do with property assessment.

You can obtain a Parcel Register Report for a property for a small fee ($33). This is payable by credit card at the time of ordering. It is like conducting a title search from the comfort of your office. It provides a passel of interesting information as outlined below.

- **LRO.** The number of the Land Registry Office of the subject property.
- **PIN.** The Property Identification Number of the subject property.
- **Assessment Roll Number.** The identification number used for property assessment purposes, associated with the subject property.
- **Registration Type.** LT for Land Titles or R for Registry.
- **Land Registry Status.** This indicates whether the property is active or inactive. Active properties are those that are "live" in the Land Registration System. Inactive properties have been retired due to consolidations with other properties, or that have been split into new properties. In some cases properties have been made inactive as part of the Land Registry Automation process. Land Registry Status does not refer to the status of any listing on MLS systems.
- **Municipality.** The municipality in which the subject property is located.
- **Address.** The municipal address for the subject property.

- **Area.** Area in square metres. To convert it into square feet, multiply by 10.76 and divide the result by 43560 if you want acres.
- **Perimeter.** This is the sum of the individual boundary elements that bound a property (in metres).
- **Description.** The legal description of the subject property.
- **Party to.** Those parties that have interest in the subject property.
- **Sales History.** Note: this area lists the prior sales on the property, where available in the GeoWarehouse database. Not all sales are available due to the nature of the automation process.
- **Instrument Number.** This is the registration number of the document.
- **Registration Date.** This is the date (dd-mm-yyyy) as specified on the last registered transfer document for the subject property.
- **Instrument Type.** Identifies the instrument type. Listed below are the transfer types of documents:
  - T: Transfer
  - TPSA: Transfer Under Power of Sale (Grant)
  - TRAPL: Transmission by Personal Representative (Land)
  - TLP: Transfer by Partnership
  - TPR: Transfer by Personal Representative
  - TTRBK: Transfer by Trustee in Bankruptcy

8.10.2 REALNET

Realnet covers commercial real estate transactions in the Greater Toronto (less than $1,000,000), Calgary (less than $500,000), and Greater Vancouver (less than $250,000) market areas. They offer several modules that cover office, retail, industrial, apartment, hotel, industrial and commerical, and residential land. In the Greater Toronto Area only, they may report on residential lot sales.

8.10.3 REALTRACK

Realtrack covers only sold commercial properties. It gives many more details than Geowarehouse on the sale itself, as outlined below under the various service categories.

- **With full service.**
  - full contact info: name, address, phone number, etc.
  - surveys
  - full copies of deeds, mortgage documents, etc.
  - photographs
  - site area, and
  - building area, clear heights.
- **For summary service.** It is similar to Geowarehouse.
  - vendor, purchaser
  - price
  - property type, and
  - size, ceiling heights.

Both services are fully searchable.

Figure 8.10
RealTrack Sales Report

1 Jun 05	**10 KODIAK CRES** North York, Metro	$2,265,000
Vendor	354401 Alberta Ltd Attn: Michael Platz 403-531-6157 Xentel DM Inc 417 Fourteenth St NW, Ste 300 Calgary, Alberta T2N 2A1	
Purchaser	1434532 Ontario Ltd Attn: Lawrence Blankenstein 416-789-0699 10 Kodiak Cres, Ste 200 Toronto, Ontario M3J 3G5	
Description	Office/Industrial Bldg - 16 ft clr; 22,160 sf @ $102 80% office Last sold in Feb 98 for $1,200,000	
Site	Map Plan 66R-14381, Part 3 Plan 66R-13545, Part 2 Area: 1.14 Ac	
Assessment	Roll No: 19 08 052 170 00500 97 Detail	99 Detail	
Consideration	Cash: $2,265,000 Mortgage(s): Nil	
Registration	Date: 1 Jun 05 Deed(s): AT-818446 Last Conveyance: E-151717	
Contact	CB Richard Ellis: Frank Protomanni, 416-633-4646	
Documents	Deed [31K] Request RT42199	◄

Home | Status | Recent Sales | Search Database | Contact Us

Source: Reproduced by permission of RealTrack Inc.

In both cases, generally, there is a setup fee. Realtrack covers only larger Ontario cities, such as the Greater Toronto Area, Windsor, Barrie, London, Hamilton, Ottawa, etc. Figure 8.10 shows a typical sales report from Realtrack.

These three services, GeoWarehouse, RealTrack, and Realnet, overlap in some areas (see Figure 8.11). Real estate specialists, including investors, could use these services for the following:

- to discover if a property has sold, where and for how much
- to find names of buyers and vendors
- to compare sold property prices to asking prices of listings
- to select sites
- to get information on market activity and values, and
- to view aerial photos of properties of interest.

Figure 8.11
Summary of Real Estate Information Services

Item / Feature	Geowarehouse (Teranet)	Marsh Report	MLS	Realnet	RealTrack
Geographic Coverage	Ontario	Greater Toronto Area, York, Durham, Peel, Halton	Approx. 90 km. Radius around Toronto	Ontario -GTA, Calgary -GCA, Vancouver -GVA	Ontario
$ value of sales reported	All amounts	$1M+, but as of March 2005, sales under $1.5M noted in summary form only	All amounts	$1M+ in Ontario $500K+ in Calgary $250K+ in Vancouver	$500K+
Details of sales	Limited	Some	Extensive	Extensive	Extensive
Type of properties	All	All, except houses	All	Commercial	All, except private homes
Proximity sales report	Yes	No	Yes	No	No
Name of Vendor	Yes	Yes if company, not individ.	Yes	Yes	Yes
Name of Buyer	Yes	Yes if company, not individ.	No	Yes	Yes
Sale price	Yes	Yes	Yes	Yes	Yes
Date of sale	Yes	Yes (date of registration)	Yes	Yes	Yes
Picture of buildimg	No	Yes	Yes	No	Yes
Colour aerial photos	Yes (low resolution)	No	No	No	When available
Mortgage information	No	Yes	Sometimes	Yes	Yes
Historic information	Yes	Sometimes	Yes	Yes	Yes
Building description	No	Yes	Yes	Yes	No
Sale analysis	No	Yes	No	Yes	Yes
Land area	Yes	Yes	Yes	Yes	Yes
Property map	Yes	No	Sometimes	Yes	No
GIS	No	No	No	Yes	Yes
Parcel register	Yes *	No	No	No	No
Website	www.geowarehouse.ca	www.marshnet.com	www.torontomls.net	www.realnet.ca	www.realtrack.com
Available to	Certain industries: Financial, Gov., Legal, Health Care, Real Estate, Utility. Others can apply.	Government and Real Estate professionals	Realtors only, but public can access an abridged version at www.MLS.ca	Everyone	Everyone
Cost (yearly)	$2,250/user * $28/parcel register ordered	$3,400 (includes 6% GST & quarterly hard copy books) $3,100 for internet only	Covered by Realtors' Toronto Real Estate Board membership fees	Principals: $995 / month Service Providers: $1,023 / month	Limited access: $1,995 Full access: $2,995 Setup fee: $295
Note			All info here is provided by a Realtor, based on the data he receives from his client, so listings may be incomplete	Above prices are for the GTA Also covers new home sales	

PART 3

Finance

Chapter 9 – UNDERSTANDING REAL ESTATE FINANCIAL TERMINOLOGY

Chapter 10 – FINANCIAL ANALYSIS

Chapter 11 – UNDERSTANDING REAL ESTATE FINANCING

Chapter 12 – APPLYING FOR A MORTGAGE

CHAPTER

9

Understanding Real Estate Financial Terminology

By the end of this chapter you will be able to:
- Use the three-variable formulas common in real estate practice.
- Explain GIM's limited use.
- Employ NIM to determine your offering price.
- Understand how PGI, V&BD, and GOI are connected.
- See the relationship between the OE and NOI and how they relate to GOI.
- Calculate the various debt factors: ADS, DSCR, and DR.
- Use CFBT and CFAT to refine the concept of cash flow.
- Distinguish between an exceptional and a low OER.
- Identify ROE as the key factor.
- See how capital improvements impact your OE.
- Calculate BCR and compare it to the zoning by-laws.

As with every business, commercial real estate practitioners use a number of terms and acronyms particularly related to financial analysis. This chapter presents these terms, often along with an example, to help you become familiar with their usage.

9.1 THE THREE-VARIABLE FORMUALS

Use the three-variable formulas common in real estate practice.

In real estate, you will frequently have to use three-variable formulas, such as the Income Formula and the Property Tax Formula. If you know the formula, when you have any two of the variables you will be able to find the third.

9.1.1 INCOME FORMULA

We refer to the Income Formula as IRV, where Income (I) equals the Net Operating Income (NOI), Rate (R) equals the Cap Rate, and Value (V) equals the asking (or selling) price. We present it as follows:

$$\frac{I \times R}{V}$$

Using the Income Formula, you can manipulate it as follows: I = V x R, or R = I ÷ V or V = I ÷ R. For example if you know that Income is $50,000 and the Cap Rate is 8%, you can find Value as follows using the Income Formula, I = V x R:

$$
\begin{aligned}
\$50,000 &= V \times 0.08 \\
V &= \$50,000/0.08 \\
&= \$625,000
\end{aligned}
$$

9.1.2 PROPERTY TAX FORMULA

The other three-variable formula commonly used is the Property Tax Formula, where Property Tax (T) = Assessed Value (A) x Property Tax Rate (R). In this case, if you were calculating Value, the formula would be V = I/R, whereas the formula to find the Property Tax Rate would be R = I/V.

9.2 GROSS INCOME MULTIPLIER (GIM)

Explain GIM's limited use.

The Gross Income Multiplier (GIM) is a very imprecise tool; however it can be used, guardedly to estimate the value of small residential units, such as a triplex. To find the GIM, you divide the asking price by the gross income. The quotient provides semi-valid information only if one finds enough truly comparable sales (at least five or, preferably, more) in the same market. To illustrate how dangerous it is to rely on the GIM, let's compare two buildings where the asking price of each is $700,000. In both cases the gross income is $100,000 and the GIM is 7 ($700,000/$100,000).

Property 1

An older building and the landlord pays all expenses.

Gross income	$100,000
Expenses	$ 52,000
Net income	$ 48,000

Property 2

A newer building and the tenants pay their own heat and electricity.

Gross income	$100,000
Expenses	$ 32,000
Net income	$ 68,000

Although both properties have a GIM of 7, property 2 generates a net income of $68,000 versus $48,000 for property 1. Clearly, it wouldn't make sense to price the two properties at the same value for sale.

9.3 NET INCOME MULTIPLIER (NIM)

Employ NIM to determine your offering price.

The Net Income Multiplier (NIM) is another financial tool, a factor, that is used to estimate the market value of an Income-Producing Property (IPP). The NIM is the inverse of the Cap Rate and Cap Rate can be used to find NIM.

The NIM is obtained by dividing the Asking Price or Market Value (MV) by the Net Operating Income (NOI). Some, but not many buyers have a NIM value in mind as a benchmark when considering a property for purchase.

$$\frac{\text{Asking Price (or Market Value (MV))}}{\text{Net Operating Income (NOI)}} = \text{NIM}$$

Example

$$\frac{\$3,650,000}{\$346,000} = 10.55 \text{ (not 10.55\%)}$$

Using the three-variable formula, you could use the NIM when buying a property to determine how much you want to offer. If, for example, you wanted an NIM of 10.55 on every property you purchased, you could determine the amount you would offer for a property based on the Net Operating Income. In a case where the property has a Net Operating Income of $346,000, you would determine your offering price, or what you view as the market value, by

Learn the lingo: NIM, GIM, PGI, GOI, NOI, etc., etc.

reversing the formula as follows: NOI x NIM or $346,000 x 10.55 = $3,650,300. As mentioned earlier, you could also use the NIM to find the Cap Rate (and vice versa). In this case, Cap Rate = 100/10.55 or 9.48%.

9.4 POTENTIAL GROSS INCOME (PGI)

Potential Gross Income (PGI) refers to all revenues generated by a property during a one-year period, assuming there are neither vacancies nor bad debts. This figure is useful because it is the foundation used to arrive at the all-important and universal value approach, the Cap Rate. Occasionally, you will also encounter the expression "contractual income", which refers to income generated only by spaces that are occupied by a tenant under a lease or contract. For example, income that is not considered "contractual", because it is not covered by a lease or contract, is laundry room or parking income.

Understand how PGI, V&BD, and GOI are connected.

9.5 VACANCIES AND BAD DEBTS (V&BD)

Generally, vacancies and bad debts (V&BD) are expressed as a percentage of the gross income. Most properties incur vacancies and bad debts, unless they have long-term lease(s) with a strong covenant tenant, such as a government.

9.6 GROSS OPERATING INCOME (GOI)

Appraisers call this term "Effective Gross Income". It is the Potential Gross Income (PGI), less an allowance for vacancies and bad debts.

9.7 OPERATING EXPENSES (OE)

Operating expenses (OE) are the expenses incurred while operating the property. They generally include property taxes, insurance, utilities, and repair and maintenance costs. Figure 9.1 is a Sample Annual Income and Expense Statement for a multi-family building.

Figure 9.1

Sample Annual Income and Expense Statement for a Multi-Family Building

Assumptions:

Property value:	$2,200,000
Down payment:	$ 800,000
Mortgage (at 8%), interest only:	$1,400,000
Mortgage interest	$ 112,000/year
Land value:	$ 650,000
Building value:	$1,550,000
CCA (disregarding the 50% rule)	$1,550,000 x 4% = $ 62,000

1. Potential Gross Income (rentals & other miscellaneous income): $427,000

Less:	Vacancy allowance (3%)	$12,810		
	Bad debt allowance (1%)	$ 4,270	$ 17,080	
			$409,920	
Plus:	Other income:			
	Laundry	$ 3,600		
	Bulletin Board	$ 4,200		
	Parking	$ 3,100	$ 10,900	

Gross Operating Income (GOI) $420,820

2. Less: Operating Expenses (OE)

Property taxes	$120,000
Building insurance	$ 12,000
Electricity	$ 18,000
Heating	$ 13,000
Waste removal	$ 4,000
Window cleaning	$ 1,000
Security system monitoring	$ 360
Advertising	$ 1,000
Outside maintenance	$ 6,000
Repairs	$ 4,000
Building staff	$ 2,400
Accounting and legal fees	$ 1,800
Auto expenses	$ 1,200
Management fee (4% of PGI)	$ 16,833
Office expenses	$ 3,000

Total Operating Expenses (OE): $204,593

Net Operating Income = GOI – OE
= $420,820 - $204,593
= $216,227

9.8 NET OPERATING INCOME (NOI)

See the relationship between the OE and NOI and how they relate to GOI.

Net Operating Income (NOI) is the Gross Operating Income (GOI), less operating expenses (OE). It disregards debt service and income taxes. Using the numbers from the sample in Figure 9.1, we calculate it as follows:

$$
\begin{aligned}
\text{NOI} \quad &= \quad \text{Gross Income} - \text{Operating Expenses} \\
&= \quad \$420{,}820 - 204{,}593 \\
&= \quad \$216{,}227
\end{aligned}
$$

9.9 ANNUAL DEBT SERVICE (ADS)

Annual Debt Service (ADS) represents the yearly amount paid to the lender/mortgagee. It includes both principal and interest. Note that while ADS does not include property taxes, for single-family units and small commercial properties the mortgagee pays the property taxes directly to the municipality and adds the tax amount to the monthly mortgage payments.

9.10 DEBT SERVICE COVERAGE RATIO (DSCR)

The Debt Service Coverage Ratio (DSCR) measures a property's ability to cover the mortgage payments, including both interest and principal. It is obtained by dividing the Net Operating Income (NOI) by the mortgage payments. An acceptable DSCR ranges from 1.20 to 1.40. For example, on a property where the Net Operating Income (NOI) is $275,000 and the mortgage payments are $200,000, the result is a very comfortable DSCR.

$$
\begin{aligned}
\text{DSCR} \quad &= \quad \frac{\$275{,}000}{\$200{,}000} \\
&= \quad 1.38
\end{aligned}
$$

Calculate the various debt factors: ADS, DSCR, and DR.

9.11 DEFAULT RATIO (DR)

The Default Ratio (DR) is used in financial analysis to compare the Gross Operating Income (the rents) to the Operating Expenses plus the Annual Debt Service. If the occupancy level does not generate a Gross Operating Income that is at least equal to Operating Expenses (OE) + Debt Service (DS), the owner will not be able to make the mortgage payments without injecting funds from another source. Also called the Breakeven Point, the Default Ratio is used to measure the degree of risk. DR = Operating Expenses (OE) + Annual Debt Service (ADS)/Gross Operating Income (GOI)

For example (using the numbers from Figure 9.1):

$$
\begin{aligned}
\text{DR} \quad &= \quad \$204{,}593 \text{ (OE)} + \$112{,}000 \text{ (DS)} \\
&= \quad \$316{,}593/\$420{,}820 \text{ (GOI)} \\
&= \quad 0.75 \text{ or } 75\%
\end{aligned}
$$

9.12 CASH FLOW BEFORE TAXES (CFBT)

Cash flow is usually used to refer to the amount of money left before income taxes, but less the Annual Debt Service (ADS). In other words CFBT = Net Operating Income (NOI) less Annual Debt Service (ADS). Using the Sample Income and Expense Statement from Figure 9.1, we can calculate the CFBT as follows:

$$
\begin{aligned}
\text{CFBT} \quad &= \quad \text{Net Operating Income} - \text{Annual Debt Services} \\
&= \quad \$216{,}227 - \$112{,}000 \\
&= \quad \$104{,}227
\end{aligned}
$$

Use CFBT and CFAT to refine the concept of cash flow.

9.13 CASH FLOW AFTER TAXES (CFAT)

The Cash Flow After Taxes (CFAT) refines the concept of cash flow even further. To obtain CFAT it is necessary to consider both Capital Cost Allowance (CCA) and income taxes.

Consider the example below, based on a $1,600,000 property with a $155,000 Cash Flow Before Taxes (CFBT) and an allocated building value of $1,300,000, leaving a land value of $300,000.

Cash flow after Capital Cost Allowance (CCA)

Cash Flow Before Taxes (CFBT)		$ 155,000
$1,300,000 (building value) x 4% (CCA rate)	=	($ 52,000)
Income after CCA, for income tax purposes	=	$ 103,000

Income taxes payable

$103,000 x 43% (estimated income tax rate)	=	$ 44,290

CFAT

$155,000 (CFBT) – $44,290 (Tax)	=	$ 96,290

9.14 OPERATING EXPENSE RATIO (OER)

Distinguish between an exceptional and a low OER.

Frequently financial statements provided by a vendor are inaccurate. For example, an owner of a multi-family building may show Operating Expenses of $75,000 on gross income of $300,000, or an Operating Expense Ratio (OER) of 0.25 or 25% (Expenses/Gross Income ($75,000/$300,000)). This is a very low ratio for an apartment building and should raise alarm bells if you are reviewing such an income statement. The OER is generally between 30% (which is exceptional and only found if tenants pay for their utilities) and 55%. It will vary depending on the quality of the building construction, particularly insulation, windows, and energy-efficient plumbing fixtures, and on whether the landlord or the tenants pay for heating and electricity. In the case of older, poorly insulated apartment buildings, where the owner pays for everything, this ratio can be as high as 60%, even 65%. This indicates an opportunity for renovation, particularly to save energy. After spending the money required for renovations and adding the purchase cost of the property, the investor should have a property worth more than the sum of the two.

Figure 9.2 is an example of an Income Statement less Total Expenses that is somewhat typical for a 210-suite multi-family property with underground parking, taken from a recent Toronto listing.

Annual operating costs per apartment unit generally range from a low of $1,300 or less for new or renovated buildings to as high as $3,000 for older ones, and depend on a number of factors such as location, age, unit size, etc.

Figure 9.2
Income Statement Less Total Expenses

A 2007 Toronto listing for a 210-unit multi-family property with underground parking.

Gross Income (GI)		$1,780,000
Net Operating Income (NOI):		$ 906,000 (50.9% of GI)
3% of GI allowed for property management:	$ 53,400	
$650/unit for Maintenance x 210 units:	$ 136,500	
$400/unit for Wages x 210 units:	$ 84,000	
$50/unit for Insurance x 210 units:	$ 10,500	
$50/unit for Miscellaneous x 210 units:	$ 10,500	
Total:	**$ 294,900**	
Balance: $906,000 - $294,900 =	**$ 611,100**	

Yearly Expenses/Unit = $611,100/210 units = $2,910

9.15 RETURN ON EQUITY RATE (ROE)

Identify ROE as the key factor.

Some investors are only interested in considering the return on their invested capital or Return on Equity Rate (ROE), also referred to as "Cash-on-Cash Return". This should not be confused with the Return on Investment (ROI), which is based on the total value of the property. ROE is expressed as a percentage and indicates the return on the cash invested. The formula is:

ROE = Cash Flow Before Taxes (CFBT)/Equity (amount of cash invested)

In other words, on an $800,000 cash investment, where the Cash Flow Before Taxes (CFBT) is $86,000, the ROE would be $86,000/$800,000 = 10.76%.

To be really thorough one should add to the Cash Flow Before Taxes (CFBT) the amount of the principal paid off the mortgage in that year, which is also called "equity build-up". You may hear the end result called the "broker's rate of return".

There is a complication with this approach. Even if annual income and expenses remain virtually the same (which they never do), this "modified Cash-on-Cash return" will increase each year, as the amount of the mortgage principal is increasingly paid off. Some people, who have no intention of selling their property, simplify the process considerably by taking the principal amount of the mortgage and dividing it by the amortization period (assuming that we are dealing with a new mortgage), and use this figure to represent the overall yearly increase in equity build-up.

For example, with a $3,000,000 mortgage with a 20-year term and amortization, you would have an annual equity build-up of $3,000,000/20 = $150,000.

The ROE is, in fact, much more complex than it appears. In reality, it is made up of four components. As an example, an 8% ROE could be broken down arbitrarily as follows:

Return *of* the investment (principal)	2%
Return *on* the investment (interest)	2.5%
Inflation rate	3%
Money management "fee"	0.5%

The ROE is very sensitive to the percentage of equity (LTV ratio) and the rate, amortization, term, and amount of the mortgage, making it far from ideal for comparing properties.

9.15.1 RETURN ON EQUITY RATE AFTER FINANCING

Example

Price (P):	$100,000
Net Operating Income (NOI):	$11,000
Cap Rate (CR):	11%
Down Payment (DP):	$25,000
Mortgage (interest only) (M):	$75,000
Mortgage Interest Rate (I):	8%
Mortgage Payments:	$6,000
Income after Financing:	$11,000 - $6,000 = $5,000
ROE (Return on Equity):	$5,000/$25,000 = 0.20 or 20%

Formula for ROE after Financing

$$ROE = \frac{(P \times CR) - (M \times I)}{DP}$$

$$= \frac{(\$100{,}000 \times 11\%) - (\$75{,}000 \times 8\%)}{\$25{,}000}$$

$$= \frac{11{,}000 - 6{,}000}{25{,}000}$$

$$= \frac{5{,}000}{25{,}000}$$

$$= 0.20 \text{ or } 20\%$$

9.16 CAPITAL IMPROVEMENTS

See how capital improvements impact your OE.

Capital improvements are major improvements, often replacements, but also new construction. For example an improvement to a building will contribute value to the property for many years, such as a new roof or a driveway. Canada Revenue Agency (CRA) demands that capital improvements be amortized, due to depreciation, over a period of years (theoretically, over their lifetime). Conversely, maintenance items and repairs are written-off as an expense for the year in which they are incurred.

For example, if an air conditioning unit commonly lasts 15 years, it is considered a capital improvement and, put simply, you would depreciate 1/15 of its cost each year. If it costs $150,000, $10,000 should be set aside each year, as a reserve for its replacement. However, CRA is "allergic" to simplicity and mandates that you use the Capital Cost Allowance (CCA) class table, class 8 for air conditioning units, which is 20% per year on the declining balance (see Chapter 5 at Figure 5.6).

9.17 BUILDING COVERAGE RATIO (BCR)

Calculate BCR and compare it to the zoning by-laws.

Building Coverage Ratio (BCR) refers to the percentage of the land that is covered by the building. For example, a 1,860 m^2 (20,000 sq ft) building situated on a 5,575m^2 (60,000 sq ft) site, has a coverage ratio of 1,860/5,575 = 0.333 or 33.3%. For industrial uses, most municipal zoning by-laws impose a maximum coverage of 50%. For strip plazas, the coverage runs from 20-30% due to parking requirements.

Some people have difficulty separating coverage and density. To be very specific, site coverage refers only to the ground floor area of the building divided by the area of the site, whereas density refers to the total gross floor area of all the floors of the building divided by the area of the site.

Example
1,860 m^2 (20,000 sq ft)/floor x 8 floors = 14,880 m^2 (160,000 sq ft)
14,880 m^2 (160,000 sq ft)/5,575 m^2 (60,000 sq ft) = 2.669 or 266.9% density

CHAPTER 10

Financial Analysis*

By the end of this chapter, you will be able to:

- Collect and analyze the information about a property to begin in-depth financial analysis.
- Precisely measure your rate of return on an investment and your cost to borrow.
- Understand the limitations of the payback method.
- Recognize the importance of the Cap Rate and calculate the value of a property.
- Define the various terms used in financial analysis.
- Manipulate the Net Present Value to calculate and analyze other financial factors.

* The authors express their gratefulness to Dr. J. Douglas Timmons, Economics and Finance Department, Middle Tennessee State University, for his review of this chapter.

Buying real estate is complicated. There are many things to consider and analyze before you make a purchasing decision. Even large real estate investment corporations who employ phalanxes of financial and real estate analysts, MBAs, lawyers, and more can only analyze a certain percentage of all the facts involved in a purchase. When the analyses are done (the "science"), which may amount to 90-95% of the decision-making groundwork, the decision-makers must turn to the "art" to judge the final 5% or 10%, leading to a yes or no buying decision.

The weakness of the small investor is that he will never be able to reach as high a percentage of sophisticated analysis as the specialists. Hence, his strength (typical of small investors) must be in the art, the so-called "nose" for a great investment. Successful entrepreneurs are often people who can look at a situation, project, or deal and quickly say "I like it" or "I don't like it" and be right most of the time. Over time, you may develop this "nose", but in the meantime there are a number of steps that will take you well along the way in your analysis of a property to help you make sound decisions.

10.1 STEP-BY-STEP ANALYSIS OF A PROPERTY

Collect and analyze the information about a property to begin in-depth financial analysis.

There are five main steps in acquiring a property. The outline below provides an overview of the process so you can see where financial analysis fits. Then, we'll use an industrial building as an example.

Step 1 – Data Gathering
Obtain all facts from the vendor or agent.
- Total area of building.
- Area of office space.
- Clear ceiling height in the plant/warehouse.
- Land acreage (calculate the building coverage ratio to see if any expansion is possible).
- Lease details – having a copy of the lease(s) is essential.
- Name of tenant(s) and details on the company.
  - Lease start and end date.
  - Were there any leasehold improvements?
    - paid by tenant or by landlord?
    - if by landlord, were improvements paid for in cash or amortized over length of the lease?
- Any free rent? When?
- Net rental/year (NOI) (you may have to check several documents to ascertain it).
- What repairs and replacements are the landlord's responsibilities?
- Any rental increases/decreases (ascertain why any decreases have been given)?
- Special clauses regarding renewal, right of first refusal, or right to buy?

Step 2 – Visit the Property
If you like what you've learned so far, then visit the property and ask plenty of questions of the listing agent during the tour. Most have to do with the property, but some will be aimed at judging the agent's real estate knowledge and experience, business common sense, and personality. It is not uncommon to find agents that do not

pass muster, mainly because they are not qualified commercial specialists, and this situation can make negotiations very difficult. You may have to abandon a potential deal if, in your opinion, the agent is going to be difficult to deal with. If you decide to do this, but really like the deal, try to find out when the listing expires and get as much information about the vendor as possible. Then you can contact the vendor directly when the listing expires and explain that you would like to deal directly with him. Do be careful in doing this. You will not be very popular with the agent, if he finds out.

During the initial visit, ask about the age of the building, the roof, and if any repairs or replacements have been made recently or are required. You should also ask for complete details about existing financing, a floor plan, survey, photos, rental schedule, etc. It is surprising how often this basic data is not available.

Try to find out the following:
- why the vendor is selling
- how urgent the sale is (motivation), and
- if there have been any offers (at what price, with what conditions).

Most vendors have an unrealistic idea of their property value. Reaching a deal is difficult with them, if you happen to arrive at the beginning of their sales effort. Many vendors need to witness the response from the market before they lower their expectations to realistic levels.

Step 3 – Analysis
Armed with the data you have collected, you can begin to compare and analyze.
- Verify if there is data available on the property from sources such as Geowarehouse and the Multiple Listing Service (MLS).
- Try to find comparable sales and rentals from other sources and determine what the Cap Rate of the sales were.
- Calculate the asking Cap Rate for the property. If it is not commensurate with other Cap Rates you found (above point), call the vendor or agent, tell him what other Cap Rates you've found, and ask why their rate is so much lower. Often, this call reveals interesting details.
- Adjust the asking price, based on what you discover (e.g., extra land, repairs).
- Calculate the existing mortgage Loan-to-Value (LTV) ratio. If it is too low, call a mortgage broker and ask him, in broad terms, what the likely terms of a new mortgage would be.
- Also ask the vendor/agent if a Vendor-Take-Back (VTB) mortgage is possible.
- Calculate the Return on Equity Rate (ROE), based on the asking price and the one you intend to offer, if appropriate.

Step 4 – Letter of Intent
If you like the property, present a Letter of Intent, based on your desired Cap Rate. If it comes back with a lower Cap Rate (higher price) or other terms you do not like, you can negotiate verbally or in writing. If you cannot obtain what you want, you must decide if you like the property enough to pay the price or if you prefer to look for another one.

Step 5 – Offer
At this stage, if you are still interested and not too far from what the vendor wants, you can present an offer. A first offer's primary goal should not be to make a deal (great, if it does), but to get things out in the open and force the vendor to think and make decisions. Most vendors have not fully contemplated all aspects of a poten-

tial sale. They have not given much thought to "details" such as: VTB financing, financial statements (existing and reconstructed), survey, mortgage balance and discharge, roof age, environmental report, guaranties, deferred maintenance. The offer should cover as many of these things as possible so that the negotiations quickly move to key terms.

Often, when we prepare the offer, we have to alter the asking price based on a myriad of factors, some raising the Cap Rate ratio and some lowering it. When we are satisfied with it, we ask our lawyer to review it.

10.1.1 TEN-POINT SUMMARY

Below is a ten-point summary of the financial analysis process.

1. Gather all data available from the vendor, but checking accuracy in great detail is not necessary at this point (you can do it at a later stage, if you pursue the deal).
2. Property visit.
3. Analysis. Find out which items add value to the property and those that make it less attractive, in your opinion.
4. Determine what the Cap Rate is supposed to be.
5. Come up with your value.
6. Present a Letter of Intent.
7. Negotiate the terms.
8. Present an Offer conditional on due diligence.
9. Conduct due diligence (see Chapter 16, Buying and Selling).
10. Request a price adjustment if there are any surprises.

10.1.2 FINANCIAL ANALYSIS – EXAMPLE

Now let's apply the theory to a possible purchase. As an example, we will use a leased industrial building, considered for purchase in May 2007.

Step 1 – Data Gathering
- Total area of Building: 16,722 m² (180,000 sq ft) located in Barrie, Ontario
- Area of Office Space: 929 m² (10,000 sq ft)
- Clear Ceiling Height: 6.7 m (22 ft)
- Land Acreage: 11 acres or 44,515 m² (479,160 sq ft)
- Building coverage ratio: 16,722 m²/44,515 m² = 0.376 or 37.6%
  - Land required for a 50% (typical) coverage ratio: 16,722 m² x 2 = 33,444 m²
  - Extra land: 44,515 m² – 33,444 m² = 11,071 m²/4,047 m² = 2.73 acres
  - Market value of extra land: $100,000/acre x 2.73 acres = $273,000
  - Combined Net Rental of building, including the extra land is: $43 x 16,722 m² = $719,046 or rounded to $720,000
- Lease details:
  - Land required for a 50% (typical) coverage ratio: 16,722 m² x 2 = 33,444 m²
  - Number of tenants: 3
  - Leases: Start and end date:

– Unit A = July 1, 2006 to June 30, 2013
– Unit B = August 1, 2004 to July 31, 2009
– Unit C = February 1, 2005 to January 31, 2010

Step 2 – Visit the Property
- Two of the three tenants are small, but strong corporations in business for over 20 years. The third one is a charitable, not-for-profit corporation in existence for over 50 years.
- Building is 35 years old and well maintained.
- Roof is 9 years old and in good condition.
- No clause in the lease that could negatively affect value, except rights to renew at market rentals.
- The asking price is $9,400,000.

Step 3 - Analysis
- Cap Rate is: $720,000/$9,400,000 = 0.0766 or 7.66%
- Upon inquiry, the agent explained that a Cap Rate of 8% is desired, but the vendor added $200,000 for the extra land.
- The existing financing will be discharged by the vendor (treat as clear).
- Our enquiries showed that the Cap Rate should be between 8.5% and 8.75% ($8,470,600 and $8,228,600) plus the extra land, if we want to consider it an asset. In fact, most of this extra land is used by two of the tenants for semi-trailer storage. Therefore, its value is reflected in the rentals.

While one lease expires in 3 years, one in 4 years, and the last one in 7 years, they are staggered, which is a big advantage if one tenant decides to move out. However, it will be a disadvantage for the financing. Because of that situation, we will probably ask the vendor for a 20% LTV ratio by way of a VTB at the same rate (or better) and expiring on the same date as the new mortgage we will arrange, but running for no more than 5 years.

10.2 MEASURING RETURN ON INVESTMENT

Precisely measure your rate of return on an investment and your cost to borrow.

The concept of rate of return has many variations — GIM, NIM, Cap Rate, IRR, MIRR. We included Gross Income Multiplier (GIM) and Net Income Mulitplier (NIM) in Chapter 9 (Understanding Real Estate Financial Terminology), instead of here, because we want to show you that they do exist, but we hold them in low esteem and unworthy of real comparison with Cap Rate and even Internal Rate of Return (IRR) or Modified Internal Rate of Return (MIRR). We even consider IRR calculations unreliable because they require you to divine values 10 or 20 years into the future. In our opinion, only the Cap Rate can be trusted as a conservative measure of rate of return.

To understand rate of return, imagine that you put $100 in a savings account and 1 year later it was worth $106. What was your rate of return on that $100? It is calculated by dividing the amount earned (in this case, $6) by the amount of the original investment.

$$
\begin{aligned}
\text{Rate of return} \;\; &= \;\; \text{amount earned/amount invested} \\
&= \;\; (\$106 - \$100)/\$100 \\
&= \;\; \$6/\$100 \\
&= \;\; 0.06 \text{ or } 6\%
\end{aligned}
$$

A rate of interest is always quoted as a percentage and on a yearly basis, regardless of the period of time involved. In other words, if you want 2.5% per month, you must specify per month.

If you are a borrower, the same concept applies. Let's suppose that you borrow $5,000 for 1 year and the lender wants you to repay him $5,700 at the end of that year. Your interest is $700. The cost of borrowing, in percentage terms, is the amount of interest divided by the amount borrowed.

$$
\begin{aligned}
\text{Cost to borrow (interest rate)} \;\; &= \;\; \text{interest amount/amount borrowed} \\
&= \;\; \$700/\$5,000 \\
&= \;\; 0.14 \text{ or } 14\%
\end{aligned}
$$

10.3 PAYBACK METHOD

Understand the limitations of the payback method.

The payback method is rarely used by sophisticated investors because, usually, gross income and expenses vary from year to year, making this an unreliable method. It is, however, the simplest of tools for measuring investment returns. Basically, it consists of taking the amount of money invested in a property (the equity) and dividing it by the Net Operating Income (NOI). The result is the payback factor, that is, the number of years it will take to recover your investment. For example, if you invest $1,000,000 in a property and the NOI each year is $250,000, the payback factor is $1,000,000/250,000 = 4. The investor will say, "I will get my money back in 4 years." This method is generally used only by inexperienced real estate investors because it assumes that both income and expenses remain constant over the years, which is very rarely the case.

10.4 CAPITALIZATION RATE (CAP RATE OR CR)

Recognize the importance of the Cap Rate and calculate the value of a property.

"Yield" and "Cap Rate" are often used synonymously. The Cap Rate is a ratio expressing the logical relationship between the value of the property and the net income it produces. A Cap Rate comparison is the most common method used to compare income properties and it is a simple formula: NOI divided by the Asking (or selling) Price or Market Value. The Cap Rate is always expressed as a percentage and it disregards any financing. The greatest advantage of the Cap Rate is that it permits financial comparison of markedly different investments. For example, if an $800,000 property generates $100,000 in annual rental income, the Cap Rate would be 12.5% as in the following example:

$$\text{Cap Rate} \ = \ \frac{\text{NOI}}{\text{Market Value}}$$

$$= \ \frac{\$100{,}000}{\$800{,}000}$$

$$= \ 0.125 \text{ or } 12.50\%$$

Because income can take different forms there are actually different Cap Rates applicable to various forms of income. Generally when you hear the term "Cap Rate", the speaker is referring to the Overall Cap Rate. This is the Cap Rate for an improved property, also called "blended" because it includes two components — the rate of return on the money invested in both the land and the building (Discount Rate (DR)) and a rate of return of the money invested in the building alone, which is a wasting asset (recapture rate).

The blended rate:
- expresses the relationship between the current year's net income and the property value
- represents a blend of the rate of return on the investment and of the rate of return of the investment
- disregards debt and income tax, and
- assumes an all-cash purchase.

This formula can also be used to calculate the value of property if you have the other two variables. Drawing from the previous example, where the NOI is $100,000 and the Cap Rate is 12.5% or 0.125, the value of the property is calculated as follows:

$$\text{Value} \ = \ \text{NOI/Cap Rate}$$

$$= \ \$100{,}000/.125$$

$$= \ \$800{,}000$$

Selecting the most appropriate Cap Rate is the most important step in determing an accurate value for a property. Consider the impact of the Cap Rate in the following two scenarios, assuming a Net Income of $500,000.

Scenario #1 - Value, using a Cap Rate of 7%
= 500,000/0.07
= $7,142,857

Scenario #2 – Value, using a Cap Rate of 8%
= $500,000/0.08
= $6,250,000

By using the higher Cap Rate, the value of the property (what you would pay for it) has decreased by $892,857.

10.4.1 DETERMINING CAP RATES

Finding accurate Cap Rates is one of the most difficult tasks facing newcomers to commercial real estate. One part of determining an accurate Cap Rate is to compare the Cap Rates for properties sold of a similar type, similar age and condition, in a similar area, and in a similar time period. You must also know the details of the sale.

This information can be difficult to obtain because details of the sale of a commercial property are often confidential. You may find the sale price, but details of the Income and Expense Statement, financing, guarantees, down payment, lease details, etc., are often not available. As a note of caution, if you are unable to obtain all the details of a sale, consider the sale price unreliable. As the saying goes, "the devil is in the details", and without all the details there is a danger of making assumptions that can lead to large errors.

Special circumstances are common in real estate. A vendor may be desperate for a deal because his bank is pressuring him; the building may need expensive repairs, such as a new roof; a neighbour may badly need to expand his property; the buyer may be the brother-in-law of the vendor; financing may be exceptional; or economic conditions may be exceptionally good, or very poor, etc. The Cap Rate of a specific property virtually always reflects special circumstances that warrant adjustments because they can markedly affect the sale price and, hence, the Cap Rate. For example, if the building has an assumable first mortgage with excellent terms, or the vendor takes back a mortgage at a favourable interest rate, the purchaser will pay more for the property, rather than arrange new financing, and incur the inherent expenses.

Finding actual Cap Rates requires a lot of effort because a rate is of limited value unless you obtain all the related information, and you must always be on the lookout for special circumstances that could affect, or have affected, the end result.

We wish to stress the importance of adjusting the income and expense figures supplied by most vendors in order to determine an accurate Cap Rate. In most cases, reported Cap Rates are derived from the NOI being generated at the time of the sale. The rate is then applied to an income statement that has been reconstructed and stabilized, with allowances made for vacancies, reserves, and management fees.

To reiterate, to obtain an accurate Cap Rate, one must be able to check all the details of a sale to determine their influence on the sale price, including the following:
- location (similar properties located in different areas of the city may have different Cap Rates)
- cash or vendor's financing amount, including rate of interest
- quality of building
- vacancies (accidental or chronic)
- guarantees by vendor, if any
- age and condition of the building and the roof
- quality and length of tenancies
- periodic rental increases, if any (sometimes called "income bumps")
- upsides, such as extra land, vacancies, low rental leases coming up for renewal in the near future, and
- risk factors (evidently, riskier properties command higher returns).

Only when you have all these details can you feel certain that you have the true Cap Rate. And, once again, this can be very difficult to achieve.

The Cap Rate should not be used as a basis for decision making if rents are expected to decline. A Cap Rate is similar to an Internal Rate of Return (IRR) because the assumption is that the property is never sold.

There are guides to Cap Rates published for various markets, sectors, etc., but they are not very precise, out of necessity, and, therefore, of limited value. Indeed a 10% difference in a Cap Rate, for example 8% versus 8.8%, means a 10% or more difference in the price!

You can gather fairly accurate Cap Rate information from appraisers, lenders, and real estate agents. One of the easier ways to find rough Cap Rates for properties is to use the Multiple Listing Service (MLS) market data for sold properties and compare buildings similar to the one that interests you. Keep in mind that the details of sales are very limited. There are also other sales reporting services available for large cities in specialized libraries, as well as a number of private database services to which you can subscribe, such as The MARSH Report <www.marshnet.com>, in Toronto. These services can range in cost from $998 to $3,400 annually (see Figure 8.11).

The most difficult factor in determining Cap Rates, and the one that affects them most, is risk. It all boils down to one consideration — if a tenant is lost, how easy or difficult will it be to find another? Investors tend to think that a property located in Toronto, Vancouver, or Calgary presents less risk than one in Lindsay, Sudbury, or Regina. Or that a property leased to a government is less risky than one leased to Jane Doe Tanning Salon.

In considering the investment risk of Ontario towns some of our investors noted the following concerns:

1. Lindsay
- Population of 17,000 people
- Limited industry
- Far from any freeway or major transportation corridor.

2. Kirkland Lake
- Population of 9,900
- Extremely dependent on the mining industry
- Far from any major freeway
- Far from any major city.

3. Sarnia
- Population of 71,000
- Too dependent on the oil industry, which sooner or later is going to decline.

4. Oshawa
- Population of 146,000
- Too dependent on one industry and one company: automotive and GM. If GM ever closes its plant, which directly employs over 20,000 people and many more, indirectly, it will be an economic debacle.

10.4.2 THE CAP RATE/PRICE CORRELATION

The general opinion is that when income property Cap Rates are low, property prices are high. And when mortgage rates fall to low levels, there is a window of opportunity for owners to sell at higher prices because there is a parallel between loan rates and Cap Rates, the former pushing the latter downward. However, some professional appraisers maintain that this is not necessarily so. They say that cap rates are driven primarily by demand and that demand drives cap rates down, whereas lower mortgage rates allow buyers to pay more for a property and still maintain a positive cash flow.

Low interest rates represent a terrific opportunity for the buyer to borrow at low cost, enhancing returns considerably.

What is clear is that low interest rates represent a terrific opportunity for the buyer to borrow at low cost, enhancing returns considerably. This window of opportunity favours both vendor and borrower, to the relative detriment of the lender.

Example

Assume a mortgage of:	$2,500,000
Mortgage payments at 10% interest:	$250,000
Mortgage payments at 6% interest:	$150,000

Once again, this points out the impact of selling when mortgage rates are low. Timing can be critical.

10.4.3 THE RELATIONSHIP BETWEEN THE CAP RATE AND NET INCOME MULTIPLIER (NIM)

It may be helpful to remember that the NIM is the reverse of the Cap Rate. In other words, whereas Cap Rate = NOI/Asking Price, NIM = Asking Price/NOI. Another way of expressing this is:

$$NIM = \frac{1}{Cap\ Rate}$$

$$or\ Cap\ Rate = \frac{1}{NIM}$$

As an example, if the NIM is 13, the Cap Rate is:

$$Cap\ Rate = \frac{1}{13} = 0.0769\ or\ 7.69\%$$

In the past, both the Cap Rate and the NIM were used to estimate market value, but in the last few decades the Cap Rate has become the universal tool. Both provide the same estimate of market value.

10.4.4 REMAINING ECONOMIC LIFE

A building has what is called a "remaining economic life", which is considered to be the period over which a prudent investor would expect to recapture his investment in the wasting asset. There is not necessarily any relationship between physical wear on a building and rate of return of capital. Twenty years ago a building might have had a Cap Rate of 8%, but the same building today may have a cap rate of 7%, 8% or 9%.

Investors do not necessarily agree on the length of time in which a building investment should be recaptured. However, generally speaking, land has a lower Cap Rate than a building because a building's value is lost over the years, while land value generally remains constant or even increases. In fact one must realize that two factors contribute to real estate appreciation — construction cost and land value. In terms of construction cost, if a new door today costs $400, the $100 door installed 40 years ago is also worth $400 today (assuming it is in good condition) because it fulfills the same function. Land value is always dependent on supply and demand.

10.5 CAPITALIZATION TERMINOLOGY

Define the various terms used in financial analysis.

There are investors of all kinds. Some, who are mathematically inclined, will want to get deeper into the mathematical concepts. The following few pages are for them.

10.5.1 DEFINITION OF TERMS

1. **Present Value (PV).** This is the current, or discounted, value of a future sum or annuity. The value is discounted back to a given interest rate for a specified time period.
2. **Future Value.** The value that an amount of money invested now will have in the future, after a certain number of periods. This is also called "compound value".
3. **Compounding.** This is the process of interest being earned on interest. It is the procedure used to convert an amount from its PV to its future value. For example, $1,000 invested at 8%, is worth $1,080 ($1,000 + (1,000 x .08)). At the end of year two, it is worth $1,166.40 ($1,080 + (1,080 x .08)). At the end of year three it is worth $1,259.71 ($1,666.40 + (1,166.40 x .08)). Note that if the interest had not been reinvested with the principal each year, in year three we would be earning only $80 in interest versus $93.31, when the interest is compounded.
4. **Discounting.** It is the reverse of the compounding procedure. It is used to determine the original principal amount required or to reduce a future amount to its PV.
5. **Period.** The compounding, or discounting, intervals: months, quarters, years, etc.
6. **Ordinary Annuity.** A series of payments, which are paid at the end of each period.
7. **PV of an Ordinary Annuity.** How much should be invested now, to receive a future series of payments? Conversely, how much a future series of payments is worth today.
8. **Annuity Due.** It is the same as an ordinary annuity except that the payments are made at the beginning of each period.
9. **Future Value of an Annuity.** Its purpose is to discover how much a series of payments will be worth in the future. The calculation of the payment is a sinking fund amount.
10. **Interpolation.** Many tables give only even interest rates. To get interest rates between the rates given, one must use straight-line interpolation. For example: to get the factor for 9%, add the factors for 8% and 10%, then divide by two. This assumes linear interpretation. There may be very slight differences because the tables are actually curvilinear.

10.5.2 TIME VALUE OF MONEY

To understand the Net Present Value method (NPV) and other concepts that follow, you must consider the Time Value of Money. Basically, the concept presents money as a tool, in the same way as a delivery truck, a welding machine, or a computer. A tool must earn its keep or there is no point in owning it (investing in it). Therefore, you use a tool (money) in order to produce, that is, you expect this tool to generate a positive cash flow for you.

Given the fact that we can safely assume inflation will continue, if you have $1,000 today and can buy a suit with it, you will not be able to buy the same suit for the same amount of money in 5 years. Your money will have depreciated (lost some of its value). In other words, you could take $1 today and put it in a sock under your mattress, after 10 years you will still have a dollar, but it would buy less than today's dollar. If this money had been invested, it could return 10% per year or even better if the investment was in real estate. If you look at a table of PV (Figure 10.2), a dollar, the dormant dollar (literally) received 10 years from now, discounted at 10%, will have declined in value to only $0.386.

The formula is:

$$PV \ = \ \frac{(1+r)-n}{r} \times FV$$

where:
$$
\begin{aligned}
PV &= \text{present value (\$ worth today)} \\
1 &= \text{dollar amount} \\
r &= \text{the Discount Rate (DR) (interest rate)} \\
n &= \text{the number of periods} \\
FV &= \text{Future Value}
\end{aligned}
$$

Annuities deal with the same concept as above, but to your original $1, another dollar of principal is added every year. The correct label is "Present Value of an ordinary annuity of $1, discounted at selected rates of interest". Therefore, to your first $1 in the sock, you add another one every year and they all lose value (since they are discounted) at the same rate of interest. Figure 10.3 shows that at 10%, after 10 years, you will have put $10 into the sock, and the initial $1, and its siblings, will be worth only $6.14.

The formula to calculate annuities is:
$$\frac{(1-(1+r))n}{r}$$

Note that r (rate) and i (interest) can be used interchangeably.

10.5.3 USING COMPOUND INTEREST FUNCTIONS

There are six compound interest functions that are commonly used in real estate appraisal practice.
- Future worth of 1
- Future worth of 1 per period
- Present worth of 1
- Present worth of 1 per period
- Sinking Fund Factor
- Periodic Repayment

Figure 10.1 (Condensed Explanation of Compound Interest Tables) provides the terms commonly applied to each function.

Figure 10.1
Condensed Explanation of Compound Interest Tables

(Examples are calculated with an Effective Rate of 10%, 5th Year)

Future Worth of $1			Present Worth of $1		
1	2	3	4	5	6
$(1 + i)^n$	$\dfrac{(1 + i)^n - 1}{i}$	$\dfrac{i}{(1 + i)^n - 1}$	$\dfrac{1}{(1 + i)^n}$	$\dfrac{1 - \dfrac{1}{(1 + i)^n}}{i}$	$\dfrac{i}{1 - \dfrac{1}{(1 + i)^n}}$
$1.10^5 = 1.6105$	$\dfrac{1.6105 - 1}{.10} = 6.1051$	$\dfrac{.10}{1.6105 - 1} = 0.1637$	$\dfrac{1}{1.6105} = 0.6209$	$\dfrac{1 - 0.6209}{.10} = 3.7097$	$\dfrac{.10}{1 - 0.6209} = 0.2637$
FUTURE WORTH OF 1	FUTURE WORTH OF 1 PER PERIOD	SINKING FUND FACTOR	PRESENT WORTH OF 1	PRESENT WORTH OF 1 PER PERIOD	PERIODIC REPAYMENT
Referred to as the future worth of $1, amount of $1, growth of $1, how $1 left at compound interest will grow, the future worth of $1 with interest, and the compound amount of $1.	Referred to as the amount of 1 per period, how $1 deposited periodically will grow, growth of $1 per period, the future worth of $1 per period with interest, the future worth of 1, and the future worth of an annuity of 1.	Referred to as the amortization rate – sinking fund, and as the periodic deposit that will grow to $1 at a future date.	Referred to as the present worth of 1, what $1 due in the future is worth today, the present value of a reversion of 1, and the reversion factor.	Referred to as the present worth of $1 per period, what $1 payable periodically is worth today, the present worth of an annuity of 1, present worth of $1 per annum, and the Inwood Coefficient.	Referred to as the periodic repayment (partial payment), installed to amortize $1, and as an ordinary annuity which has a present value of $1.
FUNCTION	FUNCTION	FUNCTION	FUNCTION	FUNCTION	FUNCTION
Indicates growth at compound interest of a single initial deposit or investment. Deposits are made at the beginning of the period.	Indicates growth at compound interest of level series of periodic deposits. Includes principal and interest. Deposits are made at the end of the period.	Indicates the amount of periodic deposit required which will grow at compound interest to a specified future amount. Deposits are made at the end of the period.	Inndicates the present value of a single future income payment. Used in estimating the value of a reversionary interest.	Indicates the present value of a series of future income payments. Used in estimating cash equivalents. Deposits are made at the end of the period.	Indicates the amount of periodic payment required to amortize a loan. It is used primarily in the mortgage equity appraisal technique. Used to determine what payments are necessary to amortize a loan. Has application in estimating cash equivalents.

10.6 NET PRESENT VALUE (NPV)

Manipulate the Net Present Value to calculate and analyze other financial factors.

The Net Present Value (NPV) is the total PV of all future cash inflows and outflows, discounted at the investor's required rate of return. Generally, it is used to evaluate the project's cash flows, not the income such as the one shown on an income tax statement, which takes into account building depreciation (Capital Cost Allowance (CCA)).

The amount in current dollars that is equivalent to an amount to be received later is called the "Present Value (PV)" of that future amount. Present dollars and future dollars are equated by using a rate of interest. Thus, the PV of $1.00 can be thought of as the amount that must be invested now in order to accumulate $1.00 at the end of a certain number of years, at a given rate of interest. To calculate it is a three-step process.

Figure 10.2
Present Value of $1 Per Year (Present Value of Annuity of $1)

year	2%	3%	4%	5%	6%	7%	8%	9%	10%	12%
1	0.9804	0.9709	0.9615	0.9524	0.9434	0.9346	0.9259	0.9174	0.9091	0.8929
2	0.9612	0.9426	0.9246	0.907	0.89	0.8734	0.8573	0.8417	0.8264	0.7972
3	0.9423	0.9151	0.889	0.8638	0.8396	0.8163	0.7938	0.7722	0.7513	0.7118
4	0.9238	0.8885	0.8548	0.8227	0.7921	0.7629	0.735	0.7084	0.683	0.6355
5	0.9057	0.8626	0.8219	0.7835	0.7473	0.713	0.6806	0.6499	0.6209	0.5674
6	0.888	0.8375	0.7903	0.7462	0.705	0.6663	0.6302	0.5963	0.5645	0.5066
7	0.8706	0.8131	0.7599	0.7107	0.6651	0.6227	0.5835	0.547	0.5132	0.4523
8	0.8535	0.7894	0.7307	0.6768	0.6274	0.582	0.5403	0.5019	0.4665	0.4039
9	0.8368	0.7664	0.7026	0.6446	0.5919	0.5439	0.5002	0.4604	0.4241	0.3606
10	0.8203	0.7441	0.6756	0.6139	0.5584	0.5083	0.4632	0.4224	0.3855	0.322
11	0.8043	0.7224	0.6496	0.5847	0.5268	0.4751	0.4289	0.3875	0.3505	0.2875
12	0.7885	0.7014	0.6246	0.5568	0.497	0.444	0.3971	0.3555	0.3186	0.2567
13	0.773	0.681	0.6006	0.5303	0.4688	0.415	0.3677	0.3262	0.2897	0.2292
14	0.7579	0.6611	0.5775	0.5051	0.4423	0.3878	0.3405	0.2992	0.2633	0.2046
15	0.743	0.6419	0.5553	0.481	0.4173	0.3624	0.3152	0.2745	0.2394	0.1827
16	0.7284	0.6232	0.5339	0.4581	0.3936	0.3387	0.2919	0.2519	0.2176	0.1631
17	0.7142	0.605	0.5134	0.4363	0.3714	0.3166	0.2703	0.2311	0.1978	0.1456
18	0.7002	0.5874	0.4936	0.4155	0.3503	0.2959	0.2502	0.212	0.1799	0.13
19	0.6864	0.5703	0.4746	0.3957	0.3305	0.2765	0.2317	0.1945	0.1635	0.1161
20	0.673	0.5537	0.4564	0.3769	0.3118	0.2584	0.2145	0.1784	0.1486	0.1037
21	0.6598	0.5375	0.4388	0.3589	0.2942	0.2415	0.1987	0.1637	0.1351	0.0926
22	0.6468	0.5219	0.422	0.3418	0.2775	0.2257	0.1839	0.1502	0.1228	0.0826
23	0.6342	0.5067	0.4057	0.3256	0.2618	0.2109	0.1703	0.1378	0.1117	0.0738
24	0.6217	0.4919	0.3901	0.3101	0.247	0.1971	0.1577	0.1264	0.1015	0.0659
25	0.6095	0.4776	0.3751	0.2953	0.233	0.1842	0.146	0.116	0.0923	0.0588
26	0.5976	0.4637	0.3607	0.2812	0.2198	0.1722	0.1352	0.1064	0.0839	0.0525
27	0.5859	0.4502	0.3468	0.2678	0.2074	0.1609	0.1252	0.0976	0.0763	0.0469
28	0.5744	0.4371	0.3335	0.2551	0.1956	0.1504	0.1159	0.0895	0.0693	0.0419
29	0.5631	0.4243	0.3207	0.2429	0.1846	0.1406	0.1073	0.0822	0.063	0.0374
30	0.5521	0.412	0.3083	0.2314	0.1741	0.1314	0.0994	0.0754	0.0573	0.0334
31	0.5412	0.4	0.2965	0.2204	0.1643	0.1228	0.092	0.0691	0.0521	0.0298
32	0.5306	0.3883	0.2851	0.2099	0.155	0.1147	0.0852	0.0634	0.0474	0.0266
33	0.5202	0.377	0.2741	0.1999	0.1462	0.1072	0.0789	0.0582	0.0431	0.0238
34	0.51	0.366	0.2636	0.1904	0.1379	0.1002	0.073	0.0534	0.0391	0.0212
35	0.5	0.3554	0.2534	0.1813	0.1301	0.0937	0.0676	0.049	0.0356	0.0189
36	0.4902	0.345	0.2437	0.1727	0.1227	0.0875	0.0626	0.0449	0.0323	0.0169
37	0.4806	0.335	0.2343	0.1644	0.1158	0.0818	0.058	0.0412	0.0294	0.0151
38	0.4712	0.3252	0.2253	0.1566	0.1092	0.0765	0.0537	0.0378	0.0267	0.0135
39	0.4619	0.3158	0.2166	0.1491	0.1031	0.0715	0.0497	0.0347	0.0243	0.012
40	0.4529	0.3066	0.2083	0.142	0.0972	0.0668	0.046	0.0318	0.0221	0.0107

Figure 10.3
Compound Amount (Future Value) of $1

year	2%	3%	4%	5%	6%	7%	8%	9%	10%	12%
1	1.02	1.03	1.04	1.05	1.06	1.07	1.08	1.09	1.1	1.12
2	2.0604	2.0909	2.1216	2.1525	2.1836	2.2149	2.2464	2.2781	2.31	2.3744
3	3.1216	3.1836	3.2465	3.3101	3.3746	3.4399	3.5061	3.5731	3.641	3.7793
4	4.204	4.3091	4.4163	4.5256	4.6371	4.7507	4.8666	4.9847	5.1051	5.3528
5	5.3081	5.4684	5.633	5.8019	5.9753	6.1533	6.3359	6.5233	6.7156	7.1152
6	6.4343	6.6625	6.8983	7.142	7.3938	7.654	7.9228	8.2004	8.4872	9.089
7	7.583	7.8923	8.2142	8.5491	8.8975	9.2598	9.6366	10.0285	10.4359	11.2997
8	8.7546	9.1591	9.5828	10.0266	10.4913	10.978	11.4876	12.021	12.5795	13.7757
9	9.9497	10.4639	11.0061	11.5779	12.1808	12.8164	13.4866	14.1929	14.9374	16.5487
10	11.1687	11.8078	12.4864	13.2068	13.9716	14.7836	15.6455	16.5603	17.5312	19.6546
11	12.4121	13.192	14.0258	14.9171	15.8699	16.8885	17.9771	19.1407	20.3843	23.1331
12	13.6803	14.6178	15.6268	16.713	17.8821	19.1406	20.4953	21.9534	23.5227	27.0291
13	14.9739	16.0863	17.2919	18.5986	20.0151	21.5505	23.2149	25.0192	26.975	31.3926
14	16.2934	17.5989	19.0236	20.5786	22.276	24.129	26.1521	28.3609	30.7725	36.2797
15	17.6393	19.1569	20.8245	22.6575	24.6725	26.8881	29.3243	32.0034	34.9497	41.7533
16	19.0121	20.7616	22.6975	24.8404	27.2129	29.8402	32.7502	35.9737	39.5447	47.8837
17	20.4123	22.4144	24.6454	27.1324	29.9057	32.999	36.4502	40.3013	44.5992	54.7497
18	21.8406	24.1169	26.6712	29.539	32.76	36.379	40.4463	45.0185	50.1591	62.4397
19	23.2974	25.8704	28.7781	32.066	35.7856	39.9955	44.762	50.1601	56.275	71.0524
20	24.7833	27.6765	30.9692	34.7193	38.9927	43.8652	49.4229	55.7645	63.0025	80.6987
21	26.299	29.5368	33.248	37.5052	42.3923	48.0057	54.4568	61.8733	70.4027	91.5026
22	27.845	31.4529	35.6179	40.4305	45.9958	52.4361	59.8933	68.5319	78.543	103.6029
23	29.4219	33.4265	38.0826	43.502	49.8156	57.1767	65.7648	75.7898	87.4973	117.1552
24	31.0303	35.4593	40.6459	46.7271	53.8645	62.249	72.1059	83.7009	97.3471	132.3339
25	32.6709	37.553	43.3117	50.1135	58.1564	67.6765	78.9544	92.324	108.1818	149.3339
26	34.3443	39.7096	46.0842	53.6691	62.7058	73.4838	86.3508	101.7231	120.0999	168.374
27	36.0512	41.9309	48.9676	57.4026	67.5281	79.6977	94.3388	111.9682	133.2099	189.6989
28	37.7922	44.2189	51.9663	61.3227	72.6398	86.3465	102.9659	123.1354	147.6309	213.5828
29	39.5681	46.5754	55.0849	65.4388	78.0582	93.4608	112.2832	135.3075	163.494	240.3327
30	41.3794	49.0027	58.3283	69.7608	83.8017	101.073	122.3459	148.5752	180.9434	270.2926
31	43.227	51.5028	61.7015	74.2988	89.8898	109.2182	133.2135	163.037	200.1378	303.8477
32	45.1116	54.0778	65.2095	79.0638	96.3432	117.9334	144.9506	178.8003	221.2515	341.4294
33	47.0338	56.7302	68.8579	84.067	103.1838	127.2588	157.6267	195.9823	244.4767	383.521
34	48.9945	59.4621	72.6522	89.3203	110.4348	137.2369	171.3168	214.7108	270.0244	430.6635
35	50.9944	62.2759	76.5983	94.8363	118.1209	147.9135	186.1021	235.1247	298.1268	483.4631
36	53.0343	65.1742	80.7022	100.6281	126.2681	159.3374	202.0703	257.3759	329.0395	542.5987
37	55.1149	68.1594	84.9703	106.7095	134.9042	171.561	219.3159	281.6298	363.0434	608.8305
38	57.2372	71.2342	89.4091	113.095	144.0585	184.6403	237.9412	308.0665	400.4478	683.0102
39	59.402	74.4013	94.0255	119.7998	153.762	198.6351	258.0565	336.8824	441.5926	766.0914
40	61.61	77.6633	98.8265	126.8398	164.0477	213.6096	279.781	368.2919	486.8518	859.1424

1. Discount all of the future cash flows at the investor's required rate of return (DR) to determine their total PV.
2. From the above result subtract the initial cost of the investment to determine the NPV.
3. If the NPV is positive, the investment exceeds his required rate of return. If the NPV is negative (if the present worth of future benefits is less than the present cost), the investment falls short of the investor's criteria, assuming, of course, that there are no extraneous factors affecting the results.

Commonly, anyone buying an income-producing property does so because he is interested in future income. NPV is one of the most popular methods used by sophisticated investors to evaluate investments. A buyer who discounts the expected earnings to arrive at his NPV decides how much the property is worth to him and to him only, because one of the key factors in the approach will be his choice of the DR. Indeed, one buyer may think that a particular property deserves a Cap Rate of 7%, while another will think 8% is more appropriate. The difference, as previously shown, is enormous. As you can see, the valuator has to make assumptions, including the projections of earnings, and these projections could be very different from those made by another person.

NPV gives a PV to future cash outlays and income receipts, which take place over different time periods. In other words, the PV of each cash inflow is added together and the PV of each cash outflow is subtracted from the total PV of cash inflows. If the result is zero or positive, the project should be retained but if the result is negative, it should be rejected. The NPV shows the hypothetical increase or decrease in wealth at the time of investing, which will occur if cash flows play out as forecasted.

Figure 10.4 provides an example that compares two investments of $10,000 each.

Figure 10.4
Present Value Comparison

Year	Cash Flow	Investment A Disc. Factor @ 10% See Figure 10.3	Present Value	Cash Flow	Investment B Disc. Factor @ 10% See Figure 10.3	Present Value
0	-$10,000	1	-$10,000	-$10,000	1	-$10,000
1	5,000	0.909	4,545	1,500	0.909	1,364
2	5,000	0.826	4,130	2,000	0.826	1,652
3	2,000	0.751	1,502	2,500	0.751	1,878
4	0	0.683	-	5,000	0.683	3,415
5	-	0.621	-	5,000	0.621	3,105
NPV @ 10% Discount Rate			$177			$1,414

If the amount to be invested differs considerably from one project to another, the best project may not be the one with the highest NPV. (Note: most academics will not agree with that statement. They consider the NPV technique as the best one to maximize investors' wealth.) The rate of the return on investment should also be considered. As a consequence, analysts generally calculate not only the NPV but also the rate of return that makes the NPV equal to zero. This rate is called the Internal Rate of Return (IRR). See section 10.6.1(b), below.

The IRR is the compound average annual rate of return estimated for a project. The appeal of the IRR method is that rates of return are more intuitive than NPVs. Investors can compare an IRR to other rates of return on other investments.

To be able to calculate NPV and IRR we will, again, define a few terms.

1. **Present Value (PV)** is either the receipt or expenditure of a sum today or the present worth of future benefits (cash flows) discounted at an arbitrarily chosen (some say "appropriate") DR.
2. **Discount Rate (DR)** is the rate used to calculate the PV of cash flows. Theoretically, the initial DR is the rate of return required by the investor. Practically, it is the best rate the investor is able to find within his property acquisition parameters.

10.6.1 DISCOUNTED CASH FLOW ANALYSIS (DCFA)

Sometimes the discounted cash flow methods are used to determine the value of a property (NPV and IRR are discounted cash flow methods). In general, it is a useful tool in the valuation of large investment properties such as office buildings and multi-tenant industrial buildings. It allows investors to consider the impact of different tenants paying different rents for different periods of time. In reports, the analysis incorporates various parameters, including a growth rate to be applied to rents and estimated operating costs, a capitalization rate to be applied to the income at the end of the investment term (reversionary capitalization rate), and the DR/Internal Rate of Return. As mentioned earlier, these parameters are obtained primarily through investment surveys and by looking at comparable sales.

The DCFA process consists of three steps.

1. Add the discounted cash flow, after tax, for each of the years one considers owning the property, to the expected value of the property after the same number of years.
2. Compare the sum to the purchase price.
3. Use the rate shown on the table of Present Value in Figure 10.1 to determine the PV.

An example puts the DCFA process into practice.

DCFA Example

Assumptions

Asking price: $800,000

NOI: Year 1: $40,000; Year 2: $42,000; Year 3: $44,000; Year 4: $46,000; Year 5: $48,000

Value of property after 5 years: $1,000,000

Required rate of return: 10%

Number of years	After-Tax Cash Flow	Present Value of $1 at 10% Cash Flow	Present Value of After-Tax Cash Flow
1	$40,000	0.909	$36,360
2	$42,000	0.826	$34,692
3	$44,000	0.751	$33,044
4	$46,000	0.683	$31,418
5	$46,000	0.621	$28,566
Sale Price at Year 5: $1,000,000		0.621	$621,000
Present value of property:			$785,080

There is a difference between the asking price and the PV of the property of: $800,000 - $785,080 = $14,920. A buyer can probably negotiate such a discount on the asking price. It is only 1.87% and, commonly, discounts on the asking price of an Income-Producing Property (IPP) run between 2-10%. If the vendor is firm on his asking price, the buyer will have to walk away or accept a lower return.

"Discounting" (you take away) is the opposite of "compounding" (you add).

As you can see, this is a good method of evaluating a property, but it has a glaring weakness — the selection of the DR. "Discounting" (you take away) is the opposite of "compounding" (you add).

(a) Selecting a Discounted Cash Flow Rate

Discounting consists of converting future amounts into their PV by choosing an appropriate DR. Input all income and expenses, including an assumed sale price (reversion) for a given period. It is generally done before tax.

One school of thought contends that the rate selection can be made by using Comparison of Quality Attributes. It allows each person to analyze returns differently, weighing various components according to one's desires, opinions, and analysis of the property. For example (rates have been arbitrarily selected):

Reliability of income prediction	15%
Reliability of expense prediction	10%
Likelihood of competitive construction	15%
Saleability of property	15%
Expense to income ratio	20%
Stability of value of property	15%
Burden of Management	10%
Total	100%

Using these components, a quality rating or weighting of the rates found in the market, brings the true rate into line. It is obvious that there is no standard interest rate for capitalization of income. Each property or investor has its own rate depending on the particular risk inherent in it. Rates may vary from time to time for the same property.

In fact, the DR is made up of four components (the percentages are arbitrary):

Safe Rate (e.g., Treasury Bills)	5.5%
Risk (re: property and market place)	3%
Lack of liquidity (difficulty of selling)	1%
Management (of money and assets)	0.5%
Discount Rate	10%

Note that the aforementioned percentages will vary from investor to investor, from time to time, and from property to property. For example, management demands are drastically different for an industrial building net leased for 10 years to a single tenant and a multi-family property, of the same value that has 15 tenants.

The risk rate will vary depending on the way the investor perceives the risk to himself. Other factors affecting risk in real estate may be:
- LTV ratio
- financial strength of tenants
- amortization period (the cash flow may be tight for a 10-year amortization period, which is unusually short), or
- construction of an addition to the building.

(b) Internal Rate of Return (IRR)

Technically speaking, the IRR is a DR at which the before-tax net PV of both an investment and the returns on this investment are equal. The IRR represents the relationship between the income earned and expenses incurred during a specific time period and the purchase price and the proceeds of the sale when the property is sold. The IRR is somewhat useful in the valuation of single- or multi-tenant properties where there is no variation in the net income from year to year.

It is the DR at which the PV of future cash flows and the sales proceeds (also considered cash flows) are exactly equal to the initial capital invested or at which the PV of cash flows equals zero. In capital budgeting, it is called the "hurdle rate". It concerns itself only with revenues and expenses and assumes that the project's cash flows are reinvested at x%. Funds are borrowed at the same rate, in case of losses. The higher the IRR is, the more attractive the project becomes.

In theory, a property requires one initial outlay, which is the purchase price (negative cash flow), and generates a number of positive cash flows (such as rentals) over the term of the investment, plus the sale value. Hence, there is only one change in cash flows from negative to positive. However, this theory is upset if, for example, you unexpectedly have to replace the roof of your building after 5 years or have a serious fire or tax laws change, turning the results of that year into a negative cash flow. Or, suppose you have to replace the asphalt of the parking lot in year 7, again generating a negative cash flow year. In these cases the IRR results generated could be gently called "doubtful".

This scenario can cause multiple IRRs. The Modified Internal Rate of Return (MIRR) (see 10.6.1(d)) eliminates the possibility of multiple IRRs and allows the investor to choose a more realistic reinvestment rate — good reasons to use MIRR instead of IRR.

The IRR is a screening tool, but it is far from perfect. Its main problem lies with the subjective assumptions that must be made regarding reinvestment (or borrowing) rates. One person may choose 6% and another may choose 8%. Academics would say that the assumption implied in the IRR model is that cash flows are being reinvested over the project's remaining life at the same rate as the calculated IRR. This assumption is one of the weaknesses of the model. These assumptions can outweigh the mathematical calculations. This is also true of other DCF models (NPV and MIRR). It also depends on the assumed selling price (usually many years down the road), which is virtually always different from the asking price and from the price a financial analyst used for his projections. Furthermore, it can lead to ambiguities if one has to deal with positive and negative cash flows, particularly if the negative cash flows exceed the value of the initial investment. MIRRs can result. Indeed, the analyst must decide today which rate of interest he will obtain when he reinvests excess income over the next 240 months (assuming a 20-year period of ownership) for each month, and what the sale price of the property will be in 20 years. It seems that a crystal ball would be useful, too.

Still thinking that we exaggerate? In another vein, Figure 10.5 contains an article from the *McKinsey on Finance* newsletter, published by the prestigious firm of McKinsey & Company (85 offices in 47 countries).

Figure 10.5
IRR Article from the McKinsey on Finance Newsletter

16 | **McKinsey on Finance** | Summer 2004

Internal rate of return: A cautionary tale

Tempted by a project with a high internal rate of return? Better check those interim cash flows again.

John C. Kelleher and Justin J. MacCormack

Maybe finance managers just enjoy living on the edge. What else would explain their weakness for using the internal rate of return (IRR) to assess capital projects? For decades, finance textbooks and academics have warned that typical IRR calculations build in reinvestment assumptions that make bad projects look better and good ones look great. Yet as recently as 1999, academic research found that three-quarters of CFOs always or almost always use IRR when evaluating capital projects.[1]

Our own research underlined this proclivity to risky behavior. In an informal survey of 30 executives at corporations, hedge funds, and venture capital firms, we found only 6 who were fully aware of IRR's most critical deficiencies. Our next surprise came when we reanalyzed some two dozen actual investments that one company made on the basis of attractive internal rates of return. If the IRR calculated to justify these investment decisions had been corrected for the measure's natural flaws, management's prioritization of its projects, as well as its view of their overall attractiveness, would have changed considerably.

So why do finance pros continue to do what they know they shouldn't? IRR does have its allure, offering what seems to be a straightforward comparison of, say, the 30 percent annual return of a specific project with the 8 or 18 percent rate that most people pay on their car loans or credit cards. That ease of comparison seems to outweigh what most managers view as largely technical deficiencies that create immaterial distortions in relatively isolated circumstances.

Admittedly, some of the measure's deficiencies are technical, even arcane,[2] but the most dangerous problems with IRR are neither isolated nor immaterial, and they can have serious implications for capital budget managers. When managers decide to finance only the projects with the highest IRRs, they may be looking at the most distorted calculations—and thereby destroying shareholder value by selecting the wrong projects altogether. Companies also risk creating unrealistic expectations for themselves and for shareholders, potentially confusing investor communications and inflating managerial rewards.

We believe that managers must either avoid using IRR entirely or at least make adjustments for the measure's most dangerous assumption: that interim cash flows will be reinvested at the same high rates of return.

The trouble with IRR

Practitioners often interpret internal rate of return as the annual equivalent return on a given investment; this easy analogy is the source of its intuitive appeal. But in fact, IRR is a true indication of a project's annual return on investment only when the project generates no interim cash flows—or

EXHIBIT 1

Identical IRRs, but very different annual returns

Internal-rate-of-return (IRR) values are identical for 2 projects ...

Project A							IRR
Year	0	1	2	3	4	5	
Cash flows, $ million	−10	5	5	5	5	5	**41%**

Project B							IRR
Year	0	1	2	3	4	5	
Cash flows, $ million	−10	5	5	5	5	5	**41%**

... however, interim cash flows are reinvested at different rates

Key assumption: reinvestment rate = IRR

Project A							CAGR[1]
Year	0	1	2	3	4	5	
Value of cash flows at year 5 if reinvested at 41%		5 → 20					41%
			5 → 14				41%
				5 → 10			41%
					5 → 7		41%
						5	

Key assumption: reinvestment rate = cost of capital

Project B							CAGR[1]
Year	0	1	2	3	4	5	
Value of cash flows at year 5 if reinvested at 8%		5 → 7					8%
			5 → 6				8%
				5 → 6			8%
					5 → 5		8%
						5	

Year 5 value of $10 million investment = **$56 million** 41% CAGR[1]

Year 5 value of $10 million investment = **$29 million** 24% CAGR[1]

True return is nearly 50% less because of lower reinvestment rate

[1] Compound annual growth rate.

when those interim cash flows really can be invested at the actual IRR.

When the calculated IRR is higher than the true reinvestment rate for interim cash flows, the measure will overestimate—sometimes very significantly—the annual equivalent return from the project. The formula assumes that the company has additional projects, with equally attractive prospects, in which to invest the interim cash flows. In this case, the calculation implicitly takes credit for these additional projects. Calculations of net present value (NPV), by contrast, generally assume only that a company can earn its cost of capital on interim cash flows, leaving any future incremental project value with those future projects.

IRR's assumptions about reinvestment can lead to major capital budget distortions.

Consider a hypothetical assessment of two different, mutually exclusive projects, A and B, with identical cash flows, risk levels, and durations—as well as identical IRR values of 41 percent. Using IRR as the decision yardstick, an executive would feel confidence in being indifferent toward choosing between the two projects. However, it would be a mistake to select either project without examining the relevant reinvestment rate for interim cash flows. Suppose that Project B's interim cash flows could be redeployed only at a typical 8 percent cost of capital, while Project A's cash flows could be invested in an attractive follow-on project expected to generate a 41 percent annual return. In that case, Project A is unambiguously preferable.

Even if the interim cash flows really could be reinvested at the IRR, very few practitioners would argue that the value of future investments should be commingled with the value of the project being evaluated. Most practitioners would agree that a company's cost of capital—by definition, the return available elsewhere to its shareholders on a similarly risky investment—is a clearer and more logical rate to assume for reinvestments of interim project cash flows (Exhibit 1).

When the cost of capital is used, a project's true annual equivalent yield can fall significantly—again, especially so with projects that posted high initial IRRs. Of course, when executives review projects with IRRs that are close to a company's cost of capital, the IRR is less distorted by the reinvestment-rate assumption. But when they evaluate projects that claim IRRs of 10 percent or more above their company's cost of capital, these may well be significantly distorted. Ironically, unadjusted IRRs are particularly treacherous because the reinvestment-rate distortion is most egregious precisely when managers tend to think their projects are most attractive. And since this amplification is not felt evenly across all projects,[3] managers can't simply correct for it by adjusting every IRR by a standard amount.

How large is the potential impact of a flawed reinvestment-rate assumption? Managers at one large industrial company approved 23 major capital projects over five years on the basis of IRRs that averaged 77 percent. Recently, however, when we conducted an analysis with the reinvestment rate adjusted to the company's cost of capital, the true average return fell to just 16 percent. The order of the most attractive projects also changed considerably. The top-ranked project based on IRR dropped to

the tenth-most-attractive project. Most striking, the company's highest-rated projects—showing IRRs of 800, 150, and 130 percent—dropped to just 15, 23, and 22 percent, respectively, once a realistic reinvestment rate was considered (Exhibit 2). Unfortunately, these investment decisions had already been made. Of course, IRRs this extreme are somewhat unusual. Yet even if a project's IRR drops from 25 percent to 15 percent, the impact is considerable.

What to do?
The most straightforward way to avoid problems with IRR is to avoid it altogether. Yet given its widespread use, it is unlikely to be replaced easily. Executives should at the very least use a modified internal rate of return. While not perfect, MIRR at least allows users to set more realistic interim reinvestment rates and therefore to calculate a true annual equivalent yield. Even then, we recommend that all executives who review projects claiming an attractive IRR should ask the following two questions.

1. *What are the assumed interim-reinvestment rates?* In the vast majority of cases, an assumption that interim flows can be reinvested at high rates is at best overoptimistic and at worst flat wrong. Particularly when sponsors sell their projects as "unique" or "the opportunity of a lifetime," another opportunity of similar attractiveness probably does not exist; thus interim flows won't be reinvested at sufficiently high rates. For this reason, the best assumption—and one used by a proper discounted cash-flow analysis—is that interim flows can be reinvested at the company's cost of capital.

2. *Are interim cash flows biased toward the start or the end of the project?* Unless

EXHIBIT 2

A rude surprise

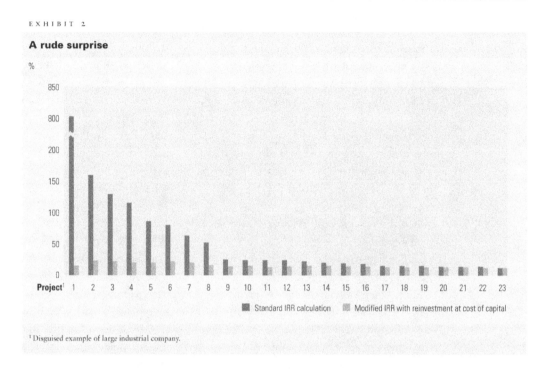

%

850

800

200

150

100

50

0

Project[1] 1 2 3 4 5 6 7 8 9 10 11 12 13 14 15 16 17 18 19 20 21 22 23

◼ Standard IRR calculation   ▪ Modified IRR with reinvestment at cost of capital

[1] Disguised example of large industrial company.

the interim reinvestment rate is correct (in other words, a true reinvestment rate rather than the calculated IRR), the IRR distortion will be greater when interim cash flows occur sooner. This concept may seem counterintuitive, since typically we would prefer to have cash sooner rather than later. The simple reason for the problem is that the gap between the actual reinvestment rate and the assumed IRR exists for a longer period of time, so the impact of the distortion accumulates.[4]

Despite flaws that can lead to poor investment decisions, IRR will likely continue to be used widely during capital-budgeting discussions because of its strong intuitive appeal. Executives should at least cast a skeptical eye at IRR measures before making investment decisions. **MoF**

The authors wish to thank Rob McNish for his assistance in developing this article.

John Kelleher (John_Kelleher@McKinsey.com) and **Justin MacCormack** (Justin_MacCormack@McKinsey.com) *are consultants in McKinsey's Toronto office.*

[1] John Robert Graham and Campbell R. Harvey, "The theory and practice of corporate finance: Evidence from the field," Duke University working paper presented at the 2001 annual meeting of the American Finance Association, New Orleans (available at http://ssrn.com/abstract=220251).

[2] As a result of an arcane mathematical problem, IRR can generate two very different values for the same project when future cash flows switch from negative to positive (or positive to negative). Also, since IRR is expressed as a percentage, it can make small projects appear more attractive than large ones, even though large projects with lower IRRs can be more attractive on an NPV basis than smaller projects with higher IRRs.

[3] The amplification effect grows as a project's fundamental health improves, as measured by NPV, and it varies depending on the unique timing of a project's cash flows.

[4] Interestingly, given two projects with identical IRRs, a project with a single "bullet" cash flow at the end of the investment period would be preferable to a project with interim cash flows. The reason: a lack of interim cash flows completely immunizes a project from the reinvestment-rate risk.

(c) Calculating the IRR

To reiterate, the IRR is the DR that makes the present worth of the future cash flows equal to the present cost. By comparing the numbers generated by each property, the investor should select the one that best matches his criteria.

Example

An investment, represented by a real property, bought today for $150,000 at a 12% return (net income of $18,000) will be worth, 1 year later: $150,000 + $18,000 = $168,000, assuming that the $18,000 is received 365 days after purchase.

$168,000, discounted at 12%, has a PV of $150,000.

Therefore, we have a PV of the future cash flow: $150,000

Less the cost of the initial investment: $150,000

NPV equals $0

Therefore, the IRR is equal to the DR of 12%.

Calculating the IRR "by hand" is a process marked by tedious repetitions. One starts by discounting the cash flows to their PV by using a trial rate, which the books will tell you is the "required" rate of return of the investor. The process uses different DRs, but this is done to find the IRR, which is the DR that causes the PV of cash flows to equal the initial investment.

If you hit too high, or too low, continue to try rates until you find an NPV of zero by using a rate that makes the PV of the cash flows equal to the cost of the property.

Here is an explanation of IRR from The National Center for Environmental Decision-Making Research:[1]

Internal Rate of Return. It is often difficult to determine the rate at which future benefits should be discounted to today's dollars. In addition, decision makers are often more comfortable with value expressed in percentage terms rather than some other metric. The internal rate of return (IRR) is a method for determining value that does not depend on the determination of a discount rate and that expresses value in terms of a percentage. Essentially, the method requires the calculation of a discount rate such that the discounted value of future cost-benefit flows exactly equal the initial investment. In other words, the present value of costs minus the present value of benefits equals zero. Let's look at these projects C and D.

| | | Project C | | Project D |
Year	Net Benefit	Discounted Cost-Benefit Flow	Net Benefit	Discounted Cost-Benefit Flow
0	-$10,000	-$10,000	-$10,000	-$10,000
1	$5,000	$4,545	$1,000	$909
2	$5,000	$4,132	$1,000	$826
3	$5,000	$3,757	$1,000	$751
4	$5,000	$3,415	$20,000	$13,660
Net Present Value		$5,849		$6,146

1. The National Center for Environmental Decision-Making Research at <www.sunsite.utk.edu>.

To calculate the IRR it is necessary to find the discount rate that would equate the initial investment with the future cost-benefit flows. This can be expressed mathematically as:

$$\$10{,}000 = \$5000 \left(\frac{1}{1+r}\right)^1 + \$5000 \left(\frac{1}{1+r}\right)^2 + \$5000 \left(\frac{1}{1+r}\right)^3 + \$5000 \left(\frac{1}{1+r}\right)^4$$

This calculation requires a financial calculator, computer, or trial and error. The answer is slightly greater than 35%. To determine whether or not project C is a winner, the calculated IRR must be compared to a minimum acceptable rate of return that should reflect the time value of money, risk, etc. The minimum acceptable rate of return is referred to as the hurdle rate. The decision to accept or reject project C depends upon whether or not the IRR exceeds the hurdle rate.

IRR is based on the assumption that the cost-benefit flows are reinvested at the internal rate of return. If we are examining projects that are mutually exclusive, IRR may yield results that are inconsistent with a ranking based on the NPV method. For example, if we calculate the IRR of project D, we find it to be roughly 25%. Given this result, we would choose C over D. ... One should note the effect of the timing of the cost-benefit flows on the IRR calculation. Any project that has relatively large positive cost-benefit flows early in its life will generate a relatively large IRR.

Finally, the use of IRR as a measure for choosing between projects is inappropriate when capital rationing exists. This problem is again due to the assumption that the cost-benefit flows are reinvested at the internal rate of return rather than at the cost of capital as in NPV. What this implies for the decision maker is that the ranking of projects will depend as much on their relative size and the timing of their cost-benefit flows as it will on the actual cost-benefit flows, where the actual flows should be the only determinant of acceptance or rejection.

(d) The Modified Internal Rate of Return (MIRR)

It is the imperfection of the IRR that led investors to come up with the MIRR. With this approach, one arbitrarily sets aside a virtual reserve, a certain amount of money that can be easily accessed to compensate for negative cash flows, if need be, such as cash held in a Money Market Account or Treasury bills. The usually positive cash flows are considered reinvested at a risk rate that is similar to one that is generated by similar investments.

The MIRR is a little better than the IRR to accurately predict returns. It should be used if more than one negative-to-positive cash flow change takes place. The MIRR produces two cash flows — all of the positive ones and all of the negative ones. The latter are discounted to PV by using a safe rate, and then added to the initial investment. The positive cash flows are compounded to Future Value, at the end of ownership, using a reinvestment rate chosen by the investor. This rate reflects a rate of return that the investor assumes cash flows can earn over the life of the project.

Note that your selection of valuation tools should take into account their suitability for your purpose. For example, the IRR may suit an investor buying for cash flow but will not suit one who is looking for faster and higher returns, based on selling the property quickly after improving it and taking advantage of appreciation. In this case, through his work and talent, the investor has created added value that was not present at purchasing date that markedly will impact the sale value.

(e) Calculating the MIRR

To arrive at the PV of future negative cash flow, one discounts them at the safe rate (e.g., 90-day Treasury Bills). This determines the amount that must be set aside to meet these cash outlays. The future value of the positive cash flows is then calculated at the risk rate to the end of the investment term. All cash flows are then reduced to one negative cash flow at time zero and one positive cash flow at the project termination date. The IRR of these two cash flows is then computed.

The excerpt below should provide further enlightenment.[2]

MIRR - Example Problem & Solution

To calculate the MIRR, ... the cash flow for any year t given in the table below is multiplied by the value of the $FVIF6.365,20-t =(1.06365)20-t$ factor given for year t to obtain the value of the cash flow at the end of year 20 assuming that it is reinvested for 20-t years at the cost of capital 6.365%. The resultant values of the cash flows at the end of the investment's life (shown in the rows labeled "FV-CASH FLOWS" and "FV-CF") are summed over all years 1 to 20 to obtain the total future value of the reinvested cash flows.

Year	0	1	2	3	4	5	6	7	8	9	10
Cash Flow	-6000	1259	1309	1362	1417	1473	1533	1594	1658	1725	1794
FVIF	-	3.23	3.037	2.855	2.684	2.523	2.372	2.23	2.097	1.971	1.853
FV-Cash Flow	-	4065	3976	3888	3802	3718	3636	3556	3477	3400	3325
	11	12	13	14	15	16	17	18	19	20	
	1866	1941	2019	2100	2184	2271	2362	2457	2555	2657	
	1.743	1.638	1.54	1.448	1.361	1.28	1.203	1.131	1.064	1	
	3252	3180	3109	3040	2973	2907	2843	2780	2718	2657	

That sum is $66301. The MIRR is the interest rate which equates the present value of $66301 to the initial investment of $6000 and is determined by calculating MIRR = $(66301/6000)^{(1/20)}$ = 12.76%.

Determining the Interest Factors

The values of the interest factors $PVIF_{k,n}$, $PVIFA_{k,n}$, and $FVIF_{k,n}$ used in the equations for NPV, IRR, and MIRR may be determined in a number of ways:

1. They may be calculated directly from the formulas for the interest factors given above.
2. They may be found in interest tables at the back of any text on financial management or engineering economy or in the CRC Handbook.
3. They may be computed using a financial calculator.
4. They may be determined from a spreadsheet program. In Lotus the function @PV(payment, interest, term) calculates the present value of an annuity (a sequence of uniform annual cash flows), @NPV(interest, range) determines the present value of series of non-uniform cash flows located in the given range, and @IRR(guess, range) calculates the internal rate of return on an investment whose cash flows (including the initial cost as a negative cash flow) are found in the given range. The function argument "guess" is an initial interest rate (expressed as a decimal fraction) used by the program to begin the iterations to solve for IRR.

2. Douglas Woods, *Handbook for IQP Advisors and Students* (Worcester Polytechnic Institute: 2004), chapter 12. Reprinted with permission Worcester Polytechnic Institute, Worcester, MA, USA.

Future Net Cash Flows

All of the steps required to conduct a cost/benefit analysis or life cycle cost study have been outlined above except for two. The two remaining are, first, the estimation of a project's future net cash flows taking into account inflation and taxes where appropriate. The second is the determination of the cost of capital, k, taking into account inflation, taxes and, most importantly, risk.

The critical rule in estimating future cash flows is to include all incremental cash flows, both inflows and outflows, that are expected to occur as a result of the initial investment, except the interest payments on borrowed capital. The key consideration is the difference the investment makes. All changes in future cash flows that occur as a result of the investment must be identified. Interest payments are not treated as cash flows because their cost is included in the cost of capital, k, used to discount the future cash flows.

The procedure for calculating cash flows varies depending on whether or not the investment will produce taxable income or savings in the future.

When income taxes are involved, as in the case of a business investing in plant and equipment, F_t, the net cash flow in any year t provided by a non-financial investment, is given by

$$F_t = (S_t - O_t - D_t)(1-T) + D_t, F_t + (S_t - O_t)(1-T) + TD_t, \text{ or}$$
$$F_t = S_t - O_t - T(S_t - O_t - D_t)$$

where
$S_t = \Delta$ benefits (revenue or savings) generated in year t
$O_t = \Delta$ out-of-pocket expenses in year t
$D_t = \Delta$ depreciation expense in year t
T = marginal income tax rate.

The first of these three alternative formulas for Ft states that the net cash flow is the incremental after tax income plus depreciation expense resulting from the investment. The second gives the cash flow as the incremental after tax gross profit before depreciation plus the tax shield of depreciation (the reduction in income tax liability due to the depreciation charge). The third definition simply states that the net cash flow is revenue minus cash expenses and income tax payments. All three definitions are mathematically identical.

When an individual, a non-profit institution or government agency invests in a physical asset, such as a new heating system or public facility, taxable income is typically not generated and the calculation of the future annual cash flows simplifies to just

$F_t = S_t - O_t$.

10.6.2 FINANCIAL MANAGEMENT RATE OF RETURN (FMRR)

Our third approach to analyzing returns is the Financial Management Rate of Return (FMRR), which is a variation of the MIRR. With this approach, positive cash flows are used to pay for upcoming negative cash flows. To determine what portion of a positive cash flow is needed to meet a future outlay, the negative cash flow is discounted at the safe rate that is available to the investor, to the date the positive cash flow is received. The calculations become more and more complex as cash flows move from positive to negative and vice versa and their numbers increase.

Here is how Don Epley of the University of South Alabama describes it:[3]

The FMRR is structured to include many of the unique characteristics of a real estate investment and market. It is a specialized version of the geometric rate of return.

The assumptions are the following:

1. Only after-tax cash flows are used.
2. Cash may be withdrawn or invested at any time in any amount at the safe investment rate.
3. If cash accumulations are greater than or equal to a pre-determined amount, they can be withdrawn and invested in another project of comparable risk at a "run of the mill" (market) rate above the safe rate.

The rules to follow in the calculations are the following:

1. Remove all future negative cash outflows by utilizing prior positive cash inflows where possible.
2. Discount all remaining negative cash outflows to the present value at the safe after-tax rate.
3. Compound forward to the end of the holding period all remaining positive cash inflows at the after-tax market rate.
4. Compute the FMRR by,

$$FMRR = (FVn / PVo)^{1/n} - 1 \qquad \text{where n = holding period}$$

Example:

year		after-tax cash flow
0	0	(10,000)
1	1	(50,000)
2	2	(50,000)
3	3	30,000
4	4	(20,000)
5	5	30,000
6		250,000

The after-tax safe rate = 5%
The market rate = 10%
Minimum accumulation of cash = 0

---

3. Courtesy of Don Epley, Ph.D., CCIM, MAI, Director, Center for Real Estate Studies, University of Alabama, email: depley@usouthal.edu.

Example 2:

year		after-tax cash flow
0	0	(125,000)
1	1	(35,000)
2	2	(10,000)
3	3	50,000
4	4	(15,000)
5	5	(25,000)
6	6	55,000
7	7	25,000
8	8	(10,000)
9	9	(5,000)
10	10	550,000

The after-tax safe rate = 8%   The market rate = 12%

We include the FMRR to complete the trilogy, but it is not used much. Like the MIRR, it is an exercise in trying to find the right rate for the model. The weakness of these three approaches (IRR, MIRR, and FMRR) is that the analyst must make subjective assumptions (in terms of possible consistency of income, expenses and "accidents", interest rates and property values) as to what will happen 10, 15, 20 years into the future, which is almost impossible to do.

10.6.3 FINANCIAL ANALYSIS SOFTWARE

Mortgage calculators and financial analysis software have become indispensable to the real estate professional and there are many choices and variations. Perhaps the best resource to find all kinds of real estate software is <www.recenter.tamu.edu/soft>, the site of the Real Estate Center at Texas A&M University. Please note that the prices listed were correct at the time of writing.

One of the programs is Amortization (loan) software by Real Benefits. It appears to be very useful and very reasonably priced. It has received various awards and the most sophisticated version costs $50 USD. It is not Canadianized, that is, it does not calculate CCA according to Canada Revenue Agency (CRA) rules and does not compound the interests "half yearly, not in advance". The end result is that it will prove to be slightly better for the borrower than the printouts show and slightly worse for the lender. Despite this drawback, the company says that they have quite a few users in Canada.

Another product is MORTGAGE2 PRO. This software package calculates several types of amortization schedules. They offer a mortgage calculator and amortization spreadsheet on the same screen. It costs $39 CDN and information can be found at <www.amortization.com>.

A third choice is a US program found at <www.pine-grove.com>. This company offers three calculators that are bundled together:
- Loan Calculator! Plus (free, without time limitation),
- AmortizeIt! The complete loan solution, and
- SolveIt! The financial calculator.

This package lets you choose Canadian compounding and is available for a free 21-day evaluation period.

A fourth option is a born- and made-in-Canada program and is a serious contender in this field: InvestIt. It is powerful, very versatile, convenient to use and reasonably priced at an introductory cost of $325 for the new version 2.0 (early 2007). It goes much further than just financial calculations. You can conduct many analyses, such as:

- investment analysis
- buy versus lease analysis
- lease analysis – landlord
- lease analysis – tenant
- development analysis, and
- hotels.

The calculator section lets you calculate:

- time value of money
- standard mortgage
- vendor take-back mortgage (cost/benefit)
- imperial/metric conversion
- APR/effective interest rate
- mortgage take over (cost/benefit)
- commercial building breakeven analysis
- area calculator, and
- discounted cash flow.

You can try the program for 21 days (see <www.investit.ca>).

Finally, the heavy duty champ, ARGUS, is one of the better known programs for analyzing real estate. The company describes its program as follows:

> ARGUS, by Realm Business Solutions, is the commercial real estate industry's most popular valuation tool with over 15,000 users in 39 countries. ARGUS is extremely easy-to-use, while comprehensive enough for even the most sophisticated analytical requirements encountered in today's transactions.
>
> ARGUS models all aspects of the real estate life cycle-from initial acquisition, though development, to lease up, and disposition. ARGUS can also be used to value assets and analyze partnership structures and debt financing.

However, it is expensive, at $3,500 USD and it takes quite a long time for a person to become proficient with it. It is not for the occasional user.

Often, if you search online for these kinds of programs, you can tell by the number of pages that are linked to a program that it is popular. Similarly, if people have had a bad experience with a piece of mortgage software, you will probably read about it.

For very occasional uses, a more economical approach is to use a calculator offered on the site of various Canadian banks. The calculators are usually found under Tools.

CHAPTER 11

Financing

By the end of this chapter, you will be able to:
- Use leverage to your advantage.
- Distinguish between senior and junior mortgages, open and closed mortgages, and the various mortgage components.
- Determine the advantages of compounded interest and use Rule of 72.
- Interpret a mortgage amortization schedule and the effects of EIR and the Mortgage Constant Factor.
- Measure and distinguish between the benefits of the many different types of mortgages.
- Demonstrate your understanding of the influence of bonds and other alternatives for financing real estate investments.
- Understand the intricacies of setting mortgage amounts, including LTV, DSR, and mortgage interest averaging.
- Be knowledgeable about bank investment theory.
- Use CMHC as it benefits your investments.

Financing can be a powerful tool but it must be used intelligently, like a craftsman uses his tools.

11.1 LEVERAGING

Use leverage to your advantage.

Few people buy real estate without borrowing against it. The process is called "leverage". Leverage is using borrowed funds for an investment with the expectation that the profits from the investment will be greater than the interest payable. In real estate, leveraging can substantially increase your return on equity (ROE). As long as the Cap Rate (Net Operating Income (NOI)/Market Value) is higher than the mortgage constant factor, the leverage is positive. Leverage is negative when the Cap Rate is lower than the constant mortgage factor (see section 11.4.2).

Let's look again at the example given in Chapter 2 (section 2.5.2) that illustrates the impact of leveraging. In that example a property is purchased for $1 million and the Cap Rate (return before financing) is 10% or $100,000.

Option 1

The purchase price is $1,000,000, and you pay cash.

Your direct return is 10% ($1,000,000 x .10):	$100,000
Plus appreciation of 6% ($1,000,000 x .06):	$60,000
Total return:	$160,000
Total annual rate of return on your equity ($160,000/$1,000,000)	0.16 or 16%

Option 2

You pay $400,000 cash and borrow 60% of the purchase price ($600,000) at 7% interest, paying $42,000 per year, interest only.

Your direct return is ($100,000 - $42,000):	$58,000
Rate of return ($58,000/$400,000):	14.50% return
Plus appreciation (indirect return) of 6% ($1,000,000 x .06):	$60,000
Total return (direct return + appreciation):	$118,000
Total rate of return ($118,000/$400,000)	0.295 or 29.50%

At the bottom of the real estate cycle, you can borrow up to 80% of a property's value (known as the "loan-to-value" or LTV ratio) with limited risk, in some cases. At the top of the cycle, when it looks like prices may be peaking or due to decline, 50% is the maximum you should borrow to control risk. Another primary consideration is the quality of the tenant(s).

This is in theory, of course. In real life, many budding investors with limited cash will take chances borrowing as much as they can and hope that nothing will go wrong. Thanks to appreciation, most succeed. Note that under the law, banks are not permitted to provide financing in an amount greater than 75% of the value of the property, or of the purchase price, unless the mortgage is insured (see section 11.9).

Financing a property at 100% should be done with extreme care. In principle, you would go this route only in the following situations:

1. when buying a building that is in bad shape or poorly leased, but you know that by spending some money and time, you will markedly increase the income from what it is today; or
2. when the tenant on the property is a no-risk tenant due to its financial strength, such as IBM or the federal government.

11.2 UNDERSTANDING MORTGAGES

Distinguish between senior and junior mortgages, open and closed mortgages, and the various mortgage components.

A mortgage is a legal document or contract signed by a borrower when a loan is made and secured against a property, specifying the borrowing terms between the borrower and lender. Technically, the money involved is a loan, not the mortgage itself, although the two are commonly equated. In Ontario legal parlance, the mortgage is also called a "charge." The lender (mortgagee) registers the mortgage document in the Land Registry System after the borrower (mortgagor) has signed it. In Canada, the mortgage business is regulated by provincial legislation that defines the rights and obligations of both lender and borrower and key terms such as, mortgage, mortgagee, and mortgagor.

A mortgage is a claim or encumbrance on the real property given by the owner as security for a loan. All mortgages contain remedies for non-payment or default. A mortgage can be non-recourse, which is common in the US but rare in Canada, whereby the only security that the vendor has is the real property itself. A non-recourse mortgage prevents the lender from taking action against other assets of a defaulting borrower. In Canada, Alberta is the only province where mortgages are automatically non-recourse (except those that are CMHC insured). Unfortunately (if you are a borrower), lenders often require a personal guarantee from the borrower in addition to the security represented by the real property, which is the case in a recourse mortgage.

The main difference between loans in general and a mortgage loan is how the interest is calculated. In Canada, interest on an amortized mortgage is almost always compounded every 6 months (it cannot be more often), not in advance, and the payments are blended. This means that while the monthly payments remain constant, with every payment a greater percentage of the payments goes toward the principal repayment. The law permits mortgages to be calculated annually, too, but this is very rare because lenders are not keen to do it.

11.2.1 SENIOR AND JUNIOR MORTGAGES

Frequently, you will hear mortgages referred to as "senior" or "junior" mortgages, or "first" or "second" mortgages. These terms relate to the order in which multiple mortgages on a property were registered.

(a) Senior Mortgages

A senior mortgage is the first mortgage registered on title and, due to this fact, is commonly called a "first mortgage". All subsequent mortgages are second, third, etc., unless the owner of the previous mortgage allows a subsequent lender to register the mortgage in front of his, which is called a Subordination of Mortgage or Postponement Privilege. Therefore, what makes a mortgage first, second, or third is the sequence in which it is registered; that is, the date and time of registration.

(b) Junior Mortgages

Junior mortgages are registered on title in second, third, etc., position after a senior mortgage. Also called "equitable mortgages", junior mortgages theoretically, but not necessarily, represent an increased risk for the lender. Which would you rather have in the following scenario, where the property is worth $1,000,000?

Situation "A"

Mortgage amount:	$750,000
Equity amount:	$250,000
Loan-to-Value ratio:	75%

Situation "B"

1st mortgage amount:	$300,000
2nd mortgage amount:	$100,000
3rd mortgage amount:	$125,000
Total mortgage amount:	$525,000
Equity amount:	$475,000
Loan-to-value ratio:	52.50%

In situation B, the third mortgage lender has a safety cushion of $475,000, while in situation A, the first mortgagee's cushion is only $250,000.

11.2.2 OPEN VERSUS CLOSED MORTGAGE

An open mortgage is one that can be repaid at any time before its expiry date with, or sometimes without, a penalty or bonus. Unless you obtain an open Vendor-Take-Back (VTB) mortgage, in all likelihood you will pay a premium on top of your rate of interest for this privilege, as much as 1% or more. Some lenders, particularly for residential mortgages, allow earlier repayment of up to 20% of the principal of the loan at no cost.

A mortgage that is locked, or closed, cannot be repaid before the end of its term, at least according to the terms of the mortgage agreement. In reality, virtually all mortgages can be repaid (except conduit loans, discussed in section 11.6.2(a)), but at a cost. Most lenders of a closed mortgage paying 6% interest will be delighted to be repaid early if the going mortgage rate at the time is 12%. On the other hand, if current interest rates are lower than the rate on the mortgage, most lenders will require the borrower to pay a penalty for repayment that is equal to the interest rate differential between the interest of the existing mortgage and the current interest rate. To figure out the penalty, subtract the current interest rate from the actual interest rate and multiply the result by the principal balance of the mortgage. If, for example, the contract rate is 7% and the current rate is 5.5%, the rate differential is 1.5%. This is multiplied by the remaining principal amount of the mortgage and the number of years remaining on the term of the mortgage to establish the penalty for repayment.

In reality, virtually all mortgages can be repaid, but at a cost.

There are some additional expenses associated with such an approach, such as lender's fees and legal fees, but discharging a mortgage can be advantageous in some sales situations so the buyer can arrange a higher LTV ratio.

Example

Sale price:	$2,000,000
Existing mortgage:	$500,000 (25% LTV rate)
Cost to discharge:	$50,000
Total cost:	$2,000,000 + $50,000 = $2,050,000
Potential new mortgage:	$1,600,000
Down Payment required:	$2,050,000 - $500,000 = $1,550,000
Potential new price:	$2,100,000
Down Payment required:	$2,100,000 - $1,600,000 = $500,000

11.2.3 COMPONENTS OF A MORTGAGE

Typically, when a lender, borrower, or real estate agent talks about a mortgage, he is interested in knowing the following:

- **Principal.** The amount being borrowed;
- **Rate of Interest on the Loan;**
- **Amortization.** The number of years necessary to pay off the mortgage, usually when the borrower makes equal (generally, but not always) monthly payments. Most amortization terms are for between 20 and 25 years;
- **Term.** The length of time the money is loaned to the borrower; and
- **Loan-to-Value (LTV) Ratio** The amount of the loan divided by the value of the property.

11.3 INTRODUCTION TO INTEREST

Determine the advantages of compounded interest and use Rule of 72.

Think of interest as the payment for the use or rental of money for a specified period of time; in other words, the cash received or repaid over and above the principal. When discussing interest in this book the basic assumptions are that the rate is always for a one-year period and, virtually always, the rate remains constant during that period.

Most lenders base the interest charge for mortgage lending on the yield of the Government of Canada bonds for the mortgage term contemplated and add a premium. Occasionally, a lender establishes its interest rates using the prime lending rate,[1] usually adding a premium. The prime lending rate plus the premium is called the "floor" or "base" rate.

There are two kinds of interest: simple interest, which is computed on the amount of the original principal only; and compound interest, which is the interest charged or paid on the initial principal amount for the current period and on the interest amounts earned or accumulated in previous periods. Put simply, compound

---

1 Prime is the interest rate charged by lenders (banks, lending institutions and others) to their most credit-worthy (lowest-risk) commercial customers, for short-term, unsecured loans. The prime rate is very important because many other interest rates for mortgages, credit card, business loans are often based on the prime rate, plus or minus certain percentage points. Each bank sets its own prime rate, but they are generally very close to one another. Traditionally, the prime rate changes when the Bank Rate set by the Bank of Canada changes. The Bank Rate is closely related to the Target for the Overnight Rate, which is the main tool the Bank of Canada uses to establish monetary policy. The Bank Rate, which is the rate of interest that the Bank of Canada charges on one-day loans to financial institutions, is part of a range called the Operating Band for the overnight rate. The overnight rate is the rate at which major financial institutions borrow and lend one-day funds among themselves.

interest is interest on the initial amount, plus interest on this interest in subsequent periods. Compound interest is calculated at specified intervals, such as daily, monthly, quarterly, or yearly. It is also called "interest on interest".

11.3.1 Compounding Example

To understand compounding, let's look at an example where 3 years ago you put $100 into a savings account that offered interest compounded annually.

Example

Amount invested (principal):	$100.00
Interest earned first year at 6% (6% x $100):	$6.00
Total amount invested end of year 1:	$106.00
Interest earned second year at 6% (6% x $106.00):	$6.36
Total amount invested end of year 2:	$112.36
Interest earned third year at 6% (6% x $112.36):	$6.74
Total amount invested end of year 3:	$119.10

If we had not used compounding interest, we would have earned only 6% per year on the principal (6% x $100) or $6.00 per year for a total interest at the end of 3 years of $18. That would mean our original $100 would grow to $118 at the end of the 3 years, instead of $119.10.

Besides the interest rate and length of time over which the loan will be repaid, when doing calculations with compound interest bear in mind the frequency of the compounding. The example below shows the same $100 at the end of 3 years if the interest, still 6%, had been compounded semi-annually. For semi-annual compounding (the shortest term allowed for calculating Canadian mortgages), use one-half of the annual rate for each six-month period. The calculations for the above example would look like this.

Example

Amount invested (principal):	$100.00
Interest earned during first 6-month period at 3% (3% x $100):	$3.00
Total amount invested at end of first 6 months:	$103.00
Interest earned during second 6-month period (3% x $103):	$3.09
Total amount invested at end of first year:	$106.09
Interest earned during third 6-month period (3% x $106.09):	$3.18
Total amount invested at end of the third 6-month period:	$109.27
Interest earned during fourth 6-month period (3% x $109.27):	$3.28
Total amount invested at end of second year:	$112.55
Interest earned during fifth 6-month period (3% x $112.55):	$3.38
Total amount invested at end of fifth 6-month period:	$115.93
Interest earned during sixth 6-month period (3% x $115.93):	$3.48
Total amount invested at end of third year:	$119.41

Although these amounts may not seem significant, consider that if your investment was $100,000 instead of $100. It would have grown to $119,010 over a 3-year period with the interest compounded annually and to

$119,410 with the interest compounded semi-annually versus only $118,000 if there had been no compounding at all. Where you really see the benefit of compounding is over a long-term investment and for large amounts of money. To help you calculate the effects of compounding, you can find a number of tools on the Internet by searching "Mortgage Calculator" or "Interest Calculator".

Moral: Avoid borrowing money (excluding mortgages) that is compounded daily, but it is okay if you lend on this basis!

11.3.2 RULE OF 72

This handy rule of thumb lets you calculate how many years it will take for a given amount of money to double in value at a given interest rate. The rule is simple:

Divide 72 by the interest rate (you are paying or receiving).

Example 1
72/7.2 (rate of interest) = 10 years
The money will double every 10 years.

Example 2
72/13 (rate of interest) = 5.54 years
The money will double every 5.54 years.

11.4 MORTGAGE AMORTIZATION

Interpret a mortgage amortization schedule and the effects of EIR and the Mortgage Constant Factor.

The amortization period refers to the length of time it will take for the principal amount to be repaid, while the term refers to the length of time for which the money is lent. A mortgage payment schedule, also called a "Mortgage Amortization Schedule", is a list of numbers showing the number of payments, their amount, the respective amount of the principal and of the interest, and the balance still owing after each payment.

It is important, if not vital to your financial health, to understand mortgage amortization. In the first few years of a loan, a mortgage amortized over 20 years (paid off over 20 years), for example, pays little principal but a lot of interest. When looking at returns, generally most people look at the NOI less mortgage payments. Truly, one should add the principal repaid.

For example, a $4,000,000 mortgage at 6.5% amortized over 25 years has blended payments (principal and interest) of $321,515 per year. The principal paid in year 1 is $66,912 and the interest is $254,603, but in year 25 the principal paid is $310,620 and the interest is $10,897. Figure 11.1 shows the first and last pages of a mortgage payment schedule. For a more visual representation, see Figure 11.2.

Figure 11.1
Interactive Amortization Schedule

(Semi-Annual Interest Compounding)

Mortgage Amount:	$4,000,000.00	Payments Displayed:	1 - 300
Interest Rate:	6.50%	Payment Frequency:	Monthly
Initial Amortization Period:	Months	Initial Payment:	$26,792.95

Period		Total Paid	Interest	Principal	Balance
Pmt:	1	$26,792.95	$21,378.96	$5,413.99	$3,994,586.01
Pmt:	2	$26,792.95	$21,350.02	$5,442.93	$3,989,143.08
Pmt:	3	$26,792.95	$21,320.93	$5,472.02	$3,983,671.06
Pmt:	4	$26,792.95	$21,291.69	$5,501.26	$3,978,169.80
Pmt:	5	$26,792.95	$21,262.28	$5,530.67	$3,972,639.13
Pmt:	6	$26,792.95	$21,232.72	$5,560.23	$3,967,078.90
Pmt:	7	$26,792.95	$21,203.01	$5,589.94	$3,961,488.96
Pmt:	8	$26,792.95	$21,173.13	$5,619.82	$3,955,869.14
Pmt:	9	$26,792.95	$21,143.09	$5,649.86	$3,950,219.28
Pmt:	10	$26,792.95	$21,112.90	$5,680.05	$3,944,539.23
Pmt:	11	$26,792.95	$21,082.54	$5,710.41	$3,938,828.82
Pmt:	12	$26,792.95	$21,052.02	$5,740.93	$3,933,087.89
Year 1 Totals		$321,515.40	$254,603.29	$66,912.11	$3,933,087.89

Period		Total Paid	Interest	Principal	Balance
Pmt:	289	$26,792.95	$1,660.18	$25,132.77	$285,486.96
Pmt:	290	$26,792.95	$1,525.85	$25,267.10	$260,219.86
Pmt:	291	$26,792.95	$1,390.81	$25,402.14	$234,817.72
Pmt:	292	$26,792.95	$1,255.04	$25,537.91	$209,279.81
Pmt:	293	$26,792.95	$1,118.55	$25,674.40	$183,605.41
Pmt:	294	$26,792.95	$981.32	$25,811.63	$157,793.78
Pmt:	295	$26,792.95	$843.37	$25,949.58	$131,844.20
Pmt:	296	$26,792.95	$704.67	$26,088.28	$105,755.92
Pmt:	297	$26,792.95	$565.24	$26,227.71	$79,528.21
Pmt:	298	$26,792.95	$425.06	$26,367.89	$53,160.32
Pmt:	299	$26,792.95	$284.13	$26,508.82	$26,651.50
Pmt:	300	$26,793.95	$142.45	$26,651.50	$0
Year 25 Totals		$321,516.40	$10,896.67	$310,619.73	$0

Totals: $8,037,886.00 $4,037,886.00 $4,000,000.00

Figure 11.2
Mortgage Calculator

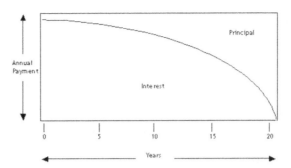

Payment #	Principal Paid	Interest Paid	Principal Left
1	$248.51	$1489.04	$274651.49
2	$249.86	$1487.70	$274401.63
3	$251.21	$1486.34	$274150.41
4	$252.57	$1484.98	$273897.84
5	$253.94	$1483.61	$273643.90
6	$255.32	$1482.24	$273388.58
7	$256.70	$1480.85	$273131.88
8	$258.09	$1479.46	$272873.79
9	$259.49	$1478.07	$272614.30
10	$260.89	$1476.66	$272353.41
11	$262.31	$1475.25	$272091.10
12	$263.73	$1473.83	$271827.37

Continue monthly payments and by year 10, your payments would look like this:

120	$472.64	$1264.91	$233049.57
121	$475.20	$1262.35	$232574.37
122	$477.78	$1259.78	$232096.59
123	$480.37	$1257.19	$231616.23
124	$482.97	$1254.59	$231133.26
125	$485.58	$1251.97	$230647.68
126	$488.21	$1249.34	$230159.46
127	$490.86	$1246.70	$229668.60
128	$493.52	$1244.04	$229175.09
129	$496.19	$1241.37	$228678.90
130	$498.88	$1238.68	$228180.02
131	$501.58	$1235.98	$227678.44

Continue monthly payments and in the final year (year 30) your payments would look like this:

349	$1628.49	$109.06	$18506.24
350	$1637.31	$100.24	$16868.92
351	$1646.18	$91.37	$15222.74
352	$1655.10	$82.46	$13567.64
353	$1664.06	$73.49	$11903.58
354	$1673.08	$64.48	$10230.50
355	$1682.14	$55.42	$8548.36
356	$1691.25	$46.30	$6857.11
357	$1700.41	$37.14	$5156.70
358	$1709.62	$27.93	$3447.08
359	$1718.88	$18.67	$1728.19
360	$1728.19	$9.36	$0.00

Source: Mortgage Calculator used by permission of Advanced Access, a division of Dominion Enterprises.

The amortization period is important from an income tax viewpoint because only the interest on a mortgage is tax deductible. Therefore, when you start paying more principal than interest, you may be better off refinancing, to put fresh money in your pocket that, hopefully, you will use to buy another property.

11.4.1 EFFECTIVE INTEREST RATE (EIR)

The true rate charged on a mortgage loan is known as the Effective Interest Rate (EIR). The EIR allows you to compare apples and oranges or in this case to compare a loan compounded monthly with a mortgage compounded semi-annually. EIRs are always quoted on an annual basis. A mortgage has, in fact, two rates: the nominal or stated rate, for example 8%, and the EIR, which is the nominal rate affected by the frequency of compounding (how often the interest is calculated). Note that no amortization is involved.

The federal *Interest Act* (R.S.C. 1985, c. I-15) requires that loans on property be calculated only one of two ways: annually or semi-annually. And, because lenders are not philanthropists, they always choose the most frequently allowed compounding period. To be more constructive, lenders should quote the EIR of a mortgage loan, but they generally quote the nominal rate. If we take a one-year, interest-only $100,000 mortgage, at 8%, our interest payments will be $8,000 or 8% if compounded annually and $8,160 or 8.16% if compounded semi-annually.

The interest received by the lender due to the two compounding periods (instead of one) was $8,160. Therefore, the EIR on the $100,000 borrowed was 8.16%

The formula to calculate the effective rate is $A = P (1 + I)^N$, where

A = Amount of payment

P = Principal amount (the loan amount)

N = Number of compounding periods, expressed as a power

1 = A unit of value

I = Interest rate per compounding period.

Example

$A = P (1+0.40)^2$ (1 unit + 0.40 (rate for 2 years)^2

$A = 100,000 (1.04)^2$

$A = 100,000 (1.0816)$

It is important to understand the EIR concept because that is the true cost to be used when comparing financing options. If you know the annual interest rate and the compounding frequency then you must be able to convert it to an EIR. The table in Figure 11.3 demonstrates that the more frequent the compounding, the larger the monthly interest factor and thus the larger the yield (EIR) for the lender. In this example the yield ranges from 12-12.75% depending on the compounding frequency. This emphasizes why an annual interest rate alone is not sufficient to accurately spell out the yield. The EIR is a much more meaningful measure, unfortunately rarely used.

Figure 11.3
Annual Interest Rates Showing Effect of Compounding

Annual Interest Rates (AIR) of 12% showing the effect of
compounding on the monthly interest factor and thus the
Effective Interest Rate (EIR).

Compounding	Monthly factor	EIR%
Annual	0.0094888	12
Semi-annual	0.0097588	12.36
Quarterly	0.0099016	12.55
Monthly	0.01	12.68
Semi-monthly	0.0100258	12.717
Biweekly	0.0100269	12.72
Weekly	0.0100385	12.73
Daily	0.0100485	12.75

11.4.2 MORTGAGE CONSTANT FACTOR

In appraisal parlance, the Mortgage Constant Factor is called the "Mortgage Capitalization Rate". It is the percentage of a loan that must be paid periodically, monthly for example, to pay off the debt.

It is the sum of 12 equal monthly payments (including principal and interest) expressed as a factor to be applied to a principal loan amount that is to be amortized over a certain term.

The constant factor for a new, fully amortized loan is obtained by dividing yearly principal and interest payments by the amount of the mortgage. For example, if you have a $4-million mortgage at 6.5%, amortized over 25 years, the constant factor would be calculated as below.

$$\text{Constant factor} \ = \ \frac{\text{Yearly payments (as required/calculated by the lender)}}{\text{Amount of the mortgage}}$$

$$= \ \frac{\$321,515}{\$4,000,000}$$

$$= \ 0.08037 \text{ or } 8.04\%$$

An amortized mortgage has, in fact, two rates.

1. The annual interest rate provides the lender with the return on his money. In this case, this component would be: $4,000,000 x 6.5% = $260,000.
2. The annual capitalization rate provides the lender with the return on (see section 10.4), and of (blended rate) his money (capital).

If we wanted to find an average, we would make the following calculation: $4,000,000/25 years = $160,000. However, if we subtract $260,000 from $321,515, we obtain $61,515 because, starting with the first payment, there is some principal repaid.

Loan amortization calculations can be performed using an equation that says that the present value of all payments is equal to the amount of the loan, then solving for the payment amount. Many mortgage constant factor tables give monthly figures that must be multiplied by 12 to obtain the annual constant.

11.4.3 BALLOON PAYMENT

If the amortization period of a mortgage is longer than its term, when the mortgage is due (at the end of the term) a large amount of principal called a "balloon payment" will have to be paid as a lump sum to the lender. For example, this commonly happens when one has a 25-year amortization period but only a 5- or 10-year term.

11.5 TYPES OF MORTGAGES

Measure and distinguish between the benefits of the many different types of mortgages.

11.5.1 VENDOR-TAKE-BACK OR PURCHASE MONEY MORTGAGE

As the name implies, a Vendor-Take-Back (VTB) mortgage, also called a "Purchase Money" mortgage, is taken back by the vendor when he sells a property. This may be a first or a second mortgage and is advantageous for the buyer because it saves him considerable time and money (e.g., lender's fee, legal fee, survey, inspection, insurance demands). Its terms are usually more flexible than those of a financial institution and the interest rate may be lower. Some vendors like VTB mortgages because they know their property represents good security and they want the benefit of a steady cash flow. A VTB's LTV ratio may be similar to that of a conventional mortgage (60-80%), but most frequently will be below 50%. It may take the form of a second mortgage, usually with a higher LTV ratio.

It is rare that a vendor will take back a mortgage representing a large portion of the purchase price. In real life this happens only if the buyer is willing to pay above-market value for the property. More commonly, a vendor will take back a second mortgage in

A VTB is advantageous for the buyer because it saves him considerable time and money.

order to make the property more attractive. It is usually for 10-40% of the price. It does happen when an existing mortgage represents a relatively low LTV ratio and the vendor takes back a mortgage so that the two loans give a good LTV ratio.

Recently, we came across a typical example of a VTB for a multi-family building. The vendor agreed to a price of $3,300,000. The balance of the principal of the existing first mortgage was $870,000 and due in 3 years.

This represented a LTV ratio of $870,000/$3,300,000 = 26.36%, which was considered far too low by the potential buyer, who wanted a 70-75% LTV ratio, representing a mortgage of $3,300,000 x 70%= $2,310,000, or $3,300,000 x 75% = $2,475,000.

The vendor agreed to take back a second mortgage of $1,500,000 at the same interest rate as the first and due on the same date, bringing the total amount of mortgages to $2,370,000. By doing that, the vendor avoided having to discharge the $870,000 and pay the penalty involved. This approach made his property much more appealing to buyers and he was able to obtain a higher price.

A vendor will take back a purchase money mortgage for one, or more, of the following reasons:
- there is one, or more, existing locked-in loans on the property
- the vendor is anxious to sell, but can only find a buyer with a small down payment or one with a relatively weak covenant (so the buyer will have trouble finding additional financing)

- the vendor wants top dollar and is firm on his price, but is flexible as to the terms of the sale
- the buyer wants to keep the benefit of the existing low-interest loan
- there is not enough time to shop for loans or little likelihood of the new buyer qualifying for same, or
- the down payment offered is insufficient.

(a) Advantages of the VTB Mortgage

The advantages of a VTB mortgage are many for both the vendor and the buyer. The vendor gains the following advantages:

- retains the advantageous terms of the existing financing, if the buyer/borrower defaults
- is able to sell a property that has a locked-in loan, without having to negotiate with the lender for a higher loan amount or for permission to assign or repay the loan, which usually implies expenses
- sometimes obtains a higher effective interest rate on the new mortgage
- sells his VTB mortgage at a lower rate, hence discounting it to an investor
- obtains a better price for his property because he gives better terms, and
- obtains a higher price and benefits from favourable capital gains tax rates, ultimately saving money (versus obtaining a lower price and investing his money and paying regular income tax rates).

On the other hand, the purchaser has the following advantages:

- can buy a larger property for the same, or smaller, down payment
- can buy a property even if he would not qualify for a high LTV ratio on a new mortgage
- can find greater tax benefits through adjustments of price and terms
- saves the cost of new loan requirements: appraisal, loan points, survey, reports, etc.
- saves considerable time
- can afford to pay more for the property, by getting a better (lower) interest rate and securing a bigger mortgage, and
- is responsible for only one loan payment (if there is no mortgage in front of the VTB), instead of two or more.

(b) Selling a VTB Mortgage

As vendor, there may be times when you have taken a VTB on a property, but find you need to free up your equity. You may have come across the "deal of a lifetime" and need to sell this mortgage to a third party (an investor who buys mortgages). Usually, you will have to discount the remaining amount due on the mortgage, therefore increasing its yield for the purchaser of the mortgage. This means you will need to sell the mortgage today for a price less than the sum of all the payments that the new mortgage owner will receive over the years before the mortgage is due. Often the selling price for the mortgage is less than the amount of the principal remaining due. However, the price at which a mortgage is sold varies, depending on the payment schedule. The more years remaining on the term of the mortgage — that is, the more time it will take the lender to recover his money — the greater the discount. The factors influencing the selling price of a mortgage are:

- terms (amortization and date due)
- credit history of the owner (buyer) of the property
- amount of down payment, which showed the LTV ratio at closing date
- type, condition, and desirability of the property serving as collateral, and
- location of the property.

The vendor of a mortgage on a commercial property may be asked to pay expenses inherent with this kind of transaction, which can cost up to $10,000 for such things as a property appraisal, mortgage registration expenses, legal fees, environmental report, and/or an up-to-date survey.

11.5.2 BLANKET MORTGAGE

A blanket mortgage is a single mortgage registered against more than one property or that "blankets" several buildings. With a blanket mortgage the lender is better protected by having recourse against several properties. A common example of this occurs when a house builder secures a loan covering the construction of several houses. When each individual house is completed and sold, the new owner, once approved by a lender, signs a mortgage document covering the purchase and the builder is then released from his obligation for that house.

11.5.3 WRAP-AROUND MORTGAGE

Also called an "umbrella mortgage", a wrap-around mortgage is a junior mortgage (usually a second, but it could be a third or fourth mortgage) that wraps around the existing first, leaving it in place. The new lender assumes the payment obligations for the first mortgage and receives payment for both loans from the borrower. The wrap-around mortgage is held by the lender as security for the total mortgage debt.

A wrap-around mortgage is attractive to lenders because usually they can increase the yield on the new (second) mortgage. When the lender is the vendor of the property, commonly he is not after a higher yield for the second mortgage, although never opposed to it! What a vendor realizes is that this type of financing will allow him to obtain a higher sale price and usually a faster sale for the property. Obviously, this approach works well only if the existing first mortgage is at a reasonably low rate. Obviously again, if mortgage interest rates increase, wrap-arounds become more interesting from the lender's viewpoint because the spread between the old mortgage and the new one will be greater.

In some situations, the wrap-around mortgage document says that the mortgage payments made by the property owner/borrower must go to a third party (the lender of the new mortgage) who is supposed to forward them to the original lender. This is a very dangerous practice that should be opposed by the borrower, as he cannot control whether the third party makes the payments or not, unless the second lender signs a covenant.

In theory, only assumable loans may be wrapped around. In practice, a wrap-around mortgage can be used to circumvent restrictions in assuming existing loans. However, in reality, if the existing lender discovers the wrap-around mortgage, he could declare the first mortgage in default and require immediate payment of the loan principal. In real life, when most lenders are unaware of a new wrap-around mortgage and discover one in place, they think twice about upsetting the status-quo if payments are made faithfully. However, some lenders will call the loan or, more likely, demand an increase in interest rate. Some will also want to charge an assumption fee. Let's look at an example.

Example

John Dandy wants to buy a building for $5,000,000. This property already has an existing mortgage with an outstanding principal balance of $1,500,000 at 7%. John does not have $3,500,000 to pay cash to the existing (1st) mortgage. He has only $1,000,000 and knows that his financial situation would make it difficult, if not impossible, to secure new financing.

John contacts a couple of lenders and finds out that for a 2nd mortgage he would have to borrow at 13.5%. John contacts a 3rd lender, who suggests a wrap-around mortgage. He will loan John $2,500,000 at 11%, with a term expiring on the same day as the existing mortgage. The lender will sign a covenant, whereby he will be responsible for making the payments on the existing mortgage. The new mortgage will automatically be a 2nd mortgage, since it will be registered behind the existing one. The lender lends John money by way of a 2nd mortgage, with a twist.

1. He lends John $2,500,000 at 11%.
2. He covenants to make the payments on the 1st mortgage.
3. John will make only one monthly payment, covering the 1st and 2nd mortgage, to the new lender.

The numbers are as follows:
1. For John:
Selling price: $5 million
Down payment: $1 million
New financing arrangement: $4 million ($1.5 million + $2.5 million) at 11% = yearly payments of $440,000

2. For the lender:

Payments from John =	$440,000
Payments for 1st mortgage of $1,500,000 x 7% =	$105,000
Left over for new lender = $440,000 - $105,000 =	$335,000
Interest earned on the new $2.5M mortgage = $335,000/$2,500,000 = 13.40%.	

3. For existing lender:
No change.

In other words, John and the new lender are taking advantage of the existing mortgage to secure lower-priced financing for John and increase the yield for the new lender. John is delighted with this arrangement. He is able to buy the property with a down payment of only 20% and, if he had gone the conventional 2nd mortgage route, his payments would have been:

1st: $1,500,000 x 7% =	$105,000
2nd: 2,500,000 x 13.5% =	$337,500
Total:	$442,500

Therefore, he saves $2,500 per year, in addition to a low down payment and the ability to arrange financing. This example assumes mortgages paying interest only. If the 1st mortgage was amortized, the new lender could benefit from principal repayments since the monthly cheques made out by John would include, for the 1st mortgage, interest plus principal. If the first mortgage is in the later years of amortization, the principal repayment portion could be considerable, perhaps even greater than the interest portion.

11.5.4 PIGGYBACK MORTGAGE

Like the wrap-around mortgage, the piggyback mortgage is a junior mortgage. With this approach, a new first mortgage is arranged, which closes the original first mortgage simultaneously with the piggyback mortgage. Commonly, there are two lenders, with the second acting as a contact or conduit for paying the first mortgagee (after receiving payments from the mortgagor). Contrary to the wrap-around mortgage, the subsequent (usually second) mortgagee does not assume responsibility for the prior mortgage.

The interest rate is often one or two percentage points higher than that of the first because of the greater risk. In the event of default, it gets paid after the first. With high-ratio mortgages (above 75%), some call the wrap-around mortgage a substitute for mortgage insurance, when a buyer has less than 25% of the purchase price for the down payment. Indeed, some investors cannot qualify for mortgage insurance.

Piggyback mortgages are used more frequently in the US for personal, residential mortgages, as the borrower can deduct the interests paid from his income tax. It is easily encountered in construction projects, where a lender would issue a commitment letter for the permanent loan, at an interest rate of 12%, for example. A construction lien is then stacked (high rate on top of low rate) on top of the permanent loan commitment, ensuring the lender that the money of the permanent loan will be borrowed, even if rates are lower when the construction loan is repaid.

11.5.5 CONSTRUCTION LOAN (MORTGAGE)

Construction loans or mortgages are used by builders and are granted for a short period of time by a lending institution (12-24 months is typical). Generally, only monthly interest is payable. Construction loans have higher interest rates than regular mortgages because they are considered high risk, and they have stringent requirements. For example, for a new condo project, a lender may demand that 50% of the apartments be pre-sold. Hence if a condominium building comprises 230 units, a lender will grant the builder a mortgage, conditional upon the builder pre-selling at least 115 units. Only when this number of pre-sales has been achieved will the lender disburse mortgage money. Money is disbursed in slices, upon receiving a Progress Estimate Certificate signed by an architect or engineer.

These loans are repaid when construction is complete and the units in the building are sold. At that time, they are replaced with new permanent financing in the name of the apartment buyer. The rules are somewhat different for buildings erected to be leased, but the same general concept applies.

11.5.6 BRIDGE FINANCING

Bridge financing usually refers to a short-term loan that is used to cover the time gap that exists when a person has bought a property and sold another one, both firm sales, but must close on his purchase before the property he has sold closes. Most bridge loans are at 2% or 3% over prime, in addition to a bank fee.

11.5.7 PARTICIPATION MORTGAGE

Where a lender receives a portion of the profits (sometimes in the form of the increase in value of the property) when the mortgage is due, you have a participation mortgage. It can also be called a "Shared Appreciation Mortgage". Since anything legal can be put into a contract, a lender could also require participation in the income of the property. In a participation mortgage, the interest rate itself is usually lower than it would have been otherwise.

11.5.8 DEVELOPMENT LAND LOAN

The developer of a piece of land who has received Draft Plan of Subdivision Approval, but has yet to have the land parcelled into lots and serviced, will generally sell the to-be-serviced site to a home builder on the following basis:

- down payment: 10-35% of purchase price,
- six to 12 months later: 10-20%, and
- two months later: the balance.

While this is customary, interest rates can vary drastically. They are generally low and sometimes no interest at all is paid, until the loan is repaid or for a period of time. For example 6 months may be interest-free on a 2-year VTB. Usually, this builder will want to borrow to satisfy the Conditions of Draft Plan Approval and to service the land. He has three choices.

1. He can convince the vendor to postpone the first mortgage so that the new lender is in first position. Few vendors are willing to do so because of the risk involved.
2. He can borrow enough money from the new lender to be able to pay off the existing first mortgage, which in all likelihood was a VTB.
3. He can find a construction loan from a lender who does not mind being in second position (behind the first mortgage) and charges accordingly.

11.5.9 LEASEHOLD MORTGAGE

A leasehold mortgage is a mortgage on improvements (buildings) when the land is leased (not owned). These mortgages must be amortized over a period that is shorter than the length of the land lease, even if it is just by one day.

11.5.10 COLLATERAL MORTGAGE

A collateral mortgage is one backed by two securities — a promissory note signed by the borrower and the property offered (as security for the mortgage).

Typically, this type of loan is made to a property owner who has owned said property for a while, but needs money for another purpose, such as the purchase of another investment property or a business. This is also called "refinancing".

11.5.11 BOND CHARGE/MORTGAGE OR TRUST DEED

These special types of mortgages are usually for large sums of money (many millions of dollars) and are given by the borrower to a trustee who holds title to the property in trust for several lenders. On repayment the borrower is given a re-conveyance and a release and a standard Discharge of Charge/Mortgage is registered. The borrower's corporate seal must be affixed.

11.5.12 ADJUSTABLE RATE MORTGAGE (ARM)

An Adjustable Rate Mortgage (ARM) is an interesting mortgage that is rarely used in commercial real estate, particularly if the rates are going down. The rate is based on the prime lending rate, less a certain percentage. If the prime changes, the interest on the mortgage is adjusted, usually monthly. The principal payments remain constant and only the interest portion changes. Virtually all ARMs can be converted to conventional mortgages.

11.6 BONDS, COMMERCIAL PAPER AND CONDUIT FINANCING

Demonstrate your understanding of the influence of bonds and other alternatives for financing real estate investments.

Prima facie, it might appear to some readers that an understanding of bonds is not necessary in real estate. However, anyone looking for a mortgage on a commercial property will promptly understand that a basic knowledge of bonds is useful if he calls a lender. The first question that he is likely to ask is: "What will the interest rate be"? To which the lender will retort: "It will be approximately xx base points over the bond rate."

Therefore, an understanding of bonds is very useful to a real estate investor, particularly if he wants to be considered knowledgeable about real estate financing. In addition, this section gives you the basics about commercial paper because it is a necessary introduction to understanding conduit financing, another important alternative for financing real estate investments.

11.6.1 BONDS

There are three main categories of fixed income securities: bills, which mature in less than 1 year; notes, which mature in 1 to 10 years; and bonds, which mature in more than 10 years. Bonds are fixed income securities (because their cash flow is fixed) that pay interest and are generally issued for periods of 10 to 30 years. A basic understanding of bonds is important because most lenders arrive at their rate of interest by using the Government of Canada bond rates as their base benchmark. For example, the rate for a 5-year term might be fixed at the bid side yield on the 4.25% coupon Government of Canada bond maturing September 1, 2008, plus 1.75%, and for a 10-year term, the interest rate might be fixed at the bid side yield on the 5.25% coupon Government of Canada bond maturing June 1, 2013, plus 1.85%.

Large companies and governments need to borrow money to expand their business operations or infrastructure and social programs. Typically, they need far more money than the average bank is willing to provide. The solution is to raise money by issuing bonds. In reality, a bond is nothing more than a loan of which you, the investor, are the lender. The entity that sells a bond is known as the issuer.

A bond is secured by the physical assets of the issuer. It gives the bond holder a financial claim on the issuer and its assets. If the issuer defaults on its payments, the trust indenture provision allows certain specified assets to be seized by bondholders and sold to recover their investment. Typically, bonds are issued by financially substantial and solid entities, such as governments and major corporations. Bonds are not risk free. It is always possible that the borrower will default on the debt payments, particularly for corporate bonds.

A bond is characterized by its face value, coupon rate, maturity, and issuer (the borrower). The issuer of a bond must pay the investor interest at a predetermined rate and schedule. The interest rate is often referred to as the "coupon". The date on which the issuer has to repay the amount borrowed (known as face value) is called the maturity date. If, for example, you buy a bond with a face value of $1,000 (price of most corporate bonds at the start of their life), a coupon of 8%, and a maturity of 10 years, you will receive $80 ($1,000 x 8%) of interest per year for the next 10 years. Because most bonds pay interest semi-annually, you will receive two payments of $40 a year. When the bond matures, you will get your original $1,000 back.

Bonds are graded by rating agencies, based on their issuer's strength. The main rating agencies are Moody's, Firth, and Standard & Poor's. The ratings rank from AAA, AA, A to BBB. These are considered investment grade and then they go on down to BB and C, which are considered junk bonds.

To estimate the selling price of a bond you divide the annual interest income yield by the current interest rate (coupon amount). For example, the selling price of a $1,000 par value bond, paying 4.75% or $47.50 annually when the current interest rate is 6%, would be $47.50/6% = $791.67.

If one buys a bond at its par value, the yield is equal to the interest rate. If the price changes, the percentage yield will too. Let's take a $1,000 bond yielding 10% or $100 (yield = coupon amount/price). However, if the value of the bond becomes $750, the yield will become $100/$750 = 13.33%. Conversely, if the value of the bond increases to $1,100, the yield will be down to $100/$1,100 = 9.09%. When price goes up, which happens in times of declining interest rates, the percentage yield goes down and vice versa. A variation of a typical bond is one that makes no coupon payment, but instead is issued at a large discount to par value.

Bonds imply covenants. A covenant is a pledge or undertaking by the issuer to do, or not do, certain things. With bonds, commonly the covenant will be of a financial nature. For example, the issuer will promise to maintain a debt service coverage ratio of 1.10 to 1.25. There will also be additional debt tests

> *A covenant is a pledge or undertaking by the issuer to do, or not do, certain things.*

based upon cash flow and balance sheet ratios. While these restraints, which force financial prudence, please the bond buyers, they limit the operational flexibility of the issuer. In fact, most recent bond issues have not had covenants.

Another kind of bond is the debenture. It is a corporate bond backed only by the credit standing of the issuer, not by any specific property. It is also called an unsecured bond.

11.6.2 COMMERCIAL PAPER (CP) AND ASSET-BACKED COMMERCIAL PAPER (ABCP)

Asset-backed Commercial Paper (ABCP) started in Canada in 1989, probably in response to a shortage of unsecured corporate Commercial Paper (CP). ABCP is a short-term unsecured promissory note issued both by financial and non-financial corporations. CP can be issued for any term, typically with maturity dates of 30-60 days, but sometimes as high as 364 days. Overall, ABCP offers many advantages.

In Canada, CP and ABCP are priced in the same way, that is, by using the Canadian Dollar Offered Rate (CDOR) as the benchmark. For example, mid-rated ABCPs will be priced at 6 to 12 basis points (1/100th of 1% or 0.01%) above CDOR, while CP may be priced at 5 basis points.

The CDOR is the recognized benchmark index for the banker's acceptance (BA) with a term-to-maturity of 1 year or less. BAs are short-term non-interest bearing notes created by a non-financial firm and guaranteed by a bank. They are sold at a discount from their face value and redeemed by the accepting bank at maturity for the full face value. Technically, a BA is a draft, or bill of exchange, generated from foreign or domestic trade and stamped "accepted" by a bank. The bank's acceptance makes the BA an irrevocable primary obligation of the accepting bank.

The CDOR is determined daily from a survey of nine market makers in BA. The daily survey of money market rates is derived from bid side prices, provided by survey participants. Here is an example of rate fixing based on a specific day for CDOR:

Term	CDOR
1 month	2.76286
2 months	2.71571
3 months	2.69429
6 months	2.70000
1 year	2.76143

(a) Conduit Financing

Conduit financing, which falls under ABCP, can be described as a channel or conduit through which mortgage lenders distribute mortgages to the secondary mortgage market. The channel is made up of the various participants required to accomplish the task and through which the paper flows. Conduit financing is a financial vehicle that pools individual mortgages, then securitizes them. This pool is then sold by large investment dealers to institutional investors. It can be said that the genius of conduit financing is its ability to make illiquid (and generally private) assets liquid, by packaging them into securities that are made available to a broad range of investors.

The program takes place thanks to the services of financial packagers, such as a major bank that determines the feasibility of the transaction and arranges the credit enhancements. The title to the assets changes hands and is transferred to a Special Purpose Entity (SPE). The assets are thus turned into a low-risk, commercial paper bought by investors at very low interest rates. As more and more mortgages become part of asset pools, it is important to understand this process so you will be able to talk intelligently with issuers.

Asset Securitization

Conduit financing depends on securitization for its very existence. Securitization, in its most simplistic terms, transfers financial assets from their owner (a vendor, or a lessor in the case of a leasing transaction) to a SPE that in turn funds the acquisition by issuing highly rated public securities (notes) to various parties (investors).

The vendor of the assets becomes the mortgagor and acts as the servicer of these assets on behalf of the SPE. For example, Boeing Aircraft may lease an airplane to Air Canada. Boeing would then be responsible for collecting the payments (usually monthly) from the user/lessee and watching over the proper maintenance of the aircraft. In addition, the vendor participates in the future excess profit spread generated by these assets. This spread is equal to the difference between the interest earned on the assets (i.e., the rental charged to a lessee) and the interest paid on the notes held by the investors and used to fund the purchase (the security, for example the mortgage).

The process of securitization transfers the credit risk from the vendor to the actual assets sold. The structure is such that investors need be concerned only with the credit worthiness attributed to the asset pool held in the SPE.

Securitization can also be defined as "the issuance of securities payable primarily from the cash flow from a pool of self-liquidating assets, where the credit worthiness of the securities 'does not depend' on the credit worthiness of the seller of the assets." Asset securitization involves pooling groups of ABCP, such as mortgages, trade or credit card receivables, automobile leases, consumer loans, etc., and financing them with securities that are sold to investors.

Steps Involved in an Asset Securitization Transaction

The process of asset securitization involves many steps and entities. The typical step-by-step process is outlined below.

1. The holder of the conventional commercial paper, the vendor (who will later become the servicer of the assets and report to the SPE), approaches an investment-banking firm (ibank) to discuss the securitization transaction of the assets. These assets are usually numerous but could be only one unit, for example, a credit card portfolio or one large mortgage.
2. The ibank will assess the eligibility of the vendor and its assets.
3. The ibank will arrange for securitization of the loan by a credit enhancer who may be asked to put up of a letter of credit amounting to 5% of the pool value, as credit enhancement. Under Canadian Generally Accepted Accounting Principles (GAAP), 10% is the maximum acceptable or the transaction will not be considered a true sale, but rather a loan.
4. The rating agency will rate the commercial paper, by looking at the collateral, structure of the transaction, and strength (credit evaluation, past performance and reliability of the vendor) and advise what amount of credit enhancement is required to raise the rating of the assets.
5. The ibank will sell the assets to a SPE, usually a charitable trust, although SPEs can also be corporations or partnerships.
6. The investors will buy the notes from the SPE.
7. The SPE will pay the vendor, less a small piece of the portfolio (1-5%) to help in case of problems.
8. Periodically, the vendor will make scheduled payments to the SPE.
9. When a mortgage is paid off, the vendor receives the 1-5% security that was held back and the property is re-conveyed to him.

For a fee, the SPE will pay the investors and do all the bookkeeping, tax returns and other regulatory duties. Figure 11.4 charts a typical securitization transaction.

Figure 11.4
Sample Securitization Transaction

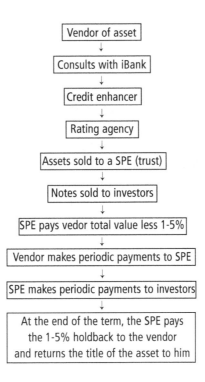

Typically, the vendor who uses securitization is a large, established corporation that has a solid infrastructure in place to support the reporting requirements of the SPE. However, more and more, one can see lenders offering this approach to smaller clients.

(b) Benefits and Drawbacks of Conduit Financing for the Vendor/Borrower

As with any process that requires the participation of many, there are many advantages and disadvantages to the various players. The benefits are:

- alternate source of funding
- balance sheet leverage (the assets are removed from the balance sheet of the vendor, often permitting increased return on equity)
- lower cost of funds (even with the costs involved in using securitization, the cost of the funds to the vendor is lower than with conventional direct borrowing)
- potential tax savings (tax savings may be possible for the vendor, depending on the securitization structure used)
- invisibility (customers of the vendor are unaware of the transaction; that is, that the asset has changed hands)
- higher LTV ratio than conventional mortgages (80% or higher, instead of 60-65%)
- lower DSR requirement (1.20 times minimum, for retail, multi-family, and industrial)
- generally, these loans are non-recourse, and
- longer amortization period (up to 30 years).

The drawbacks are:

- the asset class must be acceptable to the rating agency
- difficult packaging (a considerable amount of time and resources are required of the vendor)
- cost of setting up the structure (the cost can be high and this precludes that small amounts be considered; $25 million is probably the realistic minimum for a typical conduit deal and it can be made up of one or several mortgages)
- ongoing reporting issues (a report is required monthly; others are required quarterly and annually)
- amount must be for, at least, $1 million per participant
- rigidity of the business terms
- quasi-impossibility of early repayment (discharge)
- generally not assumable
- more restrictive underwriting procedures (the loan prohibits the sale of the mortgaged property and secondary financing, for example), and
- the property will be labelled as "impaired" because under this approach there are serious restrictions regarding what the vendor/borrower/servicer can do with it.

The typical requirements for a conduit commercial mortgage may be:

- 10-year term and 20-year amortization
- 1-5% replacement reserve holdbacks
- yield maintenance prepayment clause, or
- 2% prepayment penalty (if permitted).

However, suppose, for example, that 5 years down the road, you would like to sell or make extensive renovations, perhaps necessary to secure a AAA tenant. With a typical mortgage, you could probably re-negotiate the loan, arrange a second mortgage, or re-finance. This would be highly unlikely with a conduit loan at this time. However, the flexibility of this type of financing is improving all the time.

(c) Credit Ratings in the Securitization Process

In the securitization process, the rating agencies create a hierarchy from AAA down to BB, based on degree of risk of a given pool of assets. This allows investors, such as pension plans, money-market funds, and financial institutions, to invest according to their appetite for risk. These different categories are called "tranches" (from the French, meaning "slices") or pieces or segments. In Canada, Dominion Bond Rating Services gives its highest rating, R-1 to 95% of ABCP.

Defaults are very rare, with ABCP performing much better than CP. In Canada, since 1989, there has been no default or downgrade in the ABCP market. Conduits prefer standard 10-year term loans and they are open to all types of loans.

Securitization requires the segregation (true sale) of the assets away from the originator/vendor/servicer so that the financial health of the originator will not affect the investor's right to retrieve the cash flow produced by the assets. Almost always, the originator retains a residual interest in the performance of the assets and is forced to cover losses in the pool up to a certain percentage. If losses exceed that percentage, and any guarantee that was provided by the credit enhancer, the lower-rated tranches absorb them. This implies that conduits must assemble the loans according to the standards imposed by the rating agencies. The loans of a given pool must be compatible and structurally similar. For example, fixed-rate loans cannot be in the same pool as floating-rate loans. As a consequence, most conduits offer only fixed-rate loans.

In Canada, since 1989, there has been no default or downgrade in the ABCP market.

(d) Securitization Example

An example will clarify the process of securitization.

1. A vendor sells a pool of selected assets consisting of $200 million of commercial and residential mortgages to the trust (ibank).
2. The trust arranges credit enhancements, such as letters of credit or insurance, and arranges reserve accounts.
3. The trust issues $190 million of highly rated commercial paper to investors.
4. The trust pays $190 million to the vendor of the assets. Hence, at this stage the vendor has already received most of the money.
5. Using the income generated by the assets, the trust repays the investors and then pays the balance of $10 million to the vendor, either over a period of time or at the end of the term, when he once again owns the property free and clear.

(e) Logistics of Securitization

Organizing a securitization transaction is typically lengthy (up to 6 months), but in rare cases it can be handled in 1 to 1.5 months. It is also costly. Indeed there are multiple costs:

- structuring fee of the originator
- vendor's legal fees
- trust's legal fees
- rating agency fees

- credit enhancement fees (guarantees from other entities, letter of credit, cash deposit in trust funds), and
- program administration fees.

These costs preclude loans for small amounts, with $1 million being the minimum. The logistics involved in assembling, for example a pool of mortgages, are complicated. Indeed, it is obvious that if you have 200 or 500 mortgages in a pool, they were not created the same day. As a consequence, large financial conduits accumulate and hold loans during a 6- to 12-month period before they are securitized.

For additional info, see the Royal Bank site for conduits (<www.rbconduits.com>), the Merrill Lynch site (<www.gmi.ml.com/canada>), or First National Commercial Mortgage (<www.fnfc.com/conduit/>).

11.7 HOW LENDERS SET MORTGAGE AMOUNTS

Understand the intricacies of setting mortgage amounts, including LTV, DSR, and mortgage interest averaging.

When commercial mortgage lenders look at a mortgage application, they consider many factors. The most important are outlined below.

- **Type of Property.** Some lenders may lend on industrial properties, but not on other types.
- **Size of Mortgage Requested.** For some lenders a mortgage amount may be too small, but it may be too big for others.
- **Location of the Property.** Some lenders specialize in specific areas or in larger cities, others in small towns.
- **Use of the Property.** Some lenders will refuse to finance hotels, for example.
- **Availability and Timing of Funds.** Some lenders may have deposits to invest for 5 years, some for 10, some for 20, and their rates may vary somewhat as a result.
- **Experience and Credibility of the Borrower.** Many lenders are nervous lending large amounts to an investor who has never owned an income-producing property or is unproven as a business person.
- **Financial Means of the Borrower.** Lenders like people who have reserves.
- **Amount Requested.** The higher the LTV ratio requested, the more the lender will scrutinize the deal.

11.7.1 LOAN-TO-VALUE RATIO (LTV)

The LTV ratio compares the value of the property (as chosen by a mortgage lender) to the amount of the mortgage. It is used to determine the maximum amount of money the lender is willing to lend. The formula for calculating the LTV Ratio is:

$$LTV = Mortgage/Value\ of\ Property$$

For example, if a mortgage is for $2,000,000 and the property value is $3,000,000, LTV = $2,000,000/$3,000,000 = 66.67%.

Over the years, what is considered a typical LTV ratio has changed based on the perception of lenders regarding the state of the economy and of the real estate market in general. Because value is set by the lender, the type of property and, of course, the quality of the project and of the borrower, all affect the LTV ratio. In the case of apartment buildings in Canada, the Central Mortgage and Housing Corporation (CMHC), a governmental entity, permits higher LTV ratios (as high as 95%, depending on the number of units) because it insures the loan. For this, depending on the LTV ratio, CMHC charges a fee of 1.75% to 4.50% of the total loan amount, not only of the portion above 75%, the limit above which a loan becomes a

One borrower of large amounts of money never borrows more than the amount needed to reach a 75% LTV ratio because he feels the CMHC insurance premium is too high.

high-ratio loan. We know of one borrower of large amounts of money who never borrows more than the amount needed to reach a 75% LTV ratio (premium of 2.25%) because, beyond that, he feels the CMHC insurance premium is too high.

11.7.2 DEBT SERVICE RATIO (DSR)

Also called "Debt Coverage Ratio" (DCR), the DSR is the relationship between the NOI and the loan payment (principal and interest). The formula used to calculate DSR is:

$$\text{DSR} = \text{Net Operating Income/Annual Debt Service (principal and interest)}$$

It is used by the lender to determine the margin of safety in a loan. Put in a simplistic way, if you borrow $1,000 for a 12-month period at 10% interest only ($100) and tell the lender that you will earn $300 over 12 months, the lender has a cushion of $200, or a DSR of $300/$100 = 1.3.

For example, where the yearly mortgage payments are $160,000 and the NOI is $300,000, the DSR is:

$$\begin{aligned} \text{DSR} &= \$300{,}000/\$160{,}000 \\ &= 1.88 \end{aligned}$$

Many lenders require a minimum DSR ranging from 1.1 (rare) to 1.35 or higher. From their perspective, if the situation is less risky they will accept a higher loan amount and lower DSR. In the above example the income can drop from $300,000 to $160,000 and the cash flow will still be able to service the debt. Because of the high DSR, this property could probably also be refinanced, if the terms of the existing mortgage document allow it.

Lenders always include a property management fee in the expenses, even if no outside property manager is involved, because if the borrower defaults on the loan, the lender will have to take over the property and pay for the services of a property manager. Similarly, lenders feel it prudent to include a maintenance reserve in their calculations even though investors rarely include this when preparing financial statements. In fact, it is wise to think like a lender when preparing your financial statements to apply for a loan and include the following:

- vacancies and bad debt allowance, regardless of the quality and term of tenancies (it can go from 1% of GPI for top-quality properties to as high as 10% for poor quality properties)
- property management fees, ranging from 2-5% of the gross operating income
- maintenance reserve (2% of potential gross income is reasonable, but this will vary depending on the age and condition of the building and its components), and
- any additions or adjustments to the Income and Expense Statement received from the vendor because many entries will be incorrect, or not quite correct.

Lenders are conditioned to receiving optimistic financial statements that they must adjust. Make it your goal to present them with realistic statements that they will be able to trust.

11.7.3 MORTGAGE INTEREST AVERAGING

Quite often, a property will have two mortgages with different interest rates and you will want to know the combined rate. To find out the average rate, you have two options: use the mortgage amounts or use the percentages that the mortgages represent of the total mortgages. Let's look at an example where there are two mortgages, one for $1 million at 7% interest, and the second for $500,000 at 9% interest, bringing the total of the two mortgages to $1.5 million.

Option A: Using mortgage amounts

Average Mortgage Rate

$$= \frac{\text{(Amount of Mortgage 1 x Interest Rate)} + \text{(Amount of Mortgage 2 x Interest Rate)}}{\text{Total of All Mortgages}}$$

Average Mortgage Rate

$$= \frac{\$1,000,000 \times 7\% + \$500,000 \times 9\%}{\$1,000,000 + \$500,000}$$

$$= \frac{\$70,000 + 45,000}{\$1,500,000}$$

$$= \frac{\$115,000}{1,500,000}$$

$$= .07666 \text{ or } 7.67\%$$

Option B: Using percentage of mortgages

$$= \left(\frac{\text{Amount Mortgage 1}}{\text{Total all Mortgages}} \times \frac{\text{Interest Rate}}{\text{Mortgage 1}} \right) + \left(\frac{\text{Amount Mortgage 2}}{\text{Total all Mortgages}} \times \frac{\text{Interest Rate}}{\text{Mortgage 2}} \right)$$

Average Mortgage Rate

$$= \left(\frac{\$1,000,000}{\$1,500,000} \times 7\% \right) + \left(\frac{\$500,000}{\$1,500,000} \times 9\% \right)$$

$$= (0.6666 \times 7\%) + (0.3333 \times 9\%)$$

$$= 0.04666 + 0.02999$$

$$= 4.67\% + 3.0\%$$

$$= 7.67\%$$

11.8 BAND OF INVESTMENT THEORY

Be knowledgeable about band of investment theory.

The band of investment theory considers the risk-free rate of return, adds market risk to this amount, and then adds property risk to determine the overall capitalization rate. It is used by a few large investors/financial analysts to analyze a property. It is the synthesis of mortgage and equity rates. Using the example in section 11.7.3 and adding the total price of the property of $2,000,000 means that the equity in the property is 25% of the total price, whereas Mortgage 1 (M1) of $1,000,000 represents 50% of the price, and Mortgage 2 (M2) of $500,000 represents 25% of the price.

Assuming we want a Return on Equity (ROE) of 12%, to obtain the weighted rate average we need to multiply each percentage of monetary contribution by the rate.

	% of value		Rate		Product
M1	50%	x	7%	=	3.50%
M2	25%	x	9%	=	2.25%
Equity	25%	x	12%	=	3.00%
Weighted rate average					**8.75%**

If the desired ROE was 18%, we would change the last line to: 25% x 18% = 4.5%, giving us a weighted average of 10.25%. This average can be compared to the Cap Rate to see if the price of the property in question will give the buyer the ROE that he wants, or rather wishes.

11.9 CMHC AND MORTGAGE INSURANCE

Use CMHC as it benefits your investments.

The Canada Mortgage and Housing Corporation (CMHC) can be of great help to the investor. CMHC is the Crown corporation responsible for administering Canada's *National Housing Act* (R.S.C. 1985, c. N-11). It can assist investors in the three following ways:

1. information on all matters relating to housing (single and multi-family properties only) in Canada
2. publications (research and technical), and
3. rental mortgage insurance.

CMHC Mortgage Loan Insurance protects approved lenders against losses. With CMHC-insured loans, borrowers can obtain mortgage financing of up to 95% of the value of the property, without a maximum dollar amount, if they live in the property and it has no more than three units, or 85% if they do not live in it. However, CMHC provides mortgage loan insurance only for residential rental properties (apartment buildings, retirement homes, condominiums, mixed use buildings, and, of course, houses). Mortgage financing is insurable for a variety of purposes, including the purchase of existing property, new construction, renovations/conversions, restructuring of existing debt, and equity transfer to assist in the purchase or construction of another multi-unit residential project.

Many people assume that all CMHC-insured mortgages are non-recourse. This is not true.

The non-recourse option is possible only for loans not exceeding 60% of the lending value, as determined by CMHC. Since one can borrow up to 75% without the mortgage being considered high ratio, CMHC guarantees are rarely used below this LTV ratio. The guarantee/insurance is voided in case of environmental liability and fraud.

Here is some additional information.

- CMHC requires that the borrower have a net worth equal to as least 25% of the loan amount, with a minimum of $100,000.
- When the borrower is a corporate entity, additional personal and/or corporate guarantees are required over and above the loan covenants. The amount of additional guarantee required is 2% of the loan amount for each percentage in LTV ratio above 60%.

For example, at 78% LTV the additional guarantee is 36% of the loan amount (78 – 60 = 18 x 2%) and at 85% LTV the additional guarantee is 50% (85 – 60 = 25 x 2%) of the loan amount.

For insured loans for construction of new rental buildings, the additional guarantee during construction will be 100% of the loan amount, until stabilized rents are achieved, at which time the guarantee will be reduced to the amount based on the formula described above.

By reducing the risk to lenders, due to loan insurance, borrowers benefit from lower interest rates. Borrowers also receive favourable interest rates at renewal times since the insurance remains in force for the full amortization period of the loan. This insurance program also improves cash flow because mortgage loan insurance application fees and premiums are considered "soft" costs that may be added to the mortgage loan as a non-cash transaction. In fact, it is best to pay them separately, as explained at 12.3.1. As previously mentioned, the premium is a percentage of the total loan amount and goes from 0.05% (65% LTV ratio) to 2.9% (85% LTV ratio). Go to <www.cmhc-schl.gc.ca> and type "CMHC Quick Reference" in the search box. The rules for multi-family buildings are similar, but more complicated.

CMHC's Internet site offers a rental mortgage insurance calculator <www.cmhc-schl.gc.ca>. You can also contact CMHC at:

Ontario Business Centre -Toronto
130 King Street West, Suite 1000, P.O. Box 448
Toronto, Ontario, M5X 1E5
Tel: (416) 218-3368   Fax: (416) 218-3309

The only other company (to our knowledge) that offers mortgage insurance in Canada is GE Canada (<www.gemortgage.ca>).

11.10 THE FEDERAL INTEREST ACT

You may become involved in a situation where money is lent without the protection of a mortgage. Note that under the federal *Interest Act*, if the interest is specified to be for a monthly, weekly, or any period shorter than 1 year, the maximum interest that can be charged is 5%, unless the loan document says to which yearly rate it is equivalent. Note, too, that the maximum legal yearly rate of interest that can be charged is 59.99%.

CHAPTER 12

Applying for a Mortgage

By the end of this chapter, you will be able to:

- Know the many resources available to approach for a mortgage.
- Identify the advantages of working with a mortgage broker.
- Determine which fees are required and the correct way to pay them.
- Recognize the risks in mortgage transfers.
- Pose and answer all the questions regarding the terms of the mortgage.
- Understand and work within the negotiating process.
- Collect and organize the documentation required for existing and new properties.
- Navigate the standard industry-wide process of the mortgage application.
- Understand the Power of Sale concept within the default process and what happens upon foreclosure.

Without doubt, mortgages are of paramount importance to the real estate investor. Not only do they allow investors to purchase more expensive properties than if paying cash, but they offer the additional benefits of leveraging their investments. It is therefore critical that the investor know what's involved in the mortgage application process, how to negotiate with the vendor, critical terms to watch out for, and what to do if you run into problems with your mortgage. For an in-depth look at mortgage terms, see also Chapter 7, Contracts and Other Legal Details.

12.1 SOURCES OF MORTGAGES

Know the many resources available to approach for a mortgage.

The first step in getting a mortgage is to decide who you want to approach. If you are working with a broker, he will be the one deciding which lenders to approach. If you have decided to handle the mortgage search on your own, you will have to do some fact checking to decide the most likely lenders.

There are several potential lenders you could approach, including:
- chartered banks
- savings institutions
- life insurance companies
- trust companies
- retirement and pension funds
- finance companies
- real estate investment and mortgage trusts
- credit unions
- individuals, and
- vendors – the best source to facilitate a sale is by taking back a mortgage, which is called a Vendor-Take-Back (VTB) or Purchase Money Mortgage.

Note that all of the above lend money, but each with its own standards and idiosyncrasies.

12.2 DEALING WITH MORTGAGE BROKERS

Identify the advantages of working with a mortgage broker.

The very tempting advantage of dealing directly with a lender is to save on origination fees or sometimes to obtain a lower interest rate. However, the advantage of using a broker is that he is independent and knows the market and the lenders who are most likely to be interested in providing the kind of loan you are seeking. To obtain the name of top-calibre mortgage brokers, ask developers who frequently arrange mortgages.

Lenders tend to specialize in the types of loans they offer, in terms of loan size, type of real estate, kinds of mortgages offered, geographical market covered, and security required. A broker can save you a considerable amount of time and, in the end, it may cost you no more than dealing directly with a lender. Furthermore, mortgage brokers are required by law to give their clients detailed and complete disclosure regarding the mortgage transaction, notably the amount of the fee he receives and whether it is paid by the borrower or the lender. Obviously the broker must also indicate to which party (the borrower or lender) his first duty lies. A mortgage development officer who is an employee of the lender is not under this obligation. The ideal situation is to find a top-notch mortgage development officer at a lending institution or a top-notch mortgage broker.

It is logical to use a mortgage broker under the circumstances described below.

- You are not familiar with the mortgage field, the lingo, and the "jungle out there".
- You do not have the time or the inclination to do the legwork involved to research a number of lenders.
- Your property is one that is difficult to finance or you need a Loan-to-Value (LTV) ratio higher than "normal".
- You are pressed for time (which is almost always the case).
- You do not have credibility at this point in your commercial real estate investment career.

The *Mortgage Brokers Act* (R.S.O. 1990, c. M.39) of Ontario defines a mortgage broker as "a person who carries on the business of lending money on the security of real estate, whether the money is the person's money or that of another person". The typical mortgage broker (who generally does not lend his own money) will canvas the main banks and other institutions. If he does not meet with success, he will go to secondary lenders and/or private money, whose appetite for both risks and returns is generally higher.

The big advantage that mortgage brokers have over individuals seeking a mortgage directly is that they are familiar with many lenders and their lending policies. They know which lender has a lot of money on hand to lend, for how long, and on what types of properties it likes to lend. Note that brokers are not obligated to find the best deal for you unless they have contracted (signed a contract) with you to act as your agent.

12.2.1 BROKER'S FEES

For simple or rubber-stamped types of mortgages, the mortgage broker usually receives his commission as a referral fee from the lender, who builds it into his rate. However, in a more difficult situation, such as if the borrower does not qualify for a traditional (institutional) mortgage, the mortgage broker will have to go the secondary financing route. In this case, the borrower will have to pay the broker a fee for his services. Depending on the difficulty of the task at hand, a broker may ask for a non-refundable fee with the application. However, in most situations, you will not be asked for a fee at the outset.

Be sure to find out whether you are dealing with a lender or a broker, which may not always be clear. Some financial institutions operate as both lenders and brokers. This is important because the broker may be paid a fee for his services that is separate from, and in addition to, the lender's origination or other fees. For most conventional (primary) lenders, the borrower is not asked to pay a broker's fee. A broker's compensation may be paid at closing or be added to your mortgage, or both. You may negotiate with the brokers as well as the lenders regarding fees and expenses.

12.3 MORTGAGE FEES

Determine which fees are required and the correct way to pay them.

Mortgage fees are usually quoted as points (also called "basis points") and are often linked to the interest rate; usually the more points you pay, the lower the rate. One hundred points equals 1%. For example, on a loan from a financial institution for $5,000,000 you would probably pay 100 basis points (1%) of the loan amount, but a private lender would charge you 2-3%. The concept is similar to the leasing of a car. The more cash you pay, the lower the monthly payments will be. If you borrowed $500,000 and are asked for a fee of 300 basis points (3%), you would need to pay $15,000. Ask for points to be quoted to you as a dollar amount, rather than just the number of points, so that you will know exactly how much you will have to pay.

A loan often involves many expenses for the borrower, such as loan origination or underwriting fees, broker fees, registration and closing costs, legal fees, plus related expenses due to the lender's demands for a survey, appraisal, building condition, and environmental reports. Some fees are paid when you apply for a loan (such as application and appraisal fees) and others are paid at closing. In many cases, you can borrow the money needed to pay these fees, but doing so will increase your loan amount and total costs.

When the lender issues a letter of intent, usually he will require a commitment fee in the range of 1-3% of the loan amount, which can range from $1,000 to $50,000 and even more. This fee will either be refunded when the loan is funded or retained by the lender if the borrower does not complete the transaction through no fault of the lender, perhaps because he fails to pursue the application by providing the information requested by the lender. Basically, the lender wants to be protected from frivolous applicants. If the lender declines the application, the fee will be refunded.

Below, we explain in detail the various fees and expenses a commercial borrower may have to pay. We say "may" because it varies with the situation.

- **Origination or Sourcing Loan Fee.** This is typically 1-3% of the loan amount, paid to the mortgage broker.
- **Administration Fee.** This euphemism is encountered in some cases. This is just an extra charge, payable to the lender. Other fees that must be paid directly by borrowers or are added by lenders to the cost can include an appraisal fee, ranging from $300 for a small house to several thousand dollars for a large commercial building, survey fees ($500 to $5,000), legal fees ($1,000 to $100,000 or even more for large loans), and mortgage registration fees, which are billed by the lawyer and not very high.
- **Broker's Fee.** Usually brokers' fees must be paid in full when the loan is granted (they are often deducted from the loan amount). They are negotiable and depend on the intricacies and complexities of the application and desirability of the deal for the lender. The borrower's ability to negotiate them will depend on the appetite of the lender for the specific deal, and the level of desperation of the borrower. Usually, lenders who provide money for construction projects charge points, amounting from 1-3%, or even higher in special circumstances. Fees can also be charged for an existing property and vary according to the loan amount, property type, location, market conditions, and other factors.

Every lender has different policies, but most loans are available at a higher interest rate with no points and no fees. As a general rule, the borrower is better off not paying points, hence accepting to pay a higher interest rate (or to pay interest on a larger amount) because it can take years before the additional costs involved with fees paid upfront can be recovered.

12.3.1 THE RIGHT WAY TO PAY FEES

In principle, for income tax purposes, you cannot deduct finance charges (fees) from the initial amount of a loan. If, for example, you borrow $1,000,000 and must pay $3^{1}/_{2}\%$ in fees ($35,000), the lender may agree to withhold this amount thus deducting the fees from the loan. In this case, you would receive only: $1,000,000 - $35,0000 = $965,000.

Canada Revenue Agency (CRA) could contend that these fees are not deductible because they were not in actuality paid, just that the amount of the loan was smaller. To avoid this problem, borrow and receive the full amount of the loan and pay the fees ($35,000, in this case) by separate cheque.

12.4 DANGERS OF MORTGAGE TRANSFER

Recognize the risks in mortgage transfers.

If you sell a property with an existing mortgage, both you and the buyer might want to have that mortgage transferred to the buyer. For the buyer, it makes the deal easier and less onerous, both in time and money. For you, the vendor, it seems simple and you can avoid paying what can be a significant penalty to discharge your mortgage before it comes due. Also, if your mortgage is below the current market rate this can be a powerful appeal to the buyer.

However, remember that when you sign on the dotted line of a mortgage document, you frequently sign a personal promise to pay (this varies with the LTV ratio requirement and the lender). This means that if somewhere down the road the buyer defaults after you have assigned the loan to the buyer, the original mortgagor (you) will still be liable for payment and bound to be sued by the lender, even if the buyer has assumed responsibility for the mortgage. This is called a "personal recourse" mortgage. Ideally, you would secure a release from the lender before completing a mortgage transfer, but that is highly unlikely because there is absolutely no incentive for the lender to do so.

So, if you decide to transfer a mortgage, bear in mind the risk associated with this action and be diligent in inquiring about the character and resources of the buyer to whom you will be making the transfer.

It is possible to find non-recourse mortgages, but the LTV ratio is about 10% to 15% lower.

12.5 CLARIFYING AND COMPARING MORTGAGE TERMS

Pose and answer all the questions regarding the terms of the mortgage.

As mentioned in 11.2.3, frequently, borrowers who are not familiar with mortgages and are eager to find one concern themselves only with the major points:
- amount and, therefore, LTV ratio
- term
- amortization
- interest rate, and
- debt service ratio.

Unfortunately, mortgage borrowing has become very complicated and, as usual, the devil is in the details. Here are other points that you should clarify and plan for at the very beginning. If you do not, they will likely come back to haunt you later.

12.5.1 QUESTIONS TO CONSIDER BEFORE APPROACHING A LENDER

There are many questions to ask yourself and the lender. We've grouped them into three categories. First are questions regarding your financial requirements.

- Will the lender hold back money, for example, to pay for a roof that needs to be replaced in a few years? If yes, it means that you may have borrowed $2,000,000, but receive only $1,800,000 if the lender puts $200,000 aside and will release it only if/when you replace the roof.
- Are there reserve build-ups required, for example, to replace appliances in the case of a multi-family property?
- What is the loan's Annual Percentage Rate (APR), which includes points, fees, and other expenses that the lender may ask you to pay? The nominal interest rate alone does not permit a valid comparison between mortgages, unless all extra expenses are identical, which is rarely the case. The APR instead is calculated on the amount borrowed plus expenses, such as loan origination fees, title insurance, appraisal, mortgage insurance, and legal fees. If a bank offers to charge 8% and no fees of any kind, the nominal interest rate and APR are the same – 8%. If a private lender offers to charge 7.5% and 3% in fees, the amount borrowed increases by 3%.

  Example
  $1,000 x 8% = $80
  APR= $80/$1,000= 0.08 or 8%
  $1,000 + 3% = $1,030 x 7.5% = $77.25
  APR = $77.25/$1,000 = 0.077 or 7.7%

- What fees will be charged (as mentioned earlier)? These could include legal fees, registration fees, appraisal fees, processing fees, documentation fees, and fees that may be charged by a third party.
- Will the lender let you add all the expenses incurred in servicing the mortgage to its principal amount or will you have to pay them out of your pocket, or from the loan proceeds, lowering the effective mortgage amount?
- Does the lender require recourse (a guarantee besides the real property itself)?

With your financial requirements solved, we move on to the lender's documentation requirements.

- How much weight and emphasis does each lender place on the financial strength of your tenants? Usually lenders do not demand a minimum credit rating for the tenants, but they do take into account the size and financial strength of tenants to determine the risk (as they perceive it) they are taking in making the loan. Lenders do not think like borrowers. They wonder about things such as: what will happen if the borrower mismanages the property or loses a major tenant and the lender has to take it over; or how likely is the tenant(s) to still be in business before the mortgage is repaid; or, if this tenant defaults, how likely is it that it will be replaced by one with a similar credit rating, how good a businessperson is the president of the tenant ABC Gadget Company?
- Does the lender require specific formats for appraisals, building condition inspections, environmental reports, etc.? Which suppliers will it accept? If it is a small list of acceptable suppliers, the cost will likely be higher than normal.

- How picky is the lender regarding the insurance (coverage, terms, etc.)? Some lenders expect very extensive coverage of everything, such as mortgage insurance, business interruption insurance, and rental guarantee insurance.

- Is there a balloon payment? This is a mortgage loan, the principal of which will not be fully repaid at the end of the term. It can be an amortized mortgage with a term shorter than the amortization period, or an interest only mortgage (the whole amount of principal is due at the end of the term). Example: a 10-year term mortgage with a 25-year amortization period will have a large balloon to be paid at the end of the 10 years.

- Will the lender permit prepayment, meaning will you be allowed to pay all or part of the balance outstanding at any point in time? A typical clause regarding prepayment reads as follows: "This Mortgage can be prepaid, in whole or in part, at any time or times, without penalty or bonus." You will find this clause acceptable to the lender usually only in the case of a VTB.

- The big advantage of assuming a mortgage and/or a VTB is that the new borrower saves time and does not have to pay various expenses such as mortgage, environmental reports, or appraisals. You should negotiate strongly for this clause. It gives you the flexibility to pay off some of the principal, if you have extra cash at some point in time. It also permits you to refinance whenever it is beneficial for you. Finally, if you want to sell the property and the buyer wants to pay cash or arrange his own financing, you will be in a position to do so. However, if prepayment is not allowed in the mortgage document, which is usually the case with Income-Producing Properties (IPP) (except with private mortgages), the lender may demand a penalty for early repayment. This, too, can be a point of negotiation. Will the lender permit assumption of the mortgage by a new purchaser? That is, the new buyer would "inherit" the mortgage with all its terms (no change). This implies that the buyer would assume all liabilities. Usually the lender must approve the new borrower before it releases the vendor from liability, if it does. There may be an assumption fee. On what basis?

- At this juncture we must cover in more detail the often overlooked — by the borrower, never by the lender — question of early loan repayment (prepayment) of a conventional mortgage. Lenders like to place restrictions on early repayment. This is understandable, since prudent money management on their part makes them match their borrowing terms with their lending terms. Some lenders, though not many, accept early repayment with a 3-month interest prepayment penalty. However, most will talk about yield maintenance, which is also a penalty because it financially penalizes the borrower for repaying the mortgage early. Simply stated, a lender takes the rate of the actual mortgage and compares it to the present mortgage rate, then calculates the difference of income over the balance of the term, and adds to this amount an administrative fee to allow for repaying the mortgage early. We have seen prepayment terms cause a transaction to be aborted when the LTV ratio of the remaining balance of the principal of the mortgage is 30% or 40% while the purchaser wants a minimum 60%. The situation is much worse with a conduit loan, where a borrower must purchase bonds to guarantee constant yield to the lender.

  Don't forget to address the question of early loan repayment — often overlooked by the borrower, but never by the lender.

- Will the terms of your loan limit your ability to sell the property? Some lenders insist that the mortgage be repaid if the property is sold. This due-on-sale clause is included to protect the lender from a subsequent owner who may be a higher risk.

- Does the mortgage contain a clause allowing the lender to assign it to another party? Sometimes a mortgage will contain an assignment clause, which means that the borrower may find himself having to send his cheques to a new mortgagor. This is the assigning (passing on) of a mortgagee's interest in a mortgage to a new mortgagee (investor). It could almost be said that it is the contrary of the assumption. Assumption is when the new property owner takes over the existing mortgage, whereas assignment is when the mortgagor sells the mortgage to a new investor.

- Does the lender grant borrowers the right to renew or renegotiate the mortgage? This privilege is easier to obtain with private lenders, but there are always fees attached to it.
- What remedies are expected in case of default? An actual clause will best explain this:

> RENT AND MANAGEMENT
> PROVIDED also, and it is hereby further agreed by and between the Borrower and Lender, that should default be made by the Borrower in the observance or performance of any of the convenants, provisos, agreements of conditions contained in this Mortgage, the Lender reserves the right to enter into said lands and premises and to receive the rents and profits to be entitled to receive in addition to all other fees, charges and disbursements to which the Lender is entitled, a management fee so as to reimburse the Lender for reasonable time and trouble in management of said lands and premises it being understood and agreed that in the circumstances a management fee equal to 2.0% of the gross receipts (net of the Loan monies of this letter of Finance), in the management of the said lands and premises is a just and equitable fee, having regard to all the circumstances.

- Does the lender have demands regarding rental income? For example, if the income falls below a certain level, the lender may request that you build-up reserves from other sources, or that the rents be deposited in a lockbox account at a bank, or they will impose certain standards for new tenants.
- Will the lender limit/prohibit changes to the property?
- Will the lender prohibit or reserve the right to permit/approve secondary financing? In other words, will he permit the borrower to borrow more money by way of a second or third mortgage?

Finally, you should also ensure that you are informed of the lender's financial status.

- At this point in time, does the lender have much money to invest or, on the contrary, have more requests for loans than money available? If it is the latter, it will likely be more difficult to negotiate favourable terms.

Collect this information from at least three lenders so that you can compare. Tell the lenders that you are talking to other lenders and, after you have chosen a lender, ask that lender to provide you ahead of time with the loan documents (commitment letter and other documents) you will have to sign. This may enlighten you on how this lender treats borrowers.

12.6 NEGOTIATING MORTGAGE TERMS

Understand and work within the negotiating process.

To be able to negotiate intelligently, you must read the commitment letter (some call it the Letter of Finance) from start to end. It you ask for ten changes to it, expect two or three to be accepted. Once you know what each lender has to offer, negotiate for the best deal you can. On any given day, lenders and brokers may offer different rates for the same loan terms to different customers, even if those borrowers have the same loan qualifications and characteristics. The most likely reason for the difference is that loan officers and brokers are allowed some latitude in negotiating and may be allowed to keep some, or all, of the difference they negotiate over a lender's basis rate as extra personal compensation.

An effective negotiating technique is to ask the lender or broker to send you a letter outlining all the costs associated with the loan. Then ask him to waive or reduce one or more of the fees or agree to a lower rate. Do not hesitate to ask lenders or brokers if they can give better terms than those first quoted or than those you have found elsewhere.

12.7 GATHERING INFORMATION TO APPLY FOR A MORTGAGE

Collect and organize the documentation required for existing and new properties.

When looking for a mortgage, we suggest that the first step be to prepare a Data Sheet, such as the one shown in Figure 12.1. A Data Sheet has many purposes.
- You and the lenders can refer to it easily.
- It will speed up the process for the lender.
- It makes you appear professional.

12.7.1 LENDER DOCUMENTATION REQUIREMENTS FOR EXISTING BUILDINGS

When applying for a mortgage on an existing building there is certain information that lenders of mortgages typically require.
- **Summary Statement of Objectives (use of the funds).** For example, to pay 60% of the purchase price and use another 10% to replace the roof.
- **Site Description and Relevant Data.** For example, the 3.42-acre site fronts on two roads. It comprises a swimming pool and a tennis court.
- **Tenancies Data.** A rent roll showing tenants' names, area, unit number, lease start and expiry date, rental and other payments, and options (to renew, etc.).
- **Improvements.** A detailed description of existing or planned improvements.
- **Financial Profile and Financial Statement.** The personal and/or corporate assets and liabilities of the borrower.
- **Details of the Requested Mortgage.** This should include the amount, terms, etc.
- **Appendix.** Supporting documentation, such as mortgage application, credit references, and financial information.

Figure 12.1
Sample Data Sheet

INFORMATION FOR MORTGAGE PURPOSES

1- Address: 145 Any Boulevard, Brantford, Ontario
                                 Between Hwy 403 & Another Rd

2- Type of Property: Industrial manufacturing/warehousing building

3- Building Area: 120,000 sq.ft. including 10,000 sq.ft. of office space. Sprinklered

4- Ceiling Height: 20' and 24'

5- Bay sizes: 50' x 40' and 50' x 60'

6- Land Area: 12 acres

7- Services: Municipal

8- Electrical service: 1,500 Kva in 600 volts

9- Zoning: M-2, General Industrial

10- Type of transaction: Sale and Lease back, with sister company Large Properties Inc. as Buyer/Landlord and Begood Inc. as Vendor/Tenant

11- Rental [NOI]:   10 year entirely net Lease. 5 years @ $432,000. Second 5 years @ $480,000

12- Purchase Price: $3,650,000

13- ROI: First 5 years: 11.84%. Second 5 years: 13.15%

14- Closing Date: September 9, 2006

15- Purchaser: Large Properties Inc.

16- Details on Tenant: Begood manufactures farm hardware and does O.E.M. forging, stamping, machining and wire forming. They control 80% of the Canadian market. In addition, they have recently signed a contract with Super Tractors to do their forging.
                                 The company has been in business since 1920
                                 Number of employees: 127
                                 Annual sales: $19 million

17- To be provided :   - Agreement of Purchase and Sale
as requested   - Site Plan/survey
                                 - Registry Plan
                                 - Appraisal –August 2006
                                 - Phase One Report. Dated April 2004 –Updated in August 2006
                                 - Building Inspection report –August 2006

18- Amount requested: $2,190,000, or more

Remarks:
The one-storey building is 16 years old. While it is now occupied by one tenant, it would be easy to divide into 3 or 4 units, thanks to the building configuration and the large site.

Bear in mind, however, that there is no standard application. Within the general guidelines, each lender will have its own personal demands. See also Mortgage Letter of Intent (section 12.8.1) and Mortgage Commitment Letter (section 12.8.2).

If you give your personal financial statement to a lender, it is a given that he will request a credit report from a credit bureau. The two main credit bureaus in Canada are TransUnion Canada <www.transunion.ca> and Equifax Canada <www.equifax.ca>. They independently maintain files on borrowers that may include a payment history of credit cards, loans for cars, appliances, mortgages, and more.

The end result is that you are given a credit score, which is a credit measurement tool. It is either a FICO score (developed in 1950 by Fair Isaac & Co) from TransUnion or a BEACON score from Equifax. Both are based on a computer analysis of your financial activity to-date. They have different names, but use identical approaches. The criteria are current level of indebtness (30% of the overall score), length of credit history (15% of the overall score), new credit being applied for (10% of overall score), type of credit used (10% of overall score), and payment history (35% of the overall score).

Before you start on your real estate investing journey, request a copy of your credit report for a small fee. You can obtain this online. Equifax charges $24 for a combined credit score and credit report and $15.50 for the latter alone. TransUnion is less expensive at $15 and $8. Carefully check the contents of the report because errors are not uncommon and you want to identify any mistakes and have them corrected, if possible before you approach a lender for a mortgage. You can request that a lender correct information with the credit bureaus, if it is indeed inaccurate.

12.7.2 LENDER DOCUMENTATION REQUIREMENT FOR NEW PROJECTS

When applying for a mortgage on a new (to-be-built) commercial project, most lenders require the information outlined below.

- **Feasibility Report (Typically, $3,000 to $10,000).** Prepared by a consultant, this report can range from a letter to a fully detailed report on the economic, market, and physical characteristics of the venture.
- **Construction and Site Analysis.** This analysis is a complete documentation regarding the property, architectural drawings, detailed construction plans, utilities, landscaping, parking, buffer zones, adjacent zoning, and zoning amendments required. Obviously, this involves an architect, but it may also involve a quantity surveyor, frequently called a cost consultant.
- **Borrower Information.** Include the financing record on past projects with addresses of lenders who were involved with the project, financial statements for the past two to three years, credit check, and background of the company/individual with supporting documents for this information.
- **Estimated Income/Operating Expenses.** This provides full details of estimated gross income, projected vacancy rates, expenses (excluding debt service), and net operating income.
- **Appraisal ($3,000 to $8,000).**
- **Up-to-date survey ($500 to $2,500).**
- **Environmental Report.** A Phase 1, Environmental Site Assessment (ESA) report, will cost between $2,000 and $4,000.

12.8 MORTGAGE APPLICATION PROCESS

Navigate the standard industry-wide process of the mortgage application.

Once you have your documentation prepared and have approached three lenders, at this stage a fairly standard industry-wide process usually begins.

12.8.1 MORTGAGE LETTER OF INTENT

When a lender is interested in making the loan, it provides a Letter of Intent (or of interest), often called a "term sheet", subject to satisfactory title searching and other conditions that it may specify. The term sheet identifies the basic terms of the transaction, either already discussed with the borrower or which the borrower will request. It shows the intention of the lender and is a non-binding document. If the borrower signs this Letter of Intent, he is required to pay the lender an application processing fee. Be careful, however, because this Letter has conditions in it, which means that the lender can back out of it as shown in the letter in Figure 12.2, but keep the fee. Furthermore, it always has an expiry date of, at the most, a few weeks.

Mortgaging a property is as complicated as selling it. Using a lawyer is an absolute must.

12.8.2 MORTGAGE COMMITMENT LETTER

Once the Letter of Intent is signed by the borrower and sent back to the lender with the processing fee, the data requested in this letter must be provided to the lender by the borrower. The lender will review this material and almost always ask for some additional information. Once satisfied, the lender will issue a Mortgage Commitment Letter, which is a legally binding contract between lender and borrower. You will find an example in Figure 12.3. We have changed names and addresses to protect the privacy of the parties involved. The original letter was 13 pages long, plus three schedules, which have been omitted (Rent Roll, Estoppel Certificate, and Acknowledgement of Assignment, Attornment and Non-Disturbance).

Figure 12.2
Mortgage Letter of Intent

September 10, 2005

XYZ PROPERTIES INC.
C/o Broker & Company Limited
90 University Avenue,
Toronto, ON M5J 1S3

Attention: Mr. Jolly Guy

Dear Sirs:

Re: Potential Mortgage Financing
        999 Terry St., Brantford, Ontario

Pursuant to our discussions regarding your mortgage requirements for the referenced property, the intent of this Application is to summarize the terms and conditions under which Lending Corp will consider your request. This letter is not a commitment to provide financing. If this Application is approved, a formal commitment letter will be issued specifying the terms and conditions of the approval.

Applicant:	XYZ PROPERTIES INC.
Loan Amount:	$2,375,000
Term:	5 or 10 Years
Amortization:	20 Years
Interest Rate:	To be established following acceptance of a commitment, no earlier than 60 days nor later than 10 business days prior to the funding date.
	For a 5-year term, the interest rate would be fixed at the bid side yield on the 4.25% coupon Government of Canada bond maturing September 1, 2010 plus 1.75%.
	For a 10-year term, the interest rate would be fixed at the bid side yield on the 5.25% coupon Government of Canada bond maturing June 1, 2015 plus 1.85%.
Security:	The property to be financed is known municipally, as 999 Terry St., Brantford, Ontario.
	The site contains a total area of 11.19 acres and is improved with a 120,000 square foot single-tenanted industrial building.

As security, Lending Corp will require:
- A freehold first mortgage/charge
- General Assignment of Rents and Leases
- Specific Assignment of Leases for tenants contributing more than 20% of the gross income of the property. These tenants must have acknowledged the assignment and agree to attorn to Lending Corp upon default under the Mortgage.
- Other documentation that Lending Corp or its solicitors deem necessary

Information to be provided with Application:

- Property Rent Roll signed and certified correct by Applicant. Rent Roll to include Tenant Name, Area Leased, Lease Start and End Dates, Current and Future Contractual Income, and Expense Recoveries.
- Property Operating Statement (Income & Expense) for the past three years, signed and certified as correct by Applicant.
- 2005 and 2006 Operating budget for the property.
- Property Tax Statement and paid receipt for the most recent year.
- Applicant's Financial Statements (last 3 years; signed and dated).
- Summary of Applicant's Ownership, History and current Business Plan.
- Bank Letters of Reference.
- A copy of the Purchase and Sale Agreement.
- Copies of the Lease with ABC Manufacturing.
- Background information on the tenant.
- Informative profile on the property manager for the subject property.
- Contact name and phone number to arrange for an inspection of the subject property.

Additional information may be required.

A processing fee of $7,500.00 will be required with the return of this Application. Lending Corp may take up to 21 days from receipt of all information requested to process the Application. If the Applicant fails to provide the required Information or refuses to accept a Commitment that is substantially on the terms of this Application, then the processing fee shall be retained by Lending Corp. If this Application is declined the fee will be refunded.

General Conditions:

In making this Application, the Applicant hereby represents the security to be:
   a) free from environmental contamination;
   b) structurally sound and without material deferred maintenance;
   c) valued at no less then $3,640,000.

If this Application is approved and a Commitment is accepted, Lending Corp will verify the representations of the Applicant by:

- retaining an environmental consultant to complete an Environmental Site Assessment (ESA). The cost of this report is to be paid by the Applicant.

- retaining a building inspection consultant to complete a Building Condition Assessment. The cost of this report is to be paid by the Applicant.

- retaining one of our approved appraisers to prepare a Full Narrative Appraisal Report. The cost of this report is to be paid by the Applicant. Lending Corp acknowledges receipt of a copy of the Appraisal Report dated August 21, 2005 completed on the subject property by OPQ & Associates Inc. Lending Corp will require an original copy of the subject report along with a reliance letter allowing Lending Corp to review and rely on the contents of said report.

   Lending Corp will pay the cost of the assessments/reports from the Commitment Fee.

The receipt of satisfactory assessment/reports confirming the Applicant's representations is a condition precedent to proceeding with a loan.

If an Application is approved and a Commitment is accepted, Lending Corp. will require:

- an original or certified copy of policies for all risk, boiler and pressure vessels, business interruption, and, general liability. All insurance policies are to be in a form and with insurers satisfactory to Lending Corp. Our solicitors shall employ the services of an insurance consultant to review the Mortgagor's policies and the cost will be included in our solicitors account.

- a current survey satisfactory to our solicitor.

- a certified cheque for $47,500 (the Commitment Fee) with the return of the accepted Commitment. In lieu of a cheque, we will accept an Irrevocable Letter of Credit in a form and content satisfactory to Lending Corp. The Commitment Fee, net of any applicable assessment/report costs, will be refunded to you when the loan is funded.

- other information that is reasonably required to complete the loan transaction.

The Applicant acknowledges:

- Lending Corp's solicitor will prepare the mortgage documentation and all costs in this regard are to be paid by the Applicant.

- Lending Corp's standard Mortgage requires financial statements of the Borrower(s), a rent roll and a property operating statement be submitted annually to Lending Corp. It will also contain a due on sale and further encumbrance clause.

The Applicant hereby:
  a) warrant that they are not experiencing financial difficulties and they are not parties to any special financial arrangements with other creditors to solve such difficulties; and,
  b) give Lending Corp the authority to obtain corporate and personal credit and banking reports or references from all sources deemed necessary by Lending Corp in connection with this Application.

It the above terms and conditions are acceptable, please sign and return a copy of this letter to our offices. Please enclose the Processing Fee and all requested information to ensure timely processing of your Application,

Yours very truly,

Lending Corp

Regional Director

We hereby apply to Lending Corp for mortgage financing on the terms and conditions stated herein.

Signed this ___ day of _____ 2005.

XYZ PROPERTIES INC.

(Applicant) per:

RENT ROLL

Tenant	Leased Area	Rent/Sq.Ft.	Annual Rent
ABC Manufacturing	120,000 sq ft	$3.60/sq ft (Yr 1-5)	$432,000
		$4.00/sq ft (Yr 6-10)	$480,000

Figure 12.3
Mortgage Commitment Letter

LENDING CORP

VIA COURIER & FACSIMILE (416) 597-1234

November 21, 2005

COMPANY TO BE FORMED
C/o Broker & Company
9 University Avenue
Toronto. ON M5J 6T1

Attention: Mr. Jolly Guy

Dear Sir:

Re: Mortgage Loan #98429,   123 Best Street, Kitchener

Enclosed herewith please find two copies of our Commitment for a freehold first mortgage on the above-referenced property for your consideration and execution.

Please, call should you have any question; otherwise, please have a fully executed (and initialed) copy faxed to our office by no later than 3:00 p.m., on November 26, 2005 and then have the two originally executed (and initialed) copies among with the commitment fax returned to our office by November 27, 2005. Please make a copy for your own records.

I trust I will find this satisfactory.
Yours truly,

Lending Corp

John Doe
Regional Director

LENDING CORP

VIA COURIER & FACSIMILE (416) 597-1234

November 21, 2005

A COMPANY TO BE FORMED
C/o Broker & Company
90 University Avenue
Toronto, ON M5J 1S3

Attention: Mr. Jolly Guy

Dear Sir:
Re: Mortgage Loan #98429
         123 Best Street, Kitchener

The Lending Corp (hereinafter "the Mortagee") hereby offers you a first mortgage loan on the following terms and conditions:

1.   Loan Amount: $5,500,000.00

2.   Interest rate: The interest rate will be compounded semi-annually, not in advance, and be fixed no earlier than 60 days, nor later than 10 business days prior to the Funding date, at the sum of a) the bid side yield on the 4.25% coupon government of Canada bond maturing September 1, 2005, and b) 1.7%. The interest rate will be fixed at 11:00am EST on the next business day following receipt of written notice from the Mortgagor. If the Mortgagee has not received written notice to fix the interest rate 1 business day prior to the Funding Date, or, the fixed rate would exceed 9.25% at any time, the Mortgagee may, at its option, fix the rate without further notice to the Mortgagor.

3.   Term: 5 years

4.   Amortization: 20 years

5.   Monthly Payment: The Monthly Payment will be calculated by the Mortgagee following the Interest Rate being fixed and will be based on the Loan Amount, the Interest Rate and the Amortization.

6.   Repayment: The Mortgagor will pay accrued interest up to and including the first day of the month following the advance funds. Thereafter, the Monthly Payment will be due on the first day of each month until the maturity date of the Mortgage. On the maturity date, the outstanding principal balance together with any outstanding interest and charges will be due.
      The loan is closed for the term and there are no prepayment privileges.
      All payments in connection with this loan are to be made to:

      Lending Corp. Mortgage Administration
      P.O. Box 3412, Station "B"
      Toronto, Ontario M2Y 3Z1

7.   Taxes: All property taxes are to be paid directly by the Mortgagor, or the Mortgagor's tenant(s), to the municipality on, or prior to, the due date and receipted property tax bills are to be submitted to the Mortgagee no more than 30 days following the due date. The Mortgagee reserves the option to require monthly payments be made to the Mortgagee in amounts sufficient to meet the property taxes.

8.   The Mortgagor: The Mortgagor is a company to be formed (herein "the Mortgagor" or "you"). This commitment is

neither assignable nor transferable by the Mortgagor. The Mortgagor represents and warrants that it is not a non-resident, as defined under the Income Tax Act of Canada. As a condition of this Commitment, our solicitor must review and be satisfied with the terms and conditions of the Limited Partnership Agreement. The corporate documents and documents relating to the authority and capacity of the Mortgagor to make this loan must be approved by our solicitor.

9. Non-Recourse Limitations: Except as provided herein, collection of the Indebtedness shall be enforced solely against the Security. The Mortgagor and any beneficial owner of more than 15% of any subject property shall indemnity and save harmless the Mortgagee, on a joint and several basis from all liabilities, obligations, claims, demands, losses, damages, actions, proceedings, costs and expenses arising from:
   a. Environmental contamination of the subject property;
   b. All fraud, misrepresentation and the misapplication of funds by the Mortgagor or its agents.
   The Indemnity shall be unlimited as to time or amount and shall be satisfactory to the Mortgagee and its solicitors.

10. Security: The Mortgagor will provide to the Mortgagee, prior to any advance of funds hereunder, the following security (collectively "the Security"):
   a. A freehold first mortgage/charge on a 9.36 acre site located on the west side of Best Street in the City of Kitchener.
   b. A general assignment of all leases and rents that will be registered on title and under the Personal Property Security Act (P.P.S.A.) for a term of not less then the Amortization.
   c. The Mortgagor will execute such other collateral security documents as the Mortgagee's solicitor may reasonably require.

11. Rents and Leases: The Mortgagor hereby warrants the Information on Schedule "A" to the true and correct as of the acceptance date of this commitment and, must re-certify prior to closing.

At least 30 days prior to the Funding Date, the Mortgagor shall provide copies of executed Leases, for the Tenants occupying 5% or more of the net rentable area of the subject property, that verify the Information on Schedule "A". The form and content of all leases must be satisfactory to the Mortgagee and its solicitors acting reasonably, and at the option of the mortgagee, must be postponed to the Mortgage. You hereby warrant that all rents reserved thereby have not been, and shall not be demanded, collected, accepted or paid in advance of the time for the payment thereof, or other than in the manner set forth therein.

The Mortgagor will make commercially reasonable efforts to obtain and provide estoppel Certificates (substantially in the attached form) from all tenants occupying 5% or more of the net rentable area of the subject property.

Specific Assignments of Leases of all tenants occupying 20% or more of the rentable area, or paying 20% or more of the gross income of the subject property, are required and these tenants must provide an Acknowledgement, Attornment and Non-Disturbance Agreement (substantially in the attached form) to the Mortgagee.

All documents must be in our solicitor's hands in 10 days prior to funding.

Throughout the term of this loan, and any renewals thereof, for all tenants occupying 20% or more of the net rentable area, or paying 20% of more of the gross income of the subject property, the Mortgagor will provide the Mortgagee, within 30 days of completion, copies of all lease renewals or leases for new or replacement tenants, and an Estoppel Certificate (substantially in the attached form), as well as an Acknowledgement, Attornment and Non-Disturbance Agreement (substantially in the attached form).

12. Survey: The Mortgagor shall provide a survey prepared by an Ontario Land Surveyor that is satisfactory to the Mortgagee and its solicitors at least 30 days prior to the Anticipated Funding Date. The survey must show the location of buildings and boundaries of the lands to be mortgaged as well as the location of all rights of way and easements, and contain sufficient detail to ascertain whether there are any zoning or building bylaw violations.

13. Insurance: Satisfactory evidence of insurance must be provided to the Mortgagee's solicitor at least 30 days prior to the Funding Date. All insurance policies referred to herein shall be in form and with insurers reasonably acceptable

to the Mortgagee. In the event that the insurance policies are not available, the Mortgagee will accept bonders or certificates of insurance, in form acceptable to the Mortgagee. Evidence of property insurance on a CSIO form Accord Form 25a, or their equivalents, is not acceptable.

All policies will name the Mortgagor as a Named Insured or Additional Named Insured and will include the interests of all entities for whom the Mortgagor has contractually agreed to insure as their respective interests may appear. All property and, where applicable, boiler and machinery policies shall show the Mortgagee as First Mortgagee and Loss Payee and contain a standard mortgage clause in favor of the Mortgagee. All policies shall be permitted to contain reasonable deductibles.

All policies must not contain an exclusion for terrorism or terrorist acts, provided that such coverage is obtainable at a commercially reasonable cost, as determined by the Mortgagee. In the event such coverage is not available at a commercially reasonable cost but later becomes available, then the Mortgagor shall promptly obtain and retain such coverage upon written notification by the Mortgagee. The Mortgagee acknowledges that terrorism coverage will not be required prior to funding this loan, however, retains the right to require terrorism coverage during the term of this loan, and extensions.

All policies of insurance, and interim evidence thereof, shall provide 30 days prior notice to the Mortgagee of any adverse material change or cancellation or non-renewal.

If the Mortgagor fails to take out and keep in force such minimum insurance as is required hereunder, then the Mortgagee may, but shall not be obligated to, take out, for the sole benefit of the Mortgagee, and keep in force such insurance at the immediate sole cost and expense of the Mortgagor plus costs incurred, or use other means at its disposal under the terms of the Mortgage.

The Mortgagee's solicitor will employ the services of an insurance consultant, Risk Management Inc., to review the Mortgagor's Insurance evidence to determine the acceptability of the coverages, limits, insurees and the policies and to outline any changes required to meet the Mortgagee's requirement's. The consultant's fee, which will not exceed $360.00 plus GST, will be added to our solicitor's fee. By executing this commitment the Mortgagor agrees to the use of the consultant, to bear the cost thereon and authorizes its insurance broker or agent to release insurance information on a confidential basis to Risk Management Inc.

The Insurance Requirements contained herein are a minimum guide, and although they must be adhered to throughout the life of the Mortgage, in no way represent an opinion as to the full scope of insurance cover a prudent owner would arrange to adequately protect its interests and the interests of the Mortgagee and the Mortgagor must govern itself accordingly.

Specific Insurance Requirements –
  a. Property Insurance, with respect to the improvements and betterments (including foundations and footings) and all personal property relating thereto, insuring against any peril now or hereafter included with the classification "All Risks of Physical Loss or Damage" (and including the perils of earthquake, flood, sewer back-up, and collapse) to a limit representing 100% of the full replacement cost thereof. The insurance must include:
     • A replacement cost endorsement with no restriction to repair or replace on the same or adjacent site.
     • A Stated Amount endorsement to waive the co-insurance provisions, or not be subject to co-insurance.
     • Full by-laws extensions, including the increased cost of construction, cost of demolition of the undamaged portion of the Project, resultant loss of income;

  b. Broad Form Boiler and Machinery Insurance (without exclusion for explosion) written on a comprehensive repair and/or replacement cost basis covering all boilers, pipe turbines, engines and all other pressure vessels, machinery and equipment located in, on or about the Project with the same limits and By-laws extension as the "All risks" Property Insurance described above;

  c. Business Interruption Insurance (written on a gross rents or gross profits basis) to cover any abatement or loss of income resulting from an insured peril with a minimum period of indemnity of 12 months, or such longer period as the mortgagee may require;

d. Commercial General Liability Insurance with a limit of not less than $5,000,000 CAD on a per occurrence basis, or such higher limit as the Mortgagee may require. Such policy shall name the Mortgagee as an Additional Insured and shall include all legal liability to the extent insurable and imposed upon the Mortgagee and including all court costs, fees and expenses of legal counsel. The policy will include coverage, which a prudent owner of similar security would purchase and maintain, or cause to be purchased and maintained throughout the life of the Loan;

e. Such other insurance as the Mortgagee may reasonably require, given the nature of the security and that which a prudent owner of similar security would purchase and maintain, or cause to be purchased and maintained throughout the life of the Loan.

14. Environmental: The Mortgagor represents and warrants that to the best of its knowledge no material or substance determined to be an environmental contaminant by any government body having jurisdiction is now in the soil, ground water or improvements, or will be used in any new construction at the subject property.

The Mortgagee will obtain a Phase 1 Environmental Site Assessment (ESA1) of the subject property that will be conducted in accordance with the most recent version of CSA Standard Z768. The findings of the ESA (1) must be acceptable to the Mortgagee in every respect, failing which, the Mortgagee may, in its absolute discretion, terminate this commitment or request a Phase II Environmental Site Assessment ESA(II) and such other investigations as may be recommended in the ESA (I). Should the ESA (II) identify the presence of environmental contaminant then the Mortgagee may, in its absolute discretion, terminate this commitment. If the Mortgagee elects to proceed with the loan, 125% of the cost to remedy the contamination will be deducted from the loan proceeds and held in escrow with our solicitor pending removal or repair of the contamination.

The Mortgagor warrants that it will take all commercially reasonable steps to ensure that the subject property remains free from environmental contaminations throughout the term of this mortgage and any extension therof. The Mortgagee, or its agent, may enter the subject property at reasonable times, with notice to the Mortgagor and respecting at all times the rights of tenants, for the purpose of conducting environmental assessment or testing procedures deemed necessary by the Mortgagee. The presence of any contamination that exceeds Provincial environmental regulatory criteria and requires remediation, and is kept uncured will be a default under the mortgage.

The Mortgagor (and Guarantor(s) if applicable) shall indemnify the Mortgagee against all costs, suits and damages arising from environmental contamination and this indemnity shall be unlimited as to time or amount.

The Mortgagor is responsible for the cost of all ESAs. If an ESA (II) is required the Mortgagor will increase the Commitment Fee, upon request, by the estimated cost of the ESA (II).

15. Building Condition: The Mortgagor represents and warrants, to the best of its knowledge, that the subject property has no material structural or mechanical deficiencies defined as repair costs exceeding 5% of the value of the improvements.

The Mortgagee will obtain a Building Condition Assessment (BCA) of the subject promptly that will be completed in accordance with the most recent version of ASTM Standard E2018. The BCA must conclude that the subject property has no material structural or mechanical deficiencies or the Mortgagee may, in its absolute discretion, terminate this commitment. If this commitment is not terminated, the Mortgagor will deposit 125% of the cost to repair all deficiencies, material or otherwise, into an escrow account with our solicitor, or alternatively provide an equivalent letter of credit acceptable to the Mortgagee, pending completion of the repairs.

The Mortgagor warrants it will take all necessary steps to ensure the building components and mechanical systems are well maintained throughout the term of this mortgage and any extension thereof. The Mortgagee, or its agent, may enter the subject property at reasonable times, with notice to the Mortgagor and respecting the rights of tenants, to inspect the improvements. The presence of any material structural or mechanical deficiencies that the Mortgagor does not make reasonable commercial efforts to cure, will be a default under the mortgage.

The Mortgagor (and Guarantor(s) if applicable) shall indemnify the Mortgagee against all costs, suits and damages arising from all structural or mechanical failure and this indemnify small be unlimited as to time or amount.

The Mortgagee is responsible for the cost of the BCA.

The Mortgagee acknowledges receipt of a copy of the Building Condition Assessment Report dated October 2, 2005 completed by Carson Dunlop Weldon & Associates Ltd. An original copy of said report along with a reliance letter permitting Lending Corp to review and rely on the contents of same must be provided to the Mortgagee as a condition of this Commitment.

16. Appraisal: The Mortgagee will obtain a Full Narrative Appraisal in accordance with CUSPAP Standards. The Appraisal must conclude that the Market Value of the subject property is not less than $8.600.000.00 or the Mortgagee may, in its absolute discretion, terminate this commitment or reduce the Loan Amount.

The Mortgagor is responsible for the cost of the Appraisal.

17. Reports – General: All reports ordered by the Mortgagee are intended for the Mortgagee's use only. These reports are not intended as certification to the Mortgagor of the value or soundness of the property to be mortgaged.

All reports must include a statement that 1) the report may be relied upon by the Mortgagee in determining whether to make a Mortgage loan secured by the Property, 2) the report may be relied upon by any assignee or purchaser of the Mortgage and by any agency rating securities or representing an interest in the Mortgage, and 3) the report may be referred to in and/or included with materials offering the Mortgage or securities for sale.

18. Documentation: This commitment letter and all subsequent documentation shall be governed by the laws of the Province of Ontario. Time shall be of the essence in this commitment and the provisions and conditions of this commitment shall survive the execution and registration of the security documentation and there shall by no merger therein. Should any inconsistencies arise between this commitment and the security documents, then the security documents shall prevail.

The benefit of all or part of the Mortgagee's rights, or any interest in or power relating to all or part of the Mortgagee's rights, under this agreement or under any existing or future security guarantee or other right relating to the subject matter of this agreement, may be transferred or otherwise dealt with, free of any set-off, counterclaim or other equity or claim. Any information received may be disclosed to others. Everything to facilitate a transfer or dealing that may be requested in writing will be done at the expense of the person requesting it a transfer of all or part of the Mortgagee's rights agrees to assume any of the Mortgagee's obligation relating to those rights, the Mortgagee will be released from liability for the obligation.

The security documents, copies of which are available upon request, are to be prepared by the Mortgagee's solicitors:

John Doe
2 Division Street East, Kitchener, ON N5J 4B8
Tel. (519) 579-0000 Fax. (519) 579-9999

All documentation shall be in form prescribed by the Mortgagee and as approved by its solicitor. All documentation presented by the Mortgagee's solicitor for execution by the Mortgagor must be executed and returned to the Mortgagee's solicitor at least 5 business days prior to the Funding Date.

19. Payment of Fees: The Mortgagor will pay to the Mortgagee a processing and inspection fee of $15,000,00. This fee was received with the application and, with the insurance of this commitment, is non-refundable.

The Mortgagor shall be responsible for all fees and disbursements incurred by the Mortgagee's solicitor with respect to this loan. The Mortgagee's solicitor's fees and disbursements will be paid with the Advance of Funds. If the commitment is canceled, the Mortgagor will be billed separately for the Mortgagee's solicitor's fees and disbursements.

20. Commitment Fees: A commitment fee of $110,000.00, by certified cheque, is required with the return of this commitment. The Mortgagor may substitute an irrevocable and unconditional standby letter of credit for the certified cheque. The letter of credit must have an expiry date at least 30 days after the Commitment Expiry Date and be able to be drawn, in whole or part, on demand at a Canadian Schedule I Bank located in Toronto. The form and content of the letter of credit must be satisfactory to the Mortgagee and its solicitors. The commitment fee, less the cost of any applicable environmental building or appraisal reports, will be refunded, without allowance for interest thereon, in conjunction with advance of the full loan proceeds.

21. Financial Statements: Financial Statements of the Mortgagor (and Guarantor(s) if applicable), prepared by an independent firm of chartered accountants, as well as operating statements and a current rent roll for the subject property, are to be submitted to the Mortgagee each year during the term of the loan, within one hundred and twenty (120) days of the Mortgagor's and Guarantor's fiscal year end.

22. Due On Sale and Further Encumbrance: Should the Mortgagor directly or indirectly sell, convey, transfer, or dispose of the subject property, or any part thereof, or any interest therein, or should the Mortgagor further encumber the subject property with additional debt, without the written consent of the Mortgagee (not to be unreasonably withheld) being first obtained, then, at the Mortgagee's option, the entire principal balance, along with accrued and unpaid interest due thereon, shall be immediately due and payable.

23. Advance of Funds: The Mortgagee will fund the loan in one advance when all security documentation and legal work have been completed to the satisfaction of the Mortgagee and its solicitor, and all requirements of this agreement have been satisfied.

    All liens, unpaid taxes or existing charges or mortgages registered on title will be discharged out of the proceeds of the advance so that this loan will constitute a first mortgage/charge.

    A written request for closing must be given to the Mortgagee's applicator by the Mortgagor, or its solicitor, at least five (5) business says prior to the funding date, at which time all legal work must be completed and all fully executed documentation must be in the hands of the Mortgagee's applicator.

24. Compliance Clause: Should you fail, or be unable or unwilling for any reason whatsoever, to fulfill or comply with any of the terms and conditions set forth in this letter of commitment, or should you fail or refuse to sign the security documents prepared by our solicitors or to accept the funds to be advanced, or should any information supplied by you or any representations or warranties made by you to the Mortgagee be found incorrect in any material respect, or should you or any other person or corporation whose covenant is required become bankrupt or otherwise subject to any bankruptcy or insolvency proceedings, then the Mortgagee may, at its option, cancel this commitment.

    If cancellation or expiry of this commitment occurs prior to the advance of the full loan amount, the Mortgagee will retain the full Commitment Fees as liquidated damages, and not as penalty or payment of the above-mentioned costs. It is hereby agreed that the Commitment Fees represents a fair pre-estimate of the Mortgagee's damages.

25. Funding Date: Mortgagor and Mortgagee anticipate funding of the loan will be on January 15, 2006.

26. Commitment Expiry Date: This commitment will automatically expire on January 29, 2006, if the loan proceeds have not been fully advanced.

27. Acceptance: Acceptance hereof shall constitute a binding contract. Please signify your acceptance of this commitment by executing where indicated below, initialing each page, and returning same, together with the required fees, to this office by no later than 3:00 p.m. on November 26, 2005, after which this commitment will be null and void and may not be accepted without the further written concurrence of the Mortgagee.

Yours truly,

LENDING CORP

_____   _____

Mortgage Officer   Regional Director

(E.&O.E.)

ACCEPTANCE

WE ACCEPT THE ABOVE TERMS AND CONDITIONS THIS _____ day of_____, 2005.

Mortgagor: A COMPANY TO BE FORMED

_____

Authorized Signing Officer,
(please print name below line)

Mortgagor's solicitor for this loan transaction

Solicitor name: _____

Solicitor address/phone number: _____

12.8.3 CHARGE/MORTGAGE OF LAND

In Ontario, the *Land Registration Reform Act* (R.S.O. 1990, c. L.4) provides that a lender has the right to file a set of Standard Charge Terms with the land registrar. This specific set is given a unique number by the registrar and circulated to all land registry offices. A lender no longer has to file a lengthy document with every mortgage, but can refer to the charge number instead. The number is referenced in the Charge/Mortgage of Land Form 2, and the set of terms is deemed to be part of the mortgage document. Dye & Durham Co. Inc.'s set of terms are presented in Figure 12.4. They are probably the most widely used.

Figure 12.4
Set of Standards Charge Terms

Land Registration Reform Act
SET OF STANDARDS CHARGE TERMS
(Electronic Filing)

	Filing Date: November 3, 2000
Filed by Dye & Durham Co. Inc.	Filing number: 200033

The following Set of Standard Charge Terms shall be applicable to documents registered in electronic format under Part III of the Land Registration Reform Act, R.S.O. 1990, c. L.4 as amended (the "Land Registration Reform Act") and shall be deemed to be included in every electronically registered charge in which this Set of Standard Charge Terms is referred to by its filing number, as provided in Section 9 of the Land Registration Reform Act, except to the extent that the provisions of this Set of Standard Charge Terms are modified by additions, amendments or deletions in the schedule. Any charge in an electronic format of which this Set of Standard Charge Terms forms a part by reference to the above-noted filing number in such charge shall hereinafter be referred to as the "Charge".

Exclusion of Statutory Covenants	I. The implied covenants deemed to be included in a charge under subsection 7(1) of the Land Registration Reform Act as amended or re-enacted are excluded from the Charge.
Right to Charge the Land	2. The Chargor now has good right, full power and lawful and absolute authority to charge the land and to give the Charge to the Chargee upon the Covenants contained in the Charge.
No Act to Encumber	3. The Chargor has not done, committed, executed or wilfully or knowingly suffered any act, deed, matter or thing whatsoever whereby or by means whereof the land, or any part or parcel thereof, is or shall or may be in any way impeached, charged, affected or encumbered in title, estate or otherwise, except as the records of the land registry office disclose.
Good Title in Fee Simple	4. The Chargor, at the time of the delivery for registration of the Charge, is, and stands solely, rightfully and lawfully seized of a good, sure, perfect, absolute and indefeasible estate of inheritance, in fee simple, of and in the land and the premises described In the Charge and in every part and parcel thereof without any manner of trusts, reservations, limitations, provisos, conditions or any other matter or thing to alter, charge, change, encumber or defeat the same, except those contained in the original grant thereof from the Crown.
Promise to Pay and Perform	5. The Chargor will pay or cause to be paid to the Chargee the full principal amount and interest secured by the Charge in the manner of payment provided by the Charge, without any deduction or abatement, and shall do, observe, perform, fulfill and keep all the provisions, covenants, agreements and stipulations contained in the Charge and shall pay as they fall due all taxes, rates, levies, charges, assessments, utility and heating charges, municipal, local, parliamentary and otherwise which now are or may hereafter be imposed, charged or levied upon the land and when required shall produce for the Chargee receipts evidencing payment of the same.

Interest After
Default

6. In case default shall be made in payment of any sum to become due for interest at the time provided for payment in the Charge, compound interest shall be payable and the sum in arrears for interest from time to time, as well after as before maturity, and both before and after default and judgement, shall bear interest at the rate provided for in the Charge. In case the interest and compound interest are not paid within the interest calculation period provided in the Charge from the time of default a rest shall be made, and compound interest at the rate provided for in the Charge shall be payable on the aggregate amount then due, as well after as before maturity, and so on from time to time, and all such interest and compound interest shall be a charge upon the land.

No Obligation
to Advance

7. Neither the preparation, execution or registration of the Charge shall bind the Chargee to advance the principal amount secured, nor shall the advance of a part of the principal amount secured bind the Chargee to advance any unadvanced portion thereof, but nevertheless the security in the land shall take effect forthwith upon delivery for registration of the Charge by the Chargor. The expenses of the examination of the title and of the Charge and valuation are to be secured by the Charge in the event of the whole or any balance of, the principal amount not being advanced, the same to be charged hereby upon the land, and shall be, without demand therefore, payable forthwith with interest at the rate provided for in the Charge, and in default the Chargee's power of sale hereby given, and all other remedies hereunder, shall be exercisable.

Costs Added
to Principal

8. The Chargee may pay all premiums of insurance and all taxes, rates, levies, charges, assessments, utility and heating charges which shall from time to time fall due and be unpaid in respect of the land, and that such payments, together with all costs, charges, legal fees (as between solicitor and client) and expenses which may be incurred in taking, recovering and keeping possession of the land and of negotiating the Charge, investigating title, and registering the Charge and other necessary deeds, and generally in any other proceedings taken in connection with or to realize upon the security given in the Charge (including legal fees and real estate commissions and other costs incurred in leasing or selling the land or in exercising the power of entering, lease and sale contained in the Charge) shall be, with interest at the rate provided for in the Charge, a charge upon the and in favour of the Chargee pursuant to the terms of the Charge and the Chargee may pay or satisfy any lien, charge or encumbrance now existing or hereafter created or claimed, upon the land, which payments with interest at the rate provided for in the Charge shall likewise be a charge upon the land in favour of the Chargee. Provided, and it is hereby further agreed, that all amounts paid by the Chargee as aforesaid shall be added to the principal amount secured by the Charge and shall be payable forthwith with interest at the rate provided for in the Charge, and on default all sums secured by the Charge shall immediately become due and payable at the option of the Chargee, and all powers in the Charge conferred shall become exercisable.

Power Of Sale

9. The Chargee on default of payment for at least fifteen (15) days may, on at least thirty five (35) days' notice in writing given to the Chargor, enter on and lease the land or sell the land. Such notice shall be given to such persons and in such manner and form and within such time as provided in the Mortgages Act. In the event that the giving of such notice shall not be required by law or to the extent that such requirements shall not be applicable, it is agreed that notice may be effectually given by leaving it with a grown-up person on the land, if occupied, or by placing it on the land if unoccupied, or at the option of the Chargee, by mailing it in a registered letter addressed to the Chargor at his last known address, or by publishing it once in a newspaper published in the county or district in which the land is situate; and such notice shall be sufficient although not addressed to any person or persons by name or designation; and notwithstanding that any person to be affected thereby may be unknown, unascertained or under disability. Provided further, that in case default be made in the payment of the principal amount or interest or any part thereof and such default continues for two months after any payment of either falls due then the Chargee may exercise the foregoing powers of entering, leasing or selling or any of them without any notice, it being understood and agreed, however, that if the giving of notice by the Chargee shall be required by law then notice shall be given to such persons and in such manner and form and within such time as so required by law. It is hereby further agreed that the whole of any part or parts of the land may be sold by public auction or private contract, or partly one or

partly the other; and that the proceeds of any sale hereunder may be applied first in payment of any costs, charges and expenses incurred in taking, recovering or keeping possession of the land or by reason of non-payment or procuring payment of monies, secured by the Charge or otherwise, and secondly in payment of all amounts of principal and interest owing under the Charge; and if any surplus shall remain after fully satisfying the claims of the Chargee as aforesaid same shall be paid as required by law. The Chargee may sell any of the land on such terms as to credit and otherwise as shall appear to him most advantageous and for such prices as can reasonably be obtained therefore and may make any stipulations as to title or evidence or commencement of title or otherwise which he shall deem proper, and may buy in or rescind or vary any contract for the sale of the whole or any part of the land and resell without being answerable for loss occasioned thereby, and in the case of a sale on credit the Chargee shall be bound to pay the Chargor only such monies as have been actually received from purchasers after the satisfaction of the claims of the Chargee and for any of said purposes may make and execute all agreements and assurances as he shall think fit. Any purchaser or lessee shall not be bound to see to the propriety or regularity of any sale or lease or be affected by express notice that any sale or lease is improper and no want of notice or publication when required hereby shall invalidate any sale or lease hereunder.

Quiet Possession

10. Upon default in payment of principal and interest under the Charge or in performance of any of the terms or conditions hereof, the Chargee may enter into and take possession of the land hereby charged and where the Chargee so enters on and takes possession or enters on and takes possession of the land on default as described in paragraph 9 herein the Chargee shall enter into, have, hold, use, occupy, possess and enjoy the land without the let, suit, hindrance, interruption or denial of the Chargor or any other person or persons whomsoever.

Right to Distrain

11. If the Chargor shall make default in payment of any part of the interest payable under the Charge at any of the dates or times fixed for the payment thereof, it shall be lawful for the Chargee to distrain therefore upon the land or any part thereof, and by distress warrant, to recover by way of rent reserved, as in the case of a demise of the land, so much of such interest as shall, from time to time, be or remain in arrears and unpaid, together with all costs, charges and expenses attending such levy or distress, as in like cases of distress for rent. Provided that the Chargee may distrain for arrears of principal in the same manner as if the same were arrears of interest.

Further Assurances

12. From and after default in the payment of the principal amount secured by the Charge or the interest thereon or any part of such principal or interest or in the doing, observing, performing, fulfilling or keeping of some one or more of the covenants set forth in the Charge then and in every such case the Chargor and all and every other person whosoever having, or lawfully claiming, or who shall have or lawfully claim any estate, right, title, interest or trust of, in, to or out of the land shall, from time to time, and at all times thereafter, at the proper costs and charges of the Chargor make, do, suffer, execute, deliver, authorize and register, or cause or procure to be made, done, suffered, executed, delivered, authorized and registered, all and every such further and other reasonable act or acts, deed or deeds, devises, conveyances and assurances in the law for the further, better and more perfectly and absolutely conveying and assuring the land unto the Charges as by the Chargee or his solicitor shall or may be lawfully and reasonably devised, advised or required.

Acceleration of Principal and Interest

13. In default of the payment of the interest secured by the Charge the principal amount secured by the Charge shall, at the option of the Chargee, immediately become payable, and upon default of payment of instalments of principal promptly as the same mature, the balance of the principal and interest secured by the Charge shall, at the option of the Chargee, immediately become due and payable. The Chargee may in writing at any time or times after default waive such default and any such waiver shall apply only to the particular default waived and shall not operate as a waiver of any other or future default.

Unapproved Sale

14. If the Chargor sells, transfers, disposes of, leases or otherwise deals with the land, the principal amount secured by the Charge shall, at the option of the Chargee, immediately become due and payable.

Partial Releases

15. The Chargee may at his discretion at all times release any part or parts of the land or any other security or any surety for the money secured under the Charge either with or without any sufficient consideration therefore, without responsibility therefore, and without thereby releasing any other part of the land or any person from the Charge or from any of the covenants contained in the Charge and without being accountable to the Chargor for the value thereof, or for any monies except those actually received by the Chargee. It is agreed that every part or lot into which the land is or may hereafter be divided does and shall stand charged with the whole money secured under the Charge and no person shall have the right to require the mortgage monies to be apportioned.

Obligation to Insure

16. The Chargor will immediately insure, unless already insured, and during the continuance of the Charge keep insured against loss or damage by fire, in such proportions upon each building as may be required by the Chargee, the buildings on the land to the amount of not less than their full insurable value on a replacement cost basis in dollars of lawful money of Canada. Such insurance shall be placed with a company approved by the Chargee. Buildings shall include all buildings whether now or hereafter erected on the land, and such insurance shall include not only insurance against loss or damage by fire but also insurance against loss or damage by explosion, tempest, tornado, cyclone, lightning and all other extended perils customarily provided in insurance policies including "all risks" insurance. The covenant to insure shall also include where appropriate or if required by the Chargee, boiler, plate glass, rental and public liability insurance in amounts and on terms satisfactory to the Chargee. Evidence of continuation of all such insurance having been effected shall be produced to the Chargee, at least fifteen (15) days before the expiration thereof; otherwise the Chargee may provide therefore and charge the premium paid and interest thereon at the rate provided for in the Charge to the Chargor and the same shall be payable forthwith and shall also be a charge upon the land. It is further agreed that the Chargee may at any time require any insurance of the buildings to be cancelled and new insurance effected in a company to be named by the Chargee and also of his own accord may effect or maintain any insurance herein provided for, and any amount paid by the Chargee therefore shall be payable forthwith by the Chargor with interest at the rate provided for in the Charge and shall also be a charge upon the land. Policies of insurance herein required shall provide that loss, if any, shall be payable to the Chargee as his interest may appear, subject to the standard form of mortgage clause approved by the Insurance Bureau of Canada which shall be attached to the policy of insurance.

Obligation to Repair

17. The Chargor will keep the land and the buildings, erections and improvements thereon, in good condition and repair according to the nature and description thereof respectively, and the Chargee may, whenever he deems necessary, by his agent enter upon and inspect the land and make such repairs as he deems necessary, and the reasonable cost of such inspections and repairs with interest at the rate provided for in the Charge shall be added to the principal amount and be payable forthwith and be a charge upon the land prior to all claims thereon subsequent to the Charge. If the Chargor shall neglect to keep the buildings, erections and improvements in good condition and repair, or commits or permits any act of waste on the land (as to which the Chargee shall be sole judge) or make default as to any of the covenants, provisos, agreements or conditions contained in the Charge or in any charge to which this Charge is subject, all monies secured by the charge shall, at the option of the Chargee, forthwith become due and payable, and in default of payment of same with interest as in the case of payment before maturity the powers of entering upon and leasing or selling hereby given and all other remedies herein contained may be exercised forthwith.

Building Charge

18. If any of the principal amount to be advanced under the Charge is to be used to finance an improvement on the land, the Chargor must so inform the Chargee in writing immediately and before any advances are made under the Charge. The Chargor must also provide the Chargee immediately with copies of all contracts and subcontracts relating to the improvement and any amendments to them. The Chargor agrees that any improvement shall be made only according to contracts, plans and specifications approved in writing by the Chargee. The Chargor shall complete all such improvements as quickly as possible and provide the Chargee with proof of payment of all contracts from time to time as the Chargee requires. The Chargee shall make advances (part payments of the principal amount) to the Chargor based on the progress of the improvement, until either completion and occupation or sale of the land. The Chargee shall determine whether or not

any advances will be made and when they will be made.

Whatever the purpose of the Charge may be, the Chargee may at its option hold back funds from advances until the Chargee is satisfied that the Chargor has complied with the holdback, provisions of the Construction Lien Act as amended or re-enacted. The Chargor authorizes the Chargee to provide information about the Charge to any person claiming a construction lien on the land.

Extensions not to Prejudice

19. No extension of time given by the Chargee to the Chargor or anyone claiming under him, or any other dealing by the Chargee with the owner of the land or of any part thereof, shall in any way affect or prejudice the rights of the Chargee against the Chargor or any other person liable for the payment of the money secured by the Charge, and the Charge may be renewed by an agreement in writing at maturity for any term with or without an increased rate of interest notwithstanding that there may be subsequent encumbrances. It shall not be necessary to deliver for registration any such agreement in order to retain priority for the Charge so altered over any instrument delivered for registration subsequent to the Charge. Provided that nothing contained in this paragraph shall confer any right of renewal upon the Chargor.

No merger of Covenants

20. The taking of a judgment, or judgments on any of the covenants herein shall not operate as a merger of the covenants or affect the Chargee's right to interest at the rate and times provided for in the Charge; and further that any judgment shall provide that interest thereon shall be computed at the same rate and in the same manner as provided in the Charge until the judgment, shall have been fully paid and, satisfied.

Change in Status

21. Immediately after any change or happening affecting any of the following, namely: (a) the spousal status of the Chargor, (b) the qualification of the land as a family residence within the, meaning of Part II of the Family Law Act, and (c) the legal title or beneficial ownership of the land, the Chargor will advise the Chargee accordingly and furnish the Chargee with full particulars thereof, the intention being that the Chargee shall be kept fully informed of the names and addresses of the owner or owners for the time being of the land and of any spouse who is not an owner but who has a right of possession in the land by virtue of Section 19 of the Family Law Act. In furtherance of such intention, the Chargor covenants and agrees to furnish the Chargee with such evidence in connection with any of (a), (b) and (c) above as the Chargee may from time to time request.

Condominium Provisions

22. If the Charge is of land within a condominium registered pursuant to the Condominium Act (the "Act") the following provisions shall apply. The Chargor will comply with the Act, and with the declaration, by-laws and rules of the condominium corporation (the "corporation") relating to the Chargor's unit (the "unit") and provide the Chargee with proof of compliance from time to time as the Chargee may request. The Chargor will pay the common expenses for the unit to the corporation on the due dates. If the Chargee decides to collect the Chargor's contribution towards the common expenses from the Chargor, the Chargor will pay the same to the Chargee upon being so notified. The Chargee is authorized to accept a statement which appears to be issued by the corporation as conclusive evidence for the purpose of establishing the amounts of the common expenses and the dates those amounts are due. The Chargor, upon notice from the Chargee, will forward to the Chargee any notices, assessments, by-laws, rules and financial statements of the corporation that the Chargor receives or is entitled to receive from the corporation. The Chargor will maintain all improvements made to the unit and repair them after damage. In addition to the insurance which the corporation must obtain, the Chargor shall insure the unit against destruction or damage by fire and other perils usually covered in fire insurance policies and against such other perils as the Chargee requires for its full replacement cost (the maximum amount for which it can be insured). The insurance company and the terms of the policy shall be reasonably satisfactory to the Chargee. This provision supersedes the provisions of paragraph 16 herein. The Chargor irrevocably authorizes the Chargee to exercise the Chargor's rights under the Act to vote, consent and dissent.

Discharge

23. The Chargee shall have a reasonable time after payment in full of the amounts secured by the Charge to deliver for registration a discharge or if so requested and if required by law to do so, an

assignment of the Charge and all legal and other expenses for preparation, execution and registration, as applicable to such discharge or assignment shall be paid by the Chargor.

Guarantee

24. Each party named in the Charge as a Guarantor hereby agrees with the Chargee as follows:

(a) In consideration of the Chargee advancing all or part of the Principal Amount to the Chargor, and in consideration of the sum of TWO DOLLARS ($2.00) of lawful money of Canada now paid by the Chargee to the Guarantor (the receipt and sufficiency whereof are hereby acknowledged), the Guarantor does hereby absolutely and unconditionally guarantee to the Chargee, and its successors, the due and punctual payment of all principal moneys, interest and other moneys owing on the security of the Charge and observance and performance of the covenants, agreements, terms and conditions herein contained by the Chargor, and the Guarantor, for himself and his successors, covenants with the Chargee that, if the Chargor shall at any time make default in the due and punctual payment of any moneys payable hereunder, the Guarantor will pay all such moneys to the Chargee without any demand being required to be made.

(b) Although as between the Guarantor and the Chargor, the Guarantor is only surety for the payment by the Chargor of the moneys hereby guaranteed, as between the Guarantor and the Chargee, the Guarantor shall be considered as primarily liable therefore and it is hereby further expressly declared that no release or releases of any portion or portions of the land; no indulgence shown by the Chargee in respect of any default by the Chargor or any successor thereof which may arise under the Charge; no extension or extensions granted by the Chargee to the Chargor or any successor thereof for payment of the moneys hereby secured or for the doing, observing or performing of any covenant, agreement, term or condition herein contained to be done, observed or performed by the Chargor or any successor thereof; no variation in or departure from the provisions of the Charge; no release of the Chargor or any other thing whatsoever whereby the Guarantor as surety only would or might have been released shall in any way modify, alter, vary or in any prejudice the Chargee or affect the liability of the Guarantor in any way under this covenant, which shall continue and be binding on the Guarantor, and as well after as before maturity of the Charge and both before and after default and judgment, until the said moneys are fully paid and satisfied.

(c) Any payment by the Guarantor of any moneys under this guarantee shall not in any events to be taken to affect the liability of the Chargor for payment thereof but such liability shall remain unimpaired and enforceable by the Guarantor against the Chargor and the Guarantor shall, to the extent of any such payments made by him, in addition to all other remedies, be subrogated as against the Chargor to all the rights, privileges and powers to which the Chargee was entitled prior to payment by the Guarantor; provided, nevertheless, that the Guarantor shall not be entitled in any event to rank for payment against the lands in competition with the Chargee and shall not, unless and until the whole of the principal, interest and other moneys owing on the security of the Charge shall have been paid, be entitled to any rights or remedies whatsoever in subrogation to the Chargee.

(d) All covenants, liabilities and obligations entered into or imposed hereunder upon the Guarantor shall be equally binding upon his successors. Where more than one party is named as a Guarantor all such covenants, liabilities and obligations shall be joint and several.

(e) The Chargee may vary any agreement or arrangement with or release the Guarantor, or any one or more of the Guarantors if more than one party is named as Guarantor, and grant extensions of time or otherwise deal with the Guarantor and his successors without any consent on the part of the Chargor or any other Guarantor or any successor thereof.

| Severability | 25. It is agreed that in the event that at any time any provision of the Charge is illegal or invalid under or inconsistent with provisions of any applicable statute, regulation thereunder or other applicable law or would by reason of the provisions of any such statute, regulation or other applicable law render the Chargee unable to collect the amount of any loss sustained by it as a result of making the loan secured by the Charge which it would otherwise be able to collect under such statute, regulation or other applicable law then, such provision shall not apply and shall be construed so as not to apply to the extent that it is so illegal, invalid or inconsistent or would so render the Chargee unable to collect the amount of any such loss. |

| Interpretation | 26. In construing these covenants the words "Charge", "Charges", "Chargor", "land" and "successor" shall have the meanings assigned to them in Section 1 of the Land Registration Reform Act and the words "Chargor" and "Chargee" and the personal pronouns "he" and "his" relating thereto and used therewith, shall be read and construed as "Chargor" or "Chargors", "Chargee" or "Chargees", and "he", "she", "they" or "it", "his", "her", "their" or "its", respectively, as the number and gender of the parties referred to in each case require, and the number of the verb agreeing therewith shall be construed as agreeing with the said word or pronoun so substituted. And that all rights, advantages, privileges, immunities, powers and things hereby secured to the Chargor or Chargors, Chargee or Chargees, shall be equally secured to and exercisable by his, her, their or its heirs, executors, administrators and assigns, or successors and assigns, as the case may be. The word "successor" shall also include successors and assigns of corporations including amalgamated and continuing corporations. And that all covenants, liabilities and obligations entered into or imposed hereunder upon the Chargor or Chargors, Chargee or Chargees, shall be equally binding upon his, her, their or its heirs, executors, administrators and assigns, or successors and assigns, as the case may be, and that all such covenants and liabilities and obligations shall be joint and several. |

| Paragraph Headings | 27. The paragraph headings in these standard charge terms are inserted for convenience of reference only and are deemed not to form part of the Charge and are not to be considered in the construction or interpretation of the Charge or any part thereof. |

| Date of Charge | 28. The Charge, unless otherwise specifically provided, shall be deemed to be dated as of the date of delivery for registration of the Charge. |

| Effect of Delivery of Charge | 29. The delivery, of the Charge for registration by direct electronic transfer shall have the same effect for all purposes as if such Charge were in written form, signed by the parties thereto and delivered to the Chargee. Each of the Chargor and, if applicable, the spouse of the Chargor and other party to the Charge agrees not to raise in any proceeding by the Chargee to enforce the Charge any want or lack of authority on the part of the person delivering the Charge for registration to do so. |

DATED this   day of   ,   .

Source: The Set of Standard Charge Terms is reproduced with the permission of Dye & Durham, a division of The Cartwright Goup Ltd. (1-800-668-8208, www.dyedurham.ca)

In addition to the standard charge terms, the *Land Registration Reform Act* ensures that essential covenants are implied in any mortgage document. There are three implied covenants, sometimes called "usual covenants", in subsection 7(1) of the Act:

7. (1) A charge in the prescribed form shall be deemed to include the following covenants by the chargor, for the chargor and the chargor's successors, with the chargee and the chargee's successors and assigns:

Usual covenants

1. In a charge of freehold or leasehold land by the beneficial owner:
    i.   That the chargor or the chargor's successors will pay, in the manner provided by the charge, the money and interest it secures, and will pay the taxes assessed against the land.
    i.   That the chargor has the right to give the charge.
    ii. That the chargor has not done, omitted or permitted anything whereby the land is or may be encumbered, except as the records of the land registry office disclose.
    iv. That the chargor or the chargor's successors will insure the buildings on the land as specified in the charge.
    v.   That the chargee on default of payment for the number of days specified in the charge or in the Mortgages Act, whichever is longer, may on giving the notice specified in the charge or required by that Act, whichever is longer, enter on and take possession of, receive the rents and profits of, lease or sell the land.
    vi. That where the chargee enters on and takes possession of the land on default as described in subparagraph v, the chargee shall have quiet enjoyment of the land.
    vii. That the chargor or the chargor's successors will, on default, execute such assurances of the land and do such other acts, at the chargee's expense, as may be reasonably required.
    viii. That the chargee may distrain for arrears of interest.
    ix. That on default of payment of the interest secured by the charge, the principal money shall, at the option of the chargee, become payable.

Covenant re freehold

2. In a charge of freehold land by the beneficial owner, that the chargor has a good title in fee simple to the land, except as the records of the land registry office disclose.

Covenant re leasehold

3. In a charge of leasehold land by the beneficial owner:
    i.   That, despite anything done, omitted or permitted by the chargor, the lease or grant creating the term or estate for which the land is held is, at the time the charge is given, a valid lease or grant of the land charged, in full force, unforfeited and unsurrendered, and that there is no subsisting default in the payment of the rents reserved by or in the performance of the covenants, conditions and agreements contained in the lease or grant at the time the charge is given.
    ii. That the chargor or the chargor's successors will, while the money secured by the charge remains unpaid, pay, observe and perform all the rents reserved by and all the covenants, conditions and agreements contained in the lease or grant and will indemnify the chargee against all costs and damages incurred by reason of any non-payment of rent or non-observance or non-performance of the covenants, conditions and agreements.

12.9 MORTGAGE DEFAULTS

Understand the Power of Sale concept within the default process and what happens upon foreclosure.

When a mortgagor (borrower) defaults under a mortgage, the mortgagee (lender) usually has several remedies he can use, but he will almost always sell the property, either under Power of Sale legislation or after foreclosing on the mortgage (see sections 12.9.1 and 12.9.2). Some of the other remedies available to the lender upon default are described below.

1. **Acceleration.** Move the due date of the debt forward by requesting payment of the interests past due and the whole of the principal.

2. **Possession.** If a mortgage is in default, a mortgagee may obtain possession of the property by removing the owner mortgagor from the property and taking possession, while leaving the tenants in place. Usually, a writ of possession obtained from a court (see Figure 12.5) is required to gain possession.

3. **Attornment of Rents.** An attornment is a written order issued by a court, commanding the party to whom it is addressed to perform or cease performing a specific act. Frequently, a mortgagee does not want to remove the owner and take his place. Usually, when there are tenants, a mortgagor is forced under the implied charge terms to "attorn" to the mortgagee. This consists of the mortgagor becoming the manager of his building for the mortgagee and turning over to the mortgagee the rentals received from the tenants. It requires the serving of a notice to the mortgagor and his tenants. Under the circumstances of possession and attornment, mortgagees are said to be "mortgagees in possession".

4. **Action on the Covenant (to pay).** The mortgagee (lender) can sue the mortgagor for payments and generally obtain a judgment quickly. Indeed, the mortgagor who signed the mortgage document remains liable on his obligation to repay the loan, but most of the time he has no money. It is one of the remedies, among several, that a mortgagee may use in the case of non-payment of a mortgage.

Figure 12.5
Writ of Possession

Courts of Justice Act
WRIT OF POSSESSION
(General heading)

(Court seal)

WRIT OF POSSESSION

TO the Sheriff of the *(name of county or district)*

   Under an order of this court made on *(date)* in favour of *(name of party who obtained order)*, YOU ARE DIRECTED to enter and take possession of the following land and premises in your county or district: *(Set out a description of the land and premises.)*

   AND YOU ARE DIRECTED to give possession of the above land and premises without delay to *(name of party who obtained order)*.

Date ....

Issued by ....

Local registrar

Address of
court office ....

....

Renewed by order made on *(date)*.

....

Local registrar

RCP-E 60C (November 1, 2005)

12.9.1 POWER OF SALE

Also called a "Contractual Power of Sale Clause", a Power of Sale Clause is one that a lender uses to protect himself, in case of default. Basically, when a mortgagor is in default (usually of mortgage payments), it allows the lender to sell the property in order to clear the mortgagor's debt, without the lender taking ownership of the property. These clauses vary from lender to lender but are typically as found in item 9 of the Set of Standard Charge Terms (see Figure 12.4) as follows:

Power of Sale

9. The Chargee on default of payment for at least fifteen (15) days may, on at least thirty-five (35) days' notice in writing given to the Chargor, enter on and lease the land or sell the land. Such notice shall be given to such persons and in such manner and form and within such time as provided in the Mortgages Act. In the event that the giving of such notice shall not be required by law or to the extent that such requirements shall not be applicable, it is agreed that notice may be effectually given by leaving it with a grown-up person on the land, if occupied, or by placing it on the land if unoccupied, or at the option of the Chargee, by mailing it in a registered letter addressed to the Chargor at his last known address, or by publishing it once in a newspaper published in the county or district in which the land is situate; and such notice shall be sufficient although not addressed to any person or persons by name or designation; and notwithstanding that any person to be affected thereby may be unknown, unascertained or under disability. Provided further, that in case default be made in the payment of the principal amount or interest or any part thereof and such default continues for two months after any payment of either falls due then the Chargee may exercise the foregoing powers of entering, leasing or selling or any of them without any notice, it being understood and agreed, however, that if the giving of notice by the Chargee shall be required by law then notice shall be given to such persons and in such manner and form and within such time as so required by law. It is hereby further agreed that the whole or any part or parts of the land may be sold by public auction or private contract, or partly one or partly the other; and that the proceeds of any sale hereunder may be applied first in payment of any costs, charges and expenses incurred in taking, recovering or keeping possession of the land or by reason of non-payment or procuring payment of monies, secured by the Charge or otherwise, and secondly in payment of all amounts of principal and interest owing under the Charge; and if any surplus shall remain after fully satisfying the claims of the Chargee as aforesaid same shall be paid as required by law. The Chargee may sell any of the land on such terms as to credit and otherwise as shall appear to him most advantageous and for such prices as can reasonably be obtained therefor and may make any stipulations as to title or evidence or commencement of title or otherwise which he shall deem proper, and may buy in or rescind or vary any contract for the sale of the whole or any part of the land and resell without being answerable for loss occasioned thereby, and in the case of a sale on credit the Chargee shall be bound to pay the Chargor only such monies as have been actually received from purchasers after the satisfaction of the claims of the Chargee and for any of said purposes may make and execute all agreements and assurances as he shall think fit. Any purchaser or lessee shall not be bound to see to the propriety or regularity of any sale or lease or be affected by express notice that any sale or lease is improper and no want of notice or publication when required hereby shall invalidate any sale or lease hereunder.

Figure 12.6
Recommended Power of Sale Clause

<u>SCHEDULE "A"</u>

It is further understood that, on the date of acceptance of this Offer, there is default under the terms of the mortgage that entitles the Vendor to exercise the Power of Sale.

The only evidence of the default, which the Purchaser may require, shall be a statutory declaration by the Vendor setting forth the facts entitling the vendor to sell under the Power of Sale, including the particulars of the notice of exercising the Power of Sale, the names of the persons upon whom service of the notice has been effected and declaring that default under the Mortgage entitling the Vendor to exercise the Power of Sale has continued up to and including the date of acceptance of this Offer and to the time of closing.

The Purchaser understands and agrees that the Mortgagor has the right to redeem the property up to the time of waiver or expiration of all rights of termination and fulfilment of all conditions and this Agreement is subject to that right.

In the event of redemption by the Mortgagor, this Agreement shall be null and void and any deposit monies paid will be refunded in full without interest.

Where a court of competent jurisdiction prevents the completion of the within sales by an interim interlocutory or permanent injunction or otherwise, then the Vendor (Mortgagee) is not obliged to complete the said transaction and the Agreement shall be terminated and the deposit shall be returned to the Purchaser in full without interest. In no event shall the Vendor be responsible for any costs, expenses, loss or damages incurred or suffered by the Purchaser and the Vendor shall not have any further liability to the Purchaser whatsoever.

Notwithstanding anything contained in paragraph 10 B (reference to Agreement of Purchase and Sale, Form 101) B of this Agreement, the Vendor shall not be required either on or before closing to discharge its own Mortgage or any existing Mortgages, liens or other encumbrances subsequent in priority to the Vendor's Mortgage, which may be registered against the property.

The Purchaser also acknowledges that the Vendor makes no representation and/or warranties with respect to state of repair of the premises, inclusions of chattels or fixtures, or ownership of fixtures or appliances, and the Purchaser agrees to accept the property as is and the attached Agreement ordinarily warranted by the Vendor.

Chattels and fixtures on the premises may or may not be included with the premises but the Vendor shall not be obliged to remove any chattels or fixtures.

All the provisions or the Mortgage Act shall supersede any part of this Agreement that may be in variance thereof or in conflict therewith.

Source: Recommended Power of Sale Clause used by permission of the Ontario Real Estate Association.

(a) Schedule "A"

When a property is sold under Power of Sale, in addition to the usual terms of an Agreement of Purchase and Sale, specific clauses must be included or attached to the agreement or offer. In the real estate business, this is often referred to as Schedule "A" because, commonly, these clauses are attached to the contract as Schedule "A". The contents and exact wording of a Schedule "A" vary from lender to lender, however an example, developed by the Ontario Real Estate Association, is presented in Figure 12.6. As you can tell, a lawyer prepared this document. To make it more readable, we broke the text down into several paragraphs.

(b) Certificate of Power of Sale

Figure 12.7 presents an example of a Certificate of Power of Sale.

Figure 12.7
Certificate of Power of Sale

CERTIFICATE OF POWER OF SALE

We, <u>Boiron National Trust</u>, do hereby warrant that by reason of default under a <u>Second</u> mortgage which we hold on <u>#793 Best Drive, Ontarioland, Lot 01 Plan M1000</u>, dated <u>February 2, 2000</u> and registered as <u>number 723521</u>, we now have the power and authority under the provisions of our mortgage, and the *Mortgages Act* of Ontario, to list the property for sale.

SIGNED at <u>Ontarioland</u>, this <u>21st</u> day of <u>February 2007</u>.

DATE

(Mortgagee or Authorized Representatives)   (Witness)

(c) The Power of Sale Process

The Power of Sale consists of many steps and sub-steps. These are outlined below.

1. The mortgagor (borrower) defaults. Failure to make the mortgage payments is the most common cause of default, but there are others, such as failure to have proper insurance, or pay property taxes, leaving the building vacant for a long period of time, damaging the building, or using the property for unlawful purposes.
2. The mortgagee (lender) must wait 15 days after the default started, then sends a Notice of Default (or Notice of Sale under Mortgage) to the borrower informing him that the lender intends to exercise his right to sell under Power of Sale. This notice gives the borrower approximately 1 month (as per the mortgage agreement) to pay or remedy the default. If the borrower does not correct the default, the lender may sell the property.
3. After the time period in the notice has expired, the mortgagee places the property for sale, virtually always with a real estate agent (direct sales are rare). Mortgagees do this to protect themselves because the law says they must do all they can to obtain the best possible price for the property on behalf of the owner. For the same reason, most Power of Sale properties are placed on the Multiple Listing Service

(MLS), generally at too high a price to start, so that the mortgagee can retort, if examined in court, "We tried our best, Your Honour." Furthermore, if the mortgagees are seen to be giving a "sweet deal" to someone, they can be fairly sure to be sued by the mortgagor. The mortgagor is not entitled to receive any monies from the sale over and beyond what the mortgage can claim as principal, interest, and expenses.

> *If the mortgagees are seen to be giving a "sweet deal" to someone, they can be fairly sure to be sued by the mortgagor.*

Prior to listing a property with a real estate professional, most mortgagees also secure at least one appraisal, and often two if the value of the property warrants it, to use as a guide in setting the asking price and as protection against a critical mortgagor. The first asking price is usually above market value, even if the property is fully leased and in good shape, but since the mortgagor has run out of money, the property almost always has problems, such as vacancies, quality of tenants, deferred maintenance, etc. It is sold as is with no guarantee or representation. Frequently, the property's listing expires and it is re-listed, often several times, at a lower and lower price. Because of this, a property for sale under Power of Sale can offer a good opportunity for the smart investor, who will frequently have to roll up his sleeves and take risks to turn the property around and make it profitable.

Note that the borrower has a Right of Redemption, whereby he may pay all monies due, including principal, interests, and mortgagee's expenses, before the mortgagee sells the property and all the rights of ownership will be reinstated in the borrower. The redemption period, once the Notice of Sale has been sent, is 45 days. Courts have repeatedly decided that when a Sale Agreement is firm (no condition), the sale is effective on the date it is signed (not registered in the Registry Office) and no Right of Redemption is possible.

4. Once an Offer has been accepted, the legal process of the sale takes place. Out of the proceeds of the sale, the vendor/mortgagee pays, in this order:
   - construction liens, if any
   - property taxes that are in arrears
   - condominium fees, if applicable
   - costs incurred by the vendor/mortgagee to sell the property, such as legal and other professional fees, including fees for appraisers, lawyers, consultants, receivers, real estate commission, and any expenses incurred in managing the property (generally, receivers are used by mortgagees to sell properties, which distances them further from the process)
   - interest due under the mortgage
   - principal due under the mortgage
   - registered encumbrances, such as other mortgages, encroachments, rights-of-way, easement fees, and
   - rent deposits, if any.

5. If the net proceeds exceed the amount owed the vendor/mortgagee after all expenses are paid, the balance is paid to the borrower/mortgagor. If the net proceeds of the sale do not cover the money due, the lender can sue the borrower, the corporation itself and/or the guarantor personally, unless it is a non-recourse mortgage. In a foreclosure situation, this does not apply.

(d) Advantages of the Power of Sale Option

In a good market, a property can be sold under Power of Sale fairly quickly, usually in three to six months. This process is also relatively cheap because there is no requirement for any court proceedings. Another benefit is that no Land Transfer Tax (LTT) is payable by the lender/vendor. LTT will be paid by the buyer when the sale is registered.

(e) Disadvantages of the Power of Sale Option

The lender must make every effort to obtain a fair price for the property, to be responsible to all parties involved, to conduct the sale properly, and to give details, upon request. This requires that the lender keep accurate bookkeeping of all transactions.

(f) Tenants' Rights in Power of Sale

In most instances, if there are tenants after a property has sold under a Power of Sale transaction, they maintain the same rights with the new owner as they had with the vendor. This leads some mortgagors, who see a default situation brewing, to lease space in the building to another entity associated with them, for a long term, at a ridiculously low rental. In principle, the mortgagee selling under Power of Sale can fight this in court and is virtually assured of winning. Unfortunately, some mortgagees are neglectful, or indifferent, and the lease stands. We know of a situation where the mortgagor signed such a lease for 10 years at a rate of approximately one-third of the rental value of the space, and when his property was sold under a Power of Sale, the tenant continued to benefit from the lease for the balance of the term of the lease.

12.9.2 FORECLOSURE

Foreclosure requires a court hearing at which the court generally imposes a delay, usually of 60 days, to give the mortgagor the opportunity to redeem his equity by selling the property himself or finding money elsewhere. After 60 days, the mortgagee may apply for a Final Order of Foreclosure. When this is registered, the mortgagee becomes the new owner. Unlike in the US, in Ontario, foreclosure is only used, and very rarely at that, when there is significant equity in the property.

(a) Advantages of the Foreclosure Option

The lender becomes the new owner and does not have to sell the property. It may keep it as an investment. This would be an advantage when it is a desirable property or it is fully or almost fully leased. If there is considerable equity in the property and the lender can have a judge agree to a favourable price, it can't lose, whether it elects to keep it or to resell it.

(b) Disadvantages of the Foreclosure Option

Foreclosure is more expensive than the Power of Sale route because it must go through the courts and is subject to court supervision. It may take a long time, usually six months or more, and sometimes even years. In addition to high legal costs and delays, the lender must pay the LTT when it becomes the new owner.

Unlike Power of Sale, the lender cannot sue the borrower for shortfalls if it sells it after foreclosing on a property. There is also the danger that, due to the time it can take for the foreclosure to be completed, the property may deteriorate or be vandalized (sometimes by the borrower). In a foreclosure situation, the tenants keep their rights.

PART 4

Buying, Selling and Leasing

CHAPTER

13 Real Estate Agencies

By the end of this chapter you will be able to:

- Appreciate the differences between real estate agents, "Realtors", and real estate brokers.
- Define the agency relationship and know which agreement is most appropriate to sign.
- Feel comfortable locating and hiring an agent.
- Understand the significance of maintaining a good rapport with a reputable agent.
- Calculate an agent's payment.
- Determine which listing type is best for you.
- Understand the workings and policies of the MLS system.
- Assist your agent to better market your property.
- Decide whether getting a real estate license is right for you.

13.1 UNDERSTANDING THE ROLES

*Appreciate the differences between real estate agents, "Realtors",
and real estate brokers.*

There is no law that says that a vendor, buyer, landlord, or tenant must use a real estate agent when buying, selling, or leasing property, but most transactions are made through agents. The profession is heavily regulated and, considering the huge number of transactions that take place every year, there are very few problems.

Real estate sales professionals are regulated by provincial legislation. In Ontario the *Real Estate and Business Brokers Act*, 2002 (S.O. 2002, c. 30, Sched. C) (REBBA) regulates the industry. REBBA is administered by the Real Estate Council of Ontario (RECO), which keeps a tight leash on all licensed real estate agents. As a federally incorporated entity, RECO has its own corporate by-laws. REBBA, which came into effect on March 31, 2006, incorporated consumer protection programs put in place since 1997 through member-approved RECO by-laws, which provided an interim solution to real estate act reform. These included items such as continuing education requirements, insurance requirements, a code of ethics, and the complaint process. The law says that no one can trade in real estate (sell or lease) as a brokerage, broker, or salesperson, if he is not registered. To verify that a person or company is indeed registered you can contact RECO or check on its Web site <www.reco.on.ca> and click on "Registrant Search".

13.1.1 REAL ESTATE AGENTS

A real estate agent or salesperson is a person licensed by the government to assist buyers and vendors transacting in real estate. Agents represent their clients when buying, selling, and/or leasing property. The agents who deal in commercial properties are said to be in Industrial, Commercial, and Investment (ICI) real estate.

Agents are not necessary to conduct a real estate transaction, but they are extremely helpful. One of our clients put it to us very well. "I consider using an agent the same as buying insurance. I prefer to suffer when I write a commission cheque than to find myself in court or taken advantage of by a dishonest person."

The life of agents is not easy. They must continually attend and pay for courses, seminars, and training sessions. They read industry books and periodicals. They are members of associations with expensive dues. They subscribe to expensive online services in order to properly serve their clients. They must be knowledgeable about marketing, prospecting markets, real estate legislation, board regulations, photography, new real estate projects, zoning by-laws, schools, neighbourhood trends, computer usage, etc. A few agents are stars, but many just make a living, as in any profession.

A real estate agent is a consultant who provides a service, just like a lawyer or an accountant. He should react quickly to any request, telephone call or message, appointment, etc. He should be an efficient "go-getter" and knowledgeable. In addition, he should be pleasant and diplomatic since he is the glue in the transaction, and the cushion between the parties involved in a transaction. Often an agent will hear a party say, "Tell the buyer to go to hell," which he will translate for the other party as, "The vendor felt that this was a little unreasonable." Finally, a good agent will put his client's interest ahead of his commission.

When teaching Commercial Real Estate for the Ontario Real Estate Association, we are often asked by students whether it is better to seek out listings or buyers. Our answer is that if you believe that when a vendor signs a listing with you for the sale of a $3-million property, he is entrusting you with this amount of money for the duration of the listing, you would do well seeking listings. If not, you should work with buyers.

Treat your real estate agent as you do your lawyer. Give him an idea of what you want and put it on paper. He will tell you if you are being reasonable or unreasonable and what would be more realistic expectations.

13.1.2 REALTORS

The term "Realtor"[1] refers to real estate professionals who are members of the Canadian Real Estate Association (CREA) by virtue of holding membership in a local real estate board. The term "Realtor" is often incorrectly used to designate all real estate salespeople and brokers, even those who are not members of CREA.

As members of a real estate board, Realtors present several advantages.

- They have access to a lot of expensive information, including the Multiple Listing Service (MLS) and other electronic data bases, which would be beyond the means of an individual who is not a member of CREA.
- They have access to and are required to take part in ongoing professional training.

Dealing with Realtors offers clients better protection since they must abide by the professional standards, rules, and regulations of the board of which they are members, as well as provincial laws and regulations.

13.1.3 REAL ESTATE BROKERS

Only a broker can open his own brokerage firm and employ other agents or be a manager in a larger brokerage. To become a broker, an agent must have been licensed for at least 2 years and have taken additional courses. Brokers may, or may not, opt to join the local real estate board. If they do, they subject themselves to additional controls and regulations and all their sales representatives must join too.

13.2 THE AGENCY RELATIONSHIP

Define the agency relationship and know which agreement is most appropriate to sign.

When a vendor or a buyer enlists the help of a real estate salesperson, an agency relationship is created. Agency relationships must be outlined in writing.

13.2.1 DEFINING THE RELATIONSHIPS

It is important to be clear who an agent is representing — the buyer/tenant, the vendor/landlord, or both. All three scenarios are permitted.

1. **Vendor/Landlord.** This is commonly done by way of a listing agreement, either an exclusive agreement or an MLS authority to sell or lease a property. In this case the agent's responsibility is to serve the vendor/landlord's best interests.
2. **Buyer/Tenant.** An agent is engaged by way of a Buyer Agency Agreement to work on behalf of the buyer/tenant.

---

1 The term "Realtor" is trademarked by the Canadian Real Estate Association.

3. **Dual Agency.** Under a Dual Agency Agreement the agent represents, at the same time, the interests of the vendor and of the buyer. This situation usually occurs when a listing agent (who is contracted to represent the vendor) is approached directly by a buyer to represent him in making an offer on the listed property. In this case it can become tricky for the listing agent to serve both parties well. Although procedures for dealing with this situation are provincially regulated, generally the agent can elect to:
   – tell the buyer that he represents only the interests of the vendor, but still deal with the buyer,
   – tell both vendor and buyer that he will act as a dual agent; he must then "walk a clearly defined ethical line" to be fair to both parties, or
   – bring in a second agent to represent the buyer.

Within this context of agency agreements you may hear many terms being used.
- **Prospect.** This is a person who may buy or lease a property.
- **Customer.** This is a person who wants to buy or lease a property, but has not committed to working with a specific agent. Good agents do not work with customers. Their position is that if a person expects them to spend considerable time and money to find a property, he should view the agent for what he is — a consultant. No consultant will work with a person who is not committed to using his services exclusively.
- **Client.** The person a real estate agent represents is a client.

In every situation, the agent must:
- obey the instructions received from his client
- not reveal special knowledge he has regarding his client
- perform his duties with great care and loyalty, and
- account for all monies received from his client.

A broker, and the agents he has working for him, must be protected in writing because under the law he cannot sue for commission unless there is a written promise to pay commission. The protection is obtained in one of three ways.

1. A Buyer's Representation Agreement
2. A MLS Listing Agreement
3. A Commission Agreement

(a) Buyer's Representation Agreement

A Buyer's Representation Agreement is signed by a buyer asking the real estate broker to find him a property to buy or lease (see Figure 13.1). This gives the agent the exclusive right to work on behalf of the client. The concept of exclusive representation to find a property was a long time coming. We are now on the verge of a situation where investors will hire real estate brokers in the same way as they hire a lawyer, architect, or engineer. Although many investors will still say to a real estate agent, "I don't want to limit myself to only one agent. I will buy from the one who brings me a property I like," this represents the old times. If an investor wants a real estate agent to work diligently to find a property, he has to commit himself to that agent. It is true that occasionally an agent will talk to an investor and, by coincidence, come across a suitable property two days later, but this is rare. Most of the time, an agent must do a lot of work before finding the right property.

Figure 13.1
Buyer Representation Agreement – Commercial

Buyer Representation Agreement – Commerc
Mandate for Purchase or Lease

Commercial Division
Toronto Real Estate Board

This is an Exclusive Buyer Representation Agreement

BETWEEN:

BROKERAGE: REALTY EXPERTS, BROKERAGE ...., Tel.No. (905) 882-8800

ADDRESS:...

.... Fax.No. (905) 882-9742 ....

hereinafter referred to as the Brokerage.

AND:

BUYER(S)..., hereinafter referred to as the Buyer,

ADDRESS:...

The Buyer hereby gives the Brokerage the **exclusive and irrevocable authority** to act as the Buyer's agent
commencing at........................a.m./p.m.   on the..day of.., 20..............,
and expiring at 11:59 p.m. on the..day of.., 20..............(Expiry Date).

Buyer acknowledges that the time period for this Agreement is negotiable between the Buyer and the Brokerage, however, in accordance with the
Real Estate and Business Brokers Act of Ontario (2002),
If the time period for this Agreement exceeds six months, the Brokerage must obtain the Buyer's initials.

(Buyer's Initials)

for the purpose of locating a real property meeting the following general description:

Property Type (Use):...

....

Geographic Location:..

....

**The Buyer hereby warrants that the Buyer is not a party to a buyer representation agreement with any other registered real
estate brokerage for the purchase or lease of a real property of the general description indicated above.**

1. **DEFINITIONS AND INTERPRETATIONS:** For the purposes of this Buyer Representation Agreement ("Mandate"), "Buyer" includes purchaser,
lessee and tenant and a "seller" includes a vendor, a lessor, a landlord or a prospective seller, vendor, lessor or landlord. A "real property" includes real
estate as defined in the Real Estate and Business Brokers Act (2002). A purchase shall be deemed to include the entering into of any agreement to
exchange, or the obtaining of an option to purchase which is subsequently exercised, or an agreement to purchase or transfer shares or assets, and a
lease includes any rental agreement, sub-lease or renewal of a lease. A "real estate board" includes a real estate association. This Agreement shall be
read with all changes of gender or number required by the context. For the purposes of this Agreement, the definition of "Buyer" in the phrase "any
property of interest to the Buyer that came to the Buyer's attention from any source whatsoever" shall be deemed to include any spouse, heirs, executors,
administrators, successors, assigns, related corporations and affiliated corporations. Related corporations or affiliated corporations shall include any
corporation where one half or a majority of the shareholders, directors or officers of the related or affiliated corporation are the same person(s) as the
shareholders, directors, or officers of the corporation introduced to or shown the property.

2. **SERVICES PROVIDED BY THE BROKERAGE:** It is understood that the Brokerage may assist the Buyer with any or all of the following
services, and any other services, as agreed to between the Buyer and the Brokerage:
   - to identify the needs of the Buyer.
   - to locate available properties that may meet the Buyer's needs.
   - to assist the Buyer in negotiations for the purchase or lease of any property of interest to the Buyer (subject to the special provisions for
Multiple Representation described below).
   - Other: (Attach Schedule if additional space is required)..

3. RESPONSIBILITIES OF THE BUYER: In consideration of the Brokerage undertaking to assist the Buyer, the Buyer agrees to:
- co-operate with the Brokerage with respect to the Brokerage providing any or all of the services described above, as agreed to between the Buyer and the Brokerage.
- work exclusively with the Brokerage for the purchase or lease of a real property that meets the Buyer's needs.
- advise the Brokerage immediately of any property of interest to the Buyer that came to the Buyer's attention from any source whatsoever during the currency of this Agreement.
- submit through the Brokerage all offers by the Buyer during the currency of this Agreement to purchase or lease a real property of the general description indicated above.
- submit through the Brokerage all offers by the Buyer within.................days after expiration of this Agreement for the purchase or lease of any property that came to the Buyer's attention from any source whatsoever during the currency of this Agreement.

The Buyer agrees the Brokerage is entitled to be paid a commission of...

....

....

The Buyer authorizes the Brokerage to receive payment of commission from the seller of the property or the seller's agent. Should the Brokerage be unable to obtain an agreement in writing from the seller or the seller's agent to pay the full commission described above, the Buyer will be so informed in writing prior to submitting an offer to purchase or lease and the Buyer will pay the commission for the transaction, or any deficiency in the amount of commission described above, directly to the Brokerage.
The Buyer agrees to pay such commission as described above even if a transaction contemplated by an agreement to purchase or lease agreed to or accepted by the Buyer or anyone on the Buyer's behalf is not completed, if such non-completion is owing or attributable to the Buyer's default or neglect. The Buyer understands that a failure to negotiate and submit offers through the Brokerage as described herein will make the Buyer liable for payment of commission to the Brokerage. The payment of commission by the seller to the Brokerage will not make the Brokerage the agent for the seller. All amounts set out as commission are to be paid plus applicable federal Goods and Services Tax (GST) on such commission.

4. REPRESENTATION: The Buyer acknowledges that the Brokerage has provided the Buyer with written information explaining agency relationships, including information on Seller Representation, Sub-Agency, Buyer Representation, Multiple Representation and Customer Service.
The Brokerage shall assist the Buyer in locating a real property of the general description indicated above and shall represent the Buyer in an endeavour to procure the acceptance of an agreement to purchase or lease such a property.
The Buyer acknowledges that the Buyer may not be shown or offered all properties that may be of interest to the Buyer.
The Buyer hereby agrees that the terms of any buyer's offer or agreement to purchase or lease the property will not be disclosed to any other buyer.
The Buyer further acknowledges that the Brokerage may be entering into buyer representation agreements with other buyers who may be interested in the same or similar properties that the Buyer may be interested in buying or leasing and the Buyer hereby consents to the Brokerage entering into buyer representation agreements with other buyers who may be interested in the same or similar properties without any claim by the Buyer of conflict of interest.
The Buyer hereby appoints the Brokerage as agent for the purpose of giving and receiving notices pursuant to any offer or agreement to purchase or lease a property negotiated by the Brokerage.

MULTIPLE REPRESENTATION: The Buyer hereby acknowledges that the Brokerage may be entering into listing agreements with sellers of properties the Buyer may be interested in buying or leasing. In the event that the Brokerage has entered into or enters into a listing agreement with the seller of a property the Buyer may be interested in buying or leasing, the Brokerage will obtain the Buyer's written consent to represent both the Buyer and the seller for the transaction at the earliest practicable opportunity and in all cases prior to any offer to purchase or lease being submitted or presented.

The Buyer understands and acknowledges that the Brokerage must be impartial when representing both the Buyer and the seller and equally protect the interests of the Buyer and the seller in the transaction. The Buyer understands and acknowledges that when representing both the Buyer and the seller, the Brokerage shall have a duty of full disclosure to both the Buyer and the seller, including a requirement to disclose all factual information about the property known to the Brokerage.

However, The Buyer further understands and acknowledges that the Brokerage shall not disclose:
- that the seller may or will accept less than the listed price, unless otherwise instructed in writing by the seller;
- that the Buyer may or will pay more than the offered price, unless otherwise instructed in writing by the Buyer;
- the motivation of or personal information about the Buyer or seller, unless otherwise instructed in writing by the party to which the information applies or unless failure to disclose would constitute fraudulent, unlawful or unethical practice;
- the price the Buyer should offer or the price the seller should accept; and
- the Brokerage shall not disclose to the Buyer the terms of any other offer.

However, it is understood that factual market information about comparable properties and information known to the Brokerage concerning potential uses for the property will be disclosed to both Buyer and seller to assist them to come to their own conclusions.

MULTIPLE REPRESENTATION AND CUSTOMER SERVICE: The Buyer understands and agrees that the Brokerage also provides representation and customer service to other buyers and sellers. If the Brokerage represents or provides customer service to more than one seller or buyer for the same trade, the Brokerage shall, in writing, at the earliest practicable opportunity and before any offer is made, inform all sellers and buyers of the nature of the Brokerage's relationship to each seller and buyer.

5. FINDERS FEE: The Buyer acknowledges that the Brokerage may be receiving a finder's fee from a lender in the event that a new mortgage or an increase in financing is required for a transaction contemplated by this Agreement, and the Buyer consents to any such fee being retained by the Brokerage in addition to the commission as described above.

6. ENVIRONMENTAL INDEMNIFICATION: The Buyer agrees to indemnify and save harmless the Brokerage from any liability, claim, loss, cost, damage or injury as a result of any property of interest to the Buyer being affected by any contaminants or environmental problems.

7. USE AND DISTRIBUTION OF INFORMATION: The Buyer consents to the collection, use and disclosure of personal information by the Brokerage for such purposes that relate to the real estate services provided by the Brokerage to the Buyer including, but not limited to: locating, assessing and qualifying properties for the Buyer; advertising on behalf of the Buyer; providing information as needed to third parties retained by the Buyer to assist in a transaction (e.g. financial institutions, building inspectors, etc...); and such other use of the Buyer's information as is consistent with the services provided by the Brokerage in connection with the purchase or prospective purchase of the property.

INITIALS OF BROKERAGE: ⬭   INITIALS OF BUYER(S): ⬭

Form 540   2008

The Buyer agrees that the sale and related information regarding any property purchased by the Buyer through the Brokerage may be retained and disclosed by the Brokerage and/or real estate board(s) (if the property is an MLS® Listing) for reporting, appraisal and statistical purposes and for such other use of the information as the Brokerage and/or board deems appropriate in connection with the listing, marketing and selling of real estate, including conducting comparative market analyses.

8. CONFLICT OR DISCREPANCY: If there is any conflict or discrepancy between any provision added to this Agreement and any provision in the standard pre-set portion hereof, the added provision shall supersede the standard pre-set provision to the extent of such conflict or discrepancy. This Agreement, including any provisions added to this Agreement, shall constitute the entire Authority from the Buyer to the Brokerage. There is no representation, warranty, collateral agreement or condition, which affects this Agreement other than as expressed herein.

9. ELECTRONIC COMMUNICATION: This Buyer Representation Agreement and any agreements, notices or other communications contemplated thereby may be transmitted by means of electronic systems, in which case signatures shall be deemed to be original. The transmission of this Agreement by the Buyer by electronic means shall be deemed to confirm the Buyer has retained a true copy of the Agreement.

10. SCHEDULE(S)...attached hereto form(s) part of this Agreement.

THE BROKERAGE AGREES TO REPRESENT THE BUYER IN LOCATING A REAL PROPERTY OF THE GENERAL DESCRIPTION INDICATED ABOVE IN AN ENDEAVOUR TO OBTAIN THE ACCEPTANCE OF AN AGREEMENT TO PURCHASE OR LEASE A PROPERTY ON TERMS SATISFACTORY TO THE BUYER.

.... DATE.................................... ....
(Authorized to bind the Brokerage)   (Name of Person Signing)

THIS AGREEMENT HAS BEEN READ AND FULLY UNDERSTOOD BY ME AND I ACKNOWLEDGE THIS DATE I HAVE SIGNED UNDER SEAL AND HAVE RECEIVED A TRUE COPY OF THIS AGREEMENT. Any representations contained herein are true to the best of my knowledge, information and belief.

SIGNED, SEALED AND DELIVERED I have hereunto set my hand and seal:

....
(Name of Buyer)

....   ● DATE..................................   ....
(Signature of Buyer/Authorized Signing Officer)   (Seal)   (Tel. No.)

....   ● DATE..................................   ....
(Signature of Buyer/Authorized Signing Officer)   (Seal)

DECLARATION OF INSURANCE

The broker/salesperson **PIERRE BOIRON (Tel: 905-882-8800)** ....
                                                        (Name of Broker/Salesperson)

hereby declares that he/she is insured as required by the Real Estate and Business Brokers Act (REBBA) and Regulations.

....
(Signature(s) of Broker/Salesperson)

Form 540   2007   **Page 3 of 3**
                                                                                                           WEB*Forms*™ Dec/2006

Source: Buyer Representation Agreement – Commercial (Form 540) is used by permission of the Ontario Real Estate Association.

Contrary to what some people think, it is a lot of work to find properties and it does take considerable time. For most of our Buyer Representation Agreements, we want our assignment to be for 6 months. Clause 3 of this agreement states that the buyer agrees that the brokerage is entitled to be paid a commission by the vendor and should the vendor refuse to pay this commission, then the buyer will pay it. This clause often makes buyers nervous. It should not, however, as a buyer will always know before signing an offer if a vendor refused to pay a commission (it happens very rarely). In such a situation, the buyer has the option to pay the commission himself or to walk away from the deal. Note also that this agreement can be assigned by the initial broker to another broker, with the signed consent of the buyer.

(b) MLS Listing Agreement

An MLS, or exclusive, Listing Agreement is signed by the vendor of the property, who can sign with only one real estate agent at one time (see Figure 13.2). For people used to buying or selling real properties, there is little to discuss in the Listing Agreement. It is fair to both the vendor and the broker. There is, however, one thing to which a few vendors object — the length of the holdover period in clause 2 (see section 13.6.3). Some vendors are artful at avoiding paying a commission by waiting until the holdover period expires. Then they approach the buyer of the aborted transaction that the real estate agent had brought to them and try to make a deal without paying commission.

For most residential listings, the holdover clause runs for 90 days. For many commercial listings, if there is a standard, it is 180 days, but we have seen it as long as 5 years. A lot depends on the property itself and how difficult it is to sell.

In clause 3, the commission offered to cooperating brokers must be indicated. Traditionally, brokers split the commission on a 50/50 basis, but during a vendor's market, which makes finding properties for sale a difficult and very time- and money-consuming endeavour, we see more and more situations where the selling broker (buyer's agent) receives less than half of the commission paid to the listing agent.

(c) Commission Agreement

A Commission Agreement is signed by a vendor promising to pay an agreed upon commission if this specific agent sells the property. Note that in this case a vendor could sign a Commission Agreement with many different agents, but pay only the successful one. See Figure 13.3 for a sample agreement.

Figure 13.2
Listing Agreement – Commercial

OREA Ontario Real Estate Association · **Listing Agreement – Commercial**
Authority to Offer for Sale

Commercial Division
Toronto Real Estate Board

MLS
This is a Multiple Listing Service® Agreement ◯ (Seller's Initials)   OR   **This Listing is Exclusive** ◯ (Seller's Initials)

BETWEEN:

BROKERAGE: REALTY EXPERTS, BROKERAGE
....(the "Listing Brokerage")

SELLER(S):...(the "Seller")

In consideration of the Listing Brokerage listing the real property **for sale** known as.........................
....(the "Property")

the Seller hereby gives the Listing Brokerage the **exclusive and irrevocable** right to act as the Seller's agent,
commencing at 12:01 a.m. on the.....................................day of.............................., 20..........,
until 11:59 p.m. on the.....................................day of.............................., 20.......... (the "Listing Period"),

Seller acknowledges that the length of the Listing Period is negotiable between the Seller and the Listing Brokerage and, if an MLS® listing, may be
subject to minimum requirements of the real estate board, however, in accordance with the Real Estate and Business Brokers Act of Ontario (2002),
if the Listing Period exceeds six months, the Listing Brokerage must obtain the Seller's initials. ◯ (Seller's Initials)

to offer the Property **for sale** at a price of:

....Dollars ($Cdn ....)

and upon the terms particularly set out herein, or at such other price and/or terms acceptable to the Seller. It is understood that the price and/or terms set
out herein are at the Seller's personal request, after full discussion with the Listing Brokerage's representative regarding potential market value of the Property.

**The Seller hereby represents and warrants that the Seller is not a party to any other listing agreement for the Property or
agreement to pay commission to any other real estate brokerage for the sale of the property.**

1. **DEFINITIONS AND INTERPRETATIONS:** For the purposes of this Listing Agreement ("Authority" or "Agreement"), "Seller" includes vendor and a
"buyer" includes a purchaser or a prospective purchaser. A purchase shall be deemed to include the entering into of any agreement to exchange, or
the obtaining of an option to purchase which is subsequently exercised, or the causing of a First Right of Refusal to be exercised, or an agreement to
sell or transfer shares or assets. "Real property" includes real estate as defined in the Real Estate and Business Brokers Act (2002). The "Property" shall
be deemed to include any part thereof or interest therein. A "real estate board" includes a real estate association. This Agreement shall be read with
all changes of gender or number required by the context. For purposes of this Agreement, anyone introduced or shown the property shall be deemed
to include any spouse, heirs, executors, administrators, successors, assigns, related corporations and affiliated corporations. Related corporations or
affiliated corporations shall include any corporation where one half or a majority of the shareholders, directors or officers of the related or affiliated
corporation are the same person(s) as the shareholders, directors, or officers of the corporation introduced or shown the property.

2. **COMMISSION:** In consideration of the Listing Brokerage listing the Property for sale, the Seller agrees to pay the Listing Brokerage a commission
of..........................% of the sale price of the Property or...

for any valid offer to purchase the Property from any source whatsoever obtained during the Listing Period and on the terms and conditions set
out in this Agreement **OR** such other terms and conditions as the Seller may accept.

The Seller further agrees to pay such commission as calculated above if an agreement to purchase is agreed to or accepted by the Seller or anyone on
theSeller's behalf within...................days after the expiration of the Listing Period (**Holdover Period**), so long as such agreement is with anyone
who was introduced to the property from any source whatsoever during the Listing Period or shown the property during the Listing Period.
If, however, the offer for the purchase of the Property is pursuant to a new agreement in writing to pay commission to another registered real estate
brokerage, the Seller's liability for commission shall be reduced by the amount paid by the Seller under the new agreement.

The Seller further agrees to pay such commission as calculated above even if the transaction contemplated by an agreement to purchase agreed to or
accepted by the Seller or anyone on the Seller's behalf is not completed, if such non-completion is owing or attributable to the Seller's default or neglect,
said commission to be payable on the date set for completion of the purchase of the Property.

Any deposit in respect of any agreement where the transaction has been completed shall first be applied to reduce the commission payable. Should
such amounts paid to the Listing Brokerage from the deposit or by the Seller's solicitor not be sufficient, the Seller shall be liable to pay to the Listing
Brokerage on demand, any deficiency in commission and taxes owing on such commission.

In the event the buyer fails to complete the purchase and the deposit becomes forfeited, awarded, directed or released to the Seller, the Seller then
authorizes the Listing Brokerage to retain as agreed compensation for services rendered, fifty (50%) per cent of the said deposit (but not to exceed the
commission payable had a sale been consummated) and to pay the balance of the deposit to the Seller.

All amounts set out as commission are to be paid plus applicable federal Goods and Services Tax (GST) on such commission.

INITIALS OF LISTING BROKERAGE: ◯   **INITIALS OF SELLER(S):** ◯

3. REPRESENTATION: The Seller acknowledges that the Listing Brokerage has provided the Seller with written information explaining agency relationships,including information on Seller Representation. Sub-agency, Buyer Representation, Multiple Representation and Customer Service.

The Seller authorizes the Listing Brokerage to co-operate with any other registered real estate brokerage (co-operating brokerage), and to offer to pay

the co-operating brokerage a commission of.................% of the sale price of the Property or ....

....

out of the commission the Seller pays the Listing Brokerage. The Seller understands that unless the Seller is otherwise informed, the co-operating brokerage is representing the interests of the buyer in the transaction. The Seller further acknowledges that the Listing Brokerage may be listing other properties that may be similar to the Seller's Property and the Seller hereby consents to the Listing Brokerage acting as an agent for more than one seller without any claim by the Seller of conflict of interest. Any commission payable to any other brokerage shall be paid out of the commission the Seller pays the Listing Brokerage.
The Seller hereby appoints the Listing Brokerage as the Seller's agent for the purpose of giving and receiving notices pursuant to any offer or agreement to purchase the Property.

MULTIPLE REPRESENTATION: The Seller hereby acknowledges that the Listing Brokerage may be entering into buyer representation agreements with buyers who may be interested in purchasing the Seller's Property. In the event that the Listing Brokerage has entered into or enters into a buyer representation agreement with a prospective buyer for the Seller's Property, the Listing Brokerage will obtain the Seller's written consent to represent both the Seller and the buyer for the transaction at the earliest practical opportunity and in all cases prior to any offer to purchase being submitted or presented.

The Seller understand and acknowledges that the Listing Brokerage must be impartial when representing both the Seller and the buyer and equally protect the interests of the Seller and buyer. The Seller understands and acknowledges that when representing both the Seller and the buyer, the Listing Brokerage shall have a duty of full disclosure to both the Seller and the buyer, including a requirement to disclose all factual information about the property known to the Listing Brokerage.

However, the Seller further understands and acknowledges that the Listing Brokerage shall not disclose:

- that the Seller may or will accept less than the listed price, unless otherwise instructed in writing by the Seller;
- that the buyer may or will pay more than the offered price, unless otherwise instructed in writing by the buyer;
- the motivation of or personal information about the Seller or buyer, unless otherwise instructed in writing by the party to which the information applies or unless failure to disclose would constitute fraudulent, unlawful or unethical practice;
- the price the buyer should offer or the price the Seller should accept; and
- the Listing Brokerage shall not disclose to the buyer the terms of any other offer.

However, it is understood that factual market information about comparable properties and information known to the Listing Brokerage concerning potential uses for the Property will be disclosed to both Seller and buyer to assist them to come to their own conclusions.

MULTIPLE REPRESENTATION AND CUSTOMER SERVICE: The Seller understands and agrees that the Listing Brokerage also provides representation and customer service to other sellers and buyers. If the Listing Brokerage represents or provides customer service to more than one seller or buyer for the same trade, the Listing Brokerage shall, in writing, at the earliest practicable opportunity and before any offer is made, inform all sellers and buyers of the nature of the Listing Brokerage's relationship to each seller and buyer.

4. REFERRAL OF ENQUIRIES: The Seller agrees that during the Listing Period, the Seller shall advise the Listing Brokerage immediately of all enquiries from any source whatsoever, and all offers to purchase submitted to the Seller shall be immediately submitted to the Listing Brokerage by the Seller before the Seller accepts or rejects the same. If the Seller fails to advise the Listing Brokerage of any enquiry during the Listing Period and said enquiry results in the Seller's accepting a valid offer to purchase during the Listing Period or within the Holdover Period after the expiration of the Listing Period described above, the Seller agrees to pay the Listing Brokerage the amount of commission set out above, payable within five (5) days following the Listing Brokerage's written demand therefor.

5. MARKETING: The Seller agrees to allow the Listing Brokerage to show and permit prospective buyers to fully inspect the Property during reasonable hours and the Seller gives the Listing Brokerage the sole and exclusive right to place "For Sale" and "Sold" sign(s) upon the Property.
The Seller consents to the Listing Brokerage including information in advertising that may identify the property. The Seller further agrees that the Listing Brokerage shall have sole and exclusive authority to make all advertising decisions relating to the marketing of the Property during the Listing Period. The Seller agrees that the Listing Brokerage will not be held liable in any manner whatsoever for any acts or omissions with respect to advertising by the Listing Brokerage or any other party, other than by the Listing Brokerage's gross negligence or wilful act.

6. WARRANTY: The Seller represents and warrants that the Seller has the exclusive authority and power to execute this Authority to offer the Property for sale and that the Seller has informed the Listing Brokerage of any third party interests or claims on the property such as rights of first refusal, options, easements, mortgages, encumbrances or otherwise concerning the property, which may affect the sale of the Property.

7. INDEMNIFICATION: The Seller will not hold the Listing Brokerage responsible for any loss or damage to the Property or contents occurring during the term of this Agreement caused by the Listing Brokerage or anyone else by any means, including theft, fire or vandalism, other than by the Listing Brokerage's gross negligence or wilful act. The Seller agrees to indemnify and save harmless the Listing Brokerage and any co-operating brokerage from any liability, claim, loss, cost, damage or injury, including but not limited to loss of the commission payable under this Agreement, caused or contributed to by the breach of any warranty or representation made by the Seller in this Agreement or the accompanying data form. The Seller agrees to indemnify and save harmless the Listing Brokerage and any co-operating brokerage from any liability, claim, loss, cost, damage or injury as a result of the property being affected by any contaminants or environmental problems.

8. FAMILY LAW ACT: The Seller hereby warrants that spousal consent is not necessary under the provisions of the Family Law Act, R.S.O. 1990, unless the Seller's spouse has executed the consent hereinafter provided.

9. FINDERS FEES: The Seller consents to the Listing Brokerage or co-operating brokerage receiving and retaining, in addition to the commission provided for in this Agreement, a finder's fee for any financing of the property.

10. VERIFICATION OF INFORMATION: The Seller authorizes the Listing Brokerage to obtain any information from any regulatory authorities, governments, mortgagees or others affecting the Property and the Seller agrees to execute and deliver such further authorizations in this regard as may be reasonably required. The Seller hereby appoints the Listing Brokerage or the Listing Brokerage's authorized representative as the Seller's attorney to execute such documentation as may be necessary to effect obtaining any information as aforesaid. The Seller hereby authorizes, instructs and directs the above noted regulatory authorities, governments, mortgagees or others to release any and all information to the Listing Brokerage.

INITIALS OF LISTING BROKERAGE: ( )   **INITIALS OF SELLER(S):** ( )

Form 520   2008   **Page 2 of 3**

11. USE AND DISTRIBUTION OF INFORMATION: The Seller consents to the collection, use and disclosure of personal information by the Brokerage for the purpose of listing and marketing the Property including, but not limited to: listing and advertising the Property using any medium including the Internet; disclosing property information to prospective buyers, brokerages, salespersons and others who may assist in the sale of the Property; such other use of the Seller's personal information as is consistent with listing and marketing of the Property. The Seller consents, if this is an MLS® Listing, to placement of the listing information and sales information by the Brokerage into the database(s) of the appropriate MLS® systems(s) and acknowledges that the MLS® database is the property of the board(s) and can be licensed, resold, or otherwise dealt with by the board(s). The Seller further acknowledges that the board(s) may: distribute the information to any persons authorized to use such service which may include other brokerages, government departments, appraisers, municipal organizations and others; market the Property, at its option, in any medium, including electronic media; compile, retain and publish any statistics including historical MLS® data which may be used by board members to conduct comparative market analyses; and make such other use of the information as the Brokerage and/or board deems appropriate in connection with the listing, marketing and selling of real estate.

In the event that this Agreement expires and the Property is not sold, the Seller, by initialling,

$\bigcirc$ **Does** $\bigcirc$ **Does Not**

consent to allow other real estate board members to contact the Seller after expiration of this Agreement to discuss listing or otherwise marketing the Property.

12. SUCCESSORS AND ASSIGNS: The heirs, executors, administrators, successors and assigns of the undersigned are bound by the terms of this Agreement.

13. CONFLICT OR DISCREPANCY: If there is any conflict or discrepancy between any provision added to this Agreement (including any Schedule attached hereto) and any provision in the standard pre-set portion hereof, the added provision shall supersede the standard pre-set provision to the extent of such conflict or discrepancy. This Agreement, including any Schedule attached hereto, shall constitute the entire Authority from the Seller to the Brokerage. There is no representation, warranty, collateral agreement or condition, which affects this Agreement other than as expressed herein.

14. ELECTRONIC COMMUNICATION: This Listing Agreement and any agreements, notices or other communications contemplated thereby may be transmitted by means of electronic systems, in which case signatures shall be deemed to be original. The transmission of this Agreement by the Seller by electronic means shall be deemed to confirm the Seller has retained a true copy of the Agreement.

15. SCHEDULE(S)...and data form attached hereto form(s) part of this Agreement.

THE LISTING BROKERAGE AGREES TO MARKET THE PROPERTY ON BEHALF OF THE SELLER AND REPRESENT THE SELLER IN AN ENDEAVOUR TO OBTAIN A VALID OFFER TO PURCHASE THE PROPERTY ON THE TERMS SET OUT IN THIS AGREEMENT OR ON SUCH OTHER TERMS SATISFACTORY TO THE SELLER.

....   DATE.....................................   ....
(Authorized to bind the Listing Brokerage)   (Name of Person Signing)

THIS AUTHORITY HAS BEEN READ AND FULLY UNDERSTOOD BY ME AND I ACKNOWLEDGE THIS DATE I HAVE SIGNED UNDER SEAL AND HAVE RECEIVED A TRUE COPY OF THIS AGREEMENT. Any representations contained herein or as shown on the accompanying data form respecting the Property are true to the best of my knowledge, information and belief.

SIGNED, SEALED AND DELIVERED I have hereunto set my hand and seal:

....
(Name of Seller)

....   ● DATE.............................   ....
(Signature of Seller/Authorized Signing Officer)   (Seal)   (Tel. No.)

....   ● DATE.............................   ....
(Signature of Seller/Authorized Signing Officer)   (Seal)

SPOUSAL CONSENT: The undersigned spouse of the Seller hereby consents to the listing of the Property herein pursuant to the provisions of the Family Law Act, R.S.O. 1990 and hereby agrees that he/she will execute all necessary or incidental documents to further any transaction provided for herein.

....   ● DATE.............................
(Spouse)   (Seal)

DECLARATION OF INSURANCE

The broker/salesperson **PIERRE BOIRON (Tel: 905-882-8800)** ....
                                                              (Name of Broker/Salesperson)

hereby declares that he/she is insured as required by the Real Estate and Business Brokers Act (REBBA) and Regulations.

....
(Signature(s) of Broker/Salesperson)

Source: Listing Agreement – Commercial (Form 520) is used by permission of the Ontario Real Estate Association.

Figure 13.3
Commission Agreement

COMMISSION AGREEMENT

We, _____, Vendor(s)

                            (name of vendor(s))

of the property known as _____,

                   (municipal address or property description)

hereby agree to pay to <u>Coldwell Banker Commercial Terrequity Realty</u> on closing, a commission

                        (Real Estate broker)

equal to _____six_____% of the selling price of the property, in the event that said broker obtains an

offer which is accepted by us, or by anyone on our behalf.

Such commission shall be paid to you upon completion of any such transaction. This agreement shall not

be construed as an "exclusive listing" and shall remain valid for 365 days from the date of registration of a

prospect.

The heirs, executors, administrators, successors and assigns of the undersigned shall be bound by the

terms hereof.

The Vendor acknowledges that the broker may be acting as dual agent of the Vendor and Purchaser.

This agreement may be transmitted by fax.

Dated at _____ this _____ day of _____, 200__

Company: _____   Tel: _____

Witness: _____   Signature: per _____

                        (I have the authority to bind the corporation)

                        Name of Company Officer Signing this agreement:

                        _____

13.3 HOW TO SELECT A REAL ESTATE AGENT

Feel comfortable locating and hiring an agent.

If you are lucky, you have a friend who knows, and has used, an expert real estate agent. If not, here are some ways to find a good agent.

- Ask commercial real estate lawyers for recommendations and enquire as to why they think the commercial agent they recommend is good.
- Ask appraisers for recommendations and the reasons for those recommendations.
- If you know a good residential agent, ask him to lend you a commercial or industrial MLS book and let you peruse it or, ideally, sit down with him at his computer. By studying the listings, you will notice a few names that are prevalent and, in particular, how well the listing agents complete and use the marvellous MLS marketing tool.
- Buy a business paper, such as the *Financial Post* or the *Globe and Mail* (find out which day(s) of the week the commercial real estate display ads appear). Look for an agent whose ads appeal to you. You will need to see several days' worth of ads to get a good sense of the agent's style. Keep in mind that many outstanding agents do not use newspaper ads.
- If you are fixed on a specific area, drive around that area and call on the real estate signs offering properties for sale or for lease.
- Visit the managers of the commercial real estate companies active in the area or types of properties in which you are interested. Tell them your reasons for wanting an agent (i.e., to purchase, lease, sell, etc.) and for which specialty (e.g., office, retail, etc.). Ask them to give you the names of their top two or three producers in that field.

Next, call these agents and ask them to send you their resume, references, and testimonials from previous clients. After reviewing their material, select at most three agents that you want to meet. Have a meeting with each one face to face. If you feel particularly comfortable with one, you do not need to meet more. After the meeting, you should be in a position to pick one of the three, an agent *After the meeting, you should be in a position to pick one of the three, an agent with a solid reputation with whom you feel comfortable working.* with a solid reputation with whom you feel comfortable working. Remember: It is the person who counts; not the firm and its number of agents or offices. The office is not the one fighting in the trenches. It is your agent who is out there doing his best to get you the best price, terms, and conditions.

13.4 HOW TO WORK WITH AN AGENT

Understand the significance of maintaining a good rapport with a reputable agent.

For most people, buying a real property is one of the most important financial decisions of their lives. Make sure you choose a real estate professional to guide you. "Licensed Real Estate Professional" means that the person to whom you are entrusting your business is licensed by the province, trained to represent you, protecting your interests, and, particularly important, insured. Most real estate brokers and agents belong to a local real estate board, provincial and national real estate associations, and abide by a strict code of professional standards. They live by the rules and regulations governing the profession.

A real estate agent will:
- explain the market to you
- give you a good indication of values
- explain real estate terminology
- provide the necessary forms and contracts, and explain them to you
- select properties and help you screen them
- help you determine what the price range is, or the type of property you need
- help you to price and sell your properties, ideally using the MLS of their real estate board
- inform you of additional expenses involved in a transaction
- provide you with the names of suppliers you may need, such as lawyers, lenders, contractors, and
- last, but not least, prepare and negotiate offers.

From the agent's point of view, a cardinal mistake made by investors is failing to give the agent feedback when he presents a property to a buyer for consideration. Many people do not realize that the lack of feedback discourages an agent from continuing to work for the investor. It dulls his enthusiasm and motivation. Agents always prefer to work with people who let them know why they are not interested in a particular property.

The smart investor will find it advantageous to build strong working relationships with real estate professionals. Too many people who use the services of real estate agents have a condescending attitude towards them, perhaps due to bad experiences or stories they have heard. No doubt, some agents demonstrate a lack of ethics and some provide poor service due to lack of time, motivation, or knowledge. And a few will try to make a deal at any cost, pressuring the vendor to accept an offer with which he is uncomfortable, but for the most part, agents are well trained professionals who are very client-oriented and provide an excellent and valuable service.

Some clients resent the fact that a commission can represent a very large amount of money, however, professional investors who buy and sell properties frequently do not make this mistake. They know the value of a good agent, and when they find one they treat him with respect. They never haggle over the commission because they know how important the agent is to their success. In fact, when selling, many large landlords pay a higher than usual commission, particularly for a property on MLS, to motivate co-brokers.

The key to working well with real estate agents is to respect their time. Agents, like other professionals, do what they do to make money, and their time is money. The way you treat an agent will determine, to a great extent, if you are top-of-mind when he has properties that could be of interest to you. The more highly real estate agents think of you, the more opportunities you will have to make money.

13.4.1 THE POWER OF THE AGENT

The power of a real estate agent takes two forms. First, he should have considerable expertise acquired through courses, books, and, most of all, experience. Every good agent will have:
- knowledge of the community in which you are buying or selling property
- knowledge of the market (values, trends, supply and demand, available financing, etc.), and
- knowledge of the particular type of real property in which you are interested. Real estate is a vast busi-

ness, with many specialties, some fairly unusual, such as trailer parks, mini-warehouses, bars, hotels, golf courses, etc. An agent who specializes in the residential market, for example, should not touch these properties because his knowledge will be too limited. Most agents specialize in one geographical market and in one or two types of property.

In addition to their expertise, agents can exert considerable influence over their clients. A client, who has an open and trusting relationship with an agent, turns to that agent for guidance when making an investment decision. Good agents will answer honestly when asked if a property is a good deal, if it will lease easily, or if it is realistically priced, etc. Most sophisticated clients will not go against their recommendations. This is another reason that large, sophisticated investors, builders, and developers make sure that they maintain good rapport with agents.

13.4.2 THE AGENT'S IMPACT ON PRICE

Many vendors seem to believe that a property will fetch a certain price regardless of who markets it. This idea is absolutely wrong. The difference in the selling price can be as high as 20% depending on who markets a property. Here are two examples from personal experiences:
  - The vendor thought a 1340 m² (14,400 sq ft) industrial building was worth $400,000 and would have accepted that price. The agent sold it for $495,000, for a difference of $95,000 or 19.20%.
  - The vendor sold a 18,580 m² (200,000 sq ft) warehouse privately for $4,400,000, but the condition was not met. The agent then sold it for $6,000,000, less commission of $300,000 = $5,700,000, for a difference of $1,300,000 or 22.80%.

Remember: Because the amounts of money involved in real estate are so large, mediocrity can be very costly. An expert agent's commission may be higher than that of an ordinary agent, but the expert will undoubtedly obtain a higher price, more than making-up for the difference in commissions and the avoidance of problems. A real estate agent who knows his job can increase the value of the properties that he is marketing, which can markedly affect the Cap Rate.

13.5 HOW AGENTS ARE PAID

Calculate an agent's payment.

Agents are generally paid by commission, which is a percentage of the selling price or the rental. Listing and selling brokerages usually split the commission 50/50 between them, sharing their portion of the commission with the respective agent that did the work. An agent may receive only 20% to 30% of the total commission, often less, in a typical Industrial, Commercial and Investment (ICI) transaction.

The commission is established in the listing agreement and is almost always paid by the vendor/landlord. There is no agreement or collusion among agents to charge the same commission, in fact, the *Competition Act* (R.S.C. 1985, c. C-34) prohibits them from doing so. Although rare, an agent can be paid a fixed sum of money, regardless of the sale price, instead of a percentage.

Note that the agent is prohibited from accepting an agreement whereby he is paid a commission that varies depending on the sale price. For example, he cannot agree to:

- 4% if the price is $4 million
- 5% if the price is $4.25 million, or
- 6% if the price is $4.5 million.

Even if an agent acts as a buyer's agent, his broker will receive the commission from the listing brokerage company.

Typically, agents cooperate willingly and with pleasure among themselves. They must cooperate on MLS listings and they do so 95% of the time on non-MLS listings.

Many listing agreements provide that "the commission is due and payable upon acceptance of an offer." This means that the commission is payable even if, due to extraordinary circumstances, the transaction does not close. The intent is to prevent some vendors from playing tricks with the agent. This does happen, but rarely. More frequently, a buyer will back out and lose his deposit. Personally, we feel that it is not fair to ask a vendor to pay for a sale that did not take place. A compromise used by some agents is to agree with the vendor that if a sale does not take place, the deposit will be split equally between them. Again, note that to be able to sue for commission, an agent must have an agreement in writing from his client that is signed under seal if it is to stand up in court.

The listing broker receives the money from the vendor on closing and pays the selling broker his share. Since 2003, a new practice has developed in connection with real estate commissions for investment properties, undoubtedly due to the limited supply versus the high demand. In the past, listing agents almost always cooperated by splitting their commission 50/50 with the selling agents. It is now more common for a listing agent to cooperate with the selling agent but not agree to pay any, or only a small part, of the commission to him, expecting instead that the buyer will pay his agent's commission, or at least part of it.

Sophisticated agents working on behalf of the buyer now generally inform their clients that this practice is becoming more common and say, "Subject to your agreement, I will not ignore any property because of the commission rate and potentially miss a good deal for you. However, when I find the commission too low, I will ask you to budget my commission into the offering price or decide to pass on the property. You will always know before making any offer if I expect any commission payment from you."

The majority of commercial properties sell with a commission ranging from 6% for smaller properties to 2-3% for very large ones. On lower-priced properties (less than $5-$6 million) the commission is usually 4-6%. Many first-time investors and vendors think these commission rates are outrageously high. However, you will find that frequently, in fact almost always, lower commissions mean lower expertise and lower quality of service.

The majority of commercial properties sell with a commission ranging from 6% for smaller properties to 2-3% for very large ones.

In the end, a good agent will be far less expensive than a poor one; his knowledge, expertise, intelligence, and hard work will generally sell a property at a lower Cap Rate, that is, at a higher price. The following example illustrates the difference a slightly higher Cap Rate can make to the selling price.

NOI	$500,000	$500,000
Cap Rate achieved	9 1/2%	9%
Selling price	$5,263,000	$5,555,555
Difference		**+ $292,556**

An expert real estate agent will properly position the property and ensure that it is well showcased. The result is, invariably, that a top agent increases the sale price of a property.

13.6 HOW TO LIST A PROPERTY

Determine which listing type is best for you.

There are three types of listings: non-exclusive or open, exclusive, and MLS.

13.6.1 NON-EXCLUSIVE LISTING

This is, in fact, a Commission Agreement. The vendor permits several agents to market the property for sale and the one who sells it is paid a commission. Good agents rarely work on this basis.

13.6.2 EXCLUSIVE LISTING

Only one agent has the right to market and sell the property and there is no obligation to co-operate with other agents (honesty and common sense should motivate an agent to do so). Generally, an exclusive listing is signed to focus the marketing of the property on a few prospects, rather than peddling it to many. Some vendors are very sensitive and like this approach because the property is not peddled all over the place. Indeed, a property that stays on the market too long becomes stale and can discourage buyer interest. In rare circumstances and with particularly attractive properties, an agent may recommend an exclusive listing if he believes there will be hundreds of agents wanting additional information on a given listing or if the vendor wants anonymity or discretion.

13.6.3 MLS LISTING

One agent is the listing agent and has the right to market and sell the property, but he must co-operate with all other members of the real estate board, and pay the successful co-operating agent a share of the commission. The listing agent decides what he offers, but commonly it is 50%. The property is placed in a database available to all members of the local real estate board.

As a rule, exclusive and MLS listing forms contain a holdover clause, most frequently for 180 days, but its length is agreed to between client and agent. Even when an agent does not introduce a buyer to the property or vendor during the currency of the listing, the agent is entitled to his commission if any buyer makes a deal with the vendor during the holdover period. Note that a listing must have a specific expiry date and that a copy of it must be delivered to the vendor when he signs it.

13.7 THE MULTIPLE LISTING SYSTEM

Understand the workings and policies of the MLS system.

The Multiple Listing System (MLS) operated by real estate boards has drastically changed the marketing of real properties. It has made the process more efficient, more flexible, and allows agents to better service their clients.

Each board decides what broad geographical area it will cover, then divides the whole area into districts, which are further broken down into sub-areas. The board produces maps for use by its members showing the districts and sub-areas.

The Toronto Real Estate Board (TREB) is the largest real estate board in the world (27,000 members as of this writing) and we will use it as an example to explain how the MLS works. (For a map, go to <www.MLS.ca> and click on the map repeatedly until you find the one of interest to you.) While TREB's main service area is centred around Toronto, in fact, it accepts listings anywhere in the world. It also has four districts – C-Central, E-East, W-West, and N-North (nothing to list in Lake Ontario). Outside of these GTA districts, TREB uses the following abbreviations to represent the different areas: X01-X98 for the 35 additional districts in the rest of Ontario, X99 represents the rest of Canada, and districts outside Canada are represented by Z.

When an agent places a listing on MLS, two forms must be completed: a Multiple Listing Agreement (see Figure 13.2), which is the contract that the vendor signs to grant the listing broker authority to place the property on the MLS system, and a MLS Data Information Sheet, completed by the listing agent, for the benefit of all the other members of the board. One copy goes to the owner, one to the board, and one to the listing broker.

A property placed on MLS is exposed to all members of that board and only them. Any member of that board can sell or lease an MLS listed property and the listing agent must cooperate. Listing agent and selling agent share the commission.

A member can access MLS listings either by subscribing to the "dailies," which is now rare, or accessing them online. These ICI listings are broken down into the following categories:

- commercial/retail
- farm
- industrial
- land
- office
- sale of business, and
- store with apartment or office.

To access out-of-town listings, that is, properties listed on boards other than his, an agent can subscribe either for online access or to the MLS books. These are thick books showing the listings by categories. Depending on the real estate board, they are published monthly or more frequently.

Agents can access the board's database that includes not only all active listings, but also sold and expired listings. Agents can search listings based on type (industrial, land, investment, etc.), size (building area, acreage), price, address, and listing number or using the MapArt map coordinates. They can also program the software to notify them daily of new listings based on one or more of the aforementioned criteria. The disappearance of the dailies and the MLS books looms large. It is likely that within a few years only the electronic version of listings will be available.

Members can also search sold or leased MLS listings using the same aforementioned criteria. Also agents have access to other TREB subscribed databases showing, for a specific property, assessment data by address or by owner's name and Land Registry Data for sales showing vendor, buyer, and price.

Because the MLS system exposes all listings to such a broad and deep market we find it incomprehensible that agents of many Class AAA, AA, A, or B office buildings in Toronto do not place their listings on the service. The only logical explanation is that these agents are placing their own interests ahead of that of their clients, hoping to double end their commission, that is, keep both the listing end and the selling end of the commission for themselves and their firms.

Please note that although you may sign an exclusive listing with an individual agent, the party you sign with is, in fact, the brokerage company (or possibly, an independent broker). Indeed, it is the brokerage firm (the broker) that decides to become a member of the board. If it does, as mentioned previously, all the agents employed by that firm must also join the board. Members from other boards cannot place a listing on the MLS of a board to which they do not belong. However, it is customary for agents to co-operate with agents from any board.

13.7.1 STEPS TO AN MLS LISTING

Below is the step-by-step process for registering a property on MLS. While this description applies to TREB, it serves as a good example for most boards.

1. When an agent has listed a property, he sends the two forms (MLS Agreement and MLS Data Information Sheet) to the board for processing (generally, it is done electronically and known as "Broker Load"). A board's courier also visits each broker's office daily to pick up and deliver material. The listing data is in the board's office by the next day. Data is checked for completeness and entered as a listing into the database.
2. The listing is published (made available to members), minus the photograph, unless the listing agent supplied one.
3. A photographer receives an order to photograph the property. A large board, such as the TREB employs many photographers, each covering one area. They go out every day to photograph properties.
4. The photograph is incorporated with the listing, the following day. An example of an MLS listing is shown in Figure 13.4.
5. Listings can be accessed through dailies, MLS books, or online.
6. When a property is sold or leased the listing broker reports it to the board and it is moved to the sold category. If the listing expires without being sold, it is moved to the expired category.

13.8 THE AGENT AS MARKETER

Assist your agent to better market your property.

In addition to listing your property on MLS, your real estate agent may have a number of other strategies to market your property. We prepare data sheets and property briefs for virtually all of our listings.

13.8.1 DATA SHEET

A data sheet, also called "Executive Summary", "Summary Sheet", or "Salient Facts", is a short description of the property, be it for lease or for sale, that accomplishes two things. It gives the potential buyers and other agents a quick but solid understanding of the property and of the details for sale or lease, and it provides something that the interested party or his agent can consult later. See Figure 13.5 for a sample Data Sheet.

Figure 13.4
Sample MLS Listing

12 Retail Ave	**Sold:** $1,500,000 For Sale
Ajax, Ontario L1S2H5 Dist: E14 Map: 267-13-S	**List:** $1,595,000 For Sale
Sold Area: **32010 Sq Ft** Sale	**94% List**
Dir/Cross St: Harwood & 401	DOM: 177 Last Status: **Sld**
	Taxes: $0.97/1999/Ann

Industrial			Lease Term:	
Factory	Freestanding:	**Y**	Holdover:	**80**
Factory/Manufacturing	Occup:	**Tenant**	SPIS:	**None**
Possession: **July 31,2000**			Franchise:	

MLS#: AI2278   Seller:
PIN#:

Total Area:	**32,010 Sq Ft**	Survey:	**Y**	**Public Transit**	
Ofc/Apt Area:	**4,000 Sq Ft**	Lot/Bldg/Unit/Dim:	**353.5X260 Feet Lot**		
Indust Area:	**28,010 Sq Ft**			Soil Test:	
Retail Area:		Lot Irreg:	**2.11 Acres, Fenced**	Outside Storage:	**N**
Apx Age:	**16-30**	Crane:	**N**	Rail:	**N**
Volts:	**600**	Bay Size:	**37X30**	Basement:	**N**
Amps:	**300**	%Bldg:	**100**	Elevator:	**None**
Zoning:	**M1/Com**	Washrooms:	**4**	UFFI:	**No**
Truck Level:	**2**	Water:	**Municipal**	Assessment:	
Grade Level:		Water Supply:		Chattels:	
Drive-In:	**1**	Sewers:	**San+Storm**	LLBO:	
Double Man:		A/C:	**Part**	Days Open:	
Clear Height:	**14' 0"**	Utilities:	**Y**	Hours Open:	
Sprinklers:	**Y**	Garage Type:	**None**	Employees:	
Heat:	**Gas Forced Air Open**	Park Spaces:	**100**	Seats:	

Bus/Bldg Name:	**Bldg In Great Shape. Minutes To 401**		For Year:	Financial Statement:
Actual/Estimated:				
Taxes:	Heat:	Gross Inc/Sales:		Est Value Inv At Cost:
Insur:	Hydro:	- Vacancy Allow:		Com Area Upcharge:
Mgmt:	Water:	- Operating Exp:		Percentage Rent:
Maint:	Other:	= Net Income B4 Debt:		

Note Very Low Taxes (Property & Business) Skylights In Factory. Hydro Can Be Increased To 500 Amps, Cheaply. L/A Has Interest.
Recently Reno. Energy Efficient Lighting. New Hvac In Office. Factory Flr, Walls & Ceiling R Painted. 1 Minute 2 401/Harwood Interchange. 3 Minutes To Go Station. 10 Min. To Scarb. 0.65 Acres Of Extra Land For Expansion Or Prkg. Lot Is Fenced. Great Labour Pool.

Mortgage		**Other Encumbrances**	
Amt:	Int%:	Amt:	Int%
Payment:	Incl:	Payment:	Incl:
Freq:	Maturity Date:	Freq:	Maturity Date:
Lender:		Lender:	
Tac *$2,500			

Contract Date:	**6/7/2000**	List: <u>COLDWELL BANKER TERREQUITY</u> (416) 496-9220 Fax:	
Expiry Date:	**12/31/2000**	**PIERRE BOIRON** (905) 882-0622	
Sold Date:	**12/1/2000**	Co-Op: <u>SUTTON GRP-CLASSIC RLTY INC</u>	CB Comm: 2%*
Closing Date:	**12/1/2000**		
Last Update:	**12/1/2000**	Leased Terms:	
Original Price:	**$1,700,000**	Comments:	

Source: Used with permission of the Toronto Real Estate Board.

Figure 13.5
Sample Data Sheet

INDUSTRIAL BUILDING FOR SALE

ADDRESS: 12 Retail Avenue, Ajax
Wonderful location, 1 minute from Highway 401, 10 minutes to Scarborough.

LAND DETAILS:

Total area:	2.11 acres (91,912 sq.ft.)
Parking:	Paved and fenced.
Zoning:	The actual zoning is M1, which allows for many commercial uses: Office, bank, restaurant, funeral home, school, church, theatre, hospital, nursing home, car sales, club, etc. and, of course, industrial uses.

BUILDING DETAILS:

Area:	32,010 sq.ft.
Office Area:	4,000 sq.ft. (air conditioned)
Bay Size:	37' x 30'
Ceiling Height:	14'
Shipping:	2 T.L. doors [new], with dock levellers and 1 large drive-in door.
Heating:	Suspended Gas[new]
Power:	600 volt - 300 amps
Sprinklers:	Yes
Age:	30 years

PUBLIC TRANSPORTATION: GoBus terminal and Ajax public transit are 3 minutes away (on foot).

SHOPPING: Harwood Shopping Centre is across the street.

REALTY TAXES (1999): $0.97 per sq.ft. (property and business)

POSSESSION: July 31, 2006

PRICE: $1,595,000

REMARKS: Clean facility, recently renovated: new overhead doors; new man doors; new office heating and air conditioning systems; new suspended gas heaters in factory; new energy efficient lighting; new skylights, etc. Plenty of electrical outlets and floor drains. Office, factory's walls, ceilings and floors recently painted.
A pleasure to show.
6 miles to Scarborough (10 minutes). Note the very low taxes.
A self contained office suite of 1,380 sq.ft. can be rented separately, 0.65 acres of extra land.

13.8.2 PROPERTY BRIEF (PB)

A Property Brief (PB), also called "marketing package" or "property brochure", is a package prepared by a real estate agent to showcase a property at its best and demonstrate its appeal to potential purchasers. It can range in length from 10 to 100 pages, and can take a lot of time and money to produce, which is why one is generally not prepared for small or inexpensive properties. The impact and, therefore, the power of a PB on buyers or tenants can be incredible, resulting in a much faster sale and higher price for the property than without one. Invariably, a strong PB helps an agent to sell a property faster and for more money. The Property Brief Checklist (Checklist 13.1) would be used by a real estate agent in preparing the Property Brief.

In these days of globalization, a strong PB is especially important. We know of one situation where the property was located in San Diego, CA; the listing agent was in New York, NY; and the selling agent was in Seattle, OR. The buyer? From India. Without an informative, detailed PB, this deal would never have come together.

13.9 GETTING A REAL ESTATE LICENSE

Decide whether getting a real estate license is right for you.

Some readers may wonder if they should obtain a Real Estate License and, once registered with a broker, save most of the commission when buying or selling a property. A word of warning: It is not an easy job. It is very time consuming to get a license and to stay on top of a market, and can be emotionally draining. Furthermore, you will have to split the commission with your broker and pay for many expenses.

If you are licensed it follows that you would present offers where you are the buyer. This might elicit some distrust on the part of vendors. However, experience has taught us that once the decision to sell has been made, most vendors have one paramount thing in mind — a sale. They don't worry too much about who the buyer is. They want to sell.

As an agent in Ontario, if you buy a property, you are supposed to present a form "in accordance with the requirements of the Real Estate and Business Brokers Act and Code of Ethics Regulations of the Province of Ontario". In this form, you must state that you will be acquiring an interest, directly or indirectly, in the property. If your interest is indirect, such as in the case of your brother-in-law being the buyer, you must explain the connection. This form must be presented to the vendor before the offer itself. Personally, we have never understood the logic of this. Indeed, only a fool would sign an offer to sell his property without reading the offer or having his lawyer read it. Therefore, if the offer explains that you are buying for yourself or representing your brother-in-law, it seems to us that the offer should suffice.

The Ontario Real Estate Association (OREA) estimates that 180 to 200 hours are required to complete the course requirements for a Commercial Real Estate License. And at the time of the writing this book, the total cost of the OREA courses to become a registered salesperson was approximately $1,700. If you join a broker who is a member of a real estate board, you will also pay to join his real estate board, plus yearly membership fees ($1,000 per year in Toronto), and many various additional expenses.

For more information regarding the Licensing Process, visit the Web site of your local real estate association.[2]

---

2 This book is only a solid introduction to the world of real estate investing. It is far from being all-inclusive. Real estate agents use a real estate encyclopae-dia published by the Ontario Real Estate Association. It comprises 1100 pages and even it does not cover everything. The public can buy it for $60 and this is a true bargain. See <www.orea.com>, or call (800) 265-6732, extension 233.

Checklist 13.1
Property Brief Checklist

PROPERTY BRIEF CHECKLIST

Used by a listing agent to prepare a Property Brief to aid in selling (or leasing) a property.

Property Address:
- ❑ Give a number to the presentation, preceded with the letter L for Land or B for Building or O for Others. Example: B103, and enter it, with the address in your "Property Brief" list
- ❑ Check the assessment rolls. We do it using the Toronto Real Estate Board's Database
- ❑ Obtain last tax bill or tax assessment
- ❑ Get surveys and building plans
- ❑ Secure relevant maps (regional, municipal, local / neighbourhood)
- ❑ Make a list of important neighbours and amenities
- ❑ Gather transportation data, driving times, distances, time tables, etc.
- ❑ Take / secure photographs: Aerial, (colour if possible), exterior and interior
- ❑ Write the letter of accompaniment (if you intend to send the Brief to different people, which is likely)
- ❑ Write an Area Analysis
- ❑ Write a Neighbourhood Analysis
- ❑ Write a Property Analysis

Property Specifications and Other Details:
- ❑ Location
- ❑ Land details
- ❑ Building details
- ❑ Construction details
- ❑ Possession date
- ❑ Realty taxes
- ❑ Insurance
- ❑ Heating costs
- ❑ Utilities costs
- ❑ Public transit
- ❑ Remarks
- ❑ Price/rental
- ❑ Show possible Building divisions on the floor plan or sketch
- ❑ List the advantages of locating at .....

    EXHIBITS
    A =   Location map
    B =   Map showing highways
    C =   Map showing main points of interest
    D =   Land sketch or survey
    E =   Building plan
    F =   Office plan
    G =   Photos
    H =   Zoning By-law map
    I =   Zoning By-law excerpts
    J =   Toronto Transit Corporation (public transportation)
- ❑ You Are Working with ... your name (resume +)
- ❑ A Company is Known By the Company It Keeps .....(names of previous clients)
- ❑ City map or key map
- ❑ Include: "Submitted subject to change in price, errors, omissions and withdrawal without notice".

CHAPTER 14

Appraisals and Feasibility Studies

By the end of this chapter, you will be able to:

- Recognize the purpose of an appraisal and know who can prepare one.
- Distinguish between the types and uses of different appraisals.
- Identify the various aspects that are considered when placing a value on a property.
- Differentiate between market factors and productivity and their impact on the value of a property.
- Appreciate the different approaches appraisers use to evaluate a property.
- Understand which method to use in which circumstances to value land.
- Recognize the shortcomings in the appraisal process.
- Determine if your project is economically feasible.

14.1 WHAT IS AN APPRAISAL?

Recognize the purpose of an appraisal and know who can prepare one.

An appraisal is the analysis of a property for the purpose of determining its value. This value can vary, depending on the purpose of the appraisal. Virtually all appraisals can be criticized because throughout the process there are a number of judgement calls the appraiser must make. These include adjusting the value of the appraised property to that of comparable properties with regard to age, condition, quality of design and construction, deferred maintenance, state of the neighbourhood, and more. Another major factor is the choice of Cap Rate. Ask ten appraisers to give you the Cap Rate for a certain property and you may end up with three to five different rates.

Real estate appraisals can be prepared by real estate agents, mortgage lenders (occasionally), and professional appraisers, but only the latter will provide the most complete and sophisticated reports. Many financial institutions have a list of appraisers acceptable to them and will refuse appraisals done by people not on that list.

The Appraisal Institute of Canada (AIC) is responsible for granting three designations: Accredited Appraiser Canadian Institute (AACI), Canadian Residential Appraiser (CRA), and Professional Appraiser (PA). It has standards for the preparation of appraisals that are essentially a variation of the Uniform Standards of Professional Appraisal Practice (USPAP) established by The Appraisal Foundation in the US. These standards allow for a wide range of formats by which to convey a value estimate, with the most common being the full narrative report. With proper disclosure, however, shorter reports are permitted and many appraisal firms use a shorter report for small properties and residential properties.

14.2 USES OF APPRAISALS

Distinguish between the types and uses of different appraisals.

The three main reasons to have an appraisal completed, related to investing in commercial real estate, are the following:
- to satisfy the requirement of a lender
- to have information to guide you in establishing a price when selling or buying a property, and
- to be protected for income tax purposes, for example, to determine the value of a property at a given date, say 30 years prior, for capital gain or other purposes.

In this context, there are three kinds of appraisals.

1. **A Formal Appraisal.** Also known as a "full narrative appraisal", this type comprises all the details in a nice presentation and is conducted by an accredited appraiser who is a member of the AIC. Such an appraisal will cost $3,000 to $8,000 and will usually be accepted in court. A formal appraisal will comprise six main sections:
   - definition of the purpose of the appraisal and value appraised, as of a specific date
   - physical description of the property

- legal description and rights involved
- listing and description of comparable properties, if the direct comparison approach, also called "market data approach", is being used
- reconciliation of value, and
- property value.

2. **An Informal or "Summary" Report.** This one- to two-page appraisal or "Summary Report" includes only the essential elements necessary to determine a value quickly and is usually prepared by real estate agents and consultants. This will not stand up as well (if at all) in court, if challenged by the opposing party. The report will briefly describe land, building, zoning, and uses. The author will indicate what he thinks the property is worth without extensive research and supporting data.

3. **A Form Report.** This type of appraisal is usually used for residential properties by lending institutions for the financing of residences and smaller properties. They are usually conducted by an accredited appraiser, such as an AACI. An example of a form report supplied by the Ontario Real Estate Association (OREA) to real estate agents is shown in Figure 14.1. Although it is designed for a single family home, it illustrates the appraisal process well.

Figure 14.1
Standard Appraisal Report

OREA Ontario Real Estate Association   **Standard Appraisal Report**
Single Family   **Form 700**
for use in the Province of Ontario

CLIENT: .... Client Ref No: ....

Client: Phone No: (............)................................. Fax No: (............)................................. E-mail: ....

Client's Customer: .... Appraiser: .... Appraiser's Ref No: ....

GENERAL APPRAISAL AND PROPERTY INFORMATION

Property Address: ....

Municipality: ....

Full Legal Description: ....

Owner: .... Assessment: Total .... Taxes $ .... Year ....

This Appraisal is to estimate **MARKET VALUE** for a: ☐ Sale   ☐ Financing   ☐ Other ....

Effective Date of Appraisal: .... Date of Inspection: ....

Highest and Best Use is: ☐ Current   ☐ Other (*) ....

Zoning: .... Occupancy: ☐ Homeowner ☐ Tenant ☐ Vacant

SUBJECT & MARKET HISTORY

Subject Last Sold	Subject Currently Listed	Property Values	Demand/Supply
Date:	☐ Yes ☐ No	☐ Stable	☐ In Balance
Sale Price: $	Current List Price $	☐ Increasing	☐ Under Supply
Days on Market:	Days On Market	☐ Decreasing	☐ Over Supply

Typical Exposure Time Required for Properties to Sell in Subject Neighborhood is: ....
Typical Exposure Time Required for Properties to Sell on Subject Street is: ....

NEIGHBOURHOOD INFORMATION

Type		Trend	Subject For Area is	Adjoining Homes
☐ Rural	☐ Prestige	☐ Improving	☐ Comparable	☐ Comparable
☐ Residential	☐ Average	☐ Stable	☐ Superior *	☐ Superior
☐ Commercial	☐ Starter	☐ Declining	☐ Inferior	☐ Inferior
☐ Industrial				

Neighbourhood is: ....% Developed

Distance to
Elementary School   ....
Secondary School   ....   Age Range of Typical Property in Neighbourhood: .... to .... Years
Public Transit   ....
Shopping   ....   Age Range of Typical Property on Subject Street: .... to .... Years
Downtown   ....
Recreational Facilities   ....   Price Range of Properties on Subject Street: $....................... to $.......................

Price Range of Properties in Neighbourhood: $....................... to $.......................

Comments: (include any positive or negative factors that will have a measurable impact on the subject's marketability and value - items with an * should be discussed) ....
....
....
....

SITE INFORMATION
Utilities & Services

Street		Drainage		Water		Utilities
☐ Paved	☐ Gravel	☐ Open Ditch	☐ Storm Sewer	☐ Municipal	☐ Private Well	☐ Hydro
☐ Municipal	☐ Private	☐ Sanitary Sewer	☐ Septic Tank	☐ Cistern	☐ Shared Well	☐ Gas
☐ Sidewalks	☐ Curbs	☐ Other		☐ Other		☐ Telephone
☐ Street Lighting		....		....		☐ Cable
☐ Underground Wiring						
☐ Aboveground Wiring						

Site Dimensions: ....   Encroachments: ☐ Yes*   ☐ No

Total Site Area: ....   Easements: ☐ Yes*   ☐ No

Site Shape: ....

Topography: Lot in relation to street grade: ☐ Even   ☐ Above   ☐ Below

Parking
Driveway   **Garage (Indicate # of cars):**

Driveway		Garage (Indicate # of cars):
☐ Laneway	☐ None	☐ Attached # ....
☐ Private	☐ Paved	☐ Detached # ....
☐ Mutual	☐ Gravel	☐ Built In # ....
☐ Other		☐ Carport # ....

Site Appeal

☐ Excellent	☐ Fair*	Landscaping Includes: ....
☐ Good	☐ Poor*	....
☐ Average		....

Comments: (include any positive or negative factors that will have a measurable impact on the subject's marketability and value - items with an * should be discussed) ....
....
....

INFORMATION ON IMPROVEMENTS (BUILDINGS)

Building Type: Sq. Ft. (Above Grade)

Building Type:			Sq. Ft. (Above Grade)	
☐ Detached	☐ High Ranch	☐ 1 Storey	Level 1	Level 4 ....
☐ Semi-detached	☐ Apartment	☐ 1 1/2 Storey	Level 2	Level 5 ....
☐ Attached Row	☐ Split	☐ 2 Storey	Level 3	
☐ Other		☐ 3 Storey	Total	

Actual Age ....Years   Effective Age ....Years   Total Economic Life ....Years

Exterior Finish   Roof Material   Foundation

Exterior Finish		Roof Material		Foundation
☐ Brick Veneer	☐ Vinyl Siding	☐ Asphalt Shingle	☐ Wood Shingle	☐ Poured Concrete
☐ Solid Brick	☐ Wood Siding	☐ Cedar Shake	☐ Slate	☐ Concrete Block
☐ Stucco	☐ Solid Stone	☐ Metal	☐ Tar & Gravel	☐ Brick
☐ Alum. Siding	☐ Artificial Stone	☐ Other		☐ Stone
☐ Other				☐ Preserved Wood
		Age of Roof ....Years		☐ Other ....

Window Type

Window Type				
☐ Single	☐ Thermal	☐ Wood Frame	☐ Aluminum	☐ Vinyl
☐ Other:				

Evidence of UFFI   ☐ Yes *   ☐ No

Construction Quality   ☐ Excellent   ☐ Good   ☐ Average   ☐ Fair   ☐ Poor*

Exterior Condition/Appeal   ☐ Excellent   ☐ Good   ☐ Average   ☐ Fair   ☐ Poor*

INFORMATION ON IMPROVEMENTS (INTERIOR)

Rooms	Living	Dining	Kitchen	Family	Beds	Bath	Wash	Rec	Other
Basement									
Main									
Second									
Third									

Room Sizes   ☐ Large   ☐ Medium   ☐ Small

Additional Information on Room Sizes (Optional): ....
....
....

Kitchen
☐ Modern
☐ Average
☐ Outdated

Bathrooms
☐ Modern
☐ Average
☐ Outdated

Closets/Storage
☐ Excellent
☐ Adequate
☐ Inadequate

Basement
☐ None
☐ Full
☐ Partial

☐ Crawl Space
    % Finished ....

Floors
☐ Carpet
☐ Hardwood
☐ Vinyl Tile
☐ Ceramic
☐ Other ....

Walls/Ceilings
☐ Drywall
☐ Plaster
☐ Panelling
☐ Tile
☐ Other ....

Heating
☐ Forced Air
☐ Hot Water
☐ Baseboard
☐ Other ....
....

Fuel
☐ Gas
☐ Oil
☐ Electricity
☐ Other ....
....

Plumbing
☐ Copper
☐ Plastic
☐ Lead
☐ Galvanized
☐ Other ....

Electrical
☐ Fuses
☐ Circuit Breakers
☐ Aluminum Wiring*
☐ Copper Wiring
☐ Other ....
    Amps ....

Floor Plan
☐ Excellent   ☐ Good   ☐ Average   ☐ Fair   ☐ Poor*

Interior Condition
☐ Excellent   ☐ Good   ☐ Average   ☐ Fair   ☐ Poor*

Equipment/Built-Ins/Chattels Remaining With Property:

☐ HWT   ☐ Fridge   ☐ Central Vac   ☐ Wood Stove   ☐ Elect Air Cleaner
☐ Central Air   ☐ Washer   ☐ Humidifier   ☐ Hood   ☐ Garburator
☐ Heat Pump   ☐ Dryer   ☐ Security System   ☐ Oven   ☐ Water Purifier/Filter
☐ Stove   ☐ Dishwasher   ☐ Dehumidifier   ☐ Range   ☐ Central Intercom
☐ Fireplace(s) ....
☐ Other: ....
....

Equipment/Chattels Leased or Rented

....
....

Special Features

....
....

Comments: (include any positive or negative factors that will have a measurable impact on the subject's marketability and value - items with an * should be discussed) ....
....
....
....

COST APPROACH TO VALUE

Improvements	Cost New	Depreciation	Current Value
Building.............Sq. Ft/Mtr x .... $/Sq. Ft/Mtr.	$.................................	$.................................	$.................................
Garage:	$.................................	$.................................	$.................................
....	$.................................	$.................................	$.................................
....	$.................................	$.................................	$.................................
....	$.................................	$.................................	$.................................

Total Current Value of All Improvements $.................................

Plus Land Value $.................................

Indicated Value by the Cost Approach $.................................

Value Rounded to $.................................

DIRECT COMPARISON APPROACH
Competitive Listings

Item	Subject	Listing #1	Listing #2	Listing #3
Address				
Distance To Subject				
Original List Price				
Current List Price				
Original List Date				
Date Price Last Revised				
House Style				
Lot Size				
Building Size				
Age				
Condition				
Beds				
Baths				
Listing is: Inferior/Similar/Superior				

Comments:..
....
....
....
....

Sales Analysis

Item	Subject	Comparable 1		Comparable 2		Comparable 3	
Address							
Distance To Subject							
Date Sold							
Sale Price							
Days On Market							
Time Adjustment							
Time Adjusted Price							
Location							
Lot Size							
House Style							
Age of House							
Total Sq. Footage							
Family Room							
Bedrooms							
Bathrooms							
Basement/% Finished							
Rec Room							
Garage/Parking							
Interior Condition							
Exterior Condition							
Total Adjustments							
Totally Adj. Sale Price							

Comments, Reconciliation And Estimate Of Value By The Direct Comparison Approach

....
....
....
....
....
....
....

Based on the above information and analysis, a value by the Direct Comparison Approach is estimated to be: ($..)

Form 700   01/2004

FINAL RECONCILIATION, CERTIFICATION AND FINAL ESTIMATE OF VALUE

Given the nature of the subject property, the level and quality of information, the reliability of the necessary adjustments, and the actions of typical buyers

in the subject neighbourhood, most weight has been given to the value arrived at by the .... Approach.

- This valuation and report is subject to the attached assumptions and limiting conditions.
- This valuation and report has been completed in accordance with the Canadian Real Estate Association's Code of Ethics and Standard of Business Practice, as well as the RECO Code of Ethics and Guiding Principles.
- I confirm that I personally inspected the subject property and that I have no current or contemplated interest or bias (positive or negative) towards the subject property.
- Unless otherwise detailed in writing within this report, I can confirm that I have no personal relationship or bias (positive or negative) towards any of the parties using or affected by this valuation and report.
- I can confirm that my being employed and paid to complete this valuation is not conditional on the amount of the valuation or on any specific information being included or excluded in this appraisal report.

Therefore, based on a .... day marketing period, a reasonable market value for the subject property as at

................................, 20.............. is estimated to be:

.... Dollars ($...)

Appraiser's Signature: ....   Date of Signature: ....

Appraiser's Name: ....   Company: ....
Appraiser's Address: ....   Phone No: ....
....   Fax No: ....
....   E-mail: ....

ATTACHMENTS

☐ Neighbourhood Map   ☐ Additional Information/Analysis: ....
☐ Copies of MLS Listing/Sales   ☐ Additional Assumptions/Limiting Conditions: ....
☐ Site/Building Sketch   ....
☐ Photos   ☐ Other: ....
☐ Survey   ....

ASSUMPTIONS AND LIMITING CONDITIONS

1. This report may not be read or used by anyone other than the client without the written authorization of the appraiser. This report should only be used for the property and purpose identified within it. The appraiser accepts no responsibility or liability should the information contained within this report be used by anyone other than the client (or other authorized user) or for any other purpose or property other than that specified within this report.

2. Values are subject to varying and continual changes in market conditions and neighbourhood factors. Accordingly, the value presented in this report can only be relied on as the value estimated as of the effective date of appraisal specified in this report. Should the user of this report wish to know the value of the subject property as of another date, the appraiser will need to complete an update or a new appraisal report.

3. A search on title and ownership has not been performed. A good title with respect to the subject property has been assumed. Therefore, other than what is noted in this report, the appraiser assumes no responsibility for matters legal in nature that may affect the subject property's title, ownership, marketing or value.

4. Any sketches in this report are included solely for the purpose of assisting the reader in visualizing the property.

5. The appraiser has carried out a visual cosmetic inspection of the subject property only. This inspection and the ensuing appraisal report is not and should not be considered a structural, environmental or mechanical inspection and report. Accordingly, unless stated otherwise in this appraisal report, the appraiser is unaware of any hidden or not apparent structural, environmental or mechanical defects or problems and assumes for the purposes of this report and valuation that there are none. Therefore, should it subsequently become known that there is a structural, mechanical or environmental problem or defect, then the appraiser reserves the right to alter the value given in this appraisal report.

6. This appraisal has been based on the assumption that the subject property is in compliance with the applicable zoning, building codes, by-laws, and environmental regulations. Should this in fact turn out not to be so, the appraiser reserves the right to make any necessary changes to the final estimate of value.

7. This valuation has been based on the assumption that the information collected from industry recognized sources and professionals is in fact correct and can be relied upon for the purpose of this appraisal.

Source: Standard Appraisal Report is used by permission of the Ontario Real Estate Association.

14.3 PRINCIPLES OF VALUE

Identify the various aspects that are considered when placing a value on a property.

Appraisers concern themselves with several principles of value to establish the value of a given property. They include the following:

- supply and demand
- substitution
- contribution
- conformity
- anticipation
- change in the neighbourhood
- highest and best use
- quality of the site
- quality of the building
- quality of the tenants, and
- quality of property management.

We'll discuss each separately in the following sections.

14.3.1 SUPPLY AND DEMAND

Supply and demand rarely keep pace with each other and then, only for a brief period of time. Generally, the real estate market has short periods of under-supply and longer periods of over-supply. Evidently, the economy is its great master with supply and demand being driven by the economic cycles. When supply is high, values decline; and when supply is low, demand increases, pushing prices up. For the appraiser, there is always an element of guess work. Typically, appraised values are derived from past sales; however, when it comes to judging where the market is in the real estate cycle, it becomes an imperfect art or a guess.

Another factor affecting supply and demand is market growth. For example, if the appraised property is a shopping centre and a new development of 3,000 homes is planned nearby, it will have a considerable impact on the centre's future value.

14.3.2 SUBSTITUTION

If several properties offer the same utility, that is, offer the same benefits from a buyer's viewpoint, the lower priced one will sell first because it will be seen as the better deal.

To present this in a simplistic way, let's look at two stores of similar frontage, area, and condition. If one is offered at $799,000 and another one at $749,000, the latter will sell first. Therefore, the appraiser should lower the value on the higher-priced property to make it competitive with the other one.

14.3.3 CONTRIBUTION

A property is composed of many elements. The two main ones are land and improvements.

The building itself has many components: foundation, roof, walls, insulation, windows, design, etc. Generally, the components are fairly compatible in a new building. However, in the case of a renovated building, materials and equipment may have been used that were either an under-improvement (e.g., replacing American Standard toilets with cheap imports) or an over-improvement (e.g., a marble floor in a second hand clothing store). This is intertwined with the principle of conformity (see section 14.3.4). Over-improvement can be a bad thing as it may scare buyers away, such as in the case with an air-conditioned plant manufacturing wooden trusses. It represents an extra cost that lowers the property return but does not contribute to a higher value. Therefore, a property should fit its neighbourhood and the type of users as closely as possible.

14.3.4 CONFORMITY

Maximum property value is obtained when the property conforms to rules, whether formal or informal. This can refer to zoning or to the colour of your roof. If all the roofs on the street are black and yours is red, it does not conform. If you have a 28,000 m² (300,000 sq ft) warehouse, in a street of industrial buildings not exceeding 900m² (10,000 sq ft), yours does not conform. A given piece of land may be over-improved relative to its neighbourhood, for example, when a luxury apartment is erected or located next to a multi-unit industrial building or low-income housing. A synonym for "conformity" could be "compatibility" with neighbouring properties.

14.3.5 ANTICIPATION

Basically, anticipation refers to the fact that any buyer foresees deriving future benefits from the property and it is the appraiser's job to anticipate the quality, quantity, and duration of these benefits and calculate their impact on the value of the property.

14.3.6 CHANGE IN THE NEIGHBOURHOOD

In a real estate appraisal, this value would typically apply to the evolution of neighbourhoods (improving, stable, or deteriorating). The appraiser's role is to anticipate the change and factor this into the value. If, for example, a neighbourhood begins to decay, the value of all its real estate will decline progressively, but dramatically; conversely, if a neighbourhood is beginning a cycle of renewal, the values can be expected to rise.

The appraiser's role is to anticipate the change in a neighbourhood and factor this into the value of the property.

14.3.7 HIGHEST AND BEST USE

The use of the property that will bring the greatest net return over a given period of time and, therefore, be its highest value is the highest and best use value. The use must be physically and financially feasible, as well as legal. For example, a building may have been a nightclub that represented the highest and best use at the time, but because the neighbourhood is deteriorating, the highest and best use of the building may now be that of a second-hand store. The appraiser must analyze the neighbourhood and the demand for it and determine the value based not on what was, but on what is today. It can also happen that, due to external forces, the highest and best use consists in redeveloping the site (demolishing existing buildings and erecting new ones).

14.3.8 QUALITY OF THE SITE

The appropriateness of a site to the use (and vice versa) defines the value of the site's quality. Obviously, a large, marvellous office building in the middle of a potato farming community would have less value than it would have in the financial area of a large city. For example, in the case of a retail developer, he would value and be willing to pay a premium for four main things:

1. a good address, on a well-known street
2. exposure to traffic, meaning visibility from passersby and vehicular traffic (this can be achieved from a long distance (e.g., CN Tower in Toronto))
3. high traffic count — the number of vehicles driving by and seeing the property over a 24-hour period, and
4. a strong anchor nearby (a major tenant in the centre that is able to generate much shopper traffic).

14.3.9 QUALITY OF THE BUILDING

The value of a building is also influenced by the quality of the building itself, including:
- design
- architecture
- visual appeal
- construction materials
- workmanship, and
- maintenance.

4.3.10 QUALITY OF THE TENANTS

The quality of the tenants' covenant can also affect value. For example, a building tenanted by Roots, GAP, Eddie Bauer, or William Sonoma has a greater value for retailers than one tenanted by John Doe Companies. When it comes to retail tenants, their marketing ability, that is, their ability to attract repeat consumers, also impacts on appraised value.

14.3.11 QUALITY OF PROPERTY MANAGEMENT

A good property management firm will keep the building in good repair and ensure that the tenants' house-keeping does not detract from the building.

14.4 MARKET VALUE VERSUS VALUE IN USE

Differentiate between market factors and productivity and their impact on the value of a property.

A property has more than one value. The market value is the most probable price a property should bring in a competitive and open market, as of the specified date and under all conditions requisite to a fair sale. Implicit in this definition is the consummation of a sale as of a specified date, and the passing of title from vendor to

buyer under all conditions whereby:
- buyer and vendor are typically motivated
- both parties are well informed or well advised and acting in their own interests
- a reasonable time is allowed for exposure to the market
- payment is made in cash in Canadian dollars or in terms of financial arrangements comparable thereto, and
- the market value price represents the normal consideration for the property sold, unaffected by special or creative financing or sales concessions granted by any one associated with the transaction.

In addition to market value, a property can have a value in use that is based on the productivity a user can derive from a given property. For example, let's take two identical units of an industrial condominium building. The vendor of unit A has installed a large cooler, a large freezer, and a commercial kitchen. To the average buyer, someone who sells automobile parts, this represents a serious drawback because he will have to remove the cooler, the freezer, and the commercial kitchen. However, if someone can use all of these improvements, he will pay a premium for the property; the property has a value in use. On the other hand, the vendor of unit B in the same building offers no office, no sprinklers, only one washroom and one double man-door for shipping. For most users, this unit would require a considerable investment to upgrade it, therefore, it will have a lower value than a better finished one. Similarly, if a transport company finds a property located close to the intersection of two important freeways, it will pay a premium for the location.

14.5 APPRAISAL APPROACHES

Appreciate the different approaches appraisers use to evaluate a property.

There can be no intelligent application of the appraisal process without knowing the reasons for making the appraisal. An appraiser may be asked to find:
- value for a basis of taxation
- market value
- sales value
- fair rental value
- book value (This is the fiscal value of what is left after Capital Cost Allowance over the years. For example, a property bought for $1,000,000 a good many years ago may have an undepreciated value of only $575,000.)
- value as a basis for fair compensation, in expropriation proceedings, for whole or partial takings, or
- value for fire insurance. (This is often called "replacement value" or what it would cost to replace a building if it burned to the ground.)

A different approach to the appraisal is required for each of the above values. Thus, the reason an appraisal is being done points to the path to be followed in the accumulation, analysis, and interpretation of data.

The appraisal work may consist of all or part of the following:
- inspection of the property and of the neighbourhood

- data gathering — plans, specifications, survey, photographs, land registration data, leases, etc.
- choosing and using the appropriate approach, and
- street inspection of comparable properties.

There are three approaches generally used when doing an appraisal: the direct comparison, based on market data; the cost approach; and the income approach. Appraisers endeavour to use at least two of these three approaches whenever possible, depending mainly on the property itself. Here are a few typical examples.

- For an empty industrial building, use market data and cost approaches.
- For a leased building, such as a strip plaza, multi-family, or industrial building, use market data and income approaches. Note that the cost approach could also be used, but is generally considered redundant.
- For land only, use market data approach.
- For toll freeway, use income approach.

Ideally, any appraisal should be supported by at least one other appraisal approach, preferably the direct comparison approach.

14.5.1 DIRECT COMPARISON (MARKET DATA) APPROACH

This approach consists of finding comparable sales or leases to establish value. It is based on the concept of substitution, which states that a property has approximately the same value as another property that offers similar utility and benefits. Indeed, buyers are guided by what takes place in the market. They do not want to pay more for a property than what others paid for comparable properties. In the same vein, vendors are not generally willing to sell for less than owners of comparable properties did.

14.5.2 COST APPROACH

The goal of the cost approach is to find the cost of reproducing the building, less the accrued depreciation. The concept of substitution is at work here, too: a purchaser will not pay more for an existing building than it would cost to replace it. In fact, he would pay less, since there is always a degree of obsolescence and deferred maintenance to an existing building. The cost approach is also called the "summation" approach. It comprises a number of steps.

1. Estimate the value of the land as if vacant.
2. Determine the cost of the improvements if they were built today.
3. Deduct from step 2 the estimated depreciation in value (deferred maintenance, physical, and economic obsolescence). This has nothing to do with Capital Cost Allowance (CCA).
4. Add the values in steps 1 and 3.
   Example

Land value: 4 acres at $450,000 per acre =	$1,800,000
Building's (7,400 m² (80,000 sq ft)) replacement value at $480 per m² =	$3,552,000
Less building depreciation =	$2,200,000
Building value =	$1,352,000
Property Value: $1,800,000 + $1,352,000 =	$3,152,000

14.5.3 INCOME APPROACH

Generally people buy real estate for future benefits, for use, or for the income the property will generate. It is similar to buying a TV set or a car. You expect future benefits. The income approach is by far the most important for assessing leased income-producing properties. In fact, it is often the only approach used. For this, the appraiser finds the Net Operating Income (NOI) and applies a Cap Rate.

It is frequently not easy to arrive at an exact NOI, but the main difficulty with this approach is choosing the proper Cap Rate. Appraisers often use the Cap Rates found in the sale of several comparable properties and increase or decrease them to take into account various factors.

Appraisers also use published Cap Rates, such as those found in the *Marsh Report* (<www.marshnet.com>). In the end, there is a natural tendency to average, by using the Cap Rate of several properties. For instance they may show a Cap Rate of 10%, but the lowest one of the group may have been 8% and the top one 11%. This averaging should be avoided.

14.5.4 RECONCILIATION OF VALUE

The reconciliation of value (also called "correlation of value") is when the appraiser compares the values from the market comparison, cost, and income approaches, and decides which one is the most logical to use for that specific property. More precisely, he decides which one should be given the greatest weight and which one the lowest. The reconciliation of value should never be arrived at by averaging the values obtained through the three appraisal approaches. The appraiser should make reference to the comparable sales to support the Cap Rate he uses.

14.6 LAND VALUATION

Understand which method to use in which circumstances to value land.

Commonly encountered situations occur when land appraisers are required to include estate, partnership dissolution, and land development financing. There are three methods of land valuation: the abstraction method, the development method, and the residual method. In addition to these three methods, the direct comparison method is also used.

14.6.1 THE ABSTRACTION METHOD

With the abstraction method of land valuation, a value is allocated to the improvements (buildings) in a recent sale of another property and, after subtracting this value from the overall price, the remainder is attributed to the land. This is useful in areas where there are few land sales to use for comparison purposes.

14.6.2 THE DEVELOPMENT METHOD

The development method is typically used in the valuation of subdivision land. In this case the gross revenue from the sale of a lot(s) is established. A deduction is then made for all development costs, such as servicing (water, sewers, and utilities), roads, etc., and the residual value is an indication of the value of the vacant site.

14.6.3 THE RESIDUAL METHOD

The residual method is used when the appraiser assumes that the property will be developed to its highest and best use. The net income is subsequently capitalized to provide a value estimate and the cost of completing the proposed development is then subtracted from the capitalized value in order to provide a residual value to the land. This is useful in the valuation of commercial sites to be developed with income-producing buildings.

There are situations where it is very difficult to place a value on land, such as a water-fronting site with the right to develop a marina or the land under the CN Tower.

14.7 CRITICIZING APPRAISALS

Recognize the shortcomings in the appraisal process.

Like everything else in life, appraisals are imperfect. Here are the main criticisms that can be levelled against them.

- They use figures from the past, for example, sales that have taken place. Sometimes, when there is a paucity of recent comparables, an appraiser may have to go back several years to find a sufficient number of comparables.
- The appraiser can rarely find identical properties and choosing the right comparables can be very difficult. He must decide how much a given comparable is superior, or inferior, to the subject and this can be quite subjective.
- The appraiser has a number of methods to use to complete an appraisal. Sometimes this choice is quite difficult. He may select not to use one of them as the most appropriate method, although it may have been the best approach.
- The appraiser chooses the Cap Rate and if he is off by .5% it can make a dramatic difference.
  Example
  N.O.I.: $1,000,000
     Cap rate of:
     9% = $11,111,111
     9 1/2% = $10,526,316
     Difference = $584,796
- When the appraiser does the reconciliation of value he, subjectively, decides which approach should be given the greater weight. Again, note that the final reconciliation should never be arrived at by averaging.

In spite of these criticisms, we recommend that vendors have their properties appraised before placing them on the market. The appraisal, while imperfect, will give them 90-95% of the data needed to determine value, which is a lot more than they would have without an appraisal. An appraisal is an expense, but it makes sense to spend $5,000 on a $1,000,000 property, especially if it means the vendor then feels comfortable and justified in asking $50,000 or $100,000 more in his price. Figure 14.2 illustrates the salient facts of an appraisal as they would be received from an appraiser retained by the buyer to satisfy the requirements of a mortgage lender.

Figure 14.2
Salient Facts of an Appraisal

Super Appraisals Ltd.
123 Weber Street West Kitchener, Ontario   January 23, 2007

SALIENT FACTS

Municipal Address: 123 Weber Street West, Kitchener, Ontario

Legal Description: FIRSTLY, Part of Lot 4, Plan 567, Part of Lot E, Plan 890, Part of Lot 12, Compiled Plan of Subdivision of Lot 2, German Company Tract, in the City of Kitchener in the Regional Municipality of Waterloo, SUBJECT to an easement to Bell Canada, as outlined in Instrument No. 123456 and designated as Part 1 on Reference Plan 58R-7890

DESIGNATED as Part 1 on Reference Plan 58R-12134 and Part 1 on 58R-7890

Registered Owner: Seller Inc.

Effective Date: July 1, 2007

Property Rights Appraised: Leased fee

Site Size: 11.059 acres

Building Size: 135,311 square feet plus basement of 4,450 square feet

Municipal Plan (Kitchener):   General Industrial (M-2)

Official Plan (Waterloo):   Industrial

Zoning: General Industrial (M-2)

Highest and Best Use
  As though vacant: Mixed use, possibly multi-family (with land use approvals necessary), or an office/commercial use.

  As improved: The continuance of the office use with the conversion of part of the remaining warehouse area to office use

Estimates of Market Value:
  Cost Approach: N/A
  Income Approach
    Income Capitalization Method: $9,220,000 to $9,670,000
    Discounted Cash Flow Analysis: $9,355,000 to $9,533,000
  Direct Comparison Approach: $9,300,000

Final Estimate of Prospective Value: $9,400,000

14.8 FEASIBILITY STUDIES

Determine if your project is economically feasible.

The investor who wants to change markedly the use of a building or develop a site will want to secure a feasibility study. As the words imply, the intention is to discover if the use to which one intends to put a property is economically feasible. Feasibility studies are conducted by consultants who tend to specialize in particular property uses, such as high-rise residential condominiums, retirement homes, golf courses, etc.

There are only a few of these true specialists in the larger urban centres, probably no more than a dozen in Toronto (although many others purport to be). A few real estate agents, very few, are qualified to conduct them. In special circumstances a real estate agent may conduct such a study for a fee prior to a property being offered for sale, but offer to deduct all or part of the fee from the commission if he sells the property.

As part of the feasibility study, a consultant will do a market study to look at the proposed project, which may be little more than an idea, and make a survey of the demand and competition. This market study will be broken down by the type of comparable properties similar to the one contemplated for the property under study. For example, for a multi-family project, the type of apartments, such as one-bedroom, two-bedroom, and three-bedroom units, will create the categories. A study of the competition by the consultant will reveal the rentals in competitive buildings, vacancy rates, and absorption rates if other buildings have been recently constructed. He will then comment on the adequacy of the project and may suggest changes to the original plan.

A different kind of market study would be one conducted for a retailer. It would evaluate the desirability of the following factors:

- address
- location
- exposure (of the retail centre and of a specific store)
- vehicular traffic count
- pedestrian traffic count
- quality of and compatibility with the other tenants
- ability of the anchor(s) to generate high traffic
- family income in the market area, and
- ethnicity of the neighbourhood.

It would also look closely at the demographics within a certain radius, based on the type of retailing or product offered, and the potential customers' spending habits. This radius of influence (or appeal) is sometimes called "the trading area" and it will vary depending on the type of business. For example, the trading area for a car dealership and a dry-cleaning store will be very different. As always, the consultant will also look at the competition — existing, announced, or likely.

In the second step of the feasibility study the consultant will determine the cost of the finished project (land and building) and, based on the finding of the market study, will project the income, expenses, and profit. To give you an idea of what to expect, Figure 14.3 presents the table of contents and introduction of a feasibility study for a new project, comprising 70 townhouses, 160 condominium apartments, and 188 retirement beds on a 22-acre site.

Figure 14.3

Feasibility Study – Sample Pages

MARKET ASSESSMENT STUDY

Table of Contents

INTRODUCTION AND SCOPE OF STUDY

In February 2006, Friends Associates were retained to prepare an assessment of the market and financial feasibility of the development of two phases of the proposed Cote d'Azur Retirement Communities – Newmarket, being the residential retirement centre and the assisted care centre. Both aspects of the community provide support for seniors in the aspects of daily living and nursing care. In April 2006, the firm was retained to prepare an updated assessment of the market feasibility of these two phases of the development.

Methodology

Our feasibility study encompassed the following methodology:

- An analysis of the characteristics of the Town of Newmarket, York Regional Municipality and the Metropolitan senior's retirement accommodation markets;
- An analysis of the site to ascertain its suitability for successful operations in terms of success, visibility, surrounding uses, relationship to existing and emerging demand generators and other relevant factors;
- A market study to determine whether there is a need for the proposed project and the potential market segments the proposed facilities could capture;
- An analysis of the seniors' retirement residence market to determine whether there are or will be shifts in demand which could potentially impact the subject property;
- An examination of the existing supply of competitive retirement residence facilities and an investigation of projects rumoured or proposed for development;
- Preparation of estimates of daily rate, fill rate and occupancy.

During the course of the study, the location was evaluated with respect to the operation of a retirement residence and an assisted care centre. The study also included an analysis of daily rates and occupancies in the market area and the ability of existing facilities were visited and evaluated.

Members of municipal and government offices, retirement facility operators, and other interesting parties were interviewed to discuss the requirement for seniors' housing in the area.

Although the physical characteristics of the site are discussed, it is expressly understood that the scope of the study and report thereon does not include the possible impact of zoning regulations, licensing requirements and other related restrictions. It is expected that the operation will conform to all such regulations and legislation.

In the following sections, the study findings and conclusions are presented.

In the recommendations section (usually one or two pages), the consultant will advise whether or not to proceed with the contemplated project, suggest changes to it, or propose drastically different concepts (for example, build a hotel instead of residential condominiums).

Many projects are planned and built without the help of a feasibility study, but no large, sophisticated project builder would go ahead on any project without one. To summarize, feasibility studies and market studies comprise:

- a description of the planned development
- the methodology used to conduct the study
- the body of the report, the lengthy part, that covers the fine details of the study
- a thorough survey of the competition, and
- the recommendations, the part to which every client jumps first.

CHAPTER 15

Points to Consider Before Buying Each Property Type

By the end of this chapter, you will be able to:

- Speak the same language as your real estate colleagues when discussing rental rates.
- Evaluate the land and the interior and exterior of the building, including fencing, parking ratios, loading docks, security, ceiling height, electrical supply, and everything in between.
- Recognize the current practices and future trends in the retail business and evaluate a retail property accordingly.
- Distinguish between the classes of office buildings and determine which would make an appropriate investment for you.
- Inspect a multi-family building and know which factors to improve in order to attract desirable tenants.
- Compare and contrast the principlal factors for investing in the various types of income-producing properties.
- Appreciate the information and analysis IPD can provide.

When purchasing a particular type of income property — whether industrial, office, retail, or multi-unit residential – there are a number of factors to bear in mind related to location, land size, building exterior, and building interior. By assessing the strengths and weaknesses of the property and comparing it to other properties you will get a clear picture of the opportunities for improving the building (and thus the value of the property) and a sense of what is an appropriate purchase price.

When you acquire a property or are assessing its future, remember that most owners are reluctant to demolish any part of an empty building, especially one they have just acquired. However, many times they should, if by doing so they can create additional parking, improve access and shipping, or render the remaining space more attractive and usable. The result may be that they find tenants more rapidly and tenants who are willing to pay more for the space for lease in the building.

15.1 QUOTING COMMERCIAL RENTS

Speak the same language as your real estate colleagues when discussing rental rates.

To be able to communicate clearly, real estate practitioners have developed a well-accepted way of quoting rentals. For office, industrial, and retail spaces, rentals are almost always quoted on a per square metre (square foot) per year net basis. Net means that the tenant will be charged taxes, maintenance, and building insurance (TMI) or Common Area Maintenance (CAM) in the form of additional rent. Also they will pay for utilities. Occasionally, for smaller spaces (under 300 m² (3,000 sq ft) the rental may be quoted "gross", which includes the net rental and the TMI or CAM and sometimes the utilities.

Note that TMI is used mainly with industrial buildings. For office buildings and retail space, the additional rent is called CAM. Sometimes a landlord will quote taxes (T) separately without an amount for maintenance and insurance.

Let's look at an example where the rental is $216 per m² and CAM is $150 per m², for a total of $366 per m² net. If we had a 4,645 m² (50,000 sq ft) building space, the rental would be: 4,645 x $366 = $1,700,070 per year. Usually rentals are paid monthly, so in this case it would amount to $141,672.50.

The rental is fixed for the term of the lease, unless there is a clause in the lease agreement for adjusting it (usually upward). The TMI or CAM is adjusted yearly, based on actual costs, and landlords are supposed to show proof of expenses.

15.2 INDUSTRIAL BUILDINGS

Evaluate the land and the interior and exterior of the building, including fencing, parking ratios, loading docks, security, ceiling height, electrical supply, and everything in between.

15.2.1 AN OVERVIEW

Industrial buildings are used for everything from manufacturing to a plumber's shop to a warehouse and can vary from 50 to more than 100,000 m² (roughly 500 to 1,000,000 sq ft). Generally, your investment will be most secure if you buy an industrial property suited for a variety of potential uses. Checklist 15.1 itemizes the dozens of factors you should consider before purchasing an industrial property.

There are two main types of industrial buildings of interest to commercial real estate investors — single tenant and multi-tenant. Some developers offer a type of space called "flex space" that combines industrial and office use, which is permissible even up to 100% of the premises, if the zoning allows it and if there is sufficient land for parking. That is where the shoe pinches. Given the high price of industrial land, it is very rare to find a developer who does not build up to the maximum land coverage permitted under the zoning. In fact, with rare exceptions, most regular investor-owned buildings can be considered flex space, except that limited parking availability excludes them from that category. One exception is an owner-occupied building that is constructed for a specific (special) purpose, such as a flour mill, a metal stamping factory, a high volume warehouse with very high ceilings (more than 8 m (26 ft)). There are fashions and fads in everything and we believe that in a few years, flex space will be considered a fad that has passed out of favour.

15.2.2 LOCATION

Regarding location of the property, there are a number of points to consider.

- **Labour Pool.** The property should be located close to an abundant source of labour or should have easy access to public transportation.
- **Freeways.** It is ideal to be located close to a freeway.
- **Airport.** Proximity to an airport is a great advantage for many companies.
- **Neighbours.** Investigate the neighbours that you have or are likely to have in the future. Are the premises used as a stamping plant, which is undesirable because your whole building vibrates while the plant is in use, a rendering plant, which smells awful, or a food manufacturer whose products you smell every day, for better or for worse? Talk to your potential neighbours and ask what they think of the property and neighbourhood.

Checklist 15.1
Acquisition Checklist for Industrial Property

ACQUISITION CHECKLIST FOR INDUSTRIAL PROPERTY

Property address: _____

Square Footage: _____

Type of property / Present use / Highest and best use _____

1- OWNERSHIP
- ❏ Owner's name
- ❏ Listed by
- ❏ Previously listed / how long / at what price
- ❏ Reason for disposition / degree of urgency

2- LOCATION
- ❏ Determine boundaries of neighbourhood
- ❏ Proximity to nearest city or metropolitan area
- ❏ Proximity to major freeways / closest one / distance
- ❏ Railroad siding
- ❏ Trucking services / availability / rates / schedules
- ❏ Distance to major airport / port
- ❏ Proximity of raw material sources / delivery / storage
- ❏ Nature of industry in area
- ❏ Proximity of major markets
- ❏ Radius of overnight shipping / distance / population
- ❏ Public transportation
- ❏ Location Rating: 1 to 5 (best)
- ❏ Neighbours: types / compatibility

3- LAND
- ❏ Lot size / survey
- ❏ Coverage
- ❏ Expansion possible to
- ❏ Zoning
- ❏ Legal description
- ❏ Parking / number of spaces
- ❏ Topography
- ❏ Truck turning radius
- ❏ Landscaping
- ❏ Lawn sprinklers
- ❏ Easements / covenants
- ❏ Pavement / type / condition

4- BUILDING
- ❏ Building dimensions and square footage / number of stories
- ❏ Office dimensions and square footage / number of private offices / condition
- ❏ Expansion potential
- ❏ Floor plans
- ❏ Multiple uses or special purpose
- ❏ Age of building
- ❏ General condition / functional obsolescence
- ❏ Type of construction: concrete, concrete block, tilt-up, corrugated metal, other
- ❏ Type of roof / condition / age / insulation
- ❏ Type of floors / condition / thickness / load capacity / metallic hardener / sealant / densifier
- ❏ Ceiling height under joists
- ❏ Clear span / column spacing
- ❏ Skylights / number / sizes / single or double pane

- ❏ Exhaust vents
- ❏ Air make-up units
- ❏ Wiring / voltage / amps
- ❏ Lighting / type / outside lights / photocells / foot candles
- ❏ Drains / number / size
- ❏ Toilets / number / location
- ❏ Sprinkler / fire protection system
- ❏ Burglar alarm / special locks
- ❏ Number of truck level doors / size / levellers / door cushions / condition / manual / electric
- ❏ Number of drive-in doors / size / manual / electric
- ❏ Number of rail doors / distance between each door
- ❏ Dock height / excavated loading dock (ramp) / covered (canopy)
- ❏ Inside shipping bay / depth / width / dock height / leveller
- ❏ Building rating: 1 to 5 (best)
- ❏ Energy saving fixtures / systems

5- COMMUNITY

- ❏ Property tax system and assessment rules
- ❏ Closest police department / fire station
- ❏ Closest medical and hospital facilities
- ❏ Schools, churches, universities, libraries, recreation facilities, etc.
- ❏ Business amenities / banks / restaurants / various suppliers
- ❏ State of neighbourhood / stable / deteriorating / improving

6- DEMOGRAPHICS

- ❏ Present population of area ethnicity
- ❏ Average income per family and family size
- ❏ Population growth trend / past 5 years / projected

7- LABOUR MARKET

- ❏ Total estimated employment
- ❏ Availability of skilled and unskilled labour / abundant / average / tight
- ❏ Union or non-union / history of strikes
- ❏ Wage rates / hours overtime / fringe benefits

8- CLIMATE AND NATURAL HAZARDS

- ❏ Temperatures / average / minimum / maximum
- ❏ Rainfall in inches / rainy season
- ❏ Humidity / average / minimum / maximum
- ❏ Prevalent winds
- ❏ Fog conditions
- ❏ Fire hazards
- ❏ Inundation hazards

9- SERVICES, UTILITIES AND FUEL

- ❏ Electrical power / connected / availability / connection charges / rates
- ❏ Natural gas / available / capacity / rates
- ❏ Water / source / flow / pressure / rates / chemical analysis
- ❏ Telephone / number of lines in place
- ❏ Oil / cost
- ❏ Internet (T1, high speed, dial-up)

10- EQUIPMENT

- ❏ Cranes / type / capacity in tons / height under hook
- ❏ Heating / type / age
- ❏ Air-conditioning
- ❏ Boiler(s) / type / BTU's / backup fuel
- ❏ Piping / air / steam / pressure
- ❏ Electrical substation / transformers / size / capacity / location / owned by / bus ducts
- ❏ Back up electrical generator / make / type / capacity / fuel
- ❏ Condition of equipment / obsolescence

11- INCOME

- ❏ Tenant's name(s) / tenant or sub-tenant
- ❏ Type of business / how long
- ❏ Capitalization of business
- ❏ Dun & Bradstreet rating
- ❏ Banking information
- ❏ Other financial and/or credit information
- ❏ Number of years remaining on lease / rent escalation / option to renew, at what rent
- ❏ Tax escalation clause in lease
- ❏ Exterior maintenance (by owner / tenant)
- ❏ Other clauses in lease (Option to Buy, Right of First Refusal)
- ❏ Annual gross / net income

12- EXPENSES

- ❏ Property taxes / date last appealed?
- ❏ Hazard, public liability and rental income insurance (classification) / coverage / premium / insurer
- ❏ Utilities / deferred maintenance / cost to remedy / reserves for replacements
- ❏ Legal and accounting fees
- ❏ Others

13- EXISTING FINANCING

- ❏ Original mortgage amount / term / amortization / starting date / due date / balloon payment
- ❏ Mortgage(s) balance / As of what date / monthly payments / Interest rate
- ❏ Yearly debt service / interest payments / principal re payments
- ❏ Lender / address / phone / fax
- ❏ Loan number
- ❏ Prepayment penalty, and special provisions, if any
- ❏ Loan locked in / until when
- ❏ Loan transferable / assumption fee
- ❏ Any second loan? Can it be bought at a discount? If so, what discount?

14- POTENTIAL FINANCING

- ❏ Mortgage commitment / amount / interest / term / payments / loan fees / loan points / lender
- ❏ Will Vendor take back a mortgage / amount / interest / due date

15- PRICE

- ❏ Asking price / total / per square foot
- ❏ Price per square foot of comparable buildings recently sold
- ❏ Likely sale price and Cap Rate

16- EXHIBITS

- ❏ Survey / site plan
- ❏ Building floor plan
- ❏ Photographs
- ❏ Area map with property shown
- ❏ Inspection reports (pest control, roof, building condition, environmental, mechanical systems)
- ❏ Certified operating statements for last 3 years
- ❏ Copies of leases and rental agreements
- ❏ Copies of management contracts

NOTE

Inspect property carefully. Talk to neighbours. The bulk of the outside information can be obtained from 3 major sources: Planning Department, Chamber of Commerce, and Public Libraries.

Remarks:

15.2.3 LAND

You may think the only thing to confirm about the land is the area or size of lot, but you also must check things like the condition of the parking lot as well as the parking ratio, fencing, and trees on the land.

(a) Expansion Potential

If there is land to expand the building, the property is more attractive. For the landlord it offers the potential for higher income and for the tenant the comfort of knowing he will have extra parking or no need to move if more space is required.

(b) Trees

If there is space surrounding the building, plant trees if there aren't any or not enough of them. You can start with very small trees; they'll grow. In southern Ontario, crab apple and red maple trees are particularly attractive.

(c) Fencing

If your site is not fenced, install, at a minimum a 2 m (6 ft) high chain link fence, on at least three sides of the lot. It decreases theft and vandalism and gives the tenant a feeling of security.

(d) Parking

Check the condition of the parking lot by locating holes, cracks, and sunken areas.

If the warehouse area where semi-trailers have their legs lowered is damaged, plan to replace the area (called "the apron") with reinforced concrete. Ensure there is adequate parking space in the lot, driveway, and entrance. Make sure all spaces are wide enough and are satisfactory for very long semi-trailers. If not, they will destroy your curbs and your lawn.

(e) Parking Ratio

Space for parking is generally not a problem with industrial properties because most buildings cover only 50% of the site. Usually, you find a parking ratio of one space per 95 m² (1,000 sq ft) of building. It can be less if there is no office space and depending on the use of the building. Make sure that there is enough parking, particularly if there is a high percentage of office space. In other words, the zoning by-law will have minimum requirements, but common sense may suggest more parking spots, as would be the case in a very labour-intensive manufacturing business.

15.2.4 BUILDING EXTERIOR

Investigating the exterior of the building includes checking the condition of the roof, windows, the extent of outside lighting, and the status of security systems. Depending on the use, you will also need to look at elements like shipping doors, dock levellers, and dock seals.

Depending on how an industrial building is used, the items to check can extend to loading dock facilities.

(a) Overhead Doors/Shipping Doors

For truck level doors (docks), it is an advantage if the doors themselves are of the type that rise almost vertically (full vertical lift), instead of the ones that roll over the head of the user (standard lift), similar to residential garage doors. They should measure 2.44 m (8 ft) x 3.36 m (10 ft) high; the 2.44 m x 2.44 m ones are obsolete. You will need to ensure the ceiling height is sufficient (at least 4.5 m (15 ft)) to permit vertical lift doors. Full vertical lifts present two advantages. There are no railings that stand in the way, which can be damaged by fork-lifts, and one gains additional floor space.

Ideally, the doors should be the newer kind of insulated doors (double skin of aluminum or steel). Aluminum doors weigh about half as much as steel and promise a longer hardware life and easier handling. The insulating agent is either panels of polystyrene foam (R-value of 3.5 to 5 per 2.5 cm (1 in)) glued to the skin, or polyurethane foam, which is a better choice with an R-value of 6 to 8 per 2.5 cm (1 in), injected between the two skin sides. There are two advantages to insulated doors.

1. Because they are better insulated, they cut down considerably on the cost of heating.
2. They are sturdier than the old thin plywood doors, the panels of which could be kicked-in very easily in a break-and-enter.

It is best to have a window or row of windows in the door at eye level because it permits the person inside to see if a truck is at the door. The height of the truck level doors should be 122 cm (48 in) from grade to top of the building floor.

(b) Dock Leveller

A dock leveller is a device used to bridge the gap between the dock and the platform of the truck or trailer and to adjust for height difference. Generally there are two kinds in use. The pull-chain mechanical style is the most common one because it is cheaper to buy, install, and maintain. It is satisfactory for most situations, except docks that are used very frequently, where a hydraulic type is superior. The hydraulic version uses an electric pump and hydraulic piston to operate the dock leveller. A very important consideration when choosing a dock leveller is the length of the horizontal plate. As a rule, the longer the plate, the better it is because the angle of incline for the forklifts is gentler. The cost of a simple mechanical dock leveller, installed, is $3,500 to $5,000.

(c) Dock Seal

An added convenience to a shipping dock is a dock seal or dock cushion. The former is a fabric that fits around the door frame. The cushion is more popular. It is made of thick foam covered with a tough plastic fabric. The cushions are affixed to the top and sides of the door opening, preventing air, debris, birds, rain, and snow to enter the building when a truck is at the dock. When backing up, the trucks or semi-trailers squeeze them to achieve a good seal. Dock seals or cushions are also a great help to improve comfort inside the building and save on heating or cooling.

(d) Truck-Level Door Versus Drive-In Door

Sometimes a building or unit is perfect for a tenant, but he needs a truck-level door and the building offers only a drive-in door. A solution is to buy an elevating dock that is hydraulically operated. This device rests almost flush with the ground and can be raised to truck-level height. With this dock, for example, one can roll a pallet onto it and raise it for loading on a truck or lower it to floor level for unloading. This is practical only for a company that has limited shipping and receiving needs.

A drive-in door is at driveway level, although occasionally one can find such doors at the top of a ramp, which transforms a truck-level door into a drive-in door. As the name indicates, these doors are supposed to permit vehicles to be driven inside the building. We suggest that the minimum size of drive-in doors should be 3.6 m wide by 4.3 m high (12 ft x 14 ft).

There are times when a tenant requires more truck-level doors than are available. Frequently, the only way to install more doors is to dig along the wall of the building to create a ramp that allows the dock to be at the ideal height of 122 cm (48 in). The problem is that generally there are no sewers nearby to which rain waters can be directed. The solution is to install a sump pump.

Sump (pits that receive drainage) pumps are not expensive ($200-300), but their installation can be. The most common type of sump pump is the submersible one, which is usually installed in a hole below ground level. The above ground-level type is usually inside the building and close to the truck level doors. Whether in a masonry-lined hole or a plastic tank placed in the ground, a sump pump must be constructed at the lowest point in a drainage area system. Most sump pumps can lift water over 7.5 m (25 ft) and have a flow capacity of 90-114 litres (20-25 gallons) per minute.

Sump pumps are a compromise. They are far from being the perfect solution as they, or the water, can freeze, and abrasives (sand, silt, and the like) can find their way into the hole and wear out the pump. If there is no electricity, there is no pumping, although there are sump pumps that work on batteries. Finally, sump pumps require periodic cleaning, which is often overlooked.

(e) Turning Radius

The distance in front of truck shipping doors is called the "turning radius". Nowadays, a tractor and semi-trailer can be more than 21 m (70 ft) long; therefore a turning radius of 27.5 m (90 ft) is considered the minimum, while 36.5 m (120 ft) is ideal.

(f) Signage

The building should have a large, attractive, illuminated sign where the occupant can put its name.

(g) Security

Anything that increases security will be welcome by tenants. The options are virtually endless, including push-button numerical access control pads, programmable locking systems, surveillance cameras, alarm-monitored fencing, outside lighting, etc.

(h) Outside Lighting

Outside lighting should be bright enough and controlled by photocells, not timers. This means that the lights come on at dusk and turn off at dawn automatically, regardless of the season. In many situations, motion sensors should be used in conjunction with photocells.

(i) Building Corner Protection

Every corner of the building, next to which there is vehicular traffic, should be protected by a bollard. Commonly, this is a pipe filled with concrete that may be painted or galvanized. Its diameter, where there are trucks, should be 20.5-25.5 cm (8-10 in) with 1.2 m (4 ft) under the ground and 1.2-1.5 m (4-5 ft) above ground. Where there are only cars, the diameter should be 15.25 cm (6 in) with 1 m (3 ft) below, and 1-1.2 m (3-4 ft) above ground. They should be covered with a metal cap to prevent water seeping into them because the concrete does not fully protect the metal pipe against water penetration and, hence, rust. Make sure that bollards are installed on each side of a drive-in door and also to protect fire hydrants.

There are now bumper post sleeves that slide over existing bollards (of smaller diameter) to give a clean, new look and extend the life of the bollard. They cost approximately $150 and are made of polyethylene. Custom colours and logos can be moulded into the sleeves, which make great gifts for tenants.

If there are no bollards, which are expensive (close to $1,000 installed for big ones), heavy angle irons (preferably galvanized) should be installed to protect the bricks on each side of drive-in and truck level doors. If the building walls are made of corrugated steel, a protective, galvanized railing (security guardrail) about .6-1 m (2-3 ft) off the ground should be used along the building wherever vehicles can cause damage to the siding. These are available commercially or can be custom fabricated. The same protection should be used with fences or they will be damaged by vehicles.

(j) Jersey Barriers

Since we are on the subject of protection, we must mention jersey barriers. The full name is New Jersey Concrete Safety Shape Barrier. You've seen jersey barriers in many highway medians, where they divide the flow of traffic going in opposite directions. The standard barrier weighs 2,620 kg (5,780 lbs) and measures 3.8 m (12.5 ft) in length and costs in the range of $300-400. The height is just over 1 m (42 in) and the thickness is 61 cm (24 in) at the bottom and 24 cm (9.5 in) at the top. The barrier's sophisticated shape was designed to redirect a vehicle that hits it. They can be a blessing to property owners for construction sites or when their fences or other barriers tend to get cut or pushed out of place. Nobody pushes a barrier weighing as much as two mid-sized cars.

(k) Roof

Inquire about the age of the roof. A typical tar and gravel roof has a 20-year life expectancy, although with care, it can last 25 to 30 years.

15.2.5 BUILDING INTERIOR

The elements to investigate on the interior of the building are just as varied as the exterior and include items like ceiling height and floors as well as lighting, column spacing, and cafeterias or lunch rooms.

(a) Ceiling Height

Nowadays buildings are also arbitrarily divided into two segments based on their ceiling heights (clear, under joists).
- **Under 5.5 m (18 ft).** These are generally older buildings.
- **Over 5.5 m (18 ft).** Some will be as high as 10.4 m (34 ft).

Often you will hear people say that industrial buildings with 4.2-4.8 m (14-16 ft) ceilings are obsolete. This is untrue unless a building is to be used for warehousing, where high ceilings are needed to house large quantities of bulky and relatively light items, such as empty plastic bottles, cartons, plastic parts, toys, etc. Even in warehousing, it depends on the type of use. For example, we have a customer who uses a 4,650 m² (50,000 sq ft) building with 4.5 m (14.75 ft) ceilings for public warehousing. He specializes in smaller customers (100-500 pallets) and in maritime container de-stuffing. But, generally, warehousing implies large spaces and a 2,800 m² (30,000 sq ft) warehouse is a very small one.

Most users of space under 2,800 m² (30,000 sq ft) use very little of it for warehousing, but rather to store raw products or components and finished goods. For manufacturing or assembly, for shipping, etc., they do not need high ceilings. In fact, high ceilings can present a number of drawbacks, including higher property taxes, heating, and lighting costs. Somebody storing heavy steel plastic injection moulds or ball bearings does not need and does not want high ceilings, nor does a manufacturer of cheese, sausage, or heavy metal parts. We even know of a large furniture manufacturer that occupies a 21,400 m² (230,000 sq ft) plant that has 4.2 m (14 ft) ceilings, although he would probably prefer that 20% of the space had higher ceilings. At the most, only 50% of industrial users need high ceilings. However, for the business that needs a lot of space, and can stack goods high, either on top of one another or by using pallet racking, high ceilings (over 6 m (20 ft)) make sense because it will save on property taxes, lighting, heating, and less aisle space will be required.

(b) Bay Size

Another requirement of warehouses is large bay sizes, which are referred to by the distance between columns that support the roof structure. The fewer columns there are the better it is because there is more flexibility in how the building can be used, particularly if the user makes use of pallet racking. The fewer the number of columns, however, the higher the construction cost of the building. A bay size of 9 m x 9 m (30 x 30 ft) is a minimum requirement; 9 m x 15.2 m (30 x 50 ft) or 12.2 m x 12.2 m (40 x 40 ft) is much better. Very old buildings may have columns spacing of 3 m x 3.6 m (10 x 12 ft) while modern, high-ceilinged warehouses can have a distance of 15.25 m x 18.3 m (50 x 60 ft) between columns.

(c) Insulation

Few industrial buildings are properly insulated, even newer buildings. It is always a compromise between more insulation and cost. The more insulated the building is, the more comfortable it is to use and economical to operate. The loss of heat through the roof can be as high as 40% of the total heat loss. Therefore, it is important to discover what kind of insulation is on the roof of a building before deciding to buy it. Older buildings didn't have any roof insulation whereas newer buildings have some, but generally not enough. If the roof has been leaking, some kinds of older insulation will be rotten and will need to be replaced (see Chapter 19). A specialist with a thermographic camera can take photographs of your roof and walls and reveal the most significant areas of thermal loss.

(d) Floors

Industrial building floors are generally 12.7 cm (5 in) thick and poured over wire mesh. Buildings with high ceilings, say, over 7.3 m (24 ft) have at least 15.25 cm (6 in) floors. Some built for a specific user will have 20.3 cm (8 in) thickness or more (we have seen 30.5 cm). Some floors appear to have shiny particles in them, called "metallic hardener". Particles of metal are sprinkled over the wet cement before final trowelling. This process is used when the floor will be abused such as in steel fabricating. Pure warehouses never have metallic hardener. All factories and warehouse floors will generate dust, if not treated. The treatment, if any, usually consists of a urethane coating (generally two coats) or special wear-resistant paint. These need to be reapplied after several years of use. A better solution is not a coating but a product that causes a chemical reaction within the concrete itself, called "concrete densifier". It lasts forever.

It is natural for concrete floors to have some fine hairline cracks, but they should not be overly wide. Cracks are caused by shrinkage as the concrete dries. To control cracking concrete, floors are sawed into large areas (6 m x 6 m (20 x 20 ft) sections for example) to a depth of approximately 2.5-3.8 cm (1-1.5 in). These are called "expansion joints", improperly named since it is not expansion that is the problem, but contraction. Even with these joints, hairline cracks may still occur. Also some floors may have sunken or heaved-up. Both are expensive to repair and can create problems for the user. See Chapter 19 at section 19.2.1 for remedies.

You will see a variety of ceiling heights, floor thickness, column spacing, etc., depending on the age of the building.

Depending on the uses contemplated, it is advantageous to have floor drains and running water in some areas of the plant.

(e) Dividing Walls

In a multi-tenant building, the wall dividing the tenants' units is generally built with concrete blocks to resist abuses, mainly from lift trucks. Technically, it is only called a wall if it bears weight from above, such as a second floor or roof joists. If it is not weight bearing, it is called a partition. In office buildings, partitions are usually just two sheets of drywall (with or without insulation in between) attached to studs (wood or metal).

(f) Lighting

In today's plants and warehouses, the ideal lighting for high ceilings is either metal halide or T5 fluorescent (best) or low-pressure sodium systems (see Chapter 19). If you have ordinary (T12 lamps) fluorescent lighting, bear in mind that relatively frequently the lamps (tubes) will have to be replaced and you should attempt to have an electrical energy retrofit conducted, so that you go from T12 lamps (which are 3.8 cm (1.5 in) in diameter) to T8 lamps (which are 2.54 cm (1 in) in diameter) or T5 (1.27 cm (0.5 in)). (See Chapter 19 at section 19.3.9.)

(g) Painted Walls and Ceilings

It is much better if walls and ceilings are painted, for cleanliness, better lighting, and attractiveness. If painted white, as they should be, the lighting will be less costly because a lower foot-candle value will be required due to the reflective factor.

(h) Electrical Supply

If you do not have a long-term tenant in place and, therefore, may have a new tenant every 5 years, check the electrical power supply. Is it sufficient for the most common potential uses? If not, how much would it cost to increase the power supply? Only the tenant can tell you exactly how many amps he needs and if he needs it in 120/240 volts or 600 volts. And it will vary from tenant to tenant, sometimes markedly. For industrial buildings, the electrical service is usually a three-phase system, instead of the single-phase systems that are used in homes.

(i) Cafeteria/Lunchroom

Depending on the size of the building and the tenant's business, whether the building has a cafeteria or lunchroom goes from convenient to necessary.

(j) Sprinkler Systems

Every building should have sprinklers (see Chapter 19 at section 19.3.6).

(k) President's Office

It is nice if the president's office includes a private washroom, shower, kitchenette, etc., to please the boss and flatter his ego.

15.2.6 SPECIAL PURPOSE BUILDINGS

Often industrial buildings are erected to suit a specific use. For example, a building with the following features would denote a special purpose building:

- very high ceilings, cranes and clear span (no columns)

- different floor levels
- many solid partitions (bearing walls)
- much heavy-duty mechanical equipment such as air make-up units, air conditioning, bus ducts (electrical distribution system), cranes, etc., and
- freezer space (insulated walls, floors and ceilings).

Unless you are a sophisticated investor, it is best to avoid this type of building. This applies, too, to mini-warehouses that are more business than real estate, hotels, and medical buildings that are very property management intensive.

15.2.7 GUIDE TO OCCUPANCY COSTS

Occupancy costs, which are all the costs borne by the tenant, vary by the type of commercial property. However, to give you an idea of these costs, this section discusses occupancy costs for industrial buildings.

Most owners and occupants know the total of the many cheques they sign each month, but few know it on an area basis, the common denominator whereby they can compare it with other buildings. To determine this number a tenant needs to consider all of the costs discussed below.

"Net" rental means the amount paid to the landlord by the tenant over the term of the lease, with all other costs, such as property taxes, maintenance, building insurance, and utilities, being covered directly by the tenant. Depending on the lease, the landlord may be responsible for structural repairs and wear and tear.

(a) Rental Cost

The rental cost is normally quoted on a per square metre (square foot) basis and payable in monthly instalments. For example, if we take a 1,860 m² (20,000 sq ft) manufacturing building that is 10 to 20 years old with 5.5-6 m (18-20 ft) ceilings and 10% office space, located in Mississauga, the rental may be $65 per m² ($6 per sq ft) net, or $120,900 per year, which means the tenant would pay $10,075 per month to the owner.

(b) Property Taxes

The taxes are based on the Current Value Assessment of the property and updated every 4 years (see section 5.1.1(c)). Typically, the market value will be 10% to 20% higher than the Current Value Assessment. It is impossible to give an exact figure for property taxes because a myriad of factors intervene, such as age, ceiling height, percentage of office, quality and condition of the building, amount of land, uses, etc., and varies from municipality to municipality.

(c) Building Insurance

Insurance costs also vary, ranging from $.85-$1.30 per m² ($0.08-$0.12 per sq ft), for an occupied building and jumping drastically for a vacant one. Most of the time, if a property is vacant for more than 30 consecutive days, the insurance policy indicates that all insurance coverage stops. You should check with your insurance carrier, as this depends on the wording in your policy. According to the Agreement of Purchase and Sale, all vendors are supposed to have the building insured until closing. However, this is practically never checked and some vendors do not have insurance.

(d) Exterior Maintenance (landscaping and snow removal)

Exterior maintenance refers to landscaping and snow removal. As you can imagine, these costs can vary greatly depending on the amount and style of landscaping and the area in which you are located. In the southern Ontario area it can range from $2.15-$5.40 per m² ($0.20-$0.50 per sq ft).

(e) Lighting

Again lighting costs within the warehouse area will vary greatly. However, we can estimate that the cost of lighting the office area will range from $4.30-$12.90 per m² ($0.40-$1.20 per sq ft).

(f) Heating

The heating costs can vary enormously, depending on uses, building quality, insulation, ceiling height, heating system, etc. Commonly, costs go from $6.45-$12.90 per m² ($0.60-$1.20 per sq ft) for industrial buildings.

(g) Management

Most landlords do charge tenants a management fee. Landlords consider this management cost an expense that has nothing to do with the investment they made when buying the property, so do not want their return diminished by it. The amount varies a great deal. For example, it can be 15% of the total additional rental (property taxes, insurance, maintenance, and repairs) or 2-5% of the total rental (rental and additional rental).

Some landlords of multiple-occupancy buildings pay the costs of regular maintenance and repairs and recover these expenses by apportioning all repairs made in a unit to the whole building. For example, if a 5,575 m² (60,000 sq ft) building has six units and a heating and ventilation air-conditioning (HVAC) unit must be changed in unit #3, each tenant in the building would be charged 1/6th of the cost involved.

Generally, these landlords do not place the onus on the tenants to look after the maintenance because many are neglectful and it can turn into a nasty dispute when the tenant moves out. When landlords take care of maintenance, this practice ensures it is done, and done properly, by qualified and conscientious trades and preventive maintenance is ongoing.

15.3 RETAIL BUILDINGS

Recognize the current practices and future trends in the retail business and evaluate a retail property accordingly.

15.3.1 AN OVERVIEW

Retail buildings are buildings used to sell merchandise to the consumer for his personal use, not for re-sale to others. Retailers include all kinds of stores, such as Canadian Tire, Staples, the Shoe Company, Eddie Bauer, Honest Ed's, and the corner convenience store.

While changes are constant in any field, the retail business has seen more than its share, especially since the 1970s. In retail, it has been more like a revolution, which is far from over yet. The two main causes of this revolution are Home Depot, based in Atlanta, Georgia, and Wal-Mart, based in Bentonville, Arkansas.

5.3.2 THE REVOLUTION IN RETAIL

Home Depot's premise is that everything that has to do with the physical house should be under one roof. They built huge warehouse stores, offered good service, and, through their buying power, low prices. Home Depot was the creator of the Big-Box concept in North America. To understand the impact of a Home Depot store on regional retail sales, you should know that most of their stores do a minimum of $50 million in sales per store and a few do more than twice that much. They prefer to locate in residential areas with a lot of owner-occupied, single-family houses.

A big box is a huge building, frequently over 1,000 m² (107,000 sq ft), built as a warehouse (no marble on the floors here), and very functional. In theory, they are generally located on low-priced land that was previously zoned industrial.

Wal-Mart was created by the colourful Sam Walton who, after challenging Wal-Mart's Associates to make 1984 an exceptional year, was forced (to keep his word) to don a grass skirt and lei and dance on Wall Street because the challenge had been met. Sam Walton had been a Ben Franklin franchisee and he followed the same location rule when he started Wal-Mart. He located his stores in small American towns and that generally brought about the demise of many Main Street retailers because he brought lower prices, greater choice, and often better service.

His method of conducting a market study was unusual and lofty. He would jump in his plane, which he loved to pilot, and scout out the real estate. In his book, *Made in America*, Sam Walton explains:

> From the air, we could check out traffic flows, see which way cities and towns were growing, and evaluate the location of the competition, if there was any. I loved doing it myself. I'd get down low, turn my plane over on its side, and fly over a town. Once we had a spot picked out, we'd land, go find out who owned the property, and try to negotiate the deal, right then.

Wal-mart, the big-box giant, accounts for almost half of the department store sales in Canada. Each Wal-Mart store has sales between $40 and $60 million per year.

From the big box stores we moved into the next revolution — the power centre. This concept started in Canada in the early 1990s, in spite of the real estate market downturn and thanks to the powerful team of Wal-Mart and First Professional Realty (now Smart Centres) and went on to explode on the retail scene. We have in 2007, nearly 3 million m² (32 million sq ft) of power centre retail space in the Greater Toronto Area alone.

A power centre is a group of large format (big box), open-air strip layout retail stores that share a common parking area. In a short 15 years, it has become the preferred form of shopping space for numerous consumers. Many shoppers prefer the design of power centres to that of conventional malls with kilometres of corridors, in spite of a peculiarity of power centres, which is frequently the need to drive from store to store. It is also often the preferred investing vehicle for many large real estate investors, surpassed only by Tier 1 regional malls and, on a much different scale, food anchored strip plazas.

The advent of power retailing, best exemplified by Wal-Mart, has had two major impacts.

1. **Loss.** The increased and ferocious price competition has forced many small retailers out of business.
2. **Gain.** The consumer has been offered goods at unbelievably low prices.

This form of power retailing should, in fact, be broken down into three categories; in a way similar to traditional shopping centre formats.

1. **Self-Standing Big Box Stores.** This category includes retailers like Home Depot or Canadian Tire.
2. **Power Centres.** These are made up of several big-box stores and some smaller (but not small) retailers.
3. **Regional Power Nodes.** These retailers exert a shopping draw similar to those of regional shopping centres, such as Yorkdale Mall. An example is the area of highways 400 and 7 in North Toronto. On each of the four corners, one can find a power node:
   - Highway 7 and Jane Power Centre
   - The Interchange
   - Colossus Entertainment Centre, and
   - Seven and 400 Power Centre.

The proof of the present superiority of power centres lies in the fact that no regional centres have been developed in Canada in the last few years, with the exception of Vaughan Mills, which has several big-box stores around it.

Frequently referred to as category killers, power centres seem to have stabilized to an area of about 37,000-74,500 m² (400,000-800,000 sq ft). Also the pace of construction of power centres has slowed down in recent years, in part, because of the volume of available retail space and the difficulty of finding suitable sites (most are located on old industrial sites). And they have forced conventional centres to revisit and change their tenant mix. Whenever possible, these centres now add one or more big-box style stores.

The predominant tenants (over 50%) in power centres are US retailers (Wal-Mart, Staples, Best Buy, Home Depot, Williams Sonoma, and many more). This has led some people to talk of the Americanization of the Canadian retail scene. Most US retailers' strategy is to offer an extensive choice of merchandise at low prices. The power centre concept is ideally suited for them due to large size, major retail presence, and a format offering lower construction and operating costs than traditional centres, and flexible units.

The formidable competition that power centres represent to the traditional retailing format reinforces the need for real estate investors to select carefully conventional shopping centre acquisition candidates in this sector by checking that they follow the fundamental rules.

- **Large Centres.** These are regional centres of more than 37,000 m² (400,000 sq ft) and super-regional centres of more than 74,500 m² (800,000 sq ft). Larger centres must be anchored by at least two department stores, one department store and one large supermarket, or a big-box outlet. They are usually located at the intersection of major arterial roads with heavy exposure and ideally at intersections with traffic signals. They have multiple road access points and are serviced by several public transportation routes. Most of these centres focus on fashion.
- **Medium-sized Centres.** These are community centres that range from approximately 14,000 m² to 37,000 m² (150,000-400,000 sq ft). Medium-size centres are anchored by one department store with, ideally, a supermarket or a big-box store. They should be exposed to heavy road traffic, serviced by at least one public transportation route, and located on a major artery with signal lights as access points. They are the most vulnerable of this group due to competition from regional centres and neighbourhood centres.
- **Small Centres.** These are neighbourhood centres that range from 2,800 m² to 14,000 m² (30,000-150,000 sq ft) in size. They are anchored by at least a supermarket or drugstore, with many service-oriented stores. Ideally, they are located at the intersection of major arteries and they should have exposure to traffic on major collector roads, offer easy vehicular access, be on a public transportation transit line, and have good pedestrian traffic.

At this time, the three most obvious trends in retail development appear to be:

1. mixed uses (retail and office, often in the same building)
2. parking away from the street, with building facades close to the street frontage (an aberration for suburban centres), and
3. the influence of the sunny climate architecture of the southern US.

New trends are emerging and it seems that the next regional shopping centres may be unanchored in the traditional way, relying instead on peripheral big-boxes to generate traffic.

Regardless of the kind of retail concept, in all cases three items always have a huge impact on success: well-designed and sufficient parking, good tenant mix, and varied merchandising mix. In this three-point formula you can find the main reasons for the turnaround successes enjoyed by some sophisticated shopping centre landlords. Any landlord of retail properties should be a member of the Retail Council of Canada (40,000 members) and encourage his tenants to join <www.retail.council.org>.

The crush for the owners of strip plazas, open shopping centres, and even shopping malls will probably come around 2010 to 2015, when some conventional retail centres will sit empty or have very high vacancy rates. Many of these properties will lose some value and new uses will have to be found for them. Not all will suffer. The survivors will be the centres that have a strong anchor, a good tenant mix (compatible and complementary), limited competition, and located in an area that naturally insulates them from big boxes and other centres. The investor who is interested in retail should keep this in mind when he is considering buying a retail property. It will become increasingly important to commission quality market studies (see Chapter 14 at section 14.8) before making investment decisions.

Checklist 15.2 itemizes the dozens of factors you must consider before purchasing a retail property.

15.3.3 RETAIL CENTRE CLASSIFICATIONS

There are two broad types of retail stores: destination and impulse. Destination retail is that which attracts buyers who have a specific purchase in mind, such as an automobile, furniture, computer, clothing, garden supplies, or lumber. Impulse, on the other hand, refers to retailers who cater to unplanned purchases, such as gasoline, coffee shops, muffin shops, convenience stores, and ice cream stores. For some uses, the distinction is hazy, such as antique stores. When it comes to retail centres or malls, there are four general classifications.

(a) Power Centres

Extensively covered in section 15.3.2, power centres share many characteristics of the regional malls, in terms of area and market radius, but are composed of larger size stores (big box stores) and, therefore, fewer tenants. Usually they have no interior corridors.

(b) Regional Malls

Ranging in size between 28,000 m² to nearly 140,000 m² (300,000-1.5 million sq ft), regional malls draw customers from a 15- to 50-kilometre radius, designed to serve a trade area of 200,000 people and over. They are anchored with more than one department store, which can occupy from one-third up to one-half of the total space.

Checklist 15.2
Acquisition Checklist for Retail Property

ACQUISITION CHECKLIST FOR RETAIL PROPERTY

Property address:_____

Type of property: _____

Square footage: Gross _____   Rentable _____   Usable_____

Number of Tenants _____   Building Name _____

1- OWNERSHIP
- ❑ Owner's name
- ❑ Listed by
- ❑ Previously listed / how long / at what price
- ❑ Reason for disposition / degree of urgency

2- LOCATION
- ❑ Population of town
- ❑ Quality of address 1-5 (best)
- ❑ Exposure 1-5 (best)
- ❑ Signalized corner
- ❑ Median strip / left turn lane
- ❑ Public transportation
- ❑ Proximity to: main arteries / freeways / large apartment buildings
- ❑ Traffic patterns / planned streets / street widenings
- ❑ If Shopping Centre: neighbourhood / community / regional
- ❑ Location rating: 1 to 5 (best)
- ❑ Is area, neighbourhood, or street deteriorating / improving / stable

3- LAND
- ❑ Lot dimensions / size
- ❑ Coverage
- ❑ Zoning
- ❑ Legal description
- ❑ Easements / covenants
- ❑ Parking lot / number of cars / location / paving / condition
- ❑ Access for customers / shipping / receiving
- ❑ Landscaping
- ❑ Expansion / possible acquisition of extra land

4- BUILDING
- ❑ Square footage / frontage / depth / layout / % of rentable area
- ❑ Number of stories or levels
- ❑ Basement / foundations
- ❑ Use restrictions, if any
- ❑ Expansion potential / how much
- ❑ Age of building
- ❑ Architectural appeal
- ❑ Condition / functional obsolescence
- ❑ Type of construction
- ❑ Exterior finish / condition
- ❑ Exterior signage / pilons / fascia
- ❑ Roof / type / condition / age
- ❑ Floors / size / number / type / condition / load capacity of each floor

- ❏ Clear ceiling height
- ❏ Electrical service / wiring / voltage, amperage
- ❏ Lighting / intensity level in foot candles / kind of fixtures / lamps
- ❏ Backup power generator / make / type / capacity / fuel
- ❏ Type of HVAC / age / condition
- ❏ Toilets / type / number / location
- ❏ Sprinklers and fireproofing system
- ❏ Energy retrofit
- ❏ Burglar alarm / special locks / surveillance cameras
- ❏ Special equipment / garbage compactor
- ❏ Loading dock(s) / height / dock leveller
- ❏ Internet (T1, dial-up, high speed)
- ❏ Energy saving measure / systems

5- INCOME

- ❏ Rent Roll of triple A tenants
- ❏ Income from parking and others
- ❏ Sales per square metre (square foot)
- ❏ Type of businesses / how long in business / Dun & Bradstreet rating / quality of tenant mix and merchandising mix
- ❏ Other financial / credit information
- ❏ Centre total yearly rental (net or gross) per square foot / per front foot of store / expenses / NOI
- ❏ Percentage leases / overage / how calculated
- ❏ Overage of last 3 years
- ❏ Number of years remaining on lease(s) / rent escalation / renewal option, at what rent
- ❏ Tax escalation clause in lease
- ❏ Responsibility for exterior maintenance: owner/tenants
- ❏ Other terms of net lease (including Option to Buy, Right of First Refusal)
- ❏ Management fee charged to tenants

6- EXPENSES

- ❏ Property taxes / date last appealed?
- ❏ Hazard, liability, and rental income insurance (classification) / coverage / premium
- ❏ Services
- ❏ Utilities
- ❏ Garbage collection
- ❏ Salaries / number of staff
- ❏ Maintenance / repairs / deferred maintenance / Cost to remedy / reserve for replacements
- ❏ Leasing commissions payable
- ❏ Promotions
- ❏ Legal and accounting fees
- ❏ Merchant association
- ❏ Others

7- EXISTING FINANCING

- ❏ Original mortgage amount / term / amortization / starting date
- ❏ Due Date / balloon payment
- ❏ Mortgage(s) balance / as of what date
- ❏ Monthly payments
- ❏ Interest rate and due date
- ❏ Annual debt service / interest payments / principal repayments
- ❏ Lender / address / phone / fax
- ❏ Loan number
- ❏ Prepayment penalty, and special provisions, if any
- ❏ Loan locked in / until when
- ❏ Is loan transferable / assumption fee
- ❏ Any second loan? Can it be bought at a discount? If so, what discount?

8- POTENTIAL FINANCING

☐ Mortgage commitment / amount / interest / term / amortization / loan fee / loan points / lender

☐ Will Vendor take back a mortgage / amount / interest / due date

9- PRICE

☐ Asking price / total / per square foot / Cap Rate

☐ Estimated selling price and Cap Rate

10- AREA SURVEY

☐ Determine boundaries / neighbourhood / market area

☐ Traffic count in front and at nearest intersection (per day, week, month, year)

☐ Distance to nearest competitive centres / businesses (if only a few)

☐ Estimated population within market area / ethnicity

☐ Average income per family

☐ Population growth / past 5 years / projected

☐ Is area, neighbourhood or street / deteriorating / improving / stable

12 – COMMUNITY

☐ Property tax system and assessment rules

☐ Closest police department / fire station

☐ Closest medical and hospital facilities

☐ Business amenities / banks / restaurants / various suppliers

13- EXHIBITS

☐ Survey / Site plan

☐ Floor plan

☐ Photographs

☐ Area map with property shown

☐ Inspection reports (pest control, building condition, environmental, roof, HVAC systems, sprinklers, security, elevators, etc.)

☐ Certified operating statements for last 3 years

☐ Copies of leases and rental agreements

☐ Copies of management contracts

☐ Inventory of personal property

NOTE: *Inspect property carefully. Talk to neighbours. The bulk of the outside information can be obtained from 3 major sources: Planning Department, Chamber of Commerce and Public Libraries*

REMARKS:

(c) Community Shopping Centres

Generally community shopping centres are in the 14,000-37,000 m² (150,000-400,000 sq ft) range and anchored with a small department store or a large supermarket. When there is a supermarket, the centre is said to be "grocery store anchored". The trade area population is from 5,000 to 50,000 people.

(d) Neighbourhood Shopping Centres

From 2,800-14,000 m² (30,000-150,000 sq ft), neighbourhood shopping centres are a group of retail stores providing convenience to the people living nearby and include enterprises such as hair salons, barbers, dry cleaners, banks, convenience stores, video rentals, etc. As a rule, they have no department store, but are sometimes anchored with a small supermarket.

15.3.4 LOCATION

In retail, the concept of the trade area is of paramount importance. This is the area around the retail store from which the retailer draws it customers. It does not refer to a perfect circle drawn around a centre point, since geographical obstacles, such as a river or an international boundary, for example, can interfere. Another obstacle to the trade area expanding in a given direction could be the presence of a competing centre or retailer and customer's driving time, more important than distance in terms of attracting customers. A trade area can encompass a very large territory in sparsely populated areas or a very small one (a few blocks) in a large city. It is expressed as the number of potential customers.

Most successful retailers or retail businesses, such as banks, Home Depot, Linen'n' Things, Shoppers Drugmart, TD Canada Trust, use sophisticated market research consultants to choose new locations. Depending on the depth of analysis required, a location study can be quite expensive but it is well worth doing for a retailer, developer, or investor before spending millions of dollars on a new centre or store.

Few investors, outside of large, sophisticated landlords, ever order a location study, but they should for a number of reasons.

1. It is virtually impossible for the ordinary investor to buy properties only in prime locations.
2. In a vendor's market, it is even more difficult, which means that investors need to look at less-than-ideal properties.
3. Centres less than 10 years old, particularly those in secondary locations, do not always attract the traffic that the plaza builder/developer had hoped. Therefore, some tenants will stay, grumbling and disheartened, till the end of their lease, and then vacate with delight. Other, more substantial tenants, such as supermarket chains, will move out of a poorly performing store, but pay the rent until the end of the lease term, which may be several years.
4. Retailing concepts change.

Imagine the financial catastrophe if you buy a centre and a few months later your anchor tenant closes down. The implications are huge, even if it continues to pay rent.
- The smaller retailers in the centre will suffer markedly because of lower sales.
- Some tenants will declare bankruptcy.
- Other tenants will simply move out over a weekend and tell you, "Sue me".
- Still others will demand a rental reduction.

There are two conclusions. After you have a conditional offer to buy accepted:

- conduct a location or market study and/or order an appraisal, and
- talk to the tenants in the centre: "I like this centre and I may try to buy it, but first I would like to ask you a few questions. How is business? Do you see any problem in the future? Will you renew your lease?" In addition, there is no harm done in talking to neighbourhood retailers.

A location study will look at many factors, including access, traffic count, and demographics.

(a) Access

The ideal location for a shopping centre is on the right side of the "going home" street at an intersection with traffic lights. Because it must be as easy as possible for shoppers to enter and exit the centre, it is even better if you have access to a second or third street. Ideally, the centre should have multi-family buildings as neighbours, within a reasonable distance.

(b) Address

Your shopping centre should be on a well-known street so that shoppers finding the address in the Yellow Pages, on a flyer, or on a Web site know right away where it is located.

(c) Exposure

If your centre or its sign can be seen from heavily travelled arteries, such as a freeway, it will attract more shoppers.

(d) Traffic Count

This is an essential consideration for any retail business. The number of vehicles passing on all streets, in all directions on which the centre has entrances, should be as high as possible, preferably above 20,000 per 24-hour period. For example, highway 401 near Jane Street in Toronto carries over 160,000 cars per day, whereas highway 400 near Dunlop Street in Barrie sees 88,000 cars per day. One of Toronto's best known streets, Yonge Street, south of Sheppard Avenue, carries over 60,000 per day; one of the higher traffic counts for a city street in the area. Traffic counts can be obtained (generally for a charge) from the municipality for municipal roads and streets, and from the province for provincial ones.

(e) Demographics

Demographics are the characteristics of human populations and population segments, which are especially important when used to identify consumer markets. Demographic requirements, such as income bracket, occupation, ethnicity, age, and percentage of home owner and of tenants, vary from one retailer to another. For example, banks, car washes, restaurants, movie theatres, and building supply retailers are unlikely to want identical demographics. Virtually all sophisticated retailers use demographics as a component of the data they analyze to select locations.

Virtually all sophisticated retailers use demographics as a component of the data they analyze to select locations.

15.3.5 LAND

As with industrial property, you will want to review the parking conditions and landscaping, but you may evaluate them differently.

(a) Parking

It is critical that a retail property have enough parking and that the parking be located between the stores and the access road. Never buy a retail property where the bulk of its parking is at the back of the building. Shoppers don't like that situation because they can't see if parking spaces are available and they don't know how far they will have to walk from their cars to the store. In newer centres, front-of-building parking may be difficult to find because some municipalities' planners have embarked on a crusade aimed at forcing parking behind stores, moving the storefronts closer to the street. Ensure that the parking is well-laid-out and practical, that is it meets the following criteria:

- access lanes are wide and convenient so that you do not back out of your spot onto a heavily trafficked road
- spaces are wide enough
- there is angled parking where it is more convenient, and
- the rows of spaces are not exceedingly long without a cross-road.

Function is more important than form, except in a work of art.

(b) Trees

Trees are very pleasing but you should have only a few of them between the street and the stores, so that they do not block visibility. If they are demanded by local by-laws, trim branches 3-4.5 m (10-15 ft) off the ground and plant ones that grow tall with a small crown.

(c) Pads

A pad is a small piece of land (280-2,800 m² (3,000-30,000 sq ft)) used by a retailer to erect a small, customized building that caters mainly to drive-through customers. Some retail centres that are set well back from the roads lease or sell pads closer to the street, for small freestanding buildings such as a donut shop, a restaurant, or even a service station. While this brings additional income, if it is not done well, it can be a dangerous strategy because it can lessen the desirability of the other stores and, hence, their rental value, due to their diminished visibility.

15.3.6 Building Exterior

While not many factors need to be considered for the exterior of a retail building, they are of utmost concern. Review the list below.

- **Signage.** The storefronts of a shopping centre should be uniform and convenient for the stores to use and should display their names prominently. Because beauty is in symmetry, all signs should be reasonably similar, at least in size and shape, while respecting the logo or name design of the tenants. There should be one, or more if possible, large lit pylon sign close to the street, listing as many of the tenants' names as possible.
- **Awnings.** Awnings or a recessed front forming an exterior open corridor that allows shoppers to walk from one store to another without being exposed to rain or snow improve the appeal and, hence, the value of a retail centre.

- **Aesthetic Appeal.** People prefer to shop at an aesthetically appealing centre. This can be accomplished with decorative elements and with landscaping, but your primary concern should be proper function.

15.3.7 BUILDING INTERIOR

As each tenant will have different needs for the interior of his unit, you need only be concerned with ceiling height and the basement.

- **Ceiling Height.** It is ideal to have a ceiling height of at least 3 m (10 ft) for small stores and much higher for the anchor tenants and other large stores.
- **Basements.** Few shopping centres have basements because of building costs but they are a blessing for the tenant as a retail store never has enough storage space. Some centres have very high ceilings 5.5 m (18 ft) or more, which tenants appreciate as they can have a mezzanine used either for office, storage or for additional shopping area.

15.3.8 OTHER FACTORS FOR CONSIDERATION

Retail buildings have a few special features and requirements to be contemplated.

(a) Office Space

It can be very tempting for a developer to build a second storey on a shopping centre or strip plaza for office space. However, this space is almost always difficult to rent unless it is part of a very large centre, a mall, or in a terrific area with limited competing office buildings. Offices over strip malls frequently have a very high vacancy rate. The vacancy rates for second- and third-storey apartments built over malls are much lower, but the commercial appeal of the stores seems to suffer from the presence of the apartments.

(b) Security

It is a great advantage if your centre is located close to a police station or if you arrange to have it patrolled. Some police forces will do this on written request. Hold-ups and night robbery are a real curse for retailers, particularly small ones. A retail centre landlord using video recording surveillance cameras will appeal more to tenants.

(c) Name

All centres should have an attractive, intelligent, short, and easily remembered name, just as most large office or condominium buildings have a name (with the exception of single-use industrial buildings). If you name a building, trademark the name with the Canadian Intellectual Property Office in Ottawa. You do not need to hire a lawyer to do this. Go online at <www.cipo.gov.ca>. The cost is approximately $250.

(d) Anchor Tenants and the Tenant Mix

There are different kinds of anchor tenants but all have one thing in common — they generate traffic for the centre. Typical anchors are:

- department stores: The Bay
- supermarkets: Loblaws
- drugstores: Shopper's Drug Mart
- banks: TD Canada Trust, and
- restaurants: Tim Hortons.

The last two are not technically anchors, but they do generate considerable traffic, particularly Tim Hortons.

If you are considering buying a shopping centre, in all likelihood it will be leased, at least in large part. If there is an anchor tenant, study carefully its ability to generate traffic. For example, all supermarkets know how many receipts their cash registers have issued in the last week and their total sales for that week. From these numbers they can find the average ticket sale (total sales/number of sales) and sales per area (total sales of 52 weeks/area of store). This is the key to the centre's success. Not all anchors are good anchors. Landlords accept that anchors pay a lower rent for their space because of the contribution they make in generating traffic for the centre, so if they are not doing this well, they may hurt the entire centre.

The smaller stores are "traffic users". Their success will be due, in great part, to the quality of the anchor and its ability to attract customers. Smaller stores pay higher rentals than the anchor, but you can't get money where there is none. If the traffic is poor, they won't survive. The ideal combination for maximum income is to include a national chain store and local tenants.

To complicate things further, the merchandizing of the centre must be sound. This is achieved by selecting a proper combination of tenants, based on their specialty and a complimentary mix of merchandising aligned with customers' needs and acceptance. A sound approach is to give very long-term leases to large, Triple A tenants, and short ones (1 to 3 years) to the small stores.

(e) Retail Rentals
Retail rentals are generally quoted per square metre (square foot) net plus Common-Area Maintenance (CAM). In retail buildings, CAM includes not only the maintenance (cleaning, repairs, etc.), but also every other expense in connection with the common areas, such as property taxes, security, building insurance, HVAC, parking lot, cleaning, etc. Most centres have a merchant's association in charge of public relations and promoting the centre. This is an additional cost borne by all tenants.

5.4 OFFICE BUILDINGS

Distinguish between the classes of office buildings and determine which would make an appropriate investment for you.

15.4.1 AN OVERVIEW
In principle, an office building is one used exclusively for offices, although in many cases, in heavily populated areas there may be retail stores on the main floor. Typical ceiling height will be 2.5-3 m (8-10 ft). Most office buildings, even with just two floors, have one or more elevators if they are large floors (large floor plate). Commonly, office buildings offer such features as broadloom, thermopane (multi-pane) windows, and air-conditioning. The majority of office buildings have multiple tenants.

For small buildings, office rentals are frequently quoted as gross, meaning the rental includes all additional expenses such as property taxes, CAM and building insurance, plus utilities and, frequently, office cleaning (janitorial service). If they are quoted on a net basis, the additional expenses usually are paid by the landlord but are recovered, generally at 100%, from the tenant.

These expenses can be very high. For example, an office building rental may be $161.50 per m² ($15 per sq ft) net and the expenses — frequently labelled "additional rent" by lawyers — may be $193 per m² ($18 per sq ft). Generally, this does not include parking, which can be as high as $120 to $300 per car per month for an underground parking space in a major city. There is almost never enough parking available with office buildings, except for suburban ones, where parking (commonly surface) is sometimes free — a major attraction for tenants.

As with all commercial properties, there are dozens of factors you must consider in purchasing an office property, as shown on Checklist 15.3.

Checklist 15.3
Acquisition Checklist for Office Building

ACQUISITION CHECKLIST FOR OFFICE BUILDING

Property address: _____

Type of property: _____

Square footage: Gross _____   Rentable_____   Usable_____

                     Number of Tenants_____ Class (A, B, C, D)_____   Building name _____

1- OWNERSHIP
- ❏ Owner's name
- ❏ Listed by
- ❏ Previously listed / how long / at what price
- ❏ Reason for disposition / degree of urgency

2- LOCATION
- ❏ Population of town
- ❏ Quality of address 1-5 (best)
- ❏ Quality of location 1-5 (best)
- ❏ Exposure
- ❏ Public transportation
- ❏ Amenities
- ❏ Proximity to freeways
- ❏ Potential changes in desirability of location
- ❏ Parking / on site / nearby
- ❏ Is area, neighbourhood, or street / deteriorating / improving / stable
- ❏ Competition

3- LAND
- ❏ Lot dimensions / size
- ❏ Coverage / density
- ❏ Zoning
- ❏ Legal description
- ❏ Easements / covenants
- ❏ Parking / number of cars / location / paving / condition
- ❏ Shipping / receiving facilities
- ❏ Landscaping
- ❏ Expansion / possible acquisition of extra land

4- BUILDING
- ❏ Square footage / frontage / depth / layout
- ❏ Number of stories or levels
- ❏ Size of floor plate
- ❏ Basement / foundations
- ❏ Use restrictions, if any
- ❏ Age of building
- ❏ Architectural appeal
- ❏ General condition / functional obsolescence / view
- ❏ Type of construction
- ❏ Type of entrance and lobby
- ❏ Exterior finish / condition
- ❏ Exterior signage / pilons / fascia
- ❏ Roof / type / condition / age
- ❏ Floors / condition / load capacity of each floor / coverings

- ❑ Type of windows / size / opening or not
- ❑ Ceiling type / height
- ❑ Electrical service / wiring / voltage, amperage
- ❑ Backup power generator make / type / capacity / fuel
- ❑ Toilet facilities / number and location
- ❑ Lighting / intensity level in foot candles at desk height / kind of fixtures / lamps
- ❑ Type of HVAC / age / condition / ventilation
- ❑ Sprinklers / fireproofing
- ❑ Energy retrofit
- ❑ Elevators / number / speed / service elevators
- ❑ Shipping and receiving facilities / loading dock(s) / how many / height
- ❑ Burglar alarm / special locks / security
- ❑ Storage facilities for tenants
- ❑ Special equipment
- ❑ Common facilities: meeting rooms, cafeteria, concierge, etc.
- ❑ Internet (T1, dial-up, high speed)
- ❑ Building rating within its class (1-5 best)
- ❑ Energy saving features / systems

5- INCOME

- ❑ Rent Roll / % of Triple A tenants
- ❑ Annual gross / net income
- ❑ Income from parking and others
- ❑ Yearly rental (net or gross?) per square foot
- ❑ Rents / higher / lower / similar to competition
- ❑ Tax escalation clause in leases
- ❑ Other terms of leases (including Option to Buy, Right of First Refusal)
- ❑ Management fee charged to tenants

6- EXPENSES

- ❑ Property taxes / date last appealed?
- ❑ Hazard, liability, and rental income insurance (classification) / coverage / premium
- ❑ Services
- ❑ Utilities
- ❑ Garbage collection
- ❑ Salaries / number of staff
- ❑ Janitor / window cleaning
- ❑ Maintenance / repairs / deferred maintenance / cost to remedy / reserve for replacements
- ❑ Leasing commissions payable
- ❑ Reserve for personal property items (e.g., fridges)
- ❑ Legal and accounting fees
- ❑ Others

7- EXISTING FINANCING

- ❑ Original mortgage amount / term / amortization / starting date / due date / balloon payment
- ❑ Mortgage(s) balance / as of what date
- ❑ Monthly payments / interest rate
- ❑ Annual debt service / interest payments / principal repayments
- ❑ Lender / address / phone / fax
- ❑ Loan number
- ❑ Prepayment penalty, and special provisions, if any
- ❑ Loan locked in / until when
- ❑ Transferable / assumption fee
- ❑ Any second loan? Can it be bought at a discount? If so, what discount?

8- POTENTIAL FINANCING

- ❑ Mortgage commitment / amount / interest / term / amortization / loan fee / loan points / lender
- ❑ Will Vendor take back a mortgage / amount / interest / due date

9- PRICE

- ❏ Asking price / total / per square foot and Cap Rate
- ❏ Price per m² (sq ft) of comparable buildings recently sold
- ❏ Estimated selling price and Cap Rate

10 – COMMUNITY

- ❏ Property tax system and assessment rules
- ❏ Closest police department / fire station
- ❏ Closest medical and hospital facilities
- ❏ Business amenities / banks / restaurants / various suppliers
- ❏ State of neighbourhood / stable / deteriorating / improving

11- EXHIBITS

- ❏ Survey / site plan
- ❏ Building floor plan
- ❏ Photographs
- ❏ Area map with property shown
- ❏ Inspection reports (pest control, building condition, environmental, roof, HVAC mechanical systems)
- ❏ Certified operating statements for last 3 years
- ❏ Copies of leases and rental agreements
- ❏ Copies of management contracts
- ❏ Inventory of personal property

NOTE: *Inspect property carefully. Talk to neighbours. The bulk of the outside information can be obtained from 3 major sources: Planning Department, Chamber of Commerce and Public Libraries.*

REMARKS:

15.4.2 OFFICE BUILDING CLASSIFICATIONS

Office buildings are classified into three main categories and evaluated on factors such as quality and maintenance of structure, elevator service, parking facilities, security systems, and building mechanics. The Durham Region Real Estate Board's Web site provides a good outline <www.durhamrealestate.org/resource_centre/tenants.htm>, researched in May 2007.

Office buildings are often referred to as "Class A" or "Class B" buildings. This is a good quick comparison tool to define the value of a quoted rental rate. A higher quality building commands a corresponding higher NET RENTAL rate. However the ADDITIONAL RENT component for a higher quality building may be similar to that of a nearby lower quality building thus representing better value for the tenant.

Class A Buildings

Distinct or prestige image due to its location, major tenant(s), architecture and landscaping, etc.
Stability of ownership and quality management services
High or highest quality materials and finishes throughout
Recent date of construction and state-of-the-art heating, air-conditioning and ventilation (HVAC), and advanced security systems
Sufficient high-speed elevators
Underground parking
Unique on-site amenities: ground floor retail, services and restaurants
Information desk
Larger than normal floor plates; column-free floors
High ratio of window to building fabric

Class B Buildings

Well located and managed
Better quality building materials and finishes
Somewhat older building (although many older buildings still remain Class A)
HVAC not state-of-the-art; good security system
Slower elevators, often not upgraded
Some on-site and tenant amenities
Often less than six storeys
Lower ratio of window to building fabric

Class C Buildings

Usually brick and mortar construction and less than 100,000 square feet
Not planned for today's telecommunications requirements
Slow elevators, or walk-up
Little or no security system
No underground parking: often no parking at all
Minimal on-site amenities
Less than four storeys (higher if urban)
Low ratio of window to building fabric

In large cities, class A and B buildings represent the bulk of the market, in terms of the number of buildings. This classification has been further expanded through familiar common usage (there are no formal rules, except on an international level) and one can now see some offices labelled AA, and even AAA. As usual, things can get further refined, and you will hear of A- or C+, etc. These lettered classes are used very frequently with office buildings, more rarely with multi-family buildings, and rarely with industrial or retail buildings.

15.4.3 LOCATION

Three locations have particular characteristics to bear in mind when choosing an office building location.

1. **Downtown Financial Core.** These buildings are close to large corporations' headquarters, libraries, government offices, and, frequently, universities, exclusive stores, banks, law firms, and financial institutions. They have excellent public transportation.
2. **Near an Airport.** This situation is important for people flying frequently. Being near an airport also has many of the advantages listed under suburbs.
3. **Suburbs.** These buildings are close to many workers' homes, which means there is less traffic to fight and frequently parking is free. They generally have a less imposing size and less expensive rental. Easy everyday shopping is close by as are freeways for easy access and excellent exposure.

Three locations have particular characteristics to bear in mind when choosing an office building location.

Ideally two very different types of housing are nearby — expensive to very expensive for the executives, and middle to low class for the staff.

15.4.4 LAND

In cities, most white-collar workers drive to work, but this varies greatly depending on the availability of convenient public transportation, particularly subways in large cities. If the building is located where workers can easily come to work by public transport, parking requirements will be lower on the priority list than for office buildings with inconvenient or no public transportation.

The parking ratio is based on a certain number of spaces per 95 m² (1,000 sq ft) of rentable office area, which includes washrooms, storage, corridors, lobbies, etc. If every employee drives to work, four to six parking spots per 95 m² will be required.

15.4.5 BUILDING EXTERIOR

The building must be attractive or it must be possible to make it attractive at a reasonable cost. Some buildings are poorly designed, poorly situated on the site, and cannot be made appealing, economically. The following suggestions are aimed at the upper end of office buildings, but it is reasonable to use select ideas for class B or C buildings too.

As with most things in life, the owner of an office building must consider the following points:
- the cost of a given feature, and
- the benefit the feature will bring to the building.

As a fantastical example, if an owner aims at the top end of users, he may consider having the doors of the main entrance and the elevators made of solid gold. Such a building will receive tremendous public relations reviews and, as such, will attract prestigious tenants. However, the extra rental achievable will not be sufficient to justify the many millions of dollars that the doors will cost. Therefore, the typical approach used by developers is to build a quality building that is functional, but as inexpensive as possible, then to add luxurious touches (such as gold plated front door handles).

Typically, a class A office building wants to make a visual impact from a certain distance (90-900 m (300-3,000 ft)) for drivers and from a few metres for pedestrians (or drivers in congested downtown streets). There are two different approaches to achieve this effect. For distance viewing the best material (in fact, colour) to use is white, such as the marble used on First Canadian Place in Toronto (but it does get dirty and is costly to clean). It is not the material that creates the visual impact, it is the colour. The other way to achieve a visual impact is to use coloured glass windows, such as the Royal Bank of Canada did, across the street from First Canadian Place. To impress the pedestrian, materials (marble, granite, even stainless steel) do a good job and need not go above the three or four lower floors.

The name of the building should be prominent, extremely well designed, made of expensive material, and well illuminated at night. In fact, all building signage should be well designed and homogenous (for example only one sort of material or typeface).

Finally, lobbies are often closed in with large expanses of glass, so lobby counters, seats, and wall treatments (e.g., expensive hand-woven carpets) should reflect and even surpass the class of the building. Benches for convenience and statues or other *objets d'art* for aesthetic pleasure, placed just in front of the building, contribute powerfully to the image it projects.

15.4.6 BUILDING INTERIOR

The average area used by an office worker can be as low as 7.5 m^2 (80 sq ft) where cubicles are cramped and as high as 28-37 m^2 (300-400 sq ft) in a situation with many managers and executives and few staff. The average is 14-23 m^2 (150-250 sq ft), although this has come down in the last few years. But beyond space, there are many details to be concerned about with office building interiors.

(a) Air Quality

Most modern office buildings, particularly high-rises, have windows that cannot be opened. Despite sophisticated ventilation systems, the air quality can be sub-par and some sensitive people suffer from it, which can lead to more serious problems, such as mold and subsequent fights with unions.

(b) HVAC Units

Some office buildings have low Heating, Ventilating, and Air-Conditioning (HVAC) units that protrude inside beyond the outside walls up to 46 cm (18 in) and run around the perimeter of the building, under the windows. This is an awful waste. An office that measures 26 m^2 (280 sq ft) will have 6 m (20 ft) of windows and 2.8 m^2 (30 sq ft) or 11% of space wasted by these units. If the total occupancy costs are $375 per m^2 ($35 per sq ft), this wasted space is costing $1,050 per year for this office alone.

(c) Elevators

Some buildings, particularly class B and C, do not have enough elevators at peak hours. Elevators are costly to install, but they cost even more in maintenance contracts, which are compulsory in most jurisdictions. In Toronto, it amounts to $200 to $500 per month per elevator or more, depending on the number of floors.

Virtually all landlords have an elevator maintenance contract with a specialized company for several of the following reasons:

- liability
- reliability of service, and
- cost of repairs (the replacement of an elevator motor can cost $15,000 to $25,000). If a complete modernization (cabin, mechanical, and control components) is required, your bank account will be lowered by $75,000 to $150,000. On the plus side, considerable energy savings (up to 40%) can be achieved with a retrofit and waiting times reduced by up to 25%.

(d) Corner Protectors

There are plenty of corridors in buildings and, therefore, corners. These should be protected with corner protectors against damage by delivery carts, movers, etc. The stronger angle protectors are made of stainless steel. If you object to the appearance, you may use self-adhesive transparent plastic protectors, but they are far less durable.

15.4.7 ZONING

By checking the zoning, you may discover that different and more remunerative uses of a building, for example one currently used as an office, are permitted, such as retail stores on main floors, mezzanines, or even basements.

15.5 MULTI-FAMILY BUILDINGS

Inspect a multi-family building and know which factors to improve in order to attract desirable tenants.

15.5.1 AN OVERVIEW

Multi-family buildings can range from low (one to four storeys) to very tall (30 to 40 stories, or even more) and from apartment buildings, to townhouses, to garden homes. To be called multi-family, a complex would have to comprise over three units (a two-unit building is called a duplex). Residential condominium buildings are multi-family, but the form of ownership falls into a different category. Small multi-family buildings (from 3 to 12 units) are frequently called "x"-plex. For example, a six-apartment building will be called a "six-plex". Checklist 15.4 shows the dozens of factors that must be considered before purchasing a multi-family building.

Checklist 15.4
Acquisition Checklist for Multi-Family Building

ACQUISITION CHECKLIST FOR MULTI-FAMILY BUILDING

Property address: _____

Number of units: _____

1- OWNERSHIP

- ☐ Owner's name
- ☐ Listed by
- ☐ Previously listed / how long / at what price
- ☐ Reason for disposition / degree of urgency

2- LOCATION

- ☐ Population of town
- ☐ Proximity to Downtown / employment (type) / schools / shopping
- ☐ Public transportation
- ☐ Access to street, arterial roads, distance to closest freeways, etc
- ☐ Nearby amenities
- ☐ Area recreational facilities
- ☐ Location rating: 1 to 5 (best)
- ☐ Is area, neighbourhood, or street / deteriorating/improving/stable

3- LAND

- ☐ Lot dimensions / size
- ☐ Zoning
- ☐ Legal description
- ☐ Parking: surface #... underground #...Total...
- ☐ Lawn sprinklers
- ☐ Condition of grounds
- ☐ Expansion potential

4- BUILDING

- ☐ Builder's name
- ☐ Age of building / roof
- ☐ Number of stories
- ☐ Type of construction
- ☐ Square footage
- ☐ Floor plate area
- ☐ Type of roof / condition / age
- ☐ Exterior finish / condition
- ☐ Basement / foundations
- ☐ Storage lockers
- ☐ Laundry facilities (owned / leased)
- ☐ Garbage chutes
- ☐ Elevators
- ☐ Individual meters - gas / electricity
- ☐ Wiring / type / condition
- ☐ Backup power generator make / type / capacity / fuel
- ☐ Plumbing (copper / galvanized) / condition
- ☐ Heating / type / age / condition
- ☐ Air-conditioning / age / condition
- ☐ Sprinklers and fireproofing system
- ☐ Interior corridors / type of floor covering / condition
- ☐ Is property up-to-date regarding government regulations: fire, etc.
- ☐ Deferred maintenance
- ☐ Internet (dial-up, high speed)

❑ TV cable
❑ Energy saving / features / systems

5- APARTMENTS

❑ # of each type: bachelor / ....1BR / ....2BR / ....3BR   OTHER.............   Total:..........
❑ Views / number of suites with / quality of
❑ Broadloom
❑ Drapes
❑ Stoves / built-in / condition / age
❑ Refrigerators / brands / condition / age
❑ Dishwashers / brands / condition / age
❑ Garbage disposals
❑ Bathrooms / tubs / showers over tub / stall showers
❑ Storage space and closets
❑ Intercom system
❑ Cable TV / Satellite dish / cost / paid by
❑ Decks, balconies, patios
❑ Condition of apartments: 1 to 5 (best)
❑ Size of rooms (large / average / small)
❑ Quality of interior finishes (deluxe / average / economy)
❑ Typical occupants / families / couples / singles / age groups / occupation / economic level

6- RENTALS

❑ Using 2 to 3 apartments of each type, show: apartment number, number of bedrooms, number of bathrooms, rent per month / per square foot, square footage, and potential rental (if logical)
❑ Scheduled annual gross income
❑ Vacancies & Bad Debts, in $
❑ Vacancy factor in percent of annual gross income
❑ Income from garages and/or laundry and/or _____
❑ Last 3 year audited rental income statements
❑ Are rents comparable, higher or lower than average rents of similar units in neighbourhood?
❑ Possible conversion to condos?

7- EXPENSES

❑ Property taxes / date last appealed?
❑ Hazard insurance: premium / coverage
❑ Liability insurance: premium / coverage
❑ Rental income insurance
❑ Electricity
❑ Gas
❑ Water
❑ Sewer charge
❑ Garbage collection
❑ Elevator maintenance service
❑ Pool maintenance service
❑ Janitor and/or gardener
❑ Resident caretaker / salary or rent allowance
❑ Rental agent / salary or rent allowance
❑ Legal and accounting fees
❑ Administrative expenses / salaries
❑ Reserves: maintenance / repairs / replacements
❑ Maintenance: Are there signs of substandard maintenance / what needs to be done soon / cost?
❑ Reserve for replacement of personal property / what needs to be replaced soon / cost?
❑ Are expenses in keeping with similar buildings in the neighbourhood?

8- EXISTING FINANCING

❑ Original mortgage amount / term / amortization starting date
❑ Due date / balloon payment
❑ Mortgage(s) balance / as of what date
❑ Monthly payments
❑ Interest rate and due date

❏ Annual debt service / interest payments / principal repayments
❏ Lender / address / phone / fax
❏ Loan number
❏ Prepayment penalty, and special provisions, if any
❏ Loan locked in / until when
❏ Is loan transferable / assumption fee?
❏ If there is a second loan? Can it be bought at a discount / if so, what discount?

9- POTENTIAL FINANCING

❏ Loan commitment / amount / interest / term / payments / loan fee / loan points / lender
❏ Will Vendor take back a mortgage / amount / interest / due date

10- RETURN FOR FIRST YEAR

Scheduled and additional (garages, laundry) Annual Income
❏ Less   Vacancy and bad debt allowance
❏ Equals   Gross Operating Income
❏ Less   Operating Costs
❏ Equals   Net Operating Income
❏ Less   Annual Debt Service (payments on principal and interest)
❏ Equals   Cash flow (gross spendable income)
❏ Plus   Annual principal payments
❏ Equals   ROE

11- NEIGHBOURHOOD AND MARKET ANALYSIS

❏ Determine boundaries of neighbourhood and analyze it
❏ Economic level of people in area (typical occupations)
❏ Average income / per family / per person
❏ Typical family size
❏ Ratio of homeowners to tenants
❏ Population growth / past 5 years / projected
❏ Number of competitive apartment buildings within neighbourhood / # of apartments
❏ Rents in comparable buildings
❏ Cap Rates of comparable properties recently sold
❏ State of neighbourhood / stable / deteriorating / improving

12- PRICE

❏ Asking price, Cap Rate
❏ Likely sale price, Cap Rate
❏ Income / *Be aware of higher than average rents due to excellent management, special deals on leases, or expenses kept artificially low, and of lower than average rents due to poor management*

13 – COMMUNITY

❏ Property tax system and assessment rules
❏ Closest police department / fire station
❏ Closest medical and hospital facilities
❏ Shopping amenities / supermarkets / banks / restaurants / various
❏ State of neighbourhood / stable / deteriorating / improving

14- EXHIBITS

❏ Survey / site plan
❏ Floor plans
❏ Photographs / ground / aerial
❏ Area map with property shown
❏ Rent rolls
❏ Inspection reports (pest control, roof, building condition, environmental, mechanical systems, elevators, etc.)
❏ Certified operating statements for last 3 years
❏ Copies of leases and rental agreements
❏ Copies of management contracts
❏ Inventory of personal property

NOTE: *Inspect property carefully. Talk to neighbours and to a few tenants. The bulk of outside information can be obtained from 4 major sources: Planning Department, Chamber of Commerce, CMHC (Central Mortgage and Housing Corporation (in Canada)) and Public Libraries.*

For multi-family buildings, the rentals are quoted per unit per month gross, meaning that all expenses are included in the rent, except when the tenants pay for their own utilities, thanks to sub-metering. To check the accuracy of the rents, some buyers calculate the rent per month per area. For example, rent: $885/67 m² (720 sq ft) = $13.21 per m² ($1.23 per sq ft) (gross, of course).

The main advantage of owning multi-family buildings is that the risk for the investor is very low in comparison to single-tenant properties. This is due to the number of tenants. Frequently, however, the credit rating of the tenants is also low. An investor must be very cautious, organized, and alert to avoid being taken advantage of by some tenants. In addition, property management needs are much more intensive than in any other class of real estate investments.

On the other hand, one is virtually assured of yearly rental increases. (For example, the Ontario government ruled that in 2002 the increase would be 3.0%; in 2003, 2.9%; in 2004, 2.09%; in 2005, 1.5%; in 2006, 2.1%; and in 2007, 2.7%.) Industrial, office, or retail rental increases take place only at lease renewal time (usually every five years), unless you are able to negotiate some periodical increases.

We believe that a common mistake on the part of some residential landlords is that they think tenants want the following and in this order: a roof over their head and four walls around them, a decent level of comfort (cleanliness, no roof leaks, hot water, parking, etc.), and reasonable to low rental rates. In our opinion most tenants are looking for the following, in order of priority: a roof over their head and four walls around them, a decent level of comfort

Most tenants are looking a roof over their head and four walls around them, a decent level of comfort, ego flattering features, and an almost reasonable rental rate.

(cleanliness, no roof leaks, hot water, parking, etc.), ego flattering features, and an almost reasonable rental rate.

The significant difference is in the ego business, at least in middle and upper class buildings. The ego can be stroked, for example, by way of quasi or outright luxurious lobbies with fancy lighting, wall décor or hangings, plenty of mirrors, the presence of a concierge, etc., or by the individualized treatment of every apartment entrance door. For example, instead of a plain door, you could apply a three-dimensional wood sculpture or some nice moulding. In addition to the apartment number, you could paint or apply the tenant's name, so that he can explain to a friend: "My suite is #211; my name's on the door." These types of extras are usually paid for by the tenants with pleasure, when they are about to sign the lease, if they are shown the end result beforehand on other apartment doors or with a computer rendering.

The basic philosophy of the two approaches is totally different: one is to provide shelter, while the second one is to make each tenant proud of living in that particular building. You can imagine similar approaches used with other types of properties.

15.5.2 LOCATION
Some of the same factors regarding location are considered for multi-family buildings as for all other types of properties, but the criteria are different.

(a) Public Transportation
Multi-family buildings should be located close to public transportation, near shopping (at least a supermarket) and close to places of employment. You want to avoid main arteries with heavy (and noisy) vehicular traffic. Many tenants are willing to pay more for a quiet environment; however, it does help if the building is within minutes of a freeway.

(b) Community Amenities

A building will be more desirable if it is within easy walking distance of a community centre, tennis courts, churches, a park, etc., as well as schools (primary and secondary) if you have apartments with several bedrooms. Proximity to water (a lake, river, ocean) also adds desirability for many people.

15.5.3 LAND

Sufficient parking is the major factor to consider when evaluating the land use for a residential building, but other amenities can attract more desirable tenants.

(a) Parking

There should be parking spaces in sufficient number for tenants and for visitors. This is often not the case. The ratio, that is the number of parking spaces per apartment, varies with the level of luxury and type of apartments (one bedroom, two bedrooms, three bedrooms) and the requirements of the municipal zoning by-law.

(b) Underground Parking

If there is underground parking, make sure that before you buy such a building you check the condition of the parking structure. Up to a few years ago, particularly in cold countries such as Canada or the northern US, when concrete floors of parking garage structures were poured during winter months, additives frequently were mixed with the cement in order to prevent it from freezing. Many of these additives were salt based that, over many years, led to corrosion of the reinforcing steel bars (rebar) inside the concrete. Also, the surface of any multi-level parking garage should be treated so that it is impervious to water and salt, if any is used in that area. To avoid this problem today, contractors use epoxy coated rebar, galvanized rebar, or stainless steel rebar.

(c) Other Amenities

There are a number of other amenities that make an apartment more attractive to tenants, including things as simple and inexpensive as picnic tables. If the property allows it, it is ideal to have a few picnic tables and bar-becues on the lawn. It is even more ideal if there are trees to protect tenants from the sun. People will also pay a premium for a view, particularly over greenery and water. In fact, rentals or prices for suites with a view increase with the height of the apartment or condominium.

15.5.4 BUILDING EXTERIOR

The exterior of a multi-family building needs to include practical, safe, and pleasing features.

(a) Balconies

If there are balconies, it is ideal that the vertical portion, facing the street, be made of either solid material or translucent (not transparent) glass with a space of no more than 2.5 cm (1 in) between the floor of the balcony and the fronting. Most apartment dwellers use their balcony as storage and it makes for unsightly views and, as a consequence, detracts from the aesthetic appeal of the building. A further improvement, pioneered by a Finnish company, is a retractable glazing system that permits enclosing balconies. The safety glass panels can be partially or completely opened, as desired.

(b) Access Control System

The building should have an electrically controlled front door latch so that strangers cannot walk in (unless, of course, they follow right on the heels of a tenant). It is ideal that there be an intercom system allowing the visitor to call a tenant and announce himself in order to have the door opened.

(c) Safety

A useful and very reassuring feature is a network of surveillance cameras.

(d) Name

All apartment buildings should have an attractive, intelligent, and easily remembered name.

15.5.5 BUILDING INTERIOR

While you will want to be able to check on the condition of individual units, the areas that will concern you most in a multi-family building will be the common areas. You want to see if these areas are practical, need work, or allow for renovations, such as the addition of a laundry room.

(a) Lobby

An attractive lobby is a big asset to an apartment building, as is a concierge/security guard, if the size of the building justifies it.

(b) Building Amenities

There are many amenities that can be added to a building in order to attract tenants.

- **Fitness Centre.** If the building's size can justify it, a fitness room attracts many tenants, even if it is small and equipped with only a few treadmills and exercise bikes. Since many tenants will not use it more than four times per year, the upkeep is minimal.
- **Party Room.** Again, if the building is large enough to permit it, a party room will attract tenants.
- **Swimming Pool.** A swimming pool is usually considered an asset to attract tenants, however, it presents a number of concerns for a landlord. If it is outdoors, it can be used only a few months of the year in northern climates and becomes a costly expense. This frequently means it is poorly maintained. If indoors, a pool is expensive to maintain and can cause corrosion and humidity in the building. It also drives up insurance rates because of public liability, which is why diving boards are often eliminated.

(c) Hallways

Hallway appearance is difficult to treat in a building. In a large building, they can be very long and almost unpleasant. Quality broadloom design, painting, and lighting can make a big difference. Most buildings use very low wattage, incandescent bulbs in their hallways and the result is poor. It is much better to use energy efficient fluorescent lamps of sufficient wattage, which give off a brighter light at a lower cost.

(d) Utilities

Ideally, as a landlord you want each apartment to have separate electrical and gas meters. Insulation, for both temperature and noise, should have good values.

5.5.6 OTHER FACTORS FOR CONSIDERATION

(a) Walk-up Buildings

Buildings of two, three, or four storeys that are not equipped with elevators are called "walk-ups". They are much less desirable than buildings with elevators because they are usually older and physically challenged people and the elderly cannot rent the upper floor apartments.

(b) Suite Mix

The ideal mix of suites (e.g., one bedroom, two bedrooms, etc.) will vary with the type and location of the building. Most landlords prefer a large majority of two-bedroom units. However, suites can range from mini-bachelors (32.5 m^2 +/- (350 sq ft)) to four bedrooms, which are rare. Most commonly, in apartment buildings one finds one- and two-bedroom suites. If you are considering buying a building, find out the average area of the suites. Some older apartments have huge suites, while some newer suites are so small that one can hardly put a chair in the bedroom.

15.6 COMPARING THE TYPES OF INCOME-PRODUCING PROPERTIES

Compare and contrast the principal factors for investing in the various types of income-producing properties.

There are advantages and disadvantages to investing in each type of commercial property. Figure 15.1 notes a number of factors to be considered before deciding which property type appeals most to you. The explanation of these factors that follows will help to clarify the rankings on the chart.

1. **Management Intensity.** The greater the number of tenants in a property, *Generally, the greater the number of tenants in a property, the more work is required.* the more property management is required. While there is a fixed amount of work for each property, such as paying property taxes, insurance, and utilities, a certain amount varies according to the number of tenants. A multi-family property with 100 tenants will require many more hours of work that an industrial building leased to one tenant. Another factor is that residential tenants move frequently.

2. **Risk Level.** In case of economic downturn, people still need to live somewhere, so a multi-family landlord will not suffer too much. However, tenants in an office building will behave very differently. They may reduce their staff and tell the landlord, "The lease for our 930 m^2 (10,000 sq ft) space is up in 18 months. Now, we need only 370 m^2 (4,000 sq ft). We want to start paying on that basis now, and we will extend the lease for another 3 years. If you do not accept this, we will move out in 18 months." Or, they may choose to leave the building and move to a class B or C building, negotiating a penalty with the landlord or letting him sue them. Others will say to the landlord, "Times are tough. We are paying $270 per m^2 ($25 per sq ft) net. If you do not want us to declare bankruptcy, you will need to reduce the rent to $110 per m^2 ($10 per sq ft)."

Figure 15.1
Advantages and Disadvantages of Types of Properties

Scale: 1 to 5 (5 being highest, or most important)

#	Factor	Industrial	Retail	Office	Multi-family
1	Management Intensity	1	3	4	5
2	Risk Level	3	4	5	1
3	Level of Real Estate Sophistication	3	5	4	2
4	Stability of Income	3	4	3	5
5	Returns	3	4	4	2
6	Legal Complexity	3	5	5	2
7	Difficulty of Entry	2	2	3	1
8	Tenant Turnover	3	2	3	5
9	Sensitivity of Location	3	5	4	1
10	Public Transportation Requirements	2	3	4	5
11	Highway Access	4	3	4	1
12	Cash Required (LTV ratio)	4	3	3	1
13	Expenses Incurred for Leasing	2	4	4	1
14	Proximity to Airport	4	1	4	1
15	Government Controls	2	3	3	5
16	Wear and Tear on the Property	4	3	3	2
17	Level of Due Diligence Required	3	4	4	2
18	Environmental Risks	5	3	2	1
19	Liquidity	2	4	3	5

3. **Level of Real Estate Sophistication.** Managing a retail centre of more than a few hundred square metres requires more sophistication than managing a multi-family building. Skill as a landlord as well as retail knowledge are required, including knowing how to carefully select tenants to achieve the optimum merchandising mix; set price point levels; ensure little overlap of merchandise among merchants; design great signage; work with a merchants' association; design common advertising; and understand sophisticated leases.

4. **Stability of Income.** As explained earlier, for multi-family buildings, the greater the number of tenants, the more stable the income. It is quite stable in retail, too, because retailers are loath to move if business is good, whereas most office and industrial tenants move relatively easily.

5. **Returns.** Returns, in good or average times, will be higher with retail and office properties due to the factors explained in #3 above.

6. **Legal Complexity.** Retail and office leases are the most complicated. Those for multi-family buildings are simple.

7. **Difficulty of Entry.** It is possible to buy small multi-family buildings, but it is very difficult to find small office, retail, or industrial properties.

8. **Tenant Turnover.** Most residential tenants, as mentioned earlier, move easily. A pick-up truck and a Saturday is all most of them need. It is much more complicated, disruptive, and costly for a retailer to move.

9. **Sensitivity of Location.** To be successful, a retail centre must be in a good location. Multi-family buildings can be, and are, located almost everywhere.

10. **Public Transportation.** It is mainly residential tenants who use public transportation, followed closely by office and residential workers. It helps for an industrial building to be located near public transportation, but for most companies it is not a crucial factor, particularly now that a great deal of labour-intensive manufacturing is done overseas.

11. **Highway Access.** Industrialists love to be in close proximity to highways. Office users like it too, but it is not a big factor for residential tenants.

12. **Cash Required (LTV ratio).** Because multi-family properties are easier to finance, an investor can buy his first property with less money than is required for other types of income producing properties.

13. **Expenses Incurred for Leasing.** Complicated leases cost money. We have seen a situation where a tenant negotiating a lease took an exceptional and erroneous position in connection with an insurance clause. It cost the landlord an extra $25,000 in lawyer's fees.

14. **Proximity to Airport.** Retailers and residential tenants do not care how far they are from an airport. Industrial, and even more so, office tenants do.

15. **Government Controls.** Rent controls and residential tenants' rights are two reasons some investors refuse to buy multi-family buildings.

16. **Wear and Tear.** Some industrial buildings (far from the majority) accommodate some uses that can be rough on the building, resulting in major renovating expenses for the landlord when the tenant leaves.

17. **Level of Due Diligence Required.** When buying a property, details are more numerous and complicated in retail and office properties.

18. **Environmental Risks.** Multi-family users are not a source of contamination, but industrial buildings can be. Only a few retailers are a source of contamination (dry cleaners, for example).

19. **Liquidity.** Multi-family buildings are the easiest class of properties to sell with some industrial ones being the most difficult.

A multi-family property appears to be the winner in this figure, based on the risk level, relatively low level of real estate sophistication required, stability of income, potential high Loan-to-Value (LTV) ratio, the greater ease to secure financing, very low risk due to the large number of tenants, and ease of selling. However, this property type has a number of major drawbacks, as follows:

- it is management intensive, often having to do with myriads of minor details
- it is subject to rent controls, hence limiting the landlord's control of tenant abuses
- it has high tenant turnover, relative to the other types of properties, and
- most tenants are far from being financially strong.

Figure 15.2 shows the impact that various LTV ratios and management fees have on the Return on Equity (ROE) for multi-family and other IPPs. Again, the winner is the multi-family building with a LTV ratio of 85% and a 57% ROE. The laggards are other IPPs with 23.90% ROE. However, keep in mind that this is simply a financial picture for a number of situations. Many investors put greater weight on some of the other factors in Figure 15.2 when making their investment decisions.

Figure 15.2

Financial Analysis of Types of Properties

	LTV Loan	CMHC fee	Total mortgage amount	Mtge rate nominal real[1]	Mortgage Payments (int. only)	Less management fee[2]	Plus 15% mgt fee charged on additional rent	Cash flow ROE	Appreciation (6%)	Total (ROE)
Note: These expenses disregard legal fees, land transfer tax, and financing fees.										
Property Value: $1,000,000, 8% Cap Rate ($80,000) - Mortgage: 10-year term										
Multi-family - 1	85%	4.50%		5.50%	$48,875	on $140,000	N/A	$25,525	$60,000	$85,525
	$850,000	$38,250	$888,250	5.75%		= $5,600		17.02%		57%
Multi-family - 2	75%	2.25%		5.50%	$42,178	on $140,000	N/A	$32,222	$60,000	$92,222
	$750,000	$16,875	$766,875	5.62%		= $5,600		12.89%		36.89%

However, the above is not quite correct because the NOI on multi-family is at least 1% lower. Therefore #3 & #4 must be studied, too.

Property Value: $1,000,000, 7% Cap Rate ($70,000) - Mortgage: 10-year term

	LTV Loan	CMHC fee	Total mortgage amount	Mtge rate nominal real[1]	Mortgage Payments (int. only)	Less management fee[2]	Plus 15% mgt fee charged on additional rent	Cash flow ROE	Appreciation (6%)	Total (ROE)
Multi-family - 3	85%	4.50%	$888,250	5.50%	$48,875	on $140,000	N/A	$15,525	$60,000	$75,525
	$850,000	$38,250		5.75%		= $5,600		10.35%		50.35%
Multi-family - 4	75%	2.25%	$766,875	5.50%	$42,178	on $140,000	N/A	$22,222	$60,000	$82,222
	$750,000	$16,875		5.62%		= $5,600		8.89%		32.89%
Other IPP's - 1	75%[3]	N/A		6%	$45,000	on $20,000	$3,000	$35,600	$60,000	$95,600
	$750,000		$750,000			= $2,400		14.24%		38.24%
Other IPP's - 2	60%[4]	N/A		6%	$45,000	on $20,000	$3,000	$35,600	$60,000	$95,600
	$600,000		$600,000			= $2,400		8.90%		23.90%

[1] Includes CMHC insurance premium, which is expected to decline.
[2] The management fee is on the gross income - 4% on residential, 2% on industrial
[3] Recourse loan
[4] Non-recourse loan

15.7 INVESTMENT PROPERTY DATABANK (IPD)

Appreciate the information and analysis IPD can provide.

The Investment Property Databank (IPD) is an interesting tool for comparing large properties available to big investment companies. It shows the total return, income return, and capital growth. It was created to provide property owners with an industry measurement against which they can compare the returns they achieve on their investments and evaluate their performance. The IPD annual database is the most reliable benchmark of direct property performance in the 20 countries it covers. (See <www.ipindex.co.uk/results/indices/canada/index_canada.asp>.)

IPD is a London (UK)-based corporation that collects, analyzes, and publishes data to direct investments in property. IPD services outside the UK are run in conjunction with partner organizations in each country. In Canada, IPD's partner is Clayton Research. Although IPD's clients are mainly pension and life fund companies, smaller investors should fare as well, if not better, consulting it.

CHAPTER 16

Buying and Selling

By the end of this chapter, you will be able to:

- Investigate location, financing, and timing, as well as other factors, to buy a solid investment property.
- Make a realistic Offer to Purchase having performed your due diligence, understood the concept of conditions, and gotten to know the vendor.
- Win most negotiations with vendors by focusing on the issues, remaining unemotional, and preparing wisely.
- Project the additional expenses involved in closing the deal.
- Navigate the many steps to finalize your purchase, including completing and registering the various forms and documents.
- Understand the implications of not performing an environmental site assessment and know the phases and responsibilities involved.
- Be aware of the availability of contamination clean-up insurance.
- Make the shift to the vendor's side of the table and consider the unique details of the vendor's world.
- See the advantages of the Lease-Purchase Option for both the tenant/buyer and landlord/vendor.
- Project costs and benefits with the aid of four investing scenarios.

Buying and selling are two sides of the same coin, meaning you need to assess market conditions and compare other properties on the market to determine the value of a property, whether you are buying or selling. If you have a thorough understanding of buying, you can transfer that knowledge across to selling, which is why most of this chapter deals with buying. However, this doesn't mean that all wise buyers are wise vendors. Rational thinking goes out the window for many when they become vendors, so we have also included some advice on how to maximize your selling price.

16.1 BUYING A SOLID INVESTMENT PROPERTY

Investigate location, financing, and timing, as well as other factors, to buy a solid investment property.

You have now decided in which type of property you are interested in investing, in which geographical area(s), and how much you are prepared to spend. You are working with a knowledgeable real estate agent that you trust and have an experienced lawyer on your team of professional advisors. Keep in mind that it is important to use the right lawyer for the right situation. There are lawyers who specialize in real estate in general, retail leasing, land development, municipal law, corporate law, residential transactions, libel, and many other areas of the law. You need a lawyer who specializes in the type of commercial real estate in which you are dealing. The best way to find the right lawyer is to ask a lawyer you know or a business associate for a reference.

Although, at times, you may be tempted to work without a lawyer because of the expense involved in retaining one, not using a lawyer is false economy. There are too many unpredictable people out there and our society is very litigious. View your lawyer as an insurance premium — an expensive, but necessary, insurance premium.

In a perfect world, choosing a good property for investment would be a simple matter of intelligence backed by knowledge. Unfortunately, it is not that easy because no two properties are identical, there are a myriad of details to consider, and there are a number of factors beyond your control that influence success. In the end, you must make your decisions based on the best information you can gather about the property at the time, with consideration of the current and anticipated social, economic, and political events that may influence the market. In other words, when you buy a property there is always a certain amount of uncertainty.

At the same time, you should keep in mind that no property is ever perfect, and if you keep waiting for the perfect property, you will never get started as a real estate investor. You always have to compromise on something that is on your list of desired features and accept some you would prefer not to have.

Your first step is obviously to find properties for sale. To refresh your memory on how to go about it and of what to be mindful, you may want to refer to Chapter 13 (Real Estate Agencies), and Chapter 15 (Points to Consider Before Buying Each Property Type). To make your life easier, you should use the Data Gathering Checklist (Checklist 16.1) every time you receive information. Using this checklist for each property will keep you organized during the information-gathering process.

If you don't use this form, or a similar one, you will end up with the data for each property under consideration being presented differently, making comparison difficult. Another advantage of this form is that it reminds you to ask the proper questions.

After a few days, you will want to separate your Data Gathering Checklists into two piles — interesting and not interesting. Take the interesting pile and, using the Property Analysis Checklist (Checklist 16.2), gather as much additional information as possible for each property. This will increase your knowledge of each property so that you will be comparing apples to apples. This second checklist will help you narrow your search to the few properties that you think will merit further investigation.

Given the number of factors that are specific to each particular type of property (as discussed in Chapter 15), you will appreciate why the wise investor works with real estate professionals who are specialists in the property type and areas in which the investor is trying to buy. That said, there are still a number of factors that generally go through the mind of sophisticated investors who are considering the purchase of an investment property.

16.1.1 FACTORS TO CONSIDER WHEN BUYING

A wise investor will avoid a property having one or more of the following drawbacks, unless the price is exceptionally attractive:

- next to a freeway, railroad tracks, high tension (power) electrical lines
- risk of flooding, stemming from the relative proximity to a river or the inability of the sewers to evacuate all the water, in case of a torrential rain (this refers to underground apartments, garages, or basements)
- in a deteriorating neighbourhood
- in, or near, a high crime area
- near an industrial area, unless you are buying an industrial property
- near a source of odour or noise, such as the back of a large retail store or not far from a wind turbine
- in a neighbourhood with poorly maintained public roads
- with exceptionally high property taxes
- on a dead-end street (poor for industrial or commercial uses, but ideal for multi-family)
- with any major structural problems, such as failing foundations, and
- with no or too little parking.

You should watch for properties that offer the following desirable qualities:

- opportunity to improve income from the property or add value to it, for example, by turning one three-bedroom apartment into two one-bedroom apartments
- potential to convert usage from one use to a more desirable use, such as from industrial to office or retail
- extra land for expansion
- opportunity for renovations
- opportunity for additional income, for example, by adding a laundry room in a multi-family building
- in a hot rental market with low-rental leases expiring soon (commercial, retail, and industrial)
- opportunity to improve tenant mix and merchandising mix in retail plazas
- opportunity for, and benefits of, an energy retrofit
- visual appeal suited to the expected use
- appropriate traffic flow for the contemplated use, access to transportation, freeways, etc.
- quality construction, structurally sound
- low down payment required (usually), and
- good existing or potential mortgage terms.

Checklist 16.1
Data Gathering Checklist

DATA GATHERING CHECKLIST

Property Address: _____

Listed with:_____   Tel: _____

1- Land:
- ☐ Dimensions
- ☐ Area
- ☐ Access
- ☐ Drainage
- ☐ Sunlight
- ☐ Services
- ☐ Survey
- ☐ Environmental condition

2- Building:
- ☐ Dimensions
- ☐ Area
- ☐ Construction (brick, frame, other)
- ☐ Number of stories
- ☐ Basement (height and access)
- ☐ Units (#, type, area)
- ☐ Present vacancies
- ☐ Physical condition
- ☐ Work needed
- ☐ Anything unique?
- ☐ Fire retrofit (multi-family)

3- Transportation:
- ☐ Traffic count
- ☐ Exposure
- ☐ Transportation
    - Public
    - Freeway within: minutes;   km/miles

4- Others
- ☐ Appliances (type, brand, condition, age)
- ☐ What work needs to be done?
- ☐ How much would it cost?
- ☐ What would you do, or change, if you bought it? At what cost?
- ☐ Who are the immediate neighbors? Anything negative (odor, noise, light)?
- ☐ Is it offered at a very firm price?
- ☐ How was the price arrived at?
- ☐ Why is the vendor selling?

Checklist 16.2
Property Analysis Checklist

PROPERTY ANALYSIS CHECKLIST

A checklist is a terrific tool that is useless if it is not used

[Rate all 1 to 5 (best) – attach listing and Data Sheet if you have a copy of them]

Building/Owner's Name:_____   Date: _____

Property Address: _____

Gross Building Area: _____   Land Area: _____   Type of IPP: _____

1- IN BRIEF
- ❑ Visual appeal
- ❑ Gut feeling (am I turned on?)
- ❑ Neighbourhood
- ❑ Building condition
- ❑ Parking
- ❑ Usability
- ❑ Address
- ❑ Exposure
- ❑ Ease of division
- ❑ Traffic count (if retail)

2- ANALYSIS
- ❑ What is good with the property (what turns me on)
- ❑ What is bad with the property (what worries me, is dangerous)
- ❑ What are the "unique selling propositions" (the something(s) special)
- ❑ What is the worst that can happen
- ❑ Best uses
- ❑ What will we do once we own, or control, the property
- ❑ Upsides
- ❑ What are our ways out of the deal
- ❑ Overall rating

3- HISTORY OF THE PROPERTY AND COMMENTS

4- UPSIDE CHECKLIST
- ❑ Extra land (how much)
- ❑ Forthcoming change (zoning, highway, servicing, nearby development, etc.)
- ❑ Re-zoning potential
- ❑ Change of use
- ❑ Land assembly potential
- ❑ Partnership with neighbour(s)

5- LIST POSSIBLE DOWNSIDES

6- STRATEGY CHECKLIST

❑ Resell as-is
❑ Clean-up and sell
❑ Clean-up and lease
❑ Renovate and sell
❑ Convert to
❑ Demolish in total and sell land
❑ Demolish and rebuild for lease or sale
❑ Convert to condos
❑ Raise roof
❑ Re-zone
❑ Assemble with neighbours
❑ Option it
❑ Lease with option
❑ Joint venture
❑ Take through planning process for re-zoning and sell
❑ Others

7- SAFEST WAYS TO ACQUIRE CONTROL OF THE PROPERTY (1 to 5 (best))

❑ Lease
❑ Option
❑ Buy
❑ Lease-Purchase Option
❑ Buy a business that has a tenant in the property

8- ECONOMICS

❑ Asking Price
❑ Likely sale price
❑ Additional expenses

- Financing

- Repairs, changes, renovations

- Carrying

- Planning work

❑ Others
❑ Time to bring on stream
❑ Expected income/profit

9- REMARKS

In broad terms, the main factors to consider when analyzing Income-Producing Properties (IPP) are: location, price, real NOI (meaning the NOI determined by your own analysis, not the vendor's), the building condition (including HVAC, parking, fences, etc.), financing terms, risk, and the people involved. Life is too short to deal with unpleasant or dishonest people and you will be sorry every time you do.

16.1.2 LOCATION

"Location, location, location" is a tired, over-used saying in the real estate business, but there is no doubt that location is a major consideration when choosing a property. However, it is important to keep in mind that factors related to location vary according to use. For example, for office tenants the quality of the address is significant, while this is less significant for an industrial tenant, and for retail tenants the quality of address counts but public exposure and high traffic counts are of greater importance.

In broad terms, one could say that there are four kinds of locations:

1. **Superior.** For example, an office building should be located on one of the better arteries in town, with no negative impact neighbours, at or near public transit, with good amenities and shopping, and in a good-quality neighbourhood (e.g. Bay and Bloor in Toronto).
2. **Ordinary.** For example, a multi-family building should be located on a good, but secondary artery, with decent neighbouring uses, not too far from public transportation, and with good amenities and shopping.
3. **Marginal.** For example, an industrial property location can be a step below ordinary (2), with acceptable but barely satisfactory factors.
4. **Horrible.** For example, a contractor's yard can be next to railway tracks, freeways, airports, noisy or smelly factories, etc.

At the beginning of an investor's career, he may have to buy properties in marginal locations when funds are limited, however, avoid this category as much as possible because:
- finding tenants (and subsequently, buyers) will be more difficult
- usually, tenants of a marginal building are not of the best quality
- your mortgage will likely be at a higher rate and difficult to arrange, and
- overall, you will have more problems with a marginal building in a marginal location.

Once you are established, make every effort to buy only in superior locations to avoid these problems. It is, of course, more difficult to find properties in good locations because their owners tend to hold on to them, but it pays in the long run. Remember also, when it comes to considering location, a nation, province, neighbourhood or property can only be in one of three states: improving, neutral (stable), or deteriorating. Your analysis as to which applies to the property under consideration will determine how the future value of that property can be affected and the return you earn on your investment.

> *When it comes to considering location, a nation, province, neighbourhood or property can only be in one of three states: improving, neutral (stable), or deteriorating.*

16.1.3 THE FINANCING OPTIONS

There are many options open to you in financing your property acquisition as covered in Chapter 11 at section 11.5, but generally it is to the buyer's advantage to either take on existing financing or get financing from the vendor.

(a) Assuming Existing Financing

Always try to assume existing financing — Vendor-Take-Back (VTB) — for the reasons noted below.
- If you assume the existing mortgage and secure a VTB, you will have more cash available to improve the property or buy another one.
- If the term of the existing mortgage is at least 10 years, the amount of principal repaid each month can be quite significant.
- Almost all the expenses shown at section 16.1.3(b), Vendor's Financing, will not be incurred. You may have to pay an assumption fee if you assume an existing mortgage, but it is often low or reasonable.
- You will save a considerable amount of time and aggravation.
- When you want to refinance, you and the property will have a history of successful management.

(b) Vendor Financing (VTB)

If possible, arrange for the vendor to provide the financing when you buy a property by having him take back the mortgage (VTB). Going to an outside lender to finance a property is costly. Frequently, you will have to pay for the following:
- processing fee
- loan origination fees (to the lender or broker for arranging the mortgage)
- appraisal fees
- surveying fees
- fees for the preparation of financial statements
- lawyer's fee
- registration fee, and
- discharge fee.

Most of these expenses do not exist with a VTB mortgage. In addition, many vendors will accept that you pay interest only, with the whole amount due at the end of the term of the mortgage. The absence of amortization will make your payments lower. This is why it is always worth asking for vendor financing.

(c) Buying "Subject To"

If you buy a property and write in the offer "Subject To", it means that you are buying subject to the existing mortgage. In other words, you are not assuming the loan. The original mortgagor is responsible for any deficiency should you default. By comparison, if you are assuming the mortgage and if it is a recourse loan and you default, the buying entity and you, if you guaranteed payment, can be sued for any shortage of funds.

16.1.4 BEST TIME TO BUY

If a property has been on the market for more than 6 months, the best time of the year to present an offer is in the winter: November, December, and even January and February. Many vendors are feeling more stressed at this time of year, influenced by the cold grey days. This often leads them to accept offers more readily, rather than put up a fight to get a higher price. Conversely, the best period to sell is in the spring, when the sap is rising (in trees and people) and purchasers are feeling more optimistic.

Since we are talking about bargains, remember that, as a rule, the dirtier the building, the better the deal for the buyer (if you are the type who will do the hard, manual work yourself or supervise it closely) because a dirty property tends to discourage most people, meaning there will be fewer buyers to compete with. Always keep in mind that you are the one putting your money into the deal. The vendor needs to sell this property but you can buy this one or another. Remain in the driver's seat. Buy on your terms or walk away.

16.2 MAKING AN OFFER

Make a realistic Offer to Purchase having performed your due diligence, understood the concept of conditions, and gotten to know the vendor.

Ideally, before you present an offer to buy a property, you will have the following ideas in mind:
- an approximate value for the type of properties in the area in which you are buying (If you do not, don't be lackadaisical. Do some due diligence.);
- an idea of the improvements you can make to the property to increase its value (If you are an entrepreneur and a bargain seeker); if you can't improve it, don't buy it;
- a starting price for your offer;
- the top price that you are willing to pay; and
- a few items/requests that are not very important to you, but that you will put in the offer to give the other party the pleasure of taking some of them out, while accepting most of what is important for you.

Refer back to your Property Analysis Checklist (Checklist 16.2) for assistance with some of these items.

The first step in purchasing a property — determining value — is more difficult than it sounds because at the outset you usually do not have all the information required to establish a precise value. This includes knowing the idiosyncrasies that every property possesses, like a living being. You may know 75% of what you should know about the property. And you can usually learn about 20% more through the vendor's counter-offer and your own due diligence, but you will never know 100% about a property, unless you own it. Even then, you'll discover new quirks frequently.

This is why you should always present an offer conditional upon due diligence. It may take as little as one week for simple situations and as much as several months for complex ones.

16.2.1 EXERCISE DUE DILIGENCE

"Due diligence" is defined as "the steps a prudent person might be expected to take in the examination and evaluation of risks affecting a business transaction" (Dictionary.com). In the case of real estate transactions, this refers to doing your own investigation into the financials provided by the vendor and completing a formal or informal appraisal of the property, an environmental inspection, and a building inspection. Figure 16.1 is an excerpt from a building inspection report (sometimes called an "Engineering Report").

Figure 16.1
Excerpt from Building Inspection Report

October 22, 2006
Property Condition Assessment Report
Property: 123 Best Street, Kitchener, Ontario
1.0   SUMMARY

This is a typical commercial building that, for the most part, has been well maintained.

No major structural deficiencies were noted.

The electrical system was generally found to be in satisfactory condition. Cleaning and lubrication of the electrical equipment in the warehouse portions of the building should be undertaken. Some improvements to the distribution wiring are also required.

The majority of the roof-mounted heating and air-conditioning units are in satisfactory condition, for the most part. However, one rooftop unit is approximately 15 years into a 15-to-20-year life expectancy. The compressor at this unit was replaced in 2002. Therefore, eventual replacement of the heat exchanger at this unit may be required within the next few years.

Another rooftop unit appears to be at least 20 years into a 15-to-20-year life expectancy. One compressor at this unit is 12 years old, the second compressor appears to be over 15 years old. Therefore, eventual replacement of this rooftop unit may be required within the next few years.

The hot water boilers providing perimeter heat for the office portion of the building are 19 years into a 20-year or more life expectancy. Eventual replacement of these boilers may be required within the next few years.

The ventilation systems are in serviceable condition. Two of the three roof-mounted exhaust fans appear to be 15 to 20 years into a 20-year life expectancy. Eventual replacement of these exhaust fans maybe required within the next few years.

The plumbing system was generally found to be in satisfactory condition.

The roofing system is serviceable to satisfactory condition. The built-up asphalt and gravel membrane at the north end of the warehouse roof level and mechanical penthouse roof will require replacement within the next year. Replacement of the acrylic-dome glazing on the skylights will be required within the next few years.

The exterior walls, windows and doors were found to be in satisfactory condition, for the most part. Ideally, the older wooden overhead doors in the north façade should be replaced within the next few years.

The tubular steel handrail secured to the top of the concrete retaining wall is in serviceable repair. Severe deterioration at several locations was noted. Replacement with galvanized tubular steel is recommended and replacement over the next few years should be anticipated.

The asphalt paving is satisfactory condition, for the most part. Replacement of the asphalt paving at several localized areas will be required within the next two years. The remaining asphalt paving requires crack sealing to ensure the integrity of the pavement base.

The concrete pavement at the north entrance is in fair condition. Replacement in the next few years should be anticipated. Consideration should be given to replacing the concrete pavement with asphalt paving.

1.1   Summary of Necessary Repairs

The following table summarizes the recommendations made in this report that are of an immediate, necessary nature.

Table of Repairs

Recommendations	Report Reference	Budget Cost (2006 Dollars)
Service and clean main electrical equipment throughout the warehouse portions of the building	3.2.3, 3.2.4	$2,000 and up
Verify proper grounding of elctricial system and transformers	3.2.5	Minor
Repair leak at one circulating pump	4.2.3	Minor
Provide high water level alarm for sump pump	7.2.3	Minor
Plumbing fixture improvements	7.2.5	Minor
Replace roof membrane, mechanical room	8.2.1	$7,000 to $9,000
Replace north warehouse roof membrane	8.2.1	$180,000 to $230,000
General EPDM roof membrane improvements	8.2.3 and 8.2.6	$1,500 and up
Provide missing doorway lintel	11.2.3	Minor
Recaulk west expansion joints	12.2.5	Minor
Asphalt paving crack sealing	12.2.8	$8,000 to $10,000
Replace concrete curb	12.2.9	$2,500 to $3,000
Replace portion concrete retaining wall	12.2.11	Minor
Replace tubular steel rail, retaining wall	12.2.12	$4,000
Total		**$205,000 to $259,500**

Today, it is particularly accepted practice that few buyers of property present an offer without including a condition for due diligence. For the buyer this should translate into, "I will leave no stone unturned".

Due diligence actually starts before you present your offer (every time you discover something new) and continues throughout the due diligence period. Give the vendor an idea of what information you will require to finalize your offer. Unless he understands what you are going to be asking for, there may be difficulties in securing the materials you need. It would be ideal to include a list of required documentation with the Offer to Purchase; however, the danger with this approach is that you may scare away the vendor. You and your buying agent must decide how to approach this issue on a case-by-case basis based on your knowledge or understanding of the type of vendor (sophisticated and organized, or unsophisticated and disorganized, accommodating or reluctant).

In any case, for typical transactions, provide ample time in the Offer (at least 30 days after delivery of all documents) to complete due diligence. The ideal approach is for you, the buyer, to be required to give written notice before the expiry date of the condition, that all due diligence is complete and satisfactory, based on your sole discretion. Rather than using a specific date, keep any time limits

Literally, every document concerning the building and its operation must be examined.

tied to the delivery date of the last document from the vendor, with provisions for extensions based on the discovery of any non-disclosed defects with the information supplied.

Literally, every document concerning the building and its operation must be examined. This list includes leases with all extensions; insurance policies; building modifications; mortgages, whether you are assuming them or not; title insurance policy, if any; certificates of occupancy; insurance policy(s); elevator maintenance and service contracts; property tax notices of assessment, bills, and history; licenses, if required; parking lot contracts; etc. Also check the following: HVAC systems, security systems, fire sprinkler systems, and telephone systems. Checklist 16.3 presents a Due Diligence Building Acquisition Checklist that will give you an idea of the depth and breadth of information you need to try to collect to make informed decisions.

There is no property without some hidden defects. Some investors are so professional in their due diligence that they routinely make full asking price offers, knowing that they are going to beat the vendor down with the due diligence information. There are even professional due diligence firms that are paid, in part, by a percentage of the savings (lower price) realized by the buyer.

Leases and insurance policies are the most important documents you will have the opportunity to review. When you study these carefully you will frequently be pleasantly surprised by what you discover because many vendors and agents do not understand, or know, or point out what can be a real advantage for a buyer. A typical miss is a rental increase that is to come into effect soon.

(a) Leases

Read every word of every lease. Run through Checklist 17.2 Building Lease Review Checklist (also found in Appendix 1). Make note of anything that appears unclear or is not mentioned in the lease, including an exact description of the leased premises and extra land involved (if any), security deposits and interest payable on them, renewal rights, options to buy or right of first refusal, rights to common areas use, sublease clause, level of carefree lease (that is, anything that the tenant does not pay) to the landlord, insurance and demolition clauses, free rental period granted by the vendor, etc. Have somebody else read every word of every lease, make notes, and then compare notes. This is so crucial that you should do it yourself; do not delegate it to anyone else unless you are a very wealthy investor with trusted advisors. (See Chapter 17 at section 17.7.2 for comments on lease clauses.)

Ask questions and then ask more. At the same time, assess the quality of the tenants. Ask for the payment history on each tenant. If the vendor says that he doesn't have detailed payment records or bank statements verifying deposits, explain to him that the property just became more risky and, hence, is worth less. He may then find additional data.

(b) Insurance Policies

The insurance policy is a gold mine of information as is the last risk assessment prepared by the insurer, who uses it to determine the premium. The insured (generally the owner) has to request the risk assessment from his agent, but as a buyer you should insist on getting a copy if the vendor has it. You can also request the claim history for the property and require an affidavit from the owner that says he attests to the list of claims being complete, to the extent of his knowledge.

Insurance matters have become more and more complicated, so much so that it is a nightmare for a person who is not an insurance specialist to read and understand the policy. Truly, when studying a policy, the ideal is to use a reliable and qualified insurance agent to review it and advise you.

However, it is incumbent upon an owner to contribute to the review of the policy. Let us tell you the story of one of our clients.

Checklist 16.3
Due Diligence Building Acquisition Checklist

DUE DILIGENCE BUILDING ACQUISITION CHECKLIST

Conducting your due diligence stems from two needs:the need to control the natural tendency of many Vendors to use "Caveat Emptor" (let the buyer beware) and to take advantage of the Buyer, and to the need to know perfectly well what you are buying so that there will be no surprise.

No one will find all the answers to everything (most of the times), but he, who seeks, shall find.

The key to due diligence is a checklist. Use this one to develop your own, and keep on tweaking it.

PRELIMINARY DUE DILIGENCE CHECKLIST
(For use before presenting the offer or during the due diligence period)

Property Address: _____

Date: _____

- ❑ 1- Yearly profit and loss statements: past 3 years minimum; 5 years, if possible. One year, monthly; two years, if possible.
- ❑ 2- Balance sheet (3 years)
- ❑ 3- Rent Roll including, for each tenant: term, options, deposit, and payment history.
- ❑ 4- Tax returns: 3 years
- ❑ 5- Insurance: Insurance policy; including all riders, risk assessments, and disclosure affidavits for the insurance company
- ❑ 6- Mortgage documents: including Charge form, closing statements, title policy, rate riders, etc., and contact names and numbers.
- ❑ 7- Deed
- ❑ 8- Leases with any addendum, letters or riders.
- ❑ 9- Service or advertising contracts: garbage, pest control, maintenance, management, vending, billboard, pay telephone, etc. and any contract to be assumed by Buyer
- ❑ 10- Commission agreements from Leasing agents
- ❑ 11- Copies of all available reports: building inspection, appraisals, engineering, environmental, fire system inspection.
- ❑ 12- Survey and site plan
- ❑ 13- Architectural and engineering plans (as-built) and specifications.
- ❑ 14- List of employees, including name, position, date of hiring, salary, and benefits.
- ❑ 15- Inventory of furniture, fixtures, equipment, and supplies.
- ❑ 16- Utility bills: water, sewer, gas, electricity (at least two years of monthly statements) or letter report from supplier showing usage and cost
- ❑ 17- Bank: statements showing deposits for last 12 months
- ❑ 18- Phone system specs
- ❑ 19- Computer system specs
- ❑ 20- Property tax bills for the past three years
- ❑ 21- Legal problems: details of any past or pending litigation, or affidavit of owner stating that there isn't any.

DETAILED DUE DILIGENCE PRIOR TO CLOSING

- ❑ 1- Engineering Inspection and Survey
- ❑ 2- Environmental Inspection: wetlands, open space
- ❑ 3- Environmental Assessment Phase One report: asbestos, lead paint, PCBs
- ❑ 4- Environmental Phase Two Report, if available
- ❑ 5- LUST (Leaking Underground Storage Tank) Report
- ❑ 6- Financial Audit
- ❑ 7- Property tax verification
- ❑ 8- Tenant Estoppel letters
- ❑ 9- Mortgagee Estoppel letters
- ❑ 10- Legal Verifications: licenses, permits, zoning.

He leased a commercial building and the landlord's estimate of the insurable replacement cost, as provided by his insurance agent, was $543,984, or $1,280 per m² ($119 per sq ft). This appeared high to our client and he asked for details, which the landlord requested from his insurance agent and passed on to our client. Our client found out that the half-page report had been produced using a computer program made by Swift/Boeckh Systems. When queried about the method used by the program, the landlord's insurance agent replied that he had no idea how the program worked.

Our client discovered that the square footage used to calculate the replacement value of the property was $543,984/$1,280 per m² ($119 per sq ft) = 425 m² for 3 floors = 142 m² per floor. Trouble was that the actual floor plate area was 100 m² (1,080 sq ft), which when multiplied by 3 floors = 300 m², or a difference of 125 m² (29.4%).

(c) Land Surveys

Before you buy or sell a property you will need to examine the survey of the property to ensure that the area of the land is what you were told or you thought it was (many owners do not know the precise area). If a survey is not available and you need to have one done, in Ontario you must use the services of an Ontario Land Surveyor (OLS), who must follow strict guidelines when preparing surveys, as recommended by the Association of Ontario Land Surveyors (AOLS) (<www.aols.org>). There are several types of surveys available.

1. **A Plan of Survey.** A Plan of Survey (see Figure 8.6 in Chapter 8) is the most common type of survey to which one refers in offers when one asks the vendor to provide a survey. This survey will show the corners and boundary lines of your site. The OLS will usually go to the registry office to verify that the data (the land boundaries and area) you give him is correct.

   A more complete version of this type of survey is a Surveyor's Real Property Report (SRPR). This is a legal document that shows the location of improvements in relationship to property boundaries. It generally takes the form of a plan of the various features of the property along with a written report highlighting the surveyor's opinion and concerns, if any.

   According to the AOLS, the survey report will require the OLS to do the following:
   - a search of title of the subject and abutting properties;
   - a search of all encumbrances registered against the title of the subject property;
   - a search of other surveyor's offices to obtain all plans relating to location of boundaries of the subject property;
   - a field survey to determine the actual dimensions of the property, the location of improvements, and the setting of corner markers;
   - an analysis of research and field data;
   - the preparation of the plan based on the results of the field survey and the title research; and
   - the preparation of a written report providing the surveyor's opinion about any negative issues that may have been found during the survey.
2. **A Construction Layout Survey.** A survey made prior to construction or when construction is underway is a construction layout survey. The OLS checks elevation, horizontal position, dimensions, and configuration (i.e., stake out of line and grade for buildings, fences, roads, etc.).
3. **As-Built Survey.** Commonly, an as-build survey is used to locate physical structures and improvements. It is often required for mortgage purposes.

4. **Topographic Survey.** A topographic survey is required for all new subdivisions. Without it, proper grading of the land would be impossible and servicing (water, sanitary and storm sewers) would be installed haphazardly. A topographic survey shows:
   - lines of contours (vertical elevations)
   - watercourses, and
   - trees, if the person requiring the survey requests that they be shown, etc.
5. **Quantity Survey.** Technically, a quantity survey is not a land survey, but we mention it as it comes up during this process. A quantity survey is done to obtain measurements of quantities, such as soil, fences, concrete, etc., in conjunction with a construction process. It may be done on behalf of a lender to assist in determining when progress payments should be made to a builder.
6. **Site Plan.** A site plan is a survey that usually combines a plan of survey and a topographic survey. It shows improvements, such as buildings, driveways, parking areas, fences, municipal services, etc. It is a plan to be used on occasion for designing proposed improvements or developments, and obtaining building permits.

16.2.2 CONDITIONS IN AN OFFER

As a real estate investor, you will deal with a number of contracts and agreements. Many of them will contain conditions, probably several of them. As defined in Lectric Law Library (<www.lectlaw.com>), "[in] its most extended meaning, a condition is a clause in a contract or agreement which has for its object to suspend, rescind or modify the principal obligation; or in case of a will, to suspend, revoke, or modify the devise or bequest." In addition to a due diligence condition in your offers, we recommend you include conditions for financing, property inspections, and/or an appraisal (see Chapter 14, Appraisals and Feasibility Studies). If you like a property, you may need to move very fast. In a vendor's market, quick action becomes imperative. While a less experienced buyer spends time checking all the details and performing due diligence before making an offer, a more practiced buyer will swoop in with a conditional offer and perform his due diligence while the less experienced buyer is left wondering what happened when he's told that the desired property was sold to someone else. In these cases you can present a Letter of Intent or a quickly prepared offer, and use the conditional period to do your research.

16.2.3 LETTER OF INTENT TO BUY A PROPERTY

We like to use a Letter of Intent as the first step towards acquiring a property. Indeed, we find that preparing an offer is a waste of time and money for the parties involved, if the key business points cannot be agreed upon. The only purpose of a Letter of Intent to Buy (see Figure 16.2) is to determine if agreement can be reached on four important points.

1. Price
2. Down payment (sometimes)
3. Financing (conditional on arranging financing or VTB)
4. Condition(s)

Figure 16.2
Letter of Intent to Buy

Thursday, October 27, 2005

Mr. John Doe
Real Estate Broker
00 Yonge Street, Suite 100
Toronto, Ontario M1A 1A1

Dear Mr. Doe:

<u>Re 1234 Industry Street, Toronto</u>

We have been instructed by our client to write you a letter outlining the main points of an offer to buy that he would be prepared to present on this property.

Price:	$5,100,000
Down payment:	$1,100,000, payable:
- Deposit:	$ 200,000
- On closing:	$ 900,000

Mortgage taken back by Vendor/mortgagee:
$4,000,000, at prime, payable quarterly, interest only, and due in 5 years, open.

Conditional period for due diligence: 30 days.

Closing: 60 days after removal of condition.

We trust that the above is of interest to your clients. If it is so, and to avoid misunderstandings, please ask them to sign below and return to us a copy of this letter, which is not a binding document. It will be the basis to prepare an offer.

Yours truly

<u>We agree with the above</u>

By_____   Date _____

We find the Letter of Intent approach a much more elegant, efficient, and intelligent way to explore the potential success of an Offer. It opens the dialogue between the parties and flushes out details. Furthermore, it forces the vendor to think things through and come up with answers. It is surprising to see that most vendors don't make a decision on price until they see something on paper. Many see the vending process as two steps.

1. I decide on an asking price when I list the property.
2. I decide on the price I will accept and terms of an offer when I have one in my hand.

Additionally, while it is not a binding document, most vendors who are dealing with a buyer who has submitted a Letter of Intent are unlikely to start negotiating very seriously with another party.

16.2.4 ALLOCATION OF PURCHASE PRICE

When a property changes hands, the price must be broken down into two components: land, which is not depreciable; and the building, which is depreciable. Typically, the interests of the buyer and vendor are opposite. The buyer wants the highest possible value allocated to the building so as to have a higher starting figure for the Capital Cost Allowance (CCA), whereas the vendor wants that figure to be as low as possible so as to pay a lower recapture amount. Note: This problem does not exist with properties sold under power-of-sale or by a receiver!

There is a further refinement to value allocation. Once a buyer and vendor have agreed on the land/building allocation, the buyer can go further, obtain his accountant's advice, and break down the building value into smaller components. The idea, here, is to isolate components that depreciate faster than the building as a whole (4% per year on the declining balance). As discussed in section 5.2.2, Chapter 5, it is possible to place, in a separate CCA class, allowable items that have a shorter economic life, such as fences, outdoor advertising signs (billboards), roads, exterior lighting, sidewalks, landscaping, storage areas, and chattels. However, Canada Revenue Agency (CRA) says that you may not include in these classes the parts that make up the building, such as: electric wiring, lighting fixtures, plumbing, sprinkler systems, heating equipment, air-conditioning equipment (other than window units), and escalators. In fact, there are many grey areas when it comes to asset definitions and if the sums are large it is a good idea to consult a tax specialist to ensure you take advantage of all opportunities available to you.

Some lawyers insist that the Offer contain the land/building value allocation, while others do not. Usually, vendor and buyer agree on the value, but not always. If they do not, there is no value shown on the offer and each is free to use the numbers as he wants. If this happens, however, it is more likely to trigger a review and possible reassessment by CRA. A review and reassessment is still possible, even if vendor and buyer agree on the figures, but it is less likely since their opposing interests are more likely to result in a realistic allocation. Obviously, CRA is more concerned with the vendor's numbers since they are the ones that will be used for recapture.

16.2.5 UNDERSTAND THE VENDOR

To a certain extent, you are making an educated guess when you present an offer or letter of intent. You do not know everything about the following:
• the price the vendor will accept;
• the reality of the expenses and, sometimes, even of the income; or

- the terms that the vendor will accept, including:
  - down payment
  - VTB mortgage
  - amount, term, and interest of the VTB, and
  - other concessions.

You also don't know the mindset of the vendor on a given day. This is impossible to discover because the individual himself often does not realize when he is completely motivated to sell or tired of waiting for an acceptable offer. All you can do is present an Offer. If the vendor is not ready to be realistic, forget about this property and look for another one. The next investor may come at a more opportune time.

A vendor who has had his property on the market for a few months, sometimes even years (remember that the main drawback of real estate is that it is not very liquid), may be ready to negotiate in a more flexible way. For example, a vendor who wanted all cash might consider a VTB mortgage or accept that the down payment be paid in two halves, a few months apart.

By the way, don't feel bad for the vendor if he, perhaps with the help of his agent, mis-prices the property to less than its market value. (It does not happen often, but it does happen). Your job is not to make the world an ideal place to live, devoid of inequities, but to make money in real estate investing.

16.2.6 FINANCIAL PROJECTIONS

One of the fascinating aspects of real estate investing is that all projects are similar, yet no two are identical. Sometimes, one needs to make sure that, at first glance, the project will work. Think of this as a sort of pre-screening to get a sense of the numbers. Financially speaking, there are two main hurdles. Will we have a positive cash flow, plus some cushion? Will we make money, after taxes?

One of the fascinating aspects of real estate investing is that all projects are similar, yet no two are identical.

Figure 16.3 shows a rough projection for a warehouse, net leased for 10 years, based on the assumptions outlined. As can be seen, the concerns addressed are year 1 cash flow, year 1 profit, and year 10 profit.

Figure 16.3
Financial Projections for Warehouse

39 REVEL ST- PROJECTIONS

Assumptions
Purchase Price ($4,600,000) paid as follows:

Down payment (cash):	$1,100,000
1st mortgage for 5 years, 15 year am. @ 7.5%:	$2,500,000
2nd (VTB) at 5%, interest only:	$1,000,000
Total:	$4,600,000

1st mortgage payments

1st year interest:	$ 181,442
1st year principal:	$ 94,712
Total:	$ 276,156

Cash required (down payment):	$1,100,000
Less net rental for year 1:	$ 675,000
Balance required:	$ 425,000

Net Rental (years 1-5):	$ 550,000
Net Rental (years 6-10):	$ 675,000
Rental Deposit:*	$ 675,000

*Deposit made by the existing tenant and equal to one year rental. It would be paid by the vendor to the buyer on closing.

Income and Expenses

CCA: On the surface, this leaves only $200,000 as land value. However, because the property was acquired from a receiver representing the interests of a bankrupt company, the seller did not care about the building and land allocation of value. As mentioned earlier, this is not the case in a regular sales situation where the seller wants a very high value for the land, while the buyer wants one as low as possible.

Cash flow – Year 1

Income:		$550,000
Expenses		
1st Mortgage payments:	$276,156	
2nd Mortgage payments:	$ 55,000	
Rental Deposit interest at 4%:	$ 27,000	$358,156
Cash flow:		$191,844

Income and Expenses – Year 1

Income:		$550,000
Expenses		
1st Mortgage interest:	$181,442	
2nd Mortgage interest:	$ 55,000	
Rental Deposit interest at 4%:	$ 27,000	$263,442
Balance:		$286,558
CCA** on $4,400,000 x 4%*=		$176,000
Taxable profits:		$110,558
Income Tax at 23%:		$ 25,428
Profit after tax:		$ 85,130

Income and Expenses – Year 10

Income:		$675,000
Expenses		
1st Mortgage interest:	$ 68,663	
2nd Mortgage interest:	$ 60,000	
Deposit interest at 4%:	$ 27,000	$155,663
Profit:		$519,337
CCA (balance of CCA basis: $2,906,207):		$124,425**
Taxable profit:		$394,912
Income Tax at 23%:		$142,168
Profit after tax:		$252,744***

* Disregarding the 50% rule.

** It will be higher, through building component breakdown.

*** Cash flow will be lower than that, due to mortgage principal payments.

Note: After closing, should the down payment be converted to a 3rd mortgage, with the shareholder(s) of the owning corporation as mortgagee?

As a business owner there may be ways to improve your financial projections. Many business owners start their road to real estate investing by acquiring a property to house their business. If you own a business that requires space, buy a larger building in your name (or your spouse if you feel very secure in the strength of the relationship) or in that of a separate corporation that you own personally. Rent the whole building to your business. It is the business that will be responsible for any losses, should they occur, all repairs, etc. When the mortgage is fully paid, you own the property and all the risk has been assumed by the corporation while you have benefited from the yearly deduction of the building depreciation to shelter part of your income. An additional advantage of this approach is that you and your business may pay less in income tax. You also have a lot of flexibility to change the amount of rent paid, up or down according to your tax needs, if you create a monthly or yearly lease.

If your business makes important improvements to the building, it can deduct some of the expenses over the expected life of the improvement or over the length of the lease, if it is a short-term lease (2 or 3 years). However, if you decide to make the improvements for the tenant (your business), you may deduct the cost from the net income of your building amortized over the length of lease, too. This means that with an arm's-length tenant with a 10-year lease, you would have to amortize any improvements made for him over this period of time. However, if you, as owner of the building, sign a 3-year lease with your business, you would amortize the expenses incurred over three years. This provides plenty of room for creativity. This expense can create a loss that can be used to reduce the personal income you receive from the corporation.

16.2.7 THE HIGH COST OF "MISSING THE DEAL"

We see many investors miss deals because of a small difference in the purchase price. We, too, have heard the saying, "You make your money when you buy the property", but many people interpret this to mean you must pay as little as possible when you buy. There is another possible interpretation, and that is: "You must acquire the property in order to be able to make money."

In 2004, most people with short-term money invested earned slightly over 2.15%, before taxes, for 30 days or approximately 1% after taxes. The following mini-study, which was prepared for a client who could not bring himself to pay a little more for a property, demonstrates the opportunity lost by not buying.

Example
Assumptions
$100,000 property (allocated building value: $80,000; land: $20,000)
$30,000 down payment
mortgage of $70,000 at 6% (principal only), paying interest of $4,200/year

Scenario #1
With an 8% Cap Rate

Net Operating Income (NOI) =	$8,000
Less mortgage interest (6% x $100,000)=	$4,200
Income before CCA:	$3,800
CCA: $80,000 x 4% =	$3,200
Taxable income:	$ 600
Taxes (corporate) at 40.79%:	$ 244.74
Cash flow after tax: $3,800 - $244.74 =	$3,555.26

Add the appreciation of 6% on $100,000 = $6,000
Total direct and indirect returns: $3,555.26 + $6,000 = $9,555.26.
     ROE after taxes: $9,555.26/$30,000 cash investment = 31.85%

Scenario #2
With a 7% Cap Rate

NOI =	$7,000
Less mortgage interest (6% x $100,000)=	$4,200
Income before CCA:	$2,800
CCA: $80,000 x 4% =	$3,200
Taxable income:	$ 0
Cash flow after tax:	$2,800
Add 6% appreciation on $100,000 =	$6,000
Total direct and indirect returns: $2,800 + $6,000 =	$8,800

     ROE after taxes: $8,800/$30,000 cash investment = 29.33%

In both cases the results are considerably better when investing in real estate, versus the 1% return after taxes earned by putting your money in the bank, as noted above.

16.3 NEGOTIATING WITH A VENDOR

Win most negotiations with vendors by focusing on the issues, remaining unemotional, and preparing wisely.

Win-win negotiating depends on the willingness of each side to be truly empathetic to, or at least understanding of, the other side's position. There are many books on negotiating strategies but each person has to find what works for himself. Here are a few tips that have worked well for us over the years.

16.3.1 PREPARE A REPAIR/REPLACEMENT LIST

If you and the vendor are far apart on price, prepare a list of needed repairs or replacements. If you can price them, all the better. Better still is to have a contractor give you a written estimate based on the list you give him or that you prepare with his help. Another strategy is to enlist the help of the vendor's agent by discussing the list before making an Offer. The agent will share it with the client, thus allowing the vendor time to think over his position on price before you present your Offer. Often this is done after due diligence has been conducted.

A typical list for an industrial building might include the following:

1. **Repairs Needed.**
   - roof leaks in several places; additional downspout heads required
   - one dock leveller does not work
   - sprinkler check — should be done every year, but has not been done in last three years

- outside walls need tuck pointing and redecorating
- outside lights are not working, and
- roof flashing missing in several places.

2. **Replacements**

- overgrown bushes must be removed and new ones planted
- old single-pane, steel frame windows need replacing
- concrete curbs to the parking lot entrance are broken and cracked and need replacing
- the 20-ton office air conditioning unit is 19 years old and needs replacing
- ceiling tiles in offices need replacing, and
- parking lot asphalt needs replacing in five areas.

This list can provide great leverage in your negotiations. For example, you could tell the vendor or his agent that, "Due to the considerable amount of money required to correct these problems, I will be able to pay only a small down payment and I must also ask you for a VTB mortgage. However, bear in mind that when I have corrected these problems, the rental value of the building will increase and when the lease comes up for renewal in 15 months, I will be able to increase the rental, refinance, and pay off your second mortgage." Or, you could use the list to negotiate a lower price. The point is that being armed with the list before you enter negotiation gives you something concrete in support of your Offer.

16.3.2 USE A LETTER OF SATISFACTORY PAYMENT

If you intend to ask the vendor to carry some financing and you own, or have owned, several properties with mortgages on them, it is a good idea to ask each lender to give you a Letter of Satisfactory Payment to show that you are a good risk. Include these letters with the list you give the vendor's agent when asking for a VTB.

16.3.3 CONCENTRATE ON THE ISSUES

Do not be distracted by the actions of the other person. Sophisticated negotiators concentrate on the issues, not on the personalities. You should always be thinking, "Where are we now, compared to where we were an hour ago, or yesterday, or last week?" Also, frequently ask yourself what it is you want to achieve.

16.3.4 DON'T LET YOUR EMOTIONS GET IN THE WAY

Emotions have no place in real estate because they lead to mistakes. Never "tell" yourself any of the following:

- I love this property
- I must have this property, or
- I know that this property is bound to perform marvellously.

You must try to make your decisions objectively, based on the data at hand, and disregarding your emotional response to a property. Try to view a property as you would a shovel or other tool. It is a tool used to make money. Never fall in love with it because this would, undoubtedly, affect your judgement.

16.3.5 ALWAYS CONGRATULATE THE OTHER SIDE

When you have finished negotiating, you should always congratulate the other side. Say, "You did do a fantastic job negotiating that. I realize that I didn't get as good a deal as I could have gotten, but frankly, it was worth it because I learned so much about negotiating. You were great." Great negotiators always want the other parties thinking that they won in the negotiations. It starts by asking for more than you expect to get. It continues through all of the other mini-concessions you make that are designed to give the perception that they are winning.

> *Great negotiators always want the other parties thinking that they won in the negotiations.*

16.4 CLOSING COSTS

Project the additional expenses involved in closing the deal.

The additional expenses or closing costs involved in buying a property can be significant. Figure 16.4 provides a list of the range of costs you may face when closing on a sale in Ontario. Figure 16.5 shows as an example – a $875,000 purchase of land that took place in 2001; in that case, the legal fee was $1,500, the disbursements totalled $1,055, plus the Land Transfer Tax (LTT) of $11,600, giving a total of $14,155, which is 1.62% of the purchase price.

LTT can be avoided if the vendor is a corporation. Indeed, if the buyer acquires the shares of a corporation, the property is still owned by the same entity. Hence, no LTT is owed. This situation is rare because most buyers are reluctant to enter into these deals since they are afraid they will inherit some hidden liabilities in the corporation.

If you buy the shares of a corporation that owns a building, you do not start the CCA process anew. You continue the CCA calculations, using the balance of the vendor's CCA account, instead of starting with a figure that is usually substantially higher (assuming the vendor has owned the property for several years).

Figure 16.4
Closing Costs Worksheet

AN ONTARIO PROPERTY

Not all items will apply to every sale in every jurisdiction.

Amounts vary greatly with difficulties encountered (especially legal) and the size of the property.

Disbursement	Range
Legal	$800 - $5,000
Survey	$300 - $4,000
Appraisal	$1,000 - $6,000
Loan	
Application fee	$235
Mortgage insurance fee	0.50% - 3.5%
Mortgage broker's fee	0.5% - 2%
Lender's fee	$1,000 - $10,000
Lender's legal fee	$1,500 - $6,000
Assumption of an existing mortgage	$750 - $4,000 + legal ($1,000 - $3,000)
Discharge costs for existing financing	$0 - $300,000
Credit Report	$100
Building inspection	$250 - $5,000
Pest control inspection	$100 - $1,000
Environmental audit	$600 - $3,000
Land Transfer Tax[2]	< 1.5%
GST (Goods and Services tax)	6%
Adjustments regarding Vendor's prepaid expenses	
Property taxes	
Service contracts	
Insurance	
Credit regarding deposits held by the Vendor	

Note that the amounts will vary dramatically based on many factors, the three most important ones being the size of the building, the value of the property, and the amount of the mortgage.

1 This figure includes the legal fees, but also the cost of disbursements which may include agents' fees, certification of cheque, Conservation Authority clearance, courier and delivery, faxes, photocopies, postage/registered mail, printing/binding, document registration, subsearch of title, tax certificate, telephone charges, and transaction levy surcharge.

2 The formula for commercial properties for amounts greater than $250,000 is: Amount x 0.015 - $1,525. For example: $1,600,000 x 0.015 = $24,000 - $1,525 = $22,475.

Figure 16.5
Closing Costs on $875,000 Property in 2001

IN ACCOUNT WITH
XYZ Law Firm
First Canadian Place
Toronto, Ontario, Canada M1M 2N2
Telephone: 416-864-9700 Fax: 416-123-4567
www.xyzlawfirm.com

October 1, 2001

To ....

Our File: A1234/567890

Purchase From The Estate of ...., Pickering, Ontario

TO ALL PROFESSIONAL SERVICES RENDERED on your behalf in connection with this matter including: Review - file on July 12, 200 1; Review - title. 6- requisition on July 16, 200 1; Review requisition letter on July 18, 200 1; Telephone to ....July 23, 2001; Telephone to ....July 23, 200 1; Letter to .... on July 24, 2001; Review - file; search; letter to .... on July 27, 2001; Review - closing documents on August 9, 200 1; Review file & Letter to......... on August 13, 2001; Review file and fax waiver on August 23, 2001; Document preparation closing docs on August 27, 2001; Meeting MM review docs. on August 28, 2001; Telephone solicitor for vendor, review statement of adjustments on August 28, 200 1; Review conservation clearance letter, discuss with MM, letter to client on August 28, 200 1; Telephone on August 28, 200 1; Document preparation - borrower's resolution on August 28, 200 1; Review CLOSING DOCS ETC. on August 29, 200 1; Other - call LTT, amend Assignment Agt, meeting with client etc. on August 30, 2001; Review draft reporting letter on September 25, 2001; and all other matters, communications and attendances incidental to the foregoing but not specifically enumerated herein;

OUR FEE HEREIN: $1,500.00

Disbursements
Taxable   Agents' Fees $262.00
Taxable   Certification of Cheque $ 4.25

Taxable   Conservation Authority
          Clearance $100.00
Taxable   Courier & Delivery $155.55
Taxable   Faxes $ 81.25

Exempt   Non-Taxable Other $125.00
Taxable   Photocopies $ 29.38
Taxable   Postage/Registered Mail $ 2.80
Taxable   Printing/Binding $ 40.30
Exempt   Register Document $ 70.00
Taxable   Staff Overtime $ 35.00
Taxable   Subsearch of Title $ 20.00
Taxable   Tax Certificate $ 65.00
Taxable   Telephone $ 14.47
Taxable   Transaction Levy Surcharge $ 50.00
                Total Disbursements $1,055.00
Total Fees and Disbursements $2,555.00
GST on Fees and Taxable Disbursements $ 165.20
Total Fees, Disbursements and GST this Bill $2,720.20
Less payment from Funds held in Trust   ($2,491.39)
Balance Due: $ 228.81

This account bears interest, commencing one month after delivery, at the rate of 6.25% per annum as authorized by the *Solicitors' Act*. Any disbursements not posted to your account on the date of this statement will be billed later. GST No. R098765432.
Please return a copy of this account with your payment. Thank you.

16.5 TYPICAL STEPS TO COMPLETING A PURCHASE

Navigate the many steps to finalize your purchase, including completing and registering the various forms and documents.

16.5.1 DEPOSIT

Usually when a buyer presents an Agreement of Purchase and Sale (commonly referred to as an "offer") it reads, "Deposit payable on acceptance". In most cases, the vendor makes changes to the offer, which, in turn, will cause the buyer to make changes. If the parties come to an agreement, typically the buyer gives a certified cheque or bank draft to the real estate agent, if one is involved, or to the vendor's lawyer. The cheque is deposited in a trust account and the money can be disbursed only if the deal closes. If the deal does not close, a Mutual Release Form must be signed by both parties. If one of the parties refuses to sign, the money will be disbursed as directed by the court.

16.5.2 TITLE SEARCH

The buyer's solicitor conducts two title searches. The first is to unearth any title problems such as encumbrances, encroachments, restrictive covenants, or expropriations. To ensure the property complies with the requirements of the *Planning Act* (R.S.O. 1990, c. P.20), he will also investigate adjoining land ownership.

The second title search (sub-search) is conducted just hours before closing to ensure that nothing negative that could affect the buyer has taken place, such as a new mortgage, work orders, cautions, or liens.

16.5.3 NON-TITLE SEARCHES

There are many non-title searches that the buyer's lawyer must also conduct, such as: work orders, deficiencies, zoning, easements, *Personal Property Security Act* (R.S.O. 1990, c. P.10), property taxes, executions, and more. This varies from property to property. The lawyer will also send letters to ascertain compliance, for example, to the health department, zoning department, or fire department (see Figure 16.6). Normally, there is a clause in the offer requesting the vendor to sign letters of authorization to ask government authorities to release information to the buyer.

16.5.4 REMOVAL OF CONDITIONS

Typically, the buyer's lawyer will send a letter to the vendor's lawyer notifying him that the buyer is waiving the conditions (see Figure 16.7).

Figure 16.6
Vendor Authorization Letter

TO: Fire Department

RE: Grammy Inc.
        987 Great Street West, Kitchener (hereinafter referred to as the "Property")

You are hereby authorized to release all information which you may currently have on file regarding the above-noted property to My Properties Inc. and/or its solicitor, Marvin S.N. Brown at 1234 Hwy. No. 7, Suite 200, Vaughan, Ontario, L4K 4M3, and for so doing this shall be your good and sufficient authority.

Nothing in this authorization shall permit or authorize, or shall be construed to request that you conduct any inspection or physical examination of this property.

Dated this 16th day of October, 2007

                                      Grammy Inc.

                                      Per:_____
                                        Name: John Doe
                                        Title: President

                                        I have authority to bind the Corporation.

Figure 16.7
Notification: Buyer Waiving Conditions

MARC BOIRON
Barrister & Solicitor
63 Johnson Street, Thornhill, Ontario L3T 2N9
Telephone: 416-985-5985 Fax: 416-985-6985
E-Mail: m.boiron@marcboiron.ca

December 5, 2006

Long, Wide & Thin
Barristers & Solicitors
35 Peace Street
Waterloo, Ontario
N2J 4B9
<u>Attention: Larry Gunick</u>

Dear Sir:

RE: SMALL PROPERTIES INC, IN TRUST NOW ASSIGNED TO
        12345678 ONTARIO INC. purchase from SANDBILL INC.
        (Agreement of Purchase and Sale dated October 7, 2006)
        322 Leslie Avenue, Kitchener ON
        Closing Date: January 9, 2007
        My File No.: 9876-06

Please be advised that we act for the Purchaser with regards to the above-captioned matter and that, pursuant to the terms and conditions of the Agreement of Purchase and Sale and the agreed to amendments made between our respective clients, we are pleased to advise that those conditions as set out in paragraph 3.1 of the Agreement of Purchase and Sale are hereby waived.

We further enclose herein Assignment reflecting the Purchase being 12345678 Ontario Inc. Would you kindly amend your file accordingly. We look forward to closing the within transaction on January 9, 2007.

We thank you for your co-operation and anticipated co-operation.

Yours truly,

Marc Boiron

Encls

16.5.5 REQUISITIONS

The buyer's lawyer will request many items and guarantees by forwarding a letter to the vendor's lawyer. Some of the items include the vendor's residency status, property tax payment, certificate of taxes, arrears, expropriation, construction liens, GST exemption, direction for payment, compliance with the *Planning Act*, etc.

16.5.6 DRAFT DOCUMENTS

The buyer's lawyer will prepare draft closing documents and send them to the vendor's lawyer, who will review them to ensure they are in agreement with the accepted offer and will request changes he feels are necessary.

16.5.7 STATEMENT OF ADJUSTMENTS

A financial document, the Statement of Adjustments, outlines how much money is owed to the vendor, after adjustments for items such as the deposit, purchase price, mortgage, property taxes, insurance, rentals (if property is leased), and utilities. It is prepared by the buyer's lawyer a few days before closing and sent to the vendor's lawyer for approval. See Figure 16.8.

16.5.8 CLOSING THE SALE

Not so long ago, to register the sale of a property the two lawyers would meet at the registry office, conduct various checks, money would be paid, and the documents registered. Today, this is done electronically close to 90% of the time (see section 8.8 in Chapter 8).

16.5.9 LEGAL DOCUMENTS INVOLVED WHEN BUYING A PROPERTY

There are a number of legal documents that must be prepared for the purchase of a property. The most common include the following:

- Reporting Letter
- Assignment Agreement (sometimes)
- Transfer/Deed of Land
- Charge/Mortgage of Land, and
- Notice of an Agreement of Purchase and Sale (sometimes).

(a) Reporting Letter

Two to four weeks after closing, unless urgent processing is requested, the buyer's lawyer will send the buyer a letter outlining what has taken place (see Figure 16.9, for an example). The vendor's lawyer will do the same for the vendor. Usually, a bound book of documents also accompanies the reporting letter, along with the deed. Figure 16.10 presents a sample list of contents from a book of documents.

Figure 16.8
Statement of Adjustments

VENDOR: Fibreless Ltd.

PURCHASER: Dunno Investments Inc.

PROPERTY: 129 Banal Street, Mississauga, ON

Adjusted as of September 28, 2006

		Credit Purchaser	Credit Vendor
SELLING PRICE			$2,500,000
DEPOSIT		$100,000	
REALTY TAXES			
2006 Total Taxes	$32,794		
Vendor has to pay:	$32,794		
Vendor's share for 270 days:	$24,259		$8,536
TENANCIES – Rims Ltd.; Axle Ltd.			
Vendor has received for the month:	$12,500		
Vendor's share for 28 days:	$11,290		
Credit Purchaser:		$1,210	
UTILITIES			
No adjustment – metered			
TOTAL		$101,210	$2,508,536
BALANCE DUE ON CLOSING		$2,407,326	
($2,508,536-$101,210)			

Figure 16.9
Reporting Letter from Lawyer

Fogler, Rubinoff LLP
Suite 4400, P.O. Box 95, Royal Trust Tower
Toronto-Dominion Centre
Toronto, Ontario, Canada M5K I G8
Telephone: 416-864-9700 Fax: 416-941-8852
www. foglerubinoff.com

FOGLER, RUBINOFF	Reply To:	Martin L. Middlestadt
BARRISTERS & S0LICIT0RS	Direct Dial:	416-941-8833
	E-mail:	mlm@foglerubinoff.com

September 25, 2001   File No. 0 1 /2967

DELIVERED BY COURIER
Attention:

Dear Sirs:
Re: "Purchaser" purchase from "Vendor"
          Part Lot, Concession , City of Pickering (formerly Town of Pickering)
          designated as Part 1, Plan 40R- known as L Finch Avenue, Pickering, Ontario

We are pleased to report that the transaction wherein you purchased the above-noted property was completed on August 30, 2001 in accordance with the terms of an Agreement of Purchase and Sale between, in trust for a company to be incorporated, as purchaser, and as vendor, dated September 18, 1997, as amended by Amendment to Agreement dated May 8, 1998 (the "Agreement"), assigned by, in trust for a company to be as Assignor, to as Assignee, by Assignment Agreement dated August 31, 2001 and in accordance with the enclosed Revised Statement of Adjustments. The Agreement was further amended by letter agreement dated July 24, 2001 wherein the parties agreed to an extension of the closing date to August 30, 2001, the Purchaser to provide a further deposit in the sum of $40,000.00 and payment of $3,500.00 to cover interest for the one-month extension of the closing date.

REVISED STATEMENT OF ADJUSTMENTS
Included in the book of documents is a copy of the Revised Statement of Adjustments which reflects the following:

Sale Price
The Vendor was credited with the sale price of $875,000.00.

Deposit
The Purchaser was credited with the deposits aggregating $60,000.00.

Vendor-Take-Back Charge
The Purchaser was credited with the principal amount of the vendor-take-back mortgage in the sum of $655,000.00.

Realty Taxes
The realty taxes were adjusted on the basis of estimated 2001 taxes in the amount of $537.74. The Vendor's share for 241 days was $354.99 and the Vendor had paid $263.60. The Purchaser was given a credit in the amount of $91.39.

Utilities
No adjustments as there are no utility meters on the property.

Balance Due on Closing
The balance due on closing was in the amount of $159,908,61.

SURVEY
Enclosed herewith please find a Plan of Survey (Plan 40R- 1193 4) for the property dated January 26, 1989 prepared by Horton, Wallace & Davies Ltd., Ontario Land Surveyors, showing the boundaries of the property.

PROPERTY
The property which is the subject of the transaction is legally described as Part of Lot 34, Concession 2, City of Pickering (formerly Town of Pickering) designated as Part I on Plan 40R-1 1934, in the Land Registry Office for the Land Titles Division of Durham (No. 40) at Whitby, comprising the whole of PIN 26370-0014 (LT).

PRIOR ENCUMBRANCES

Our search of title reveals registrations of Cautions in favour of registered as Instruments Nos. _____ on February 7, 1989, _____ on December 5, 1991, _____ on October 17,1994 and _____ on October 21, 1997 and Last Will and Testament of registered as Instrument No. _____ which granted a life interest to
_____.

On closing, the Vendor's solicitor, Mr. _____ undertook to delete the aforementioned life interest of title to the property. A copy of this Undertaking is included in the book of documents.

Subsequent to closing, we received confirmation from the Vendor's solicitor that a Certificate of Withdrawal of the aforementioned Cautions was registered on September 14,2001 as Instrument No. _____, a copy of which is included in the book of documents.

REGISTRATION OF TRANSMISSION APPLICATION

In order to close the purchase transaction and effect the conveyance to the Purchaser by the Vendor, the Vendor's solicitor was required to prepare and register a Document General - Transmission Application wherein it contained recitals stating that, as estate trustee, was the owner entitled by law to the property and that she was appointed estate trustee with a will by the Surrogate Court of the Judicial District of York Region under File No. _____ dated October 24, 1986 and that the debts of the deceased vendor were paid in full. The said Transmission Application was registered on August 30, 2001 as Instrument No. DRI _____.

TITLE

Prior to the closing of this transaction, we searched the records of the aforementioned Land Registry Office and made searches in offices of public records, as we deemed appropriate. Based upon such searches, we are of the opinion that by Transfer/Deed of Land registered August 30, 2001 as Instrument No. DRI _____ from Estate by its Estate Trustee, acquired good and marketable title to the property in fee simple, free and clear of all liens and encumbrances except as hereinafter described:

1. Any unregistered easements, rights-of-way or other unregistered instruments or claims not disclosed by registered title although at the present time, we are not aware of any such claims.
2. The exceptions and qualifications of the Land Titles Act.
3. The reservations, limitations, provisos and conditions expressed in the original grant from the Crown of the property.
4. Any inchoate statutory liens, charges or similar liabilities and/or rights which may exist from time to time including, without limitation, liens for realty or similar taxes not yet due and payable.
5. Instrument No. DRI _____ is a Charge/Mortgage of Land registered August 30, 2001 by the Purchaser, as mortgagor, and – Estate, as mortgagee, in the principal sum of $655,000.00 as will be hereinafter reported.

Included in our book of documents is the duplicate registered Transfer/Deed of Land and copy of the vendor-take-back mortgage.

OFF-TITLE CLEARANCES

Tax Department

Prior to closing, we obtained a Certificate of Treasurer issued August 2, 2001 by the City of Pickering indicating no arrears of realty taxes.

We confirmed with the City of Pickering that the 2001 realty taxes levied were $712.5 8 of which the amount of $263.60 (interim bill) was paid by the Vendor prior to closing.You are responsible for paying the following tax instalments:
due September 26, 2001 — $224.00 due October 29, 2001 — $224.98

We enclose 2001 Final Tax Bill issued by the City of Pickering.

Building Department

Prior to closing, we received a letter dated August 8, 2001 from the Corporation of the Town of Pickering indicating that there were no records of building contraventions outstanding against _____ the property, the Zoning By-law requirements have been satisfied based from the survey submitted and that a cemetery has never been located on the property.

Conservation Authority

Prior to closing, we received a letter dated August 7, 2001 from The Toronto and Region Conservation Authority ("TRCA") confirming the following:

(a) The property is located within or adjacent to an area regulated by TRCA;
(b) In accordance with Ontario Regulation 158, a permit is required for the following works and is subject to a decision by the Executive Committee of TRCA and if development is contemplated, discussions with TRCA is recommended:
(i) The property is located within the Fill Regulation Line, a permit is required for placing, dumping of fill or re-grading within the regulated area of the property; and
(ii) The property appears to be traversed by/adjacent to a watercourse identified in the TRCA's Fill Line Extension Program, the owner may be required to produce a flood study which delineates the Regional Storm flood plain prior to further development of the property.
(c) Evaluated Wetland as identified by the Ministry of Natural Resources appears to be located within the property and if devel-

opment is proposed, an Environmental Impact Study may be required prior to development and discussion with TRCA is recommended.

(d)   There is no directive, order or breach of Ontario Regulation 158 with respect to the current use of the property.

You advised us to complete this transaction by your fax letter dated August 29, 2001 notwithstanding the TRCA report.

Copies of the above clearance letters are included in our book of documents.

VENDOR-TAKE-BACK FIRST MORTGAGE

On closing, the Purchaser gave and the Vendor took back a first mortgage against title to the property the salient provisions of which are as follows:

Chargor: _____

Chargee: _____

Principal Amount:	$655,000.00
Interest Rate:	per annum calculated annually
Interest Adjustment Date:	August 30, 2001
Payment Date:	30th day of each and every month commencing September 30, 2001
Payment Amount:	Interest Only
Maturity Date:	

Registration Particulars: Instrument No. DRI _____ registered on August 30, 2001 in the Land Registry Office for the Land Titles Division of Durham (No. 40) at Whitby.

The Chargor has the privilege of prepaying the whole or any part of the principal sum thereby secured at any time or time without notice or bonus.

The Chargor acknowledged receipt of Standard Charge Terms No. _____.

We are advised by the Vendor's solicitor that you forward all monthly interest payments payable to the Estate of

_____.

REALTY TAX ADJUSTMENT

Subsequent to closing and further to the Vendor's undertaking to readjust taxes, we enclose a trust cheque in the amount of $115.44, representing the adjusted realty taxes, as follows:

Actual 2001 realty taxes:	$712.58
Vendor's share to closing:	$470.43
Vendor paid:	$263.60
Purchaser's credit:	$206.83

You received a credit of $91.39 on closing as shown on the Revised Statement of Adjustments and the difference is $115.44 ($206.83-$91.39).

CLOSING DOCUMENTATION

On closing, and in accordance with the terms of the Agreement of Purchase and Sale, as amended, we obtained the following documents, copies of which are included in the book of documents:

1.   Statutory Declaration.
2.   Direction re: Funds.
3.   Vendor's Undertaking to Readjust.
4.   Undertaking to delete life interest as in Instrument No. _____.
5.   Undertaking to register Release of Cautions Nos. D_____, D_____, D_____ and D_____.

On closing, we delivered the following documents to the solicitor for the Vendor:

1.   Purchaser's GST Certificate and Indemnity.
2.   Purchaser's Undertaking to Readjust.
3.   Acknowledgment of Standard Charge Terms No. _____.
4.   Certificate of Incumbency and Signature.
5.   Certified copy of Resolution of the Purchaser authorizing the purchase and mortgage transactions.

This completes our report in connection with the above transaction and we trust the foregoing is clear. In the event there is any further information you require, please do not hesitate to contact the writer.

Our statement of account will follow shortly.

Yours truly,

Source: Reporting letter used by permission of Martin L. Middlestadt of Fogler, Rubinoff LLP.

Figure 16.10
Table of Contents for Books of Documents

Re: Purchase from the Estate of _____
Re: Vendor-Take-Back First Mortgage - $655,000.00
Part Lot 12, Concession 3, City of Pickering
L34 Finch Avenue, Pickering, Ontario
(File: 01/9876)

A. PURCHASE   Tab Nº

Agreement of Purchase and Sale including all amendments	1
Assignment Agreement	2
Transmission Application registered as Instrument No. DR_____	3
Duplicate Transfer/Deed of Land registered as Instrument No. DR_____	4
Revised Statement of Adjustments calculated as of August 30, 2001	5
Vendor's Direction re: Funds	6
Vendor's Statutory Declaration	7
Vendor's Undertaking to Readjust	8
Undertaking by Vendor's solicitor to delete life interest of as in Instrument No. C_____ and Cautions Nos. D_____, D_____, D_____ and D_____	9
Certificate of Withdrawal of Cautions Nos. D_____, D_____, D_____ and D_____ registered September 14, 2001 as Instrument No. DR_____	10
Purchaser's Undertaking to Readjust	11
Purchaser's GST Certificate and Indemnity	12
Certified copy of Resolution of the Director authorizing the transaction	13
Certificate of Incumbency and Signature	14
Plan of Survey dated January 26, 1989 prepared by Horton, Wallace & Davies Ltd., O.L.S.	15
Clearance Certificates/Off-Title Searches	16

- Sheriff's Certificate
- Certificate of Treasurer issued by City of Pickering
- Building/Zoning Report issued by City of Pickering
- Conservation Authority

B. VENDOR-TAKE-BACK FIRST MORTGAGE

Copy of Charge/Mortgage of Land registered as Instrument No. DR_____	17
Acknowledgment of Standard Charge Terms No. ____	18

Source: Table of Contents for Books of Documents used by permission of Martin L. Middlestadt of Fogler, Rubinoff LLP.

(b) Assignment Agreement

There will be times when one wants to buy a property in trust, for example, "John Doe, in trust for a company to be incorporated" or "John Doe, in Trust". The Agreement of Purchase and Sale can then be assigned using an Assignment Agreement (see Figure 16.11).

Figure 16.11
Assignment Agreement

ASSIGNMENT AGREEMENT

L34 FINCH AVENUE, PICKERING, ONTARIO

THIS INDENTURE made in duplicate this 31st day of August, 2001.

BETWEEN:

_____ in trust for a company to be incorporated under the laws of the Province of Ontario, (hereinafter called the **"Assignor"**), OF THE FIRST PART,

- and -

_____, an Ontario corporation, (hereinafter called the **"Assignee"**), OF THE SECOND PART.

WHEREAS:

(a) by an Agreement of Purchase and Sale dated the 10th day of October, 1997, as amended, (the "Purchase Agreement"), the Assignor, as Purchaser, agreed to purchase from the Estate of _____, as Vendor, certain lands and premises described as Part of Lot __, Concession __, City of Pickering, municipally described as L__ Finch Avenue, Pickering, Ontario (the **"Property"**);

(b) the Assignor has agreed to assign the said Purchase Agreement to the Assignee; and

(c) the Assignee has agreed to assume the payment of all monies due under the said Purchase Agreement.

NOW THEREFORE WITNESSETH THAT in consideration of the sum of **TWO DOLLARS ($2.00)** of lawful money of Canada and other good and valuable consideration (the receipt and sufficiency whereof is hereby acknowledged by the Assignor), the Assignor agrees to and with the Assignee as follows:

1. The Assignor hereby assigns to the Assignee the Purchase Agreement and its interest in the Property, to have and to hold the same as if the Assignee was named as Purchaser in the Purchase Agreement and the Assignor does hereby grant, release and quit claim unto the Assignee the Purchase Agreement and its interest in the Property, together with all appurtenances thereto belonging or appertaining and all improvements thereon and all of the right, title and interest of the Assignor therein and thereto.

2. No additional consideration has been paid by the Assignee in respect of the assignment of the Purchase Agreement.

3. The Assignor hereby covenants with, represents and warrants to the Assignee that it has done no act to encumber the Property and has done no act or has been guilty of no omission or laches whereby the Purchase Agreement has become, in part or entirety, in any way impaired or invalid.

4. The Assignee hereby covenants and agrees to and with the Assignor that it will assume, pay and discharge all monies due and to become due under the said Purchase Agreement and indemnifies and saves harmless the Assignor from all monies due and to become due under the Purchase Agreement and will indemnify and save harmless the Assignor against and from the payment of the same, or any part thereof, and will observe, keep and perform all the terms, covenants and conditions contained in the Purchase Agreement and which the Assignor has agreed to observe, keep and perform.

5. This Agreement and everything herein contained shall extend to, bind and ensure to the benefit of the successors and assigns of the parties hereto.

DATED as of the day and year first written above.

_____ **LTD.**, in trust for a company to be incorporated.

Per: _____
Name and Title:
I have the authority to bind the Corporation.

_____ **INC.**

Per: _____
Name and Title:
I have the authority to bind the Corporation.

(c) Transfer/Deed of Land

This is the document, Form 1, from the Land Registry Office, that is stamped "accepted for registration" by the Land Registrar.

(d) Statement of Adjustments

Solicitors work out what a party owes to the other party for deposit, taxes, oil, etc. This information is listed in a document called a "Statement of Adjustments" and is covered in more detail at section 16.5.7.

(e) Charge/Mortgage of Land

If a mortgage is involved, it is registered on title in the Land Registry Office by way of a Charge/Mortgage of Land (Form 2).

(f) Notice of an Agreement of Purchase and Sale

When a savvy investor buys a real property, in particular a parcel of land, if the closing is many months away, the new soon-to-be owner will have his lawyer prepare and register a Notice of an Agreement of Purchase and Sale with the Land Registry Office by way of a Document General Form (Figure 16.12). To do so, he will have to pay the LTT, which he can recover if closing does not take place. This is a great protection for the investor because it serves notice to the world that he has an interest in the property. For example, with such a notice on title, no lender would lend money to the vendor using the property as collateral.

Figure 16.12
Notice of an Agreement of Purchase and Sale

NOTICE OF AN AGREEMENT OF PURCHASE AND SALE

Notice is hereby given, of a registered Agreement of Purchase and Sale of land, dated the 10th day of October, 2006, made

BETWEEN

AS PURCHASERS

-and-

AS VENDORS

Affecting the land described in Schedule "A" appended hereto under which, (Purchaser), in Trust for a Company to be Incorporated, agreed to purchase the vacant agricultural lands described in Schedule "A", for the purchase price of $875,000.00, which purchase was to have been completed 60 days after removal of conditions, or sooner, at Purchaser's option.

The Purchaser is prepared to produce the Agreement of Purchase and Sale to which this notice relates for inspection by any person who can establish that he has an interest in the lands described in Schedule "A".

DATED at the Town of Richmond Hill this 9th day of December 2006.

The address of the Purchaser for service is _____

16.6 ENVIRONMENTAL SITE ASSESSMENT (AUDIT/REPORT)

Understand the implications of not performing an environmental site assessment and know the phases and responsibilities involved.

Environmental pollution has become a major issue in real estate transactions, particularly with factories. Some situations are so bad that the costs of removing the contamination are higher than the value of the clean property. It is impossible, today, to sell an industrial property without the Offer containing a clause requiring that the property be clean. It is frequently also required for other kinds of properties.

A powerful incentive for insisting on an Environmental Site Assessment (ESA) before you buy a property is that, for almost all properties, lenders will refuse to give financing if they are not supplied with what they consider a satisfactory Environmental Assessment.

16.6.1 OWNER'S RESPONSIBILITY

A property owner with a contaminated site is not obligated to clean it up, unless the contamination has migrated onto neighbouring properties. Indeed, in this case, there is a regulatory requirement to remedy the situation under the Ontario *Environmental Protection Act* (R.S.O. 1990, c. E.19), when the contamination is causing an "adverse effect". That definition is rather vague, so people and the Ministry of the Environment (MOE) often use the impact of off-site migration as a clearer trigger for action. Regulations aside, there is tort law that supports landowner A's right to take landowner B to court if landowner B is doing something that impacts A's property.

Owners of contaminated property can recover damages from neighbouring polluters if they can be found and have assets to pay damages. On the other hand, if you buy contaminated land, you become the owner of the contamination and you can be held responsible for remediation, even if you did not create the contamination. Sometimes, it is easy to show that you are not the one who created the contamination, but this is not always the case and often does not remove you from responsibility.

Courts may order damages based on the costs to clean up to a "pristine" state, a higher standard than required by the MOE clean-up guidelines. The stringent "pristine" standard may be invoked, even where the current land use is commercial or industrial. Once the site is in a "pristine" state or damages have been awarded, there is no stigma attached to that site for once having been contaminated. This implies that the regulations permit that a site be cleaned to a less than a "perfect" (pristine) state for certain uses.

One cannot be too cautious. In British Columbia, a real estate agent sold a site on which a service station had been located. The vendor, a large oil company, commissioned an environmental company to determine the extent of the pollution and to have the site cleaned up. When the clean-up satisfied the vendor's environmental company, the engineer in charge issued a "clean bill of health" and the sale took place and closed. The buyer then asked his own environmental engineer to review the Environmental Assessment and remediation, and to conduct additional investigation if judged necessary. This engineer determined the clean-up had not been sufficient. The end result is that the buyer went to court; he should have asked for the review before removing the conditions.

16.6.2 ENVIRONMENTAL SPECIALISTS

Because this is a complicated field, it is a good idea to get to know a good environmental specialist who does not mind spending a few minutes on the phone to answer your occasional question. See also Appendix 2 at section 2.2, Books.

ESAs are generally conducted by specialized engineers (particularly Phase I ESAs), although they can be performed by non-engineers. The specialist involved relies on governmental and lender guidelines. These guidelines generally refer to pollution in parts per million (ppm) of a given contaminant. They can, and do, vary from jurisdiction to jurisdiction. During the process the engineer must at times make subjective decisions. In Canada, the minimum requirements are set by the Canadian Standards Association (CSA), Standard #Z768 for Phase I and #Z769 for Phase II.

ESAs are generally conducted by specialized engineers who rely on governmental and lender guidelines.

16.6.3 PHASES OF ENVIRONMENTAL SITE ASSESSMENT

There are three phases of Environmental Assessment, with phases becoming progressively more in depth, more costly, and more time-consuming to complete. Phases II and III only need to be completed if recommended by the previous phase.

(a) Phase I

This phase consists of a visual inspection combined with a review of owner's documents, interviews, registry information, ministry/department records and certificates, databases, and other relevant records. Generally, this costs between $2,000 and $3,000. Commonly, it takes 2 weeks to complete, but it is wise to plan on 4 weeks. An update, for example when a tenant leaves, costs anywhere from $300 to $1,200, if done by the same company that did the original Phase I.

(b) Phase II

This phase is a more costly investigation involving various tests, including core drilling, hazardous waste assessment/analysis, and soil/water sampling. It can take 3 or many more weeks to complete and cost from $5,000 to many times that. It is necessary if Phase I determined that there are grounds to believe that contamination may exist.

(c) Phase III

The final phase involves additional sampling to delineate the boundaries of the contaminated area, laboratory analyses, remedial steps, and associated costs arising out of situations uncovered in Phase II. This phase can take a minimum of 3 months to several years to complete and costs, which vary enormously, can run into the millions of dollars for large properties.

16.7 ENVIRONMENTAL INSURANCE

Be aware of the availability of contamination clean-up insurance.

It is now possible to insure the risks associated with cleaning up a contaminated site. Insurance companies have developed sophisticated approaches and programs to allow a purchaser to acquire a brownfield (contaminated) site, the cleanup of which is guaranteed by the insurer, and paid by the vendor. Their coverage includes a Clean-up Cost Cap that protects the insurer against cost overruns associated with environmental clean-up activities due to:

- a greater extent of contamination than anticipated
- a higher level of contamination than anticipated
- changes in regulations that increase the cost of remediation, and
- discovery of other unknown pollution conditions.

It is possible to integrate this Clean-up Cost Cap with Pollution Legal Liability, which is a form of insurance designed to transfer the risk of clean-up for unknown pollution conditions, third-party toxic tort claims, waste transportation and disposal liability, and economic losses due to pollution conditions.

16.8 SELLING A COMMERCIAL PROPERTY

Make the shift to the vendor's side of the table and consider the unique details of the vendor's world.

A vendor can use many of the ideas in the preceding sections dealing with buying a property when selling a property. However, there are certain details that are unique to selling.

16.8.1 ESTABLISHING MARKET VALUE FOR YOUR PROPERTY

Pricing a property for sale may, or may not, be the most important aspect of a sale, but if it is done correctly, it will bring peace of mind to any vendor and will certainly avoid late price adjustments that can be ego shocking. Since selling price is of paramount concern for every vendor, we should start by stating that, in our experience as real estate professionals, most (except large ones) vendors are irrational when they first come up with an asking price.

No source of pricing information will be 100% accurate. However, you can usually expect to sell within 10% of a well-established asking price; depending on the market, it may be a little more. The process for establishing a solid asking price can be time consuming, but it is the best approach if you want to feel confident in the price you set.

(a) How to Place a Value on Your Property

You can use the sources described below to put a value on your property.

1. **Multiple Listing Service (MLS).** Ask a commercial real estate agent to print listings offered for sale and listings sold of comparable properties. Give him the geographic boundaries of the area of interest, using street names. You can also go to <MLS.ca>, select the properties of interest, and call the listing agents to get more information on each property. Ask that they e-mail you a copy of the listings involved.

2. **Real Estate Board Library.** Go to the local real estate board's library, if it is open to the public, and ask to consult sales history data.

3. **Signs.** Depending on the type of property you are selling, it may be of benefit to drive around the area to see if you can find signs on comparable properties for sale (or lease) or recently sold. Call the agents for information. Sold properties are especially interesting because they show you the spread between asking and selling price. If a property sells at full asking price or very close to it (1-2%), the asking price was too low, unless it was a unique situation. During a crazy vendors' market, where virtual auctions can take place, again, ask for a copy of the listings. The drawback in this approach is that many large properties go on sale without a sign being placed in front of them, such as office buildings, retail plazas, leased industrial buildings, and multi-family buildings.

4. **Real Estate Professionals.** Call a commercial real estate brokerage firm located in the area where your property is located. If you don't know any, you may call:
   – the local real estate board and ask for names of members located in your area
   – look in the Yellow Pages
   – make note of the firms' names on "For Sale" or "For Lease" signs in the area, and
   – call a large real estate developer or landlord (someone who deals with real estate agents on an everyday basis) and ask to be given a few names.

   When you call the brokerage company, ask to talk to the "broker of Record". He is the owner or manager. Tell him that you want the name of one of their top agents specializing in your type of property. Invite three such agents from different companies to come to see the property to give you a price. It is unprofessional for an agent to price a property sight unseen, so be wary if this happens.

5. **Appraisers.** If your property is large enough, for instance worth over $500,000, you should definitely secure an appraisal. It may cost you up to 1% of the value of your property, but it may result in you selling for 5-10% more. An appraisal provides you with the following:
   – reasonably accurate valuation
   – considerable data on your property (most vendors do not have all the data an appraisal will cover or uncover)
   – a professional (the appraiser) to answer your questions
   – a strong foundation for your asking price, and
   – great peace of mind.

Agents and appraisers follow a similar route to place a value on a property. They find properties that have sold recently (in the last few months, whenever possible), mark up or down adjustments to be able to compare your property to these, and come up with a value. The inherent weakness here is that they are dealing with the past. It is not too serious in a large and active market, but may be a big factor in others. Generally, real estate agents have a better understanding of specific areas, prices, and trends, but are less thorough and methodical in their approach than appraisers and have less complete databases of information, particularly for sold properties.

However, they are free. Appraisers, on the other hand, collect more data and do more in-depth analysis. Their process is more complete, but they are not free. (See Chapter 14 for a more thorough discussion of appraisals.)

(b) Reconciliation

In an ideal situation, a vendor or the vendor's agent on his behalf will then take all the data compiled on comparable properties (5-20 is ideal) and compare the selling price to the area of the property for each. Then, using the notes made throughout the process, he will adjust the values to reflect the property to be sold. For example, one property may be 80 years old and another one 40. Or the physical condition of one may rank 9/10 and another one 4/10.

Reconciliation is the difficult part of the process and is best done by an appraiser. After the adjustments, the vendor will be left with an adjusted total price and a price based on building or land area, for each property. Usually, a few comparables will be abnormally high or low, compared to the others, and should be discarded. Once again, this is where the good appraiser shines. As part of his duties, he talks to the various parties and tries to unearth all important details affecting the sale of comparable properties. Working with the adjusted prices, the vendor must then settle on an asking price.

16.8.2 MAXIMIZING YOUR SALE PRICE

There can be a huge difference between a selling price, which is after the fact, and an asking price. As a vendor, you should have only one goal — the highest possible selling price achieved in a reasonably short period. Although you can't change the basic characteristics of a property, such as location, quality of the building, or age, there are a number of

> *There can be a huge difference between a selling price, which is after the fact, and an asking price.*

things you can do to ensure you maximize your selling price and minimize the length of time your property is on the market.

(a) Tenancies

On the surface, the number of tenants, their quality (covenant), rentals, and lease terms and conditions at the time of sale are beyond your control? Not quite. You can make changes.

- **Replace a Poor Tenant (if the lease permits).** Too many landlords tolerate a poor tenant because they are apprehensive about finding a new one. For example, they keep a tenant on a montly basis or in spite of continually late payments.
- **Renegotiate Rentals.** For example you could say to your tenant, "You have 1 year left on your lease. If you wait say, 9 months to renew, I expect to charge you a rental of $51 per m² ($4.75 per sq ft). If you renew now for 5 years, I will make it $50 per m² (or give you 2 months free rent (even better option)). If you sign a 10-year lease, I will give you 3 months free rent." Note: if you are a smart landlord, you will give the 6th month of the next 3 years free, not 3 months upfront. By doing that, you have decreased two things attached to your proposal: your cost and your risk. You've also made it easy for the buyer to mortgage the property.

- **Renegotiate the Terms of the Lease.** For example, you could say to your tenant, "You have a right of first refusal (i.e., I was desperate for a tenant when I found you). I will pay you $x to cancel this clause (better to offer free rent)." The same can apply to an option to buy. Sometimes, tenants find themselves in financial straights and will welcome such a proposition with open arms.

(b) Property Condition

If the maintenance has been poor or deferred or the building is not clean, take care of what needs to be done before putting the property on the market. You are better to fix things like a leaky roof, broken windows, or holes in driveway asphalt because buyers will discount the asking price significantly for these things. If your roof is over 10 years old, obtain a roof inspection report from a roofer. And, if the building is big enough to justify the expense and its condition is decent, obtain a building condition report. If you have maintenance contracts, make a copy of them and have them ready for buyers to review.

Economic obsolescence refers to physical items that cannot be corrected at a reasonable cost, for example low ceilings or a truck turning radius that is too short. It may not be practical or financially feasible to correct these things, but be aware that they may impact the selling price.

On an everyday basis, few buildings are kept as clean as they could be. Now is the time to make a special effort until the property is sold. Remove that small mound of dirt; cut down those invasive trees; paint that rusty gas pipe in nice bright yellow; etc., and paint, paint, paint. Discard anything that is not in use. For most properties, it is best to request a large dumpster and start filling it.

(c) Financing Considerations

Here are some examples of steps you might consider taking beforehand to facilitate a sale.

- If the vendor is a partnership, the partners should give one of them the responsibility for the sale so that decisions can be made quickly by him alone, rather than having multiple meetings of the various partners or the selling agent chasing one after the other trying to get all of them to agree.
- A chartered accountant should be asked to project the fiscal and economic consequences of the sale. When armed with this information, some vendors change their mind about selling.
- Financing should be studied with a view to facilitating the sale. Possibilities are:
  – paying off a small mortgage
  – arranging a new mortgage with as high a LTV ratio as possible
  – better yet, requesting a proposal for a new mortgage to be in the name of an (acceptable) buyer, and
  – arranging leases as explained at 16.8.2(a).
- Ask your solicitor to check the property title, with an aim to ensure that there is nothing to which a buyer could object, such as an old paid-off mortgage that has not been discharged.

(d) Environmental Report

If you do not have an environmental report or it is several years old, order a new one or an update. If you have one, make at least three copies.

(e) Floor Plans and Surveys

If you have floor plans, have them reduced to legal or letter size for marketing purposes. Have five copies of floor plan blueprints made (ask people to whom you give one to sign a receipt and a promise of return within a specified number of days). If you do not have a floor plan, have one made by an architectural student or use a floor measuring company. Do the same with surveys of the property.

(f) Sales Package

Prepare a sales package to give to potential buyers. It should include, at the very least, the following items:

- a rent roll
- three years of the property's financial statements
- a data sheet
- a location map
- an aerial colour photo, and
- a few ground colour photos.

Your sales package should answer any question or meet any objection a buyer may have before it is even formulated. You want your property to project a professional, reassuring image that promises no surprises. Another advantage of this approach is that it will allow conditional periods to be shorter.

All these things should bring you a faster sale and a premium price.

16.8.3 SELLING IN A DECLINING MARKET

When there is a market meltdown, such as took place in the Greater Toronto Area in the early 1990s, it is particularly difficult to sell a property. It is human nature to see all the faults with a property when you are buying, but when selling many vendors typically think their property is worth at least 20-30% more than its real market value. It can be deadly when owners are forced to sell during a market meltdown. Here is a scenario that took place in the early 1990s.

Example

An investor purchased a property for $2 million at the top of the market in 1988. In 1990, the owner tried to sell the property for $2.2 million, then reduced it to $2 million, still refusing to accept that the market was softening. At the end of 6 months, he listed it with another broker for $1,800,000, but the value was $1,600,000. Still no sale. In 1991, he tried at $1,600,000, but the market value was $1,400,000. And so on.

The tendency to refuse to recognize the true market value of a property can cost a vendor dearly, especially when the market is declining. Very few people have the wisdom to price a property based on its current market value, without letting their egos get in the way. In fact, it is more than ego. We call it "illogical greed". It goes this way: when a buyer sniffs around a property, the human tendency seems to be to find plenty of reasons to disparage it. Yet, as soon as that same person has acquired the same property, he sees it as of such great value that it is akin to sitting on a gold mine.

16.8.4 DIFFICULT SALES

If you have trouble selling a property in a difficult market, try this approach.

1. Price the property at the top of the market.
2. Ask for a relatively low down payment (10-20%).
3. Offer a 10- or 15-year VTB mortgage, at no interest.

If you are nervous about this approach, consult with your lawyer and try to have the deed or shares of the buyer's holding corporation, if there is one, held in trust by your lawyer. In case something goes wrong, you can get the property back easily.

If you wish, ask the buyer to pay some principal every year, starting with a small percentage.

> For example: On a 10-year mortgage, he'd pay:
> Year 1: 0.5% of the principal
> Year 2: 1%
> Year 3: 3%
> Year 4: 7%
> Year 5: 10%
> And so on.

16.9 THE LEASE-PURCHASE OPTION

See the advantages of the Lease-Purchase Option for both the tenant/buyer and landlord/vendor.

Still, you may hesitate to jump into this exciting field of real estate investing. After all, the unknown always appears strewn with danger and difficulties. If you want to do it the low risk way, consider the Lease-Purchase (also called "Lease-Option") route. This is a technique to acquire, or rather to control, by way of an option, a property when one has only limited capital with which to work. An investor can use it to do the following:
- acquire a property as the tenant/buyer (T/B), or
- sell a property as the landlord/vendor (L/V).

With a typical Lease-Purchase Option a landlord/owner agrees to give a tenant (or would-be tenant) an option to buy the property for a period of time and usually at a set price. The price may also be determined at a later date based on an agreed-upon formula. Generally, a portion of the rent goes towards building the future down payment. The owner promises that he will not sell the property to somebody else. If he did, he would be in breach of contract and would expose himself to being sued. The incentive for an owner may be the sale of a hard-to-sell property, a higher price, and the guarantee offered by the consideration. The incentive for a buyer is that he controls the property, usually with little money, has lots of time to conduct his due diligence, is not obligated to buy, and can spend money to improve it if he is sure to exercise his option to purchase.

A Lease-Purchase is created by two documents, the Lease and the Conditional Agreement of Purchase and Sale (the option).

The T/B leases the property from the L/V for a minimum of one year as a rule. This is the most common term, but it can be more (2-3 years) and rarely less. The lease payments are often a little higher than market rates (10-20%). A portion of the rental, ranging from 5-25% depending on the negotiating ability and needs of the two parties, is generally credited towards the purchase price. This sum becomes the property of the L/V if no sale takes place.

At the same time (each document being conditional on the other one), an Agreement of Purchase and Sale is signed, closing (if the option is exercised) at the end of the Lease term, with no obligation by the buyer to buy. A non-refundable deposit (the option consideration) is paid by the T/B to the L/V. If you buy, the deposit could be 1-2% of the purchase price and 2-3% when you sell. The non-refundable deposit is credited toward the purchase price at closing. When negotiating, always ask the other party what figure he has in mind first. Use minimum figures with a vendor and maximum with a buyer.

If the T/B does not close, he loses the portion of his rental payments that were credited toward the purchase price and his option consideration. While an L/V may become upset if the T/B tells him that he will not close, he will come to realize that it is a blessing because he can keep the option money and start anew. If the T/B exercises the option, a typical property closing takes place.

You can also approach a vendor or a landlord to offer to lease his property on the condition that you have an option to buy in the lease for, say, two years, at a price agreed upon or to be determined by an appraisal. The difference here from a typical Lease-Purchase Option is that in this situation your option deposit (rarely there is one) is not at risk, whereas if you paid an option consideration it could be lost.

It's easy to find a T/B for your Lease-Option Properties. The cash they give you up-front is non-refundable and it is tax-deferred income because no sale has taken place yet. T/Bs who don't exercise their option to buy, routinely "forget" that the money isn't refundable. Consider tape-recording your conversation with the T/B so that you can refresh his memory or make it very clear in writing at negotiating time.

Disclosure is the name of the game in real estate today. When in doubt do it in writing.

Disclosure is the name of the game in real estate today. When in doubt do it in writing.

When you choose the Lease-Purchase Option, you should disclose to the tenant any item that may be required to be disclosed if the transaction were an outright sale.

16.9.1 THE TENANT/BUYER

Lease-Purchase Options are generally used by buyers who do not have enough money for the down payment and buying expenses, have bad or no credit, or have no proof of income that will satisfy a lender. This is often the case with contractors.

There are a number of advantages to this system for the T/Bs.

- They can move into a house or a commercial building with the certainty that it will be their property if they choose to close.
- They have the opportunity to try out the property and its location. If there is something that the T/B finds unsuitable or not up to the expected quality, they do not have to close. They will, of course, lose their option money but it may be better than being forced to close on an unwanted property.
- They have a year or more to save money for the down payment.
- After they have paid the L/V regularly for one year, they have a reference for their financing. The L/V will give the T/B a letter to this effect.

If the T/B does not have any credit rating at the end of the lease term, he can still do a Lease/Purchase if the L/V is willing to help. He can do so in two ways.

1. The L/V arranges for a new mortgage. If the latter can be assigned, all the better. If it can't, the T/B stays in the building as a 5- to 10-year tenant and pays the amount of mortgage payments to the L/V every month. At the end, the T/B's credit should be acceptable and he can close the deal.
2. The L/V takes back a mortgage for the full amount or as a second mortgage behind an existing first.

16.9.2 THE LANDLORD/VENDOR

There are two main kinds of L/V. There are those who want the top price, sometimes above market, and those whose property has problems.

The advantages of the Lease-Purchase Option for L/Vs are as follows:

- very high probability of effecting a sale
- a property offered for Lease-Purchase Option will move much faster than a regular sale
- if T/B fails to close, the L/V has received:
  - regular rentals
  - extra rentals, if they were a little higher than market, and
  - option money; and
- in addition:
  - the T/B, commonly, has taken care of all repairs and ongoing maintenance problems
  - the T/B is usually a better-quality tenant than an ordinary one, because he already views himself as the owner of the property and will take care of it, whereas an ordinary tenant may not care much, and
  - frequently, the T/B will spend money in improvements.

16.10 BUYING YOUR FIRST INVESTMENT PROPERTY

Project costs and benefits with the aid of four investing scenarios.

In order to help readers further, we are offering a few scenarios based on the amount of cash available to them. The scenarios assume that their credit is good enough to borrow. If it is not, the only hope to get started is by using the Lease-Purchase Option approach.

16.10.1 UP TO $20,000 IN CASH

The first property selected for the category is on Simcoe Street in Oshawa, Ontario. (See Figure 16.13.) It is listed on MLS at $139,900 and we are assuming that it will sell for $135,000. The vendor should be receptive to a Lease-Purchase Option deal because he is not desperate for money since he will consider a VTB.

The Gross Operating Income (GOI) is:

$909.16 + $550
= $1,459.16 x 12
= $17,510 per year

The expenses are:

Taxes of $3,000 and utilities of $1,500 = $ 4,500
The Net Operating Income (NOI) will be: $17,510 – $4,500 = $13,010

Figure 16.13
Up to $20,000 in Cash

xxx Simcoe St S	**List: $139,900 For Sale**
Oshawa, Ontario L1H4J8 Map: 269-27-R	Sale
Dir/Cross St: Simcoe/Bloor	**DOM:** 152	Sold Date:
Orig Price: $149,900 **Taxes:** $3,000/2003/Annual	**Contract Dt:** 5/20/2004

Store W/Apt/Office Store W/Apt/Office | **Lease Term:**
Commercial | **Freestanding:** N | **SPIS:** N
Store Plus Apartment | **Occup:** Tenant | **Franchise:** N
Possession: Immediate

MLS#: E123456   **PIN#:**

Total Area:	1,050 Sq Ft	**Survey:**			Public Transit
Ofc/Apt Area:	400 Sq Ft	**Lot/Bldg/ Unit/Dim:**	14.2X95.7 Feet Building		
Indust Area:		**Lot Irreg:**		**Soil Test:**	
Retail Area:	650 Sq Ft	**Crane:**	N	**Outside Storage:**	N
Apx Age:	51-99	**Bay Size:**		**Rail:**	N
Volts:		**%Bldg:**		**Basement:**	Y
Amps:		**Washrooms:** 2		**Elevator:**	
Zoning:	Comm	**Water:**	Municipal	**UFFI:**	No
Truck Level:		**Water Supply:**		**Assessment:**	
Grade Level:		**Sewers:**	San+Storm	**Chattels:**	N
Drive-In:		**A/C:**	N	**LLBO:**	
Double Man:		**Utilities:**	A	**Days Open:**	
Clear Height:		**Garage Type:**	None	**Hours Open:**	
Sprinklers:	N			**Employees:**	
Heat:	Baseboard	**Park Spaces:**		**Seats:**	

Bus/Bldg Name:		**For Year:**	**Financial Statement:** N
Actual/Estimated:			

Taxes:	**Heat:**	**Gross Inc/Sales:**	**Est Value Inv At Cost:**
Insur:	**Hydro:**	- Vacancy Allow:	**Com Area Upcharge:**
Mgmt:	**Water:**	- Operating Exp:	**Percentage Rent:**
Maint:	**Other:**	= Net Income B4 Debt:	

Seller Will Consider A Vtb 2nd, Front Tenant Appx 6 Yrs. No Survey Available. Rear Tenant Is Month To Month. Next To Pizza Pizza (Just Completed Major Reno) Feet Away From 401 Ramp. Zellers/Swiss Chalet Across The Road. Close To Municipal Pk'g Lot. Apt Has 5 Rms.

You should offer to lease it for 2 years (see the sandwich lease mentioned in Chapter 7 at section 7.4.11) for $12,500/year net with an option to buy at a price of $138,000 with a VTB, of course, at a favourable rate. The vendor may balk at that, but you might be able to pacify him by offering to pay one year's rent ($12,500) in advance.

Note that, if you assume that the market value is $135,000, in 2 years (based on a 6% annual increase in value) it will be worth: $135,000 x 1.12 = $151,200. Furthermore, the NOI will have probably increased to $14,000+/year. If you decided to sell, your profit would be $151,200-135,000 = $16,200, less selling expenses. In exchange, you would have managed the property for two years.

Assuming you have made no changes to this property, after 2 years when (and if) you exercise the option, the situation should be as follows:

Property value:	$151,000
Funded by:	
Mortgage amount (85%)	$128,500
Down payment:	$ 20,000
Savings (in two years)	$ 2,500
Total investment:	$151,000
Mortgage payments (6.25%, 25-year am.):	$ 10,095[1]
NOI:	$ 14,000
CFBT: $14,000 - $10,095=	$3,905

ROE: $3,905 / $22,650 (equity)= 0.1724 or 17.24%

16.10.2 UP TO $60,000 IN CASH

An investor who has approximately $60,000 in cash may look for a Lease/Purchase Option or for a conventional purchase. He could hope to acquire a property of approximately the following values.

1. $175,000, using conventional financing;
2. $200,000 to $300,000 if he can use conventional financing plus a VTB. The figures might look as follows:

Price:	$300,000
Funded by:	
1st Mortgage:	$180,000
VTB:	$ 80,000
Total	$260,000
Down payment (saving $10,000 for ancillary expenses)	$ 50,000
Total investment:	$310,000; or

3. $400,000, if it is a multi-family property financed at 85%. All of these options are good but, undoubtedly, the second and third ones are preferable to build your nest egg faster.

---

1 For simplicity's sake, we have purposely left out: CMHC fees and premiums, ancillary buying expenses such as, for example, the LTT and reserves for repairs and replacements. It might be possible to generate more income and, therefore increase the property value by splitting the five room back apartment into two units.

The best option seems to be number 3, but it has the drawback of dealing with residential tenants who demand more property management attention. The flip side is that residential rentals usually are increased every year and the risk is low, thanks to the large number of tenants.

The property chosen for this example is in Belleville, Ontario. It is located on Belleville's main downtown street and the large lot (1,437 m² (15,470 sq ft)) will probably one day be redeveloped for retail uses. See Figure 16.14.

The vendor paid $650,000 in 1988. The property has some deferred maintenance needing urgent attention that could be cured with around $10,000 and some elbow grease on the part of the buyer. The property GOI is $85,538[2] and the expenses are $55,649 (65%), leaving an NOI of $29,889.

The problem with the property lies mainly with the very high expenses for: electricity: $12,444; gas: $10,572; water and sewer: $9,610; for a total of $32,626 per year. If this were reduced by one-third, saving $11,000, the NOI would jump to $40,000. This can be accomplished reasonably easily and without spending a huge amount of money. We are estimating $15,000 in capital improvement costs. The picture would look as follows:

GOI:	$ 85,538
Expenses:[3]	$ 55,649 (65%)
NOI:	$ 29,889
We are assuming:	
Purchase price of:	$ 280,000
Additional expenses:	$ 15,000
Total:	**$295,000**
Funded by:	
First Mortgage (70% at 6.5%/25 years)	$ 205,500
VTB, at 6% interest only, 5 years[4]	$ 40,000
Down payment required	$ 49,500
Total investment:	**$295,000**
Mortgage payments	
1st: Constant factor: 6.69%	$ 13,845
2nd: $40,000 x 6%	$ 2,400
Total debt service	**$ 16,215**

Cash Flow Before Taxes (CFBT): $29,889 - $16,215 = $13,674

ROE: $13,674/($49,500 - $7,128[5]=) $42,372 (equity) = 0.3227 or 32.27%

2 The listing sheet shows the GOI as $83,000, but the amount has increased since that date, as per listing agent. This illustrates how difficult it is to be sure of the GOI when there are many tenants, particularly residential ones.

3 To a person used to analyzing Income-Producing Properties (IPP), it is obvious that the vendor is either very incompetent, or has fallen into a rut and, after 15 years of ownership, is disgusted with the property. A 65% ratio of expenses to GOI is almost unthinkable. A smart buyer (without much cash to work with) can bring this ratio to less than 50% within 2-3 years, having spent less than $100,000. In 5 years, assuming a 15% higher GOI, we would have $85,538 x 15%= $12,830, for a total of $98,369. Our NOI, at 50%,would be $49,184. Assuming an 8.5% Cap Rate, the property would be worth $578,639. Our cost would have been: $295,000 + $100,000= $395,000, and our profit $578,639 - $395,000= $183,639.

4 If the VTB is not possible, there are two other options: CMHC insurance or a second mortgage. This can be a VTB, a private mortgage, or one that is insured by CMHC, as they now insure second mortgages (a CMHC-insured loan cannot be more than 90%).

5 Remember that, in principle, on closing you will be credited with the tenants' last month deposit: $85,538/12= $7,128.

Figure 16.14
Up to $60,000 in Cash

xxx Front St		**List:**	$299,900 For Sale
Belleville	Map: 900-13-H	Sale	
Dir/Cross St: Bridge St./Front		**DOM:**	260
Contract Dt: 2/9/2004		**Taxes:**	$8,151.63/2003/Annual

Investment		**Lease Term:**	
Multiplex	**Freestanding:** Y	**SPIS:**	
Apartment Complex	**Occup:** Tenant	**Franchise:**	N
Possession: 60 Days/Tba			

MLS#: X987654   **PIN#:**

Total Area:	15,500 Sq Ft	**Survey:**			
Ofc/Apt Area:	85 %	**Lot/Bldg/ Unit/Dim:**	85X182 Feet Lot	**Soil Test:**	
Indust Area:				**Outside Storage:**	
Retail Area:	15 %	**Lot Irreg:**			
Apx Age:		**Crane:**		**Rail:**	N
Volts:		**Bay Size:**		**Basement:**	N
Amps:		**%Bldg:**		**Elevator:**	
Zoning:	Comm/Res	**Washrooms:**		**UFFI:**	
Truck Level:		**Water:**	Municipal	**Assessment:**	
Grade Level:		**Water Supply:**		**Chattels:**	N
Drive-In:		**Sewers:**	San+Storm	**LLBO:**	
Double Man:		**A/C:**	N	**Days Open:**	
Clear Height:		**Utilities:**	Y	**Hours Open:**	
Sprinklers:	N	**Garage Type:**	Outside/Surface	**Employees:**	
Heat:	Other	**Park Spaces:**		**Seats:**	

Bus/Bldg Name: **For Year:** 2003   **Financial Statement:** Y

Actual/Estimated: Act

Taxes:	**Heat:** $10,572	**Gross Inc/Sales:**	**Est Value Inv At Cost:**
Insur: $3,798	**Hydro:** $12,444	- **Vacancy Allow:**	**Com Area Upcharge:**
Mgmt:	**Water:** $9,610	- **Operating Exp:**	**Percentage Rent:**
Maint:	**Other:**	= **Net Income B4 Debt:**	

Investments Opportunity Apartment Bldg.Consisting Of 12 Residential Units & 2 Main Street Store Fronts. Fully Rented In Downtown Area Close To River & Lake. Gross Rental Income Over $83,000/Yr. Statements Available To Interested Parties.

Exclude: Tenants Belongings.

16.10.3 UP TO $250,000 IN CASH

An investor with $250,000 in cash (or cash plus RRSP/RRIF) available can hope to buy a property worth between $700,000 and $1,200,000, depending on whether he finds an owner agreeable to a VTB or arranges a conventional commercial mortgage. If he chooses to buy a multi-family property with CMHC insurance, the value could be as high as $1,660,000 (85% LTV). For this scenario we have chosen a property on Lake Shore Boulevard West in Toronto (see Figure 16.15).

We like the following about this property:

- reasonable Cap Rate of 8.79% on asking price, likely to be over 9% on selling price of, say, $1,350,000
- reasonable expenses (apparently)
- good address and high traffic volume
- large site (15 parking spaces on site, which is excellent for Toronto)
- 24 hour TTC (public transportation)
- mixed uses
- 18 tenants, therefore low risk
- large building of 1,256.5 m² (13,525 sq ft), and
- in a neighbourhood that is improving.

The NOI is:	$ 122,231
Assuming purchase price of:	$1,350,000
Funded by:	
Mortgage: 70% at 6.5%, 25 years	$ 945,000
VTB at 6% interest only, 5 years	$ 160,000
Down payment:	$ 245,000
Net before debt servicing:	$ 122,231
Mortgage payments	
1st: Constant factor of 6.698% =	$ 75,955
2nd: $160,000 x 6% =	$ 9,600
Total debt service	**$ 85,555**
CFBT: $122,231 - $85,555 =	$ 36,676
ROE: $36,676/$245,000 (equity) =	**0.1497 or 14.97%**

Figure 16.15
Up to $250,000 in Cash (or cash and RRSP/RRIF)

xxx Lake Shore Blvd W		**Sold: $1,275,000 For Sale**
Toronto, Ontario M8W1N5 Map: 118-5-U		List: $1,390,000 For Sale
Sold Area: 13525 Sq Ft Sale		92% List
Dir/Cross St: 33rd Street	**DOM:** 127 **Sold Date:**	8/26/2004
Orig Price: $1,490,000 **Taxes:** $37,145/2003/Annual	**Contract Dt:** 4/21/2004	

Investment Commercial/Retail		**Lease Term:**
Mixed 2+ Cat	**Freestanding:** Y	**SPIS:**
Mixed	**Occup:** Tenant	**Franchise:**
Possession: 30 Days / Tba		

MLS#: W123456   **PIN#:**

Total Area:	13,525 Sq Ft	**Survey:**			Public Transit
Ofc/Apt Area:	6,998 Sq Ft	**Lot/Bldg/Unit/Dim:**	116.75X140 Feet Lot		
Indust Area:				**Soil Test:**	
Retail Area:	6,537 Sq Ft	**Lot Irreg:**	12 Ft R.O.W. @ Rear	**Outside Storage:**	
Apx Age:		**Crane:**		**Rail:**	
Volts:		**Bay Size:**		**Basement:**	Y
Amps:		**%Bldg:**		**Elevator:**	
Zoning:	Com/Res	**Washrooms:**	18	**UFFI:**	
Truck Level:		**Water:**	Municipal	**Assessment:**	
Grade Level:		**Water Supply:**		**Chattels:**	
Drive-In:		**Sewers:**		**LLBO:**	
Double Man:		**A/C:**	N	**Days Open:**	
Clear Height:		**Utilities:**	Y	**Hours Open:**	
Sprinklers:	N	**Garage Type:**	Lane	**Employees:**	
Heat:	Gas Hot Water	**Park Spaces:**	15	**Seats:**	

Bus/Bldg Name: **For Year:** 2003   **Financial Statement:**

Actual/Estimated: Est

Taxes: $37,145	**Heat:** $15,000	**Gross Inc/Sales:**	$190,634	**Est Value Inv At Cost:**	
Insur: $3,021	**Hydro:** $3,315	**- Vacancy Allow:**		**Com Area Upcharge:**	
Mgmt: $2,500	**Water:** $2,070	**- Operating Exp:**	$68,403	**Percentage Rent:**	
Maint: $4,998	**Other:** $354	**= Net Income B4 Debt:**	$122,231		

Retrofit Completed, Roof (8Yrs), 7 Shops, 11 Apts, High Traffic Count, 24Hr Ttc, Adjacent To New Condos, Note Lot Size, Ideal Development Site, Municipal Address 3503 - 3515 Lakeshore Blvd W

11 Stoves, 11 Fridges, 2 Gb&E, 1 Ob&E, Survey 1998

16.10.4 MORE THAN $600,000 IN CASH

An investor with more than $600,000 in cash (or cash plus RRSP/RRIF) available can seek a property between $1,000,000 and $2,500,000, and even $4,000,000 if it is a multi-family property and he uses CMHC mortgage insurance (85% LTV).

We have chosen a property in Welland, Ontario. See Figure 16.16.

This property appeals to us because of the following conditions:

- has 60 units
- can be CMHC insured (mortgage can be increased or a second mortgage arranged)
- has a large site of 3.20 acres
- is a really nice property (as per listing agent) and is only 25 years old
- is in a town of 48,000 people
- is less than a two-hour drive from Toronto
- is near Niagara College
- has a mortgage with a low rate of interest of 5.51%, and
- the vendor will take back a mortgage (as per listing agent).

The NOI is:	$ 241,184 (7% Cap Rate)
Assumed purchase price of:	$3,400,000
Funded by:	
Assumption of existing first at 5.51%	$1,800,000
VTB at 5%, interest only, 5 years[6]	$1,020,000
Down payment:	$ 580,000
Mortgage payments:	
1st	$ 131,970
2nd	$ 512,000
Total debt service	**$ 182,970**
Net before debt servicing:	$ 241,184
CFBT: $241,184 - $182,970 =	$ 58,214

ROE: $58,214/$580,000 (equity) =   0.1003 or 10.03%

It is not a great return, but there are three other considerations.

1. With 3.20 acres, there is a good possibility of adding more apartments.
2. Within 2 years, the NOI will likely have increased 5% through rental increases and the cutting of expenses. This would be an additional $12,059, making the CFBT = $70,273. The Cap Rate would become 12.12%.
3. Conversion to condominiums is likely.

Most important, in these two years the property would have increased in value by: $3,400,000 x 6% (see below) x 2 = $408,000!

---

6 An alternative is to ask the first mortgagee to increase the amount of the existing mortgage to an 85% LTV ratio ($2,809,000), leaving a down payment of $510,000, or to secure a second for up to $1,090,000. In both cases, CMHC will insure the mortgage. The VTB rate is unlikely to be as favourable as that of a loan with CMHC coverage, but one never knows with vendors, and there would not be any insurance premium.

Figure 16.16
More Than $600,000 in Cash

xx-xx Glenpark Dr		**List:**	**$3,450,000 Acres**
Welland	Map: 900-9-M	Sale	
Dir/Cross St: Thorold Road		**DOM:** 76	
Contract Dt: 8/11/2004		**Taxes:** $93,759.56/2003/Annual	

Investment			**Lease Term:**
Multiplex	**Freestanding:** Y		**SPIS:** N
Apartment Complex	**Occup:** Tenant		**Franchise:** N
Possession: Immediate			

MLS#: X987654   **PIN#:**

Total Area:	3.20 Acres	**Survey:**			
Ofc/Apt Area:		**Lot/Bldg/Unit/Dim:**	3.2X0 Acres Lot		
Indust Area:				**Soil Test:**	
Retail Area:		**Lot Irreg:**		**Outside Storage:**	
Apx Age:	16-30	**Crane:**		**Rail:**	
Volts:		**Bay Size:**			
Amps:		**%Bldg:**	30	**Basement:**	N
Zoning:	R M 4	**Washrooms:**	3	**Elevator:**	
Truck Level:		**Water:**	Municipal	**UFFI:**	No
Grade Level:		**Water Supply:**		**Assessment:**	
Drive-In:		**Sewers:**		**Chattels:**	Y
Double Man:		**A/C:**	N	**LLBO:**	
Clear Height:		**Utilities:**	A	**Days Open:**	
Sprinklers:	Part	**Garage Type:**	Outside/Surface	**Hours Open:**	
Heat:	Gas Hot Water	**Park Spaces:**		**Employees:**	
				Seats:	

Bus/Bldg Name:		**For Year:**	**Financial Statement:** Y
Actual/Estimated:			
Taxes:	**Heat:**	**Gross Inc/Sales:**	**Est Value Inv At Cost:**
Insur:	**Hydro:**	- **Vacancy Allow:**	**Com Area Upcharge:**
Mgmt:	**Water:**	- **Operating Exp:**	**Percentage Rent:**
Maint:	**Other:**	= **Net Income B4 Debt:**	

Superior Loc'n,Superior Bldgs(3-20 Units On 3.2 Acs.Mediterranean Design.Excellent Res.Area.Roof 2000,Eaves 2001.Near Niagara College,Bus Routes&Shopping.Assumable 1st Mortgage At 5.51% Until Feb 2009.Owners May Assist With 2nd.Call L.A.*Full Address: 22-36-42 Glenpark Drive

Superior Loc'n&Cond'n.(3-20 Unit Bldgs On 3.2 Acs)Mediterranean Style.Roof'00,Eaves'01.Excell.Assum.1st Mtg @5.51% Til Feb/09. Owners May Assist W/2nd Mtg,60 Fridges,60 Stoves,Call L.A.**Interboard Listing: Niagara Association Of Realtors**

In other parts of this book, we have advocated great caution with the LTV ratio. Here, we have used the maximum financing we could secure for two reasons.

- All the selected properties have multiple tenants, which means low risk
- To get started in real estate investing, generally, one has to make sacrifices, roll up one's sleeves, and take some extra risks.

Three of the properties chosen are not in Toronto because the returns are much lower in, or near, the GTA. We feel that the difference justifies driving once or twice a month to inspect the property involved.

A word of caution: To make projections regarding appreciation, one has to choose a rate. We have used 6%, as shown in Chapter 2 at 2.5.1. Remember that this rate is not a straight line. It goes up and down. The charts in Chapter 2 prove it.

To get started in real estate investing, generally, one has to make sacrifices, roll up one's sleeves, and take some extra risks.

Since you do not intend to sell the property in the short term, the appreciation rate simply provides you with a window in which to refinance. You can then use that new money to finance additional property renovations or acquisitions.

CHAPTER 17

Leasing

By the end of this chapter, you will be able to:

- Assist your agent in promoting your property and find the best tenant.
- Perform many of the marketing tasks, such as preparing the information tenants want to see, advertising your property, and ensuring your property shows at its best.
- Demonstrate to potential tenants the financial and business advantages of leasing.
- Make requests of the prospective commercial tenant in order to complete your financial and background checks.
- Know what and how to check a residential tenant's financials and background.
- Watch for the warning signs that may point to a risky tenant.
- Customize a standard lease form by adding clauses that you want.
- Develop a friendly and professional rapport with your tenants.

This chapter explains how to deal with tenants, finding tenants, negotiating with them and their agents, and presents a review of the clauses and conditions that you should watch for in dealing with leases. For an understanding of the types of leases, see Chapter 7 at section 7.4.3.

17.1 FINDING TENANTS

Assist your agent in promoting your property and find the best tenant.

17.1.1 USING AN AGENT

As when you are buying and selling, when you are leasing a property you have the option of using a real estate agent or marketing the property yourself. A real estate agent worth his salt offers many advantages. He is intimately familiar with market information, other agents, and potential tenants (see Chapter 13 for more detail). It's true that you can handle many of the tasks an agent will do for you, but an agent will do them faster and probably better. The commission you pay will be well worth the time and aggravation you will avoid and will likely result in better quality tenants and faster occupancy. Again, it is worth noting that you should be sure to engage the services of a real estate agent who is experienced in dealing with the type of property you are leasing and the market area in which you are located.

In order to get quality service from an agent, an owner or landlord must give proper direction and supervision. Ask to see a written marketing plan and copies of the ads, if any, planned to promote the property. Check on the quality, type, and location of any signs erected to lease the property. Should there be more than one? Does the location of the signage permit highest visibility? Ensure your agent has informed the municipal economic development office of the availability of the property and any other agency that could generate prospects.

A good client/agent relationship requires frequent feedback; verbally every week or two and in writing, in detail, once a month. There are also a number of ways that you can help your agent get top rental and the best tenants for your property:

- Prepare the property so that it shows at its best.
- Answer any request promptly.
- Make decisions without delay.
- Meet prospects, if required to do so.

Keep in mind that an agent may have many listings and may be too busy to do justice to your listing. Remember, stay on top of your agent's activities in promoting and showing your property.

17.1.2 ACTING AS YOUR OWN AGENT

If you have the time to make marketing your property your absolute focus and the marketing expertise to do the job well, you may decide to act as your own agent. If you are unwilling to pay a commission, you may miss out on a strong tenant because agents are unlikely to show your property. On the other hand, you may decide to market the property yourself but still pay a commission to an agent who acts on behalf of the tenant. In this case, you should indicate "agents welcome" when agents call and on any written material, including signage.

17.2 MARKETING THE PROPERTY

Perform many of the marketing tasks, such as preparing the information tenants want to see, advertising your property, and ensuring your property shows at its best.

Whether you are marketing the property yourself or using an agent, there are a number of tasks that need to be completed to ensure you attract the best tenants for your property. You may also want to review selling a property in Chapter 16 at 16.8, as much of the advice given there applies here as well.

Most of what follows can be used by you directly, if you market the property yourself, or to supervise and assist your agent.

17.2.1 SURVEY THE COMPETITION

Drive around the general area of your property, jot down the telephone numbers you see on "For Lease" signs, and get the details from the listing agents.

17.2.2 FIND COMPARABLES AND SET PRICE

Select four or five buildings for lease in the area and study them carefully, visiting them if possible. Identify your property's strengths and weaknesses against the competition. You must develop the ability to find what special advantages your property offers. In other words, how is your property superior to others on the market?

Also, consider what is the best use for the property. It may not be the previous or current use. To help you in this consideration, make a list of every possible use that comes to mind, even if it appears improbable initially. Let it sit for a day or two, and then cross out what appears unfeasible or unrealistic. Finally, select the most likely one(s) and focus your marketing accordingly.

To really know your property, we suggest you analyze the area, the neighbourhood, and the property. You probably know most of the data, but even you may be surprised that you will discover new nuances. It is a certainty that it will help your prospective tenant feel more comfortable with your property. Figures 17.1, 17.2, and 17.3 present examples of these analyses for an industrial property in Toronto. These are three simple examples, but it is possible to be more extensive, to the point of exaggeration. Some inexperienced agents go overboard when doing analyses.

If you can convince a friendly real estate agent to conduct a search of comparable buildings that have leased in the past year, this can provide valuable information too. You may also approach an appraiser to obtain a list of leased buildings. Some will perform this task for free as a goodwill gesture and some will charge a modest fee. After you have completed your analysis, preferably with your agent's input, set a rental for your property (after reading about appraisals in Chapter 14). Be sure to have this rental in mind when you put your property on the market. Surprisingly, it is not uncommon to come across people, both owners and agents, who consider themselves highly sophisticated but then say, "There is no asking rental set; make an offer."

Figure 17.1
Area Analysis for Industrial Use

Area Analysis for Industrial Use

This area in Toronto is bounded by Royal York Road to the west, Highway 401 to the north, Keele Street to the east and Dundas/St. Clair on the south.

Intersected by main arteries, such as Eglinton Avenue, giving access to the Highway 427-401 basket-weave, and Jane Street, connecting the Highway 400-401 basket-weave with the Gardiner Expressway - Q.E.W. combination, it is very obvious that this area is good for the transportation-conscious business-man.

Running from the south-east to the north-west, virtually parallel to Weston Road, another major transport link is the CN-CP line providing rail service to industry. Public transportation is provided by four bus lines close by, connecting with Go Train and subway services.

Aside from the industrial-commercial features of this area, there are ample recreational spots at close quarters: the Humber River, with parkland along its banks, golf courses, community centres, and public swimming pools.

It is, to a great extent, this balance of commercial and recreational living which has attracted such a large number of national and international companies.

The ever ongoing change and modernization of this activity-filled part of Toronto is exemplified by a very recent large (30 acres) residential high-rise development on the south-west-side of Trethewey Drive. This will no doubt add both white- and blue-collar workers to an already excellent labour pool.

Figure 17.2
Neighbourhood Analysis for Industrial Use

Neighbourhood Analysis for Industrial Use

The property is located in an industrial area bounded by Trethewey Drive, Eglinton Avenue West, the CN-CP rail corridor and Jane Street.

Of this somewhat triangular-shaped pocket, virtually half is in the Borough of North York to the north, and half in the Borough of York to the south.

Neither the M2 Zoning in North York nor the M Zoning in York allows outside storage, which means that the area is kept in a clean and well-maintained state.

The mixture of structures is such that the larger ones are located at the north-west tip of Industry Street, whereas the smaller, and multiple occupancy, buildings are located towards the south-east portion of Industry Street.

Although Industry Street is "The Artery", carrying traffic to medium and heavy industry within this area, a stretch of parkland extends along its easterly border, from south of Eglinton Avenue to north of Lawrence Avenue. Presently used for recreational purposes, most of it will become the corridor for the Highway 400 extension.

Surrounding the pocket of industrial zoning and activity is a rather dense residential area with a predominantly ethnic population. This, of course, makes for a good source of labour.

Access to the subject property from, and to, Highway 401 is presently limited to only one route, Jane Street. However, as indicated on Exhibit "AA" the planned extension of Highway 400 southward, will open up the area and facilitate truck and passenger vehicle traffic, in and out of Industry Street, to connect with all other major arteries.

Companies, which found this area to be just right for them for some time now, are:
- Sprague Electric of Canada Limited
- C.P. Clare, Div. of General Instrument of Canada Limited
- Liquid Paper Limited
- Johnson Matthey & Mallory Limited
- Ferranti Packard Limited
- Continental Group of Canada Limited
- Canadian Admiral Corporation Limited
- Moore Business Forms
- Kodak Limited

Figure 17.3
Property Analysis for Industrial Use

Property Analysis for Industrial Use

This industrial building is situated on a large, flat, 14.283-acre piece of land having a frontage of 1,130' on Industry Street. The vacant 6 acres would allow for expansion to over 300,000 square feet (on one floor).

The structure is of solid brick and block construction and its saw-tooth type roof, which covers approximately 60 percent of the structure, indicates that the first stage of construction took place around the mid-1940s.

Since this building was erected in stages, it lends itself very easily to being divided into three, virtually self-contained, areas of approximately 51,000, 54,000, and 72,000 square feet. The dividing walls are already in place and the openings could be closed up very easily.

Shipping facilities, along the frontage on Industry Street, provide excellent access to the three sections.

Because of the tremendous hydro power requirements by the present occupant, there are two 1,000-KVA sub-stations. One of these sub-stations, along with a 700-square-foot area inside the building, would be leased back by the Vendor for testing purposes for a few months, up to 1 year.

Given the quality, solidity, and versatility of the facility, room for expansion, and excellent availability of employees very close by, this is a most desirable piece of real estate.

The owners are prepared to sub-divide the building as set out in the second paragraph above, to provide space as required by users, varying in size from 15,000 square feet to the entire 178,000 square feet.

Shipping doors and office space will also be constructed to suit.

17.2.3 PREPARE A DATA SHEET

Prepare a Data Sheet (see Figure 13.5) to provide basic information to a prospect, so that he can determine if the property is of interest to him. It should be two to five pages in length and include a location map and floor plan or site plan. If the space is a large one, it may be worth preparing a Property Brief (see section 13.8.2 in Chapter 13). The Property Brief is only provided to those who show a definite interest; to prospects you give only a data sheet.

17.2.4 ACQUIRE A FLOOR PLAN AND SITE PLAN

If you do not have a floor plan, make a sketch. It is essential to have one and the first thing you should do when you buy any building. A better approach is to secure a site plan from a floor measuring company.

17.2.5 PUT YOUR FLOOR PLAN IN THE WINDOW

When marketing your property, be it for sale or for lease, if you have a glass door or a window at street level and visible from the street, tape the Data Sheet and floor plan to it, preferably enlarged to 28 cm x 43 cm (11 x 17 in), so that it can be easily seen from the outside. If there is much foot traffic in and out of the building, it is a good idea to have these visible from inside and outside.

17.2.6 INSTALL SIGNS

Put up signs, more than one, if possible. If the property lends itself to it, show the floor plan and/or the site plan on the sign. Figure 17.4 shows a simple sign for a multiple-occupancy industrial building. The present fashion in real estate signs is toward huge sizes, although it certainly depends on the type of property and the building itself. Large properties may warrant two 3 m x 4.8 m (10 x 16 ft) signs, for example, but it depends how far the signs are from traffic. The minimum size we recommend is 81 cm x 121 cm (32 x 48 in).

17.2.7 TAKE PHOTOGRAPHS

Take colour photos of your property. The most flattering photos are colour aerial photos taken at an oblique angle. They can be a very powerful aid in marketing a property in ads and brochures. There are also artists in many markets who will generate colour renderings on computer, starting at as little as $300. These can show your property in a very favourable light. This is particularly helpful if the building, for example, has an addition or a major renovation planned that is not yet erected.

17.2.8 PREPARE THE BUILDING TO SHOW

As soon as you know that your tenant is moving out, thoroughly inspect the premises to make a list of items he must remedy. Once your former tenant moves out, visit the premises again and, armed with pen and paper, conduct a thorough inspection. Run through the Landlord's Post-Tenancy Checklist

As soon as your former tenant moves out, visit the premises and, armed with pen and paper, conduct a thorough inspection.

(Checklist 17.1). Also review the list under Improving a Building (section 19.6 in Chapter 19) and use every possible point to ensure your building shows at its best.

Figure 17.4
Sample Site Plan Signs

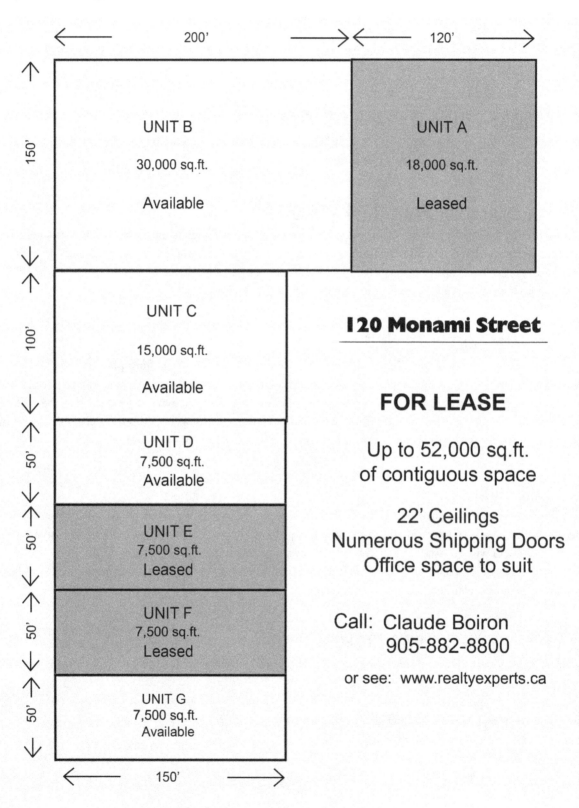

Checklist 17.1
Landlord's Post-Tenancy Checklist

LANDLORD'S POST-TENANCY CHECKLIST

Property Address: _____

This is a series of reminders of what should be done after a tenant has moved out.

- ❑ Thoroughly inspect the property and make a note of everything that should be done.
- ❑ Shampoo or replace broadlooms.
- ❑ Redecorate.
- ❑ Make sure that utilities are switched over to your name.
- ❑ You <u>must</u> keep one phone line so that the alarm system, now in your name, is operative.
- ❑ Change the outside locks.
- ❑ In winter, check that the heating units are all on, with thermostats set at 5 degrees above freezing, and that the gas is turned on, or that there is sufficient oil, or propane in the tank.
- ❑ In summer, set the circulating fans on "on", so that the air moves about.
- ❑ Remove <u>all the signs</u> from the previous occupant, inside and outside.
- ❑ Contact the fire department, regarding the sprinkler system. Has it been checked during the last year? Is it connected to a fire alarm system?
- ❑ Talk to the neighbours to ask them to keep an eye on the property.
- ❑ Talk to the police and ask them to keep an eye on the property.
- ❑ Turn off the water valve at the building entrance.
- ❑ There may be items that should be replaced, repaired, painted, etc., but that you do not want to, or cannot, do. Get an estimate for every one of them, so that you know the cost involved and can inform the new tenant, during the course of negotiations, if you are asked to do it.
- ❑ Contact your insurance agent, and be ready for a shock. Premiums for empty buildings skyrocket. The premium for an occupied building may be $5,000/year, but it may jump to $20,000-30,000 for an empty one. <u>Do not make the mistake of staying without insurance to save money.</u>

17.2.9 GATHER OPERATING COSTS

Gather together all the operating costs of the building, even if the previous tenant paid the suppliers directly. You can usually obtain the figures by calling utility companies. Show this as the total amount and the amount per square metre (square foot) of the building.

17.2.10 MAKE LOW COST IMPROVEMENTS

Buy a few hours of an architect's time. Ask how you can beautify the building at little or reasonable cost. Remember: "It is better to wear a $200, off-the-rack suit with a $100 silk tie, than a $1,000-custom-tailored suit with a $9.99 polyester tie." Similarly, a building owner can install a great entrance door with a canopy, on an otherwise run-of-the-mill building.

17.2.11 TAKE CARE OF REPAIRS AND DEFERRED MAINTENANCE

Repair what should be repaired. Clean, clean, and clean again, and as frequently as required. You may want to do some light renovating. If a tenant has been in the building for a few years, maintenance may have been neglected. Take care of anything that needs doing now to make the property show at its best.

17.2.12 PLACE NEWSPAPER ADS

Place a display ad in newspapers of appropriate size to reflect the value of your property. If your property is worth $2-million, don't buy a 2.5 cm x 3.8 cm (1 x 1½ in) ad. You would be belittling your property. It should be at least two newspaper columns in width, generally 6 cm (2¼ in), and no less than 6 cm (2¼ in) in height. When writing your ad, remember AIDA (Attention, Interest, Desire, Action). See Figure 17.5 for an example.

Figure 17.5
Sample Ad

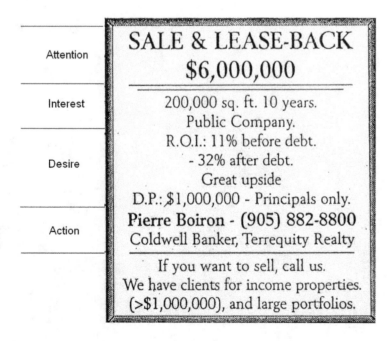

17.2.13 DO PROMOTIONAL MAILINGS

All cities of reasonable size have mailing companies. Also the post office will deliver to every address on specified streets. It is called "Letter Courier Walk". Prepare a nice mailing piece promoting your property.

17.2.14 PROMOTE TO NEIGHBOURS

Talk to the neighbours within a reasonable radius. They, their families, suppliers, and customers are the most likely prospects for your property. Because most tenants come to like an area where they do business, they will be great supporters too. Also, if they happen to be planning to expand, they will be interested as they would rather avoid major disturbances, such as losing employees, changing phone numbers or neighbourhood suppliers, by moving far away. Always leave a Data Sheet with them.

17.2.15 CANVAS BY TELEPHONE

Secure a list of possible tenants and call them or have someone call them on your behalf to let them know that your property is available. There are various sources of possible tenants. Many municipalities sell a business directory. Some Chambers of Commerce print one, too. In the Greater Toronto Area, it is possible to rent a directory from Routing Services <www.routingservices.com> or buy one from Scott's directory <www.scottinfo.com/scottshome/default.aspx>.

17.3 OWNERSHIP VERSUS LEASING

Demonstrate to potential tenants the financial and business advantages of leasing.

It is often debated whether a business is in a better position if it owns or leases its property. As a commercial real estate landlord, sooner or later you will have to discuss this issue with tenants. Hopefully, the following will help you convince them that they should lease (from you, of course).

The advocates of ownership will point to the success stories. "I know the owner of XYZ Co. They bought their building 20 years ago for $500,000 and just sold it for $1.8 million." But for the savvy entrepreneur, owning real property does not make good business sense for two main reasons.

- The equity injected into an active business (versus real estate, which is a passive investment) will generate much greater returns, after Capital Cost Allowance (CCA) and taxes, than will a real property.
- A growing business never has enough capital and investment in real estate ties up considerable capital.

In other words, the equity that would be committed to real estate would be better used to grow the business. Also, lenders generally will not lend enough capital against the real estate owned to reflect the true market value of the property. In addition to this, a mortgage shows on the corporate books as a liability, loading the company with more debt, meaning that if the business decides to sell its property, leasing the premises usually strengthens the company's balance sheet and increases the Return on Equity (ROE).

As explained earlier, based on the Toronto Real Estate Board's statistics, since the 1960s real estate values have increased at a compounded yearly rate of over 6%. In other words, it has doubled in value every 12 years

(Rule of 72: 72/6 = 12 years). On the other hand, most businesses expect a minimum ROE of 25-30% or more. Real estate will not achieve this kind of return, if bought around the 10% Cap Rate. This explains why the present trend with most companies is to focus on their core business and to outsource as much as possible, including leasing their buildings, instead of buying them.

Figure 17.6 provides a financial example of ownership compared to leasing.

In the end, the decision whether to lease or buy must be based on the person's or company's needs. Almost 90% of large corporations managed by sophisticated executives lease, rather than own, unless their buildings are used for a very special purpose. In any event, a tenant should not buy if he projects strong growth in the business and will, therefore, need capital to fuel that growth or outgrow the space in two to three years. It generally only makes sense to buy a property if the business plans to stay at least 10 years in the space.

Real estate is a passive business, while manufacturing, distributing, etc., is an active one.

17.4 BACKGROUND CHECKS ON RETAIL, OFFICE AND INDUSTRIAL TENANTS

Make requests of the prospective commercial tenant in order to complete your financial and background checks.

When you accept an Offer to Lease for a commercial space, you will want to insert a clause in the agreement that reads something along these lines:

> "The tenant shall supply to the landlord any document that the landlord may require in order to be able to assess the financial strength and suitability of the tenant. This Offer is conditional, for a period of ten business days after receipt of these documents upon the landlord being satisfied with this assessment."

If the Offer to Lease came through a real estate agent, as is likely, ask him to have the prospective tenant fill in a Credit Information Form, similar to the one shown in Figure 17.7. (Note: This simple form may not be considered detailed enough for some situations, but it does not intimidate tenants as much as a multi-page form.)

Figure 17.6
Owning Versus Leasing

B & L Company has just sold an asset and has $2,000,000 to invest. The two partners, Brian and Luke, argue as to whether they should now buy a building or lease one. They each prepare projections based on their personal preference, using the following assumptions.

Assumptions
- They are looking at a 15,240 m² (50,000 sq ft) industrial building, with a value of $2 million and a net rental value of $200,000 per year (regardless of the use: B & L Company or a tenant).
- The previous year, the business generated an income of $800,000.
- They expect a minimum ROE of 30% per year on equipment.
- Property appreciation is assumed to be 6% per year.
- Building is valued at $1,500,000 and land $500,000.
- CCA on the building is 4% and 20% on machinery .
- Building expenses (repairs, etc.) are $40,000 per year (half to be paid by the tenant).
- Corporate income tax rate is 36%.
- To invest the $2,000,000, Brian opts to buy a building, while Luke opts to buy production equipment.

Brian – Buy the Building

Business income:	$800,000
Building expenses:	($40,000)
Net income:	$760,000
CCA on $1,500,000 building at 4%:	($ 30,400)
Taxable income ($760,000 - $30,400):	$729,600
Income tax at 36%:	($262,656)
Net income after tax:	$466,944

Total income:	
Direct – after tax:	$466,944
Indirect – property appreciation ($2M at 6%):	$120,000
Total:	$586,944
Cash flow ($466,944 + $30,400)	**$497,344**

Luke – Lease the Building

Business income:	$800,000
Business income due to new machinery ($2M invested at 30%):	$600,000
Total income:	$1,400,000
Building rental:	($200,000)
Building expenses (part):	($20,000)
Total expenses:	($220,000)
Net income:	$1,180,000
CCA on machinery at 20%:	$120,000
Taxable income:	$1,060,000
Income tax at 36%:	($381,600)

Net income after tax:	$678,400
Cash flow ($678,400 + $120,000)	**$898,400**

Difference in net income after tax:

Brian:	$466,944
Luke:	$678,400
Difference:	**$211,456, in favour of Luke/Leasing**

Difference in Cash Flow:

Brian:	$497,344
Luke:	$898,400
Difference:	**$401,056, in favour of Luke/Leasing**

Figure 17.7
Credit Information Form

Ex: FRI, SIOR, Ontario Land Economist
E-mail: pini@sympatico.ca
Cell: 416-804-5555

TERREQUITY
REALTY

63 Johnson Street
Thornhill, Ontario
L3T 2N9 Canada
Bus: 905-882-8800
Fax: 905-882-9742

FINANCIAL INFORMATION

Name of business _____   Contact _____

Address _____   Tel. No. _____

Parent Co. _____   Subsidiary _____

President _____   C.F.O. _____

Public or private co., proprietorship, partnership _____

Bank 1 _____   Manager_____

Address _____   Tel. No. _____

Bank 2 _____   Manager_____

Address _____   Tel. No. _____

How long at present address? _____   OWN __RENT __

List three main suppliers:

Names	Addresses	Tel. No.	Managers/presidents
_____	_____	_____	_____
_____	_____	_____	_____
_____	_____	_____	_____

Change of ownership or management, in the last three years: _____

How long in business? _____

Type of business: _____

Type of operation to be conducted on premises: _____

Sales and profits of last three years (supply financial statements of last three years):

1._____

2._____

3._____

I authorize the prospective landlord to conduct any investigations and credit checks appropriate to accept us as a tenant

Per:_____

REMARKS:

_____

_____

Along with a credit check, you should check a tenant's references. In terms of references, ask for the name and address of the tenant's accountant, banker, suppliers, key customers, previous and present neighbouring businesses, key competitors, and previous landlords. Try to get not only the present landlord's name, but if the company has been in business for a long time, get the previous landlord's information as well. Indeed, the current landlord may be glad to get rid of this tenant and therefore not be willing to say anything negative about him. Do not expect to obtain everything you ask for from a prospective tenant, in terms of this information, but by asking for a lot you may end up with what you need.

Sophisticated tenants understand the need for a prudent landlord to conduct due diligence regarding their creditworthiness. Frequently, however, smaller, less sophisticated tenants do not. To overcome this attitude, we present things as follows:

> "The occupancy costs of this building, excluding utilities, amount to $350,000 per year. On a 5-year lease, this is $1,750,000. With this size of deal, you can understand that we need to know about you before we commit to a lease."

Basically, the landlord needs to answer certain questions with confidence.
- Will the tenant be able to pay during the whole term of the lease?
- Are there assets that can be liquidated if the tenant defaults?
- Is the tenant likely to want to move out before the end of the term?
- Is the tenant's anticipated usage of the property likely to damage the premises?
- Could the tenant be a source of problems for other tenants in the building because of noise, vibrations, odours, unusually large parking requirements, type of clients or visitors, etc.?
- Could the tenant be a source of competition for other tenants? (Even if there is no lease clause covering this, you want to think twice about displeasing a good existing tenant.)

Some landlords automatically require additional guarantees or indemnities from principal shareholders or associated companies. Others want security deposits, letters of credit, and, in rare cases, promissory notes. The assessment of a new tenant is similar to that performed by a mortgagee. The total amount of rental involved can be considerable. For example, a 6,970 m² (75,000 sq ft) industrial building with a rental of $64.50 per m² ($6 per sq ft), plus additional rent of $4 produces a total rental over 5 years of $3,750,000. This figure certainly justifies the landlord spending the time required to properly assess the creditworthiness of a prospective tenant. Also you should ask the tenant to supply you with his financial statements of the last 3 years. However, many tenants will refuse to do this before the offer is accepted.

At the same time, try to obtain a blank Letter of Authorization from the prospective tenant, reading:

> "To whom it may concern. We hereby authorize Mr. 'Landlord' to contact you and we ask you to supply him with any information he requires to help him assess the lease transaction that we are contemplating with him."

To get information released by the tenant's banker, you will need a clause in the Offer to Lease giving you permission to obtain a written reference. The bank's answer will usually take the form of a Banker's Report, such as:

"In connection with the ABC Company, we are pleased to advise the following:

This company has been a client of our bank for the last 12 years. Completely satisfactory and enjoyable relationship. No NSF activity. Mid-6-figure balances maintained. We would be pleased to recommend this company for business dealings. Considered a high-profile client of the bank."

Banks are very cautious when they give out information. You may get better results if you ask your bank to call the potential tenant's bank, but still try to obtain permission from the tenant to get more financial detail than usual. Sometimes you will have greater success in gathering financial information if you ask the potential tenant to have its accountant directly show your accountant its financial statements for the last two to three years.

Be sure to visit potential tenants at their present places of business; very few landlords take this step. Ask them to give you a tour of their premises. The staff that you see and the kind of housekeeping that you notice will tell you a great deal about how the tenant is going to keep your premises.

17.5 BACKGROUND CHECKS ON RESIDENTIAL TENANTS

Know what and how to check a residential tenant's financials and background.

The two major drawbacks to being a good landlord are lack of knowledge and lack of available time to be devoted to the role. In residential real estate, there will always be some deadbeat tenants, sometimes referred to as "professional tenants". These are tenants who know how to abuse the law to stay in a place for several months without paying a cent in rent, frequently causing extensive damage to the premises.

To avoid this, take the steps outlined here before leasing:

- Obtain a credit report for the potential tenant.
- Check references thoroughly, particularly of present and past employers.
- Demand a security deposit (only the last month is permitted).
- Make an inventory of what the dwelling contains and have the tenant sign it.
- Take digital photographs or a video showing the condition and contents of the apartment.
- Repair whatever needs to be repaired before the tenant moves in.
- Insist that no one moves in until the rental deposit cheque has cleared.
- If the prospective tenant has a car, try to see it and inspect its condition and cleanliness.
- Make every effort to visit the tenant at his current residence. Ask to use the washroom; its condition will tell you a lot.
- Be tough with tenants right from the beginning and explain clearly what kind of behaviour you expect.
- Inspect the apartment often, every room, after the tenant is living in it.

Generally, the lower the value of the property, the higher the rental is in relationship to its value. For example, for a 15-unit, multi-family building where each unit costs $50,000, you may get a rental of $800 per month, while the one across the street, which has a unit cost of $75,000 may get only $930 per month for the same amenities. On the other hand, there will be more property management required on a less expensive property, unless the latter is a prestige building.

There are a few tools that will aid the landlord in checking a potential tenant's financial and background history.

17.5.1 RESIDENTIAL RENTAL GUARANTEE PROGRAM (RENT SHIELD)

A new product appeared on the market a few years ago — tenant screening and default risk insurance. It seems to be a good idea, but only time will tell if it becomes popular. It should bring peace of mind to landlords, but at a cost. For its clients, Toronto-based Rent

A new product appeared on the market a few years ago — tenant screening and default risk insurance.

Shield Corporation <www.rentshieldexpress.com> will do the following:

- pay up to 6 months of rental if a tenant defaults within 30 days of the due date, with their core services,
- pay $10,000 for wilful damage done by a tenant, with their optional services
- reimburse reasonable legal, eviction, and administrative collection expenses
- pre-qualify prospective tenants through background and credit verification
- eliminate the need for security deposits, and
- list vacant properties <www.propertysolutions.com>.

17.5.2 LANDLORD'S SOURCE CENTRE

This company offers three levels of membership, starting from $60 per month. Among other things, they assist landlords with legal forms, laws and regulations, credit checks, eviction checks, banking and employment confirmation, tenancy history, records search, courses, rent collections, etc. Most of these come at extra cost. If you are a busy person, it is worth giving them a try (<www.landlordsinfo.com>).

17.6 TENANT DANGER SIGNS

Watch for the warning signs that may point to a risky tenant.

Even after the credit checks, the background investigations, and the inspections of current premises, there are still some warning signs of which you should be aware.

17.6.1 NEW BUSINESSES

New and untested businesses are by far the most risky tenants. Therefore, you have to be thrice (not twice) as careful in investigating them. Be particularly weary if there are few or no assets. You will have nothing to fall back on in case of problems and it is very easy for many tenants to move out over a weekend. Be leery, too, of new business concepts. They may work very well, or they may flop, but more often than not, they flop.

17.6.2 REPUTATION OF THE LEADER

The personal reputation of a business's leader is significant. Ask all the suppliers, customers, competitors, and neighbours who deal with the leader about his ethics, reputation, and any problems they may have had in the past.

17.6.3 COMPATIBILITY OF PERSONALITIES

Look for compatibility of personalities between you and the potential tenant. It is very important to receive a nice cheque every month, but you have to be able to get along with the tenant. If you feel that there might be personality conflict, forget about that tenant, regardless of how much it costs.

17.6.4 ASSOCIATION MEMBERSHIPS

A company that belongs to several professional associations is more likely to succeed than one working in a vacuum. If the prospective tenant does not belong to any association, ask why and draw your conclusions.

17.7 DEALING WITH OFFERS TO LEASE

Customize a standard lease form by adding clauses that you want.

A real estate investor must be thoroughly familiar with Offers to Lease (Chapter 7 at section 7.3), but this does not mean you can avoid involving your lawyer. Before you accept an offer, run through the Building Lease Review Checklist (Checklist 17.2) to ensure that nothing has been overlooked. It is not difficult to forget to cover one or more points in a lease — there are so many of them. The purpose of this checklist is to help you overlook as few points as possible and to make reviewing a lease less onerous. It is not intended to make a lawyer out of you. The lawyer will put in legal terms that you tell him to include. He will also suggest the clauses used 99% of the time. However, it is up to you to provide the business input, ask him the right questions, and think of the remaining 1% that should be included.

Checklist 17.2
Building Lease Review Checklist

BUILDING LEASE REVIEW CHECKLIST

This checklist can be equally helpful as a refresher for experienced landlords and aspiring landlords in performing their due diligence. This checklist is not exhaustive. There will be the odd time when you will find an item you want to add, or delete. Keep on tweaking it. Once you have taken care of one item, tick in the box.

❑ **1. Arbitration**

    Has an arbitration clause been made part of the Lease, to avoid making lawyers wealthy and happy?

❑ **2. Breaches**

    Are there damages to be paid by the Tenant if he breaches Lease conditions?

    Who pays for legal and professional fees? Why?

❑ **3. Building rules and regulations**

    What are they? They should be given to the Tenant, by the Landlord, along with a copy of the Lease.

    What happens if they are not respected by the Tenant?

❑ **4. Condition of the space**

    If a Tenant takes the building "as is", does the Landlord have to reveal in writing any problem of which he is aware?

❑ **5. Dangerous substances**

    May Tenant store dangerous/hazardous substances in his space. Any limit? Permits required?

    Does the Lease require the tenant to comply with government laws?

    Must Landlord notify Tenant if another Tenant in the building stores hazardous substances?

❑ **6. Destruction or expropriation**

    If building is destroyed, must Landlord rebuild? Define "destruction".

    Will rental be abated during "non-usability"?

    May Tenant terminate Lease if destruction occurs (total or partial)?

    Expropriation: Rights of Tenant and Landlord

❑ **7. Environmental concerns**

    Should Landlord provide Tenant with an up-to-date environmental report showing that the property is environmentally clean? Is that Tenant required to do the same, at the expiration of the Lease?

    If contamination, which existed prior to Tenant taking possession, is found in the premises later, what is the responsibility of the Landlord and that of the Tenant?

    Will there be any rental abatement if Tenant's use of premises is hindered by the contamination or removal of it?

    If more stringent laws are passed, whose responsibility will it be to do the work involved, and who pays for it?

❑ **8. Expense allocation**

    Percentage paid by Tenant.

    List of special expenses: capital expenses, equipment updating, testing Reports. Who pays for these?

❑ **9. Grace period**

    If Tenant is found in default, is there a grace period? How long?

❑ **10. Guarantor**

    Is there any guarantor to the Lease? Name? What is his "financial substance"?

    Does his guarantee cover the whole term? The whole amount due?

❑ **11. Insurance**

    Type: public liability – casualty - rental income / who pays – limits – deductible.

    What must be covered? / Is Landlord named as co-insured?

    Hold–harmless provisions (damages caused by Tenant / Landlord).

    Will Landlord be indemnified only for harm caused by the Tenant <u>within</u> the leased space?

❏ **12. Inspection**

Does Tenant have the right or the obligation to inspect, and approve, the condition of the premises, prior to signing the Lease (in case of new construction or renovation)?

Landlord's warranties: Building codes, laws. What happens if Tenant must make corrections? Who pays? What if Tenant is forbidden to use the space for a period of time?

❏ **13. Improvements**

If Tenant wants to make improvements, who pays, if it is of benefit only to this Tenant, or to any Tenant?

Landlord's restrictions on improvements.

❏ **14. Tenant's substance**

Reputation of the Tenant / Does he have the means to pay for the move and other expenses to prepare the space?

What happens if the Landlord does not maintain the building properly? What are the Tenant's remedies?

❏ **15. Lease**

When does it start? – Fixed date – Upon a previous tenant moving out – When space is ready

Any free rent period? Does Tenant pay the additional rent during this period?

Is delayed possession acceptable? Any penalty or bonus? Will it affect the termination date of the Lease? or escalation dates?

❏ **16. Options**

On adjacent space (rentals). Can adjacent tenants be moved elsewhere in the building, so that Tenant's spaces are contiguous?

On additional space in the building (rental).

Will the term for the additional space ends up on same date as the original Lease?

For more parking stalls.

To renew – At which rate – Term – Notice.

Of first refusal to lease additional space (rental) / To buy the property / At what price? When?

Landlord's fee ("out-of-pocket" expenses) for these options?

❏ **17. Parking**

Are there sufficient parking spaces available? For Tenant – for Tenant's customers.

Are any spaces reserved for Tenant/customers? How? Enforcement?

❏ **18. Premises**

Square footage. Is it Net Rentable or Net Usable Area?

The space should be measured and certified by a professional.

❏ **19. Property taxes**

Who sends the property tax cheques to the municipality?

If it is the Tenant, how does the Landlord insure that they have been paid?

If it is the Landlord, how does he collect them from the Tenant: monthly, based on previous year's amount – monthly, based on projections - invoice to Tenant, when bill is received from municipality.

Does Tenant have the right to appeal? At whose expense?

❏ **20. Rental**

Is it net or gross? / Spell out who pays what (taxes, insurances, utilities, maintenance, repairs, replacements, capital expenditures).

If it is a net Lease, can Tenant contract with any suppliers, or must he use Landlord's approved suppliers, or use the Landlord's own services?

Rental during holdover period.

Overage (percentage rental).

❏ **21. Rental escalations**

Rental deposit: Is it a rental deposit (last month?) or a security deposit?

Any escalations? – When – Fixed amount – Percentage – CPI (Consumer Price Index)

On operating expenses – actual; partial; indexed.

❏ **22. Retail Space Lease**

May Landlord lease space to a competitor (define)?

Only within a radius of… ? Remedies of Tenant if Landlord violates the restriction.

May Tenant open another store, within a radius of... Remedies of Landlord if Tenant violates the restriction.

Type of goods/services to be carried by the store. Any specific exclusions? Any specific inclusions?

What happens if a major (anchor) Tenant vacates, or the vacancy rate goes over a certain percentage of the total building square footage? Will the Tenant have the right to cancel his Lease, or will the Landlord consent to a substantial reduction of the rent?

23. Right of Entry

May Landlord enter the premises: With own key – During business hours only (unless in emergency) – Upon giving notice? Can he close the space for repairs (will Tenant be compensated, if he does, how?)

24. Services

Will existing services capacity (HVAC, water, sewers, electricity) be sufficient? What if they are not? Who does the work to correct? Who pays?

25. Sublease

May Tenant sub-lease? With, or without, Landlord's permission? All or part of the space? At a higher rental?

Reasons for Landlord to refuse a sub-Tenant.

26. Term

Possession date / How many years?

27. Termination of the Lease

At the end of the Lease, what are the Tenant's obligations? – Removal of: fixtures, chattels and improvements made by, or for, the Tenant.

Shall Tenant surrender the building in "good condition", subject to wear and tear (define), or not?

Shall Tenant redecorate? Who chooses the quality of products (i.e. broadloom) and colours?

Note: This is almost never treated properly in Leases.

28. Uses

Are there limitations to the uses of the premises by the Tenant, and all other Tenants in the building – Noise, music, vibrations, special equipment,etc.

29. Waste

If the Tenant harms the property through improper use, what are the Landlord's remedies. Will they survive a sale of the property?

30. Workletter

In many cases, work will need to be done to render the space suitable for a tenant.

The workletter specifies who does what, and who pays what, as well as the schedule and timing of Landlord's and Tenant's work / If cost overrun, who pays? If delays, any penalty?

31. Zoning

Exact designation / Any restrictions to use / May Tenant apply for re-zoning?

Does Tenant need: an occupancy permit? A letter from the municipality confirming that the use he contemplates is legal? What happens to the Lease if it is not? If use is found "illegal" later on?

Are there any easements, right-of-ways, over the property or over an adjacent one?

17.7.1 CONDITIONS IN OFFERS TO LEASE

Nowadays most offers, whether for leases or purchases, contain conditions. When you use a conditional clause ensure that it is very clear and that you say what will happen if the condition is satisfied, and what will happen if the condition is not satisfied.

As landlord, there are several conditions you should include for your protection such as those outlined below.

(a) Lawyer's Review

There may be times when your lawyer is unavailable to review an Offer to Lease, but you want, or need, to respond to it promptly. In this case, it is wise to include a condition whereby your lawyer must review and approve the Offer within, for example, 3 business days.

(b) Financial Strength

The Offer should be conditional upon the landlord being fully satisfied with the financial strength of the tenant.

(c) Leasehold Improvements

The offer should include a list of the work to be done, usually before occupancy, both by the landlord and the tenant, and that is subject to landlord's approval. Because it is not always possible to prepare lists in time, an alternative is to make it a condition to have the lists prepared within "x" days and that their contents be acceptable.

(d) Nature of a New Tenant's Business

If you have any doubt about the new tenant's business, for example a metal stamping plant, put in a condition that you are to visit the present premises of your future tenant, and that acceptance is conditional on approval of the type of business and of this inspection.

(e) Environmental Assessment

If there is any possibility of future contamination, the lease should stipulate that the landlord will provide a report at the start of the occupancy showing that the property is environmentally clean and the tenant will submit a similar report at the end of the tenancy. Evidently, this applies mainly to industrial properties.

17.7.2 RECOMMENDED LEASE CLAUSES

The vast majority of real estate leases are prepared by the landlord's lawyer. This implies that there is an inherent bias in the landlord's favour. And perhaps, there should be as he is entrusting (leasing) an expensive asset to a stranger for several years.

A lease starts with a "skeleton". Then, one builds up the rest of the body on it, and that is where differences can be considerable, depending on the landlord. A sublease clause is a typical example, as mentioned in Chapter 7 at 7.4.6. Therefore, the typical landlord uses his standard form of lease and makes changes to it, according to the terms of the agreement with the tenant (usually contained in an Offer to Lease).

The exception is when you are dealing with very large companies, such as McDonald's restaurants, General Motors, or Manulife. These companies have hordes of in-house lawyers who spend considerable time crafting a document that is biased in the tenant's favour. Most landlords grunt and squirm when confronted with these leases, but most love the safety of the strong covenant and the prestige of the name. In rare cases, when a location is outstanding and the strong-covenant tenant wants to be there badly, he will accept the landlord's lease terms (as long as they are reasonable). Following are a number of clauses to which you would be wise to pay particular attention.

(a) Deposit

In the Offer to Lease, make sure the clause dealing with the deposit does *not* read along the following lines: "A certified cheque in the amount of $x, as a deposit payable to the listing broker, shall be submitted upon acceptance and be held, in trust, until completion or termination of the agreement and is to be credited on account of the first and last month net rental." You want the lease to specify that you are to receive the first month's rental and a security deposit of an amount equal to last month rental, plus GST.

(b) Net or Gross Lease

Define very specifically what the tenant will pay and for what the landlord will be responsible. Personally, we like to say, "the lease shall be net to the landlord who shall only be responsible for Y", where the specifics are listed such as "the roof and walls". Others say, "The lease shall be a completely carefree net lease to the landlord."

(c) Lease Renewal

If the tenant has a renewal clause, demand at least 6 months' notice of an intention to renew, so you have ample time to find a new tenant.

(d) Building Alterations

Specify that any changes made to the building may not be done unless and until they are described in writing, with plans and specifications having been submitted to you, and your written permission having been secured. Make it clear that you may need to request the services of your architect, at the tenant's expense, to review the project. Also specify, "that the work performed must be done in a good workmanlike manner using new materials of a quality acceptable to the landlord."

(e) Sublease

Refer also to Chapter 7, section 7.4.6 regarding subleases. In all likelihood there will be a sublease clause in the Offer. Make sure that you make the sublease clause conditional upon credit approval and type of use of the possible sub-tenant. You may also want to add, "If the tenant subleases the space for more money than he is paying, the extra money shall be paid to the landlord."

(f) Post-dated and NSF Cheques

Put in the Offer to Lease the requirement that the tenant shall supply you with 11 post-dated rental cheques, since you will be given the first month rental with the Offer, and that the tenant will pay a healthy fee for any NSF (Not Sufficient Funds) cheques. Specify that, if during the term of the lease the landlord receives two or more cheques from the tenant that are returned by the tenant's bank for insufficient funds (or for any reason), the tenant will make all the future payments by way of certified cheques, cashier cheques, or bank drafts. Depending on the situation you may even specify that if there are three or more cheques that come back NSF during the tenancy period, this will result in "the landlord having the right to declare the lease in default, at the time of occurrence, or at any time in the future."

(g) Default of Payment

Have a clause in the lease that covers a situation that if the tenant is in default of payment for rent for a period of 15 days from the date due or if the tenant is in default of any covenant of the lease for a period of 15 days after notice is given by the landlord of such default, the landlord at his option, may re-enter the premises and terminate the Lease Agreement.

(h) Tenant Bankruptcy

Specify that if the tenant goes into bankruptcy or is otherwise insolvent, the current month rental and the following three months' rental shall immediately become due and payable and the landlord may re-enter the premises and terminate the Lease Agreement. From these 3 accelerated months' rental, the landlord must deduct any rent paid by the trustee, if the latter continues to occupy the premises. The landlord cannot cancel the lease, but the trustee has the right to do so (to disclaim it).

(i) Lease Guarantees

Because tenants do go bankrupt, try to have some kind of guarantee in the lease (such as personal guarantee of the main shareholder of the company), in addition to the company that is signing the Offer to Lease. This is quite difficult to obtain, but worth the effort in such an eventuality. Of course, put in our arbitration clause (see Chapter 7, section 7.7.)

The usefulness of guarantees was undermined in the 1960s by the infamous judgement in *Cummer-Yonge v. Fagot*, in which the judge ruled that if a tenant goes bankrupt, the guarantee no longer exists (even if it was by way of a Letter of Credit). However, a recent decision by the Supreme Court of Canada in *Crystalline Investments v. Domgroup Ltd.* appears to finally have overturned that decision. Indeed, the conclusion was that guarantors and assignors remain liable if the lease they have guaranteed fails.

(j) Landlord's Warranties

Ideally, the landlord will limit warranties with the following clause: "The landlord warrants that the existing mechanical, plumbing, and other building systems shall be in good working order upon the commencement date of the tenancy."

(k) Lease Execution

Specify that the lease shall be executed by both parties within 14 days of receipt by the tenant, subject to the tenant's lawyer's reasonable right of amendment, and that if the lease is not signed within this period of time, you, as landlord, have the option to declare the Offer null and void.

(l) Insurance Coverage (see also, Taxes and Insurance, section 17.8.2(y))

Specify that the lessee shall maintain insurance on the conveyed premises and liability insurance against claim for personal injury, loss of life, or property damage in, or about, the conveyed premises on terms, and with insurers, satisfactory to the landlord.

In connection with building insurance, you should know that if a building (a dwelling or commercial building) is vacant for longer than two days, most insurance policies specify that the insurance coverage automatically stops unless someone checks

If a building is vacant for longer than two days, most insurance policies specify that the insurance coverage automatically stops unless someone checks on the building daily.

on the building daily. If you are unaware of this circumstance, you could continue to pay premiums for many months (which the insurance company will gladly accept) and not realize that there is no coverage. If there is a fire or accident, compensation will likely be denied.

According to the Insurance Bureau of Canada <www.ibc.com> you have three options with empty buildings. You can cancel the insurance, check on the property daily, or notify the insurance company and it will ask you to pay a drastically higher premium to maintain coverage.

(m) Lease Confidentiality
To avoid problems wih other tenants, ensure this language is used in the lease:

"The landlord and the tenant agree that the terms concerning this Offer to Lease shall be treated as confidential by the lessee and neither party shall disclose to any other lessee of the building, the terms of the lessee's Offer to Lease or of the lease."

(n) Building Area
It is a good idea to have a land surveyor, an architect, or a professional building measuring company (not as accurate as the others) measure the space ahead of time and certify the area of the building that is rented. Attach the certificate to the lease.

(o) Periodic Rental Increases
Always try to have periodic rental increases stipulated in the lease either on a yearly or every second year basis.

(p) Inflation Protection
Ideally, leases that exceed 1 year in length should include a protection for the landlord against the effects of inflation and increases in taxes, utilities, etc. In a gross lease, tax and utility increases are easily covered by way of a clause stating that the tenant agrees to pay any increase in taxes or utilities over the base year (or first year) of the lease. To protect against inflation, the most common approach is to use the Consumer Price Index (CPI). Most governments publish an annual CPI showing how much prices have increased (or decreased) during the past year. The lease could include a clause providing that the rent will be adjusted as per the CPI, using the year the lease commenced as the base year. Typically, landlords use another clause that reads, "Rental cannot be less than that owing at the last rental period."

This common-sense approach is generally accepted by tenants. Another method that can be used, but it is more difficult to negotiate, requires agreed-beforehand increases at predetermined periods of time over the life of the lease. For example, in an industrial lease, you could say the rental will increase by $2.70 per m² ($0.25 per sq ft) every year. You will be much more successful at having tenants accept periodic rental increases if you are in a vendor's market.

(q) Option to Renew the Lease
Be aware that some options to renew the lease are meaningless. For example, the clause may read as follows: "If not in default, the tenant shall, upon giving 6 months' written notice, have the right to extend the lease for a further 5-year term on the same terms and conditions except for the rental which shall be arrived at by common agreement." If you stop here, the tenant may think that he has an option to renew, but in reality he does not because, if the landlord disagrees on the new rental, he cannot stay in the space. If you want a clause that is

strong and binding, and in the tenant's favour, then you have to add "or, failing so by arbitration as provided herein, based on the then current rates for similar spaces in the area".

(r) Late Rental Payment Penalties

The biggest aggravation in dealing with residential tenants is collecting the rentals on time (besides, of course hearing too often about plugged toilets). Some tenants will habitually be late paying their rent, but do eventually get it paid. Consider writing a late penalty clause into your lease, similar to the following:

> "Rent is due on the first of the month. It will be accepted through the third of the month, without penalty. Any rental payment made after the third of the month must include an additional $10.00 penalty charge."

You will be pleased to see the difference this small penalty can make. Another approach is to say to a new tenant: "Your rent is $765, but if we receive your cheque before the 1st of the month, it will be reduced to $755."

When you lease an apartment on the 15th of the month, but want to work on a calendar month, prorate the first month's rent and collect for only 15 days (the remainder of the month), with the first full month's rent due the first of the following month.

(s) Pet Problems

Many high-rise residential tenants will not tell you they have pets. If your building has balconies with metallic components, you will probably be able to find out which tenants have pets, particularly cats and dogs. Pets urinate on balconies and the consequence is that they cause any steel to rust. Hence, watch for rusted balconies.

To reduce pet problems consider the following clause:

> "Most pets are accepted, with our special lease endorsement/clause. There is an additional rental of $100 per month and an additional deposit of $500 per pet. If undeclared pets are found, the money is due from day one of the lease, plus a penalty of $500 per pet."

This may not be legal in your area, so check with a lawyer before using this clause.

(t) Work Letter

The term "Work Letter" refers to the quality and extent of standard allowances provided by a landlord to a tenant in a commercial Lease Agreement. In Canada, the standard practice with office and retail space (mainly in new buildings) is to include a schedule with the lease under the title "Landlord's and Tenant's Work" setting out the parties' responsibilities. Following are examples of three such clauses.

- "The landlord will supply outline drawings showing such things as overall dimensions, cross-sections, location of rear door (if required), and entry points for heat and air-conditioning, water, sewers, electricity, and sprinkler layout."
- "The landlord will also specify the extent of structural finishing, e.g., framing, finished roof, concrete floor, party walls, and entrance doors."
- "The tenant will submit complete drawings for the finishing of the premises, e.g., under-floor electrical or plumbing systems (if any), floor plan, ceiling plan, ductwork, electrical wiring, distribution panels, washroom facilities, interior partitions, and finishing."

(u) Landlord's Work

In commercial situations, the greatest source of problems between landlord and tenant is the completion date of work that the landlord has committed to doing. Once you have determined exactly what work has to be done and agreed to the cost, etc., the tenant should be asked to sign an agreement specifying that the landlord is relying on contractors to complete the work when they have estimated they will do so, but if the work is not finished that shall not be a reason for the tenant not to sign the lease or to declare the Offer to Lease null and void.

(v) No Occupancy Without Lease

Specify in the Offer to Lease that there shall be no occupancy, even partial occupancy, by the tenant and that you will not give a key to the tenant before the lease is signed.

If the tenant requires access from time to time, for example, to show the space to contractors, it would be wise for you, or one of your representatives, to accompany him. If he needs to move some equipment or goods into the buildings, do not allow it without a separate rental agreement, which your lawyer can prepare. Too often we have seen tenants move in before they sign the lease, then argue some points of the Lease and refuse to sign it. The relationship is then governed entirely by the Offer to Lease, which although legally binding, covers only a small fraction of the points covered in the lease, many details of which are for the protection of the landlord.

(w) Access and Visits

In the lease, as landlord, you should reserve the right to have a key to the premises, to be given the code for the alarm system, to be given new keys if the keys are changed, and to be made aware of the new code if the alarm system code is changed. Finally, reserve the right to visit the property from time to time during reasonable business hours and to have access at any time if extraordinary events warrant it, or if you want to show the property if it is offered for sale or lease.

(x) Arbitration Clause

Do not forget to include our arbitration clause in the Lease (see Chapter 7, section 7.7).

(y) Building Uses

Be specific as to the uses permitted for the building and check that the tenant is using the building as agreed. There are lots of horror stories around usage. For example, there was a case where the tenant filled an industrial building with old tires and then left the premises. Of course, the tenant was a numbered company with no assets and the landlord was saddled with the horrendous cost of removing and disposing of the tires. Be certain you know what is going on in your buildings.

Another sad story was when a client of ours learned his lesson the hard way. He owned a 4,180 m² (45,000 sq ft) industrial building where he occupied 2,322 m² (25,000 sq ft) for his own business and rented the remaining area to a food import and distribution business. During the 5 years of the lease he never visited the tenant's space. At the end of the 5 years, he refused to renew the lease because he needed the space for himself. When he entered the vacated space, he was appalled. The place was a dump, infested with rats and mice including inside the partitions. It was so bad that he had to bring in a bulldozer to demolish all the partitions, at great expense.

(z) Managing Taxes and Insurance

Even if the lease is entirely net to you, you want to be absolutely certain that the property taxes and building insurance are always paid. One of the ways to do so is for you to receive the tax bills and pass them on to the tenant, so that notification of non-payment comes to your attention. Remember, however, that if the tenant doesn't pay, you are the one responsible because the municipality will, in the end, place a lien on the building for tax arrears. If you receive the tax bill yourself, you also have the option to pay it directly and collect from the tenant. Since there is generally a reasonable lead-time from notification to due date, the lease should stipulate that upon the landlord receiving the property tax bill, it will be faxed to the tenant, who must send a cheque to the landlord within one week. If the tenant does not do so, he will be considered in default on the lease.

For the building insurance, the same process can be used. Another option is to require the tenant's insurer to provide you with a certificate of insurance and that you be a co-insured so that the insurance agent or company will notify you if the insurance is not renewed.

(aa) Property Management Fees

It is now more and more common for landlords to charge tenants a property management fee on top of the rental, usually 5% of the gross rental, with the exception being residential tenants. The reasoning is that this is an expense that has nothing to do with the space itself and should, therefore, be borne by the users. Some landlords charge 12-15% but only on the additional rental, including property taxes, and not on the rental itself.

17.8 ESTABLISHING A GOOD TENANT/LANDLORD RELATIONSHIP

Develop a friendly and professional rapport with your tenants.

Too often at the beginning of a relationship a landlord will not have direct contact with the tenant and will rely entirely on the agent as a go-between or there may be only one or two contacts with the tenant, often by fax or telephone. This is not a good idea. Get to know the tenant promptly and behave in such a way that he appreciates the efforts you are making to prepare the space rapidly and to his liking. Even before you sign the Offer to Lease, if you feel confident that you will agree on the terms of the lease and that it will be signed, provide the tenant with a Pre-Move-In Checklist such as shown in Checklist 17.3. This can be just one printed page, but it serves two valuable purposes. It shows your tenants that you care, that you are a professional landlord, and it helps your tenants make their move. Don't underestimate the value of establishing a good reputation with your tenants. Former tenants can provide excellent references and referrals for new tenants.

Checklist 17.3
Pre-Move-In Checklist

PRE-MOVE-IN CHECKLIST FOR TENANTS

This can be just one printed page, but it is a tool that serves two purposes. It positions you with your tenants; it shows your tenants that you care, that you are a professional landlord, and it helps your tenants plan their move. Don't underestimate the value of your reputation in finding good tenants. Former tenants provide excellent references in referrals.
This checklist does not pretend to cover it all. On the contrary, the intent is to focus on what is easily forgotten, not provided, or overlooked.

Property Address: _____

❑ Nearest governmental labour placement office and temporary personal placement company
❑ Postal code of the building
❑ Telephone exchange middle digit available. For example: 617-<u>457</u>-1234.
❑ Name of 2 or 3 neighbourhood locksmiths.
❑ Name of 2 or 3 janitorial (office cleaning) services.
❑ Name of 2 or 3 waste disposal suppliers.
❑ Name of 2 or 3 computer service specialists
❑ Name of 2 or 3 telephone installers
❑ Telephone number of closest police station.
❑ Telephone number of utilities suppliers.
❑ Distance to nearest freeways.
❑ Map, showing building location.
❑ Closest public transportation:

    1- bus
    2- subway
    3- rapid transit

❑ Closest "key" stores:

    1- hardware
    2- building supply
    3- banks
    4- restaurants
    5- post office
    6- hotel/motels
    7- supermarkets
    8- used office furniture
    9- service stations
    10- hospital
    11- doctor(s)
    12- office supply
    13- copying stores
    14- telephone

❑ Names of immediate neighbours: Company, president, address, telephone number.

17.8.1 SCHEDULE POST-MOVE-IN VISITS

It's a good idea to put yourself on a schedule for post-move-in visits. An example of such a schedule follows.

- **Week 1.** Drop in on the tenant, unannounced, and tour the entire building to see how it is being treated. The reasons for your visit? Perhaps it might be to give the tenant a floor plan, a rendering, a choice of colours for decorating, or to present two estimates for work to be done (one where you are willing to pay entirely yourself and a more expensive, but evidently superior, one where you will ask the tenant if he is willing to pay the difference for the superior work).
- **After 1 Month.** Your new tenant should now be almost settled in. Drop in to see if he is happy and things are going satisfactorily. Take a one-month gift along, such as a nice wine, baked goods, a decorative plant, etc.
- **Every 3 Months.** Visit the building.
- **After 6 Months.** Happy 6-month anniversary. Take a gift (only the first time, not every six months). You are building up a rapport with your tenant.
- **Annual Anniversary of Lease.** Take a gift.

Prepare a Walk-Through Form that you carry on a clipboard when you visit the property, outlining the main items you should look at, such as broadloom, lighting, painting, doors, windows, washrooms, etc. At the bottom, leave room for additional remarks. Use a form for each unit and for common areas, and keep them in each tenant's file. These forms will be priceless in helping you to monitor and maintain conditions. It is also a good idea to take a video of the building, inside and out (or at least photographs), at the beginning of the lease. If it is justified, you could also conduct an inventory. Give copies of these to the tenants so that they know you have a record of the condition of the building at the outset of your relationship.

Whatever you do, remain in frequent contact with your tenants, keeping them informed of all work that is planned or underway. If you have several tenants in one location, find a spot where you can place a bulletin board called "Intra-Tenant Communication Board". Place a note at the top: "This is for our tenants to communicate among themselves.

Whatever you do, remain in frequent contact with your tenants, keeping them informed of all work that is planned or underway.

Post a note if you have: office furniture for sale, a car for sale, if you need employees, or a used printer, etc." You can use the same idea if you have a Web site for the building.

Keep in mind that when a lease expires, landlords and tenants alike are nervous. One wants to get a high rental and the other wants to pay as little as possible. One of the better ways to prepare for a lease renewal is to gather comparable offerings, on paper. If the tenant cries "thief" when you tell him the new rental, show him the comparables, and explain why the rental is increasing relative to other properties on the market.

As a rule of thumb, try to be accommodating when dealing with your tenants, at least most of the time (and if the cost of that accommodation is justified), so that you can be firm with your tenants when the occasion warrants it. If you have developed a clear set of rules, communicated them to your tenants, and enforced them without exception but with fairness, you will be able to be a nice guy without problems.

PART 5

Managing Your Properties

CHAPTER

Property Management

By the end of this chapter you will be able to:

- Establish positive relationships with tenants to effectively manage your property.
- Plan for repairs and upgrades and establish a preventative maintenance program to ensure that your property is attractive.
- Fix cash flow problems and deal with a slow market creatively.
- Keep on top of any innovative alternate uses for your property.
- Appreciate the importance of accurate floor measurements and understand BOMA standards.
- Avoid mistakes that will cost you money when expanding, repairing, and maintaining your property.
- Build a solid team of professionals to assist with your real estate investments.
- Select a property management course that fits your needs.

Property management is a key function for any real estate investor. It consists of taking care of all details involved with an income-producing property, including establishing the best rental structures, selecting and managing tenants, negotiating leases, planning building improvements with a view to increasing income, collecting rents and paying expenses, supervising the maintenance and repairs of the buildings, and maintaining accurate accounting records.

In our experience, a very high percentage of properties are either poorly managed or not managed as well as they should be. Why? Because of a lack of discipline, organization, knowledge, commitment, and enthusiasm. The same can be said of businesses. In fact, the people who do not manage a business well are the same ones who do not manage buildings well.

Virtually all buildings offer opportunities for improvements in the following:
- property management, through upgrading the building and its components, better housekeeping, longer lasting fixtures, landscaping, building additions, creating new uses for the property, and finding new tenancies;
- cost savings through energy saving efforts and retrofits, computerization of equipment and bookkeeping, new administrative rules and systems, and more accurate area measurements; and
- Net Operating Income (NOI) through higher rentals and/or lower expenses.

Most landlords, once they have owned a building for a while, allow their alertness and enthusiasm to dull, falling little by little into the rut of poor or routine maintenance. This is why using a property management company should be viewed as a worthwhile expense, because alert oversight of the building will be maintained. In exactly the same way, a tenant's objective complaint should be given serious consideration.

There is a simple secret to good property management — your assets are not the property itself, but your tenants, who are paying off the property for you. If you remember this at all times, you will manage your properties well because you will want to please your tenants.

18.1 MANAGING YOUR TENANTS

Establish positive relationships with tenants to effectively manage your property.

One of the quintessential pre-requisites of a well-managed property is to select tenants well. This requires time but you cannot, as a landlord, invest your time better than in screening your tenants with care. See sections 17.4 and 17.5 in Chapter 17 for more details on finding good tenants. If you are negligent about this, you will pay dearly. Unfortunately, we are speaking from experience.

Once you find good tenants, treat them well. Be nice to them. From time to time, drop in with a small gift. On the yearly anniversary date of the lease, make a more sizeable gift, like a good bottle of wine, a coupon for a restaurant, tickets to a sporting event, etc, to build goodwill. This is very little to give to someone who pays you $30,000 or $300,000 per year and it works marvels at lease renewal time. Moreover, the semi-antagonistic relationship that is often typical between tenant and landlord changes, and does so markedly. See Figure 18.1 for an example of a terrific maintenance program for multiple occupancy industrial buildings that communicates to the tenants that this landlord cares.

Figure 18.1
The Platinum Maintenance Program

The hassle-free maintenance program included in the monthly common area maintenance fees

1. Lawn care (cutting, weed and fertilizer spraying). Tree and shrub care.
2. Lawn sprinkler startup and shutdown and maintenance for the greener lawn.
3. HVAC (heating/cooling equipment) complete service including heat exchangers and compressors.
4. All mechanical service calls.
5. Quarterly HVAC tune up, change filters, belts, and oil system, and complete check-up.
6. All door locking systems.
7. Fire sprinkler alarm monitoring by ULC approved service, including monthly inspections.
8. Realty and business taxes.
9. Fire insurance (content insurance and liability not included).
10. Annual roof tune-ups.
11. Roof leaks.
12. Roof and wall caulking.
13. Asphalt repairs.
14. Tax assessment appeals.
15. Parking lot line painting.
16. Exterior lighting – front door coach lamps, pot lights and shipping area HPS flood lighting all on photocell's (hydro included).
17. Driveway asphalt maintenance and repairs.
18. Snow clearing, removal and salting.
19. Plumbing, toilets, sinks and exterior hose bib maintenance.
20. Sewer and water maintenance, including sewer flushing.
21. Building directory board, signs and parking lot sign maintenance.
22. Glass break coverage.
23. Draperies in every unit.
24. Burglar alarms in every unit.
25. Quarterly window and door washing.
26. Spring clean-up and flushing of driveways.
27. Weekly grounds clean-up.
28. Ceramic vestibules and washroom maintenance, and replaced periodically.
29. Garage door weather stripping maintenance.
30. 24 hour – 7 days a week telephone call or email service.
31. Meter room access – 24/7.
32. Sidewalk and curb cleaning and maintenance.
33. Mailbox maintenance and replaced every 5 years.
34. Unit heater service and maintenance.

Our goal at Springtown is to assist you in the success of your business.

Source: The Platinum Maintenance Program used by permission of Springtown Business Parks. See http://www.businessparks.ca/platinum_program.htm.

Figure 18.2
Sample Letter to Tenant

Dear Melvin:

The attached photos show two problems that any wise landlord would want to avoid:

1. You can see a piece of cardboard squeezed between a door and its frame to keep the door open. The person who closed the door forgot to remove it. It shows that our request, made both to you and your warehouse manager, Bill, to use outside chains to keep the doors open, was not followed. This is a perfect recipe to damage doors and/or hinges. You may want to place a copy of this letter in the property file, as we will do so, with a note that you will be responsible for any damage to the doors at the end of your lease.

2. The container that was left at one of your shipping docks over the weekend has damaged the asphalt, due to bent "rocking feet plates". This is abnormal, as it is the first time that a trailer has caused this sort of damage, which you can verify by noting that there is no damage elsewhere in that shipping area. I would suggest that you get compensated for the damage by the transport company because we are hereby asking you to repair it ASAP.

We are taking care of the building for us and for you, so that you and your employees can enjoy using it. Please, help us by treating it with respect. I would suggest that you press this point with Bill. He is very pleasant and certainly not one to complain about anything, but we must protect our building against any form of misuse or abuse.

Sincerely,
Mr. Landlord

This does not mean that you should allow a tenant to disregard policies and rules. When you observe problems you should deal with them promptly. Figure 18.2 presents a letter we wrote to a tenant that noted maintenance problems and suggested solutions.

18.1.1 TENANT QUESTIONNAIRE

Probably the best way to maintain good communication with tenants is to send them a questionnaire, with covering letter, at least once per year, preferably twice (see Figure 18.3 for an example). If you are an investor who is using a property management firm, send it yourself by mail with a self-addressed, stamped return envelope. Then be sure to follow up. If you, as a landlord, don't follow up on the returned questionnaires, you are wasting your time and there is no point going through the exercise. It will take quite a few hours to review the questionnaires, but it will guarantee you better returns from your property and keep your property manager attentive and thorough.

Figure 18.3
Covering Letter and Tenant Questionnaire

Mr Tenant
Suite 125
65 Main Street
Toronto M5X 2I2

Dear Tenant: Re Suite 125

It is that time of the year again, when I write to solicit your opinion.

You will find a questionnaire with this letter. Please, take a few minutes to answer it. The more you guide me with your answers, the more satisfied you will be as a tenant.

Thank you for your input.

Yours truly,

Mr. Landlord

Questionnaire

Can you reach the property manager easily? If you have to leave a message, is your call returned promptly (within two hours, at most)?

Do you find that the maintenance and repairs are handled promptly and done well?

Do you find the property and maintenance staff responsive, courteous, and concerned?

Are there things at the property that you dislike (lobby, painting, lighting, parking, landscaping, etc.)? Why? How could we improve them?

What are the main things that you like about the building?

Do you intend to renew your lease? For how many years? 1, 2, 3, 5?

Would you feel comfortable recommending the building to a friend?

Are there any problems that you have not yet reported?

Please, feel free to write below, or on the back of this sheet, any outstanding problems you may have or any comments.

Thank you for helping us improve your building.

Comments:

Name: _____ Telephone: _____

Address: _____ Lease expiry date: _____

18.1.2 RESIDENTIAL TENANT'S RESPONSIBILITIES

It is important that you begin the relationship correctly with new tenants as many are not quite clear regarding all their responsibilities. Consider sending a letter to new residential tenants, or to potential tenants before they sign the lease, outlining their responsibilities and your commitment to them. Following are a number of points you might consider making in a letter establishing the ground rules.

- As landlords, we have only two goals — to keep our tenants happy because we value the rent you pay every month and to maintain the value of our investment in the building through good property management.
- The following rules are for the protection and happiness of all tenants, including you.
- What we expect from our tenants (some of these points are covered in your lease and this is just a reminder).
  - You will treat the space as if it were your own.
  - You will keep your unit and parking space, garage, locker, if any, clean and free from refuse.
  - You will not leave unused cars or trailers on site.
  - You will do nothing to damage the good appearance of the building.
  - You will make the small repairs that may be needed in your unit: leaking faucet, lamp replacement, malfunctioning toilet, faulty lock, dirty carpet, plugged drain, etc. The landlord will be responsible for any repair in excess of $200 in any one month.
  - If you have your own lawn area, you will treat and maintain it, as would any good homeowner.
  - When moving out, you will leave the unit in as good, or better, condition as you found it except for regular wear and tear, which does not include holes in walls or dirty paint or broadloom. If you do, we will have a gift for you.
  - If you see something wrong with the building or another tenant's behaviour, you will notify us immediately.
- This is what you can expect from us.
  - We care about our real estate. We want to keep it in great condition for you to enjoy and be proud of, and so we can rent to great tenants. These are the reasons we enforce our rules.
  - If you have a problem, tell us and we will try to solve it if possible.
  - We will treat your needs with respect.
  - We will respond promptly to any question or request.

Many tenants think that all landlords are rich people who take advantage of the tenant, "the little guy". This is untrue; 95% of landlords treat their tenants fairly. On the other hand, there are many landlords who believe that tenants are envious of the landlord's financial position and have nothing better to do than give the landlord a hard time. This too is untrue; 95% of tenants treat their landlords and their rental properties fairly. This is the message we try to communicate to our tenants.

> *There are many misconceptions on both sides of the landlord-tenant relationship. In reality 95% of landlords treat their tenants fairly and 95% of tenants treat their landlords and their rental properties fairly.*

18.1.3 TIPS FOR RESIDENTIAL LANDLORDS

Here is a list of tips to help landlords attract and retain desirable tenants.

- Whatever you do to or with a building, do it while bearing in mind the market segment that you want to reach, for example, young professionals, blue collar workers, retirees, etc.
- It is a lot more expensive to replace a tenant than to retain one, so prepare a plan to keep your tenants. Besides improving your bottom line, it will make you a better landlord.
- Encourage tenants to lease for longer terms: 2 or 3 years instead of 1, in residential; 10 or 20 years instead of 5 in retail, office, and industrial, always with rental escalations, of course. In residential buildings, you could accomplish this by, for example, implementing a "3-Star Program" through which residents are given perks, at no charge, such as minor property upgrades, on each rental anniversary for 3 years. This will create tenant loyalty and encourage residents to see themselves as 3-year residents. If there is a law that prevents this length of lease, include a clause saying that the lease is month-to-month, but that the intention of the parties is to see the tenant in place for 2 or 3 years.
- Insist on receiving rentals by way of automatic withdrawal (called "auto rent" in the US) from your tenants' bank accounts. As a rule, this is acceptable with residential tenancies.
- Try to have a guarantor/co-signer on all leases.
- Watch for innovative rental ideas from other industries and use them in your business.
- Meet with your tenants at least once a year, near the anniversary date of their lease. Before this meeting, send out an Anniversary Meeting Agenda Checklist (on your letterhead) to encourage your tenants to think about what they want to say during this meeting (see Figure 18.4 for an example).

18.1.4 DEALING WITH UNRULY TENANTS

Maybe unruly is not the right epithet, but certainly difficult is. Unfortunately, there are always some tenants who abuse the system. Here is a little tip that may come in handy. Hire a uniformed police officer for a few evening hours, the bigger and the more menacing-looking the better. Knock on the door of the difficult tenants and introduce your new associate as constable … . Explain that "he will be inspecting the building from time to time and wanted to meet a few of the tenants". Have this officer spend one to two hours in the building every two or three months. You will be surprised at the difference in attitude of most unpleasant tenants.

18.1.5 REASONS NOT TO COLLECT RENT ON THE FIRST OF THE MONTH

A US landlord, Louis Brown, who originally collected rent like everyone else — on the first of the month — realized, after a few years, there was a better way. Some residents had plenty of bills to pay with their last-of-the-month cheque. This meant that he was fronting the money for the mortgage payment instead of the property paying for itself.

From a landlord's viewpoint, if a tenant's lease expires on the first of the month, the tenant rarely moves before then, as most tenants coming from other buildings have to be out of their existing apartment by the first. There is a period of time (usually a few days, sometimes weeks) when the unit is not ready for occupancy by the next tenant. Usually this results in losing some or all of a month's rent while the unit is made ready and a new resident is approved, often for occupancy on the first of the following month.

Figure 18.4

Anniversary Meeting Agenda Checklist

Dear Ms. Tenant:

We like to meet with residents *at least* once each year to help ensure that we continue to meet your housing needs and make sure you are aware of all the housing options available to you. We want you to select the agenda for the meeting from the following list. Tell us what you would like to talk about. We can discuss as many of the topics as you select, or, if you prefer not to meet at this time, just let us know.

The meeting will take place at your residence on one of the following two dates. Please let us know which date and time is most convenient for you. Return this checklist to us within the next three days so we can schedule the meeting. Mail or deliver it to the following address:

> Mr. Landlord
> 123 Main Street
> Anytown, Ontario

Which meeting date and time is best for you? _____ or _____

Select which topics you would like to discuss at the meeting.

_____ Different rent payment plans available. Some residents prefer to pay every two weeks instead of monthly. It is possible to change the payment terms in your rental agreements.

_____ Any concerns about your current rental home?

_____ Receive 10% annual refund of your security deposit for passing semi-annual inspections.

_____ New upgrades, and service options, available for the next year of your 3-Star Program.

_____ Transfer location options if you want to consider moving to another size rental home.

_____ Prices and rental policies of other homes in area.

_____ Negotiate new rental amount for the upcoming year.

_____ Tell-A-Friend: Referral Fee program for 3-Star residents. (How to get free rent, or cash.)

_____ Your evaluation, or comments, about our maintenance guarantee program.

_____ Special services and advantages of our "VIP" Resident Programs.

_____ Other topic _____

_____ I prefer not to meet at this time. Everything is satisfactory. No topics I need to discuss.

Source: Anniversary Agenda Checklist provided courtesy of MrLandlord.com and Mr. Landlord newsletter. For a free sample issue of the Mr. Landlord newsletter, call 1-800-950-2250 or visit MrLandlord.com.

After this happened several times, this landlord started to analyze this first-of-the-month problem. To make life easier for him and his tenants he made the lease start on the 25th of the month. He found there were several great reasons to shift the rent period to run from the 25th of the month to the 24th of the next.

1. Getting paid when the tenants' middle-of-the-month cheques arrive means less competition for the money available to pay bills.
2. Getting 5-6 extra days to market the unit after a vacancy allows you to lease to someone who hasn't made a decision yet or had something go wrong with the deal they made with another landlord.
3. Getting 5-6 extra days after a vacancy allows time to make the unit ready for the new tenant who will likely need to be out of his current rental by the first of the month.
4. If a new tenant wants to move in on the first, you can say, "All our contracts begin on the 25th" and lead him gently into the realization that he will pay not only for the time he lives in the unit but for the time the landlord has the property off the market waiting for him to move in. If he does not wish to pay, then he runs the risk of someone else coming along and submitting an application to move in that very day!
5. An applicant always wants to start paying rent on the very latest date possible to save money while the landlord wants to begin the agreement as quickly as possible. The landlord may suggest that, "there's always overlap in this business" to put the tenant in the right frame of mind to negotiate days. "Today's the first. You want to move in on the first of next month, but all our contracts begin on the 25th. The owners won't allow me to take the property off the market and lose 25 days. Maybe we can meet somewhere in the middle. Let's start on the 10th. That will give you plenty of time to move small things, get utilities connected, etc. Is that fair?" Effectively you've negotiated down to one-third of the month versus what they wanted.
6. With rents due on the 25th, you will know by the 26th if there is a problem and have 5-6 days to arrange other funds to make your mortgage payment.
7. Get to the Landlord and Tenant Board (LTB) ahead of everyone else. You should begin your eviction proceedings as quickly as possible, but no later than 5 days after the rent is due (subject to residential rental laws). This gives you time for any required notice period and wait/see if their promise to pay materializes before you file.
8. Get your eviction lawsuit served quicker. When you file on the first, the Sheriff is not as busy and can get your proceeding served quicker because he is not as overloaded.
9. Get your property back on the market ahead of competing landlords. You will lessen the competition you'll have in renting your unit.

18.1.6 RESOURCES FOR LANDLORDS

Mr. Landlord/Rental Publishing is a large company that produces a wealth of materials to help landlords. Check <www.mrlandlord.com>. They have many books, supplies, software, newsletters, etc. You can join their Rental Owner Newsletter Club for free. They also publish the *Landlord Survival Handbook of Rental Forms*, which is a very handy resource. The handbook covers the following:

- application/verification (17 forms)
- leasing (16 forms)
- collection/violation notices (18 forms)
- maintenance/management (17 forms)
- turnover (10 forms), and
- supplemental rental (10 forms).

Their target market is do-it-yourself landlords in the United States, but many small and large Canadian landlords can benefit from their data and ideas by adapting them to their market.

18.1.7 TENANT PROTECTION ACT

Ontario's *Residential Tenancies Act, 2006* (S.O. 2006, c. 17) (the RTA), which came into effect on January 31, 2007, replaced the previous legislation, known as the *Tenant Protection Act*. This statute sets the rules for most residential rental housing in Ontario. Other provinces and territories are covered by different legislation, but most deal with similar points. In Ontario, there is also a Landlord and Tenant Board (LTB) (formerly the Ontario Rental Housing Tribunal) whose role is to provide information about the RTA and to resolve most disputes between residential landlords and tenants. (For more information, see <www.ltb.gov.on.ca/en/Key_Information/STEL02_111677.html>).

A summary of the key points of the RTA is provided below.

- The main exception to the regulations of the Act exists where the "owner, spouse, same-sex partner, child or parent lives in the building in which the living accommodation is provided".
- The RTA takes precedence over leases and applies even if there is no lease.
- Landlords can collect a rent deposit, paying 6% interest, of up to one month's rent. This is not a security deposit and, hence, it cannot be used to apply to damages.
- A tenant may refuse to give post-dated cheques and the landlord must give tenants a rent receipt.
- At the expiry of a lease, if the landlord and tenant can't agree on the new term, the tenancy becomes month-to-month.
- A tenant must secure the landlord's approval to sub-lease. If the landlord rejects the request the tenant may apply to the LTB.
- Tenants may not withhold rent for repairs.
- Landlords can only increase rent once each year and must use the province's guidelines, which are published in August and come into effect January 1st of the following year.
- Capital expenditures are capped at 4% above the guidelines, with any excess carried forward.
- Landlords can set rent at any level they want for a new tenant.
- Terminating a lease requires notice, the length of which varies depending on the reasons. A 60-day notice to terminate is necessary if the lease term is monthly or longer.
- One day after the rent is due, the landlord may give a notice to terminate for non-payment of rent. Tenants on monthly and longer terms have 14 days to pay. If they do not, the landlord may file an application with the LTB.
- As for evictions, here is an excerpt taken from the Canadian Mortgage and Housing Corporation's (CMHC) Web site:

There are numerous grounds for eviction but the main reason is rent arrears. Evictions for rent arrears in Ontario proceed as follows: One day the tenant is late paying rent; landlord serves notice to tenant; tenant has 14 days to pay rent; on the 15th day landlord pays a filing fee for Application to Terminate a Tenancy for Non-payment of Rent and for Collection of Arrears of Rent; Tribunal gives notice of hearing as soon as possible; landlord serves Notice package on the tenant; landlord signs the certificate as proof; tenants has 5 calendar days to file a written dispute. If a dispute isn't filed, on the 6th day a default order terminating the tenancy will be issued. If the tenant disagrees with the default order they can file a "Motion to Set Aside the Default Order". The hearing is held as soon as possible. The landlord arranges with the provincial Sheriff to evict the tenant.

- A landlord may refuse to rent to a person who smokes or has pets. However, a tenant cannot be evicted either for smoking or for having a pet, unless there are damages. The best advice is to check the prospective tenants' references and to re-read Chapter 17, Leasing.

18.2 THE APPEARANCE OF A BUILDING

Plan for repairs and upgrades and establish a preventative maintenance program to ensure that your property is attractive.

We cannot over-emphasize the importance of making and keeping your buildings attractive. You will rent them faster, for a higher rental fee, and to better tenants. Furthermore, if you decide to sell your property, you will obtain a higher price. Many landlords fail to recognize that if they keep their buildings well maintained and attractive, their tenants will respect the buildings more and also maintain them better, which keeps the landlord's expenses down over the long term. However, don't make the mistake that many landlords make of trying to be the architect or the interior designer. Hire professionals to give you good design advice and you will recoup their fees many times over.

Since we are on the subject of building appearance, we may as well broach a subject dear to our hearts — unattractive buildings. There are many things that can make a building unappealing: rusty parts, peeling paint, broken window panes, dead trees or trees in need of trimming, garbage, detritus, old cars, old pallets, cracked sidewalk, faded signs, broken doors, overgrown bushes, damaged asphalt, and many more. A smart landlord will not tolerate this. It leads to mediocre financial results and causes headaches.

Too many landlords believe that the rental amount is the top criterion that potential tenants consider when looking for a building. We have found that at least 50% of tenants will pay a little more, some of them a lot more, if the building is attractive, pleasant, and flatters their personal or corporate egos. And, these not-so-price-conscious tenants are the better tenants because most are more financially successful than those who are price sensitive.

Everything projects an image. If your commercial building is well-kept and attractive, it will appeal to quality companies that care about image. They can afford and are willing to pay more. Furthermore, their covenant is stronger than that of a tenant who is only interested in the lowest possible rental. This image depends on the basic quality, design, materials, and architecture of the building and its location, but also in great part on the standard of maintenance. There will be times when you cannot afford to do certain things. However, always try to do what will make your tenants proud to be in your building.

If you could have only one sign on the wall of your office, it should read: "Quality buildings attract quality tenants".

If you could have only one sign on the wall of your office, it should read: "Quality buildings attract quality tenants". Use huge letters, of course, so that you are constantly reminded of this cardinal principle.

We will go even further. When it comes to caring for a building, depending on your attitude vis-à-vis your building, you can turn a lousy tenant into a reasonably respectful one or, conversely, you can turn a good tenant into a lousy one. It's up to you.

18.2.1 SIGNAGE

Place an elegant and sturdy owner's sign on all your buildings. It should be very visible, but not ostentatious or overwhelming. It should read: "Owned by: ABC Company. Tel: 800-123-4567". If it is a single-tenant building, check with the tenant first. He may disagree with your placing the sign and you don't want to do anything to alienate a good tenant.

When selling a property or looking for a new tenant, do not put up a $100 sign on a $2-million building; the sign should reflect the value of the building. There are sign companies that specialize in real estate signs. For general signage, coordinate all the various signs on the property (yours, as landlord and those of the tenants), in terms of size, colour, and lettering. Pay proper attention to position, visibility, uniformity, and legibility.

If there are several units in the building, have a spot at the bottom of the directory where you can slide the heading, "Space available", plus space for a one or two line rider, providing information such as your telephone number or the area of the space.

18.2.2 PREPARING A BUDGET

You should prepare a budget for each property that you manage. If you use a professional property management company, it will prepare budgets for you. A budget does not have to be ten pages long if it is for a simple property, but preparing a budget will force you to anticipate and plan for upcoming expenses. Commonly, budgets are prepared for 1 year. There are four steps to preparing a budget.

1. Create a budget form with headings to represent the expenses you anticipate for the following year. Headings will differ from property to property. For a multi-family building, obvious headings would be:
   - property taxes
   - building insurance
   - gas (oil)
   - electricity
   - telephone
   - landscaping
   - maintenance
   - repairs
   - appliances
   - on-site manager
   - property management fee
   - legal fees
   - accounting fees
   - engineering fees, and
   - reserves (for expenses expected in future years).
2. If you have the necessary knowledge, inspect the building using the walk-through form (see section 17.8.1 in Chapter 17). Note the condition of each item that may need work in the next year. If you don't have the knowledge to identify needed repairs, hire a professional to do it for you. This could be a property manager, an architect, or a general contractor.
3. Contact suppliers and obtain estimates for the work you anticipate.

4. Fill in the cost for each heading and the total. You will then be left with the task of finding the money. If your reserves or the cash flow of the building are not sufficient, you may have to borrow or defer some of the expenses. In principle, it is worth borrowing if the planned improvements will permit you to charge higher rentals.

18.2.3 PREVENTIVE MAINTENANCE PROGRAM (PMP)

The principle behind a Preventive Maintenance Program (PMP) is that small expenses incurred at regular intervals to maintain a building and its components are preferable and more cost-effective than large expenses incurred every 10 or 20 years. A PMP is a must if you want to realize the maximum profit from your properties.

Basically, the concept is to maintain equipment on a scheduled basis, so that you don't have to repair or replace it on an unscheduled basis, which is generally more expensive. A PMP, which can be very simple or very complex, must be custom designed for each building. A simple PMP would consist of the tasks outlined below.

Basically, the concept of a PMP is to maintain equipment on a scheduled basis, so that you don't have to repair or replace it on an unscheduled basis, which is generally more expensive.

- **Visual Inspection Inside and Outside.** The frequencies of inspection will vary with the equipment involved. For example, a dock leveller or a truck level door will be inspected much more often (every 6 months) than a driveway.
- **Conversations.** Talk with your tenants on a regular basis to determine if there is anything wrong. Many will not tell you if you do not ask.
- **Inspection of the Roof.** Ideally the roof should be inspected twice a year, but many landlords do it only once a year.
- **Furnace.** Have the furnace or heaters checked once a year.

A complex PMP for a large building would be prepared by an engineer who would probably require the following documentation: as-built drawings and specifications, warranties, identification of the major building components and their life expectancies, sources, availability and cost of main parts, frequency of inspection, type of inspection technique used (either intrusive, which causes damage, or non-intrusive, such as infrared thermography).

Key data will be maintained on a computer for easy storage, update, and retrieval. Once this data has been gathered, the engineer will keep three sets of data:
- **Diary.** In the diary you will record defects, daily expenses, and injuries.
- **Maintenance Logbook.** The logbook is used to record a description of any work carried out, including date, estimated and actual cost, contractor's name, and warranties.
- **Periodic Inspection Survey.** Recording observations made at regular intervals to identify any maintenance work required, including cleaning, is the purpose of the periodic inspection survey.

The engineer will then prepare a maintenance program, which addresses two time periods. The long term is concerned with items that need to be attended to every 2, 5, 10 years, etc., while the annual period concerns items identified for annual or monthly maintenance based on the diary and the annual inspection survey.

18.2.4 ONGOING DANGER SIGNS

Visit your property regularly. Drive around it. Check for abandoned cars, trucks, semi-trailers, stacked unused pallets, old packaging, lumber, etc. Also, check for broken windows, damaged doors, outside lighting that is not working, and garbage. We've heard it said that you can tell if new tenants are going to succeed or fail in their business within two weeks of occupancy, based on how they handle their garbage. For example, if cartons are broken down flat and tied to occupy as little space as possible, the tenants are likely to succeed because they are organized and take care of details. The opposite is true of tenants who don't bother to break down cartons that take ten times more room in the dumpsters.

18.2.5 MULTI-FAMILY CARETAKER

Sooner or later you will need to consider hiring a caretaker for your multi-family residential property. This person will do regular maintenance such as cutting grass, plowing snow, completing minor repairs, keeping the building and grounds clean, watching over the property, and, of course, looking after tenants' requests.

There are two options open to you when hiring a caretaker. You can hire a local handyman/jack-of-all-trades or use one of the tenants. Both are acceptable but a tenant is preferable. Before hiring, interview the prospective caretaker carefully. Prepare a specific list of the tasks he is to perform, instructions for handling specific occurrences, and discuss the details during an interview. You can pay your tenant caretaker by the hour, an agreed upon monthly sum, or by reducing his rent. Ask other landlords in the area for the going compensation rate. As continually recommended in this book, check his references carefully.

18.2.6 INEXPENSIVE WAYS TO SPRUCE UP YOUR RESIDENTIAL RENTAL

Renovations can be costly, but there are a number of inexpensive ways you can improve the appearance of your residential property. Here is a list of ten to get you started.

1. New switch plates.
2. New or improved indoor doors.
3. New door handles.
4. Paint/replace trim (use a semi-gloss white on all the trim in your residential buildings).
5. New front door.
6. Tile the foyer entrance (the materials (e.g., Mexican tiles) for a 2.5 x 2.5 m (8 x 8 ft) area should cost about $200).
7. New shower curtains (don't be cheap; pay $50 to $100 and buy a nice rod and fancy curtain).
8. Focus on the kitchen (most people spend a lot of their time there while at home; paint kitchen cabinets using semi-gloss white paint and finish the cabinets with colourful plastic knobs; unless they are dirty, there is no need to paint the inside of them, since you are only trying to make an impression; also, a fancy modern sink faucet can make a big difference to a kitchen and most retailers run clearance sales regularly for discontinued models so it need not be too costly).
9. Add window shutters if the windows lend themselves to it (they come pre-primed at most hardware retailers; if need be, paint them a complementary colour to the outside of the house (e.g., if the house is dark, paint the shutters white; if the house is light coloured, paint them green, blue, etc.)).
10. Add a nice mailbox if you are dealing with a house (the $60 to $100 you will spend is worth it).

You have likely heard that some renovations are more recommended than others in terms of increasing the value of your property. Figure 18.5 lists the estimated recovery on renovation costs for single-family homes, but many of the items apply to commercial properties as well.

Some renovations are more recommended than others in terms of increasing the value of your property.

CMHC also offers a payback range of typical renovations on their Web site at <www.cmhc-schl.gc.ca/en/burema/repi/berereguca/berereguca_004.cfm>.

18.3 MY PROPERTY HAS PROBLEMS

Fix cash flow problems and deal with a slow market creatively.

Rarely do properties have problems; it is generally their owners that have them. Usually these problems relate to ownership indifference or a cash shortage (the former frequently leading to the latter).

Some landlords find themselves with insufficient net income to cover mortgage payments. Ideally you won't borrow so much money that you have put yourself in this position; however, if necessary, you can try one of the remedies listed below.

1. Borrow money at low or no interest (or accruing interest) from a relative or friend.
2. Enter into a joint venture with someone who will put in more cash in exchange for a percentage of ownership.
3. Renegotiate leases ahead of time. Even if you do not receive more income right away, this will give you more flexibility in dealing with the lender. For example, you could ask for a reduction in your monthly payments until the new rental(s) kick in and then make up the shortfall.
4. Ask your lender to let you skip two or three monthly payments. Yes, most of them will do that if approached properly.
5. Ask your lender to rearrange the payments. For example, you could ask for a graduated-payment mortgage, where you pay less at the beginning and more at the end. Obviously, the monthly payments will have to average the same over the length of the term.
6. Ask your lender to change your mortgage into an interest-only mortgage payment. This means you will have to pay the whole amount of the principal as a balloon payment at the end of the term.
7. Try to convince your tenant to buy an option to purchase the property by paying a higher rental (see section 16.9 in Chapter 16).
8. Study the property in detail. Are there any ways to increase the income? For example, could you lease land for parking, install a pylon to support a billboard for rent, or provide a pad for a wireless telecommunications tower, which can also be rented.

Figure 18.5
Estimated Recovery on Renovation Costs

Renovation Project	Recovery on Resale
Adding a full bath	96%
Adding a fireplace	94%
Remodelling kitchen (minor)	79%
Remodelling kitchen (major)	70%
Remodelling bathroom	69%
Adding a skylight	68%
Adding new siding	67%
Adding insulation	65%
Adding a room	62%
Re-roofing	61%
Adding a wood deck	60%
Adding a greenhouse	56%
Replacing windows, doors	55%
Adding a swimming pool	39%

Source: Estimated Recovery on Renovation Costs used by permission of Douglas Gray. All rights reserved www.homebuyer.ca.

Other landlords can pay the mortgage, but have insufficient income to cover building repairs or replace equipment, such as air-conditioning units. In that case, you can try these solutions.

1. Review the options offered in the previous scenario.
2. Ask a tenant, who is inconvenienced by the problem, to advance the money at a reasonable rate of interest, for example prime +2%. In return, the tenant pays only half of the rental until the loan has been repaid.
3. Ask a supplier (roofer, painter, etc.) to finance the cost at, say 2% over prime, and to amortize it over 2, 3, or 5 years.
4. Approach a finance company. Some will advance up to a year's worth of rentals, for a fee. Others will lease some items, such as HVAC units.

18.3.1 NEGATIVE CASH FLOW

A negative cash flow takes place when the expenses of the property, including mortgage costs, exceed the revenues. It is an unhealthy situation but not an absolute "no-no". If you are counting on inflation to pull you through, there will probably be years of losses for the prize — a sale price that is much higher than your own purchase price. It is dangerous to have a negative cash flow if your means to cover the shortfall are very limited. If anything goes awry, it could cause you to lose the property.

A negative cash flow is acceptable if you are certain that within a reasonable period of time (one year, at the most) you will have increased the revenues significantly through improvements made to the property and increased rental as a result of lease renewals, changes of use, or new tenants. This assumes that you have the means to keep paying the shortfall from other income.

> *A negative cash flow is an unhealthy situation but not an absolute "no-no".*

One advantage of negative cash flow is that you will be able to deduct the losses from other incomes. This was confirmed in the Supreme Court of Canada case of *Stewart v. R.* (May 2002). Mr. Stewart purchased four condominium units as part of a syndicated real estate development. The properties were highly leveraged. The promoters projected negative cash flow for the first 10 years of ownership and the actual losses for that period exceeded predictions. Mr. Stewart deducted his losses on the properties and such losses were denied in the taxation years 1990 through 1992 on the basis that he had no reasonable expectation of profit and, as a result, had no source of income from which to deduct expenses.

However, in 2002, the Supreme Court of Canada ruled in favour of the taxpayer, and made it clear that use of the reasonable expectation of profit test (REOP) was to be used only as a supplement to other profit analysis systems. In its judgement, the court set out a two-stage process, in place of REOP analysis, to be applied in determining whether a source of income exists for purposes of section 9 of the *Income Tax Act* (R.S.C. 1985, c. 1 (5th Supp.)).

1. Is the activity of the taxpayer undertaken in pursuit of profit or is it a personal endeavour?
2. If it is not a personal endeavour, is the source of income a business or a property?

The court concluded that "where the nature of an activity is clearly commercial, there is no need to analyze the taxpayer's business decisions. Such endeavours necessarily involve the pursuit of profit. As such a source of income by definition exists and there is no need to take the enquiry any further".

18.3.2 DEALING WITH MARKET DOWNTURNS

One of the worst problems a commercial landlord can have is not being able to lease a building. When it happens to a decent landlord, it is usually at the bottom of the real estate cycle, when the market is truly poor. At these times you need to think creatively.

(a) Partnerships

Determine what kind of business could locate in your building. Let's suppose that it is a dentist or a woodworking shop. For a dentist, place ads in the newspaper that read, "Own your own dentistry office. Little or no money required; Landlord will finance".

You will find interested parties. Make them a proposal: "I will finish the space to suit your needs and I will advance the money for the down payment on the equipment. A corporation will own the business and you will have 25% of the non-voting shares. I will have the balance. You will pay no rental for 6 months and then pay regular rental. You will pay all occupancy costs, outside of the net rental. You will give me a financial report monthly. I will keep track of all the monies I have advanced you and charge interest on it at prime +5%. You will keep the salary the business pays you as low as possible and you and I will have to agree beforehand on the amount. Once you have paid me in full, the business is yours 100% and I am out of the picture".

(b) New Businesses

If your building is in a less desirable location, let's suppose a warehouse in the middle of nowhere, turn to the Internet. There are many good marketing people who want to sell merchandise, but don't want to handle the warehousing and fulfilment of the product. Set up a good computer system, a mini-call centre, and offer to perform the following tasks:

- take telephone orders
- process e-mail, fax, and postal orders
- inventory the products
- de-stuff maritime containers
- pick, pack, and ship
- invoice and collect, and
- report results daily, or weekly, to your Internet-based merchant.

You may charge 10-20% of the selling price of the item for these services, but this is a bargain for the merchant (your client). Of course, you charge every step of the way. After a while, if the business becomes successful, you can hire a manager to run it for you or sell it to your new tenant. If you get into this kind of business, join some warehousing or logistics associations, such as International Facility Management Association (IFMA). See their Web site at <www.imfa.org.>.

(c) Existing Businesses Looking to Expand

There are almost always new businesses that are growing fast and are strapped for cash. Their profits are not able to sustain the financial needs of their growth or to pay for a move to another building. If you find it difficult to lease your building, send a letter to accountants offering to pay to move their clients and to give them 6, or more, months' free rent.

Before you think that this is crazy, let's look at what it accomplishes. Remember that we are talking about a weak leasing market for landlords, when finding a tenant is very difficult. Let's make the assumption that it may take you one year to rent the space. Figure 18.6 compares the cost of holding an empty building versus 6 months of free rental.

Figure 18.6
Empty Building Versus 6-Month Free Rental

Who pays for what: L = Landlord; T = Tenant		
Item	**Landlord Waits (hoping to find a Tenant)**	**Landlord Offers 6-Month Free Rental**
1st 6 months		
Net rental	L	L
Property taxes	L	T
Building insurance (higher for an empty building)	L	T
Occupancy costs	L	T
Maintenance	L	T
2nd 6 months		
Net rental	L	T
Property taxes	L	T
Building insurance	L	T
Occupancy costs	L	T
Maintenance	L	T

18.4 ALTERNATE USES

Keep on top of any innovative alternate uses for your property.

Always ask yourself, "To what other use could this property be put?" This can be especially relevant when you are buying a new property, but it should always be on your mind as an opportunity to increase your return on investment, especially if you are losing tenants or having difficulty leasing the building. Here is an example of how a change in usage can benefit an investor.

A Toronto property was purchased in 1981 from an institution that used it as a printing plant. It consisted of a two storey, 8,000 m² (86,000 sq ft) building. Gene, a real estate agent, was a partner in the deal. The two other purchasers intended to use about 1,850 m² (20,000 sq ft) of the building as a warehouse and planned to rent the balance for similar uses. It was Gene's responsibility to do the due diligence during the 30-day conditional period and, after studying the property and the market, he suggested that the building should be renovated for office space. His partners were skeptical about this.

To convince them Gene determined the trade area for the property and conducted a thorough market survey of all available office space in the area. He drove through the area, made a note of all the "For Lease" signs on office buildings, and called every number to find out how much area was available, the rental rate, and the total area in the building. By dividing the available space by the total building area, Gene obtained the vacancy rate. The overall vacancy rate turned out to be 4.5%. This indicated a much lower real vacancy rate because it did not include the buildings that were not for lease. The market study proved that there was a need for more office space and Gene convinced his partners to support his suggestion.

Gene chose an architect, interior designer, engineers, etc. One of the partners did the construction work. By 1986 the building was 97% leased and was sold. The cash invested at that time was $1,000,000. The property was sold for a $3,600,000 profit, 5 years after buying it — an outstanding return on investment. In the meantime, of course, there was also income from renting the space.

The real difficult work starts immediately after you buy a property. You must think about the building constantly.

There is a lesson here. The real difficult work starts immediately after you buy a property. You must think about the building constantly (keep a note pad on your bedside table) to determine what can and should be done regarding pricing it; studying the competition and their leasing rates; consulting with real estate agents, professionals, other investors and governmental agencies; and always looking for opportunities to increase the return.

It could be said that buying an income-producing property (IPP) is akin to buying a farm. You study the land, make a decision on which crop to plant, plough the land, fertilize it, plant the seeds, and then wait till harvest time. The main difference is that a farmer has to go through this process every season, whereas if a landlord has a good tenant he keeps on receiving a monthly cheque/crop with very little involvement on a monthly basis. However, if the tenant moves, the landlord must again get in the harness for another effort.

18.5 FLOOR MEASUREMENTS

Appreciate the importance of accurate floor measurements and understand BOMA standards.

Many smaller landlords do not have floor plans with proper measurements, but these are a virtual necessity for repairs, maintenance, and leasing. It is one of the most neglected aspects of property management by landlords with poorer skills.

So that everyone was using the same terminology when dealing with floor area measurements, the Building Owners and Managers Association International (BOMA) created recognized standards that have become quite complex. The first standard was published in 1915 and amended several times. The "BOMA 80" was replaced recently with the "1996 BOMA Standard". The major change, affecting primarily office facilities, is that the standards are now building-wide instead of the previous version in which they were calculated on a floor-by-floor method.

Under BOMA 80, a landlord was responsible for the costs of lobbies, mechanical rooms, and other common areas. Tenants paid for their own space plus the grossing up, which was calculated by taking the total floor area, less the space occupied by the tenants on a specific floor, and dividing the result (being the stairwells, corridors, washrooms) on a pro-rata basis among tenants. The gross-up represented from 12-30% of the office space.

BOMA 96 makes it easier and better for the landlord. The landlord now takes all these spaces in the building and divides the result on a pro-rata basis among all tenants, causing the gross-up to jump to 5-15%, quite a bonanza for landlords. Landlords, when able to switch to the new standard (based on market conditions and dealing with new tenants), will see their building value increase 3-8%.

Obviously, it is a landlord's decision to switch to the new standard or keep using the old one. However, in a tenant's market, the acceptance of BOMA 96 by a large, sophisticated tenant is unlikely. It may take the landlord many years before he is able to implement BOMA 96. For several years, most landlords will have to use the two standards for different tenants in the same building.

18.5.1 SOME BOMA DEFINITIONS

BOMA measurement methods are so complex that some specialists offer courses to demystify them. Here are some key points.

- For industrial buildings, you measure outside wall to outside wall or centre of partitions.
- For retail space, the measurements are done from the building line, if fronting on a street, to the finished surface of the store area of the corridor, or permanent walls, or centre of a partition.
- For office space, the rentable area includes the usable area plus the balance of the floor except for major vertical penetrations (atriums, elevators, stairways, etc).

A few definitions are in order, which we have borrowed from LASERtech Floorplans, the official consultant to BOMA International, because their explanations are clear.

- **Finished Surface.** A finished surface is defined as a wall, ceiling, or floor surface, including glass, as prepared for tenant use, excluding the thickness of any special surfacing materials such as panelling, furring strips, and/or carpet.

- **Dominant Portion.** The portion of the inside finished surface of the permanent outer building wall, which is 50% or more of the vertical floor-to-ceiling dimension, represents the dominant portion. For example, if a window is more than 50% of the wall height, then the inside of the glass is the dominant portion. If not, then the inside finished surface of the wall is dominant.
- **Gross Building Area.** The total constructed area of a building, as measured to the exterior of all outside walls, i.e., the building footprint is the gross building area. It is generally not used for leasing purposes.
- **Gross Measured Area.** The gross measured area is the total area of a building enclosed by the dominant portion, excluding all parking areas and loading docks (or portions of same) outside the building line. Basically, it equals the sum of floor rentable areas and the vertical penetrations. Generally, it is not used for leasing purposes and is calculated on a floor-by-floor basis.
- **Major Vertical Penetrations.** These are stairs, elevator shafts, flues, pipe shafts, vertical ducts, and the like, and their enclosing walls. Atria, light wells, and similar penetrations above the finished floor are included in this definition. Not included, however, are vertical penetrations built for the private use of a tenant occupying office areas on more than one floor. Structural columns, openings for vertical electric cable or telephone lines, and plumbing chases are not considered as major vertical penetrations.
- **Floor Rentable Area.** The floor rentable area equals the gross measured area of a floor less the major vertical penetrations for that same floor. Generally, it is fixed for the life of a building and is rarely affected by changes in corridor size or configuration, as all such corridors are included.
- **Usable Area.** The usable area is the measured area of an office area, store area, or building common area, on a floor. The total of all usable areas on a floor equals the floor usable area of that same floor. Note: The difference between rentable and usable area can be difficult to perceive. The easiest way is to think of usable area as the area within a tenant's four walls, the actual area available to him for business activities. It does not include any common areas such a restrooms, walkways, janitor rooms, nor does it include stairwells or elevators (unless a private stairwell/elevator), or void areas occupied by such things as ventilation shafts or ducts. Rentable area is always greater than usable area, and includes a tenant's pro-rated share of common areas such as washrooms, lobbies and hallways, janitor closets, and building mechanical rooms. Under BOMA Standard, rents are based on rentable area. The usable area is of most importance to a tenant in both his evaluation of a space and allocation of the space to house personnel.
- **Office Area.** This is the area where a tenant normally houses personnel and/or furniture, for which a measurement is to be computed.
- **Store Area.** The area of an office building suitable for retail occupancy is the store area and is usually included in floor usable area. Store area requires a street frontage and ground level, but does not necessarily require a separate entrance.
- **Building Common Area.** The areas of the building that provide services to building tenants but which are not included in the office area or store area of any specific tenant is the building common area. Typically included are main lobbies, atrium spaces at the level of the finished floor, concierge areas, conference rooms, lounges, food service facilities, health or fitness centres, day-care facilities, locker or shower facilities, mail rooms, and service areas, such as fully enclosed mechanical or equipment rooms. Parking areas, portions of loading docks outside the building line, and major vertical penetrations are specifically excluded.
- **Floor Usable Area.** The sum of usable areas, office areas, and building common areas on a single floor represents floor usable area. This figure can vary over the life of a building, as corridors expand and contract and floors are renovated.

- **Floor Common Area.** The floor common area is represented by the areas on a floor available primarily for the use of tenants on that floor. Examples include washrooms, janitorial closets, electrical rooms, telephone rooms, mechanical rooms, elevator lobbies, and public hallways.
- **Floor Rentable/Useable Ratio.** Basically, the floor R/U ratio is the relationship between the total floor rentable and the total floor usable, for a given floor. The resulting ratio is used to convert any usable area to a basic rentable area.

Example:	Total Rentable Area:	1,400 m² (15,000 sq ft)
	Usable Area:	1,200 m² (13,000 sq ft)
		1,400/1,200 = 1.16

  Although the tenant will use only 1,200 m², he will pay for 1,200 x 1.16 = 1,392 m².
- **Basic Rentable Area.** This is the usable area of an office, store, or building common area, plus its share of the floor common areas on that floor. The total of all basic rentable areas on a floor equals the floor rentable area of that same floor. It should be noted that under older versions of the BOMA Standard, the basic rentable area was in fact the final rentable area, as previous versions worked on a floor-by-floor basis only.
- **Building Rentable Area.** This equals the sum of all the floor rentable areas.
- **Building R/U Ratio.** This ratio represents the gross-up factor to be applied in distributing building common area over all usable areas in a building.
- **Rentable Area.** This is the usable area of an office or store area, with its associated share of both floor common area and building common area added on. Rentable area is determined by multiplying the usable area by the combined R/U ratio.
- **R/U Ratio.** The combined conversion factor, obtained by multiplying the floor R/U by the building R/U ratios, which when applied to any usable area, gives the rentable area of that office or store area. This is referred to as the combined R/U to clearly differentiate it from the other component R/U factors.

Here is a quick summary of ratios and equations as per BOMA:
- Floor R/U Ratio = (Floor Rentable Area)/(Floor Usable Area)
- Basic Rentable Area = (Usable Area) x (Floor R/U Ratio)
- Building R/U Ratio = (Building Rentable Area)/(Building Rentable Area) – (Basic Rentable Area of Building Common Area)
- Rentable Area = (Floor R/U Ratio) x (Building R/U Ratio)
- Rentable Area = Usable Area x Combined R/U Ratio

18.5.2 ACCEPTED STANDARDS OF VARIANCE

If ten professionals measure a building and calculate its rentable area, you of course will have ten different answers. No two people will measure a complex building and obtain exactly the same result. The BOMA Standard allows for this discrepancy by provision of a 2% variance when comparing site measurements. That is, if two sets of calculations are within 2% of each other, they are deemed to be equal according to BOMA. If they differ by more than 2%, BOMA International recommends the opinion of an unbiased third party be sought to assist in resolving the matter.

The standard also makes note of another important fact — it is not uncommon for an area calculated from the building's design plans to differ from the area measured on site. That is, for an accurate representation of a building's area, an "as-built plan" is required.

Note: In the fall of 2004, BOMA released the "BOMA/SIOR 2001 Standard for Measuring Floor Area in Industrial Buildings". This standard effectively covers all buildings where more than 50% of the space is non-office, thus applying to industrial, retail, and all non-office buildings. It should be adopted by The American National Standards Institute (ANSI) soon.

18.5.3 FLOOR MEASURING COMPANIES

There are companies that will measure buildings using a laser device. These machines can be accurate up to within 0.3 cm in 91.4 m (1/8 in in 300 ft), the maximum distance they can handle. They produce clean, simple plans that are very handy when marketing or making changes to a building; however, some consider them a little expensive. If pricing is based on gross building area, or an equivalent, generally prices start at $0.86 per m^2 ($0.08 per sq ft), with volume discounts available. Site plans, parking lots, and designers' preliminary plans are priced according to availability of existing plans and complexity of the final plans. We are not convinced results of these measuring companies are 100% accurate. Of course, they may be within 2% of each other, but 2% of a 92,900 m^2 (1,000,000 sq ft) building is 185 m^2 (2,000 sq ft). If total rent is $325 per m^2 ($30 per sq ft), the dollar difference in annual income is over $6,000.

Figure 18.7 presents a floor plan prepared by a floor plan measuring company. Many landlords lose money because their buildings are not measured properly. Indeed, the area of a leased space is frequently greater than what the landlord thinks. The reasons are: the landlord accepted the size shown in the lease to measure it when he bought the building or asked a maintenance person (who is not qualified in floor measurement).

Figure 18.7
Sample Floor Plan

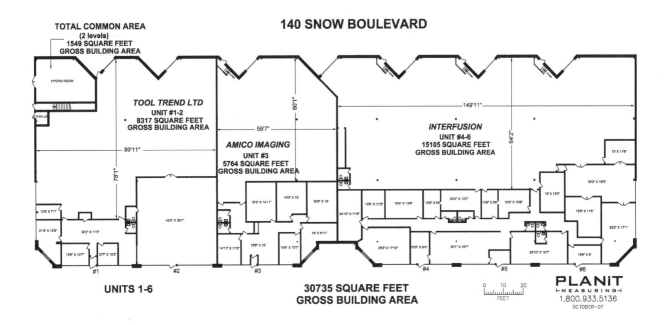

Source: Floor Plans provided by Planit Measuring.

18.6 RENOVATING AND MAINTENANCE TIPS

Avoid mistakes that will cost you money when expanding, repairing, and maintaining your property.

Here are a few ideas to avoid mistakes, which in the long run, will allow you to save money or make a larger profit.

18.6.1 BUILDING POSITIONING AND EXPANSION

If you are positioning a building on a large piece of land it should be located close to one of the lot lines; not in the middle of the site. This placement will make it easy to expand rationally or to sever the extra land. Of course, you should respect legal set-backs (set by by-law) and we recommend that you leave a good size strip of land to allow vehicle access all around the building. Personally, we find that 4.5-6 m (15-20 ft) is a good minimum and 7.5 m (25 ft) it great (but uses up a lot of land).

All building expansions should be done professionally. Below are some items to keep in mind before and during the expansion.

- If at the time of original construction an expansion in the future seems likely, ensure that the wall that will be between the original space and the expansion is not a load-bearing wall.
- Plan so that the building can be divided into independent units, if need be.
- Make sure that during the expansion, you can take advantage of opportunities to modernize parts of the old building. If, for example, you are installing metal halide lighting fixtures in the addition, do the same in the original portion. The same principle applies to the heating system.
- Materials used should be as similar to the original materials as possible. For example, avoid using corrugated metal siding on the addition if the original building was built with bricks. This is particularly important for the front of the building.
- Make certain floors are exactly at the same level.
- Keep roof types the same; for example, do not mix flat and pitched roofs.
- Ensure identical or similar windows are used for the addition.

18.6.2 THE BUILDING

For the building itself, there are a number of areas to maintain or improve, including the roof, entrances, basements, balconies, and skylights.

- Remember to inspect your roof regularly. If you must replace your roof, insulate it well (see section 19.1.6 in Chapter 19).
- Vehicle entrances from the street and access lanes are frequently too narrow. Make them very wide, particularly if semi-trailers use them.
- If you erect a new wall or roof, install a few windows, roof windows, or skylights. It is not logical to have bright sunlight outside and have the inside of your building as dark as an oven. Almost everyone is familiar with the typical square or rectangular skylight that is installed directly in the ceiling of the room. If dealing with a pitched roof, there is another type that is quite interesting. Under the skylight itself is an aluminium, pleated tube up to 55 cm (22 in) in diameter that can spread light to nearly 28

m² (300 sq ft) (based on full midday sun). The skylight can be located up to 7.6 m (25 ft) above the ceiling of the room. The tube shaft used reflects 95% of available sunlight.

Another type that deserves to be mentioned marries a window with a skylight. It is the electric venting skylight, made by Velux. What makes it very interesting is that it has a built-in motor and control system that permits the window to be opened and closed from a distance, by way of an infrared controller. It even has a rain control system for automatic closing and a battery backup option. This fancy window would make a building fairly unique, but it does not come cheap. Currently a 53 x 117 cm (21 x 46 in) base model costs $990.

- If you erect a new building, or buy one with a basement, try to install excellent access doors, lighting, and some windows. It is now possible to buy pre-cast concrete basement window wells, which permit high windows.

- If your multi-family building has balconies, try to install a railing or a railing cover to hide what most tenants leave on their balconies. It is unsightly and makes the building look less attractive.

18.6.3 THE EXTERIOR

Renovating and maintaining the exterior of your building can have a big impact — from trees to parking lots to protecting your building from damage when empty.

- Plant some saplings on your land and 20 years later your building will look much more attractive for it. You may want some advice on where to plant, but in front of the building is good, except, generally, for retail plazas (you don't want the view obstructed when they are grown).

- Repaint the parking lines every few years to keep them looking fresh. For retail uses, ensure that virtually all parking is in front of the building, provided by-laws permit.

- It is important to protect the exterior of your buildings on a regular basis. To prevent general wear and tear, place bollards at corners of your buildings, and curbs and/or guardrails along walls to protect corrugated metal siding from vehicles. In fact, the bottom 1.8-2.4 m (6-8 ft) or 1.2 m (4 ft), at least of the wall below the corrugated metal siding of your building should be concrete, concrete blocks, or bricks. You should also use curbs or guardrails to protect fences.

- If you lease your buildings to tenants, sooner or later you will have an empty one. Make sure that there are no doors, vents, or windows open and if a glass pane is broken, replace it at once. If you do not, birds will get inside. To prospective tenants, their droppings are unsightly, smelly, a potential health hazard, and you will find them very difficult and costly to clean. Avoid this situation; it is a curse.

- Whether a building is vacant or occupied, pigeons and geese on lawns, walkways, and roofs can be a real nuisance for building owners in terms of maintenance. There are now a few products to keep birds away.
  - **Spikes.** Glued or screwed to the surface to be protected, spikes are not cheap: $48 to cover a length of 3 m (10 ft), but apparently they work well.
  - **Wires.** The system consists of small vertical poles sticking up 10-15 cm (4-6 in) above the surface. A thin cable is then threaded through the holes in the poles and tensioned. They work because birds seem to find them uncomfortable.
  - **Traps.** Traps are priced from $50 (sparrows) to three compartment pigeon traps at $120. There are also nets (2.5 x 12 m (8 x 40 ft)) that cost $300.
  - **Stomach Upset Liquid.** This is used to discourage geese from frequenting your lawns and ponds. The birds eat the stuff and their stomachs protest. It costs $280 to treat one acre of turf and is probably worth every penny.

18.6.4 FUTURE USES

Whatever you do — build, enlarge, or repair a building — bear in mind that one day it will be used by a different company that will probably have very different needs. Avoid unusual shapes, specifications, materials, and designs.

Try to have a building that is as plain as possible. You can add a creative touch here and there to make a building more attractive, as explained at 17.2.10.

18.7 YOUR PROPERTY MANAGEMENT TEAM

Build a solid team of professionals to assist with your real estate investments.

Your investment team should consist of many individuals. Gather names of suitable professionals at every opportunity.

- **Real Estate Agent.** He will save you a lot of time and give you invaluable advice.
- **Lawyer.** Like it or not, we can't live without them. Pick a lawyer who does only real estate work.
- **Accountant.** There are three kinds of accountants: a "numbers" only person, a "taxes" only person, and a "numbers and taxes" person. Try to find someone in the third group. Smart tax planning is critical.
- **Land Surveyor.** As explained in section 16.2.1 (c), sooner or later, you will need to use the services of a land surveyor.
- **Architect.** An architect's services can benefit you by improving the building and making it more attractive, thus allowing a higher rental to be charged.
- **Contractor.** Try to find a builder/contractor with several years of experience, who can give you advice on most things in a building. If you hire him for repairs on a regular basis, often he will inspect for free when you are considering a property for purchase.
- **Building Inspector.** You will use a building inspector to examine a property you are considering buying. Some private building inspectors also provide long-term capital replacement studies, which are excellent when budgeting for major repairs and replacements.
- **Engineers.** Eventually, you may need to use several kinds of engineers — structural, HVAC (mechanical), environmental, civil, electrical. You will need a structural engineer if you need to open a new shipping door, make changes to your roof, or find out if your roof can support a large HVAC unit. An HVAC engineer will calculate the size of units needed. Environmental engineers will be needed if you need to produce environmental reports. Civil engineers will be needed to install new roads or services and electrical engineers will be needed if you change your incoming service or make major electrical distribution changes in the building.
- **Appraiser.** If you borrow funds from a conventional lender, you will need an appraisal on your property. When you interview an appraiser, determine in what type of property he specializes, if any (see Chapter 14). Ensure he is acceptable to the specific lender.
- **Mortgage Broker.** A good mortgage broker is almost as important to your success as a good real estate agent.
- **Insurance Broker.** His help and advice can be really valuable.

Meet each of these people before you are in need of their services, chat a few minutes with each one, ask about their hourly rate, when applicable, and decide if you are comfortable with them.

18.8 PROPERTY MANAGEMENT COURSES

Select a property management course that fits your needs.

If you decide that you want to take courses in property management, your two best options are Building Owners and Managers Institute (BOMI), an offspring of Institute of Real Estate Management (IREM) and BOMA. The courses offered by BOMA range from the Growing Concern of Mould to Improving Tenant Satisfaction and Retention to Advertising, Marketing and the Internet. See <www.bomacanada.ca> for more information, including publications, such as newsletters, office space and leasing guides, and more.

CHAPTER 19

Renovations, Repairs, and Building Components

By the end of this chapter, you will be able to:

- Maintain and improve the exterior of your building from roofs to insulation to fences and everything in between.
- Take care of the surface areas within your building, including floors, walls, and masonry.
- Understand and instruct specialists to maintain or improve your building services, such as water and sewer systems, electricity, and heating and cooling systems.
- Recognize the importance of insulation — for sound and temperature.
- Hire contractors or direct the construction or renovation of your property.
- Make a list of the work to perform inside and outside your property before putting it on the market.
- Ensure you know when and how to remove underground storage tanks.
- Keep your building safe and secure.
- Appreciate the complexities of building stairways.
- Select the features that will improve your building's efficiency.

The buildings constructed today are much more sophisticated than those of the past, but also a source of many more problems. To put it differently, to manage buildings today you require a lot more knowledge in many more disciplines. It is unrealistic for a landlord to obtain all the knowledge required, but he should have enough understanding of the various fields to ask intelligent questions of contractors and tradespeople who will complete the repairs and renovations required. To do so, you will need a basic awareness of the various products, materials, and techniques available. Not only will this help you to control your repair and maintenance expenses, but it will also ensure your buildings are more appealing to tenants. It is the intent of this chapter to bring you this knowledge.

In addition, if you are dealing with older properties, you will find that many times the greatest opportunity to increase their value is to redevelop, renovate, enlarge, or modify the building. Some unusual jack-of-all-trades can do most repair and maintenance work themselves when dealing with small buildings. However, it is very difficult to be up-to-date on all construction specialties and often what you save in labour, you may lose by not using the best products, equipment, or methods for the job.

For an investor starting with a small building, a general rule is to do the tasks that do not require specialized knowledge, such as demolition, cleaning, moving things around (including construction materials), etc., but leave the specialized work to the specialists.

It is easy for do-it-yourselfers to do poor work in the construction business. A typical example is painting. The non-professional wants to apply the paint quickly and admire the end result. Professionals know that the key to a good painting job is surface preparation, which can easily take 80% of the time required for the whole task.

First, a few words of advice about contractors. Contractors range from good (only 10-20% fall in this category) to sloppy and unqualified, with most falling in between. The ideal contractor is one who is qualified, licensed, belongs to professional associations, is clean and neat, and finishes the little details at the end of the job. He is properly insured (don't hesitate to ask to see his insurance policy), is willing to answer all your questions (educate you) about the work you want done, keeps his word, and is reasonably priced (but not cheap). He is willing to put in writing any agreement, gives you a reasonable warranty, has been in the business 10 years or more, and can give you 20 names of customers you can call for references.

If after checking references and meeting in person several times, you do not feel 100% comfortable, cross the name off your list and move on to the next contractor. Be forewarned that good contractors are busy. Be leery of anyone who can start right away. We know waiting can be a real problem. Indeed, there will be times when you sign a lease with a tenant, and the delivery date for the space is tight; however, some tenants will understand your predicament if you explain to them that you want the work done well, so they will be happy in the building.

Choosing a contractor is a time-consuming process, but, except for selecting tenants, you cannot invest your time better. If you do not do your homework at the beginning, a bad contractor will cost you a lot in the end.

This is a long chapter. To make it more easily referenced it is broken into five main categories, followed by a few miscellaneous areas.

19.1 Building Exterior – windows, walls, roofs, and land

19.2 Surface Care – cleaning, painting, etc.

19.3 Building Services – water and sewage, sprinklers, electrical, lighting, HVAC, etc.

19.4 Insulation, and

19.5 Construction and Renovation.

19.1 BUILDING EXTERIOR

Maintain and improve the exterior of your building from roofs to insulation to fences and everything in between.

19.1.1 WINDOWS

Most people like windows and the light they allow, but few know the proper window terminology. To help you become a semi-specialist, visit the Canadian Mortgage and Housing Corporation (CMHC) Web site at <www.cmhc-schl.gc.ca>. Two other informative sites are <www.innotech-windows.com/faq/intro.html>and <www.pages.drexel.edu/~jpf25/AE/5/Windows.htm>.

The old single-pane window is a thing of the past. The standard today is two panes separated with an air space (from 12-75 mm (0.5-3 in+)) acting as an insulator. Most are hermetically sealed and are called thermopane, but there are multi-pane windows available that are not sealed. The best windows today prevent heat transfer five times better than the windows of yesterday. The ideal window must transmit as much sunlight as possible, while blocking the rest of the solar radiation. A major advantage of modern windows is that they allow for smaller and less expensive Heating Ventilation Air Conditioning (HVAC) equipment.

Below are the three main types of window glazing with the amount of heat loss encountered measured in British Thermal Units per hour per square foot (BTU/H/sq ft).

- **Single Pane.** 113 BTU/H/sq ft per 100°F difference (outside temperature versus inside temperature).
- **Double Pane.** 58 BTU/H/sq ft per 100°F difference.
- **Triple Pane.** 36 BTU/H /sq. ft. per 100°F difference.

When there is more than one pane of glazing, the air space contained between the panes is hermetically sealed to prevent dust and condensation. Very modern thermopane units use an inert gas between the panes, such as argon or krypton, instead of air. The gases increase the insulating value not only for temperature, but also for noise. It is interesting to note that adding a second piece of glass significantly reduces heat loss, but adding a third one is not as effective. Out of 2,000 Canadian Window Manufacturers, less than 50 have their products rated by the Canadian Standards Association (CSA). This is probably due to the fact that CSA subjects products to thorough testing, based chiefly on CSA's A440 Standards and the process is costly. The certification program covers construction requirements and physical and energy performance, including air, water, and wind resistance. Buying CSA-certified products is a form of insurance.

The problem with some thermopane windows is that, eventually, they fail. That is, the seal between the sheets of glass is no longer airtight. Because the exterior air contains some water vapour (humidity), it will come between the sheets, eventually condense, and leave streak marks. Up to recently, the only solution to this problem was to replace the window. There is now a process that removes the moisture from between the window panes, returning it to its original state — an enclosed, sealed airspace — and restoring fully its R-value.

This process uses micro-filter vents that become active when sunlight increases the pressure between the panes. The pressure created by the expanding air expels water vapour through the vents, drying out the window. Once the vapour is gone, the filters remain dormant, sealing the enclosed air space. This process can also be used for newly installed windows to prevent future seal failures.

The cost of installing the micro-filter is about half the cost of replacing windows and is less disruptive. This is a powerful incentive, especially when combined with significant guarantees from the manufacturer. Information on one of these systems, Crystal Clear Windows Works, can be found at <www.ccwwi.com>.

(a) Window Coatings or Films

In some older buildings, particularly in summer months, solar heat gain can be very annoying to tenants. A good way to solve the problem is to replace the windows with double-pane, tinted glass. A more economical solution is to apply window film. This could be a semi-transparent metallic coating or a reflective coating for single-pane windows. Both, however, block as much, or more, daylight than they do solar heat, which is less of an issue in warm climates, given the intense sunlight. It is also possible to buy windows with spectrally selective coatings or low-emissivity, or low-e, which can minimize solar gains. Window films can reduce up to 75% of solar heat gain. The best known film is 3M's Scotchtint. Films also reduce glare considerably and block almost all UV rays. These films last between 10 and 25 years. Information can be obtained from The International Window Film Association at <www.iwfa.com>.

Other types of window film can be used with great success to rejuvenate the appearance of a building. Some are applied to large panels of glass and make them appear etched. Others are almost works of art and can depict a swan, fish, tree, etc. They can drastically change the appearance of a building.

Window films are available to retrofit existing windows as well. They are almost always applied to the interior side of the windows. Window films can reduce the temperature near the window by 13.3°C (5-8°F), considerably improving the level of comfort for people in the room.

(b) Solar Shade Fabrics

Another option for filtering out heat and glare is to use Solar Shade Fabrics, which are mounted in a system similar to opaque roll-up blinds. Most of these are made up of PVC-coated fibreglass or polyester fabrics with UV inhibitors. The fabric is a mesh and its openness goes from 3% for intense glare situations, to 14% for lighter glare situations where clarity is required. UV blockage and glare control go from 70-95% and heat transfer is reduced up to 94%.

(c) Structured Acrylic Glazing

Acrylic glazing comes in double, triple, and quadruple-skinned sheets, with the insulating capabilities of two, three, or four panes of glass. An alternative to glass, glazing was designed for overhead use and to build enclosures. The sheets measure almost 1.2 m (4 ft) wide and vary in length to more than 7 m (24 ft). They are available in clear, bronze, and light white (opal). The air space between the two panes goes from 12-25 mm (0.5-1 in).

The light weight and long span make installation a fast and easy job. They can withstand heavy live loads, such as snow. They transmit a diffused, soft, natural light and block UV rays. Uses that come to mind are patios, solariums, skylight-like roofing, and balcony coverings.

A similar product, called Pentaglas, is offered by CPI International and distributed by Architectural Plastics Ltd. This product is honeycombed, instead of having parallel walls, which the manufacturer claims makes it more solid.

(d) Condensation and Heat Recovery Ventilation Units (HRVs)

Condensation on the inside of windows during winter months can be a constant problem. In severe cases, there is so much condensation that water runs down the window. The problem is not caused by the windows, but because buildings are now constructed much more airtight than they were in the past. It is a question of air humidity and temperature control. There are several solutions. One (which seems irrational) is to open the window a little to increase ventilation. You can also lower the ambient humidity by turning off or down your humidifier and by avoiding excessive washing, cooking, and long showers or baths. Alternatively, one could buy a heat recovery ventilation unit (HRV), also called an air-to-air heat exchanger.

An HRV is a mechanical ventilation system, usually located near the furnace or in a mechanical room, that uses the outgoing air to warm up the incoming fresh air. It passes one over the other, but does not mingle them, using a heat-reclaim chamber. It provides the following benefits:

- filtered fresh air also helps asthma and hay fever sufferers
- less noise and greater security thanks to closed windows
- excellent heat recovery and greater energy efficiency
- constant air exchange, without draughts, to help remove smells and smoke, and
- a balanced ventilation system because it removes and replaces equal volumes of air from the home.

An HRV recovers 60-75% of the heat in the exhaust air and returns it to the building. A special kind of HRV, called "Energy Recovery Ventilators" (ERVs), will recover moisture from the exhausted air as well, helping to maintain indoor humidity in cold climates. A properly installed HRV is quiet. It can be installed in any kind of building. In a home, it replaces several bath and utility room fans with a single system, which may run continuously or intermittently. An HRV creates a tight, well-insulated building, which will only have a 1.1-2.2°C (2-4°F) variance of temperature between the floor and ceiling.

The installation cost of an HRV is a little high but it is recovered through the savings realized over a period of time that can be as short as 24 months. The electricity consumed by an HRV varies from 100-200 watts per hour for a small building, such as a home or small office building (for which the savings in heat loss is 25-50%). This must be compared to the cost of using 2,000-4,000 watts per hour of heating energy that is typically required and wasted with a drafty, non-airtight building. There are timers for scheduled ventilation, demand switches for high-speed ventilation of bathrooms and kitchens (a range hood is still necessary). HRVs require their own ducting system, usually 15.25-20.3 cm (6-8 in) conduits.

(e) Window Sills

Many North American buildings are designed without proper window sills. A proper sill protrudes from the face of the building or wall and beyond the sides of the window for about 10-12 cm (4-5 in). It is slanted and designed to prevent the rain from running down the wall below. It directs water away from the wall. With many, if not most, modern buildings you can see water marks, particularly below and at the sides of windows, on the exterior that are a result of this poor design.

Many North American buildings are designed without proper window sills. A proper sill protrudes from the face of the building and directs water away from the wall.

Surprisingly, up to a half century ago (1950-1960), most window sills were properly designed in Canada and the US, as can be seen with older buildings. For some reason, this changed and now, most buildings lack sills that provide this basic function. For more information about water-shedding details in general see <irc.nrc-cnrc.gc.ca/pubs/ctus/23_e.html>.

(f) Windows and Security

Windows offer easy points of entry for thieves and vandals. Of course, most commercial buildings have security systems that are triggered when a windowpane is broken. However, often this is not the case for second-storey windows. Frequently it takes a thief under five minutes to break in and steal what he wants. When it comes to retail stores, thousands of dollars of merchandise can be stolen in only minutes. There are now thick

506 | Managing Your Properties

window polyester films that can be glued to the interior side of the glass, which holds the pieces of glass together when a window is broken, making it difficult for a thief or vandal to gain entry. This offers an additional advantage for high-rise buildings in that dangerous pieces of broken glass will not fall onto cars and bystanders below. This approach is aesthetically superior to using bars and much cheaper than using very thick glass. It also can slow down bullets fired from a large-calibre handgun from nearly 8 m (25 ft) away. Because they are made with solar inhibitors, these films also reduce solar energy transmission by up to 80%, lowering energy consumption and preventing the fading of carpet, wood, upholstery, etc. These films are used on government and military buildings worldwide. They cost approximately $75 per m² ($7 per sq ft), installed.

19.1.2 EXTERIOR INSULATION AND FINISH SYSTEMS (EIFS)

Sooner or later exterior walls need repair. More and more buildings are now being erected or renovated with what is known as Exterior Insulation and Finish Systems (EIFS). The new materials, coupled with attractive mouldings, generally made with expanded polystyrene foam, can dramatically improve the appearance of a building.

EIFS are multi-layered exterior wall systems. Introduced in North America almost 30 years ago, today, EIFS account for 17% of the US commercial exterior wall market and for about 3.5% of the residential wall market. In the residential area, sales are increasing at the rate of 12-18% per year.

Typically, EIFS consist of the following:
- insulation board, made of polystyrene or polyisocyanurate foam, which is secured to the exterior wall surface with a specially formulated adhesive and/or mechanical attachment;
- a durable, water-resistant base coat, which is applied on top of the insulation and reinforced with fibreglass mesh for added strength; and
- an attractive and durable finish coat, typically using acrylic co-polymer technology, which is both colourfast and crack-resistant.

Both base and finish coats are polymer-based stuccos that are very thin compared to traditional stuccos.

The growing popularity of EIFS is due to the fact that they offer superior energy efficiency and virtually unlimited design flexibility. EIFS can duplicate the appearance of stucco or stone, but are far more versatile than these and other materials. They come in a wide variety of colours and textures, and can be fashioned into virtually any shape or design.

A word of warning: While EIFS is becoming very popular, it seems that it has serious growing pains. Apparently, many houses and small buildings finished with EIFS are prone to the wood framing rotting because some barrier EIFS products trap water between the wood sheathing and the foam insulation. In the US, there were so many cases that a legal class-action lawsuit took place against two manufacturers, Senergy and Thoro.

Originally, the material was used on commercial buildings, where it was applied over concrete blocks and masonry or other non-wood products that would not rot. It is virtually certain that a solution will be found to this problem, but in the meantime it would appear that it may be safer to stick to the original materials.

19.1.3 INSULATING CONCRETE FORMS (ICFS)

Insulating concrete forms (ICFs) are hollow blocks, panels, or planks made of rigid foam that are erected and filled with concrete to form the structure and insulation of the exterior walls of a building. Reinforcing steel bars are placed in the forms cavity (typically a gap of 5-30 cm (2-6 in) between the two layers of foam) before the concrete is poured.

Although there are no federal conformity standards, systems used in Canada must obtain product approval from the Canadian Construction Materials Centre (CCMC), which offers a national evaluation service for all types of innovative construction materials, products, systems and services (see <irc.nrc-cnrc.gc.ca/ccmc/home_e.shtml>).

ICFs offer lower (some even say much lower) energy bills, a healthier living environment, and much flexibility of design. Other advantages include the following:

- a virtually dust and pollen free environment
- reduced sound transmission
- larger windows and longer floor spans
- wide window sills
- sound resistance and quiet floors (no squeaks)
- in-floor radiant heating
- resistance to storms and high winds
- fast, year-round construction, and
- superior insulation.

Typically, ICF is 3-5% more expensive than conventional wood-frame construction. This increase in cost is offset by lower energy costs, greater comfort and higher strength of the structure. See <www.insulatingconcreteforms.ca> for more information about the Insulating Concrete Forms Association.

19.1.4 DRIVEWAYS AND PARKING LOTS

Little else diminishes the appeal of a property as much as neglected or damaged driveways and parking lots. What kind of asphalt should you be using? There are three main types.

1. HL8 is a base layer, very durable, and a great foundation for a long-lasting driveway.
2. HL3 is a finishing layer, a finer mix than HL8, used for highways and may also be used as the top layer for driveways.
3. HL3A is a finer mix than HL8, that is, there is not as much aggregate in the mix. This is the preferred mix as a finishing layer for driveways. It must be less than 5 cm (2 in) thick.

For a long-lasting performance (30-40 years), ask for a double application of HL8 base coat and one of the two finishing coats, HL3 or HL3A. Your driveways and parking lots will then be constructed like city roads and highways. Make sure that the contractor gives you clear and complete specifications for the materials to be used and a cost guaranteed in writing.

For large areas, use a consultant to write specifications and tender the specifications to contractors. If you rip out an old parking lot or install a new one, pay particular attention to the underlying stone base. Indeed, it is the foundation of the whole job. Make sure that this foundation is very strong. The following are the main causes of asphalt surface failures:

- insufficient base
- not enough granular material, resulting in poor drainage
- granular not compacted enough, which leads to insufficient strength to support the asphalt, and
- wearing out of the top asphalt layer due to misuse (excessive weight), regular wear and tear, and poor maintenance (cracks and depressions not attended to as part of the regular maintenance).

Asphalt problems start with cracks. A person who is not knowledgeable will think that the problem with cracks will be solved by applying a driveway sealer over the asphalt. It does not work. Applying a film of liquid asphalt will seal minute cracks, extend the life of the asphalt, and freshen up the appearance; however, to repair larger cracks, one needs to widen them to between 12-25 mm (0.5-1 in) in width and deepen them to 25+ mm (1+ in) with a rotating tool, blow-out the dust, and pour hot liquid asphalt in the enlarged crack.

A parking lot that is seriously cracked in multiple places cannot be repaired with resurfacing. Whatever is underneath will eventually again break through to the surface. In that case, you must cut an area that is a little larger than the affected one, remove all the layers of asphalt that are damaged, and replace them with new layers. However, if there is only surface damage, that is, no deep cracks or sunken areas, resurfacing is the cheapest form of repair. It will increase the height of the asphalt by approximately one inch.

If you own an industrial property, it is likely that the area in front of the shipping doors where the landing gear feet of the semi-trailers are dropped, called the "apron", will be damaged. You are much better to replace the asphalt with concrete (typically 20 cm (8 in), reinforced), if you intend to own the property for a long time. Another term for apron is "dolly pad". However, the term "dolly pad" is also used to describe a trailer dolly wheel pad. This is frequently made of two layers of lumber nailed or screwed to one another and placed under the semi-trailer legs to protect the asphalt.

If you are having a driveway or parking lot constructed, or the asphalt replaced, demand that particular care be paid to slope and water drainage, so that no puddles form when it rains. It is common to find areas of parking lots that do not drain properly. Roadways and other surfaces, whether paved with Portland cement, concrete, or asphalt, must withstand very harsh conditions. Wheel loads from moving vehicles cause strains, stresses and deflections in the paved surface and underlying roadbed. Additionally, pavement in most of Canada must endure significant temperature variations through the depth of the pavement, which induces internal stresses. In many areas, freezing and thawing temperature cycles cause variations in foundation support that cause additional stresses to the paved surface, particularly when moisture is present.

Driveways and parking lots need maintenance and, eventually, replacement. According to the American Concrete Pavement Association (ACPA), one technique for rehabilitating distressed asphalt is a concrete overlay, a technique often referred to as "whitetopping", which has been used in the US since 1918. An evolution of this technology, called "ultra-thin whitetopping", emerged in the early 1990s. It bonds the new concrete overlay to the existing asphalt, resulting in a composite mass rather than two independent layers. The concrete overlay can be significantly thinner (5-10 cm (2-4 in)) for the same load capacity as compared to a whitetopping with no bond to the underlying asphalt.

According to the ACPA, ultra-thin whitetopping lasts two to three times longer than asphalt overlays, having a life expectancy of 20-40 years. They derive their strength (up to 3,000 psi) from the inclusion of synthetic fibres. When comparing construction cost savings and maintenance costs, whitetopping easily wins the life cycle cost analysis. See <www.pavement.com/techserv/usUTW2.html> for more details.

19.1.5 PLASTIC PAVERS

There are many situations when we wish we had a solution to problems such as worn-out lawns, damaged driveways, parking areas that should not look like parking areas, and many more. Several companies have found a similar, but not identical, solution — plastic pavers. Basically, it is a plastic grid that is set below the finished level of the ground that can be filled with sand, gravel, or concrete, or in which one can seed a lawn. It is also possible to press some of these products into the top of existing lawns.

One application for this product is when a by-law requires that a certain percentage of a lot remain landscaped. The use of these pavers lets one have lawn that you are able to park on or drive cars over without damaging it. Other times there may be a restriction on impervious structures. The surface covered or treated with these products offers a water-pervious solution.

Here is an explanation from one manufacturer's Web site:

> [A] honeycomb cell paver product that allows light to heavy vehicular traffic to drive over turf areas. It prevents compaction allowing healthy root growth. It may also be used for erosion control. A tongue and groove latching system provides quick and secure connection between the pavers. The cell design includes more openings in the cell base allowing the paver to grip the subsurface, increase drainage, and increase oxygen transfer by 56 percent over any other honeycomb plastic paver. The smooth top surface of … eliminates sharp corners reducing liability to pedestrians.

There are a number of manufacturers for this type of product, including Eco-Grid, TeffTrack Grassroad Pavers, Gravelpave and Grasspave, and Netpave.

19.1.6 ROOFING

When it comes to roofs, too many building owners practice crisis maintenance, looking at a roof only when problems occur. It is not unusual for roofs with a theoretical design life of 20 years to survive less than 15 years. Yet, with regular inspections, proper repairs and maintenance, those same roofs can last beyond the design life — even as long as 25-30 years. There is no question that the cost of roof maintenance, which can represent up to 90% of the total maintenance cost of a building, is justified in the potential savings in longer roof service life. An additional benefit of having a roof that is free of leaks and other problems is the immense goodwill it brings to the owner, in terms of tenant satisfaction.

Roof warranties can be dangerous because they provide a false sense of security. It is crucial to investigate who provides the guarantee and the financial strength behind it. Is it the manufacturer, the roofing supplier, or the contractor? The key is that this entity should have the financial resources and probable longevity to honour the warranty, so the best option is the roofing manufacturer or an insurance company. When a warranty is written by the manufacturer, it is intended primarily to protect the manufacturer, and has strict

Roof warranties can be dangerous because they provide a false sense of security.

conditions, limitations, and maintenance requirements. Roof warranties vary, ranging from very limited to unlimited, over periods of 5-30 years. One thing that most warranties will not cover is roof negligence. A roof must be inspected a minimum of once a year, preferably twice, and kept free of debris, clogged drains, and minor damage. Reflective coatings, which are not usually covered by warranties, must be renewed periodically. Roofs that have reflective coatings should be recoated every 3-5 years. A wise owner should have a file for each roof, and keep in it all relevant information, such as photographs, bids, invoices, maintenance contracts, repairs, reports, etc., so that he has the necessary back-up material to deal with manufacturers' warranties and/or insurance companies if problems arise.

(a) Inspection and Maintenance

Without doubt the greatest threat to buildings is water penetration. If a roof is to keep water out of a building it needs regular inspection and maintenance. In this section, we are referring to inspection by the building owner, not a professional roofer. Wait for a mild day to make an inspection, wear rubber footwear, and, if the roof is covered with tiles or slate, use planks to spread your weight and prevent cracking when walking on the tiles. Stand on points of support to check roof valleys and junctions, gutters and down pipes, fixings and flashings, decorations and features. While checking for signs of deterioration, ponding, and other indications of developing problems, clean out leaves and accumulated dirt, which may clog drains.

Although all roofing systems require this sort of routine inspection, one of the major advantages of high-performance roofing systems is a lower maintenance requirement over the life of the building. When a roof has exceptional tensile and tear-strength performance, UV resistance, and the flexibility to adjust to thermal-related movement, it is far less likely to require anything more than routine maintenance.

Common entry points for water include seams and joints, especially around flues, vents, skylights, and chimneys. The problem may be as simple as a blocked gutter or the cladding itself may have corroded through to a hole. Another form of water penetration is through capillary action, when water is gradually transmitted through the cladding material itself.

With the flat roofs found on most commercial buildings, it can be difficult to find the exact location of the leak, especially if it is a multi-ply built-up roof. Indeed, you may see the water dripping from the roof at one spot but the real leak, the one in the upper layers, may be 6-9 m (20-30 ft) away and have migrated over another layer or along the roof decking.

If a roof shows signs of serious decay, you need to decide whether to repair or replace it. Small buildings, frequently covered with shingles and tiles, are relatively easy to repair, although care must be taken to match dimensions, texture, material, and repair technique. The home handyman can usually slide the odd slate or shingle back into place, but more extensive repairs are best undertaken by an experienced roofer.

If you do not know a roofer you trust and you have a large job, get an unbiased opinion from a roofing consultant that is independent from any roofing contractor or product manufacturer. Typically, the consultant will design a new roofing system, but he will do much more. He can recommend repairs, select a roofing contractor, prepare bidding documents, and evaluate bids. He can also check the work being done to assure quality (one of the weakest links in construction). Obviously, you will need a roof large enough to justify the cost of a consultant.

Often, in the case of a shingled roof, where deterioration is advanced, a new roof may be a better option than repairs. Seek expert advice before completely re-roofing or cladding over an existing roofing and see sections 19.1.6(b) and (d).

For roofing systems that are showing effects of premature aging due to ponding water or exposure to environmental contaminates, a polymer-modified compound has recently been introduced that can be used on any built-up or modified bitumen membrane system. The manufacturer suggests that one coat applied over a prepared roofing membrane forms a continuous monolithic membrane that is thicker than the typical single-ply rubber or thermoplastic roofing systems. The compound has a 2,000% elongation property and utilizes the structural qualities of the existing roof membrane as a base. That means the product should not be used if the existing roof membrane is deteriorated or damaged. This restoration system can be finished in several ways: surfaced with granules or aggregates, to match the surrounding surface, or coated with an aluminium or highly reflective white roof coating on smooth surface membranes.

(b) Roofing on Commercial Properties

Starting from the bottom, the various components of a typical flat roof are the following: the support structure (joists, on top of beams); roof decking (made of wood on older buildings and corrugated steel sheets on newer buildings); vapour barrier (to prevent condensation from occurring on the cold side of the insulation); insulation; the weatherproofing membrane; and the weather (usually ultraviolet) protection (gravel or coating). In addition, there is flashing around the perimeter of the roof and around each penetration (chimney, vent, skylight, etc.).

Roofing systems used to be relatively few and relatively simple. Now there are many and they are much more sophisticated, particularly roof coatings. Roofs can be constructed from an amazingly broad variety of materials, including metal, plastic, rubber, bitumen, fibre, glass, wood, rocks, and ceramics. Today, one also needs to be familiar with roof coatings, which are composed of metals, organics, and minerals. Applying a coating on top of a roofing system usually increases the life expectancy and the energy efficiency of a building. Coatings are commonly used to prevent direct exposure of the membrane to the sun, atmospheric elements, and to reflect the sun's rays.

The cost of a new roof can vary greatly, depending on its quality and the materials used. Unless you intend to sell a building soon, go with a quality product. Remember that the labour cost is almost the same, whether you use a product with a 10-year warranty or one with a 30-year warranty.

Before getting into too many details, review Figure 19.1, which summarizes the various roofing types.

(c) Commercial Roofing Systems

There are three major types of roofing systems, each with many sub-categories:

1. built-up bitumen (BUR)
2. modified bitumen, and
3. single-ply.

Also known as an asphalt roof, the built-up bitumen (BUR) roof is the best known and, at one point in time, was the most commonly used. The roof is made up of several layers of felt fabric, laminated together with bitumen (a resinous substance coming from various sources, including petroleum, asphalt, and coal).

There are two major drawbacks to this roofing system. It is labour intensive to install and it is susceptible to blistering and cracking.

We recommend that anyone who wants to install a new asphalt roof hire a contractor to do so and buy the NRCA (National Roofing Contractors Association) recommended installation instructions for asphalt roofing available at <www.nrca.net>.

Modified bitumen products provide excellent handling and weathering characteristics by combining modifiers with high-quality asphalt reinforced with fibreglass, polymer, or a combination of both, giving it qualities usually found in plastic or rubber. It is the material most frequently used (just under 40% of the market).

Atactic polypropylene (APP), the first modified bitumen product brought from Europe, was widely used in re-roofing sectioned, smaller buildings. This was followed by styrene butadiene styrene (SBS) hot-mopped asphalt systems that ultimately captured 50% of the overall market nationally. In addition to working as a roofing membrane system, both APP and SBS modified products have been used successfully for many years as flashing for built-up roofing systems. They can be coated with a reflecting surface.

Modified bitumen roofing membranes can be installed using a variety of methods. These two-ply roofing systems incorporate a base sheet and a cap sheet. Some sheets are self-adhesive, peel-and-stick membranes. Others may be attached to the substrate and to each other by torch, hot molten asphalt, cold adhesives, or mechanical fasteners.

Figure 19.1
Summary of Roofing Types

1. Asphalt Shingles
   Description: Most common and least expensive type of roofing material for pitched roofs
   Life Expectancy: 20 to 30 years
   Maintenance: None

2. Built Up Bitumen:
   Description: Usually referred to as hot asphalt or coal tar; ideal for low or no slope roofs
   Life Expectancy: 10 to 20 years
   Maintenance: Annual Inspections

3. Metal:
   Description: Durable, non-combustible metal panels, commonly fastened to a roof deck; available in a variety of colours and may be customized to fit your roofline; ideal for steep slopes
   Life Expectancy: 20 to 50 years
   Maintenance: None

4. Modified Bitumen:
   Description: A rolled membrane composed of reinforcing fabrics coated with a polymer modified bitumen; results in a relatively strong, heavyweight material
   Life Expectancy: 10 to 20 years
   Maintenance: Annual Inspections

5. Single Ply:
   Description: Includes membranes such as EPDM, PVC, CPA, and Hypalon; these rubber-like membranes are rolled and adhered to the roof deck; ideal for low sloped and flat roofs.
   Life Expectancy: 10 to 25 years
   Maintenance: Annual Inspections

6. Wood Shakes:
   Description: Usually cedar or Southern yellow pine; can be treated to boost fire rating and pest resistance.
   Life Expectancy: 15 to 30 years
   Maintenance: Annual washing; wood sealing treatment every four to five years

When the membrane base sheets are torch applied, the open flame from the torch may come into contact with flammable surfaces and materials supporting the roof covering. The potential for flame to travel into voids, cracks, and crevices is great and fires have become alarmingly commonplace and result in very large property losses.

The demand for cool roofs that reduce air conditioning requirements is driving the increasing use of white, thermoplastic systems, a common single-ply or flexible membrane system. Black asphalt or torch-applied systems don't have an answer for cool roofs, whereas the cooler white thermoplastic membranes will last for 15-20 years and reduce energy costs. Most big-box retailers use white thermoplastic membranes on their buildings because they can be hot-air welded. There are three main types of single-ply systems — polyvinyl chloride (PVC), thermoplastic polyolefin (TPO), and ethylene propylene diene monomer (EPDM).

- **Polyvinyl Chloride (PVC).** The popularity of this system seems to be declining, probably due to the tendency of PVC to become brittle and to the fact that it is not a green product (they contain chlorine). They can be made in a variety of colours and offer reasonable resistance to puncture and flammability. The drawback of PVC is that it is made with plastics that can leach over time, leaving the membrane weak and brittle.

- **Thermoplastic Polyolefin (TPO).** TPO is a compound of ethylene and propylene that is used as an elastomeric single-ply roofing membrane. These roofing membranes are only a few years old, but have quickly become the fastest growing type of single-ply membrane on the market. Their success seems to be due to the following:
  – they fit between PVC (vinyl) and EPDM (rubber), but do not have the drawbacks of either,
  – they have the characteristics that rubber offers, such as longevity, flexibility in cold temperatures, and chemical resistance,
  – their hot-air welded seams are stronger than vulcanized ones, and
  – they can be white, which reflects up to 80% of the sun's ultraviolet (UV) rays.

In the summer, a white roof keeps the roof and the building cooler. Ninety per cent of roofs in North America are black and their surfaces can reach 66-88°C (150-190°F), while a white roof will stay up to 70% (39°C) cooler.

TPO systems are reported to be as heat-resistant as the more commonly used EPDM and as heat-weldable as PVC. TPOs do not contain plasticizers and so avoid the problem of plasticizer loss.

The original TPO was made with a base resin of polypropylene (PP) and these systems have 15+ years of proven performance. The new type of TPO is made with a base resin of polyethylene (PE). Little is known about their durability.

- **Ethylene Propylene Diene Monomer (EPDM).** Commonly called membrane roofs or rubber roofs, the ingredients of a typical EPDM are the following:
  – clay, for fire resistance and dimensional stability
  – carbon black, to increase tear strength and resistance to UV light
  – process oils for flexibility, and
  – curing agents for vulcanization.

EPDMs, first installed in 1975, hold the lead in today's market. They withstand the assault of weather well, being very resistant to rain, sun, hail, snow, or ice. EPDMs are also resistant to UV light and to temperature extremes and are available in fire-rated types. Finally, they are easy, fast, and safe to install, requiring only adhesive application equipment. In addition, the product flexibility makes it ideal for difficult applications. The drawback is that the seams are glued or taped and degrade over time. There have also been problems with thermal shrinkage.

(d) Shingle Roofs

Shingles are used to cover small commercial buildings and houses. Few people understand shingle roofs. Many think that they contribute to the insulation of the structure. In fact, the roof's only function is to keep the building dry. Insulation is placed on top of the ceiling.

To prolong the life of these roofs, proper venting of the attic is essential. Venting allows summer heat and moisture to escape from the space below the roof and can increase the life of shingles by as much as 5 years, particularly on the warm, south-facing side. Vents along the roof ridge (top) and under the eaves (soffits) guarantee longer roof life. Here, a common mistake is not balancing the size of the soffit openings and those of the ridge vents on top.

Probably you have seen people re-roofing over older shingles. This is not recommended because it will shorten the life of the new shingles by many years. Indeed, the added thickness acts as an insulation, causing thermal shock, which occurs when shingles are warmed up quickly by the sun, expanding fast, but remaining cold underneath due to the extra insulation. This causes stress on the fabric of the shingle.

A properly installed asphalt shingle roof will last 30-40 years. An improperly installed roof will last 10-20 years — both using the same material. A good roof is one with 260 pound, or heavier, shingles, which are light in colour to reflect life-shortening sunlight. Historically, there were three types of shingles:

1. three-tab
2. laminated, and
3. wood.

Three-tab shingles are the most inexpensive of the three. They are available in different colours, with limited warranties of 20, 25, and 30 years. Their life span is reduced in dry areas because they crack due to the lack of moisture.

Laminated shingles are the most popular type. They have the look of wood shingles without the cost. They have limited warranties ranging from 25-40 years.

Wood shingles are used rarely because they are expensive, susceptible to pest damage, although as mentioned earlier they can be treated, and catch fire easily. Still, some people swear by them because of their natural look and beauty.

In addition to these three types of shingles, a new type needs to be mentioned. Fibreglass reinforced shingles carry a 50-year limited warranty. The fibreglass is supposed to help shingles resist rotting, warping, curling, and fire.

(e) Metal Roofing

Modern metal roofs are more durable than other types of roofing materials and this durability easily justifies their frequently higher cost.

A metal roof is, on average, 30-50% lighter than an asphalt shingle roof and 75% lighter than concrete tile or fibre cement shakes. A new metal roof will cost up to

Modern metal roofs are more durable than other types of roofing materials — last 40 to 60 years or longer – easily justifying their frequently higher cost.

twice that of an asphalt shingle roof, depending on the type, but it will be comparable in price to tile roofing or cedar shake roofing.

Another way to describe panel metal roofs is the method of attachment. For example, standing seam, folded seam, batten, and mechanically fastened. No matter what kind of metal roofing style you choose, you will not have to worry about your roof for a long time. Most metal roofing comes with a 30- to 50-year warranty, but lasts 40-60 years or longer.

You can expect a metal roof to last at least two to three times longer than a regular roof. To put this in context, the average lifespan of an asphalt roof is 12-20 years, but can be shorter depending on the pitch of the roof and the climate in the area. Made of oil-impregnated paper or fibreglass, asphalt begins to deteriorate as soon as you expose it to normal weather. A metal roof, however, will never decompose. Another advantage is that in case of a fire nearby, metal roofing can protect your building should burning embers land on it. Some insurance companies lower their premiums up to 10% for buildings with steel roofs. These roofs come in the following two types:

1. vertical panels,
2. tiles.

While called "vertical panels", these are metal panels installed on a pitched roof. The standing seam metal roof is designed to withstand rain, wind, and snow, and still remain weather-tight. Panels are joined together by a weather-tight seam that is raised above the roof's drainage plane. Factory-applied organic sealants are applied to the seam during roll forming of the panel. Once on site, automatic field seaming machines complete the seal.

Metal panels are attached to the roof substructure with concealed clips. These are roll formed or crimped into the panel seams without penetrating the corrosion-resistant steel weathering membrane. The clip system performs two functions; it retains the panels in position without exposed fasteners, and it allows the roof to expand and contract during temperature changes.

Tiles, also known as metal shakes, metal shingles/slate, metal tile, are primarily used for residences and they look exactly like other common roofing materials, such as asphalt shingle, cedar shake, clay tile, or slate roofing, but metal is stronger and more durable. In comparison to asphalt tiles, metal will not crack, break, warp, curl, or split. They are non-flammable, will withstand winds of over 190 kmh (120 mph), and last at least twice as long as asphalt tiles. They come with a transferable 50-year warranty, which means that in the case of a sale of the property the warranty passes to the new owner.

You may come across commercial metal roofs that are rusted. There are several ways to prolong their lifespan, including painting. Maintaining a sound paint film will prolong the life of corrugated roofing, even when much of the initial coating has been lost from the sheet. Rust converters, alkyd-based primers containing anti-corrosive pigments, and special primers for use over zinc coatings are readily available. Modern rust converters provide a ready-primed surface that accepts most types of finishing paint.

If you are trying to renovate a leaking metal roof, note that the cause is generally loosened fasteners and this problem must be addressed before painting. Additional information can be obtained from The Steel Structure Painting Council at <www.sspc.org>.

However, a better way seems to be the installation of a single-ply membrane, such as a hot air, weldable TPO, on top of the existing metal roof. The big advantage of the TPO is that it is flexible and accepts the movements of a metal roof that are caused by temperature change.

A roof has what is called a "life cycle cost". A study conducted for a 19,600 m² (211,000 sq ft) building in Reading, PA, showed a cost per m² going from a high of $159.85USD for modified bitumen down to $85.14USD for metal, due to the minimal maintenance the latter requires and its longevity.

There are many Web sites where you can find excellent information on the metal roofing industry, including:

- <www.metalroofing.com>
- <www.michaelholigna.com>
- <www.bobvila.com>
- <www.naturalhandyman.com>, and
- <www.household-helper.com>.

(f) Roofing Insulation

If you install a new roof, or replace an old one, consider improving the insulation with a minimum R-value of 11 to 13. This is achieved using extruded Styrofoam sheets that are 5 cm (2 in) thick. Roofers may say that 7.6 cm sheets will give R-20 insulation, but in reality it is closer to R-16.

There are two main types of Styrofoam insulation — expanded polystyrene (EPS), which is often called "beadboard", and extruded polystyrene (XEPS), of which the best-known is Dow's Styrofoam. Both are rigid, closed-cell thermoplastic foam materials. XEPS out-performs EPS in thermal insulating value (rough initial value of R-5.5 vs. 4.5) and moisture vapour permeance. Because XEPS has generally a higher density with a somewhat higher compressive strength, it is better suited for roof insulation.

Given the fact that heat rises, the roof can represent 40% of all heat losses of a building. Good insulation is not expensive, will save considerably in heating and cooling costs, and will increase comfort, hence tenant satisfaction, in the building.

Remember, insulation is the trapping of air that acts as a barrier to the movement of heat. With small buildings, you can improve it very cheaply if, between layers of traditional insulating material, such as Fiberglas or cellulose, you place a layer of three or four sheets of newspapers that are available for free. This approach would not be used for large commercial buildings.

For pitched roofs, the ideal under-roof ventilation system would be perforated soffits (the horizontal part under the overhang of the roof). Some people swear by turbine ventilators, while others argue against them, apparently for many reasons. Good turbines are guaranteed for life.

There are a number of common roofing insulation problems.

- **Phenolic Foam.** Phenolic foam insulation, which was previously used throughout Canada and the US, caused significant corrosion of steel roof decks if it got wet. Although production of this insulation stopped in 1994, many buildings still have it. Ask your roofer, even though there is nothing you can do until the problem presents itself. However, forewarned is forearmed.

- **Ridging.** Ridging of the membrane is the long, narrow elevation of the roofing surface (it appears as a bump 2.5-5 cm (1-2 in) wide) and is another problem that can be encountered with phenolic foam insulations and other rigid foam insulations. Some board insulations are not structurally strong enough to take the wear and tear of being walked on, particularly during the roof membrane installation, which can result in the top layer de-bonding from the core portion of the insulation panel. Because the roof membrane is adhered to the top surface of the insulation, but not structurally to the deck, any expansion or contraction of the roof membrane is not resisted, causing ridging to occur. The same effect would occur if the insulation panels were not properly adhered to the roof deck.

- **Wet Insulation Board.** If the insulation board gets wet during installation or because of a leak, it will dry at different rates, with the top surface drying faster than the core of the board. This causes the board to curl, similar to a wood shingle, which becomes a bigger problem if the long edges of the insulation board are not sitting directly on top of the steel deck flute. If the long edges are between flutes (valleys), the amount of curling and subsequent ridging of the membrane can be significant.

- **No Protection Board.** Typically, a protection board is required when installing hot asphalt onto a foam board product to prevent the foam from coming into contact with hot asphalt and melting. Without a protection board the surface of the insulation board will deteriorate and possibly bond improperly to the membrane of the insulation. Another concern is that any gasses produced by this condition may be trapped, aggravating the bonding problem.
- **Seams.** Seams are the most vulnerable part of a roof, since that's where leaks usually appear. Air-welded seams are usually used with single-ply systems because they are considered the most durable. Indeed, the welding, when properly done, makes them as strong as the membrane itself. Some specialists contend that a hot-air welded seam can be up to eight times stronger than an adhesive seam and up to three times stronger than a taped seam.

If you become obsessed with roofing, the Canadian Roofing Contractors' Association has produced the *Canadian Roofing Reference Manual*, a comprehensive, 678-page, four-volume manual. It is, in fact, a specification manual. See <www.roofingcanada.com> for more information.

19.1.7 ROOFTOP GARDENS AND GREEN ROOFS

A rooftop garden can be a marvellous addition to a building, particularly a multi-family building. Common in Europe, but used little in North America, these gardens can provide several advantages in addition to the tenants' enjoyment, including:

- increased property values
- increased durability of roof membranes, and
- reduced heat flow across the roofing system, which lowers the energy required for air conditioning during the warmer months and heating during colder ones.

Rooftop gardens are sometimes called "green roofs". Here is a sophisticated definition from "Eco-roof" by W.P. Hickman Systems (<www.ecoroofsystems.com>):

> Green roof, eco-roof, nature roof or green roofing system are general terms referring to vegetated roof coverings consisting of a thin layer of living vegetation installed on top of a modified conventional roof system with significant changes. Modern green roof systems replace traditional rooftops; flat or angled up to 45 degrees, with a series of carefully engineered layers. A water and root-repellent membrane is installed on top of a reinforced roof structure. A filter layer is placed between the base membrane and a layer of soil as thin as 1.2 inch thick. Finally the soil layer is seeded with varieties of simple durable plants- sedums, perennial grasses and other "rock garden" plants.

Green roofs are lightweight, modern versions of the sod roofs that are a centuries-old tradition in Scandinavia. Because of their relatively light weight, they require little additional load-bearing capacity from a building's structural system. Tests conducted by the National Research Council found that in the spring and summer of 2001, a green roof reduced the overall heat entering a building during the day by

A green roof reduced the overall heat entering a building during the day by more than 85% and leaving the building at night by about 70%.

more than 85% and leaving the building at night by about 70%. (See <irc.nrc-cnrc.gc.ca/newsletter/v7no1/rooftop_e.html>.) However, green roofs are not cheap, starting at around $129 per m² ($12 per sq ft).

19.1.8 DECKS, PATIOS, AND BALCONIES

If you have decks, patios, or balconies, you may find yourself having to cover or recover them. For a high quality job, you will probably want to use vinyl deck covering, which has a life span of 15-20 years. The product looks very much like indoor vinyl flooring but resists UV rays and weather. These attractive materials come in a variety of patterns, thicknesses, colours, and textures. They are maintenance free, durable (usually with a 10-year warranty), mildew and slip resistant, and stand up to tough abuse.

Installation of vinyl deck covering is not a do-it-yourself job. The seams need to be heat-sealed and special equipment is required to do it.

19.1.9 CONCRETE AND STUCCO

Although it is common for people to use the words "concrete" and "cement" interchangeably, they are entirely different products. Cement is a powder and is the most important component of concrete. Concrete is made by mixing cement with water and aggregates (sand, gravel, etc.) and allowing the mixture to dry and harden. The drying process is called curing. Stucco, on the other hand, is a mixture of cement, sand, and clay. The same mixture is called "mortar" when used in concrete block and brick masonry.

To obtain strong concrete, as little water as possible should be used. The ratio of water to cement is expressed as a decimal fraction. The longer the curing period, the stronger the concrete will be because it will have fewer capillaries, which are mini-tunnels left behind after the water has evaporated.

The most common way to use concrete is to reinforce it with steel reinforcing bars, known as rebar. This increases its strength enormously.

One of the drawbacks of conventional concrete is that it prevents the penetration of water, but is not vapour-proof. Thanks to the capillaries, formed during the curing process, water vapour is able to move through the concrete. When the vapour reaches the dew point — the temperature at which dew begins to form — it condenses into water and can cause damage to floor covering adhesives and even the covering itself. It can also lead to rust that will corrode the rebar.

Additives, such as glass fibres, air entrainers, plasticizers, latex, pigments, dyes, and sealers can be added to the basic concrete mix, producing different kinds of concrete. Each one has a specific purpose.

Concrete has evolved considerably, over the last few decades. With modern technology it can now be produced in virtually any colour, texture, or shape. Wet concrete can be stamped with a pattern to resemble stone, wood, tile, or a custom pattern. This is more commonly seen in exterior concrete applications such as patios, stairs, and the like, but it is now also common to see concrete countertops advertised as a rival to granite and Corian. Acid-stained concrete takes on a wood look or rustic patina. Although the term "acid stained" is used, acid is not the ingredient that colours the concrete. It is metallic salts in an acidic, water-based solution that react with hydrated lime (calcium hydroxide) in hardened concrete to yield insoluble, coloured compounds that become a permanent part of the concrete. Because the colour can be mixed in the concrete, a slight wear of the surface will not affect the appearance. Obviously, this is more expensive than traditional concrete.

A recently released concrete from LePage Corporation, called Ductal, derives its strength from glass fibres instead of rebar. The glass fibres, mixed with the liquid concrete, act as a crack control agent. This product is also less brittle than traditional concrete and has increased tension capability. The combination, said to be as strong as steel, is so strong that it can be cast in a thickness as thin as 2.5 mm (0.1 in).

If you are excited about concrete, go to <www.concretenetwork.com/> for more information.

19.1.10 WATERPROOFING MASONRY WALLS

Many above-ground masonry walls, whether concrete, concrete block, or brick assemblies, suffer from water penetration. Over the years (sometimes only a few years), water or water vapour travels through such materials. The result may be only a wet wall or water leaking into the building.

There are three typical solutions to this problem. You can apply metal, plastic cladding, or stucco, which contains additives for water repellence, or a water repellent product. The third option, which is most common, we will discuss here.

For water problems in existing buildings, most water repellent sealers for use on porous surfaces are usually clear, penetrating, and breathable. They must allow the substrate or wall surface to breathe and allow moisture to escape, while keeping water out. The three main categories of sealers contain silicone in some form. They are the following:

- silanes
- siloxanes, and
- silicone rubber.

An important factor with sealers is their ability to penetrate the substrate to which they are applied. Silanes have the deepest penetration, followed by siloxanes, and then silicone rubber. Silanes and siloxanes will not last beyond a few years because they are organic and, hence, susceptible to acid rain, UV rays, and salt spray. When a substrate is treated with silanes or siloxanes, a chemical reaction takes place. Therefore, they cannot be used with substrates such as wood or natural stone, unless a catalyst is added in the factory.

Silicones are oxygen-permeable, flexible, and have inert properties and the ability to seal any material, including natural stone. Today's silicones offer long-lasting protection. In vertical applications, 20-year-old treatments that are still working are not uncommon. An additional advantage of silicone is that it retains its elasticity, allowing it to accept minor structural movements.

Usually, sealers will suppress or reduce the effects of mildew, efflorescence, and stains. If you plan to use sealant on freshly poured concrete, note that concrete should not be treated for at least 28 days, more if curing is slow.

19.1.11 FENCES

A line fence, also known as a division fence, is any fence marking the boundary between an owner's property and a neighbouring property. By law (*Line Fences Act* (R.S.O. 1990, c. L.17)) an owner of land has the right to construct and maintain a fence to mark the boundary between the owner's land and adjoining lands. Virtually every municipality has rules as to the materials that can be used and the height of the fences.

Fences are frequently a source of disputes between neighbours because few people are familiar with the laws or simply choose to ignore them and proceed with erecting a fence without first obtaining the neighbour's consent. In Ontario, disputes relating to fences are municipal matters and are handled by fence-viewers that are appointed by the municipal council. An owner may request fence-viewers to view and arbitrate any dispute over a fence. There is no arbitration between November 1 and March 31.

4.(1) Where the owner of any land desires to have a fence constructed to mark the boundary between the owner's land and the land of an adjoining owner, or where such a fence exists, to have it repaired or reconstructed and where the owner has not entered into a written agreement with the adjoining owner for sharing the costs of the construction, reconstruction or repair, as the case may be, of such fence, the owner may notify in the prescribed form the clerk of the local municipality in which the land is situate that the owner desires fence-viewers to view and arbitrate as to what portion of the fence each owner shall construct, reconstruct or repair and maintain and keep up.

Because you are responsible for paying the fence-viewer, this can become quite costly. There are two possibilities.

1. If the land is in an area with municipal organization that has a by-law, passed under section 11 of the *Municipal Act*, 2001 (S.O. 2001, c. 25), for apportioning the costs of line fences, the by-law must be followed. There may be a municipal by-law regulating height, materials, etc., of the fence.
2. If the land is in an area without a municipal organization, the *Line Fences Act* applies.

During fence viewing, there are three fence-viewers who visit the property and study the location of the proposed fence or examine the state of the existing fence. They discuss the issues with each owner separately. The fence-viewers then leave and make their decision. The city clerk's office sends the decision, known as the "award," by registered mail to the owners involved. The Award specifies the following details:
- the location of the fence
- the description of the fence, including the materials to be used and the maximum height of the fence,
- who will pay for the construction and/or maintenance of the fence
- when the work should be started and completed
- who will pay the fence-viewing arbitration fee, and
- any other factors they consider relevant.

The decision of the three fence-viewers can be appealed to a referee whose decision is final. This process is not cheap. In Toronto, the application fee for a Request for Fence-Viewers costs $1,110, plus $30 per hour for each of the three fence-viewers (minimum 3 hours). This can total $1,380.

19.2 SURFACE CARE

Take care of the surface areas within your building, including floors, walls, and masonry.

19.2.1 REPAIRING AND INSTALLING FLOORS

In industrial buildings you will, unavoidably, come across damaged concrete floors. To repair them use latex concrete that forms a perfect bond with old concrete surfaces and can be feather-edged without spalling (chipping or crumbling). If forklifts are to be used on the floor, make sure you use the type of product that can withstand heavy use.

If a new floor covering, such as tile or broadloom, is going to be installed on top of a damaged floor, use an underlayment, a material laid between a subfloor and a finished floor. Ardex manufactures this type of product and offers several types (distributed in central and eastern Canada by Centura Floor and Wall Fashions (<www.centura.ca>)).

Such a product is Ardex SD-T. It can be used as a new flooring surface, as an underlayment, or for the repair and renovation of flooring surfaces in a number of warehouse and light manufacturing environments. It can be applied in thicknesses of 3.2-12.7 cm (1¼-5 in) in a single operation. It withstands heavy foot traffic — even rubber wheel forklift traffic. However, you must be careful to select the right type for your project or run the risk of being disappointed.

Another interesting product made by their company is Ardex K-15. This outstanding product can be used over concrete, metal, terrazzo, ceramic tile, wood, and old flooring adhesive residue, above or below grade. It can be applied in situations where its thickness will be anywhere from a feathered edge to 76 mm (0-3 in) (with the addition of proper aggregates). It can withstand a load of 4,100 psi.

Concrete is poured directly on base soils covered with aggregates for slab floors, sidewalks, roads, or parking lots. Sometimes, the soil on which the concrete was poured is unstable or may become so with time. In that situation, you will notice that part of the concrete surface has sunk. For many years, the only two cures were to pour more concrete over the sunken surface, hoping for proper adhesion to the old concrete and for stability of the underlying soil, or to dig out the old floor, fill where required, and pour new concrete.

Then, came mud-jacking. With this system, one injects mud under high pressure, under the slab, hence the term "slab-lifting". A Finnish firm, Uretek Canada (<www.uretek.ca>) with an office in Concord, Ontario, seems to have improved on this system by injecting a urethane foam mixture to lift the slab. We haven't used this solution but it looks promising.

If you want to create an office or a residence and need to install new floors on an existing concrete slab, the best approach is to install a layer of extruded polystyrene foam (XEPS) 2.5-5 cm thick (1-2 in) and cover it with 1.6-1.9 cm (5/8-3/4 in) plywood. The users of the space will bless you because their feet will stay warm. Furthermore, this is a good floor to avoid the problems brought about by moisture or small animals, such as mice. While on this subject, if occupants' comfort is important, for example in an office or retail store, it is recommended that there be insulation placed on the soil, prior to pouring a concrete slab.

19.2.2 CLEANING WALLS, FLOORS, AND MASONRY
Sooner or later you will need to clean floors, walls, masonry (concrete or brick), etc. The choices open to you are as follows:

1. chemical cleaners
2. blasting, washing, and steam cleaning, and
3. green cleaning.

(a) Chemical Cleaners
Your first choice, in most cases, is to try the heavy-duty champ, Trisodium Phosphate (TSP), an all-purpose cleaner and degreaser. Another name for TSP is "tribasic sodium phosphate". TSP is used primarily by painters and cleaners to remove heavy deposits of grime, smoke, grease, oil, soot, mildew, etc. If the surface involved is to receive paint, it must be rinsed thoroughly prior to painting. If the surface does not clean sufficiently well, it should be rinsed thoroughly before using another cleaning product.

The next best chemical products for cleaning concrete and grouts are those containing phosphoric acid, followed by many other commercial products, some much better than others.

Muriatic acid should not be your first choice because it corrodes. It should not be left on the surface being cleaned any longer than necessary. A drop on a natural fibre fabric will quickly burn a hole. When working with muriatic acid, wear old clothes, protective glasses and gloves, keep a bucket of water handy, and rinse your skin immediately if it comes into contact with the acid. Secure and follow instructions, particularly to dilute it (always adding the acid to the water). Also note, muriatic acid is not recommended for indoor applications due to its potent fumes.

(b) Blasting, Washing, and Steam Cleaning

Acid cleaners and blasting actually clean masonry by eating away or removing the top layer of the surface. They can leave a surface that is raw, exposed, and more prone than before to collect dirt and other impurities. They also expose the more porous inner layers of the materials to destructive elements. A number of these methods are still in use.

- **Compressed Air.** Compressed air is great if it is mainly to dislodge dust — but then you have to collect the dust.
- **Sand Blasting.** Sand blasting of exterior walls was all the rage a few years ago. This is no longer the case because people found that it could cause serious damage, particularly to brick.
- **High-Pressure Washing with Cold Water.** While very effective, high pressure washing with cold water may cause damage to wood (swelling, cracking, staining) or to very soft materials. In addition, it uses a lot of water that must then be disposed of.
- **Steam Cleaning.** Steam cleaning is more effective and will cause less damage than cold water. Steam can deliver temperatures up to 163°C (325°F), so it can be very useful when one wants to remove or destroy bacteria. Obviously, with these high temperatures, the steam also sanitizes. This system reduces cleaning costs because it obtains faster results, lowering labour costs. Steam cleaning is the only effective means to remove heavy oil, such as bunker-C, from most surfaces.
- **Dry Ice (CO_2) Blasting.** Dry ice blasting cleaning, also called CO_2 blasting, is similar to sand, bead or soda blasting, where a medium is carried in a pressurized air stream to hit the surface that is to be cleaned. In a dry ice blasting system, liquid CO_2 is converted into a kind of "snow" which is packed to an exact pressure and extruded through hundreds of holes, resulting in consistently sized pellets. On impact, the pellets vaporize into carbon dioxide gas, leaving no residue. The air supply must come from an oil-free compressor that provides a minimum of 9.9 cubic metres of air per minute (350 cfm (cubic feet per minute)), at up to 230 psi of pressure.

   Unlike the grit particles, such as sand, a CO_2 pellet striking the surface does not bounce back. It penetrates the coating, then shatters, blasting fragments laterally in all directions and releasing the contaminant from the base material. Instantaneously, the dry ice fragments turn from a solid to a gaseous state. The expansion of the CO_2 from solid to gas adds a lifting force called a "mushroom effect" to speed removal of the contaminant. The debris falls away and the CO_2 gas returns harmlessly to the atmosphere.

   While dry ice blasting equipment is more expensive than grit blasting equipment, it offers the advantage of not damaging the objects being cleaned. The second, very important advantage is that there is no problem collecting or disposing of the cleaning medium, since the CO_2 pellets disappear on contact. Dry ice blasting appears ready to replace high-pressure washing and other blasting methods as well as abrasive agents and other cleaning methods that damage the surface being cleaned.

(c) Green Cleaning

If you are environmentally conscious, you may want to use Greensolv, which is biodegradable, has a very low toxicity, and is non-carcinogenic and non-mutagenic. The manufacturer describes it as a "high performance paint stripper for wood and household applications". Greensolv works on a wide variety of coatings, such as acrylic latex, urethanes, epoxies, polyurethanes, alkyds, enamels, antifouling coatings and glues. It was developed to replace highly toxic and ozone-depleting chemicals. Unfortunately, it is not inexpensive. To our knowledge, the only place selling it is Lee Valley Tools (<www.leevalley.com>).

Greensolv — an environmentally friendly cleaner — is biodegradable, has a very low toxicity, and is non-carcinogenic and non-mutagenic.

19.2.3 PAINTING AND REMOVING PAINT

Painting serves two purposes. The first is to prevent air, sun, and water from reaching the substrate (the surface being painted). The second is to beautify the item. As mentioned earlier, if there is one thing to remember about painting, it is this — the most important, time-consuming, and costly part of painting is surface preparation (except for moisture-cured urethanes, as discussed below). This means that you need to plan on spending a lot more time and money removing old paint, plugging holes and cracks, sanding, and cleaning and protecting adjoining surfaces than on the application of the paint itself.

To do a good painting job requires knowing the kind of existing paint involved. You will probably need a professional painter's help for that task. Before stripping any surface, ask yourself if it is really necessary. Stripping may well remove earlier paint layers, however, the wrong method can damage the substrate underneath. Where old paintwork is sound, it is best left undisturbed and used as the base for new paintwork. The adhesion between coats of paint and between paint and substrate can decrease when applied over surfaces where paint strippers have been used.

(a) Moisture Cured Urethane Coatings (MC-urethanes)

For most industrial applications such as steel bridges (particularly in coastal areas) and other steel structures exposed to harsh elements, MC-urethanes do not require thorough surface preparation. The paint can be applied over rusted steel and encapsulated asbestos, concrete, and old lead paint. It easily covers nail holes and can be applied in environments with up to 99% humidity. MC-urethanes can be immersed in water 30 minutes after application and have excellent corrosion resistance. They come in primer-sealer, primer, and finishing coats. They are long-lasting (15-25 years), but not very attractive. However, they do require a relative humidity of at least 45% to cure and the containers cannot be left open for a few hours or a thick film will form on the surface. They are generally more difficult to handle that regular paints.

(b) Methods of Paint Removal

All methods of paint removal are laborious and slow. Different paints respond to different methods and it is therefore helpful to be able to identify the nature of the substrate and the thickness and the type of paint (i.e., water or solvent thinned, bitumen or polyurethane based, etc.) you want to remove before deciding upon the means of removal. Manufacturers of the paint can often provide useful advice. It may be necessary to try several techniques or a combination of methods to achieve success. Tests should be made over small trial areas to see if the paint can be lifted and to ensure that the substrate will not be damaged. A number of techniques and products are described below.

- **Water Washing.** Water washing can be helpful in removing lime washes, whiting, and soft (size-bound) distemper. However, when removing paint from plaster, keep water to a minimum; prolonged soaking will soften plaster, especially gypsum-based plasters.

- **Steam Stripping.** Steam stripping is usually undertaken using an appliance designed mainly for stripping wallpaper. It generates steam at low pressure and the steam is applied to the surface via a hose capped with a perforated metal applicator. This can also be used with water-thinned paints that are softened by steam and then removed with a sponge, brush, scraper, and water.

- **Chemical Paint Removers.** There are two main types of chemical paint removers — solvent (non-caustic) and alkaline (caustic). Both are available in liquid, gel, and poultice form. All chemical paint removers constitute a health risk. Some can burn on contact with the skin and vapour and sprays are toxic if inhaled.

  - **Solvent (Non-Caustic) Removers.** Non-caustic solvent removers are usually based on methylene chloride. They are effective in removing oil-based paints, tar, and some emulsions. They are available as either water soluble, which removes wax residues by a thorough wash down, or spirit soluble, which removes wax deposits with white spirit.

  - **Alkaline (Caustic) Removers.** Based on caustic soda, potash, washing soda, or similar material, alkaline removers should only be used as a last resort. A caustic product is one that is capable of burning, corroding, dissolving, or eating away by chemical action. They are easily absorbed by porous surfaces and the harmful residues are very difficult to remove. Application should be restricted to small areas. They are not suitable for plywood, veneers, or hardboard and can be harmful to brickwork, stonework, metal, and most types of plaster or putty. Alkaline removers may raise the grain of timber and darken or bleach some woods.

    They are effective on oil-based paints as they break down the oil or resins that bind the paint, permitting the softened paint to be removed by scraping or scrubbing with a hard brush and water. It may be necessary to subsequently neutralize surfaces with acid. This should be followed by a thorough washdown with several applications of clear water to remove all traces of alkali, which may attack subsequent coats of paint. Care must be taken to clean up carefully.

- **Manual Abrasive Removal.** Scraping, or carborundum block and water (laborious but often effective) are considered manual abrasive methods and should be used in preference to powered tools such as sanders, which tend to scratch the surface and are generally only suitable for flat surfaces.

- **Blast Cleaning.** Only to be undertaken by an experienced contractor, blast cleaning should not be used on stone and brick surfaces, which can be irreparably damaged by this process. Blasting is useful on cast iron but it will destroy a smooth surface. Priming of cast iron immediately after blasting is necessary to avoid surface rusting.

- **Hot-Air Strippers.** Hot-air strippers are not suitable for removing water-based paints, some primers and undercoats, or for removing paint from metal or plaster. They should only be used on masonry when thick layers are to be removed. Blowlamps or blowtorches are often quicker but pose a fire hazard.

(c) Removing Coverings from Brick or Stone

Most methods of removing paint from brick or stone will damage the base material to some extent and paint may be next to impossible to remove from porous brick or stone. There are a number of products used to cover brick and stone, as listed following, but there is no wholly satisfactory method for removal. Below we will discuss the best methods for removing various products.

- **Bituminous Paints and Tar.** For water-thinned bituminous emulsions, use steam cleaning in conjunction with a solvent stripper. For solvent-thinned bitumen paints and tar (solution type), naphtha will help to soften and dissolve them, but mechanical methods may be necessary to remove them.
- **Chlorinated Rubber-Based Paints.** They are difficult to remove. Consult the manufacturer, if known. Try naphtha.
- **Creosote.** Creosote is difficult to remove, however, solvent strippers in poultice form can be effective if penetration of the coating is shallow. It is usually best to allow creosote to weather and fade naturally. Bleeding can occur if it is painted over with other paints.
- **Distemper, Oil-Bound (washable distemper).** Oil-bound distemper can be difficult to remove. Hot-water washing and scrubbing, together with a non-ionic detergent, can loosen adhesion of some types of distemper. Steam stripping and scraping with a knife is usually successful.
- **Distemper, Size-Bound (soft distemper) and Whitewash.** These distempers are generally removed by washing down thoroughly with warm water. A hand-spray, to soften the coating, used prior to washing will aid removal. Keep water to a minimum and do not add alkaline soap or detergents because harmful residues can be absorbed by porous surfaces. Steam stripping may be necessary for stubborn coatings.
- **Emulsion Paints.** Emulsion paints, which are based on polyvinyl acetate (PVA) and acrylic copolymers, are used mainly for indoor surfaces. Removal depends on the type of emulsion and the number of coats. Some coatings can be softened with hot water followed by scraping and scrubbing. Others respond to a solvent stripper (non-methylene chloride based). Steam stripping and scraping is effective on one or two coats. Steam stripping in conjunction with a solvent stripper may be necessary for removing multiple layers of old paint, including polyvinyl emulsion, that have resisted other forms of treatment. A solvent stripper in poultice form is sometimes successful. Preliminary rubbing by hand will reduce encrustation and ease stripping. Paint and chemical residues on plaster should be removed with water, not turpentine.
- **Lime Wash.** Lime wash containing tallow or linseed oil can be difficult to remove. Brushing down loose, powder coatings, followed by washing, sponging and scrubbing is usually effective. Hot-water washing and steam will help to soften coatings. Old sulphated lime wash in multiple applications may respond to a wet poultice maintained in position over a long period, but a low-pressure wet abrasive cleaning system may be necessary as a last resort.
- **Masonry Paints.** This term covers a wide range of coatings of variable compositions and textures. They may be solvent or water-thinned. It is difficult to remove masonry paint without damage to the substrate. Consult manufacturers, if known, or a paint supplier regarding the best means of removal. Many types of masonry paint respond to solvent strippers in paste form, but large quantities would be required for textured masonry paint. Mechanical methods may also be necessary.
- **Oil (alkyd) Paints.** Use solvent removers, hot-air strippers, and abrasive methods.
- **Textured Coatings.** For internal plaster, see above for masonry paint. For textured, plastic coatings, gypsum based, use a hot-water solution, containing a mild detergent, in a hand-spray followed by scraping. Do not abrade dry. For emulsion-type coatings, use hot water softening or steam stripping, together with scraping.

- **Graffiti.** There is no general solution to removal of graffiti but it is important to begin treatment as soon as possible so that the paint does not have time to harden. Long-standing aerosol paints are almost impossible to remove from porous surfaces such as brickwork and stonework. There is also a risk of spreading the paint and increasing absorption in the process. Cleaning with an air abrasive pencil using a suitable fine abrasive, then toning down the cleaned patch by rubbing with stone or brick dust, may be successful. A solvent-based (non-caustic) poultice can be tried. If this fails, an alkaline (caustic) remover in poultice form might be effective. Brick and stone must be thoroughly washed after removing the paint. A second poultice (without the chemical incorporated) can be applied to help draw out the residual salts. Anti-graffiti coats are available to protect walls, but they can create problems by trapping moisture and salts behind an impermeable membrane.

(d) Sandblasting

Often, sandblasting seems to be an easy way to get rid of paint, but, as mentioned earlier, it should be avoided, particularly with brick. When you sandblast brick you actually remove some of the hard finish that protects bricks from the elements. Over time the bricks will soften and crumble. There are other ways to remove paint depending on how much area is involved. Consult your local brick supplier or building centre for suggestions. Using paint removers on brick rarely works and can make the problem worse. Brick is porous and paint removers tend to just soften the paint and encourage it to seep into the brick.

(e) Dealing with Lead-Based Paint

Exposure to lead is dangerous, particularly to children. The greatest care is needed when disturbing old, lead-based paint, especially when sandblasting.

Buildings constructed before 1960 are likely to contain lead-based paint. In all likelihood, those built after 1980 will not have lead-based paint inside, but may have some outside. Paints produced after 1992 have very low concentrations of lead or no lead. If the paint involved does not chip or flake and is not within the reach of children, it is best to leave it alone. It may be covered with wallpaper, wallboard, or panelling for extra safety.

If you must remove lead-based paint, the overriding principle is to not create dust or fumes. The best approach is to hire an expert. If you decide to do it yourself, remember:

- use a chemical paint stripper in paste form
- remove furnishings from the room or cover anything that cannot be moved
- isolate the work area by covering doorways and vents with plastic sheeting and tape to prevent scrapings, chips, and paint particles from leaving the room
- ventilate the room to the outdoors, for example, by using a fan to blow air out through a window
- wear goggles, gloves, and a mask
- take a break outside every 10-15 minutes
- do not drink, eat, or smoke while removing paint, and
- put paint scrapings in a sealed container marked "Hazardous Waste" and ask your municipality where to take it for disposal.

If you are trying to find out if your property has lead-based paint, specialized contractors have portable meters that can measure lead on paint surfaces. Paint chips can also be sent to a laboratory for analysis. A list of specialized labs can be obtained from the Standards Council of Canada or the Canadian Association for Environmental Analytical Laboratories. More information regarding lead-based paint is available from Health Canada. For extensive information about painting, go to <webpages.charter.net/foley/Painting/ProblemSolver.htm>.

19.2.4 FLOOR COVERINGS

When faced with the task of putting something on the floor, the first decision is whether hard flooring or resilient flooring is preferable.

(a) Hard Floorings

Hard floor coverings run the gamut to stone, tile, and hardwoods and laminates. We'll explore the properties of each.

- **Marble.** Marble appeals to people because of its beauty and elegance. It comes in different varieties and is often found in the common areas of office buildings. Many architects and owners who place form before function, put marble on the floors, particularly in lobbies. Frequently, this is a mistake because many kinds of marble are relatively soft and sometimes it is cut too thin to save money. You will often find old marble floors that are worn out, cracked or nicked. Many marbles are better used on vertical surfaces. For kitchen counters another natural stone option is Serpentine. Although it is sometimes called green marble due to its appearance, it is not truly a marble. It presents the huge advantage of not being sensitive to citric acid and kitchen spills.

- **Granite.** The king of hard flooring, granite is very popular and justifiably so. It presents a combination of strength, hardness, and beauty that is hard to beat. It comes in an almost infinite array of colours and patterns and can be outstandingly beautiful. In addition, granite resists heat and is one of the most bacteria-resistant kitchen surfaces available. Granite is not affected by spills of citric acid, alcohol, wine, coffee, or tea and its hardness makes it almost impossible to scratch. If you want a luxurious office lobby, granite is one of the better choices you can make.

- **Travertine, Limestone, Sandstone, and Slate.** These are also used both inside and outside buildings, but they are not in the same league as marble or granite. Travertine is a type of limestone. Limestone is popular as a building stone because it is readily available and easy to work with. Nowadays, unlike many decades ago, slate is only rarely used for roofing, due to its cost and weight. It is, however, still used for interior paving.

- **Ceramic Tile.** Ceramic tile is a mixture of clays and minerals that has been shaped, pressed, then fired at temperatures exceeding 1,000°C (1,830°F), resulting in a hard surface. A protective glaze is applied before firing to give the tile added colour and finish and to make it resistant to odours, stains, bacteria, and scratches.

- **Porcelain Tile.** Porcelain tile is a type of ceramic made of a very fine mixture of clays and minerals, similar to those found in fine dinnerware. Porcelain tiles are fired at higher temperatures than ceramic tiles, usually over 1,300°C (2,370°F). It is this higher temperature that produces a very dense (hence hard) product that resists moisture. It is 30% harder than granite. Porcelain owns 30-40% of the US tile marketplace.

  There are several grades of porcelain/ceramic tiles based on a grading system developed by the Porcelain Enamel Institute (PEI). The rating is arrived at by subjecting the tile to an abrasion test. For medium traffic, a PEI-4 grade is acceptable, while PEI-5 is recommended in a commercial setting. Originally, porcelain was unglazed, through-body tile, which meant that the colour was consistent from top to bottom. It was designed for and installed in high traffic — usually commercial — areas. However, it was later adopted for residential use. Eventually, improved technology allowed porcelain manufacturers to achieve a stone-like look by mixing additional dyes in the powder, but the absorptive quality remained. Next came double-filling, pressing different colours to achieve a more random look to replicate the appearance of stone.

Variations in technology have resulted in several types of porcelain, but they all share the 0.5% absorption rate, which is one of the key characteristics that distinguishes porcelain tiles from other porcelain-like products.

Like ceramic tile, porcelain tile is resistant to odours, stains, bacteria, and scratches. Properly installed porcelain tile is strong and durable enough to withstand even forklift traffic.

- **Concrete.** Concrete used to be strictly a utilitarian material, but it is now used everywhere. Concrete floors can be tinted and embossed to look like stone paving, for example. Concrete can also be used as counters with plain colours or varied colours mixed throughout the material. It is no longer just painted on top.

- **Terrazzo.** Terrazzo is practically indestructible (like granite, perhaps even more so). It is resistant to water, chemicals, oil, solvents, and most acids. There are two main kinds of terrazzo. The traditional one usually has metal strips that are usually used to create various shapes, while a new type, which contains synthetic binders, does not require the strips. Some terrazzo can be quite luxurious and show various designs.

- **Hardwood.** The first type of wooden floor, born in Europe, was made of wide planks. Then came narrow plank floors and parquet floors, which are made, originally, of parquetry (an inlay of wood, often of different colours, which is usually worked into a geometric pattern or mosaic).

  Many factors define the look of natural hardwood, including the species of the tree, where it grew, the rate of growth, and the part of the tree used. The closer a plank is cut to the centre of the tree, the darker its overall tone. Lighter boards come from closer to the bark. Knots indicate that a limb grew from that spot. Growth rings, determined by climate trends and mineral/nutrient absorption, determine grain pattern. Solid hardwood flooring is milled from a single 1.9 cm (3/4 in) thick piece of hardwood. Because of its thickness, a solid hardwood floor can be sanded and refinished over several generations of use. One of the characteristics of solid wood flooring is that it expands and contracts with changes in a building's relative humidity. Normally, installers compensate for this movement by leaving an expansion gap between the floor and the wall. Base moulding or quarter round is traditionally used to hide the extra space.

- **Engineered Hardwood.** Engineered flooring is actually produced with three to five layers of hardwood. Each layer is stacked in a cross-grain configuration and bonded together under heat and pressure. As a result, engineered wood flooring is less likely to be affected by changes in humidity and can be installed at all levels of a building. It comes in two different engineered constructions — with hardwood core and with high-density fiberboard core.

- **Laminate.** Laminate flooring offers a wide selection of designs that have the look and feel of beautiful hardwood, ceramic tile, and slate. It is actually a composite that is designed to endure much wear and tear. A direct-pressure manufacturing process fuses four layers into one extremely hard surface. The four layers are as follows:
  - a back layer that is reinforced with melamine for structural stability and moisture resistance
  - a fiberboard core made of ultra-dense core board that provides impact resistance and stability; it also features an edge sealing treatment that provides even further structural stability
  - a decorative layer, the source of the floor's beauty, which is actually a highly detailed photograph that gives the laminate the appearance of wood or tile, and
  - a melamine wear layer which is a tough, clear finish reinforced with aluminum oxide (one of the hardest mineral compounds available) that helps the floor to resist staining, fading, surface moisture, and wear.

The resulting floor is a technological breakthrough. There is no staining, no fading, no wear, and installation is quite easy. To maintain it, simply wipe off such problem spills as nail polish, grease, and mustard. There is one major drawback. Unlike natural wood, it cannot be sanded, which means it cannot be repaired or refinished. Just as carpet needs cushioning or an underpad, laminates need a quality underlayment between them and the subfloor.

(b) Resilient Flooring

Resilience is defined as "the physical property of a material that can return to its original shape or position after deformation that does not exceed its elastic limit." Besides being manufactured from many materials such as cork, polyurethane, rubber, asphalt, vinyl (which is by far the most common resilient flooring material), resilient flooring comes in a variety of colours, patterns, and textures and in sheets up to 3.6 m (12 ft) wide or individual tiles. The options are linoleum and commercial sheet vinyl.

- **Linoleum.** Linoleum is a durable, washable material made in sheets by pressing a mixture of heated linseed oil, rosin, powdered cork or flour, and pigments into a jute or canvas backing. It is used mainly, but not only, for floor coverings. This well proven, long-lasting material is warm and comfortable, dust-free, and 100% biodegradable. The fact that it is dust-free makes it an excellent choice for people with allergies. It can be installed with great designs to produce extremely attractive floors. These products are often chosen for heavy-traffic areas.
- **Commercial Sheet Vinyl.** Commercial sheet vinyl may have a similar appearance to linoleum, but it is made from resin compounded with plasticizers and stabilizers, and compressed under pressure and heat. Vinyl is non-porous, long lasting, resilient, and easy to maintain. It can be installed in many different patterns and colours. A testimony to its desirability and durability is the fact that it is used in airports and sports surfaces, trains, airplanes, tennis courts, hospitals, schools, hotels, and chain stores.

For an excellent website on floors, see <www.shawfloors.com.>.

(c) Carpet

The majority of commercial spaces, except for big boxes, have their floors covered with carpet (in fact, broadloom), and for good reasons. Carpet has one of the highest insulation properties of any floor covering and is more economical to maintain than most smooth floor coverings. Carpet also has great acoustical value as it absorbs sound and thus provides a positive environment, especially in workplaces that are noisy with phones, computers, or air-conditioning systems. A carpet's acoustic value varies with the nature of the pile — height, cut, or looped pile — and the method of installation.

Carpets contribute to energy conservation because of their insulating properties. They also provide a visually warm environment that is comfortable and safe because of their shock-absorbing properties and anti-skid surface, unlike hard flooring which may become very slippery when wet.

Carpeting is used in more areas and more buildings than any other type of flooring (outside of concrete, of course). It is warm, soft to the touch, comfortable, and decorative. It comes in a wide range of construction materials, styles, and colours.

There are a number of factors to consider when selecting carpet:

- **Appearance.** Appearance can be described in terms of pattern, colour scheme, shape, and size.
- **Durability.** Ask lots of questions. Can the carpet take abuse? Has it been treated with soil retardants, stain repellents, etc.? Can it resist mildew and other microbial attacks? How easy is it to clean? Are the colours fast? Is the carpet flame resistant?

- **Cost.** The purchase price is usually given in dollars per square metre (sq yd) for carpet only and cushion only. Installation may need to include the cost of removing and disposing of the old carpet, repairing cracked and worn floors, etc. Don't forget to factor in maintenance expenses (essentially the cost of cleaning and repairs).

Commercially speaking, there are two main types of carpet — wall to wall and carpet modules.

1. Wall-to-wall carpeting covers the entire floor. Its advantages include:
   - is securely anchored so it does not shift
   - maximum potential for insulation and energy conservation
   - no special treatment needed, and
   - can camouflage worn floors.

   Its disadvantages are that it must be cleaned in place and is difficult, and therefore costly, to relocate.

2. The carpet modules (or squares) are 46 x 46 cm (18 x 18 in) squares of carpet that are laid over the floor just like tiles. The advantages of carpet modules include:
   - ease of installation
   - minimum waste of material during installation
   - easily rotated to equalize traffic and soiling patterns
   - easily replaced, and
   - combinations of colour can create appealing designs.

   Disadvantages of carpet modules include:
   - initial cost can be high
   - if poorly installed, curling edges can increase the chances of tripping, and
   - joints may separate.

   Carpet tiles were not much used for many years and could be found only in commercial applications. This is changing and the residential carpet tile market is now booming. The cost is reasonable, similar to that of a top-quality broadloom and they can be rearranged easily since they have a self-adhesive or non-slip backing. A stained or soiled tile can be removed and washed easily in the sink.

(d) Types of Carpet Materials

The four main fibres used in carpet manufacturing are wool, nylon, polypropylene, and polyester.

- **Wool.** Wool is strong, comfortable, and prestigious. It naturally repels water and can be dyed easily. Wool can be cleaned easily and ages gracefully.
- **Nylon.** Nylon is a frequently used fibre that was introduced in 1938 by DuPont and started our modern era of synthetic fibres. The main brands of nylon are made by DuPont, Solutia, and Honeywell.
- **Polypropylene or Olefin Fibre.** First introduced to the carpet industry in 1950, polypropylene is naturally fade resistant. Usually found in continuous filament, it is great for outdoor as well as indoor use. The fibre is not as resilient or as expensive as nylon, but if it is properly constructed, it offers exceptional value. Most constructions for this fibre are in loop pile.
- **Polyester.** First introduced to carpeting in the 1960s, polyester is today the most commonly used synthetic fibre. Polyester is used in cut pile and textured constructions. It is not quite as resilient as nylon but will give excellent performance if properly constructed.

(e) Carpet Manufacturing

There are two ways to make carpeting today — weaving and tufting. Weaving has been used for centuries and may be done by hand or machine. The product is extremely durable and wears for as long as it is maintained. The yarns are woven through or around vertical strands of fibre called warps. The yarns are then locked into place with horizontal strands called wefts. This process goes back to the earliest manufacture of carpets.

Today, 90% of carpeting uses the tufting method, which involves gathering tufts or clumps of carpet fibre together and attaching them at the base. There are basically four processes to making tufted carpeting: processing the fibre, tufting, dyeing, and finishing.

All of the aforementioned fibres used to make carpet come in continuous filament, except for wool, which can only be made in staple.

A yarn is a continuous strand or thread made of fine fibres (filaments) that are long enough to be yarn by themselves. Short natural fibres (staple), such as wool, must be twisted together to create yarn. Synthetic and natural fibres can be blended. Tighter (more twists) produces stronger yarn while low twist produces softer yarn. The thickness of synthetic fibres is measured in denier (a thick, double-knit is about 140 denier, while a very fine one, as used in pantyhose, is 12 denier).

There are two ways to make carpeting today — weaving and tufting. Weaving has been used for centuries. Today, 90% of carpeting uses the tufting method.

A well-made yarn, whether natural or synthetic, goes through blending, carding, pin drafting, spinning, twisting, and heat setting. Twisted yarns are used in many yarn styles, like textured or cut pile.

Once the fibre is processed, it will be tufted into carpet. Much of the pattern effects, styling, and construction are done at this stage. The denser the construction is, the better the performance. This stage will determine the type of carpet style. Today, the main styles used are Frieze, Textured, Cable, Cut/Uncut, Commercial Cut Pile, Cut Pile Berber, Cut Pile Saxony, Sisal, Velvet Cut Pile, Shag, Commercial Level Loop Pile, Sophisticated Pattern, and Berber Loop Pile.

If the carpet is not using a dyed fibre, it will need to be dyed. This stage also gives the carpet colour, pattern in colour, multicolour, heather, and flecks as well as solids.

The final stage in manufacturing is where the carpeting is sheared for the best finish (higher twist products finish the best here). The carpet also receives a secondary backing, where an action back is applied to give the carpet dimensional stability and allow it to be stretched. All carpets today are also treated for stain protection.

(f) Measuring Carpet Quality

Most manufacturers have their products tested for performance. For a true comparison on each styling you must compare the twist, weight, and fibre. Twist is the single most important factor in performance, especially in any cut construction products. Use a 4.5 twist for heavier traffic and go up from there for a better performance and texture retention.

Another excellent indication of carpet quality is the density of the pile. The closer the tufts are together, the better the quality. In comparing samples of the same fibre type, note how close the individual loops or tufts are to each other. Press down on the pile with one finger and see how easy or difficult it is to penetrate to the backing; better carpet will have more closely spaced tufts and will therefore be more difficult to penetrate. Bend the carpet as it would be bending over a tread of a stair and compare the amount of backing material exposed.

For more detailed descriptions of the various types of carpets, go to <www.carpetcorneronline.com/carpet.htm>.

(g) Cleaning Carpet

There are various ways to clean carpet.

- **Hot-Water Extraction or Steam Cleaning.** Portable or truck-mounted equipment is used to spray a hot detergent solution into the carpet pile at a high pressure and extract it immediately along with the suspended soil particles. The machine may employ rotary brushes or another agitating device to work the solution into the pile and to loosen the soil.

- **Shampoo.** In this method, detergent solution is released onto the carpet through openings in a rotary brush, whose rotary action converts the solution into foam and works it into the carpet. Once dry (a long time later), vacuuming removes the residue containing loose, encapsulated soil. Chemicals may be added to the solution to reduce odours, retard soiling, brighten colours, and/or speed drying.

- **Combination Hot Water and Shampoo.** This combination uses the hot-water extraction method and shampoo and is especially effective for cleaning highly soiled carpets, with heavy oil/soil build-up. This is a two-step process: applying the shampoo using rotary brushes to loosen the soil and using hot water extraction to remove the shampoo. Some units combine both steps, which is usually better and, hence, more expensive.

- **Foams.** Foam is a variation of shampoo, generally applied onto the carpet, usually from aerosol containers, and rubbed in with a dry sponge. Once dry, the residue containing suspended soil is simply vacuumed away. Since foam uses little water, there is no danger of over-wetting and related complications. But for the same reason, this method is not as effective as the wetter methods. Some foams can leave a residue that is difficult to remove and may cause problems with subsequent wet cleaning.

- **Bonnet Cleaning.** This is another method similar to shampoo. Bonnet cleaning employs an absorbent pad (called a "bonnet") that is attached to the bottom of a rotary machine. The detergent solution is sprayed onto the carpet and the rotary pad is used to agitate and remove the soil suspended in the solution from the carpet. Once one side of the pad gets soiled, it can be reversed. And when both sides get soiled, the pad is replaced and later cleaned. This method is commonly used in the regular maintenance of commercial buildings.

- **Absorbent Dry Compound.** A dry compound detergent-solvent is sprinkled onto the carpet and worked into the pile by machines. The soil particles get encapsulated in the absorbent dry compound and are removed by vacuuming. Since this method does not use any wet process, there is no danger of over-wetting.

(h) DuPont's Resistech

Some broadlooms are subjected to heavy-duty dirt, where conventional carpet cleaning does not do a satisfactory job, and the broadloom quickly gets dirty again. DuPont Flooring Systems have patented a cleaning process, called "DuPont Resistech", that keeps carpet looking cleaner longer by reducing the resoiling. It seems to be revolutionary.

19.2.5 MASONRY TESTING

At times, one may have doubts about the integrity of masonry. It is possible to determine if there are any problems by using Non-Destructive Testing (NDT) systems that use different technologies to "see" inside masonry.

- **Acoustic Emission.** An ultrasound elastic wave is used to determine the presence of cracks, voids, or honeycombing in reinforced concrete structures.

- **Magnetic Particle Inspection.** Magnetic particle inspection uses a penetrant (liquid) that penetrates the substrate by capillary action.
- **Radiographic Testing (Radioscopy).** This is an older approach that uses x-rays to pass through the material. It has been much improved with the addition of modern computer hardware and software.
- **Ultrasonic Testing.** The test instrument, an ultrasonic flaw detector, transmits and receives ultrasonic waves. These acoustic vibration frequencies are greater than 18,000 Hertz.
- **Holography.** Holography is an imaging method that records the amplitude and phase of light reflected from an object.

Because all these methods are imperfect, usually more than one approach is utilized so you can have confidence in the results. The only other way to diagnose this kind of problem is to remove the "non" in NDT, and start hammering away. For more details, see <www.ndt.net>.

19.3 BUILDING SERVICES

Understand and instruct specialists to maintain or improve your building services, such as water and sewer systems, electricity, and heating and cooling systems.

When talking about utilities, the most common ones referred to are heat (natural gas, electric, oil or propane), water, electricity, and telephone. Many building services are related to one of these utilities.

19.3.1 WATER AND SEWER SYSTEMS

(a) Water

Typically, municipalities provide water. However, in rural areas where there is no municipal water, it is necessary to use a well. A well can be bored or drilled. A bored well has a pipe, with a pointed end, hammered down to water level. The bottom section of the pipe is perforated with small holes to let the water seep in and the pump is at ground level. A drilled well, which is the most common, is created by a rotary drill that sinks a hole to the water level. The hole is lined with a pipe and an electrical submersible pump is lowered into the pipe.

Assuming you want to buy a property with an existing well, the offer to buy should contain a condition regarding water flow, quantity, and satisfactory results upon submission of a water sample to a laboratory. It is recommended that the water be tested three times, seven-plus days apart, which means it could take 14-21 days. Water should also routinely be tested, at least once a year, because a well can become contaminated. This is a serious matter since disease, even death, can result from contaminated water. Contractors that dig water wells require a license from the provincial Ministry of the Environment. Water wells in Ontario, for instance, are regulated under the *Ontario Water Resources Act* (R.S.O. 1990, c. O.40).

(b) Sewers

There are four ways of handling rain water and sewage: storm sewers, sanitary sewers, septic systems, and holding tanks.

1. **Storm Sewers.** A storm sewer is used to collect rainwater and direct it, generally untreated, to a stream or lake. This water is not clean because it collects contaminants, such as sand, oil, rubber particles, chemicals applied to lawns, etc. Depending on the size of the property, a water retention pond, which could be located on the property itself or on public lands, may be required by the municipality.

2. **Sanitary Sewers.** Sewage, that other kind of water, is regulated under sections 53 and 53.1 of the *Ontario Water Resources Act*, except for large industrial installations, such as found in mining operations. The sanitary sewers that carry the sewage outside the building are taken care of by the municipality or the region. Generally, the water collected flows through gravity (but, occasionally, it is pumped up) to a municipal sewage treatment plant, where it is treated before being released in a watercourse.

3. **Septic Systems.** This is not a sanitary sewer system per se, but it fulfills the same function. When municipal sanitary sewers are not available, the most frequently used sewage disposal method is a septic system, which includes a septic tank and a leaching bed. The septic tank is generally a prefabricated (concrete or plastic) tank. Some authorities contend that virtually no treatment takes place in this tank and that it is only a holding or storage tank. In fact, anaerobic bacteria are furiously at work in this tank, breaking down matter and preparing it to move in a liquefied form to the leaching bed. The septic tank should be pumped every 3-5 years, at which time a specialist should inspect the entire system. Pumping-out is necessary due to the build-up of sludge, grits, or other solids in the tank.

   A leaching bed receives the clear liquid from the septic tank, either pumped or through gravity, and lets it leach out into the ground. Typically, leaching beds are made up of plastic pipes with holes in them, through which the water (effluent) can escape. The size of the bed, that is the length of pipes, will vary based on the number of users and soil conditions. The law specifies that a leaching bed must be a safe distance from anything that it could contaminate, such as a river, pond, and well. The user of a septic system must take greater care of how it's used than with a municipal sewer system.

   Do not drive over the septic tank, leaching bed, or plant trees on it. However, planting grass or small bushes over the leaching bed will assist in the evaporation of the effluent. Do not put harmful products in the system, such as non-degradable items, cigarettes, grease, diapers, or bleach, chemicals, and solvents.

4. **Holding Tanks.** As the name indicates, waste water goes into a holding tank and stays there until the tank is full, at which time it must be pumped out. The advantages of a holding tank over a septic system are the following: it never malfunctions; it doesn't prohibit any area of ground from being used (except the area occupied by the tank itself), as does the leaching bed of a septic system; and there is no leaching bed to install and maintain. The major disadvantage is that it is expensive to pump out the holding tank so that users must adjust their practices to try to limit its use. For instance, a typical four-bedroom home in southern Ontario will pay $5,000 annually to have waste water pumped from its holding tank.

19.3.2 TOILETS

Every smart building owner should pay particular attention to water consumption. Many municipalities have adopted a system whereby they charge a sewage fee based on water consumption. Take a hard look at your showerheads and toilets; these are cost-effective areas to reduce water consumption.

The average household uses between 3,182 *l* and 5,455 *l* (700 and 1,200 gal) of water per day; 60% of that is for toilet and shower, 20% for the laundry, and 20% for other uses. The kind of toilets most often found in older buildings use 13.2 *l* (2.9 gal) of water for every flush (LFP). By law, when one installs a new toilet, be it in a new building or in an existing one, it must be a low-flush toilet, using a maximum of 6*l* (1.3 gal) of water per flush. Over 50 different low-flush toilets are available.

If you prefer not to replace a toilet, you may still lessen its water consumption by replacing the original flapper of a 13.2-*l* toilet (60.5 gal) (if it is not a proprietary one) with a flapper that lets you adjust the water used with every flush. The three better known flappers are the Niagara (79%), the Fluidmaster (55%), and the Frugal (17%). The numbers in parenthesis indicate the percentage of toilets on the market that each type of flapper can fit. However, this is a compromise as sometimes solid matter will not be completely flushed out with these flappers. Since most flushings are used to evacuate urine, this compromise is an intelligent one. You can choose between almost round and elongated bowls, the latter of which is much preferable.

A study conducted by an independent company found that the absolute leader in terms of flushing efficiency was the Drake model toilet manufactured by Toto of Japan. Toto makes a range of toilets, all of them excellent. Costs range from $200 to $1,000.

The City of Toronto conducted a study of a 30-year-old multi-family building containing 413 units. The owner replaced the original 13.2-*l* toilets with ultra-low-flush, 6-*l* Toto CST-703 toilets (which are round rim — the elongated rim is a little more expensive and requires a little more space). In addition, each unit received a water-saving spa showerhead, tamper-proof lavatory aerator and a tamper-proof kitchen aerator. The project cost was $84,600 and after a rebate of $25,260, the total cost to the owner was $59,340. The annual savings were $42,126. That is a return of 71% or a payback period of just 16.8 months! The water consumption was reduced by 36%, to 444 *l* (98 gal) per suite per day. Not all renovations will achieve these savings, but it gives you an idea of what is possible.

Various types of toilets are available and more than water saving needs to be considered.

Various types of toilets are available and more than water saving needs to be considered, as can be seen from the following description of the three main types:

1. **Gravity.** Still the most common type in use, a gravity toilet is chosen if one wants quiet operation or if the water pressure is low as it can function with as little as 10 psi of pressure. Its costs start at $100, plus installation.

2. **Vacuum-Assisted.** Also very quiet, a vacuum-assisted toilet has a vacuum chamber inside the tank that siphons air out of the trap below the bowl, allowing it to fill with water quickly to clear the waste. The cost starts from $250, plus installation.

3. **Pressure-Assisted.** In the pressure-assisted system, the water filling a sealed tank compresses the air at the top of the tank, allowing a powerful flush that efficiently thrusts out the waste through the bowl. This type of toilet is best where there is frequent flushing and where plugging might be a problem, however, they are louder than the other types. They require a minimum water pressure of 25 psi and costs start at $300, plus installation.

An oddity among toilets is one made by Eljer. Their Titan 091-0777 model ($350+/-) is a gravity toilet that performs almost as well as a pressure-assisted one, but does it quietly. The champion of water economy is the Flushmate made by the Sloan Valve Company. The Flushmate IV model uses only 4 *l* (0.9 gal) per flush without sacrificing performance and saves up to 45% more water than conventional 6 *l* (1.6 gal) per flush. There are two main reasons for this amazing performance.

Flushmate-equipped bowls are hydraulically designed to push contents out of the trapway, instead of gravity siphoning them (as with traditional toilets), which requires a more complicated trapway that can impede performance. Flushmate-equipped water closets have trapways that are specifically designed to allow waste to be extracted earlier in the flush, unlike gravity trapways that require a choke area or siphon bend that, ultimately, restricts flow.

And the Flushmate system traps air and, as its reservoir fills with water, it uses the water supply line pressure to compress the trapped air inside. It is the compressed air that forces the water into the bowl, under a much greater pressure than a conventional toilet.

An additional advantage, particularly in situations where toilets are used and flushed frequently (restaurants, for example) is that the tank does not sweat due to condensation, as the water is contained not in the tank, but inside the unit, which is, itself, installed inside the tank. Many Tim Hortons restaurants are equipped with Flushmate toilets.

Flushmate can be installed in the same standard dimensional area as a conventional water closet, and all leading toilet manufacturers offer specially designed toilets with Flushmate inside, as it does not work with conventional toilets.

Flushmate is best characterized by its efficiency, speed of flushing, and whooshing noise. If you install some of these toilets, you will learn to love the noise that is saving you big money. On the other hand, there are situations where these toilets are not recommended, precisely because of the noise they generate. It could be a source of annoyance, for example, in multi-storey apartment buildings.

Another interesting toilet is one made by Caroma, an Australian manufacturer of high-performance, ecologically-friendly toilets. Their award-winning Dual-Flush toilets have two speeds, controlled with two buttons. The under-3-litre-per-flush speed is for liquid waste, while the flush for solid waste uses around 6 l of water. Another interesting hygienic feature is that they offer toilet seats that snap-on and snap-off, making cleaning very easy (see <www.energysmartcanada.com>). These two-level-of-flush toilets are common in Europe.

If performance is your number one criterion, see the Web site of the California Urban Water Conservation Council, which provides a Flush Performance Index at <www.cuwcc.org/Uploads/product/Performance-Index.pdf>.

Another elegant and efficient, but relatively expensive way to save huge quantities of water in commercial buildings is to use electronic sensor systems to control wash basins, urinals, and toilets. When the user comes in contact with an invisible infrared beam, it activates the unit and the water will run only for a determined amount of time. Again, these systems, besides permitting huge savings, rejuvenate a building.

Composting toilets provide another alternative where there are no municipal sanitary sewers. There are several manufacturers, but it seems that Sun-Mar Corp. of Burlington, Ontario, is one of the better known. Sun-Mar composting toilets use the natural processes of decomposition and evaporation to recycle human waste. Since waste entering toilets is over 90% water content, the water is evaporated and carried through the vent system, then the small amount of remaining material is converted to useful fertilizing soil by natural decomposition. Composting toilets don't generate any odour because air is being continuously drawn into the unit and up the vent stack, creating a partial vacuum in the unit. In addition, the composting drum fosters good aerobic compost, which produces no odours.

Typically, one empties some of the compost out of the drum once every few months for residential use. In cases of continuous use, one may need to extract compost more often. The compost always sits in the drawer to cure before being removed and is never disposed of as fresh waste. In other words you are never handling fresh waste when the unit is operating properly. There are no chemicals used. The only thing that is added is peat moss mixed with wood shavings.

The most common models require electricity to power a fan (30 watts continuous) and a heating element for drying that is thermostatically controlled. The average draw is about 150 watts or the equivalent of a big light bulb. Larger models may have larger power requirements. Fortunately, Sun-Mar toilets are also available in a non-electric version.

19.3.3 BIDETS

Sophisticated people enjoy a bidet. If you rent luxury residences, consider installing one. It will separate you from the competition.

Do not fret if there is not enough space. It is now possible to have a bidet on top of a toilet. It takes the place of the toilet seat and requires a water connection and an electrical plug. Once this is done, the magic comes in: the seat heats up, a spray of warm water can be commanded and a mini-blow dryer finishes the work. This style starts at $500.

19.3.4 URINALS

Urinals are frequently encountered in commercial buildings. A typical urinal, flushed after every use, is a water guzzler. Older models use 8 *l* (1.76 gal) per flush, which is more than an energy-saving toilet. To present it differently, an office building with 120 men using urinals three times per day, 220 days per year, will use 633,600 *l* (139,000 gal) of water per year or 2,880 *l* (634 gal) per day!

A new no-flush, waterless urinal is now available. The key to the system is a patented cartridge that lets the urine through, collecting sediments, and then seals it so there are no odours. It uses no water, hence, no water connection is required. It is touch-free operation. The cartridge has to be replaced two to four times per year. The liquid (3 oz) that effects the seal must be replaced every 1,500 uses. The cartridge itself must be replaced after 6,000 to 7,000 uses, at a cost of $45. The cost of the urinal itself is $400-500. See <www.waterless.com> and <www.sloanvalve.com/waterfreeindex.htm> for two companies that offer this type of product.

19.3.5 MACERATING TOILETS

As a building owner, sooner or later, you will want to add a washroom to a building. Unless you are fortunate to have a drainpipe to which you can connect easily, you will be shocked at the cost. For example, if you had a 4,650 m² (50,000 sq ft) industrial building that had been leased to one user, but you wanted to divide it into four units you would need to add several bathrooms. Inevitably, the existing bathrooms are at the front, with the office. To install new washrooms may require cutting a trench a hundred metres or longer through the concrete slab and it may not even be feasible if the required slope is not available.

There is now a system that allows you to send sewage long distances overhead called a "macerating" toilet. You could call it a toilet that flushes up. This is also a great solution if you want to install a washroom in a basement. A macerating toilet has a built-in pump and shredder that liquefies and transports all waste and wastewater to a regular plumbing drain. It can lift the waste water up to 4.8 m (16 ft) and pump it more than 45 m (150 ft) horizontally. Bathroom sinks, bathtubs and showers, and urinals can be connected to the same toilet pump, using a 1.9 cm (3/4 in) pipe to connect the unit to the sewage pipe.

The macerating system, which comes with or without a toilet, has three major components — a container that houses the pump, a pressure chamber that turns the motor on and off, and a motor that drives the shredding blades and pump assembly. The macerator motor has no gears or brushes to wear out. It is lubricated for life and needs no regular maintenance. Note that the same type of grinding (macerating) pumps, called "sewage pumps", are available, separate from a toilet.

These are accepted under the National Building Code (in the US and Canada). The CSA has standard B45.9 for macerating systems and related components. Check that they are acceptable to your municipal building department before installing one. The manufacturer of these toilets and pumps that is the best known (and perhaps the most expensive) is Saniflo, a company located in Guelph, Ontario.

19.3.6 SPRINKLER SYSTEMS

Most industrial and commercial buildings are protected against fire by a sprinkler system, which is comprised of a water supply and distribution piping under pressure. Generally the water is supplied by a municipal source, but it can be a private one, in which case it is commonly necessary to have a large pond nearby for water storage. Sprinkler heads are attached to the piping system. These are valves that are kept sealed by a fuse. These fuses — in fact a thermosensitive unit — were, in the past, made of a soft metal alloy that melted at a relatively low temperature. Modern heads utilize a 3 mm fragile glass ampoule. If there is a fire, when the hot air reaches the fuse, it melts (at between 51-141°C (124-286°F)), opening the valve and causing an alarm to sound.

Each sprinkler system is equipped with a water-flow sensing device that is generally connected to the building's fire alarm system. These devices incorporate a variable delay setting to prevent false alarms caused by changes in the water system supply pressure. Otherwise, every time the pressure surged, the detector would see a little water moving and activate the alarm.

Not all buildings require sprinklers. Besides fire control and extinguishing capabilities, the main reason to install sprinklers is to lower the building and contents insurance premium, particularly in the case of flammable products, such as paper or wood. Approximately 90% of fires are extinguished or controlled by four or fewer sprinkler heads and, within this number, 65% by a single sprinkler head. Of course, they do cause some water damage, but it is better than losing a whole building and its contents.

Sprinkler heads open one at a time, when their rated temperature is reached, not a whole building or section of the sprinkler system. Accidental discharges are very rare. Statistics show that an accidental discharge due to a manufacturing defect is 1 in 16,000,000 sprinklers per year of service.

The standards in sprinklers are established by the US National Fire Protection Association (NFPA). The NFPA recommends that a sprinkler system be checked by a professional every 3 months. Most landlords do it once or twice or year. This is, in fact, controlled by the insurance companies, as they have specific requirements (usually, once a year inspections) and with premium increases being charged if this is not done.

Some professionals recommend frequent inspections on the following basis:
- sprinkler control valves: visually inspect monthly, closed and reopened annually, and interior inspected every five years
- water flow alarms: inspected quarterly by letting water flow from the Inspector's Test connection
- valve tamper devices: tested every 6 months
- 5 cm (2 in) drain tested annually
- electrical equipment: the major cause of industrial fires and should be given an infrared test every three years; most landlords are not aware of this recommendation
- fire pumps: tested weekly, and
- full flow tested annually.

To the outsider, a sprinkler system is a simple thing. In fact, sprinkler systems are complex. Depending on the present or the likely future use of the building, you have to check that the sprinkler system is adequate. Sprinkler systems vary in two ways — the density (spacing) of the heads and the type of sprinkler systems (not heads). Most sprinklers are of the wet type (filled with water), but they may be dry if a building is not heated or, on the contrary, if it is cooled such as in the case of a freezer. In rare instances, they may even be filled with a non-freezing fluid, such as anti-freeze (Glycol). Standard sprinkler systems, meaning those before 1980, would cover ordinary and extra hazard occupancy.

- **Ordinary Hazard Occupancy.** For all types of construction the protection area per sprinkler head shall not exceed 12 m² (130 sq ft), except in buildings used for high-piled storage when the protection area per sprinkler shall not exceed 9.3 m² (100 sq ft).
- **Extra Hazard Occupancy.** The protection area per sprinkler shall not exceed 8.4 m² (90 sq ft) for any type of building construction, except that protection area per sprinkler head shall not exceed 9.3 m² (100 sq ft) where the system is hydraulically designed.

A reasonably priced sprinkler system, installed at a cost of around $21.50 per m² ($2 per sq ft) for a 4,650 m² (50,000 sq ft) industrial building, is worth the peace of mind it provides and frequently lowers insurance costs. The industry organization is the American Fire Sprinkler Association (AFSA) in the US. The Canadian Automatic Sprinkler Association (CASA) can be contacted for information.

A reasonably priced sprinkler system is worth the peace of mind it provides and frequently lowers insurance costs.

(a) Early Suppression, Fast Response Sprinklers (ESFR)

Since the late 1980s, the Early Suppression, Fast Response Sprinklers (ESFR) sprinkler heads have been the preferred choice. In warehouses, EFSR can be used for many, but not all kinds, of products. There are now six different ESFR systems.

Because of the large volume of water they deliver, ESFRs are vulnerable to obstruction such as joists, girders, pipes, lighting fixtures, and electrical conduits. They differ from standard sprinklers heads in several ways. First, ESFR heads react much faster to a fire (in half the time) and drop a larger volume of water using a larger droplet size. (Note that residential sprinklers do not require large droplets). Instead of just controlling the fire, as was usually the case with standard sprinklers, the ESFR system extinguishes it. In the past, standard sprinklers used two types of heads: one with a 1.27 cm (1/2 in) opening and one with a 1.35 cm (17/32 in) opening. The first discharges 95-114 *l* (25-30 gal) per minute, while the second discharges 212 *l* (56 gal) per minute, at 50 psi. In comparison, the ESFR has a 2.54 cm (1 in) orifice and discharges 380 *l* (100 gal).

There is a wide range of ESFR sprinkler heads. The ultimate, the ESFR-K-25 head can protect high-piled storage risk in a building that is up to 13.7 m (45 ft) high, with goods piled up to 12.2 m (40 ft) high, without requiring sprinkler leads in racking, as was necessary with standard sprinklers. The flow of a K-25 sprinkler is 675 *l* (178 gal) per minute. In comparison, according to the old standards, if pallet racking was installed in a building and reached a certain height, besides the sprinkler at the ceiling, a second one was required in the racking itself.

There are several different shapes and diameters of sprinkler heads. In fact, the three parts that can vary are the link or fuse, the deflector (there are over eight different kinds), and the diameter of the orifice. See Figure 19.2 for detailed information.

Figure 19.2
ESFR Commodities Classifications

Flammability	Available Sprinkler Temperatures	Bulb Colour	N.F.P.A. Maximum Ceiling Temperature
Ordinary	135°F/155°F 57°C/68°C	Orange/Red	100°F 38°C
Intermediate	175°F/200°F 79°C/93°C	Yellow/Green	150°F 66°C
High	286°F 141°C		225°F 107°C

A complete list can be found in the *Industrial Fire Protection Handbook* by Craig Schroll, which can be purchased at <www.materialsnetbase.com>, or in the booklet *Warehouse Fire Protection* (1999) available for free at <www.mhiastore.org/moreinfo.>.

For an investor planning to install or modify a sprinkler system, the difficulty is in indicating to the sprinkler designer the use of the building, since different tenants will occupy the buildings over the years. Different tenants will manufacture or use different products (called "commodities" by sprinkler specialists), such as metal cabinets, cardboard, or plastics, that will require specific sprinkler system designs. A wise choice is a system that is reasonably priced, but will cover as many uses as possible, so that any future tenant will be happy, and costly upgrades will be avoided at a later date. A building equipped with ESFR sprinkler offer maximum flexibility.

In new warehouses equipped with pallet racking, an ESFR system generally costs 30-50% less than a conventional in-rack system because no in-rack sprinklers are required. Of course, this is even more significant if there is the possibility that racks could be rearranged later.

Retrofitting an existing building with an ESFR system is usually not feasible from an economic viewpoint, since existing conventional pipes would be too small and, hence, need replacing.

It is important to understand that the classes of sprinklers are based on the use made of the premises. If, for example, the previous tenant required only ordinary hazard sprinklers and now you are renting the vacated building to a wood furniture manufacturer who sprays flammable varnishes, your sprinkler system would need upgrading.

Not all buildings are connected to a municipal water supply that provides sufficient pressure (commonly 75 psi). ESFR sprinklers work at pressures of 50-75 psi, but it is still possible to have ESFR if the pressure is low by installing a diesel-driven booster pump set. Sometimes a storage tank, holding enough water to last one hour, is also required.

Risk Logic Inc (<www.Risklogic.com>) of New Jersey offers a wealth of sprinkler information on their Web site.

(b) Factory Mutual

One cannot talk about sprinklers and risk insurance without mentioning Factory Mutual (FM). FM is a company that traces its roots back to 1835, when a group of mill owners created a mutual insurance company in which the policyholders would be the shareholders and would insure each other. Over the years, they decided to go further and work together to prevent and minimize losses by controlling the causes of fire. This concept was copied by other manufacturers with such success that there was a total of 42 individual companies that came to be known as the Factory Mutual. Over decades, the companies pooled their resources and consolidated into just three corporations: Allendale Insurance, Ark Wright, and Protection Mutual. Today, FM is recognized as the world leader in property loss prevention for large industrial and institutional properties, with over 2,400 employees in 33 locations. FM does not sell insurance or fire prevention equipment. Its business is to provide services, research, and resources that will help its clients prevent and control property losses. Its Web site

(<www.factorymutual.com>) offers a unique, large, and invaluable collection of loss prevention information ranging from roof specifications to preparing for earthquakes.

FM's Engineering Plan Services (EPS) Department may be the most appreciated service offered by the company, providing documentation in the form of a site plan/layout on insured locations. This documentation provides a permanent record for risk assessment by insurance company personnel, appraisers, loss adjusters, the insured, and FM itself.

Factory Mutual Research (FMR) is a non-profit research and testing organization, managed by FM Global, which is the world's largest commercial and industrial property insurance company. Virtually every large project is requested to conform to their standards. These apply, for example, to roofs, insulation, wall panels, fasteners, flame detectors, combustible gas sensors, dry pipe valves, air pressure maintenance devices, fire protection systems, diesel engine fire pump drivers and, of course, sprinklers.

The manufacturers of building components must seek FMR's approval, if they want their products to be specified for certain jobs. Their manufacturing facilities are audited periodically for product quality and consistency by unannounced FMR representatives.

An interesting booklet, *Warehouse Fire Protection*, authored by Mark Shofield of FM Engineering was published by the Material Handling Institute of Charlotte, NC, in their series "Perspective on Material Handling Practice". Building owners will find their understanding of sprinkler systems enhanced after reading this booklet. It can be downloaded for free at <www.mhia.org>.

(c) Fire Extinguishers

We would be remiss if we did not talk about fire extinguishers. It is important to understand that there are different kinds of compounds used on different sources of fires. Figure 19.3 provides a useful guide.

Figure 19.3
Portable Fire Extinguisher Guide

Class of Fire Risk	Symbol	Water	Foam	CO2	Powder
Class A: Paper, wood, cloth, rubber, and types some of plastic		I	G	NS	I
Class B: Flammable Liquids, oil, gasoline, gases, greases, paint		A	G	I	G
Class C: Flammable Gases All of the materials in Class A & B		NS	NS	I	G
Class D: Combustible Metals: Sodium, magnesium, potassium		NS	A	I	I
Electrical Hazards		NS	A	G	G
Remarks		Most effective for Class A	Seals flames; prevents re-igniting	Non-damaging; very effective;	Versatile; clean
Instructions		Direct the nozzle toward the base of the fire.	Let the foam fully cover the fire.	Direct the nozzle toward the base of the fire.	Direct the nozzle toward the base of the fire

Ideal (I)
Good (G)
Acceptable (A)
Not Suitable (NS)

19.3.7 WATER SYSTEMS PROBLEMS

Water system problems range from annoying problems like noise in the pipes to more serious concerns like rusting or freezing pipes.

(a) Noise in the Plumbing

There are situations where plumbing noise is a cause of irritation and worries. There can be four reasons for it:

1. **Hammering.** Hammering occurs when one hears a bang, similar to that caused by a hammer hitting a pipe. It tends to happen when the flow of water is stopped suddenly, as when a tap is closed. The typical remedy consists of installing a special device called a "snubber", which is an air chamber made of a short piece of pipe, 30.5-45.7 cm (12-18 in) long and 1.27-1.9 cm (1/2-3/4 in) in diameter with a cap at one end. It is mounted vertically above a "T" on the water line, reasonably close to the equipment that is causing the hammering. Another option is a cylinder similar to a propane tank. Home Depot sells different types. The air in the snubber acts as a cushion. Eventually the air will be absorbed by water. If the device stops working, the water must be emptied from the line to allow the air in the pipe to be replenished.

2. **Cavitation.** Cavitation is caused by small bubbles contained in the water that eventually explode under the pressure surrounding them, with a noise that is more akin to a whistling sound than a bang. To understand the process, watch and listen to a pot of water boiling on a stove. The main cause of cavitation is plumbing (work and components) of poor quality.

3. **Dropping.** When water drops (flows) into a basin, sink, or bathtub, the impact of the water on the fixture causes a noise. This noise can be reasonably controlled depending on how the fixture is mounted. It is difficult and time consuming to correct after the fact, but feasible. It is a question of insulating the guilty fixture. The cheapest, and often the best, approach is to control the flow of the water.

4. **Drainage.** This noise is caused by air and water rushing through the pipes. It is not economically feasible to correct this problem after the plumbing has been installed, but can be prevented by proper pipe sizing and installation. For example, metal pipes create less noise than plastic. To improve insulation, the pipes should be insulated with neoprene foam sleeves and they should be allowed to move by using fasteners that do not attach them firmly to the structure.

(b) Rusting Pipes

Up to about 1960 plumbers used galvanized water pipes, under the assumption that the galvanizing process would prevent rusting. Indeed it does, but it was also found that galvanizing lasts for only 40-50 years. Surprisingly, in a dry atmosphere, the inside of the pipe usually rusts faster than the outside.

Three problems stem from this. The first is that the rust inside can become quite thick and reduce the flow of water. The second is the risk of the rust eating and perforating the pipe. The third one is that, if the water stands in the pipes for a while, one sees the distinctive rusty colour, particularly in toilet bowls.

The water is still potable and you can tell your tenants they will not have to eat spinach since the pipes will supply them with more than enough iron, but few will like it. If you buy older buildings, you will run into this problem. The solution is to replace these pipes with copper piping, which unfortunately is expensive, or, where the building code permits, with plastic pipes.

(c) Frozen Pipes

The risk of frozen exterior water pipes is a worry in many parts of Canada. You can prevent this problem by burying pipes 1.2-1.8 m (4-6 ft) below the ground surface, which may not be economically feasible if rock is close to the surface. An alternative is to wrap electric heating cables around the pipes, which works but consumes a lot of electricity.

A new system offers a pipe with polyethylene insulation around it that contains a heating cable in the insulation. Because the insulation is very thick, the electricity consumption is quite low. A typical residential water supply system will be made up of a 1.9 cm (3/4 in) water pipe, inside a 3.8 cm (1 ½ in) polyethylene pipe, which is surrounded by the insulation that is contained within a 10 cm (4 in) diameter drain line.

19.3.8 ELECTRICITY

Because we depend so much on it, electrical power is very important to tenants. It is essential that you know how to read a meter and how to give information of an electrical nature to prospective tenants. Here is some of the terminology you should be familiar with, reprinted with permission from Richard Weldon, P.Eng., Carson Dunlop Weldon & Associates Ltd.

1. Amps vs. Volts
Think of electricity as water flowing through a pipe. The amperage is analogous to the amount of water flowing through the pipe. Amperage is also called current. Larger diameter wires can handle more current, just as larger pipes can handle more flow.

Voltage is analogous to pressure, the force, which moves the water through the pipe. A small pump (low voltage) would produce less pressure than a big pump (high voltage). In most commercial buildings the voltage will either be 208 volt (low voltage) or 600 volt (high voltage). The critical question is how much voltage and amperage is the system rated at or, in other words, how much equipment can be used in the building.

2. 208 Volt vs. 600 Volt
Most modern buildings are equipped with 600-volt services. Equipment, such as air conditioning units (over five tons), larger exhaust fans, electric heaters, and some lighting will utilize 600 volts. However, standard outlets and most lighting operate at 208 volts.

Buildings equipped with 600-volt services will always have a transformer to reduce the 600 volts to 208 volts for the main building panels. These transformers are generally located near the main electrical service entrance.

When comparing the amount of power available, a 200 amp, 600-volt service has nearly three times the power of a 200 amp, 208 volt service.

3. Three Phase vs. Single Phase
This is of less importance. All 208 volt and 600 volt services have three phases. This means there are three power wires coming into the building. Single-phase services may be found in older, smaller buildings and are found exclusively in houses. In some older buildings you can find a single phase and a three-phase service. This is usually identifiable, on the outside, by two separate services leading to the building.

Determining the voltage

When you are standing in the electrical room, the two pieces of information you are looking for are amperage and voltage. The presence of a transformer in the electrical room is usually a dead giveaway that it is 600 volts. On a very rare occasion, the transformer could be used to step up a 208-volt service to 600 volts, for a specific piece of equipment.

The ratings on the switches and splitter panels are not to be relied on; they only tell you the maximum amount of current or voltage the equipment can handle. Do not rely on the rating of the hydro meter(s), for the same reason.

The best way to verify the amperage is to open the door of the main power switch and read the rating on the main fuses. This is sometimes impossible to do without turning the power off, but it is always dangerous, unless you know what you are doing. Even with the power off, half the box is live. Your life can end, right there in an electrical room.

Reading the gauge (size) of the main power wires (in the meter cabinet or main splitter panel) can also help to determine the amperage of the service. The gauge number is typically printed on the wire sheathing. Common wire gauge sizes, for copper conductors and the allowable amperages are as follows:

Wire Gauge	Allowable Amperage
3	100 amps
000	200 amps
350MCM	300 amps
500MCM	400 amps

The amount of power available can also be determined from the KVA rating of the main building transformer; however, this information is often unknown.

(a) Main Electrical Service

Generally the main electrical service in a building consists of one main disconnect switch, the meter box containing the electrical meter, and the distribution panels feeding all the branch circuits in the building. As a rule, electrical companies do not want multiple services to a building.

By way of background, it is good that you know the types and measurements of currents you will come across. We deal with alternating current (AC) that flows between positive (+ or active) and negative (- or neutral) frequencies that are measured in hertz (H). In North America we use 60 hertz service; in England they use 50 hertz service. If you feed an electrical apparatus, especially one with a motor, into the wrong hertz service, the apparatus will burn out and be ruined beyond repair.

You may also run across direct current (DC), but it is not common. In DC, the current flows in one direction only and is of low voltage (e.g., 12-36 volts) and it is always positive. Electrical companies never distribute DC current.

When one wants to locate the main disconnect and meter, the easiest way is to follow the incoming lines from the street hydro lines. This is true, of course, only in buildings where the service comes in overhead, which is not always the case in modern industrial parks where the service may come in underground. Usually, the main service is on an outside wall and close to the street.

(b) Electrical Service Size

Once the main service has been located, an inspection of the main disconnect switch will disclose the type of service installed. There are four common types of electrical services.

- 600 volt, 3 phases, 3 wires
- 600 volt, 3 phases, 4 wires
- 120/208 volt, 3 phases, 4 wires
- 120/240 volt, single phase, 2 wires

Unfortunately, it is usually a little more complicated than this. You may find boxes, meters, etc., with voltages different from these. There are three main groups of voltage, with more than one value indicated. For practical purposes, the numbers in each of these three groups can be considered as having the same value, but the real figures are 120 volts, 240 volts, 600 volts.

- 110-115-120
- 220-230-240
- 208-550-575-600

It is one thing to know the size of the service coming into a building; it is another to know how much power the tenant will need. When new tenants move into a building, they almost always exaggerate their needs, not because they want to, but because they are not fully aware of their requirements and how that translates into usage needs. The easiest way to determine accurate need is to call the electricity supplier and ask what the tenant's peak demand has been in the past.

Quite often, you will hear the terms "single phase" or "three phase". A residential electrical system runs on single-phase power, but most commercial electrical systems have three-phase power.

(c) Commercial

A 120/240-volt service is made up of two lines with a potential difference of 240 volts between lines plus a neutral wire (ground). It has three wires. The potential difference between any of the two lines and the neutral one is 120 volts. It can also be called "Phase to Neutral".

Power is supplied at 240 volts (range of 220-240 volts). The voltage fluctuates and at any point in time could be any value from +120 to -120. The voltage could be 10 volts, 50 volts, or zero volts. The voltage fluctuates at a rate of 60 cycles per second (hertz). The frequency is fast enough that we don't notice that the voltage is fluctuating. Household appliances work well in this mode although the voltage may be zero at points in time. It is not possible to get 208 volts from a single-phase system.

A 600-volt service usually has four wires: three "hot" wires and a neutral one, except in older areas where it may have only three wires.

Note further, that 347 volts is now quite often found in industrial plants where it is used for lighting. This is 600 volts, Phase to Neutral (ground). It is not possible to obtain 240 volts from a three-phase system. You may come across 480 volts, but is not common in Canada; it is an American voltage. However, it can be found in buildings that have large, American-made, air-conditioning chillers.

Most commercial buildings have machinery that requires lots of power and are sensitive to the peaks and valleys. Full power is only obtained at the top and bottom of the cycle. Three-phase power is actually three separate power transmissions. Each of the three transmissions is similar to a single-phase transmission (it fluctuates at 60 hertz, etc.), with each of the transmissions set up to be out of phase with each other. When one is at a very low voltage, one of the others will be at a much higher voltage. In other words, when one of the phases is not supplying much power, there will be another phase coming into use to equalize, so that the machinery will not notice the fluctuations.

Finally when one says "single phase" this always means two fuses or breakers in the main disconnect, and when one says "three phases" this means three fuses.

You will find that, generally, multi-family buildings have service of 208 or 240 volts, office buildings have 208, 480, or 600 volts, retail spaces have 208, 480, or 600 volts, and industrial buildings have 480 or 600 volts. Figure 19.4 shows how the power is taken for the aforementioned phases and wires.

Figure 19.4
Electrical Phases Explained

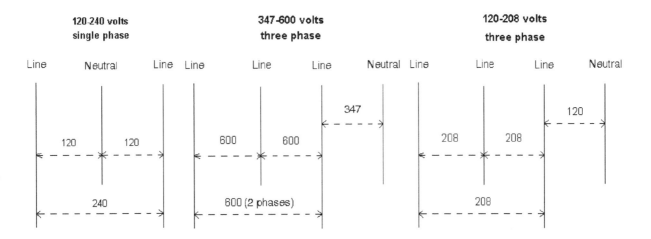

(d) Electrical Transformers

Where the main feeder lines are 600 volts, one generally finds a step-down transformer nearby to change the 600 volts to 120/208 volts (most commonly). This is necessary to allow for the installation of the branch circuits such as receptacles (outlets) and lighting. When 600 volt service is not available in the building but is required, it can be obtained by means of a step-up transformer, as long as the building is equipped with a 120/208 volt, three-phase service and has an adequate amperage rating. As mentioned earlier, this is rarely encountered.

Occasionally, an incoming 208-volt service will be stepped-up for a specific piece of equipment. Step-up and step-down transformers are the same piece of equipment except a step-down transformer will have a small, high-voltage cable on the input side (closest to the source) and a large, lower voltage cable coming out. A step-up transformer will have large, low-voltage cables closest to the source and small, high-voltage cables exiting the transformer.

(e) Electrical Sub-Station

Where the power requirement exceeds certain amperage, it is necessary to install a large exterior transformer, usually called a "sub-station". Generally, these are surrounded by fencing and are customer-owned, although some (mainly the older sub-stations) are owned by the electricity company. To find out who owns the transformer, call the utility company.

Transformers can be of the indoor or outdoor type. Indoor transformers are typically step-down and are used in buildings with 600-volt incoming services. The more common transformers are usually dry-type, which means they rely on natural air circulation for cooling. They can be identified by the many ventilation openings in the casings.

Wet-type transformers rely on a liquid coolant. These are typically larger units found outside buildings or very old units found inside. Some of the large exterior units have metal sections (similar to a heat exchanger from a furnace) and may have cooling fans to create airflow across the heat exchanger. Interior transformers, located in a locked room that cannot be opened by the owner, are typically owned by the electrical utility.

Transformers are sized by a kVA rating. This stands for kiloVolt Amperes and indicates the maximum power the transformer can handle for a prolonged period. Most transformers can handle peak demands greater than their ratings, but only for short periods of time. Common dry-type transformer sizes are 9, 15, 30, 45, 60, 75, and 112.5 kVA.

Here are some numbers to help clarify these measurements
Voltage x Amps = Watts
Watts/1,000 = kVA (kilo-volt-ampere)

Example:
220 volts x 60 amps =	13,200 watts
13,200 watts/1,000 =	13.2 kVA
800 kVA x 1,000 =	800,000 watts
800,000 watts/600 volts =	1,333 amps

(f) Determining the Line Voltage

One way to determine the line voltage is to look for a transformer. If there is one, the source voltage is generally 600 volts. The transformer is there to step the voltage down for use in the office areas, etc. If the line coming in goes straight to the panel splitters and breaker panels, then it's 208 volts, as you would not have 600 volts going to outlets, etc.

For practical purposes, the conversion factor of kVA to amps in a 600-volt system is approximately one to one. This means that, if you have a 300 kVA transformer at 600 volts, consider that you have 300 amps at 600 volts. Actually, 300 kVA usually does 400 amps; 500 kVA does 600 amps; 750 kVA does 800 amps; and 1000 kVA does 1200 amps. As you can see, it is a little complicated. The size of the sub-station or transformer depends upon the requirements of the user.

(g) Back-up Generators

The August 2003 blackout that affected 50 million people in Ontario and the northeastern US created an opportunity for landlords to make their rental spaces more attractive by buying a back-up generator, driven by a gasoline (small) or diesel (large) engine. This may not be practical for large buildings with huge power requirements, but it should be for smaller ones. The small generators are portable (or on wheels) and the user plugs equipment or lighting fixtures into its outlets.

A large generator can also be what is called a standby unit, which is connected to the electrical system and starts automatically if the electricity from the public utility is no longer available. Bear in mind that it will have to be run 30-60 minutes each month for maintenance purposes. If you do not want to spend the large amount of money required to buy a permanent emergency generator, you could enter into an agreement with a rental company that would guarantee a generator would be available to you in case of blackout. You would probably have to pay a monthly fee to secure this guarantee. Think of it as an insurance premium and as a way of making your building more attractive to tenants.

19.3.9 LIGHTING SYSTEMS AND MEASUREMENT

Some of the terminology used in lighting has been adopted into common parlance, but we want to be very specific in this section and ensure we are all speaking the same language. Here are a few definitions.

- **Fixture.** A device that is securely and permanently attached to a building is a fixture.
- **Luminaire.** A luminaire is a lighting unit consisting of one or more electrical lamps, with all the necessary parts and wiring.
- **Lamp.** A device that generates artificial light is a lamp.

You can find a more extensive glossary of lighting terms at <www.lrc.rpi.edu/programs/lightHealth/AARP/healthcare/glossary.asp#cct>.

Warning: Unless you are practically a lighting expert, the information that follows will complicate your life! Lighting can be a difficult topic and other factors also contribute to its complexity. For example, different manufacturers will obtain different levels of performance from a given lamp due to small differences in design, components used, or the manufacturing processes employed. For instance, the Osram Sylvania Capsylite e-PRO halogen PAR 38 has a rocket switch that enables the lamp to produce 35% more lumens and last 80% longer than another halogen PAR lamp of similar wattage. Therefore, most of the numbers given below are an average and will likely be a little different from one manufacturer to the next.

(a) Lighting Measurement

It is necessary to know the level of lighting you need, in order to ensure that you get or provide it. In lighting there are standards that, although too rarely used, will save you a lot of complaints from your tenants if you pay attention to them. In North America the standard unit of intensity of a lighting system is the foot candle. It corresponds to the light given out by one candle at a distance of one foot, at work height. A device called a light meter measures lighting intensity.

Under the metric system, the standard unit of measurement is the lux. The lux is the metric unit (SI) equivalent to 0.0929 foot candle. Lux represents lumens per square metre; lumen represents one foot candle per square foot. Figure 19.5 provides these equivalencies in chart form.

Figure 19.5
Lighting Measurement Equivalencies

Lumen	Unit of quantity of light, emitted on a reflecting surface. One Lumen per square foot produces a lighting intensity of one foot candle, at one foot.
Foot candle	One lumen per square foot
Lux	Metric unit equilavent to 0.0929 foot candle
Lux	One Lumen per square metre
Decalux	Ten lux
Decalux	0.929 foot candle

Note: 1 square metre = 10.76 square feet.

There are, in fact, three different lighting levels for a given room.

1. **Initial.** The initial level is displayed with new lamps.
2. **After 100 Hours of Burning.** Also called "foot candles maintained", this is always lower than with new lamps because, after a few hours of use, there is a drop in lighting intensity. Note that when a user specifies X foot-candles, he means (or should mean) the "foot candles maintained".
3. **After Several Months.** Luminaires and lamps become dirty and should be cleaned after several months of use. As an example, T12 fluorescent lamps can lose up to 40% of their original light due to lumen depreciation and dirt.

Lighting requirements vary, based on both uses and users. For example, a warehouse requires less light than a laboratory and as people age they require more light. Figure 19.6 provides information on the recommended light levels for different areas and types of use. The Illuminating Engineering Society of North America (IESNA) is to lighting what Building Owners and Managers Association International (BOMA) is to floor measurements. IESNA recommends the amount of lighting required for various situations but these numbers are average and arbitrary. Some elderly office users may want 100 foot candles, or more, lighting in their office, while you may come across warehouses where very small items are handled that require lighting levels of 80 foot candles, and other warehouses where users who are quite happy with 10 or 15 foot candles.

If you want to avoid problems later, ask your prospective tenant to show you a room with a lighting level that is satisfactory for the planned usage, then, show him what the reading is with a light meter.

There are two major types of lighting, one using incandescent, or resistance, lamps and the other using gaseous.

Figure 19.6
Recommended Lighting Levels

Location	Foot Candles
General Office	60-70
Entrance Lobby and Hallways	40-50
Conference Rooms	30-50
Washrooms	30-40
Corridors and Stairs	10-20

(b) Incandescent Lighting

The incandescent bulb is the most costly one to operate, based on the amount of light given, but it is the cheapest one to buy and install. It is used mainly in homes or where a minimum amount of light is required.

(c) Gaseous Lighting

The gaseous bulbs such as fluorescent, metal halide, mercury vapour, or sodium lamps operate when the gas they contain is ignited by an electrical current. The most commonly used gaseous lighting systems are fluorescent and high-intensity discharge (HID). The T12 is the oldest fluorescent lamp still in use, with the T8 being a newer version and the T5 the most recent. Two newer options that are gaining popularity are the light emitting diode (LED) and the induction lighting system (ILS).

In North America, the most commonly found lighting systems are fluorescent. In industrial and retail applications, 1.2 and 2.4 m (4 and 8 ft) lamps are most frequently used in fluorescent fixtures. In offices, four-lamp, 1.2 m fixtures are most common. The typical 1.2 m T12 lamp is rated at 40 watts (some are rated at 32 watts), while a 2.4 m lamp is rated at 80 watts. One encounters the 2.4 m lamps mostly in industrial and retail buildings, but many users avoid them because they are more difficult to store and to handle.

Fluorescent lighting is the most ubiquitous type used in modern countries. A fluorescent fixture is made of two key components — lamp and ballast (and two other parts, not quite as important — reflectors and lenses).

In North America, the most commonly found lighting systems are fluorescent.

Fluorescent lamps differ essentially because of their diameter, length, type of phosphor coating (the powder that can be seen if one breaks a tube), the gas used, and the starting method. An unlit, typical T5 fluorescent lamp may look the same as the next one, but there can be major differences between them, such as lumens per watt, lumens maintained (or mean) after 40% of its rated life, colour temperature, colour rendering index, and life expectancy.

A fluorescent lamp is classified according to its efficiency. One can find three types:

1. standard light output is the most commonly encountered and they are usually more efficient and cheaper to buy than the next two types and offer the widest range of colour temperatures
2. high output (HO), and
3. very high output (VHO).

Lamps are divided based on their starting speed.
- A preheat-start is rarely encountered in lamps longer than 91 cm (36 in), and the 1.22 m (48 in) fluorescents are the ones of interest to us.
- The instant-start lamps use the most efficient ballasts but usually have the shortest lamp life, particularly if the time the lamp is on is less than 3 hours (frequent on and off cycles).
- Rapid-start lamps yield the longest lamp life, but to the relative detriment of efficiency.

The ballast, the other key component in a fluorescent fixture, controls how the current is delivered to the lamp (fluorescent or HID). It could be called a regulator.

Correlated Colour Temperature (CCT) is expressed in Degrees Kelvin (°K). Based on the Celsius scale used by scientists, the Kelvin scale has no negative numbers. CCT shows how "warm" or "cool" the lamp appears to be visually. The higher the number, the cooler the lamp is, in terms of colour. Incandescent (and halogen) lamps have a CCT of 2,800°K, T5 and T8 have a CCT of 4,100°K. Daylight ranges from 5,000-10,000°K.

Within CCT the Kelvin temperature guide operates as follows:
- warm white: 2700K
- soft white: 3000K
- neutral: 3500K
- cool white: 4100K, and
- daylight: 5000K.

The Color Rendering Index (CRI) measures a lamp's ability to show colours as compared to the light of the sun, relative to a standard. This is particularly important when the quality of the light is a consideration, as it frequently is in retail stores. The CRI is measured on a scale of 0 to 100. The better CRI comes from incandescent lamps, then T12 lamps, then metal halide. Be careful, as the CRI varies within each type of lamp (such as fluorescent, metal halide, sodium). For example, a T8 fluorescent lamp can rate at only 75 CRI while a better, or more expensive, one can have a CRI of 85. In comparison, a metal halide lamp used in a parking garage will have a CRI of 70. The CRI is an important consideration for applications such as the lighting of food and vegetable products or for retail clothing stores because it indicates the lamps ability to show colours well. In these situations a CRI of 80 or higher is preferred. CRI indices are classified as follows: 60 to 70 is fair; 70 to 80 is good; and over 80 is superior. CRI is of more practical use than CCT.

There are three fluorescent lighting standard lamps.

1. The old fashioned T12 stands for 12/8 in (38 mm or 11/2 in).
2. The succeeding T8 version measures 8/8 in (25 mm or 1 in).
3. The T5 lamp, which started to be available in the late 1990s, measures 5/8 in (16 mm) in diameter.

While there are other lamps of different diameters (T17 (6.3 mm or 0.25 in), T10 (6.3 mm or 0.25 in) and T2 (6.3 mm or 0.25 in)), they are used only for special applications and will not be covered here.

Currently the T8 and T5 lamps are the darlings of users and it is almost certain that they represent the demise of the T12. Both T8 and T5 lamps are superior to a T12 lamp because they give out a better light and are more economical, due to lower electricity consumption and longer life. These T8 and T5 lamps are controlled by Programmed Start Electronic Ballasts, which don't flicker or hum, use less power, and generate less heat. The T12 uses magnetic ballasts that are much heavier. The T8 and T5 lamps are called Triphosphor Fluorescent lamps. The T5 were designed to peak in the lumen ratings at 35°C (95°F), compared to 22°C (72°F) for T12 and T8 lamps. This increase in operating temperature is an important factor to consider for use in areas where there is little or no air circulation. In addition, T5 lamps project a very bright light that can cause visual discomfort, if not shielded properly or not installed high enough.

Figure 19.7 provides a comparison of the various lamps and lighting systems, taking into consideration many variables.

Figure 19.7
Lighting System Performance Comparison

Performance Comparison	Standard T8 Lamps	T5HO (linear)	T5HO (biax)	250 Watt Metal Halide	Phillips QL 165 Watt	Genura 23 Watt	ICETRON 150-Watt
Lamp Data							
Lamp Lumens (initial)	2,950	4,450	4,800	23,000	12,000	1,100	12,000
Rated Life (hours)	20,000	20,000	12,000	10,000	100,000	15,000	100,000
Color Rendering Index (CRI)	82	82	82	65	80	82	80
Mean Lumens	2,714	4,136	4,128	17,000	9,600	935	8,880
Lumen Maintenance (40% life)	92%	93%	86%	74%	80%	85%	74%
Re-strike time requirement	None	None	None	10 min	None	None	None
System Data							
Number of Lamps	4	4	4	1	1	1	1
Ballast Factor	90%	100%	100%	94%	100%	100%	100%
Initial System Lumens	10,620	17,800	19,200	21,620	12,000	1,100	12,000
Nominal System Watts	114	234	234	289	165	23	150
Initial System Efficacy (lpw)	93	76	82	75	73	48	80
Mean System Lumens	9,770	16,544	16,512	15,980	9,600	935	8,880
Maintained System Efficacy (lpw)	86	71	71	55	58	41	59

All values were based upon manufacturer's published data.

Given their higher output, one T5HO lamp can almost replace two T8 lamps (188%) and, in practice, does. A four-lamp T5HO fixture (216 watts) can provide as much light as a 400 watt metal halide lamp. For this reason, national retail chains with large stores are removing their metal halide fixtures and replacing them with T5 lamps.

Currently, the T5 lamp costs about three times more than the T8, but the difference is narrowing and it offers several advantages:

- better optical control
- lower profile, more aesthetically attractive luminaires
- higher lumen maintenance (over 90% after 15,000 hours of use)
- higher peak operating temperature, which yields better than rated performance in most situations
- differently sized luminaires, which prevents misapplication of fluorescent type,[1] and
- available in three standard colour temperatures: cool (4100K), warm (3000K), and neutral (3500K). The CRI is greater than 80.

One additional advantage of the T5 is its ability to be dimmed from 100% to as low as 1%, which is impossible with the conventional T12 because its magnetic ballast does not allow dimming. This feature can be a considerable source of additional savings. Whenever possible, do not use fancy lamps, such as 0.6 m (2 ft), U-shaped, etc. These cost two to five times more than the typical 1.2 m (4 ft) straight lamp and do not give out more light.

There is one other type of fluorescent lamp, called the "compact fluorescent" (CF), which was designed to replace incandescent bulbs. Most CF lamps screw directly into a fixture, in place of a conventional incandescent bulb, while others need a special socket. They consume far less electricity and last far longer than incandescent bulbs. As an example, a 15-watt CF bulb has an output similar to a 60-watt incandescent bulb and is designed to last 9,000 hours instead of 1,000 to 1,500.

Natural Resources Canada conducted a comparative study over 9,000 hours (the life of a 15-watt CF bulb). The total cost of a CF lamp, with a purchase price of $7 and including electricity consumption, was $18.00 while the 60-watt bulb's cost, including changing eight bulbs at $0.50 each, was $47.50. For more info, see <www.energystar.gc.ca>.

The information in Figure 19.8 is quite revealing in demonstrating the cost of ownership of three different types of luminaires over a 15-year period.

Figure 19.8
15 Year Cost of Ownership

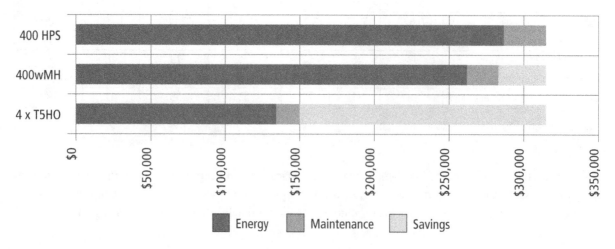

Source: 15-Year Cost of Ownership used by permission of 1st Source Lighting, Auburn, CA.

1 For safety reasons, the lamp manufacturers agreed on variances in actual lamp lengths and in socket designs, so that the T5 lamp cannot be retrofitted in existing T12 and T8 luminaires, nor can the T8 be retrofitted in existing T12s.

The next most commonly used gaseous type of lighting is the high-intensity discharge lamp (HID). Metal halide, mercury vapour, or sodium lamps are the most frequently encountered HIDs in warehouses, factories, and high-ceiling retail stores and still have the advantage over T5s for very high ceilings (higher than 6.7-7.3 m (22-24 ft)). There are sub-types within each, such as white high-pressure sodium, high-pressure sodium, and low-pressure sodium, and standard and pulse-start metal halide. Metal halide and high-pressure sodium are the most popular for indoor applications. Until a few years ago, HID luminaires were commonly used to provide better and more economical lighting in buildings where the ceiling height was in excess of 6 m (20 ft). Initially, these systems were not used with ceilings under 6 m. Now, thanks to improved reflector design, it is even possible to find some HID lamps in parking garages with only 2.4 m (8 ft) ceilings. One of the drawbacks of these lamps is that, unlike fluorescent, they need several minutes to warm up before they reach their proper lighting levels. The sodium lamp provides nearly five times the light of a standard incandescent lamp and twice that of a mercury vapour lamp for a similar consumption of electricity. However, the sodium HID system, particularly the low pressure one, emits a yellow light, making it less attractive with today's available options. The lamp life poses a drawback for the metal halide HID system. Lamp life is considered spent when 20% of the lamps in the group are not operating. Now these HID systems are frequently replaced with the T8 and even more often with the T5 lamps. T5 is the high bay lighting of the future (while waiting for LEDs or induction lighting) because, as noted earlier, the T8 and T5 offer many advantages.

A third, much less common, type of lighting is the light emitting diodes (LED). These are low-power bulbs (diodes) that are very economical in terms of consumption, commonly lasting 100,000-plus hours and offering energy savings of up to 80%. LED lamps were used for many years in electronic devices because of their small size, lightweight, and low energy consumption, but they have now penetrated the lighting market. They are usually used in groups because a sole diode is not very powerful. LED lights are great for exit signs, stairways, corridors, etc. They are being used more and more for street traffic signals, vehicle rear red lights, and even for flashlights.

The major and apparently the most advanced manufacturer of LEDs in North America is Lumileds, of California's Silicon Valley. Their LEDs, called "Luxeon" emitters, come in various colours of red, red-orange, amber, blue, cyan, green, and white. The typical LED light source uses a small LED chip mounted in an optical-grade epoxy package, whereas the Luxeon uses a totally new packaging technology consisting of a semiconductor chip mounted on a heat-sink slug, which provides much better thermal properties.

LEDs offer phenomenal advantages, including the following:
- last longer than any other light source
- are more energy efficient
- offer vibrant saturated colours, without filters
- provide direct light for increased system efficiency
- are robust and durable
- can be digitally controlled for dynamic effects
- are fully dimmable without colour variation
- have no mercury in the source
- are cold start capable (some lamps do not come on below a specific temperature), and
- operate on low DC voltages.

Only since 2006 were LEDs able to deliver up to 130 lumens per watt in white, 150 in amber and 190 in red-orange and Philips has recently produced a 1,000 lumen prototype LED. They are very small, saving space, and impervious to electrical shock, vibration, frequent switching, and environmental extremes. A further important advantage is that they retain high-lumen maintenance. Since 1998, Luxeon light sources have been used in over one million traffic signals, each signal using 12 to 18 Luxeon emitters. Because they still cost more than other kinds of lamps and only recently delivered a lumen/watt ratio that was competitive, they are still not in wide use. However, the future of most types of lighting systems seems to belong to LEDs. Undoubtedly, they will become very common.

Induction lighting systems (ILS) were introduced in the mid-90s and may soon become the second lighting system of choice, competing for supremacy with LEDs, for specific applications.

Neither LEDs nor ILS compete with T5 and T8 because their respective applications are different. The common weakness of almost all lighting systems is the lamp filament, which can easily be seen to be broken in a burnt incandescent bulb.

ILSs do not have electrodes. While there are several manufacturers of ILSs and, hence, differences in their approach to producing light, the basic operating principles are the same. The systems include a high frequency generator (a type of ballast), a power coupler (a type of induction coil that converts the current from the high frequency generator into a magnetic field within the discharge bulb), and a glass lamp housing that is called a "discharge bulb".

The discharge bulb contains the induction coil. It is filled with a mixture of gases including mercury and its inside wall is coated with rare earth phosphor. When power is supplied to the induction coil, an electromagnetic field is generated within the lamp and the light comes on immediately.

ILSs are ideal in lighting locations where relamping is inconvenient or expensive, such as streets, tunnels, work yards, parking lots, hard to access situations, facilities with high ceilings or with lights on 24 hours per day, indoor applications using incandescent lamps, signs, and freezers.

They present the following advantages:

- very long life; some manufacturers announce 100,000 hours (22 years at 12 hours per day), saving four or five relamping cycles, which offers major appeal where fixtures are very high or hard to reach
- white colour with CRI of 80+ (minimal colour shift over life)
- choice of 2,700, 3,000, 3,500 and 4,000°K colour temperatures
- instant on capabilities (no re-strike period); no flicker and no noise
- vibration resistant (no filament)
- can light at very low temperatures (-40°F)
- good lumens per watt of 59, compared to 86 for standard T8 lamps, 71 for T5HO, and 55 for metal halide
- lumen maintenance of 80%, compared to 92% for standard T8 lamps, 93% for T5HO, and 74% for metal halide, and
- savings of 33% over HIDs.

One finds the disadvantages as outlined here:

- ILSs cost two to three times more than other HID units (lamp and ballast). This will obviously change when volume of sales increases.
- They require specifically designed fixtures and cannot be used to retrofit most existing ones.
- There is limited choice, for example, the biggest lamp is 165 watts (for now) but some products, such as the Sylvania Icetron contain two lights (321 watts).
- At end of their life, the three components, high-frequency generator, power coupler, and lamp, must be replaced together.
- They run much hotter than other types of fluorescents (the lamp temperature reaches 65°C (150°F)).
- The fixtures of some manufacturers may interfere with radio signals, cordless telephones, and computers.

(d) Parking Garage Lighting

Parking garage lighting is a major consumer of electricity because most lamps stay on all the time. For many years, metal halide fixtures were the best choice for parking garages. This is no longer the case. T8 is a better choice for the reasons outlined here:

- The T8 fixture height requires little vertical space, being only 11.4 cm (41/2 in) deep, while a good quality metal halide measures a minimum of 20 cm (8 in) in height.
- T8s start instantly in temperature as low as –29°C, while metal halide requires several minutes to come up to full intensity. This is important in case of blackouts.
- T8s consume 20-60% less electricity than metal halide lamps.
- The metal halide fixture is a compact one while the T8 is almost 1.2 m (4 ft) long. This means that 15-20% more metal halide fixtures are required in order to avoid unlighted areas.
- The initial cost of the T8 is lower, starting at approximately $40 per fixture and reaching as high as $120-130, while a metal halide will start at $90-100 and can go much higher.
- Garages have low ceilings, which means that low-mounted fixtures are more susceptible to vandalism. To prevent this, manufacturers sell metal halide fixtures with tough polycarbonate plastic covers. Unfortunately, these covers yellow over time due to the high temperature, lowering the amount of light emitted.
- T8 lamps maintain higher average lumens than metal halides do.
- Typically, manufacturers warrant T8 fixtures and lamps used in parking garages for 3 years, but the guarantee is only 2 years for metal halide.

T5s should not be used in parking garages or any other situations with low ceilings.

(e) Lamp Replacement Policy

In large buildings, one of the most poorly managed aspects of lighting is the proper policy for lamp replacement. A key decision revolves around whether to practice group relamping, when a set of lamps is replaced at a scheduled time, or spot relamping, when lamps are only replaced when they burn out. This applies primarily to fluorescent and HID lamps rather than incandescents, which have much shorter lifetimes. In the article "Lighting: Spot versus Group Relamping",[2] the following reasons are listed in favour of group relamping.

Group relamping requires much less labor per lamp than spot relamping. A worker might take as long as a half hour to retrieve and install a single lamp. If all the materials were on hand for a large number of lamps, a worker could move systematically from fixture to fixture and cut the required time to about 3 minutes per lamp. The process would also be less disruptive since group relamping is usually done outside working hours.

Group relamping is easy to schedule and delegate to outside contractors, who have special equipment and training.

Group relamping provides brighter and more uniform lighting because lamps are replaced before their output has fully depreciated. Direct energy benefits result if the designer, anticipating group relamping, uses a smaller safety factor.

Group relamping offers increased control over the replacement lamps, reducing the chances of mixing incompatible lamps—such as those with different color temperatures.

2 This information is copyrighted and was provided courtesy of E Source Companies, 1965 North 57th Court, Boulder, Colorado 80301, USA, (303) 444-7788.

Economic comparisons typically show that group relamping has higher lamp costs but lower labor costs than spot relamping. ... This type of calculation is heavily dependent on the difference in labor costs between group and spot relamping. For example, if the group relamping cost of $1.50 per lamp jumps to $3.50, the balance tips in favor of spot relamping. Remember, however, the noneconomic benefits of group relamping discussed above when deciding between the two methods.

(f) Reducing Energy and Costs

Some tenants do not care very much if they are wasting utilities, especially when the landlord pays for them. It is said that in some apartment buildings, 10% of the tenants use 20-30% of the electricity. There are two viable methods available to control this situation — sub-metering and occupancy sensors.

The ideal way to control tenants' indifferent waste is to install sub-meters, which can be done by the electricity supplier through one of their sub-metering sub-contractors, but this is usually not the most economical approach. Sub-metering is done mainly for electricity, but sub-meters are also available for cold and hot water. Sub-meters vary in sophistication, from meters that require physical readings to computerized ones that automatically log the consumption of each individual tenant into a computer program. Because tenants are billed for what they consume, they tend to be more careful about waste.

In a sub-metered building, the landlord pays the utility supplier, and then invoices each tenant for individual consumption. The landlord then ends up paying for only the utility consumed for the common areas. There are companies that specialize in installing and managing sub-metering systems, but it is more economical for the landlord and for the tenants, if the landlord owns and manages the system. In most cases, a sub-metering system will pay for itself in a few years, out of the savings realized through lower consumption. Typically, the savings are more than 20% per year for electricity and up to 15% for water. It is also possible to obtain financial help with the supply and installation costs from the federal government through one of their energy saving programs.

Occupancy sensors turn lights on and off by detecting the presence of people within a space. There are three main types of occupancy sensors:

1. **Passive Infrared (PIR).** Passive infrared sensors require a direct line of sight as they sense the heat emitted by a human body. They are frequently used in private offices where they replace the light switch. They are the most widely used, but are prone to false triggering due to air movement (curtain, HVAC system). Their maximum effective range is 4.6 m (15 ft).
2. **Ultrasonic (US).** Emitting an inaudible sound pattern, ultrasonic sensors react to feedback. They detect minor motions better than most PIRs and are excellent in washrooms where the stall partitions block the line of sight, but reflect the sound pattern. They cover larger areas than PIRs.
3. **Dual (hybrid) Technology.** These sensors use both PIR (for its resistance to false triggering) and US technology (to take advantage of its sensitivity).

Sensors need to be positioned carefully. They are used most effectively in spaces that are often unoccupied, such as storerooms, conference rooms, restrooms, loading docks, stairwells, and cafeterias. Some sensors can be used in conjunction with dimming devices (to a preset level) to prevent the lights from turning off completely.

The savings realized can range from 10% in private offices up to more than 90% in restrooms, corridors, and stairwells. If this sounds enormous to you, consider that some people forget to turn off the lights at the end of the day. If this happens on a Friday night, it means that the lights will be on three nights and two days, needlessly. An extensive choice of sensors can be found at <www.wattstopper.com>.

19.3.10 FIBRE-OPTIC CABLES

For the transmission of voice or data, fibre-optic cables reign as king. It is far superior to the traditional copper cable used in the past. Fibre is lighter, faster, more stable, tougher, and more enduring than copper cable. Furthermore, it costs less to install and maintain. Here are some mind-blowing comparisons:

- Fibre is very small: a 0.95 cm (0.375 in) (12 pairs) cable can handle as much traffic as a 7.6 cm (3 in) diameter copper twisted-pair cable.
- It weighs only 57 g (2 oz) per metre versus 7.25 kg (16 lbs) for copper.
- Its bandwidth is enormous.
- Its speed is phenomenal. Theoretical rates of 50 billion bits per second are achievable. Tests have shown over 4 billion bits per second over a 100 km (62 miles) distance.
- Single–mode fibres have losses of only 0.2 dB per km, which is a very small number.
- Fibre is dielectric which means that it is not affected by electromagnetic or radio frequency interference. Copper is affected and, therefore, requires shielding.
- It is safe. It cannot generate heat or sparks or be a cause of fire.

Fibre-optic cable is lighter, faster, more stable, tougher, and more enduring than copper cable — and it costs less to install and maintain.

19.3.11 HEATING AND COOLING SYSTEMS

Conventional or typical heating and cooling systems are well known and relatively well understood by most people. Therefore, we will not cover them here. A newer system, geothermal, is very exciting and bound to become popular for two reasons. It is eco-friendly and very economical to use.

(a) Geothermal Heating and Cooling Systems

Geothermal heating and cooling systems, also known as "ground source" systems, make a lot of sense and we predict that in a matter of time, they will become very common, if not universal. The principle is simple. One needs three major components.

1. A pipe (generally of sealed polyethylene), in which a heat transfer fluid (water or glycol (an antifreeze)) circulates, must be buried underground or under water.
2. A geothermal heat pump (GHP) is needed to transfer or boost heat or cold between the building and earth.
3. A distribution and control sub-system, comprising ventilation ducting, equipment monitors, distribution fans, and system controls, is required for delivering heating or cooling.

In winter, geothermal systems bring the earth's natural warmth up into a building and augment and distribute it using heat pumps and ventilation systems. In summer they work in reverse, extracting heat from inside a building to be discharged into the cooler earth. At the same time, the cool temperature from the underground can be transferred up.

There are two main kinds of GHP systems — closed-loop (most common), where the same liquid keeps circulating in the system, and open-loop, where water from a river, well, or pond is used and then returned to a discharge area at a slightly higher, or lower, temperature. Pipe loops can be installed vertically if the site is small, or horizontally with high-density polyethylene pipe buried at least 1.2 m (4 ft) underground (below the frost line). These systems, as a rule, use an antifreeze liquid.

Today's improved GHPs circulate a non-chlorofluorocarbon (CFC) refrigerant gas inside a closed-loop cycle, either compressing or expanding it. When a refrigerant gas is expanded, it absorbs heat creating cold. If the cycle is reversed and the refrigerant gas molecules are compressed, they radiate heat, creating warmth. Heat exchangers make the temperature transfers; fans and ventilation ducts distribute the warm or cool air. Compressing or expanding a refrigerant gas within a GHP can be repeated *ad infinitum*. Consequently, earth energy extraction is pollution free and the use of this technology reduces greenhouse gases.

Geothermal is sometimes called "Ground Source Heat Pump Technology". It is the most energy-efficient technology available today. Indeed, over 70% of the system's energy comes from beneath the ground. The more extreme the climate is, the higher the benefits. In fact, energy efficiency ranges from an incredible 300-400%, compared to a 90% high-efficiency boiler. A typical 140 m^2 (1,500 sq ft) house in a moderate climate can be heated and cooled for a year-round average of $1.20 per day ($438 annually).

GHPs are not 100% green since they still use electricity to power pumps and fans, but they are much greener than traditional systems. Their operating costs are much lower (typical savings on energy consumption are 25-50%), after the initial investment, which is usually higher than regular systems. Maintenance costs are very low as are operating costs and longevity is very high (pipe warranties extend up to 55 years). The equipment also takes up less space, at one-third that required by traditional systems. An additional benefit is that if the temperature in one area of the building is too high, or too low, the excess or lack can be exchanged with other parts of the building, meaning you can simultaneously heat and cool different parts of the same building.

An existing 6,500 m^2 (70,000 sq ft) industrial building in Mississauga, Ontario, was recently retrofitted with a geothermal system. It involved drilling 28 holes, 15.25 cm (6 in) in diameter, 110 m (360 ft) deep at a cost of $600,000. The gas supply was discontinued and the only energy cost will be $6,000 of electricity per year that will be required to drive the pumps and fans. This amounts to a cost of $0.93 per m^2 ($0.086 per sq ft) versus $8.61-10.76 per m^2 ($0.80-1.00 per sq ft) for a conventional gas heating system.

The system is particularly appropriate when heating or air-conditioning is used year-round. Sweden has 176,000 geothermal units, Germany 73,455 units, and France 36,000 units. Ninety-five per cent of new homes in Sweden have heat pumps, versus 5% in France. In the US, there are over 500,000 installations and the federal government alone has installed over 10,000 GHPs. To view the savings in heating a typical home using a geo-exchange system as compared to the traditional methods, review Figure 19.9.

The City of Toronto is the site of a very large geothermal system where water from Lake Ontario is collected offshore and brought, via huge pipes, to the city's downtown to heat and cool large buildings. Enwave's Deep Lake Water Cooling Corporation owns and operates the $175 million infrastructure that will eventually pump up to 265,000 *l* (70,000 US gal) per minute of water taken 5 km offshore, deep in Lake Ontario. Enwave is a corporation owned by the City of Toronto and the Ontario Municipal Employees Retirement System. The Air Canada Centre, TD Centre, the Royal Bank Plaza, and the Metro Convention Centre were the first users connected to the system. See <www.ghpc.org> and <www.igshpa.okstate.edu> for more information.

Figure 19.9
Cost Savings Using a Geo-Thermal System

The following is a comparison of costs to heat a typical home for a month using different heat types. Compare these with a geothermal system. These are costs to produce 10,000,000 BTUs (required to heat a typcially built and insulated house of about 2,000 square feet).

EARTH COMFORT GEOTHERMAL COST: $76.63

Heat Type	Cost	Compared to Geothermal
Electric	$251.56	-$174.93
Gas	$161.26	-$84.63
High Efficiency Gas	$139.76	-$63.13
Ultra High Efficiency Gas	$123.32	-$46.69
Oil	$285.71	-$209.08
Propane	$370.70	-$294.07
High Efficiency Propane	$313.67	-$237.04
Ultra High Efficiency Propane	$271.84	-$195.21
Air Heat Pump	$142.31	-$65.68
Wood	$126.92	-$50.29

Please, note that these prices are in US$

You may access the calculator by going to: www.earthcomfort.com/new_furnace_calc.html

Source: Michigan Geothermal Energy Association <www.earthcomfort.com>.

(b) Hot Water and Steam Heating Systems

Most homes, offices, and retail buildings are heated with a forced-air system primarily because they are less expensive to install than almost anything else, except electrical heat, which is expensive to operate. Forced air has the drawback of moving around a lot of air that is loaded with dust and this dust collects in the ducts. The best way to control the dust is to clean or change the filters frequently, but unfortunately very few people do so.

Hot water heating is more appealing from a hygienic viewpoint, but water leaks, although rare, do occur. If you have hot water heating systems, here is a way to save 10% on your heating costs. Almost always radiators are placed against outside walls. Behind the radiator, against the wall, slide a sheet of corrugated Mylar film with the mirrored side facing the radiators to reflect the heat away from the wall. It's cheap and simple. You may adhere the mylar film to the wall with contact glue.

Low pressure steam heating systems (usually 6.8 kg (15 lbs)) are commonly found in older buildings. In our experience, steam systems pose many problems. If you acquire an industrial building with one, try to replace it as soon as you can with suspended forced air gas or infrared gas, if you do not or cannot go with a geothermal system. Infrared gas heating, which is a bit cheaper, is great for manufacturing uses, but not recommended for warehousing because the pipes through which the gases of combustion flow become very hot, making it dangerous to stack anything too close to them without running the risk of damage or fire.

19.3.12 TANKLESS WATER HEATERS

The heating of water requires much energy. The average household spends 20-40% of the energy consumed to heat water. A typical gas-fired storage tank water heater uses older technology that has terrible efficiencies, only about 55%.

For over 75 years, Europe and Asia have used tankless water heaters that have efficiency as high as 80%. The burner of the heater comes on automatically when a faucet is opened. The start-up process is virtually instant as it takes only 2-3 seconds. However, even the larger models do not deliver more than 12 or 15 litres per minute. The available volume does pose a drawback, but on the other hand you don't need to wait to recover hot water once it is used up. Tankless water heaters are sometimes installed with a storage tank to partially remedy this problem. Usually, one opens only one faucet at a time, although some larger models can accommodate multiple users at the same time.

The main drawback to tankless heaters is the initial higher cost, at close to $1,000 for a residence, considerably more than a typical water heater that costs from $300-500. However, the return on this investment is 20-30% per year. Tankless heaters are also supposed to last much longer than tank heaters.

There are tankless electrical water heaters, but most people prefer to install gas powered ones, as they are more economical to run.

19.3.13 LIFE EXPECTANCY OF HEATING AND COOLING EQUIPMENT

Figure 19.10 provides an indication of the average life expectancy of heating and cooling equipment. Bear in mind that it can be less, in the case of gross neglect or heavy usage, or more, in the case of light usage and/or very good maintenance.

19.4 INSULATION

Recognize the importance of insulation — for sound and temperature.

19.4.1 SOUND

Almost everyone who talks of insulation thinks about temperature. In fact, there are two kinds of insulation — one for temperature and one for sound. Sound is measured in decibels (dB). The higher the number is, the louder the sound. In certain circumstances, you may want or need to control or lower the noise level in a room. The ability of material to insulate noise is measured in Impact Insulation Class (IIC) ratings, which measure how noise travels through ceilings and floor assemblies. For example, certain vibration pads have a rating of 49 IIC to 60 IIC.

Most people will tell you that in residential or office applications a heavy-duty commercial sheetrock (drywall), 1.6 cm (5/8 in) thick versus the commonly used 1.27 cm (1/2 in), used on each side of a 5 x 10 cm (2 x 4 in) stud is a great way to cut down noise between rooms. This is true. You may also be told to place fibreglass batts between the studs to further improve sound blockage. However, in many situations, this may not suffice. There are other options.

Figure 19.10
Life Expectancy of Heating and Cooling Equipment

Air conditioning compressor – hermetically sealed	12 to 15 years
Air conditioning compressor – water-cooled	20 years
Air conditioning compressor – reciprocating	20 years
Rooftop heating and air conditioning unit	20 years
Copper core boiler – heat exchanger	15 to 20 years
Steel core boiler – heat exchanger	10 to 15 years
New cast iron core boiler – heat exchanger	20 to 25 years
Old cast iron core boiler – heat exchanger	30 to 50 years
Steel tube boiler – heat exchanger	20 to 40 years
Heat exchanger – standard rooftop unit	15 to 20 years
Heat exchanger downstream of a cooling coil (package unit)	10 to 20 years
Heat exchanger – standard indoor system	20 to 25 years
Cooling tower	20 to 25 years
Central chiller	20 + years
Air handler	20 to 30 years
Gas-fired ceiling-mount unit heater	15 to 25 years
Gas-fired ceiling-mount radiant heater	20 to 25 years

Source: Compiled by Carson Dunlop Weldon, based on historical data and company experience.

First, you can place not one, but two, sheets of sheetrock on each side of the wall. Second, you could stagger the studs in what is sometimes called a "double-stud" wall. To build this structure, use two horizontal pieces of 15.25 cm (6 in) lumber (called bottom and top plates) placed with one laying on the floor and one placed under the ceiling. One stud is nailed flush with one side of one plate and the next one flush with the other side. They are in contact with the sheetrock only on one side of the wall and there is a space of 5 cm (2 in) between the back of the studs and the back of the gypsum board of the other side of the wall. This, of course, allows for the placement of thicker insulation batts, which aids further in abating noise. The drawback is that double-stud walls reduce the size of rooms. For example, if your partition is 5.5 m (18 ft) long, you have lost 5.5 m x 5 cm (18 ft x 2 in) or 28 m² (3 sq ft). Your third option, in severe situations, is to use one of the various products manufactured to reduce sound transmission. These are frequently made of recycled rubber with binders, sometimes glued on a base of high-density fibreboard.

Finally, a fourth option is to use the other sound insulating products on the market, such as neoprene vibration pads. Toronto-based NRI Industries Inc.'s Symar Sound Down product has been engineered to provide acoustic dampening by reducing mid- to high-frequency sound transmission through concrete sub-floors. Designed for use with hard surface floor coverings like ceramic tile, hardwood, and laminate, Sound Down achieves proven IIC ratings ranging from 49 IIC to over 60 IIC.

An effective way to reduce noise across partitions, which was used in Europe for a long time, is to place a thin sheet of lead 0.8-1.5 mm (1/32-1/16 in) between the studs and the gypsum board. The weight and density of lead reduces vibrations, hence the transfer of sound.

For greater sound insulation, the accepted practice is to use resilient channels. These are thin metal channels, insulating the sheetrock from the framing woodwork. The channels are screwed onto the lumber, then the sheets of drywall are screwed on them, dramatically increasing the noise insulating value of the wall or ceiling.

Aircrete is a lightweight precast autoclaved aerated concrete material in block or panel form that has been used extensively around the world for over 60 years for sound insulation and firewalls (4-hour fire rating in a 15.25 cm (6 in) wall). It can be used as a one-step structural wall, up to seven storeys, but is frequently used as a dividing wall between units for hotels because of its sound-deadening properties. It weighs one-third the weight of regular concrete. The most commonly used block measures 20 x 20 x 61 cm (8 x 8 x 24 in). It is estimated that 40% of all housing in Great Britain is constructed using Aircrete.

Additional information can be found on the Web site of the Oak Ridge National Laboratory (Building Envelope Research), on which an interesting insulation calculator is offered (<www.ornl.gov/sci/roofs+walls/insulation/ins_16.html>).

It is possible to measure sound levels yourself with a sound level meter. But, if you find this too daunting or need a job done professionally, there are sound engineers that can be consulted. They will conduct tests in conformance with the American Society for Testing and Materials recommendations. The test should be performed both in the room where the noise is heard and in the room from which the noise seems to come. If you want to delve further into noise insulation details, see <www.csinet.org/s_csi/doc_specifier_article.asp?TRACKID=&CID=1141&DID=9948>.

19.4.2 TEMPERATURE

Heat always flows from warmer to colder areas, never in the reverse. This movement or transfer of heat occurs by one or any combination of three methods — conduction, convection, and radiation.

Conduction occurs when heat is transferred directly through materials in contact with each other. Heat transfer along a metal rod is a simple example of conduction.

Convection is the transport of heat within a gas (air) or liquid. Air, when heated, becomes less dense than the surrounding air and rises upwards. The denser and cooler air flows downwards. These air movements, known as convection currents, can occur in spaces between the framing members of ceilings or walls of buildings, causing a significant amount of heat loss.

Radiation is the transmission of rays through the air. When you warm up your hands by a fireplace, you feel the heat through radiation. Heat energy may be radiated through air space and then be absorbed by another body, such as when the sun's energy is absorbed as heat by the human body.

All three methods of heat flow occur in the wall space of buildings. Insulation will almost completely eliminate heat transfer by convection.

(a) R-Value

When it comes to temperature, the standard used to measure insulation is R-value. It is the reciprocal of the material's thermal conductance (C-value).[3] The R-value refers to the thermal resistance to heat flow (or movement of heat) of a material or assembly of materials, such as the wall of a building. The higher the R-value, the more the material insulates. Some common materials and their corresponding R-values are shown in Figure 19.11.

When it comes to temperature, the standard used to measure insulation is R-value. The higher the R-value, the more the material insulates.

3 Thermal conductance is the quantity of heat that passes in a unit of time through a plate of a particular area and thickness when its opposite face differs in temperature by one degree.

Figure 19.11
Common Materials and the R-Values

Material	Thickness in Centimetres	R-Value
Metal	N/A	0.00
Concrete	2.54	0.30
Wood	2.54	0.91
Fiberglas	2.54	3.90
Polystyrene		
Expanded (EPS)	2.54	4.00
Extruded (XEPS)	2.54	5.50
Polyurethane Foam	2.54	6.88
Sprayed Foam	2.54	7.00

Thermal Conductivity (K-value) is the measure of the amount of heat, measured in BTUs, that will be transmitted through a 2.54 cm (1 in) thick piece of homogenous material, 0.09 m^2 (1 sq ft) in size, in one hour, when there is a 1°F temperature change.

A British Thermal Unit (BTU) is the quantity of heat required to raise the temperature of 0.454 kg (1 lb) of water from 14.5-15.5°C (60-61°F) at a constant pressure of one atmosphere. A BTU is also the equivalent of 252 heat calories (one calorie is the amount of energy required to raise the temperature of 1 g of water by 1°C).

To calculate the R-value, you need to know the components of the roof or wall system and add up each individual R-value.

Insulating products such as Fiberglas, extruded and expanded polystyrene foam and cellulose are used to control the transfer of heat by way of conduction only. This type of mass insulation, which works by trying to trap the heat or cold in air pockets contained between the fibres in the product does not control heat transferred by radiation. Air is a good insulator against conduction but cannot stop radiant heat and, once the insulation is saturated with all the heat it can absorb, it then transfers it on through the wall.

As usual in our world nothing is simple and, the subject of insulation becomes a little more complicated when one gets into detail. SOLPLAN Review explains some of the complications involved in proper wall insulation and makes excellent suggestions for the better insulation of buildings.

A key factor in assessing the overall insulation factor for walls is to take account of the heat loss through all parts of the wall, not just through the insulation.

For instance, a 2 x 4 wall with wood studs at 16 inches on centre with R11 insulation batts does not have an overall R-value of R11. If we take into account the effect of the studs and wall plates, the wall insulation value falls to R 10.6. [Authors' note: The vertical studs alone represent 12.5% of the wall area. Add to it the bracing spacers, floor plates and more, and you have around 20% of the wall area that has only an R-value of 6 to 8. The only way to overcome this is to place insulation, such as Styrofoam, on the outside of the studs].

Steel studs are considerably worse than wood studs. A steel stud wall with R12 batts and studs at 16 inches on centre only has an R-value of about R7.

Here are several ways to improve the R-values of walls in new construction, relatively inexpensively. A lot of this information is quite old, but it is amazing how little of it is being applied in the field:

1- Increase the wall stud spacing from 16 inches on centre to 24 inches on centre.

On a 2 x 4 wall system, the R-value is increased from R12 to about R12.9, for a gain of 7.5% in R-value. On a 2 x 6 wall, the R-value will increase from R17.7 to R19.5. In addition, the wall will be less expensive to build.

2- Increase the R-value of the insulation used.

It is now possible to buy higher density R14 batts that will fit in 2 x 4 wall cavities. With the R14 batts and 24-inch on-centre studs, the R-value of the wall increases to R14.2, or 18% better than the base wall R-value of R12. The extra cost of the R14 batts, compared with R12 batts, is about 7%. For 6-inch studs, R22 batts are now available.

3- Replace the wall sheathing (which is often oriented-strand board or plywood) with insulating foam sheathing.

The least expensive foam is usually bead board (expanded polystyrene) with an R-value of about 3.7 per inch of thickness; the next most expensive is extruded polystyrene (R5 per inch), and the most expensive is foil faced polyurethane board (about R6 per inch). To provide racking strength for the wall, metal cross bracing will be needed. One slight disadvantage of the foam sheathing is that the wall will have less mass than the wall with OSB or plywood sheathing, and more noise transmission from outside will occur.

4- Increase the stud size.

Going from 2 x 4" to 2 x 6" studs obviously increases the cost, but the cost increase can be relatively small if some simple value engineering techniques are used. With a 2 x 6 stud, you can cantilever the bottom plate of the wall over the foundation by about 2 inches. Aligning the floor joists, the wall studs and the trusses will allow you to go to a single top plate for the walls, again saving on materials and labour. A 2 x 6 stud wall with studs at 24 inches on centre and R22 high-density batts will have an R-value of 20.8.

5- Use 2 x 3 horizontal strapping on the inside of the wall studs.

The strapping can be placed at 24 inches on centre and R8 batts used between the strapping.

To get wall R-values larger than about R27, double stud walls have been used.

In my own house, we have R60 wall insulation, which was accomplished by using two 2 x 4 stud walls in parallel with a 9-inch air space between the two walls. The insulation used was blown cellulose.

(b) Side Window Insulation

If you acquire an older industrial building (40-60 years old) that was built before energy was dear and before we were aware of the value of insulation, it could well have side windows. These typically cover the whole length of a building on both sides and are placed high, near the top of the walls, and are 0.9-1.5m (3-5 ft) tall. They are terrific for letting daylight in, but they also let in a lot of the sun's heat and let out a lot of the heated air during winter.

It is advisable to insulate the majority of these windows, keeping 5-10% of them for daylight. We have seen them insulated, from the outside. An aluminium U-shaped channel measuring 5 cm (2 in) wide is cut so as to make a rectangular frame. The best idea is to make the inside of the horizontal dimension the same length as a sheet of Styrofoam. Five-centimetre-thick Styrofoam is then placed in the frame that is fastened against the old windows. This is then covered with vinyl siding. The top of the siding is covered with a horizontal moulding (like a protective corner) to prevent water infiltration.

Five-cm Styrofoam siding will add an insulating value of R-8 to R-11. If it is not too difficult or too costly, it is even better to use 7.6 cm (3 in) Styrofoam, for a R-value of R-12 to R-16. The same system can be used for even older buildings that have saw-tooth roofs. In this case, the aesthetics do not matter, and it is possible to use a covering material that is less expensive than vinyl siding. The ROI of this insulation is 30-40% per year.

Be selective when choosing Styrofoam. Styrofoam is the brand name of the Dow Chemical Company. The generic name is polystyrene, of which there are two kinds — expanded (EPS) (also called "beadboard") with an R-value of 10.67 per cm (4.2 per in) and extruded (XEPS) with an R-value of 14 per cm (5.5 per in). The latter is denser, better insulating, and resists water absorption better. Polystyrene comes in thickness of 2.54, 3.8, 5, 7.6, and 10.2 cm (1, 1.5, 2, 3 and 4 in), but few suppliers stock them all. The sheet sizes are 1.2 x 2.4 m (4 x 8 ft) and 0.6 x 2.4 m (2 x 8 ft). In fact, 0.6 x 2.4 m sheets also come in a 60.6 cm (237/8 in) width, to fit between Z-furring channels (saving the contractor installation time).

For more detailed specifications, see <www.conservproducts.com/wall_performance.html>. There are many different types of insulation. A good source of information is the following Web site <www.theworkshop.net/CTVGoodMorningCanada/new_page_1.htm>.

19.4.3 AIR INFILTRATION

According to studies, random air leakage can account for as much as 40% of total energy loss (gaps in fibreglass insulation as small as 3% have been found to reduce performance as much as 35%). It is not surprising that more emphasis is now being placed on air leakage control, where payback on investment is far higher than the payback from increasing R-values.

Products with low air permeance, that fit perfectly into any shaped cavity and adhere to other building components, can eliminate air leakage and convection within a cavity, resulting in a higher performance than can be expected from conventional insulation material of equal R-value. Be aware that too low of an air exchange rate may be a source of problems, resulting in insufficient air replacement and mould.

19.4.4 R-2000 STANDARD

R-2000 is a voluntary Canadian national standard. It is not commonly used for commercial buildings, but it is useful to understand it.

The R-2000 Standard presents the criteria that a new house must meet to be eligible for R-2000 certification. The technical requirements of the R-2000 Standard include measures for the efficient use of energy, improved indoor air quality, and better environmental responsibility in the construction and operation of a house. This standard applies to the following:
- low-rise detached, semi-detached, and row houses covered by Part 9 of the *Building Code Act, 1992* (S.O. 1992, c. 23) that do not share heated areas, ventilation systems, or heating systems with other dwelling units, and

- multi-unit residential buildings covered by Part 9 of the *National Building Code of Canada* that share heated areas, ventilation systems, or heating systems between dwelling units must meet the requirements of the R-2000 Standard for multi-unit buildings.

To be eligible for R-2000 certification, the house must be constructed by a licensed R-2000 Builder, who built and had certified an R-2000 demonstration home before he could become licensed.

19.5 CONSTRUCTION AND RENOVATION

Hire contractors or direct the construction or renovation of your property.

Sooner or later, real estate investors must do some renovations or new construction. Using a professional is essential for peace of mind. Spend some time performing due diligence to be sure that you feel comfortable working with the contractor for an extended period of time. We'll explore the approaches that are open to you.

19.5.1 CONSTRUCTION MANAGEMENT METHODS

You can supervise sub-contractors yourself or hire a specialist who hires and supervises the sub-contractors. There are advantages and disadvantages to each approach. Choosing one approach over another will depend on your level of technical knowledge, the time you have available, and your ability to handle frustration and risk.

When you hire a corporation as a *general contractor*, it will perform the following tasks:
- finances the construction
- co-ordinates sub-trades
- is responsible for execution of project (at its own risk) to satisfactory completion
- has a contract with the owner
- usually, has at least some trades on staff
- over last few years, has become more and more of a financial operator, and
- owner's involvement and risk are limited (2/10)

On the other hand, a *construction manager* (individual) will be responsible for the construction of a building and satisfactory completion, but is not financially responsible. This approach necessitates a little more involvement and risk on the part of the owner (4/10).

If you choose to manage the sub-contractors yourself, you, as the *owner-builder*, will have total responsibility and control over timing, method, materials, sub-contractor selection, etc. You may make poor decisions, due to lack of construction and/or business knowledge and experience and your involvement and risk is substantial (8/10).

The *turn-key contractor* is the most popular approach today. This approach is used mainly with industrial or commercial buildings containing extensive improvements beyond the building itself. The owners/clients want to be given the key when they take possession of the finished building and be able to start operating their business virtually immediately. This approach offers the best efficiency in terms of marrying good design, good materials, and good results. This contractor will provide an architect; he may have one in-house or bring in an independent. The total cost is most often on a lump sum basis (fixed sum contract), but payments are made periodically by the owner, usually upon Progress Estimates certified by a professional, such as a P.Eng., construction cost consultant, or architect, if one is involved. The owner's involvement and risk is somewhat limited (3/10).

A *project manager* is responsible for the whole building, including concept design, construction, and liaison with owner. He will direct the construction manager. He has a contract with the owner, or with the party responsible for erecting the building, but usually does not have contracts with sub-trades. The owner contracts with sub-trades and this can be the source of many problems. The owner's involvement and risk is about even (6/10).

In all cases, the owner has the following responsibilities:
- chooses designs and specifications
- controls extras and credits during construction
- budgets, and
- pays the bills.

You may be tempted to select a contractor who says he will save you money by not charging you GST (6%) and perhaps save you even more, if you pay him cash. If you choose to go this route, do it with your eyes wide open because you will have little legal recourse against him in case of dispute and you may find out too late that he is not insured. Insurance is of paramount importance in construction projects because they are wrought with risks and, even with the best of luck and care, there are almost always problems that arise.

Insurance is of paramount importance in construction projects.

19.5.2 GUARANTEED MAXIMUM PRICE (GMP) CONTRACTS

When hiring a builder or a contractor, you must sign a contract. A Guaranteed Maximum Price (GMP) contract is often misunderstood. The basic concept of the GMP is that the owner and the contractor share savings. This is a powerful incentive for the contractor to come in under contract price.

The form of the contract itself is important. Some people will use a standard GMP contract, such as the 1998 Canadian Construction Documents Committee 3 (CCDC3) Cost Plus contract with a GMP option. There are other contracts, such as the CCDC2, which is far too generic. Furthermore, there are unavoidable Change Orders, often using a cost-plus formula, which means that the GMP will have to increase. (For examples of these forms, see the CCDC's Web site (<www.cca-acc.com>).)

The numbers in Figure 19.12 are valuable in demonstrating the price of renovations and maintenance relative to each other. The prices vary year over year depending on many factors, but the most important is supply and demand, that is, whether the construction market is booming or slack. Please note that the numbers are specific to southern Ontario, vary considerably by market, and quotations can vary significantly.

Figure 19.12
Building Improvement Costs for 2007

**Carson Dunlop
Weldon
& Associates Ltd.**
Consulting Engineers
Building Inspections

I C I D I W I

120 Carlton Street, Suite 212
Toronto, Ontario M5A 4K2
Tel: 416-964-3246
Fax: 416-964-2046

www.CDWengineering.com

Toronto   Vancouver

Carson Dunlop Weldon Report

Building Improvement Costs for 2007

The following are ballpark estimates for repairs and/or improvements to a typical single-storey industrial or retail structure. The costs reflect the Southern Ontario area. Our experience has shown that actual quotations can vary by as much as 300%.

Naturally, the quality of workmanship and materials will influence cost. The complexity of the job, accessibility and current local economic conditions can also affect actual costs.

ROOFING

Strip and replace built up tar and gravel roof	$7.00 - $10.00 per sq. ft.
Strip and install single ply roof membrane	$7.00 - $11.00 per sq. ft.
Strip and reroof with asphalt shingles	$3.00 - $4.00 per sq. ft.
Strip and reroof with cedar shingles	$7.00 - $10.00 per sq. ft.
Reflash typical skylight (2 ft. by 4 ft.)	$1,000
Rebuild single flue masonry chimney above roof line	$200 - $300 per linear ft of chimney height
Reroof with metal over built-up membrane, including tapered purlins	$8.00 - $11.00 per sq. ft.
Install concrete tile roofing (assuming no structural reinforcement)	$7.00 - $10.00 per sq. ft.

EXTERIOR

Resurface asphalt paving	$2.00 - $3.00 per sq. ft.
Repoint exterior wall	$6.00 - $9.00 per sq. ft.
Recaulk windows	$2.00 - $3.00 per linear ft. of caulking
Install insulated steel siding	$9.00 - $11.00 per sq. ft.
Install precast concrete panels	$25.00 - $35.00 per sq. ft.
Install shipping door cushions	$250 each
Replace 8'x10' wood sectional shipping door	$1,200 - $1,800
Install 8' high chain link fencing	$15.00 - $20.00 per linear ft.
Lay sod	$0.75 - $1.50 per sq. ft.
Replace windows – aluminum framed, double glazed	$25.00 - $50.00 per sq. ft.
Install interlocking brick walkway	$6.00 - $8.00 per sq. ft.
Rebuild masonry retaining wall	$30.00 - $50.00 per sq. ft.

Professional Engineers
Ontario

EXTERIOR Continued

Replace tarpaulin exterior cover for loading dock	$1,000 - $1,500 each
Wet sandblast concrete block (to remove ink or marker)	$2.00 per sq. ft.
Clean out catch basins in open parking lot	$150 per catch basin

STRUCTURAL

Replace corroded steel lintel (shelf angle) supporting brick veneer	$170 - $210 per linear ft.
Repair delamination of conventional concrete slab (assuming only minor corrosion of reinforcing bar)	$20.00 - $25.00 per sq. ft.
Repair crack in concrete roof or wall slab by polyurethane injection	$40.00 - $50.00 per linear ft. (Min. $800)

ELECTRICAL

Replace circuit breaker panel	$1,000 - $2,000 each
Install electrical outlets	$100 - $200 each
Replace 200 amp disconnect switch	$600 - $1,000 each
Replace 30 KVA transformer (dry type)	$2,500 - $3,000
Install lighting in office area	$3.50 - $5.50 per sq. ft.
Install lighting in warehouse area	$2.50 - $3.50 per sq. ft.
Install 2 ft. by 4 ft. light fixtures	$200 - $250 each
Replace conventional receptacle with aluminum-compatible type (CO/ALR)	$25.00 - $35.00 each (Min. 25 outlets)

HEATING, VENTILATION AND AIR CONDITIONING

Install interlocking brick walkway	$6.00 - $8.00 per sq. ft.
Replace conventional package roof top heating/cooling unit -	
ductwork already there	$2,000 per ton
ductwork required	$2,500 per ton
Replace ceiling mounted, unit heaters	$1,500 - $2,500 each
Replace ceiling concealed water source heat pumps (1 - 2½ tons)	$2,500 - $3,500 each
Replace air conditioning compressor	$700 per ton
Replace heat exchanger for roof top unit	$2,000 - $4,000 each
Clean duct system for roof top unit	$0.20 per sq. ft. of building floor area
Replace 1,000,000 BTU/hr. hot water boiler	$15,000 - $25,000 each
Replace roof top cooling tower	$150 - $250 per ton
Replace centrifugal chiller	$500 - $800 per ton (Min. 200 ton)
Retrofit centrifugal chiller from R11 to R123 refrigerant	$180 per ton
Install pumps	
5 H.P. and less	$800 - $1,600 each
5 H.P. to 10 H.P.	$3,000 each
Install roof mounted exhaust fans (<2,000 CFM)	$1,500 per fan
Install diffuser (including branch duct and damper)	$250 - $350 each
Balance air ductwork	$0.20 - $0.25 per sq. ft. of building floor area
Install flexible ductwork	$8.00 - $12.00 per linear ft.
Install electric baseboard heater	$200 - $300 each
Replace thermostat	$150 - $250 each
Replace radiator control valve with thermo actuator	$200 - $300 each
Install individual bathroom exhaust fan	$500 - $800 each
Install 1 inch diameter gas piping	$12.00 - $18.00 per linear ft.

PLUMBING

Replace water closet	$700 and up
Replace urinal	$900 and up
Replace basin and faucet	$700 and up
Replace 1/2 inch diameter copper piping	$17.00 per ft. (Min. 100 linear ft.)
Replace 3/4 inch diameter copper piping	$22.00 per ft. (Min. 100 linear ft.)
Replace storm or sanitary pipes - above grade	$25.00 - $35.00 per ft. (Min. 100 linear ft.)
Replace storm or sanitary pipes -	
underground (inside building)	$45.00 - $60.00 per ft. (Min. 100 linear ft.)
underground (outside the building)	$60.00 - $80.00 per ft.(Min. 100 linear ft.)
Insulate supply water piping	$1.50 - $2.50 per ft. (Min. 100 linear ft.)
Replace 40-gallon electric water heater	$500 - $800

INTERIOR

Install 8 inch concrete block partition wall (no doors)	$9.00 - $12.00 per sq. ft.
Install medium quality commercial broadloom	$3.00 - $5.00 per sq. ft. and up
Install vinyl composite floor tiles (no preparation)	$2.50 - $3.50 per sq. ft.
Install ceramic tile (no preparation)	$6.00 - $10.00 per sq. ft. & up
Install drywall partitions	$5.00 per sq. ft. and up
Replace suspended ceiling tiles	$1.50 - $2.50 per sq. ft and up.
Power sweep concrete floor of warehouse	$0.07 per sq. ft.

ENVIRONMENTAL

Underground storage tank removal and minor soil cleanup	$5,000 - $10,000
PCB waste disposal	
45 gallon drum of light ballast	$1,800
45 gallon drum of PCB fluid	$1,200
45 gallon drum of PCB contaminated mineral oil	$600
Hazardous waste disposal	
Oily water	$0.20 per litre
Waste oils	$0.40 per litre
Solvents/Inks	$0.80 per litre
Asbestos removal	
4 inch pipe	$25.00 per ft. (Min. 200 ft.)
Elbows and T's	$80.00 each
Bore hole sampling (including laboratory testing)	$1,200 per hole
Laboratory testing/soil sampling	$150 - $300 per test
Asbestos/Lead samples (taking sample and having tested)	$100 per sample
Phase I Environmental Site Assessment	$1,400 - $2,500

Source: Compiled by Carson Dunlop Weldon, based on historical data and company experience.

People are often in a hurry and sign contracts accompanied by specifications and drawings that are incomplete, inaccurate, or misunderstood. Unavoidably, a GMP contract requires more administrative time than a fixed price contract. An owner who enters into a GMP contract must understand that he should pay only the actual cost up to the figure shown on the contract. If there are changes, they increase or decrease the maximum figure accordingly.

The owner must also understand that he does not have to pay for additional costs incurred by the contractor. A key protection for the owner is to have a clause in the contract stipulating that the work will be evaluated by a construction cost consultant. In fact, except for very sophisticated owners, with a GMP contract it is possible to effect important savings and prudent to use a construction cost consultant. Commonly, this does not apply to small jobs.

19.5.3 UNDERGROUND PIPES AND CABLES

You have probably heard or read it often: "Call before you dig". Sometimes, investors must install posts, fences, pipes, foundations, or bollards. The law requires that one determine the location of buried pipes or lines before breaking ground.

Ontario One Call is a private, not-for-profit corporation formed to provide a call centre to receive excavation requests within the province of Ontario. Other provinces have similar services. They will contact their members, which are the most common, but not all, utility companies (Bell Canada, Enbridge Gas, Allstream, Toronto Hydro, Hydro One) and ask them to go out and mark the location of their pipes and/or cables on your property or on public property on which you need to dig.

They will then fax or e-mail you a report. Turnaround time is usually one week, but you can request urgent service and they will try to accommodate your schedule. Utilities provide this service for free, as it is cheaper for them to send someone out to locate their utilities than to repair them when they are damaged by a company or individual during digging.

Another approach to locating underground items is to use Ground Penetrating Radar (GPR) that locates almost anything underground. It makes an underground picture. GPR is a non-destructive geophysical method that produces a continuous cross-sectional profile or record of subsurface features, without drilling, probing, or digging. GPR profiles are used for evaluating the location and depth of buried objects and to investigate the presence and continuity of natural subsurface conditions and features.

GPR operates by transmitting pulses of ultra high frequency radio waves (microwave electromagnetic energy) into the ground through a transducer or antenna. The transmitted energy is reflected from various buried objects or distinct contacts between different earth materials. The antenna then receives the reflected waves and stores them in the digital control unit.

Ontario One Call is free. GPR services are not.

19.5.4 CONSTRUCTION COSTS FOR MULTIPLE-UNIT RESIDENTIAL

To give you an idea of the cost of new construction, the discussion below and the numbers in Figure 19.13 will show you the appropriate cost to construct a new condominium building of 929 m² (100,000 sq ft).

Figure 19.13
Construction Costs for Condominium Residential

	Unit Cost per square foot	Unit Cost per square metre
Apartments		
One storey (no garage)	$ 80	$ 861
Two to ten storeys (with underground garage)	$ 116	$ 1,248
Over ten storeys (with underground garage)	$ 113	$ 1,216
Townhouse (with single car garage)	$ 88	$ 947
Parking Garages		
Above ground, with ramps ($20,000+/- per stall)	$ 46	$ 495
Underground parking ($27,630+/- per stall)	$ 60	$ 646

Note: When condominium developers analyze a site for density potential, they use a figure of 74 m² (800 sq ft) per apartment.

The gross area multiplied by the unit cost (per square metre or foot) will include all the work usually included in the main building contract, including all the architectural trades: structural, mechanical and electrical work contained within the building and all site services, and soft landscaping, paving and all sidewalks within the property line. Costs are based on the use of commercial union labour.

Unit costs for apartments are for the gross liveable area. The unit rates include the cost of underground parking, but the area of underground parking should not be included when applying the unit costs.

The square metre costs of apartments vary considerably, depending on unit sizes and quality. The unit prices in Figure 19.13 are for standard rental units with one three-piece washroom and no air conditioning. Condominiums fluctuate in cost from $970 per m² ($90.00 per sq ft) and up per unit.

Costs given are for parking garages constructed solely for the purpose of parking. They should not be applied to garages built as an integral part of office buildings, apartment buildings, etc. The rate indicated for underground parking excludes such work as shoring, excavation, underpinning, adjacent structures, etc.

To get a total cost you need to add to the main building contract the cost of the following:
- special foundations, including piles, shoring caissons, underpinning, rock blasting, etc.
- architectural and engineering fees (for plans, etc.)
- site services and connections, landscaping, roads, and sidewalks outside the property
- land (don't forget this one)
- legal fees
- land surveyor's fees
- environmental site assessment fees
- developers' administrative costs

- land transfer taxes
- property taxes during construction
- sewer levies and other charges
- soil (geotechnical) tests
- brokers' commissions
- interim financing and stand-by fees
- completion appraisal
- completion surveys
- maintenance costs
- tenant inducements
- the Goods and Services Tax (GST), and
- development charges or construction levies.

In many situations, the trend is to small apartment units. An elegant way to save considerable room is to use space-saving kitchen units. Their width varies from a 76 cm (30 in) unit that contains a sink, a two-burner electric range, and an under-counter fridge to a 152 cm (60 in) unit that contains a sink, a three-burner electric range, a counter, an oven, and under-counter fridge. The cost of a large space-saving unit is approximately $750, uninstalled.

If you renovate a building with the intention of selling it reasonably fast, use residential quality items. If you intend to keep the building for a long time, use heavy duty, commercial quality products. It will, no doubt, cost you more initially, but in the long run you will be better off because you will save time (a lot of time) and you will attract better-quality tenants.

19.6 IMPROVING A BUILDING FOR SALE OR LEASE

Make a list of the work to perform inside and outside your property before putting it on the market.

To lease or sell a building faster and for more money, there are two rules:

1. This is the time when the building should look its very, very best.
2. Don't hesitate to do what should be done.

From our point of view it is financially unforgivable to list a property for sale or lease with unfinished renovations, trees untrimmed, overgrown grass, dirty windows, ripped broadloom, peeling paint, and, worst of all, birds in the buildings.

Here is a list of the typical outside work that must be completed before putting a property on the market.

- Trim trees and bushes. If you have Manitoba maples on your property, eradicate them. They are an invasive species that is an unattractive urban weed. If you do not eliminate them completely, you will forever be pulling out young ones as they are extremely prolific.

- Kill weeds around fences, trees, and along driveways. Most professional gardeners will use a pump tank sprayer to apply Roundup Super Concentrate Weed and Grass Killer after diluting it. If you do not need a lot, you can buy it ready-to-use at any garden centre. Be careful not to spray good plants; they would not survive.
- Manicure the lawns.
- Paint any item that is rusty or faded.
- Ensure all door latches and keys function perfectly.
- Repair the asphalt.
- Ensure outside lights are on photocells and working.
- Ensure windows are clean and none of them are broken.
- If you are offering the building for lease, replace single-pane windows with thermopane. This doesn't always pay from the point of view of high return, but no quality tenant today will move into a space with single pane windows.
- Install an attractive pylon sign in front of the building ready to receive the new occupant(s)' name.
- If your building is a "plain box", consider installing awnings over doors and windows.
- Install things that will flatter your tenant(s)' ego or make his life more pleasant, such as entrance door chime/alarm, an access control system, outside surveillance cameras, picnic tables, a car shelter (for the boss's car, with covered walkway, if possible), outside (protruding) lobby, flag pole, electronic running word sign, high-speed Internet connection, etc.
- Fence the land, at least on three sides. This adds a feeling of security and privacy, both of which are valued by tenants.
- Hire an architect to suggest what to paint, inside and outside, and how to paint it, to render the building more appealing.
- Hire a landscape architect to improve the appearance of the site. Attractive landscaping contributes greatly to a building's appeal. As a general rule, you get a beneficial result for the money spent.
- Redo the parking lines. (Nothing improves a property so much at so little cost). To do a great looking job, first paint or spray the asphalt with driveway sealer.
- Clean the truck level dock levellers' wells, if you have any. Typically, dirt and debris fall below the platform and few owners clean this area regularly, if at all.

There are also a number of things that must be done to the inside of the building, too:

- Ensure all interior lights are working. Replace the old incandescent and T-12 fluorescent fixtures, with T-8 lamps or, better yet, in plant or warehouse areas where height allows, replace with metal halide or T5 lamps. Retrofitting the lighting rejuvenates an older building, gives better light, and lets you recover your money in 2-5 years.
- Shampoo or, if necessary, replace the broadloom.
- Clean everything, everywhere. The whole space should be spotless.
- If not too difficult, install a light switch in every room.
- Install occupancy sensor switches in all rooms where people go only from time to time.
- Install blinds on office windows.
- Install programmable thermostats.
- If you are dealing with a luxury building, consider adding an equipped fitness room, showers, and sauna.

As a final step, prepare a Building Manual, a binder in which you gather all possible information about the building. Give a copy to potential tenants or buyers (they will be impressed) and keep a copy for yourself. It should include the following:

- survey or site plan
- floor plan, preferably as originally constructed (can be in a pouch, folded up)
- photos — street level and aerial, if possible
- building specifications, as in a Data Sheet
- equipment details, such as HVAC, water, electricity, etc., with age, size, location, etc.
- location of electrical boxes and switches and the equipment, fixtures, or outlets, they control
- useful phone numbers, including oil, gas, electricity supplier, police department, fire hall, municipal water department, post office, etc.
- property tax assessment notice and bill
- recommended suppliers for utilities, HVAC maintenance, snow plowing, grass cutting, roofing company, glass company, electrician, etc.
- guarantees and warranties
- maintenance contracts, and
- equipment peculiarities.

19.6.1 14 STEPS TO RENOVATING A BUILDING

This section assumes that you are using a general contractor.

1. **Meet with the Contractor and Define the Job (what you want done).** He contracts to sub-contractors and then relays the results of his conversations with them to you.
2. **Buy Materials and Obtain Building Permit.** A draw schedule is usually required by the lender (assuming there is one) and lists the order in which the work required must be completed. Of course, do not forget to secure a building permit.
3. **Demolition.** Demolish first. Get a dumpster at the very beginning of a job and rip everything out.
4. **Roof, Windows and Siding.** Begin with the exterior of the building.
5. **Plumbing and HVAC.** Always make contractors check out the plumbing first, including the sewer lines. Have a working heating system up front. Always install completely new systems. If the electrical system needs to be updated, do this while the HVAC system is being installed.
6. **Framing and Sub-floors.** Begin by addressing areas such as rotten wood, tearing down walls, and building new ones.
7. **Sheet Rock.** The sheet rock goes a long way toward making an old building look new. The walls are neat, clean, and they can be attractively painted.
8. **Painting.** First, apply a coat of primer or a light first coat. Have the sheet rock crew fix any flaws, and, then, apply two more coats of paint.
9. **Installing New Restrooms.** Install ceramic tile or vinyl floors in the restrooms (and in the kitchen or lunchroom if there is one), before installing the new cabinets, etc. Take kitchen dimensions to a building supply store such as Home Depot and have them design the kitchen for you.
10. **Punch Out List.** Check everything. Contractors usually refer to this as their "punch out" list. It consists of all the little details such as outlets, switch plates, and light fixtures. The punch out is the hardest part and the step that makes your renovation a good one or an excellent one.

11. **Carpeting.** Put new wall-to-wall carpeting throughout (assuming your tenant wants it).
12. **Clean Up.** Make sure that everything is absolutely spotless.
13. **Marketing.** Have the entire job finished before allowing people to see the space.

If you are dealing with a multi-family residential building that includes basement living quarters, you have your own set of problems.

The walls should be well insulated, but since it is prohibitively expensive to do it from the outside, you will probably want to do it from the inside using polystyrene (Styrofoam). The floor should be insulated with the same material. Use a minimum of 6 cm (21/2 in) polystyrene for walls, but for the floor, the thicker the better and 12.7 cm (5 in) would be ideal if the resulting clear height — and your wallet — will allow it. You definitely need thicker insulation if you are in a location with damp soils.

The ideal set-up below the insulation would be a 15.25 cm (6 in) drain rock layer that has few fine stones (you do not want sand) followed by a minimum 6-mil poly vinyl (PVC or vinyl), carefully lapped and sealed. The extruded polystyrene is then placed on top. Do not confuse it with high-density expanded polystyrene, also called "bead board", which is softer, therefore more likely to get damaged, and would have to be thicker as it has a lower R-value (15-20%). The concrete slab is poured on top of the insulation.

If you want ultimate comfort, the heating system would be an under-the-floor hot water type. If this is not possible and you use forced air heating, whenever possible, place the registers in the wall near the floor level. A hard surface flooring should be considered, such as laminate, tile, stamped/finished concrete, or linoleum. Do not use carpets; instead, use area rugs that can be removed for cleaning because concrete has a relatively high moisture content (it is never completely dry). A carpet on top of concrete acts as an insulating blanket, lowering the temperature of the surface of the concrete, so that if you are in a cool climate it is possible that it will be at, or close to, the dew point at some times of the year, which can lead to mould growth. You should insure that the basement has a good ventilation system.

19.7 UNDERGROUND STORAGE TANKS (USTS)

Ensure you know when and how to remove underground storage tanks.

In Ontario the owner of a property is responsible for removing all underground fuel tanks that have stopped being used. For commercial tanks (gas station), tanks must be removed within 1 year and for residential fuel tanks, within 2 years.

In Ontario the owner of a property is responsible for the removal of any unused tank(s), remediation or removal of any ground contamination, and filling of the resulting hole. The tank must be removed by a contractor who is registered under the *Energy Efficiency Act* (R.S.O. 1990, c. E.17).

In Ontario the owner of a property is responsible for the removal of any unused tank(s), remediation or removal of any ground contamination, and filling of the resulting hole.

The vendor of a property, who conceals the existence of an underground tank or other environmental problem or defect, may be open to legal action in the future. If there is contamination and it spreads to the surrounding areas and the leakage is traced back to that owner, usually he will be held responsible for the cleanup.

When buying a property, request a statement from the vendor that there are no USTs or any form of contamination. A Phase I Environmental Site Assessment would generally uncover the existence of USTs. When a UST leaks, it becomes a LUST (Leaking Underground Storage Tank). Even tanks in use corrode over time and need to be replaced. In Ontario, for example, if a tank is older than 25 years (or its age is unknown), regulations required that it be removed before October 1, 2006, unless it was protected from corrosion. Newer tanks must follow similar rules.

19.8 LOCKS AND SECURITY SYSTEMS

Keep your building safe and secure.

A whole book could be devoted to the various kinds of locks and security systems, but we will only make a few points concerning regular locks:
- If you do not want to have your keys multiply like rabbits, buy a lock with duplication control, such as with Medeco.
- If you install a deadbolt, make sure that you buy one with a long bolt.
- If your lock is of decent quality, the weak area will be either the door itself or, more often, its frame. So it is a good idea to reinforce door frames and, often, doors. In fact, it is an absolute must if you are serious about preventing unauthorized entrance.

19.8.1 LOCKS

Today, the most exciting developments in entry control are keyless locks. There are many types, for example, keypad, card reader, fingerprint reader, and biometric products (face or eye recognition). Some locks are connected to a central computer (a server), while others are stand-alone. Centrally controlled electronic systems have many advantages:
- Keys cannot be lost or duplicated by non-authorized persons.
- Users can have their access limited to certain times, or disallowed entirely.
- Many users can be programmed (up to 500 for most manufacturers).
- The software keeps track of who enters, and when, and can print reports.

You will eliminate annoyances and risks such as having keys hidden outside the building, as many people do for convenience, loaning keys to service people, and re-keying when a key is lost or an employee is fired.

There are also locks that are computer controlled, but these differ from the centrally controlled electronic systems. These computer-managed locks also offer terrific advantages:
- They can be programmed with software from a laptop or PDA.
- New users, access points, and access privileges can be programmed in seconds.
- The locks can be programmed to keep people out of areas or to be allowed access only at certain times.

The savings realized can be phenomenal. A good example is a school in California that installed 573 new locks. With the old, conventional system, it took a specialist 9 weeks to re-key all the doors, at a cost of $25,000. Now, it takes 2.5 hours to reprogram and replace a card for all the locks, at a cost of less than $100. Thus, these systems are suitable for larger buildings.

Yet another system is Cyberlock, a US company. Its "intelligent" lock cylinders are designed to quickly convert mechanical lock hardware into fully functioning access control systems. It can restrict users' access to specific locks at pre-selected days and times. A complete record of all entries and denied entries is stored in both the lock and the key, providing an audit trail of events for management.

One simple stand-alone system is the programmable locking system, which is an electronic keypad combined with a door lock. One sophisticated model now on the market can store up to 100 codes. It takes only 10 seconds to add or delete users. Its four AA batteries will last three years.

These devices are attractive, flexible, and economical to code, easy to install on existing doors, and make your building look modern, which increases its appeal. You can also say goodbye to visits from a locksmith every time you change tenants, fire somebody, or a tagged key is lost. Retail cost is $500-$600 per door, plus installation. Some systems with fewer features are less expensive, starting at around $200.

Another kind of lock uses a lever-shaped door handle and functions without batteries. The system generates power every time you turn the lever — no batteries to replace. It is simpler and cheaper to install than a hard-wired system, but cannot be controlled from a central computer. The lock records the last 30,000 events and the information can be retrieved easily via a PDA. It can accommodate up to 3,000 users. It is suitable mainly where only a few locks are required. The cost varies with the model, but ranges from $1,200-$1,600.

19.8.2 ALARM SYSTEMS

The problem with common alarm systems is that thieves have 5-10 minutes to grab the most valuable items and run, before police or security personnel arrive on the scene. We recommend a rarely used approach – fog systems in combination with a traditional burglar alarm system. Two Canadian manufacturers are Fog Security Systems Inc. of Winnipeg and Arias Tech Ltd. of Mississauga.

The concept of a fog system is simple and elegant. The fog system is activated by the burglar alarm system when a person enters illegally. The fog is created by introducing a fluid solution into a heater block under pressure. When the vapour is reintroduced into the atmosphere, it cools and condenses, forming fog particles that are suspended in the air. It does not soil anything and it does not interfere with any precision equipment such as computers, however, it is virtually impossible to steal from a room protected with this system. Within seconds a burglar cannot see his shoes — very uncomfortable! The fluid used is glycol, which is harmless. The fog will remain a maximum of 2 hours, less if you use a fan.

The performance of these systems is phenomenal. One of them discharges nearly 1,700 m^3 (60,000 cu ft) per minute for the basic system, and nearly 8,500 m^3 (300,000 cu ft) for the static industrial model, which will fill a room measuring (18 x 30.5 x 3 m) (60 x 100 x 10 ft).

19.8.3 FIRE DOORS

It is now compulsory to have fire-rated doors providing a minimum 20 minutes of fire resistance between residential units and corridors, and in commercial buildings. To replace an existing door with a new one costs $400-$700. It is possible to retrofit existing doors, rather than replacing them, by covering them with thin fire-resistant materials (see <www.fireskin.com> (Ever Ready Technologies: 877-600-0072)).

Check the fire rating of the doors during your due diligence period. The rating label must be visible on the edge of the door (not painted over). If no label is visible, assume that the door is not rated.

19.9 BUILDING STAIRWAYS

Appreciate the complexities of building stairways.

Stair building is never easy and a circular stairway is one of the most complex aspects of carpentry. When designing them, one must consider the following three factors — the form (appearance), the function, and the available space. If a day comes when you must build a stairway, you will be faced with two opposing forces — comfort (and safety) and cost.

It will be helpful if you are familiar with stair terminology:
- Baluster: The vertical piece that joins the handrail and base rail. Also called a spindle.
- Going: The horizontal distance between the face of the first and last risers. The total going is the total horizontal length of the stair.
- Landing: The horizontal area that can be at the end of, or part way up, the stair and acts as a resting place or permits a change of direction.
- Newell: The post at the bottom of a handrail.
- Nosing: The horizontally projecting edge (over the riser) of a stair edge.
- Pitch Line: The imaginary line connecting the nosings of all treads in a flight of stairs.
- Rake: The angle of ascent, slope, or pitch of a stairway.
- Rise: The vertical distance between the floors (or landings) connected by the flight.
- Riser: The vertical element of a set of stairs. Most frequently, it is a 2.5 x 20.3 cm (1 x 8 in) board nailed to the stringers.
- Staircase: The entire structure making up a stair.
- Stairwell: The space provided for the stairs.
- Step: The combination of tread and riser.
- Stringers: The lateral supporting pieces.
- Tread: The top, horizontal surface of a step.
- Winders: The radiating treads that are wider at one end and narrower at the other. They are used to accommodate a change in direction of 90 or 180 degrees.

The ideal step or tread is 17 cm high and 27 cm deep (6.69 x 10.63 in). This is a terrific standard, but rarely used because it requires a lot more room than, say, a 20 x 24 cm (7.87 x 9.45 in) step. In North America, the generally recommended maximum is 20 cm (7.87 in) for the height and minimum 23 cm (9.06 in) for the depth.

Let's compare 17 cm and 20 cm treads, for a ten-foot (3.05 m) high stairway:
- 3.05/.17 = 18 steps in height; 18 x 27 cm = 4.86 m (16 ft), the length of the stairway.
- 3.05/.20 = 15 steps in height; 15 x 24 cm = 3.60 m (12 ft), the length of the stairway.

The difference in the stairway length is 1.26 m (4 ft) times, say 1.26 m (4 ft) in width, equals 1.487 m² x $1,076/m² = $1,600 (16 sq ft x $100/sq ft = $1,600) more for the more comfortable, 17-cm high step.

In Canada, the recommended stairway specifications are as follows:
- riser height: maximum 20.32 cm (8 in)
- tread extension: minimum 22.86 cm (9 in)
- stair width: minimum 91.44 cm (36 in)
- head clearance: minimum 203.2 cm (6 ft 8 in). With the increasing height of the population, it would be wiser to use 208.4 cm (6 ft 10 in), and

- handrail: 86.36-96.52 cm (34-38 in) above the stair nosing
  - minimum 3.81 cm diameter (1.5 in)
  - maximum 5.08 cm diameter (2 in)
  - required at stairways having four or more risers
  - at the bottom, the handrail should extend along the pitch line one tread depth, plus 30.5 cm (12 in), horizontally, and
  - at the top, the handrail should extend horizontally 30.5 cm (12 in).

It is wise, when dealing with stairs made of concrete or tiles, to install stairs that have the edge of the steps rounded or protected in some way. If there is no protection, the edges get damaged very quickly and this can become quite dangerous. It is prudent, too, to install anti-skid products to prevent accidents. These can be cast metal, extruded aluminium, coatings, or pressure sensitive anti-skid surfaces.

Lighting is an often neglected factor in stairways. Many do not have proper lighting or properly placed switches. For more information and drawings that will help you understand better the contents of this topic, see CMHC's Web site: <www.cmhc.ca/en/burema/gesein/abhose/abhose_079.cfm>.

19.10 INTELLIGENT BUILDINGS

Select the features that will improve your building's efficiency.

There is no standard definition of what constitutes an intelligent building. The Continental Automated Buildings Association (CABA) is an industry association that promotes advanced technology for the automation of buildings in North America. Frank Spitzer, co-author of a recently released 60-page CABA document, *The Technology Roadmap for Intelligent Buildings*, suggests that an intelligent building is "a building and its infrastructure, which provides the owner, operator and occupant with an environment which is flexible, effective, comfortable and secure, through the use of integrated technological building systems, communications and controls."

The concept, therefore, is to control all operating systems, including HVAC, lighting, fire, voice, data, T.V., video, security, access, safety, and Internet, by way of one single computerized system.

On one hand, an intelligent building will cost the landlord more money because it requires more complete communication and control systems than is typical and the landlord must pay for some systems that tenants paid for themselves in the past. On the other hand, the landlord will have a more sophisticated building, will lower energy costs, higher rentals, and will be able to more easily attract tenants and, probably, better-quality tenants. For more information, see <www.caba.org>.

While it is most efficient to create an intelligent building at the initial phases of design and construction, it is possible to retrofit a building. In these instances, usually the main objective is to lower energy costs. This can be very involved and is achieved by improving the building's insulation and by using systems and strategies that are more efficient. Usually, it starts with a study conducted by a building retrofit specialist. Depending on the scope and the budget, it can be as simple as switching to T8 or T5 lamps and installing occupancy sensors where they will do the most good, or you can do the complete project and update all the building mechanicals, including the plumbing, heating, air conditioning, and electrical systems.

Buildings are commonly upgraded by the following retrofits:
* replacing outdated, inefficient boilers and cooling systems with high-efficiency units
* installing programmable thermostats
* installing reduced or flow-controlled water valves
* replacing old toilets with 6 or less litre-per-flush fixtures
* installing geothermal HVAC systems and solar walls
* changing lighting systems to high-efficiency ones, using T8 or T5 lighting with reflectors or HID lamps
* installing occupancy sensors
* installing individual electrical switches in each room
* replacing old fire exit sign bulbs with LEDs
* improving the insulation of walls and roof
* replacing old, single pane windows with thermopane units
* installing heat recovery and economizer systems, if possible, and
* installing cushions at truck level doors, in industrial buildings.

Rare is the owner who will replace or modernize everything at once, but out of the above list there are items that do not cost a lot of money and save a lot of energy. The sad part is that when an owner is trying to meet a budget, be it when constructing a new building or in an existing one, mechanical systems are historically cut first. Therefore imagine how difficult it is for a building retrofit specialist to tell a building owner, who is about to undertake renovations to improve the leasing appeal of a building, the following: "I know that your HVAC system and your toilets function properly, but we still maintain that you should replace them with more energy-efficient units".

APPENDIX

Checklists

The Checklists following can be found within the chapters indicated along with an appropriate discussion. They have been reproduced here for your convenience.

Chapter 13: Real Estate Agencies
13.1 Property Brief Checklist

Chapter 15: Considerations When Buying Each Property Type
15.1 Acquisition Checklist for Industrial Property
15.2 Acquisition Checklist for Retail Property
15.3 Acquisition Checklist for Office Building
15.4 Acquisition Checklist for Multi-Family Buildings

Chapter 16: Buying and Selling
16.1 Data Gathering Checklist
16.2 Property Analysis Checklist
16.3 Due Diligence Building Acquisition Checklist

Chapter 17: Leasing
17.1 Landlord's Post-Tenancy Checklist
17.2 Building Lease Review Checklist
17.3 Pre-Move-In Checklist for Tenants

Checklist 13.1
Property Brief Checklist

PROPERTY BRIEF CHECKLIST

Used by a listing agent to prepare a Property Brief to aid in selling (or leasing) a property.

Property Address:
- ❏ Give a number to the presentation, preceded with the letter L for Land or B for Building or O for Others. Example: B103, and enter it, with the address in your "Property Brief" list
- ❏ Check the assessment rolls. We do it using the Toronto Real Estate Board's Database
- ❏ Obtain last tax bill or tax assessment
- ❏ Get surveys and building plans
- ❏ Secure relevant maps (regional, municipal, local / neighbourhood)
- ❏ Make a list of important neighbours and amenities
- ❏ Gather transportation data, driving times, distances, time tables, etc.
- ❏ Take / secure photographs: Aerial, (colour if possible), exterior and interior
- ❏ Write the letter of accompaniment (if you intend to send the Brief to different people, which is likely)
- ❏ Write an Area Analysis
- ❏ Write a Neighbourhood Analysis
- ❏ Write a Property Analysis

Property Specifications and Other Details:
- ❏ Location
- ❏ Land details
- ❏ Building details
- ❏ Construction details
- ❏ Possession date
- ❏ Realty taxes
- ❏ Insurance
- ❏ Heating costs
- ❏ Utilities costs
- ❏ Public transit
- ❏ Remarks
- ❏ Price/rental
- ❏ Show possible Building divisions on the floor plan or sketch
- ❏ List the advantages of locating at .....

    EXHIBITS
    A =   Location map
    B =   Map showing highways
    C =   Map showing main points of interest
    D =   Land sketch or survey
    E =   Building plan
    F =   Office plan
    G =   Photos
    H =   Zoning By-law map
    I =   Zoning By-law excerpts
    J =   Toronto Transit Corporation (public transportation)
- ❏ You Are Working with ... your name (resume +)
- ❏ A Company is Known By the Company It Keeps .....(names of previous clients)
- ❏ Pouch =   City map or key map
- ❏ Include: "Submitted subject to change in price, errors, omissions and withdrawal without notice".

Checklist 15.1
Acquisition Checklist for Industrial Property

ACQUISITION CHECKLIST FOR INDUSTRIAL PROPERTY

Property address: _____

Square Footage: _____

Type of property / Present use / Highest and best use _____

1- OWNERSHIP
- ☐ Owner's name
- ☐ Listed by
- ☐ Previously listed / how long / at what price
- ☐ Reason for disposition / degree of urgency

2- LOCATION
- ☐ Determine boundaries of neighbourhood
- ☐ Proximity to nearest city or metropolitan area
- ☐ Proximity to major freeways / closest one / distance
- ☐ Railroad siding
- ☐ Trucking services / availability / rates / schedules
- ☐ Distance to major airport / port
- ☐ Proximity of raw material sources / delivery / storage
- ☐ Nature of industry in area
- ☐ Proximity of major markets
- ☐ Radius of overnight shipping / distance / population
- ☐ Public transportation
- ☐ Location Rating: 1 to 5 (best)
- ☐ Neighbours: types / compatibility

3- LAND
- ☐ Lot size / survey
- ☐ Coverage
- ☐ Expansion possible to
- ☐ Zoning
- ☐ Legal description
- ☐ Parking / number of spaces
- ☐ Topography
- ☐ Truck turning radius
- ☐ Landscaping
- ☐ Lawn sprinklers
- ☐ Easements / covenants
- ☐ Pavement / type / condition

4- BUILDING
- ☐ Building dimensions and square footage / number of stories
- ☐ Office dimensions and square footage / number of private offices / condition
- ☐ Expansion potential
- ☐ Floor plans
- ☐ Multiple uses or special purpose
- ☐ Age of building
- ☐ General condition / functional obsolescence
- ☐ Type of construction: concrete, concrete block, tilt-up, corrugated metal, other
- ☐ Type of roof / condition / age / insulation
- ☐ Type of floors / condition / thickness / load capacity / metallic hardener / sealant / densifier
- ☐ Ceiling height under joists
- ☐ Clear span / column spacing
- ☐ Skylights / number / sizes / single or double pane

- ❑ Exhaust vents
- ❑ Air make-up units
- ❑ Wiring / voltage / amps
- ❑ Lighting / type / outside lights / photocells / foot candles
- ❑ Drains / number / size
- ❑ Toilets / number / location
- ❑ Sprinkler / fire protection system
- ❑ Burglar alarm / special locks
- ❑ Number of truck level doors / size / levellers / door cushions / condition / manual / electric
- ❑ Number of drive-in doors / size / manual / electric
- ❑ Number of rail doors / distance between each door
- ❑ Dock height / excavated loading dock (ramp) / covered (canopy)
- ❑ Inside shipping bay / depth / width / dock height / leveller
- ❑ Building rating: 1 to 5 (best)
- ❑ Energy saving fixtures / systems

5- COMMUNITY

- ❑ Property tax system and assessment rules
- ❑ Closest police department / fire station
- ❑ Closest medical and hospital facilities
- ❑ Schools, churches, universities, libraries, recreation facilities, etc.
- ❑ Business amenities / banks / restaurants / various suppliers
- ❑ State of neighbourhood / stable / deteriorating / improving

6- DEMOGRAPHICS

- ❑ Present population of area ethnicity
- ❑ Average income per family and family size
- ❑ Population growth trend / past 5 years / projected

7- LABOUR MARKET

- ❑ Total estimated employment
- ❑ Availability of skilled and unskilled labour / abundant / average / tight
- ❑ Union or non-union / history of strikes
- ❑ Wage rates / hours overtime / fringe benefits

8- CLIMATE AND NATURAL HAZARDS

- ❑ Temperatures / average / minimum / maximum
- ❑ Rainfall in inches / rainy season
- ❑ Humidity / average / minimum / maximum
- ❑ Prevalent winds
- ❑ Fog conditions
- ❑ Fire hazards
- ❑ Inundation hazards

9- SERVICES, UTILITIES AND FUEL

- ❑ Electrical power / connected / availability / connection charges / rates
- ❑ Natural gas / available / capacity / rates
- ❑ Water / source / flow / pressure / rates / chemical analysis
- ❑ Telephone / number of lines in place
- ❑ Oil / cost
- ❑ Internet (T1, high speed, dial-up)

10- EQUIPMENT

- ❑ Cranes / type / capacity in tons / height under hook
- ❑ Heating / type / age
- ❑ Air-conditioning
- ❑ Boiler(s) / type / BTU's / backup fuel
- ❑ Piping / air / steam / pressure
- ❑ Electrical substation / transformers / size / capacity / location / owned by / bus ducts
- ❑ Back up electrical generator / make / type / capacity / fuel
- ❑ Condition of equipment / obsolescence

11- INCOME

- ❏ Tenant's name(s) / tenant or sub-tenant
- ❏ Type of business / how long
- ❏ Capitalization of business
- ❏ Dun & Bradstreet rating
- ❏ Banking information
- ❏ Other financial and/or credit information
- ❏ Number of years remaining on lease / rent escalation / option to renew, at what rent
- ❏ Tax escalation clause in lease
- ❏ Exterior maintenance (by owner / tenant)
- ❏ Other clauses in lease (Option to Buy, Right of First Refusal)
- ❏ Annual gross / net income

12- EXPENSES

- ❏ Property taxes / date last appealed?
- ❏ Hazard, public liability and rental income insurance (classification) / coverage / premium / insurer
- ❏ Utilities / deferred maintenance / cost to remedy / reserves for replacements
- ❏ Legal and accounting fees
- ❏ Others

13- EXISTING FINANCING

- ❏ Original mortgage amount / term / amortization / starting date / due date / balloon payment
- ❏ Mortgage(s) balance / As of what date / monthly payments / Interest rate
- ❏ Yearly debt service / interest payments / principal re payments
- ❏ Lender / address / phone / fax
- ❏ Loan number
- ❏ Prepayment penalty, and special provisions, if any
- ❏ Loan locked in / until when
- ❏ Loan transferable / assumption fee
- ❏ Any second loan? Can it be bought at a discount? If so, what discount?

14- POTENTIAL FINANCING

- ❏ Mortgage commitment / amount / interest / term / payments / loan fees / loan points / lender
- ❏ Will Vendor take back a mortgage / amount / interest / due date

15- PRICE

- ❏ Asking price / total / per square foot
- ❏ Price per square foot of comparable buildings recently sold
- ❏ Likely sale price and Cap Rate

16- EXHIBITS

- ❏ Survey / site plan
- ❏ Building floor plan
- ❏ Photographs
- ❏ Area map with property shown
- ❏ Inspection reports (pest control, roof, building condition, environmental, mechanical systems)
- ❏ Certified operating statements for last 3 years
- ❏ Copies of leases and rental agreements
- ❏ Copies of management contracts

NOTE

Inspect property carefully. Talk to neighbours. The bulk of the outside information can be obtained from 3 major sources: Planning Department, Chamber of Commerce, and Public Libraries.

Remarks:

Checklist 15.2
Acquisition Checklist for Retail Property

ACQUISITION CHECKLIST FOR RETAIL PROPERTY

Property address:_____

Type of property: _____

Square footage: Gross _____   Rentable _____   Usable_____

Number of Tenants _____   Building Name _____

1- OWNERSHIP

- ❑ Owner's name
- ❑ Listed by
- ❑ Previously listed / how long / at what price
- ❑ Reason for disposition / degree of urgency

2- LOCATION

- ❑ Population of town
- ❑ Quality of address 1-5 (best)
- ❑ Exposure 1-5 (best)
- ❑ Signalized corner
- ❑ Median strip / left turn lane
- ❑ Public transportation
- ❑ Proximity to: main arteries / freeways / large apartment buildings
- ❑ Traffic patterns / planned streets / street widenings
- ❑ If Shopping Centre: neighbourhood / community / regional
- ❑ Location rating: 1 to 5 (best)
- ❑ Is area, neighbourhood, or street deteriorating / improving / stable

3- LAND

- ❑ Lot dimensions / size
- ❑ Coverage
- ❑ Zoning
- ❑ Legal description
- ❑ Easements / covenants
- ❑ Parking lot / number of cars / location / paving / condition
- ❑ Access for customers / shipping / receiving
- ❑ Landscaping
- ❑ Expansion / possible acquisition of extra land

4- BUILDING

- ❑ Square footage / frontage / depth / layout / % of rentable area
- ❑ Number of stories or levels
- ❑ Basement / foundations
- ❑ Use restrictions, if any
- ❑ Expansion potential / how much
- ❑ Age of building
- ❑ Architectural appeal
- ❑ Condition / functional obsolescence
- ❑ Type of construction
- ❑ Exterior finish / condition
- ❑ Exterior signage / pilons / fascia
- ❑ Roof / type / condition / age
- ❑ Floors / size / number / type / condition / load capacity of each floor

- ❏ Clear ceiling height
- ❏ Electrical service / wiring / voltage, amperage
- ❏ Lighting / intensity level in foot candles / kind of fixtures / lamps
- ❏ Backup power generator / make / type / capacity / fuel
- ❏ Type of HVAC / age / condition
- ❏ Toilets / type / number / location
- ❏ Sprinklers and fireproofing system
- ❏ Energy retrofit
- ❏ Burglar alarm / special locks / surveillance cameras
- ❏ Special equipment / garbage compactor
- ❏ Loading dock(s) / height / dock leveller
- ❏ Internet (T1, dial-up, high speed)
- ❏ Energy saving measure / systems

5- INCOME

- ❏ Rent Roll of triple A tenants
- ❏ Income from parking and others
- ❏ Sales per square metre (square foot)
- ❏ Type of businesses / how long in business / Dun & Bradstreet rating / quality of tenant mix and merchandising mix
- ❏ Other financial / credit information
- ❏ Centre total yearly rental (net or gross) per square foot / per front foot of store / expenses / NOI
- ❏ Percentage leases / overage / how calculated
- ❏ Overage of last 3 years
- ❏ Number of years remaining on lease(s) / rent escalation / renewal option, at what rent
- ❏ Tax escalation clause in lease
- ❏ Responsibility for exterior maintenance: owner/tenants
- ❏ Other terms of net lease (including Option to Buy, Right of First Refusal)
- ❏ Management fee charged to tenants

6- EXPENSES

- ❏ Property taxes / date last appealed?
- ❏ Hazard, liability, and rental income insurance (classification) / coverage / premium
- ❏ Services
- ❏ Utilities
- ❏ Garbage collection
- ❏ Salaries / number of staff
- ❏ Maintenance / repairs / deferred maintenance / Cost to remedy / reserve for replacements
- ❏ Leasing commissions payable
- ❏ Promotions
- ❏ Legal and accounting fees
- ❏ Merchant association
- ❏ Others

7- EXISTING FINANCING

- ❏ Original mortgage amount / term / amortization / starting date
- ❏ Due Date / balloon payment
- ❏ Mortgage(s) balance / as of what date
- ❏ Monthly payments
- ❏ Interest rate and due date
- ❏ Annual debt service / interest payments / principal repayments
- ❏ Lender / address / phone / fax
- ❏ Loan number
- ❏ Prepayment penalty, and special provisions, if any
- ❏ Loan locked in / until when
- ❏ Is loan transferable / assumption fee
- ❏ Any second loan? Can it be bought at a discount? If so, what discount?

8- POTENTIAL FINANCING

- ❏ Mortgage commitment / amount / interest / term / amortization / loan fee / loan points / lender
- ❏ Will Vendor take back a mortgage / amount / interest / due date

9- PRICE

- ❏ Asking price / total / per square foot / Cap Rate
- ❏ Estimated selling price and Cap Rate

10- AREA SURVEY

- ❏ Determine boundaries / neighbourhood / market area
- ❏ Traffic count in front and at nearest intersection (per day, week, month, year)
- ❏ Distance to nearest competitive centres / businesses (if only a few)
- ❏ Estimated population within market area / ethnicity
- ❏ Average income per family
- ❏ Population growth / past 5 years / projected
- ❏ Is area, neighbourhood or street / deteriorating / improving / stable

12 – COMMUNITY

- ❏ Property tax system and assessment rules
- ❏ Closest police department / fire station
- ❏ Closest medical and hospital facilities
- ❏ Business amenities / banks / restaurants / various suppliers

13- EXHIBITS

- ❏ Survey / Site plan
- ❏ Floor plan
- ❏ Photographs
- ❏ Area map with property shown
- ❏ Inspection reports (pest control, building condition, environmental, roof, HVAC systems, sprinklers, security, elevators, etc.)
- ❏ Certified operating statements for last 3 years
- ❏ Copies of leases and rental agreements
- ❏ Copies of management contracts
- ❏ Inventory of personal property

NOTE: *Inspect property carefully. Talk to neighbours. The bulk of the outside information can be obtained from 3 major sources: Planning Department, Chamber of Commerce and Public Libraries*

REMARKS:

Checklist 15.3
Acquisition Checklist for Office Building

ACQUISITION CHECKLIST FOR OFFICE BUILDING

Property address: _____

Type of property: _____

Square footage: Gross _____ Rentable_____ Usable_____

Number of Tenants_____ Class (A, B, C, D)_____ Building name _____

1- OWNERSHIP
- [ ] Owner's name
- [ ] Listed by
- [ ] Previously listed / how long / at what price
- [ ] Reason for disposition / degree of urgency

2- LOCATION
- [ ] Population of town
- [ ] Quality of address 1-5 (best)
- [ ] Quality of location 1-5 (best)
- [ ] Exposure
- [ ] Public transportation
- [ ] Amenities
- [ ] Proximity to freeways
- [ ] Potential changes in desirability of location
- [ ] Parking / on site / nearby
- [ ] Is area, neighbourhood, or street / deteriorating / improving / stable
- [ ] Competition

3- LAND
- [ ] Lot dimensions / size
- [ ] Coverage / density
- [ ] Zoning
- [ ] Legal description
- [ ] Easements / covenants
- [ ] Parking / number of cars / location / paving / condition
- [ ] Shipping / receiving facilities
- [ ] Landscaping
- [ ] Expansion / possible acquisition of extra land

4- BUILDING
- [ ] Square footage / frontage / depth / layout
- [ ] Number of stories or levels
- [ ] Size of floor plate
- [ ] Basement / foundations
- [ ] Use restrictions, if any
- [ ] Age of building
- [ ] Architectural appeal
- [ ] General condition / functional obsolescence / view
- [ ] Type of construction
- [ ] Type of entrance and lobby
- [ ] Exterior finish / condition
- [ ] Exterior signage / pilons / fascia
- [ ] Roof / type / condition / age
- [ ] Floors / condition / load capacity of each floor / coverings

- ❑ Type of windows / size / opening or not
- ❑ Ceiling type / height
- ❑ Electrical service / wiring / voltage, amperage
- ❑ Backup power generator make / type / capacity / fuel
- ❑ Toilet facilities / number and location
- ❑ Lighting / intensity level in foot candles at desk height / kind of fixtures / lamps
- ❑ Type of HVAC / age / condition / ventilation
- ❑ Sprinklers / fireproofing
- ❑ Energy retrofit
- ❑ Elevators / number / speed / service elevators
- ❑ Shipping and receiving facilities / loading dock(s) / how many / height
- ❑ Burglar alarm / special locks / security
- ❑ Storage facilities for tenants
- ❑ Special equipment
- ❑ Common facilities: meeting rooms, cafeteria, concierge, etc.
- ❑ Internet (T1, dial-up, high speed)
- ❑ Building rating within its class (1-5 best)
- ❑ Energy saving features / systems

5- INCOME

- ❑ Rent Roll / % of Triple A tenants
- ❑ Annual gross / net income
- ❑ Income from parking and others
- ❑ Yearly rental (net or gross?) per square foot
- ❑ Rents / higher / lower / similar to competition
- ❑ Tax escalation clause in leases
- ❑ Other terms of leases (including Option to Buy, Right of First Refusal)
- ❑ Management fee charged to tenants

6- EXPENSES

- ❑ Property taxes / date last appealed?
- ❑ Hazard, liability, and rental income insurance (classification) / coverage / premium
- ❑ Services
- ❑ Utilities
- ❑ Garbage collection
- ❑ Salaries / number of staff
- ❑ Janitor / window cleaning
- ❑ Maintenance / repairs / deferred maintenance / cost to remedy / reserve for replacements
- ❑ Leasing commissions payable
- ❑ Reserve for personal property items (e.g., fridges)
- ❑ Legal and accounting fees
- ❑ Others

7- EXISTING FINANCING

- ❑ Original mortgage amount / term / amortization / starting date / due date / balloon payment
- ❑ Mortgage(s) balance / as of what date
- ❑ Monthly payments / interest rate
- ❑ Annual debt service / interest payments / principal repayments
- ❑ Lender / address / phone / fax
- ❑ Loan number
- ❑ Prepayment penalty, and special provisions, if any
- ❑ Loan locked in / until when
- ❑ Transferable / assumption fee
- ❑ Any second loan? Can it be bought at a discount? If so, what discount?

8- POTENTIAL FINANCING

- ❑ Mortgage commitment / amount / interest / term / amortization / loan fee / loan points / lender
- ❑ Will Vendor take back a mortgage / amount / interest / due date

9- PRICE

❑ Asking price / total / per square foot and Cap Rate
❑ Price per m² (sq ft) of comparable buildings recently sold
❑ Estimated selling price and Cap Rate

10 – COMMUNITY

❑ Property tax system and assessment rules
❑ Closest police department / fire station
❑ Closest medical and hospital facilities
❑ Business amenities / banks / restaurants / various suppliers
❑ State of neighbourhood / stable / deteriorating / improving

11- EXHIBITS

❑ Survey / site plan
❑ Building floor plan
❑ Photographs
❑ Area map with property shown
❑ Inspection reports (pest control, building condition, environmental, roof, HVAC mechanical systems)
❑ Certified operating statements for last 3 years
❑ Copies of leases and rental agreements
❑ Copies of management contracts
❑ Inventory of personal property

NOTE: *Inspect property carefully. Talk to neighbours. The bulk of the outside information can be obtained from 3 major sources: Planning Department, Chamber of Commerce and Public Libraries.*

REMARKS:

Checklist 15.4
Acquisition Checklist for Multi-Family Building

ACQUISITION CHECKLIST FOR MULTI-FAMILY BUILDING

Property address: _____

Number of units: _____

1- OWNERSHIP
- ☐ Owner's name
- ☐ Listed by
- ☐ Previously listed / how long / at what price
- ☐ Reason for disposition / degree of urgency

2- LOCATION
- ☐ Population of town
- ☐ Proximity to Downtown / employment (type) / schools / shopping
- ☐ Public transportation
- ☐ Access to street, arterial roads, distance to closest freeways, etc
- ☐ Nearby amenities
- ☐ Area recreational facilities
- ☐ Location rating: 1 to 5 (best)
- ☐ Is area, neighbourhood, or street / deteriorating/improving/stable

3- LAND
- ☐ Lot dimensions / size
- ☐ Zoning
- ☐ Legal description
- ☐ Parking: surface #... underground #...Total...
- ☐ Lawn sprinklers
- ☐ Condition of grounds
- ☐ Expansion potential

4- BUILDING
- ☐ Builder's name
- ☐ Age of building / roof
- ☐ Number of stories
- ☐ Type of construction
- ☐ Square footage
- ☐ Floor plate area
- ☐ Type of roof / condition / age
- ☐ Exterior finish / condition
- ☐ Basement / foundations
- ☐ Storage lockers
- ☐ Laundry facilities (owned / leased)
- ☐ Garbage chutes
- ☐ Elevators
- ☐ Individual meters - gas / electricity
- ☐ Wiring / type / condition
- ☐ Backup power generator make / type / capacity / fuel
- ☐ Plumbing (copper / galvanized) / condition
- ☐ Heating / type / age / condition
- ☐ Air-conditioning / age / condition
- ☐ Sprinklers and fireproofing system
- ☐ Interior corridors / type of floor covering / condition
- ☐ Is property up-to-date regarding government regulations: fire, etc.
- ☐ Deferred maintenance
- ☐ Internet (dial-up, high speed)

❑ TV cable
❑ Energy saving / features / systems

5- APARTMENTS

❑ # of each type: bachelor / ....1BR / ....2BR / ....3BR   OTHER.............   Total:..........
❑ Views / number of suites with / quality of
❑ Broadloom
❑ Drapes
❑ Stoves / built-in / condition / age
❑ Refrigerators / brands / condition / age
❑ Dishwashers / brands / condition / age
❑ Garbage disposals
❑ Bathrooms / tubs / showers over tub / stall showers
❑ Storage space and closets
❑ Intercom system
❑ Cable TV / Satellite dish / cost / paid by
❑ Decks, balconies, patios
❑ Condition of apartments: 1 to 5 (best)
❑ Size of rooms (large / average / small)
❑ Quality of interior finishes (deluxe / average / economy)
❑ Typical occupants / families / couples / singles / age groups / occupation / economic level

6- RENTALS

❑ Using 2 to 3 apartments of each type, show: apartment number, number of bedrooms, number of bathrooms, rent per month / per square foot, square footage, and potential rental (if logical)
❑ Scheduled annual gross income
❑ Vacancies & Bad Debts, in $
❑ Vacancy factor in percent of annual gross income
❑ Income from garages and/or laundry and/or _____
❑ Last 3 year audited rental income statements
❑ Are rents comparable, higher or lower than average rents of similar units in neighbourhood?
❑ Possible conversion to condos?

7- EXPENSES

❑ Property taxes / date last appealed?
❑ Hazard insurance: premium / coverage
❑ Liability insurance: premium / coverage
❑ Rental income insurance
❑ Electricity
❑ Gas
❑ Water
❑ Sewer charge
❑ Garbage collection
❑ Elevator maintenance service
❑ Pool maintenance service
❑ Janitor and/or gardener
❑ Resident caretaker / salary or rent allowance
❑ Rental agent / salary or rent allowance
❑ Legal and accounting fees
❑ Administrative expenses / salaries
❑ Reserves: maintenance / repairs / replacements
❑ Maintenance: Are there signs of substandard maintenance / what needs to be done soon / cost?
❑ Reserve for replacement of personal property / what needs to be replaced soon / cost?
❑ Are expenses in keeping with similar buildings in the neighbourhood?

8- EXISTING FINANCING

❑ Original mortgage amount / term / amortization starting date
❑ Due date / balloon payment
❑ Mortgage(s) balance / as of what date
❑ Monthly payments
❑ Interest rate and due date

- ❏ Annual debt service / interest payments / principal repayments
- ❏ Lender / address / phone / fax
- ❏ Loan number
- ❏ Prepayment penalty, and special provisions, if any
- ❏ Loan locked in / until when
- ❏ Is loan transferable / assumption fee?
- ❏ If there is a second loan? Can it be bought at a discount / if so, what discount?

9- POTENTIAL FINANCING

- ❏ Loan commitment / amount / interest / term / payments / loan fee / loan points / lender
- ❏ Will Vendor take back a mortgage / amount / interest / due date

10- RETURN FOR FIRST YEAR

Scheduled and additional (garages, laundry) Annual Income

- ❏ Less — Vacancy and bad debt allowance
- ❏ Equals — Gross Operating Income
- ❏ Less — Operating Costs
- ❏ Equals — Net Operating Income
- ❏ Less — Annual Debt Service (payments on principal and interest)
- ❏ Equals — Cash flow (gross spendable income)
- ❏ Plus — Annual principal payments
- ❏ Equals — ROE

11- NEIGHBOURHOOD AND MARKET ANALYSIS

- ❏ Determine boundaries of neighbourhood and analyze it
- ❏ Economic level of people in area (typical occupations)
- ❏ Average income / per family / per person
- ❏ Typical family size
- ❏ Ratio of homeowners to tenants
- ❏ Population growth / past 5 years / projected
- ❏ Number of competitive apartment buildings within neighbourhood / # of apartments
- ❏ Rents in comparable buildings
- ❏ Cap Rates of comparable properties recently sold
- ❏ State of neighbourhood / stable / deteriorating / improving

12- PRICE

- ❏ Asking price, Cap Rate
- ❏ Likely sale price, Cap Rate
- ❏ Income / *Be aware of higher than average rents due to excellent management, special deals on leases, or expenses kept artificially low, and of lower than average rents due to poor management*

13 – COMMUNITY

- ❏ Property tax system and assessment rules
- ❏ Closest police department / fire station
- ❏ Closest medical and hospital facilities
- ❏ Shopping amenities / supermarkets / banks / restaurants / various
- ❏ State of neighbourhood / stable / deteriorating / improving

14- EXHIBITS

- ❏ Survey / site plan
- ❏ Floor plans
- ❏ Photographs / ground / aerial
- ❏ Area map with property shown
- ❏ Rent rolls
- ❏ Inspection reports (pest control, roof, building condition, environmental, mechanical systems, elevators, etc.)
- ❏ Certified operating statements for last 3 years
- ❏ Copies of leases and rental agreements
- ❏ Copies of management contracts
- ❏ Inventory of personal property

NOTE: *Inspect property carefully. Talk to neighbours and to a few tenants. The bulk of outside information can be obtained from 4 major sources: Planning Department, Chamber of Commerce, CMHC (Central Mortgage and Housing Corporation (in Canada)) and Public Libraries.*

Checklist 16.1
Data Gathering Checklist

DATA GATHERING CHECKLIST

Property Address: _____

Listed with:_____ Tel: _____

1- Land:
- ☐ Dimensions
- ☐ Area
- ☐ Access
- ☐ Drainage
- ☐ Sunlight
- ☐ Services
- ☐ Survey
- ☐ Environmental condition

2- Building:
- ☐ Dimensions
- ☐ Area
- ☐ Construction (brick, frame, other)
- ☐ Number of stories
- ☐ Basement (height and access)
- ☐ Units (#, type, area)
- ☐ Present vacancies
- ☐ Physical condition
- ☐ Work needed
- ☐ Anything unique?
- ☐ Fire retrofit (multi-family)

3- Transportation:
- ☐ Traffic count
- ☐ Exposure
- ☐ Transportation
  - Public
  - Freeway within: minutes;   km/miles

4- Others
- ☐ Appliances (type, brand, condition, age)
- ☐ What work needs to be done?
- ☐ How much would it cost?
- ☐ What would you do, or change, if you bought it? At what cost?
- ☐ Who are the immediate neighbors? Anything negative (odor, noise, light)?
- ☐ Is it offered at a very firm price?
- ☐ How was the price arrived at?
- ☐ Why is the vendor selling?

Checklist 16.2
Property Analysis Checklist

PROPERTY ANALYSIS CHECKLIST

A checklist is a terrific tool that is useless if it is not used

[Rate all 1 to 5 (best) – attach listing and Data Sheet if you have a copy of them]

Building/Owner's Name:_____   Date: _____

Property Address: _____

Gross Building Area: _____   Land Area: _____   Type of IPP: _____

1- IN BRIEF
- ❑ Visual appeal
- ❑ Gut feeling (am I turned on?)
- ❑ Neighbourhood
- ❑ Building condition
- ❑ Parking
- ❑ Usability
- ❑ Address
- ❑ Exposure
- ❑ Ease of division
- ❑ Traffic count (if retail)

2- ANALYSIS
- ❑ What is good with the property (what turns me on)
- ❑ What is bad with the property (what worries me, is dangerous)
- ❑ What are the "unique selling propositions" (the something(s) special)
- ❑ What is the worst that can happen
- ❑ Best uses
- ❑ What will we do once we own, or control, the property
- ❑ Upsides
- ❑ What are our ways out of the deal
- ❑ Overall rating

3- HISTORY OF THE PROPERTY AND COMMENTS

4- UPSIDE CHECKLIST
- ❑ Extra land (how much)
- ❑ Forthcoming change (zoning, highway, servicing, nearby development, etc.)
- ❑ Re-zoning potential
- ❑ Change of use
- ❑ Land assembly potential
- ❑ Partnership with neighbour(s)

5- LIST POSSIBLE DOWNSIDES

6- STRATEGY CHECKLIST

- ❑ Resell as-is
- ❑ Clean-up and sell
- ❑ Clean-up and lease
- ❑ Renovate and sell
- ❑ Convert to
- ❑ Demolish in total and sell land
- ❑ Demolish and rebuild for lease or sale
- ❑ Convert to condos
- ❑ Raise roof
- ❑ Re-zone
- ❑ Assemble with neighbours
- ❑ Option it
- ❑ Lease with option
- ❑ Joint venture
- ❑ Take through planning process for re-zoning and sell
- ❑ Others

7- SAFEST WAYS TO ACQUIRE CONTROL OF THE PROPERTY (1 to 5 (best))

- ❑ Lease
- ❑ Option
- ❑ Buy
- ❑ Lease-Purchase Option
- ❑ Buy a business that has a tenant in the property

8- ECONOMICS

- ❑ Asking Price
- ❑ Likely sale price
- ❑ Additional expenses

    - Financing

    - Repairs, changes, renovations

    - Carrying

    - Planning work

- ❑ Others
- ❑ Time to bring on stream
- ❑ Expected income/profit

9- REMARKS

602 | Appendix 1

Checklist 16.3
Due Diligence Building Acquisition Checklist

DUE DILIGENCE BUILDING ACQUISITION CHECKLIST

Conducting your due diligence stems from two needs: the need to control the natural tendency of many Vendors to use "Caveat Emptor" (let the buyer beware) and to take advantage of the Buyer, and to the need to know perfectly well what you are buying so that there will be no surprise.

No one will find all the answers to everything (most of the times), but he, who seeks, shall find.

The key to due diligence is a checklist. Use this one to develop your own, and keep on tweaking it.

PRELIMINARY DUE DILIGENCE CHECKLIST
(For use before presenting the offer or during the due diligence period)

Property Address: _____

Date: _____

- [ ] 1- Yearly profit and loss statements: past 3 years minimum; 5 years, if possible. One year, monthly; two years, if possible.
- [ ] 2- Balance sheet (3 years)
- [ ] 3- Rent Roll including, for each tenant: term, options, deposit, and payment history.
- [ ] 4- Tax returns: 3 years
- [ ] 5- Insurance: Insurance policy; including all riders, risk assessments, and disclosure affidavits for the insurance company
- [ ] 6- Mortgage documents: including Charge form, closing statements, title policy, rate riders, etc., and contact names and numbers.
- [ ] 7- Deed
- [ ] 8- Leases with any addendum, letters or riders.
- [ ] 9- Service or advertising contracts: garbage, pest control, maintenance, management, vending, billboard, pay telephone, etc. and any contract to be assumed by Buyer
- [ ] 10- Commission agreements from Leasing agents
- [ ] 11- Copies of all available reports: building inspection, appraisals, engineering, environmental, fire system inspection.
- [ ] 12- Survey and site plan
- [ ] 13- Architectural and engineering plans (as-built) and specifications.
- [ ] 14- List of employees, including name, position, date of hiring, salary, and benefits.
- [ ] 15- Inventory of furniture, fixtures, equipment, and supplies.
- [ ] 16- Utility bills: water, sewer, gas, electricity (at least two years of monthly statements) or letter report from supplier showing usage and cost
- [ ] 17- Bank: statements showing deposits for last 12 months
- [ ] 18- Phone system specs
- [ ] 19- Computer system specs
- [ ] 20- Property tax bills for the past three years
- [ ] 21- Legal problems: details of any past or pending litigation, or affidavit of owner stating that there isn't any.

DETAILED DUE DILIGENCE PRIOR TO CLOSING

- [ ] 1- Engineering Inspection and Survey
- [ ] 2- Environmental Inspection: wetlands, open space
- [ ] 3- Environmental Assessment Phase One report: asbestos, lead paint, PCBs
- [ ] 4- Environmental Phase Two Report, if available
- [ ] 5- LUST (Leaking Underground Storage Tank) Report
- [ ] 6- Financial Audit
- [ ] 7- Property tax verification
- [ ] 8- Tenant Estoppel letters
- [ ] 9- Mortgagee Estoppel letters
- [ ] 10- Legal Verifications: licenses, permits, zoning.

Checklist 17.1
Landlord's Post-Tenancy Checklist

LANDLORD'S POST-TENANCY CHECKLIST

Property Address: _____

This is a series of reminders of what should be done after a tenant has moved out.

- ❑ Thoroughly inspect the property and make a note of everything that should be done.
- ❑ Shampoo or replace broadlooms
- ❑ Redecorate
- ❑ Make sure that utilities are switched over to your name
- ❑ You <u>must</u> keep one phone line so that the alarm system, now in your name, is operative.
- ❑ Change the outside locks
- ❑ In winter, check that the heating units are all on, with thermostats set at 5 degrees above freezing, and that the gas is turned on, or that there is sufficient oil, or propane in the tank.
- ❑ In summer, set the circulating fans on "on", so that the air moves about.
- ❑ Remove <u>all the signs</u> from the previous occupant, inside and outside.
- ❑ Contact the fire department, regarding the sprinkler system. Has it been checked during the last year? Is it connected to a fire alarm system?
- ❑ Talk to the neighbours to ask them to keep an eye on the property.
- ❑ Talk to the police and ask them to keep an eye on the property.
- ❑ Turn off the water valve at the building entrance.
- ❑ There may be items that should be replaced, repaired, painted, etc., but that you do not want to, or cannot, do. Get an estimate for every one of them, so that you know the cost involved and can inform the new tenant, during the course of negotiations, if you are asked to do it.
- ❑ Contact your insurance agent, and be ready for a shock. Premiums for empty buildings skyrocket. The premium for an occupied building may be $5,000/year, but it may jump to $20,000-30,000 for an empty one. <u>Do not make the mistake of staying without insurance to save money.</u>

Checklist 17.2
Building Lease Review Checklist

BUILDING LEASE REVIEW CHECKLIST

This checklist can be equally helpful as a refresher to experienced Landlords and aspiring Landlords performing their due diligence.
This checklist is not exhaustive. There will be the odd time when you will find an item you want to add, or delete. Keep on tweaking it.
Once you have taken care of one item, tick in the box.

☐ **1. Arbitration**

Has an arbitration clause been made part of the Lease, to avoid making lawyers wealthy and happy?

☐ **2. Breaches**

Are there damages to be paid by the Tenant if he breaches Lease conditions?

Who pays for legal and professional fees? Why?

☐ **3. Building rules and regulations**

What are they? They should be given to the Tenant, by the Landlord, along with a copy of the Lease.

What happens if they are not respected by the Tenant?

☐ **4. Condition of the space**

If a Tenant takes the building "as is" does the Landlord have to reveal in writing any problem of which he is aware?

☐ **5. Dangerous substances**

May Tenant store dangerous/hazardous substances in his space. Any limit? Permits required?

Does the Lease require the tenant to comply with government laws?

Must Landlord notify Tenant if another Tenant in the building stores hazardous substances?

☐ **6. Destruction or expropriation**

If building is destroyed, must Landlord rebuild? Define "destruction".

Will rental be abated during "non-usability"?

May Tenant terminate Lease if destruction occurs (total or partial)?

Expropriation: Rights of Tenant and Landlord

☐ **7. Environmental concerns**

Should Landlord provide Tenant with an up-to-date environmental report showing that the property is environmentally clean? Is that Tenant required to do the same, at the expiration of the Lease?

If contamination, which existed prior to Tenant taking possession, is found in the premises later, what is the responsibility of the Landlord and that of the Tenant?

Will there be any rental abatement if Tenant's use of premises is hindered by the contamination or removal of it?

If more stringent laws are passed, whose responsibility will it be to do the work involved, and who pays for it?

☐ **8. Expense allocation**

Percentage paid by Tenant.

List of special expenses: capital expenses, equipment updating, testing – Reports. Who pays for these?

☐ **9. Grace period**

If Tenant is found in default, is there a grace period? How long?

☐ **10. Guarantor**

Is there any guarantor to the Lease? Name? What is his "financial substance"?

Does his guarantee cover the whole term? The whole amount due?

☐ **11. Insurance**

Type – public liability – casualty - rental income / who pays – limits – deductible

What must be covered? / Is Landlord named as co-insured?

Hold – harmless provisions (damages caused by Tenant / Landlord)

Will Landlord be indemnified only for harm caused by the Tenant <u>within</u> the leased space?

☐ **12. Inspection**

Does Tenant have the right or the obligation to inspect, and approve, the condition of the premises, prior to signing the Lease (in case of new construction or renovation)?

Landlord's warranties: Building codes, laws. What happens if Tenant must make corrections? Who pays? What if Tenant is forbidden to use the space for a period of time?

☐ **13. Improvements**

If Tenant wants to make improvements, who pays, if it is of benefit only to this Tenant, or to any Tenant?

Landlord's restrictions on improvements

☐ **14. Tenant's substance**

Reputation of the Tenant / Does he have the means to pay for the move and other expenses to prepare the space?

What happens if the Landlord does not maintain the building properly – What are the Tenant's remedies?

☐ **15. Lease**

When does it start? – Fixed date – upon a previous tenant moving out – When space is ready

Any free rent period? Does Tenant pay the additional rent during this period?

Is delayed possession acceptable? Any penalty or bonus? Will it affect the termination date of the Lease? or escalation dates?

☐ **16. Options**

On adjacent space (rentals). Can adjacent tenants be moved elsewhere in the building, so that Tenant's spaces are contiguous?

On additional space in the building (rental)

Will the term for the additional space ends up on same date as the original Lease?

For more parking stalls

To renew – At which rate – Term – Notice

Of first refusal to lease additional space (rental) / To buy the property / At what price? When?

Landlord's fee ("out-of-pocket" expenses) for these options?

☐ **17. Parking**

Are there sufficient parking spaces available? For Tenant – for Tenant's customers.

Are any spaces reserved for Tenant/customers? How? Enforcement?

☐ **18. Premises**

Square footage. Is it Net Rentable or Net Usable Area?

The space should be measured and certified by a professional.

☐ **19. Property taxes**

Who sends the property tax cheques to the municipality?

If it is the tenant, how does the Landlord insure that they have been paid?

If it is the Landlord, how does he collect them from the tenant: monthly, based on previous year's amount – monthly, based on projections - invoice to tenant, when bill is received from municipality.

Does tenant have the right to appeal? At whose expense?

☐ **20. Rental**

Is it net or gross? / Spell out who pays what (taxes, insurances, utilities, maintenance, repairs, replacements, capital expenditures)

If it is a net Lease, can Tenant contract with any suppliers, or must he use Landlord's approved suppliers, or use the Landlord's own services?

Rental during holdover period

Overage (percentage rental)

☐ **21. Rental escalations**

Rental deposit: Is it a rental deposit (last month?) or a security deposit?

Any escalations? – When – Fixed amount – Percentage – CPI (Consumer Price Index)

On operating expenses – actual; partial; indexed.

☐ **22. Retail Space Lease**

May Landlord lease space to a competitor (define)?

Only within a radius of… ? Remedies of Tenant if Landlord violates the restriction

May Tenant open another store, within a radius of… Remedies of Landlord if Tenant violates the restriction

Type of goods/services to be carried by the store. Any specific exclusions? Any specific inclusions?

What happens if a major (anchor) tenant vacates, or the vacancy rate goes over a certain percentage of the total building square footage? Will the Tenant have the right to cancel his Lease, or will the Landlord consent to a substantial reduction of the rent?

❑ **23. Right of Entry**

May Landlord enter the premises: With own key – During business hours only (unless in emergency) – Upon giving notice? Can he close the space for repairs (will Tenant be compensated, if he does, how?)

❑ **24. Services**

Will existing services capacity (HVAC, water, sewers, electricity) be sufficient? What if they are not? Who does the work to correct? Who pays?

❑ **25. Sublease**

May Tenant sub-lease? With, or without, Landlord's permission? All or part of the space? At a higher rental?

Reasons for Landlord to refuse a sub-Tenant

❑ **26. Term**

Possession date / How many years?

❑ **27. Termination of the Lease**

At the end of the Lease, what are the Tenant's obligations? – Removal of: fixtures, chattels and improvements made by, or for, the Tenant.

Shall Tenant surrender the building in "good condition", subject to wear and tear (define), or not?

Shall Tenant redecorate? Who chooses the quality of products (i.e. broadloom) and colours?

Note: This is almost never treated properly in Leases

❑ **28. Uses**

Are there limitations to the uses of the premises by the Tenant, and all other Tenants in the building – Noise, music, vibrations, special equipment,etc.

❑ **29. Waste**

If the Tenant harms the property through improper use, what are the Landlord's remedies. Will they survive a sale of the property?

❑ **30. Workletter**

In many cases, work will need to be done to render the space suitable for a tenant.

The workletter specifies who does what, and who pays what, as well as the schedule and timing of Landlord's and Tenant's work / If cost overrun, who pays? If delays, any penalty?

❑ **31. Zoning**

Exact designation / Any restrictions to use / May Tenant apply for re-zoning?

Does Tenant need: an occupancy permit? A letter from the municipality confirming that the use he contemplates is legal? What happens to the Lease if it is not? If use is found "illegal" later on?

Are there any easements, right-of-ways, over the property or over an adjacent one?

Checklist 17.3
Pre-Move-In Checklist

PRE-MOVE-IN CHECKLIST FOR TENANTS

This can be just one printed page, but it is a tool that serves two purposes. It positions you with your tenants; it shows your tenants that you care, that you are a professional landlord, and it helps your tenants plan their move. Don't underestimate the value of your reputation in finding good tenants. Former tenants provide excellent references in referrals.
This checklist does not pretend to cover it all. On the contrary, the intent is to focus on what is easily forgotten, not provided, or overlooked.

Property Address: _____

❑ Nearest governmental labour placement office and temporary personal placement company
❑ Postal code of the building
❑ Telephone exchange middle digit available. For example: 617-<u>457</u>-1234.
❑ Name of 2 or 3 neighbourhood locksmiths.
❑ Name of 2 or 3 janitorial (office cleaning) services.
❑ Name of 2 or 3 waste disposal suppliers.
❑ Name of 2 or 3 computer service specialists
❑ Name of 2 or 3 telephone installers
❑ Telephone number of closest police station.
❑ Telephone number of utilities suppliers.
❑ Distance to nearest freeways.
❑ Map, showing building location.
❑ Closest public transportation:

    1- bus
    2- subway
    3- rapid transit

❑ Closest "key" stores:

    1- hardware
    2- building supply
    3- banks
    4- restaurants
    5- post office
    6- hotel/motels
    7- supermarkets
    8- used office furniture
    9- service stations
    10- hospital
    11- doctor(s)
    12- office supply
    13- copying stores
    14- telephone

❑ Names of immediate neighbours: Company, president, address, telephone number.

APPENDIX 2

Additional Resources

APP 2.1 ASSOCIATIONS AND ORGANIZATIONS

Advanced Buildings, Technologies and Practices

A building professional's guide to more than 90 environmentally-appropriate technologies and practices to improve the energy and resource efficiency of commercial, industrial, and multi-unit residential buildings through the use of technologies and practices. The following design and construction issues are covered: indoor air quality, water conservation, waste management, electricity production, non-toxic materials, recycled materials, delighting, and energy efficiency. The Web site is offered to assist building designers.

Web site: www.advancedbuildings.org

The Appraisal Institute of Canada

The Institute grants professional designations in real estate appraisal, such as Accredited Appraiser Canadian Institute (AACI).

Web site: www.aicanada.ca

Building Owners and Managers Association (BOMA)

BOMA provides resources regarding property management and their Standard Method of Floor Measurement.

Web site: www.boma.org

Canadian Legal Information Institute (CanLII)

CanLII is a not-for-profit organization initiated by the Federation of Laws Societies of Canada (there are 14 of them). Its goal is to make primary sources of Canadian law accessible for free on the Internet.

Web site: www.canlii.org

Canadian Real Estate Association (CREA)

CREA is an association of Provincial Real Estate Associations. Their Web site is the gateway to over 300,000 properties listed on the Multiple Listing Service (MLS) (<www.mls.ca>). The commercial listings can be accessed on their commercial Web site (<www.icx.ca>), which also offers additional data on demographics, labour, transportation, etc.

Commercial Investment Real Estate Institute (CIREI)

CIREI confers the Certified Commercial Investment Member (CCIM) designation and is an affiliate of the US National Association of Realtors (NAR). The CCIM movement began more than 40 years ago with commercial real estate practitioners who wanted to elevate their business practices through education and networking. A CCIM is a recognized professional in commercial real estate brokerage, leasing, asset management, valuation, and investment analysis. Only about 6,000 commercial real estate professionals hold the CCIM designation, which reflects the calibre of the program and is one of the most coveted and respected designations in the industry.

Web site: www.ccim.com

Continuing Legal Education Society

The Continuing Legal Education Society of British Columbia is rich in legal information for Canadians.

Web site: www.CLE.bc.ca

CoreNet Global

CoreNet Global is the world's premier association for corporate real estate and related professionals with a

membership base of 7,000 corporate real estate executives, service providers, and economic developers. As a global learning organization, it is the industry thought and opinion leader. CoreNet Global is the only group that convenes the entire industry and symbolizes a professionally and geographically diverse membership of more than 50 locally-based chapters in five global regions (Asia, Australia, Europe, Latin America, and North America). Programs and services are designed to meet the business needs of members' companies and the career needs of individual members.
Web site: www.corenetglobal.org

Clean Energy
Clean Energy is a technology portal for information and action on energy efficiency and conservation. Here, you'll also find practical information, tips, and links for taking action to improve energy efficiency and conservation practices.
Web site: www.cleanenergy.gc.ca

Fair Rental Policy Organization of Ontario (FRPO)
FROP was founded in 1985 by property owners and managers. The organization is a fierce opponent of rent controls. The primary goal of the association is to protect the interest of private owners of rental housing. They advise their members, organize seminars for them, and lobby governments, particularly the Ontario government, and secure discounts for their members. They also provide legal and technical advice, and publish a monthly newsletter. Of special interest to the smaller apartment owner are their member discounts on products ranging from property and liability insurance and employee benefit plans to car rental rates and office supplies. Their most successful discount is a natural gas purchase plan.
Web site: www.frpo.org

Home Builders Associations
Homebuilders associations exist in most larger municipalities. In Ontario, the biggest is BILD (up to mid-2007 the Greater Toronto Home Builders Association (GTHBA-UDI)).
Web site: www.gthba.ca

Institute of Real Estate Management (IREM)
IREM provides training, information, research, analysis, and practical advice for professionals managing all types of income-producing real estate. The institute awards the Certified Property Manager (CPM) designation to managers of commercial properties.
Web site: www.irem.org

International Council of Shopping Centers (ICSC)
ICSC is the global trade association of the shopping centre industry. The principle aims of ICSC are to advance the development of the shopping centre industry and to establish the individual shopping centre as a major institution in the community.
Website: www.icsc.org

Law Society of Upper Canada (LSUC)
The LSUC exists to govern the legal profession in the public interest for the purpose of advancing the cause of justice and the rule of law. While the primary mandate is to regulate the profession, it also offers services to the

public through a lawyer referral service and provides legal information and support for lawyers. The Great Library of the LSUC is a reference library located in Osgoode Hall in Toronto. You may consult their more than 120,000 volumes (plus many CD-ROMs), but you may not remove them.
Web site: www.lsuc.on.ca

National Association of Industrial and Office Properties (NAIOP)
NAIOP is the leading trade association for developers, owners, investors, asset managers, and other professionals in industrial, office, and mixed-use commercial real estate. Founded in 1967, NAIOP comprises more than 14,500 members in 53 North American chapters. It provides networking opportunities, educational programs, research on trends and innovations, and strong legislative representation.
Web site: www.naiop.org

National Association of Real Estate Investment Trusts (NAREIT)
NAREIT provides a strong Web site for information about REITs with links to many real estate sites.
Web site: www.nareit.com

National Association of Realtors (NAR)
This is the US equivalent to CREA. Its Web site offers information concerning real estate education, federal issues, governance, industry news, law and policy, etc. It also has listings for boards all across the US plus tips for homebuyers and sellers.
Web site: www.realtor.org

National Council of Real Estate Investment Fiduciaries (NCREIF)
This organization is the creator of the NCREIF Property Index, which includes properties treated as completely unleveraged.
Web site: www.ncreif.com

Office of Energy Efficiency (OEE)
The OEE is Canada's centre of excellence for energy conservation, energy efficiency, and alternative fuels information. One of the OEE's key tasks is managing the government of Canada's new ecoENERGY Efficiency Initiative with its programs to reduce energy use in buildings and houses, industry, retrofits, personal vehicles, and fleets. In addition, the OEE promotes other energy-efficient transportation choices.
Web site: www.nrcan.gc.ca

Ontario Real Estate Association (OREA)
OREA represents 38,000 brokers and salespeople who are members of Ontario's 43 real estate boards. The association provides all real estate licensing courses in Ontario.
Web site: www.orea.com

Santa Monica Green Building Program
The City of Santa Monica has adopted a set of requirements and recommendations to encourage the development of "green" buildings without forcing excessive costs or other burdens upon developers, building owners, or occupants. The City has also developed the Green Building Design and Construction Guidelines.
Web site: greenbuildings.santa-monica.org/

Saskatchewan Environmental Society (SES)

The SES's goal is a world in which all needs can be met in sustainable ways. Sustainability requires healthy ecosystems, healthy livelihoods, and healthy human communities with focus on Saskatchewan.
Web site: www.environmentalsociety.ca

Society of Industrial and Office Realtors (SIOR)

The SIOR is the leading professional commercial and industrial real estate association. With more than 3,100 members in 480 cities in 20 countries, SIOR represents today's most knowledgeable, experienced, and successful commercial real estate brokerage specialists. Their Web site gives you access to experts, properties, and market data. Valuable course, convention, publication, and membership information is also available.
Web site: www.sior.com

Toronto Real Estate Board (TREB)

The Toronto Real Estate Board (TREB) has 27,000 members. TREB and other local real estate boards generally have libraries that are open to the public.
Web site: www.torontorealestateboard.com

US Green Building Council (USGBC)

The USGBC is the US's foremost coalition of leaders from every sector of the building industry working to promote buildings that are environmentally responsible, profitable, and healthy places to live and work. The USGBC's core purpose is to transform the way buildings and communities are designed, built, and operated, enabling an environmentally and socially responsible, healthy, and prosperous environment that improves the quality of life.
Web site: www.usgbc.org

APP 2.2 BOOKS

Art of Worldly Wisdom, The, Baltasar Gracian (Doubleday: 1992)
Follow the timeless advice of seventeenth-century Jesuit scholar Baltasar Gracian. Each of the elegantly crafted maxims in this New York Times bestseller offers valuable insight on the art of living and the practice of achieving.

Builder's Manual, Canadian Home Builders' Association (<www.chba.ca>)
A great source of information and a marvellous resource for novice and professional alike, based on the tough Canadian climatic conditions.

Buy it, Fix it, Sell it: Profit!, Kevin C. Myers (Dearborn Financial Publishing Inc.: 1998)
A comprehensive guide to no-sweat money-making home renovations.

Encyclopaedia of Real Estate Terms, Damien Abbott (Delta Alpha Publishing: 2004)
The most comprehensive single-volume reference book on real estate terminology has 1,476 pages. It provides real estate definitions and detailed explanations on the meaning and significance of over 9,000 terms (www.deltaalpha.com).

Handbook of Environmental Compliance in Ontario, The, Brett Ibbotson and John Phyper (McGraw-Hill Ryerson: 2003)
This book is used as a manual by the University of Toronto and Queen's University.

Lease-Purchase America, John Ross (Starburst Inc.: 1993)
You will learn a lot from this book if you want to practice Lease-Purchasing.

Making Money in Real Estate, Douglas Gray (John Wiley & Sons Canada Ltd.: 2005)

Personal Finance, Garman/Forgue (Houghton Mifflin Company: 1991)
An outstanding book on how to become financially successful.

Pocket Dictionary of Canadian Law, 4th ed., Daphne A. Dukelow (Carswell: 2006)
This pocketsize legal dictionary provides quick reference to current Canadian legal definitions (<www.carswell.com>).

Pocket REF, Thomas J. Glover, 3rd ed. (Sequoia Publishing, Inc.: 2002)
An outstanding pocket technical handbook that costs under $15. They also have a PC software version of the book, called Mega Ref. (<www.pocketref.com>)

Putting a Lid on Legal Fees: How to deal effectively with lawyers, Raymond Klein (Interlink Press, Inc.: 1988)

Realty Bluebook, Robert de Heer (Professional Publishing Corporation: 1993)
An American book geared towards residential real estate but, still an excellent reference book.

Richest Man in Babylon, The, George Clason (Signet (Penguin): 1989)
The best book you can buy on personal money management, if you are not sure how to become rich or how to hang onto your money.

Ugly's Electrical References, George V. Hart (United Printing Arts, Inc.: 1996)
If you can't find the electrical info you want in *Pocket REF*, you will find it in *Ugly's*. (<www.uglys.net>)

Visual Handbook of Building and Remodelling, The, Charlie Wing (Putnam Pub Group: 1998)
This is more of a reference book than a "how-to". It is very helpful, in some areas, for small builders, do-it-yourselfers, and hands-on investors.

APP 2.3 GLOSSARIES OF RELEVANT TERMINOLOGY

www.deloitte.com/dtt/article/0,1002,%20cid%253D15162,00.html
A very complete "Glossary of Real Estate Terminology".

www.realtor.com
Provides definitions for the US real estate industry.

APP 2.4 GOVERNMENT

Federal Government (www.canada.gc.ca)

Strategis is the master depository of information regarding the federal government. This site lists, alphabetically, the various federal sites, such as advertising services, building products, business library, lease calculator, copyrights, monthly economics indicators, privacy for business, real estate developers, etc.
Web site: www.strategis.ic.gc.ca/engdoc/alpha.html

Canada Revenue Agency (CRA)

Web site: www.cra-arc.gc.ca

Central Mortgage and Housing Corporation (CMHC)

CMHC is the government of Canada's national housing agency. It provides good information on housing assistance and research into the quality and affordability of housing and new ways to finance home purchases. The CMHC also offers a downloadable publications catalogue and online versions of various local housing market reports.
Web site: www.cmhc-schl.gc.ca

Statistics Canada

In addition to a huge archive of statistics, Statistics Canada offers a free downloadable copy of "The Daily", which contains information from their latest studies and surveys. You can also find CPI (Consumer Price Index) values here.
Web site: www.statscan.ca

Ontario Government

Ontario offers a terrific 34-page booklet, "Taxation in Ontario", that can be downloaded at <www.2ontario.com/software/brochures/taxation.pdf>.
Web site: www.gov.on.ca

APP 2.5 LEGAL

ONLINE LEGAL SITES

www.quicklaw.com
Publishes Canadian cases, decisions, and court, board, and tribunal information.

www.legalline.ca/
This not-for-profit organization provides free legal information online and through telephone and Internet.

www.findlaw.com
A US site containing a wealth of information, including message boards that cover many subjects, such as real estate and property law, landlord and tenant matters, and Forms Exchange.

www.lawpro.ca
A legal site brought to you by the Lawyers' Professional Indemnity Company.

LAW FIRMS

Many law firms offer a wealth of legal information on their Web sites. Here are some Canadian law firms of particular interest.

- Borden Ladner Gervais: www.blgcanada.com/publications
- Gowlings: www.gowlings.com/resources/index.asp
- McCarthy Tetrault: www.mccarthy.ca/search/pub_search_results.asp
- Blake, Cassels & Graydon: www.blakes.com/english/publications
- Goodmans: www.goodmans.ca/index.cfm?fusefction=publicationdirectory&rs=0
- Osler, Hoskin & Harcourt: www.osler.com/resources_landing.aspx?id=8889
- Stikeman Elliott: www.stikeman.com/cps/rde/xchg/se-en/hs.xsl/1125.htm
- Torys: www.torys.com/publications

APP 2.6 INFORMATION FOR LANDLORDS AND OWNERS

www.landlordsinfo.com
"The best place for landlords to meet and share ideas with other landlords".
A one-year membership costs $90. They also offer "Commercial Tenant Investigations".

www.landlordspace.com
Dedicated to helping landlords increase profits with rental property and reduce management headaches.

REAL ESTATE INTERNET SITES

www.loopnet.com
Loopnet is a sort of privately owned MLS system, and the number one online commercial real estate site. It has more than $100 billion of properties for sale, and two billion square feet for lease.

www.realestateleasingtips.com
An interesting site dealing primarily with the leasing of properties. You will find in-depth explanations on leasing real property, what constitutes a lease from a business viewpoint, and various clauses and their implications. They also offer publications and educational resources.

www.realestatefoundation.com
The Land Centre is a terrific site covering land use and real estate information. It offers online access to thousands of documents. The focus is British Columbia.

www.homebuyer.ca
Many interesting items can be found on this site, such as useful checklists, charts, forms, articles, and educational resources. Douglas Gray, a prolific author of business, legal, and real estate books, is the site creator.

REAL ESTATE SOFTWARE

www.pine-grove.com
Loan, amortization and financial calculator.

www.martindalecenter.com/Calculators.html
Hundreds of free calculators.

www.investit.ca
Software program for investment analysis and calculators (Canadian and US).

www.onlineconversion.com
Use of conversion tables to convert just about anything to anything!

www.realm.com/en/products/argus/default.aspx
Sophisticated and expensive. Better suited for larger portfolios.

www.worldtimeserver.com
Current local time for any country or major city in the world.

www.amortization.com
Mortgage amortization.

www.recenter.tamu.edu/soft
If you want to find real estate software information, the repository seems to be the "Real Estate Center" at Texas A&M University.

www.z-law.com/zlawtoc.html
See this site for what they call "The Complete Real Estate Software Catalogue".

APP 2.7 TECHNICAL INFORMATION AND SUPPLIERS

BUILDING ADVICE

Ontario Roofing, Toronto, Ontario
Web site: www.ontarioroofing.com

Building and Renovation Advice
Ask the Builder, Cincinnati, Ohio
The Web site of Cincinnati-based Tim Carter's Home Improvement Centre offers helpful building tips about remodelling and renovations and e-books about, for example, painting kitchen cabinets and building stairs.
Web site: www.askthebuilder.com

Building Conservation, Wiltshire, United Kingdom
This site is oriented towards older or historic buildings, but the series of over 100 articles contains interesting data.
Web site: www.buildingconservation.com

BUILDING PRODUCTS

Custom Building Products, Seal Beach, California
Web site of this US Company offers good technical advice, particularly for tile and stone products.
Web site: www.custombuildingproducts.com

Copper Information, Toronto, Ontario
The first place to go to find information on copper. They also produce the newsletter "Canadian Copper".
Web site: www.ccbda.org

Plumbing Information, Chico, California
Offers a wealth of information on plumbing, kitchen, and bath.
Web site: www.plbg.com

CONSULTANTS

Environmental Consultant

Water and Earth Science Associates, Toronto, Ontario
Web site: www.wesa.ca

Architecture

Atkins Architects, Mississauga, Ontario
Web site: www.atkinsarchitects.com

Building Inspection Engineers

Carson Dunlop Weldon, Building Inspection and Consulting Engineers, in many Ontario cities (commercial and residential)
Web site: www.carsondunlop.com

Quantity Surveyor

Helyar, Toronto, Ontario
Quantity surveyors and construction cost consultants, member of the Altus Group. Publish the free Altus Helyar cost guide that can be ordered online or by telephone.
Web site: www.helyar.com

Landscape Architect

Schollen & Company Inc., Toronto, Ontario
Web site: www.schollenandcompany.com

Energy Conservation

R-2000 Quality Assurance, Ottawa, Ontario
Go to this site to understand R-2000 specifications.
Web site: oee.nrcan.gc.ca/residential/personal/new-homes/r-2000/

MAGAZINES

Building Operating Management Magazine, Milwaukee, Wisconsin
This Web site of "Building Operating Management" magazine offers a wealth of useful information, from HVAC to grounds care.
Web site: www.facilitiesnet.com/bom

EC&M

The magazine of Electrical Design Construction and Maintenance, Chicago, Illinois. Their Web site offers terrific advice and their magazine appears to be very interesting for technically minded persons.
Web site: www.ecmweb.com/news/ECM-business-advice-111904/

ROADS

The Asphalt Institute, Lexington, Kentucky (roads)
Web site: www.asphaltinstitute.org

Canadian Technical Asphalt Institute, Victoria, British Columbia (roads and driveways)
Web site: www.ctaa.ca

APPENDIX

3

Glossary of Acronyms

These are terms and abbreviations you will encounter throughout this book.

ABCP: Asset Backed Commercial Paper
ADS: Annual Debt Service
APP: Atactic Polypropylene
APR: Annual Percentage Rate

BA: Banker Acceptance
BOMA: Building Owners and Managers Association
BTU: British Thermal Unit
BUR: Built-up Roofing

°C: degrees Celsius
C (-value): Thermal Conductance
CAM: Common Area Maintenance
CCA: Capital Cost Allowance
CDOR: Canadian Dollar Offered Rate
CREA: Canadian Real Estate Association
CEO: Chief Executive Officer
CFAT: Cash Flow After Taxes
CFBT: Cash Flow Before Taxes
CFM: Cubic Feet per Minute
CFO: Chief Financial Officer
CMHC: Central Mortgage and Housing Corporation
CP: Corporate Commercial Paper
CR: Capitalization (Cap) Rate
CSA: Canadian Standards Association

DCF: Discounted Cash Flow
DR: Default Ratio
DSR: Debt Service Ratio

EIFS: Exterior Insulation and Finish System
EPDM: Ethylene Propylene Diene Monomer
EPS: Expanded Polystyrene
ESA: Environmental Site Assessment

°F: degrees Fahrenheit
FMRR: Financial Management Rate of Return

GAAP: Generally Accepted Accounting Principles
GIM: Gross Income Multiplier
GOI: Gross Operating Income
GROC: Gross Occupancy Cost

Gross: Gross Rental
GTA: Greater Toronto Area

HRV: Heat Recovery Ventilation
HVAC: Heating, Ventilation and Air-Conditioning

I: Income or Interest
ICI: Industrial, Commercial and Investment
IPP: Income Producing Property
IRR: Internal Rate of Return

K: Thermal Conductivity

LTB: Landlord and Tenant Board
LTT: Land Transfer Tax
LTV: Loan to Value

Mc-Urethanes: Moisture Cured Urethane Coatings
MIRR: Modified Internal Rate of Return
MLS: Multiple Listing Service
MPAC: Municipal Property Assessment Corporation

NDL: No Dollar Limit
Net: Net Rental
NIM: Net Income Multiplier
NPV: Net Present Value
NRC: National Research Council

OE: Operating Expenses
OER: Operating Expense Ratio
OREA: Ontario Real Estate Association

PGI: Potential Gross Income
PPSA: Personal Property Security Act
PSI: Pounds per Square Inch
PVC: Polyvinyl Chloride

R (-value): Thermal Resistance
RfR: Request for Reconsideration
ROE: Return on Equity
ROI: Return on Investment
ROR: Rate of Return

SBS: Styrene Butadiene Styrene

SI: System International (Metric System)
SPE: Special Purpose Entity
Sq ft: Square Foot

T-Bill: Treasury Bill
TIP: Tenant Information Program
TMI: Taxes, maintenance and insurance
TPO: Thermoplastic Polyolefin
TREB: Toronto Real Estate Board

USD: United States Dollar
UV: Ultra Violet

V & BD: Vacancies and Bad Debts
V: Value
VTB: Vendor Take-Back Mortgage

X EPS: Extruded polystyrene

Index

NOTES

NOTES

NOTES

NOTES

NOTES

NOTES

NOTES

NOTES

CPSIA information can be obtained
at www.ICGtesting.com
Printed in the USA
BVHW011437170420
577766BV00011B/31

9 780470 838402